FURY ON EARTH
A BIOGRAPHY OF WILHELM REICH
BY MYRON SHARAF

St. Martin's Press/Marek
New York

Grateful acknowledgment is made for permission to reprint material from the following:

Extracts of letters from Sigmund Freud to Paul Federn, reprinted by permission of Sigmund Freud Copyrights, Colchester, England. An extract from "At the Grave of Henry James" from W. H. Auden's *Collected Shorter Poems 1927–1957,* reprinted by permission of Random House. An extract from "Palimpset: A Deceitful Portrait" from *Selected Poems* by Conrad Aiken, copyright © 1961 by Conrad Aiken, reprinted by permission of Oxford University Press, Inc. An extract from *The Inmost Leaf* by Alfred Kazin, reprinted by permission of Harcourt Brace Jovanovich, Inc. Extracts from *A Book of Dreams* by Peter Reich, Harper & Row, reprinted by permission of Peter Reich. Extracts from *Wilhelm Reich: A Personal Biography* by Ilse Ollendorff Reich, reprinted by permission of the author. Extracts from *Wilhelm Reich Vs. the U.S.A.* by Jerome Greenfield, copyright © 1974, published by W. W. Norton, reprinted with the permission of Jerome Greenfield. Extracts from Wilhelm Reich's *The Function of the Orgasm, Character Analysis, The Sexual Revolution, The Mass Psychology of Fascism, Listen Little Man!,* and *The Cancer Biopathy,* originally published by Orgone Institute Press and translated by Theodore P. Wolfe, reprinted by permission of Peter Reich and Gladys Meyer Wolfe. Extracts from David Boadella, *Wilhelm Reich: The Evolution of His Work,* reprinted with the permission of Contemporary Books, Inc., Chicago; available in Dell paperback; Canadian rights held by Vision Press, London. Extracts from "The Trial of Wilhelm Reich" in *The Wilhelm Reich Memorial Volume,* Ritter Press, Nottingham, England, 1958, reprinted by permission of Paul Ritter. Extracts from Myron R. Sharaf, "Reich's Early Work on Character Analysis," reprinted by permission of *McLean Hospital Journal.* Extracts from Myron R. Sharaf, "The Great Man and Us: An Approach to the Biography of Wilhelm Reich," reprinted by permission of *Journal of Orgonomy.*

Design by Manuela Paul

Library of Congress Cataloging in Publication Data

Sharaf, Myron R.
  Fury on earth.

  Bibliography: p.
  Includes index.
  "A St. Martin's/Marek book."
    1. Reich, Wilhelm, 1897–1957. 2. Psychiatrists—
United States—Biography. 3. Orgonomy. 4. Sex
(Psychology) I. Title.
RC339.52.R44S47   150.19′5′0924 [B]   82-5707
ISBN 0-312-31370-5   AACR2

First Edition

10 9 8 7 6 5 4 3 2 1

Twenty-five years after his death in prison and the burning of his books by the Food and Drug Administration, the protean Wilhelm Reich—brilliant protégé of Freud, discoverer of orgone energy, great social and natural scientist—remains a figure of immense interest and importance ...and misunderstanding. This major biography, years in the making, takes a remarkably fresh look at his emblematic life, and includes new material on his personal development and sections on his work that are accessible to the layman, but sufficiently detailed to be instructive to the scholar.

Sharaf explodes the myths that have collected around the name "Wilhelm Reich"—the psychoanalytic myth of the early brilliant Reich, and the later insane Reich of orgone energy; the Marxist myth of the radical Reich, and the conservative

(continued on back flap)

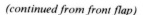

(continued from front flap)

myth of the Republican Reich. Sharaf's Reich is profoundly human: complex and contradictory, a generous, loving person capable of extraordinary bursts of bizarre ideas and impassioned cruelty. Of particular interest are the illuminations of the relationship between Reich's childhood traumas and his major concepts; and the pivotal personal and scientific significance of Freud for Wilhelm Reich.

In 1944, Sharaf met Reich and for the next decade, as student, patient, and co-worker, kept careful notes toward the eventual preparation of this biography. He has interviewed Reich's colleagues, family, friends and enemies, and gathered important papers. From these many sources he has discovered significant unpublished connections between Reich's personality, his social-intellectual milieu, and his work.

This masterful study will serve for years as the definitive biography of a man whose contradictions mirror our own contemporary schisms, whose greatness charts a future wholeness.

MYRON SHARAF received his Ph.D. from Harvard and was on the faculties of both the Harvard and Tufts Medical Schools. His articles on psychiatric subjects have appeared in many periodicals. He currently practices psychotherapy in the Boston area and lectures all over the world.

FURY ON EARTH

To my son Paul

CONTENTS

Acknowledgments ix

Part I. *The Viewpoint of the Observer*
 1. Introduction 2
 2. My Relationship with Reich 15

Part II. *The Development of the Mission: 1897–1920*
 3. Reich's Childhood and Youth: 1897–1917 36
 4. Becoming a Psychoanalyst: 1918–1920 53

Part III. *Reich as Insider—Building a Career and Marriage: 1920–1926*
 5. Reich's Work on the Impulsive Character: 1922–1924 66
 6. Reich's Early Work on Character Analysis: 1920–1926 72
 7. Reich's Work on Orgastic Potency: 1922–1926 86
 8. Personal Life: 1920–1926 106

Part IV. *The Radicalization of Reich: 1926–1930*
 9. Reich's Illness and Sanatarium Stay in Davos, Switzerland: Winter 1927 116
 10. July 15, 1927, and Its Aftermath: 1927–1928 122
 11. The Application of Sex-economic Concepts on the Social Scene—The Sex-pol: 1927–1930 129
 12. Personal Life and Relations with Colleagues: 1927–1930 145

Part V. *Liberation and Rejection—Reich's Breaks with the Communist Party and the Psychoanalytic Association: 1930–1934*
 13. The Sex-political Furor: 1930–1934 160
 14. The Psychoanalytic Furor and Reich's Break with the Psychoanalytic Association: 1930–1934 175
 15. Personal Life: 1930–1934 192

Part VI. *First Steps on the Road to Life—Reich's Experimental Work*
          in Scandinavia: 1934–1939
  16. The Bio-electrical Experiments: 1934–1935   206
  17. The Bions: 1936–1939   217
  18. Psychiatric Developments: 1934–1939   234
  19. Personal Life and Relations with Colleagues: 1934–1939   245
Part VII. *On His Own in America—Total Immersion in Studies of*
           "Life Energy" (Orgone Energy): 1940–1950
  20. Getting Settled in America: 1939–1941   262
  21. The Discovery of Orgone Energy: 1940   276
  22. The Medical Effects of the Accumulator: 1940–1948   293
  23. Psychiatric, Sociological, and Educational Developments:
       1940–1950   310
  24. Personal Life and Relations with Colleagues: 1941–1950   335
Part VIII. *The Road to Death—The FDA Campaign and Oranur:*
            1948–1957
  25. The American Campaign Against Orgonomy—The
       Beginnings: 1947–1948   360
  26. The Oranur Experiment: 1950–1953   370
  27. Personal Life and Other Developments: 1950–1954   383
  28. The FDA Injunction and Reich's Responses: 1951–1955   410
  29. Background to the Trial for Contempt of Injunction:
       1955–1956   435
  30. The Trial: 1956   446
  31. The Destruction of Orgone Energy Accumulators and
       Burning of Reich's Publications: 1956–1957   457
  32. Prison and Death: 1957   468
       Epilogue   479
       Notes   485
       Bibliography   521
       Index   525

A section of photographs follows page 174.

ACKNOWLEDGMENTS

So many people helped so much in my research and writing that in retrospect the enterprise lives for me as a cooperative venture. Its social nature was enhanced by the length of the undertaking: formal work began eleven years ago but I have been heading toward the goal of a Reich biography since 1946. Also, as I detail in Chapter 2, this project was often less the focused writing of a book than a painful process of self-discovery, requiring as much help from others as did the more intellectual components of the task.

I want to thank first those I interviewed about Reich and his work: Elsworth F. Baker, Kari Berggrav, Grete Bibring, Richard Blasband, David Boadella, Walter Briehl, Edith Buxbaum, Lilian Bye, K. R. Eissler, Ernst Federn, Margaret Fried, George Gerö, Bernard Grad, Jerome Greenfield, Nathan Cabot Hale, Sidney Handelman, Charles Haydon, Ottilie Heifetz, Morton Herskowitz, Sigurd Hoel, Grethe Hoff, Rosetta Hurwitz, Edith Jacobson, Jo Jenks, Lia Laszky, Elsa Lindenberg, Alexander Lowen, Bob McCullough, Gladys Meyer, Mitzi Mills, A. S. Neill, Ilse Ollendorff, Ernst Papanek, Ola Raknes, Chester M. Raphael, Eva Reich, Peter Reich, Tom Ross, Lore Reich Ruben, Fredrick Silber, Victor Sobey, Gisela Stein, Richard Sterba, Kenneth Tynan, Nic Waal, James A. Willie, and Lois Wyvell.

Some of these interviews were brief. Others required several sessions. The book itself will make clear, for example, how much the vivid, detailed recollections of Lia Laszky and Ottilie Heifetz, both now deceased, help me to understand the young Reich more fully. However, only here can I convey what a personal pleasure it was to get to know their lively minds and temperaments. Of those I met in the course of the research, Elsa Lindenberg also holds a special place. Between 1957 and 1978 we met five times, for several hours on each occasion. Her depth of perception and emotion enriched not only my work but also my life.

My relationship with some of the interviewees antedated the research by many years. I would like to single out a few of these old friends for special thanks. Ilse Ollendorff gave me the benefit of her warm support and was always available to discuss a troublesome point about Reich's personality or work. Also, until I made my own biographical effort I did not fully appreciate the value of her concise volume, *Wilhelm Reich: A Personal Biography.* Whenever I had a question about the facts, I could rely on her information to be accurate to the smallest detail. I am grateful for her permission to quote so extensively from her biography.

When I began my research, Peter Reich was deeply engaged in setting down his own recollections of Reich in *A Book of Dreams.* He generously helped me not only with information but by sharing the peculiar pleasure and pain of trying to capture in words one's evolving vision of an extraordinary father and teacher.

Of all those who knew and studied with Reich, Eva Reich has perhaps the most extensive knowledge of his work and life. I am forever thankful that over countless hours she shared that knowledge with an unrestrained giving-ness. Like Ilse, she had no need to try to make sure that I painted an "author-ized" portrait any more than she wanted a negative caricature. At his best, Reich desired that an entirely honest view of his work and personality should enter the historical record; that spirit seems to have rubbed off on many who were close to him.

I have known Gladys Meyer since 1946. She was helpful to me then and she has remained so during the intervening years. In numerous conversations I had the benefit of her discerning, candid mind focused on Reich and, espe-cially, the relationship between Reich and Theodore Wolfe. We have had our differences of opinion or emphasis, but to a remarkable degree she embodies the true liberal spirit, which expects disagreement. Finally, I cannot cite here her thousand acts of personal kindness on my behalf.

Elsworth F. Baker was always available to give whatever information he had that could be of use to me. However, my thanks to him center more on his intangible contributions. From the start of the project to its conclusion, he buoyed my self-confidence through his confidence in me.

Lois Wyvell played a key role in transforming the diffuse vapor of my biographical ambition into workable steam—in 1971 she recommended me to a publisher seeking a biographer of Reich. She also gave me her valuable recollections based on her association with Reich over many years.

David Boadella and I have been corresponding about orgonomy since the 1950s. I have found his book *Wilhelm Reich: The Evolution of His Work* a treasure trove of facts and interpretations.

Jerome Greenfield and I met in the early 1970s when he was working on his book *Wilhelm Reich VS. the U.S.A.* Since then we have exchanged considerable information. His meticulous research on the Food and Drug Administration's investigation of the orgone accumulator spared me much effort.

During the 1960s Nathan Cabot Hale encouraged me to begin this biography. I am also grateful to him for sharing precious data concerning the Norwegian newspaper campaign against Reich and regarding the FDA's activities. With David, Jerry, and Nathan, I have felt the joy of being present at the beginning of genuine historical scholarship in orgonomy.

I would like to thank David Blasband for his generous and astute legal counsel.

Douglas Levinson helped immeasurably with the conceptualization and writing of Chapter 16. He has also brought an informed background in orgonomy and in several academic disciplines to our long-standing dialogue about Reich's work.

An important source of encouragement and illumination was my participation in a group experience coextensive with the writing of this book. The group was made up of therapists who were also friends. During hectic periods this collectivity provided a kind of safety net for me. Most importantly, our work together facilitated my better emotional and intellectual comprehension of themes, such as the expression of negative feeling, fusion, and separation, issues that also pervaded my relationship with Reich. My gratitude to the following as members for varying periods and as steadfast friends: Sandra Fabian, Sam Fisk, Ildri Bie Ginn, Phillip Helfaer, Barbara Miller, Bob Rosenthal, Velma Sowers, and Carter Umbarger.

Phil Helfaer brought his incomparable empathy and fine mind to bear on my struggles, struggles that at times would have been too much for a less stalwart ally. Bob Rosenthal had a less intense interest in "Reichian" concepts, but precisely this distance combined with open-mindedness and strong personal involvement helped to maintain the steadiness of our valuable friendship.

A number of other colleagues and friends gave me encouragement or friendly criticism: Courtney Baker, Alvin Becker, John Bell, John Bellis, Dorothy Burlage, Judith Chadwick, Art Efron, Susan Gulick, Eva Hartmann, Barbara Koopman, Alexander Lowen, Greg Lombardo, Paul Mathews, Karl McLaurin, Jacob and Patricia Meyerowitz, John Pierrakos, Roberta Reich (no relation), Philip Reimherr, Bob Risse, Meatchie Russell, Michael Sales, Terry Santino, Gabrielle Sichel, Jean Stamps, Beth Strassberg, James Tropp, William Tropp, Kathy Vieweg, Mary Watkins, and Colin Wilson.

Bob Risse has been the kind of friend in whom I could confide doubts and anxieties I was scarcely able to acknowledge to myself.

I am grateful to several "non Reichian" colleagues I met in the 1950s at the Massachusetts Mental Health Center, my second intellectual home. First and foremost is Daniel J. Levinson, whose elegant sociopsychological approach to adult development in general and career development in particular so permeates my own thing that I cannot begin to itemize the particularities of my intellectual debt to him.

As a leader, Milton Greenblatt provided me with an example radically different from Reich's. He welcomed diversity of thought, a new experience after my total immersion in Reich's relentless pursuit of his own paradigm. His stance toward this biography—fervent support combined with informed criticism—has often renewed my spirits.

Ernest Hartmann read chapters ever since I started the writing. Like Milton, he has been a friendly critic of my interest in Reich's scientific work, thereby stimulating me to hone my arguments as sharply as I could. Ernest has also been a strong, gentle friend—a friend for all seasons.

Leston Havens and I have been carrying on a wide-ranging conversation for twenty-five years. His always stimulating and sometimes provocative mind has clarified and expanded my own position regarding Reich's psychiatric work.

An old friend and collaborator, Evelyn M. Stone, has warmly encouraged my research, writing, and speaking on Reich's life and work.

During the research phase and the writing of the first chapters, the late Larry Schiff was a precious friend and counselor. The world and I have been robbed by his untimely death of a prince of this earth—honest, enthusiastic, perceptive, and endlessly giving.

Several persons helped in an editorial capacity. Before I met my editor, Joyce Engelson, I thought the age of the great editors was over. I was wrong. She permitted me to work in peace for half a decade, putting up with delays most editors would have found intolerable. By action and word she communicated that she wanted only one thing—the best, most honest biography I was capable of writing. When I wavered from that commitment, she brought me back to first principles. As the project neared completion, she worked side by side with me in the final preparation of the manuscript. I shall never forget her tactful fervor during that difficult time.

When I was bogged down in shortening the manuscript to a manageable length, Joyce made it possible for me to obtain the help of an editorial consultant, Alison Bond. Alison helped cut the manuscript and much more. With a keen eye for confusion and holes in the story, she participated in a thorough rewriting of a number of chapters. Our correspondence and intense working days together rank among my most treasured professional experiences.

Grace M. Clark did a meticulous job of typing a clean manuscript from a cluttered draft. In the process she caught a number of my errors. Ann Adelman was a superb copyeditor; she submerged herself in the sense as well as the syntax of the pages. Erika Schmid's careful proofreading was of invaluable assistance. As managing editor for St. Martin's, Carol E. W. Edwards combined expertise with enthusiasm in a way that made working with her a great pleasure. Joyce Engelson's assistant, Jeff Pettus, had an unflappable temperament and a passion for detail that helped us through some difficult spots.

Editorially last but functionally perhaps first, I would like to thank Richard Marek, publisher of the St. Martin's/Marek imprint. He gave us steadfast, uncomplaining support, and from a position where the buck stopped.

It was my agent, Susan Ann Protter, who put me in contact with Joyce and Alison. The agent for several other books about Reich, she brought an informed awareness to my project. Through all the problems—she was a partner who showed astonishing grace under pressure. As one of the few persons who was with the project from inception to completion, she holds a special place in my affection. Susan, our long journey is over. Thanks!

My former wife Grethe Hoff participated in many of the experiences described in this book. I cherish and learned from her honesty and independence of mind toward Reich and his work. Until his death in 1979 our son Peter encouraged me with love and humor to finish the task. His support was all the more significant because the emotional entanglements among Grethe, Reich, and myself had cost him dearly.

My wife Giselle brought unusual qualities of mind and heart to the undertaking. She often had a sure instinct for lapses in tone or content in my psychological depictions. Her quiet integrity provided my grounding. Above all, she had faith in the book—and in me. The public reads a book; a wife shared the reality, often grim, of rendering that work. Giselle, my love and gratitude!

Our son Paul was five when I started the book and sixteen when I completed it. Even though its protracted labor pains often cast a shadow over his growing-up years, he gave the enterprise his warm blessing. He also provided the necessary spur, usually with a light touch but on occasion with entire frankness.

Through their efforts Eva and John Varadi, my parents-in-law, contributed greatly to the smooth functioning of our lives; through their love and solicitude to the intangible atmosphere so important for writing.

Life gave me Nathan Sharaf as a father. He has been a godsend always, but never more so than during my work on this project. I do not know how to thank him.

Finally, I would like to express my gratitude to Wilhelm Reich:

> He was blessed with an eternal childhood,
> with the givingness and vigilance of stars;
> he inherited the whole earth,
> and he shared it with everyone.
> —From "Boris Pasternak," a poem by Anna Akhmatova

Every fury on earth has been absorbed in time, as art, or as religion, or as authority in one form or another. The deadliest blow the enemy of the human soul can strike is to do fury honor. Swift, Blake, Beethoven, Christ, Joyce, Kafka, name me a one who has not been thus castrated. Official acceptance is the one unmistakable symptom that salvation is beaten again, and is the one surest sign of fatal misunderstanding, and is the kiss of Judas.

—James Agee
Let Us Now Praise Famous Men

When confronted by a human being who impresses us as truly great, should we not be moved rather than chilled by the knowledge that he might have attained his greatness only through his frailties?

—Lou Andreas-Salomé, of Sigmund Freud

PART I

The Viewpoint of the Observer

Introduction

When Wilhelm Reich died in his sleep at the Federal Penitentiary in Lewis-burg, Pennsylvania, on November 3, 1957, few people paid attention. His fellow inmates were temporarily kept waiting while a check was made to find the missing prisoner.[1] The world as a whole scarcely noticed. True, Reich's earlier prominence as a psychoanalyst merited a brief milestone in *Time:*

> Died. Wilhelm Reich, 60, once-famed psychoanalyst, associate, and follower of Sigmund Freud, founder of the Wilhelm Reich Foun-dation, lately better known for unorthodox sex and energy theories; of a heart attack in Lewisburg Federal Penitentiary, Pa.; where he was serving a two-year term for distributing his invention, the "orgone energy accumulator" (in violation of the Food and Drug Act), a telephone-booth–size device which supposedly gathered energy from the atmosphere, and could cure, while the patient sat inside, common colds, cancer and impotence.[2]

No matter that Reich never claimed the accumulator could cure colds, cancer, or impotence. What little comment his death aroused was mostly of the brief, inaccurate kind typified by *Time*'s obituary. Only a few newspapers, such as the anarchist publication *Freedom,* in London,[3] and *The Village Voice,*[4] carried more extensive, serious obituaries. Established scientific journals maintained a total silence. Not a single psychiatric journal carried any mention of his death, though "In Memoriam" statements are the rule in such publica-tions when a major contributor to psychiatry dies. Yet the received opinion about Reich was that he had indeed made very substantial contributions to psychoanalysis in the 1920s before he became "psychotic." However, it is understandable why the profession was so silent. Representatives of its organizations had been active in urging the Food and Drug Administration (FDA) to launch the investigation that ultimately jailed Reich, and they had congratulated the FDA on its successful prosecution of the case.[5]

If the world at large showed indifference or said "good riddance," about fifty persons who had studied with Reich or admired him from a distance attended his funeral, which was conducted on the grounds of Orgonon, Reich's 200-acre estate near the small town of Rangeley, Maine. The atmosphere was emotionally charged. Charles Haydon, Reich's chief legal adviser during his difficulties with the FDA, said some fifteen years later that it reminded him of the funeral of a Viking chieftain.[6] Reich's presence dominated in death, as it had in life, when the bereft community gathered to mourn him amid the falling November snow.

It was in keeping with Haydon's chieftain image that Reich should have left detailed instructions for his own funeral, specifying no religious ceremony but a record of Schubert's "Ave Maria," sung by Marian Anderson. A year earlier he had bought a coffin from a Maine craftsman.[7] He had also designated a plot of land in the woods at Orgonon overlooking the mountains and lakes, where his memorial was to consist of a simple granite slab with the words:

William Reich
Born March 24, 1897   Died____

At the funeral, Dr. Elsworth F. Baker, the physician closest to Reich in his last years, delivered the following brief oration:

"Friends, we are here to say farewell, a last farewell, to Wilhelm Reich. Let us pause for a moment to appreciate the privilege, the incredible privilege, of having known him. Once in a thousand years, nay once in two thousand years, such a man comes upon this earth to change the destiny of the human race. As with all great men, distortion, falsehood, and persecution followed him. He met them all, until organized conspiracy sent him to prison and then killed him. We have witnessed it all, 'The Murder of Christ.' What poor words can I say that can either add to or clarify what he has done? His work is finished. He has earned his peace and has left a vast heritage for the peoples of this earth. We do not mourn for him, but for ourselves, at our great loss. Let us take up the responsibility of his work and follow in the path he cleared for us. So be it."[8]

Already we note the first paradox in a life that had been full of them: the contrast between how the professional community at large regarded his work and how a small group of followers viewed his achievement. This ambiguity is compounded by the fact that what most people considered his major accomplishment, his contributions to psychoanalytic technique, Reich and his close associates at the end deemed of secondary importance. And what the received opinion regarded as a hoax or delusion, Reich's work on orgone energy, he and his associates came to believe was his truly significant set of discoveries.

Some twenty-five years later, it is clear that matters are more complicated than the standard view of 1957 portrayed them. Today, there is a surge of interest in Reich's work that is pushing hard against the stereotyped view of Reich as a "good psychoanalyst" who went astray in the late 1920s. At least some of what he "went astray" about has colored the cultural climate in a major fashion. Reich's work of the 1930s and 1940s on the muscular armor— chronic muscular spasms representing the somatic anchoring of the characterological rigidities Reich studied as an analyst—has heavily influenced a spate of therapeutic developments, including Alexander Lowen's bio-energetics, Fritz Perls's Gestalt therapy, Arthur Janov's primal therapy. And one of Reich's dominant metaphors, that of "man in the trap," the trap of his own armor, pervaded the therapeutic ambiance of the 1970s.[9]

Reich also anticipated many recent social developments. During the 1920s and early 1930s, he advocated the affirmation and social protection of healthy adolescent sexuality; the public availability, regardless of marital status or age, of contraceptives and abortion; the rights of women to their own economic independence and assertiveness; and the existence of a "biological core" in the human structure that is spontaneously social and emotionally open, not driven by the compulsive accumulation of money and status. In the early 1930s, he established a relationship between personal emotional misery, on the one hand, and submissiveness to authoritarian political regimes, on the other. Later, in his concept of "work democracy," he was to focus on building social and economic interrelationships from practical tasks and human needs rather than from the external imposition of a political ideology.

All these themes are very relevant today, often in forms quite different from what Reich was talking about, and some are still hotly contested. In subsequent chapters I shall argue that very few of the above ideas are unique to Reich. What is unique is his concept of orgastic potency and the specific way he connected a series of psychological, social, and biological findings with the presence or absence of this function.

A friendly critic might grant the legitimacy of these views of Reich's contributions. True, he might say, the earlier judgment of Reich—"good psychoanalyst, bad everything else"—was wrong. Reich did indeed contribute more to the clinical treatment of emotional problems and to sociology than the psychoanalysts realized. However, all this had nothing to do with the work that was to preoccupy Reich and be most prized by him during the last seventeen years of his life: his research on orgone energy. Cannot this work be characterized as absurd *prima facie*? For example, his claim to have "harnessed" a life energy within a simple box he alleged was helpful in the treatment of various illnesses? Is not this the reason why Reich is often regarded as a ludicrous, pathetic figure while those who utilize his psychiatric or socio-logical work but do not "dabble" in science are taken more seriously?

This revised view of Reich, making him more than a "good psy-choanalyst" but not a serious scientist, has been adopted by many. Yet one must be skeptical of facile datings of Reich's decline or glib explanations as to why he began to err. The image of him as sinister or insane was beginning to emerge long before he ventured into experimental science. Even in the 1920s when certain of his psychoanalytic contributions were applauded, colleagues mocked him for his emphasis on "orgastic potency" as the goal of psy-choanalytic treatment. In the late 1920s, many psychoanalysts and others considered him a psychopath or on the verge of psychosis, because he ad-vocated adolescent sexuality and broke all kinds of laws in his efforts to provide young people with sexological assistance (in the form of contraceptive informa-tion, counseling, and so on). In the 1930s, many dismissed him as psychotic because he spoke and wrote about the healthy person's perception of "stream-ings" in his body. Did not schizophrenics also speak of experiencing "electric currents" in their bodies?

The picture is further complicated by the fact that throughout his life Reich met with both acclaim bordering on adulation and the severest criticism. Although a controversial figure within psychoanalysis from the start, in the early 1920s many regarded him as "Freud's pet," destined for a position of leadership within the psychoanalytic movement. When his relations with his Viennese colleagues soured, he was able to surround himself in Berlin with an able group, including the analysts Otto Fenichel, Erich Fromm, and Edith Jacobson, who shared his social-political concerns. After his expulsion from the analytic organization in 1934, he developed a new circle of talented psychia-trists, psychologists, and writers in Oslo, Norway.

Reich had to leave Oslo in 1939 when his work on the bions (vesicles that he asserted represented transitional forms between the nonliving and the liv-ing) was denounced by many Norwegian scientists and Reich was accused of the grossest scientific charlatanism. These controversies led to the loss of his Norwegian support but, once again, he was able to attract a new group—this time in New York. Defying established psychiatric and medical opinion, well-regarded psychiatrists such as Theodore P. Wolfe and Elsworth F. Baker devoted themselves to learning and practicing Reich's kind of therapy and to aiding his scientific research.

In the 1940s, Reich's writings made a deep impression on the thinking of several outstanding people who were later to be very influential; they included Alexander Lowen, Fritz Perls, Paul Goodman, Saul Bellow, Norman Mailer, and William Burroughs.

Who exactly was this man whose life was filled with controversy, whom people loved and hated, who had to flee five countries, who once was regarded by many as "Freud's pet" but was excluded and hated by the psychoanalytic establishment? Why was he expelled from the Social Democratic Party in

Vienna in 1929 and from the Communist Party in 1934, after having been well regarded in both organizations? Why, in 1939, was he forced to leave Norway despite its tradition of civil liberties and after he had been so influential a teacher? Was it a sign of dilettantism, madness, or Renaissance-type genius that his work involved so many fields—psychiatry, sociology, biology, physics, meteorology? And what forces—outer, inner, or both—led to his death in an American jail?

When students were interested in Reich's scientific work, he used to say: "Try to prove me wrong." By this he meant that students should not take his theory and evidence on faith, but should scrupulously repeat the experiments with the most exact controls they could devise. Positive testimonials without firsthand critical investigation were as worthless, if not as destructive, as uninformed attacks.

My interest in Reich was and is primarily centered upon his work on human beings. Not trained as a biologist or physicist, I have never made systematic studies of his natural-scientific work. In writing this biography my first impulse was to concentrate on what I knew, not only from firsthand experience in orgonomy but from related study in psychoanalysis and sociology. However, I have decided to cover the entire range of Reich's work, although with far more concentration on its contributions to human concerns than on its experimental aspects. For one thing, it seemed desirable to have the entire range of Reich's work in a single volume, since only some of his writings are available today. Secondly, the fields with which I am most concerned—Reich's psychiatric and social concepts and findings—were from 1934 on profoundly influenced by his natural-scientific work. Finally, in the period from 1948 to 1955, when I worked with Reich, he was deeply immersed in experimentation and I had the opportunity to observe his methods of thinking and working at first hand. In order to render these experiences clearly, I have to give some picture of his experimental work. Although I have not myself repeated many of Reich's experiments, I hope to sharpen the questions that can be asked about his work, utilizing not only his own publications but also reports from and interviews with those few well-trained scientists who have replicated these experiments carefully.

A further restriction on the inclusiveness of this biography is imposed by the state of the Reich Archives. Reich's will stated that his unpublished papers were to be "put away and stored for 50 years to secure their safety from destruction and falsification by anyone interested in the falsification and destruction of historical truth."[10] Reich designated his daughter, Eva Reich, M.D., the executrix of his estate. For reasons to be discussed later, Eva Reich in 1959 appointed Mary Higgins as the executrix, a position she still maintains. Ms. Higgins has taken a strict interpretation of the "50 years" clause, reading it to mean that the unpublished papers are not to be made available even to scholars.

The inaccessibility of the archives, especially the diaries Reich kept from at least as early as 1919 until the end of his life, is a serious loss for the biographer. Nonetheless, there is sufficient evidence from a variety of sources, including interviews with people who knew him during different phases of his life, to give a picture of his personality, private life, and inner development. With any great man, but particularly with someone like Reich, character structure and work are closely interrelated. Reich himself often alluded to this relationship, as when he wrote: "The deeper the problem [of research] lies and the more comprehensive it is, the more intimately it is interwoven with the history of him who represents it."[11]

One of my chief concerns is with that "interwovenness," as he put it. The misuses of this approach are manifold. A very common one, frequently criticized but often committed, is psychoanalytic reductionism. One postulates a flaw or overemphasis in a person's work and then "explains" it on the basis of a personality conflict. Thus, Charles Rycroft has linked Reich's "idealization" of the orgasm with the "tragedies of his . . . childhood."[12]

This kind of argument is demeaning. It requires the acceptance of the original, unsupported premise that Reich did in fact "idealize" the orgasm. It leaves unexplained why others who suffered from similar childhood tragedies did *not* make of them what Reich did. John Mack has commented well on this kind of approach in the context of his biography of T. E. Lawrence:

> When I presented "psychological material" about Lawrence at conferences or meetings, my audience would inevitably offer interpretations about his psychopathology which, however accurate they may have been, left me always feeling that they had not seen Lawrence as I knew him to have been. In reading other psychological studies of historical figures I found myself becoming impatient with the failure of their authors to come to grips with the salient fact of unusual accomplishment, and kept registering the same objection that Lawrence himself had made when he commented upon a biographical essay about a famous general: that the article "left out of him his greatness—an extraordinary fellow he was."[13]

Reich was initially a psychoanalyst. We permit the artist his severe emotional problems and his wilder moments without denigrating his work. Erik Erikson has demonstrated how historical figures such as Martin Luther and Mahatma Gandhi can be seen in their wholeness, including their pathology, without demeaning their spiritual innovations.[14] Unfortunately, the fiction exists that psychoanalysts who have "completed their training" must be "well-adjusted" persons, who have "worked through" their unconscious conflicts. When they are presented otherwise, as in Erich Fromm's biography of Freud,[15] it is usually with the intention of denigrating them. Fromm's form of maligning Freud was mild, however, compared to what classical Freudians can offer in the way of psychiatric slander when confronted by theorists with differing views. It is ironic and disturbing that members of the very discipline that postulated no clear boundary between "normality" and "abnormality," between the "crazy" and the "compact majority," have so readily dismissed as "psychotic" such persons as Jacob Moreno (the founder of psychodrama), Sandor Ferenczi in his last years, and R. D. Laing, all of whom strongly diverged from classical analytic theory or technique.

But in no instance has the use of psychiatric diagnosis been as relentless or destructive as in Reich's case. During his career, rumors were rife that he had been hospitalized for mental illness, though in fact he never was. The accusation of madness—for that is what it amounted to—became a malignant legitimization for denying any aspects of Reich's work one did not like. By dating the onset of psychosis, one could neatly split Reich into a "good" pre-psychotic personage and a "bad" post-psychotic object. Depending upon one's predilections, the date of illness would vary. Thus, psychoanalysts could see Reich's character-analytic work in the 1920s as a product of his sane period, with everything after that viewed as psychotic. Some political radicals have pinpointed the illness as occurring in the mid-1930s, thereby permitting his Marxist-oriented, mass-psychological work of the early 1930s to be considered sane.

The problem is further complicated when Reich became a laboratory scientist. If a scientist's work is valued for its discoveries, we are inclined to disregard whatever pathological conflicts a Newton or Einstein manifested. Generally speaking, we are as eager to banish consideration of the relationship between personality and "objective," scientific accomplishment as we are to include it in dealing with the "subjective" work of artists. One may consider the connections between Dostoevski's attitude toward his father and *The Brothers Karamazov,* but Einstein's relationship with his father presumably has nothing to do with the theory of relativity. This attitude in part reflects our idealization of "emotion-free" science. One does not look for impure things in dealing with the cleanliness of "pure research." When, as in the case of Reich, a relationship between personality and scientific work is proposed, it is usually for the purpose of ridicule. Reich, the scientist, becomes a movie Frankenstein, a madman with a delusionary system involving the "creation of life" in his laboratory. Reich's capacity to cross scientific boundaries and to see common elements in apparently disparate realms is itself seen as a symptom of insanity; anyone who claims to work as a psychiatrist, cancer researcher, biologist, and physicist must be mad.

Nor do we do justice to Reich and his achievements, or to the connections between his personality and his work, if we obliterate the problematical elements of his character. There are indeed those among his followers who can brook no association of Reich with severe emotional conflicts. They have heard for so long the accusation that Reich was psychotic, and experienced with such pain this attempt to dismiss his work, that they refuse to examine any pathological tendencies in Reich. Often, part of their motivation is to avoid providing ammunition for his enemies. Here his followers are akin to those who, in the backlash against psychoanalytic reductionism, eliminate psychodynamics altogether in dealing with admired persons.

Reich himself did not entirely disregard the relationship between his inner struggles and his achievements, although frequently he wrote and spoke only indirectly about this "interwovenness." His first published article was a disguised self-analysis.[16] There are important similarities between his self-analysis and his description a few years later of the "impulsive character."[17] His awareness of his own problems contributed to his elucidation of authoritarianism and the "emotional plague," just as his perception of his own emotional health was crucial to his formulations concerning the "genital character" and "orgastic potency."

In a more general sense, Reich by no means wished to exclude character structure in dealing with competing scientific and philosophic "world pictures," even though he insisted that the *final* criterion in evaluating a clinical, social, or scientific finding was its objective validity. I will explore in further detail Reich's investigation of the relationship between the researcher's approach to "the problem" and his personality. My chief point here is to underscore his preoccupation with the question. As a psychoanalyst, he learned from Freud the importance of the therapist's overcoming his own repressions in order to "see" and deal sensitively with those of his patients. Later, he expanded the analytic emphasis on self-knowing to include full self-experiencing.[18] Still later, Reich stressed that the emotional, energetic openness of the observer, the "cleanliness of his sensory apparatus" was a key prerequisite for studying basic natural phenomena outside as well as inside every individual.[19]

I will argue that throughout his career, Reich struggled not only to master his unconscious in the Freudian sense but to maintain contact in the Reichian sense with the core of his being. I will contend that Reich's neurotic problems —and he had many—often creatively interacted with his emotional depth and soaring intellect. At other times, the interaction was destructive. On some occasions—during his Marxist political work in pre-Hitlerian Europe, say, or his efforts to combat the Food and Drug Administration's investigation in the 1950s—the interaction yielded a complex mixture of creativity and major errors. Such interactions embodied in so protean a figure provide lessons, writ large, for all of us who, in our own fashion, struggle with the same dialectic of health and illness.

I shall also apply Reich's concern with the interpenetration of self and society, individual character structure and social structure, toward understanding how his own struggle to further his health and master his sickness developed and evolved within particular familial, social, and historical matrices. What I will call the "core Reich"—his inner depth—interacted with external influences in ways which enriched and focused that depth and in ways which sullied and distorted it. What was true for Reich is true for all of us. To quote the psychologist Daniel J. Levinson: "Every man's life gives evidence of his society's wisdom and integration as well as its conflicts, oppression and destructiveness."[20]

In dynamic interplay with the inner Reich, then, stood the "historical Reich," the man who embodied many characteristics of the authoritarian society he so sharply and brilliantly illuminated. What was remarkable about Reich was not only his capacity to try to overcome the ways he had internalized his society's "conflicts, oppression and destructiveness," but also the way that the core Reich often creatively utilized the destructive internalizations contained in the historical Reich. For example, Reich at times was able to employ an enormous competitiveness, pride, even an arrogance very similar to his father's, as well as the vicissitudes of his own Oedipal strivings, in order to protect and fight for the insights his more modest, innocent, and deeper self had discovered.

No man, then, was more a child of his particular era; no man more engaged—always passionately, sometimes bullyingly—in the social and scientific conflicts of his time. No man was more able to transcend the destructive and erroneous in his social inheritance, to keep in touch with a depth of nature his times knew little of. To do so required relentless effort. In Nietzsche's words: "The great man fights the elements in his time that hinder his own greatness, in other words his own freedom and sincerity." Reich fought just such a battle with his age.

Through this struggle he finally saw—and saw with blinding clarity—that he had disturbed the sleep of the world more fundamentally even than Freud or Marx had done. Although his achievement was inconceivable without their precepts, he realized that he had disturbed the world not through additions to existing systems of thought but through his own unique perspective, the perspective of basic nature that the core Reich reflected. At last he could distinguish this perspective by means of his struggle, never complete but yet successful, to liberate his natural core self from the dual armor of neurotic bonds inherited from his personal life history and erroneous concepts inherited from his scientific environment.

What should our attitude be toward the emotional life of a man like Reich? As I have suggested, nothing is easier than to distance ourselves from great figures, whether through a negative interpretation or through idealization. Denigration and idealization are twins with the same basic motive: to avoid taking responsibility for the discoveries before us and to avoid taking responsibility for emulating the lives of great individuals. If we find severe flaws in the personality of the "genius," we can look upon him as some kind of genetic freak, closely linked to the madman, whose contributions were almost an incidental offshoot of his weird personality. If we consider the great man a triumphant genius with a basically unflawed personality, we can make small demands upon ourselves since we lack genius and possess flaws. Still another way of dealing with the great man is simply through indifference. One explains his loneliness and suffering through the kind of clichés Reich hated: "A genius is always one hundred years ahead of his time," or, "A genius always meets opposition in his lifetime."

The need for distance from greatness is especially intense when we are dealing with persons who make the implicit demand: You must change your life if you are truly to understand what I have discovered. In his biography of Gandhi, Erik Erikson has commented very well on the various ways of neutralizing such innovators:

> I, for one, have rarely met anybody of whatever level of erudition or information, in India or elsewhere, who was not willing and eager to convey to me the whole measure of the Mahatma as based on one sublime or scandalous bit of hearsay. And some formulas sanctify him in a manner which dispose of a true man just as totally as do the formulas which define him by what he was not—not a saint or not a statesman, not a true Indian or not a literate man. . . . *It is as though a man had passed by who simply made too great demands on all as well as himself and must, therefore, be disposed of somehow.* Thus, the funeral pyre which consumed his remains to ashes often seems to be an elemental act of piety and charity compared to the totem meal by which his memory is now being devoured by friends and adversaries alike; many feed on him, deriving pride from having owned him, from having intelligently disposed of him, or from being able to classify the lifeless pieces. But nobody thereby inherits . . . what held him together and what gave him—and through him, millions—a special kind of vitalizing aliveness which does not seem expendable in this world. (Italics mine.)[21]

Even a balanced biography of Reich, one that would neither glorify nor demean the man, would "intelligently dispose" of him. Psychobiographies in particular can isolate the message of a great person's work and life. It is all too easy to segregate him from the rest of our lives, in the manner of Sundays-only religion. We can admire the great man and see how his achievements reflected the rich texture of his health and illness. Yet we still avoid the full meaning of his life for us.

My aim is to overcome this separation of the extraordinary individual from the rest of us. I find it ironic that psychobiographers so intent upon relating a great man's life to his work rarely give specifics about the relation of their lives to their biographies. Usually they offer a quite general statement of interest and attitude, with some caveats about possible biases toward their subject. They leave aside the details of their own involvement with the person they are portraying, usually on the grounds that the reader is interested in the life of the great individual, not the life of the biographer. In so doing, they behave in a way analogous to the therapist who refuses to disclose much about his or her own feelings and experiences on the grounds that "here—in therapy —we are dealing with *your* problems, not mine."

This will not do. Just as the therapist sees the patient through the prism of his own personality and experiences, just as Reich brought all of his being to his work in a way that the reader needs to know, so I shall bring all of myself to writing about him. Since you, the reader, will be seeing Reich through my eyes as well as your own, it is important for you to know who I am.

This approach is essential not only so that we can try to make explicit the possible sources of distortion in our evaluation, but also so that we—you and I—can apply more effectively the lessons of Reich's life in living our own. Primarily for these reasons, I intend to present in the next chapter an unusually full account of my own background and involvement with Reich. I do not do this simply to help the reader watch for possible biases stemming from my ten years of association with Reich as student, patient, and assistant, and from the kind of transference I had toward him. This is important, but it is only part of the story. For as with Reich, and as with you, my biases are inextricably interwoven with my emotions and my talent. In my understanding Reich and your comprehending him, everything must rest—as it did with Reich—upon what emerges from the interaction between clear and tainted perceptions, upon what emerges from the struggle to see and experience the truth about Reich and about ourselves, free of denigration or idealization.

People often ask why there are so few "objective" studies of Reich and his work by a writer neither strongly for nor against him. They also assume more objectivity on the part of those who did not know him. Although it has merit, this approach contains major oversimplifications. It assumes the possibility of a calm objectivity toward a man whose work is profoundly subversive to much in our usual thinking and feeling about ourselves and the world. Reich and his work touch people with peculiar intensity, whether they knew him or not, whether they are favorably or unfavorably disposed toward the man and his assertions. We can try to overcome the neurotic distortions of even our deep and honest assessments. However, some elements working toward distortion will remain as they remained in Reich. We can only hope to achieve what he achieved: sufficient contact with the core of ourselves so that some of the time at least we can transform our conflicts and permit them to further rather than to impede the quest for truth.

Biographies of Reich as well as commentaries on his work present the danger that both man and work will be seen through a series of distorting mirrors. As I have made clear, distortion is as destructive in the form of deification as it is in slander. To quote James Agee: "Every fury on earth has been absorbed in time, as art, or as religion, or as authority in one form or another. The deadliest blow the enemy of the human soul can strike is to do fury honor. . . . Official acceptance is the one unmistakable symptom that salvation is beaten again, and is the one surest sign of fatal misunderstanding, and is the kiss of Judas."[22]

Reich was well aware that he was a "fury on earth" and of the fate meted out to such furies. Indeed, this very problem preoccupied him during the last years of his life—the danger of his work being transformed into the opposite of what it was intended to be, as he believed had happened to Christianity, Marxism, and psychoanalysis. It was the fear of distortion that led him to specify in his will that his archives should be "stored" for fifty years after his death.

But Reich also had a strong desire for honest scholarship, a wish that caused him in the last years, when he was virtually alone at Orgonon, to spend considerable effort arranging in clear order all the documents concerning his life and work. He often said that he himself was too involved in the events to write the history of orgonomy with sufficient detachment. What he could do was make the evidence available for others.

Reich's hopes have as clear a basis as his fears. For if there is the image of distorting mirrors, there is also the metaphor of the relay race. Great men can hand the torch on and it can then be carried further without having to wait for the next "genius" to continue the line of development.

Whether we do so or not depends a good deal on our "attitude toward greatness."[23] It depends upon whether we can cease to isolate exceptional individuals by defamation, glorification, or even the kind of accuracy that studies only their depth, their talent, their psychopathology, and the outcome of their struggle with competing inner forces, all the while neglecting these same issues within ourselves. There is much to unite us with great individuals, especially our common emotional depth and the effort we can make—as they made—to free it from distortion. In his address to the "Little Man," Reich made this point forcefully:

> You [the little man] are different from the really great man in only one thing: the great man, at one time, also was a very little man, but he developed *one* important ability: he learned to see where he was small in his thinking and action. Under the pressure of some task which was dear to him he learned better and better to sense the threat that came from his smallness and pettiness. *The great man, then, knows when and in what he is a little man. The little man does not know that he is little, and he is afraid of knowing it.*[24]

Reich here is stating an unconventional truth about how great men differ from the rest of us, a truth that helps to lessen the pernicious distance established between extraordinary individuals and other people. But Reich gives only part of the truth. Knowledge of our littleness can pave the way to removing the various methods by which we dispose of great men and their work. Used positively, it can help us to give a real response to their contributions. However, the distance between "them" and "us" consists of more than their awareness of their smallness and our denial of ours. It takes a rare combination of emotional depth, courage, and penetrating intellect to make the great leap forward in human awareness. The critic George Steiner has beautifully appreciated the right kind of distance one should feel toward individuals like Reich, a distance I shall do my best to maintain in dealing with his life and work:

> Where criticism and scholarship invoke instances of the reach of a Shakespeare . . . or a Pushkin, they have to exhibit imperatives of delicacy. They must reflect at every point of style and proposal their sense of the relevant dimensions. They must fall short of their object, but do so *by a distance of incomplete perception* so honestly defined that the object is left at once clarified and intact. The inner lives of Shakespeare and Michelangelo are our heritage; *we feed our smaller sensibilities on their donations and excess.* There can be no other thanks than extreme precision, than the patient, provisional, always inadequate attempt to get each case right, to map its commanding wealth. (Italics mine.)[25]

My Relationship with Reich

I first met Wilhelm Reich in December 1944. Eighteen at the time, I had studied for just a few months at the University of Chicago and was due to go into military service in a week or so. The only works of Reich then available in English were *The Function of the Orgasm* and several volumes of a quarterly journal. Relatively few people, perhaps several hundred, were familiar with his work in the United States. The standard psychiatric opinion of Reich was well reflected by the title of Martin Grotjahn's review in 1943 of *The Function:* "Nuttier Than a Fruitcake."

Most students and teachers at the University of Chicago knew nothing of Reich. But from my readings of what had appeared in English, I was full of enthusiasm and excitement. His whole syndrome of ideas appealed strongly to me: the concept of a deeper, more joyous sensuality; the affirmation of adolescent love life; the linking of sexual freedom with a nonauthoritarian social order; the relationship between emotional suppression and economic exploitation of submissive, "unalive" workers; the sense that "unarmored" man could experience a more vital existence; a psychiatric therapy that dealt not only with psychological complexes but also with bodily rigidities; even the notion of a universal energy identical to the energy that moved in sexual excitation. I found it all intoxicating.

To a somewhat confused, vaguely radical, sexually yearning young man it was indeed heady stuff. I had found what I wanted to do in life—I wanted to be "in orgonomy," as Reich termed his science, to help Reich in his struggles against a malignant world. The fact that he had moved from country to country, persecuted for his beliefs, was all the more enthralling. Here was a hero worth emulating, worth supporting. Here was a vision that involved no "compromise," no petty specialization in rat psychology or the trade-union movement of the nineteenth century. One could enlist in no less than the service of life against death. Little did I realize then how complicated such a service was to be, how far removed from it I was, or how many difficulties there were to be both on my side and on Reich's.

With the intention of preparing myself, I requested an interview with Reich, and this was surprisingly easily arranged. However, when the time came, I was in such a state of nervous apprehension that I was twenty minutes late getting to his home in Forest Hills, about half an hour's ride from New York City. Even in my haste and confusion, I remember being surprised by the ordinary, "bourgeois" appearance of the three-story brick house. I was struck by the idea of Reich carrying out his "cosmic" work in so unpretentious a setting; it might as well have been the home of a moderately successful lawyer or businessman.

A young assistant greeted me, and said that "Dr. Reich" was waiting for me in his basement laboratory. So I went downstairs. I dimly recall many laboratory instruments and devices but was too dazed to note them at the time.

Most striking initially was Reich's appearance. I had expected an academic, professorial-looking person, but the only thing about him typically "scientific" was a white laboratory coat. Otherwise, there was an earthy, almost peasant look to his face. He was ruddy-looking—a redness I later learned was partly due to a skin condition he had long suffered from. His dark brown eyes were mobile and sparkling, reflecting interest and amusement, impatience and friendliness. His smile was unusually open and warm as he reassured me while I apologized for being late.

This description does not do justice to a certain quality of suffering in his face. It was nothing obvious. He did not look at all depressed, nor did he put on any airs; on the contrary, he was remarkably simple and matter-of-fact. But his face looked scarred, as though he had experienced considerable turmoil, and the shock of white hair combined with his expression gave the appearance of a man much older than forty-seven. Twenty years later I would gain some real understanding of the personal tragedies as well as the scientific struggles that had already left their marks on Reich at this point.

He seemed tall to me (in fact, he was 5 feet 10 inches) and there was considerable physical strength in the oaklike frame, combined with a supple quality. The impression of largeness was intensified by his weight. Since 1940 he had acquired a distinct potbelly.

Reich asked me how I "got here." I was muttering something about a taxi when he interrupted impatiently: "No, no, no . . . I mean how did you find out about me?" When I mentioned that my mother had told me about his books, Reich looked down and his mouth fell open, the expression resembling that of a disappointed child. He simply said "Oh," in a crestfallen way, as though he had expected I had heard about him from a more academic or professional source.

Next he asked: "Are you healthy?" I remember being surprised by the question, although he asked it in a matter-of-fact way, as one might say, "How are you?" but with real interest in the answer. I was familiar enough with his writings to know that he was not referring to my everyday health, but was talking about my "genital health," my "orgastic potency." Being fairly inexperienced at the time (as well as inhibited), I replied in an embarrassed way that I didn't know whether I was healthy or not. He tactfully dropped the subject.

One of my special concerns was the sexual problems of other students at the University of Chicago. I raised the subject of how "sick" other people were, prepared to go on at length, but Reich interrupted again: "I know, I know . . . I spent much time with youth in Austria and Germany. Someone should pick up that kind of work again, I am entirely in natural science now." Typically, he was not interested in prolonged descriptions of issues with which he was already familiar or thought he was familiar.

During my stay in Chicago, I had read Korzybski's *Science and Sanity,* a book on general semantics that was causing quite a stir at the time, though one no longer hears much about it today. I told Reich I thought there were many similarities between his "theories" and Korzybski's. His reply came succinctly: "This isn't a 'theory.' The orgone is *burning* in the air and in the soil." He illustrated the "burning" by rubbing his fingers together and gestured toward his laboratory instruments to indicate the concreteness of his work. (I was later to become familiar with Reich's rubbing his fingers together whenever he wished to demonstrate something quite realistic as opposed to "words" or "theories" unsupported by facts.)

When I raised the practical issue of how I should go about preparing for work in orgonomy, Reich surprised me by questioning the whole idea. He would advise me, he said, "not to go into the work, it is too dangerous, there is too much opposition, the work is very difficult." Of course, this kind of warning only increased my zeal.

We talked for half an hour or so. Soon after I had gone upstairs, he followed, stood in the doorway, and asked his assistant to record my name and address in his files. I was very pleased that he had taken this step. Perhaps he would permit me after all to enter this "dangerous" field. I remember staring, full of admiration, as he stood there in the doorway. He noticed my stare, then assumed a "back to work" expression and returned to the basement. Later he commented that he had recognized the mystical, religious look in my eyes, the "burning eyes" he had seen so many times when people first made contact with him and his work. That same adoration, he was to say later, would often turn to hatred when the longing to be "saved" by Reich was disappointed.

At the time I knew nothing of all this. I only wanted to help, as I thought.

And I left his house exhilarated—I would convince him of my suitability. Meanwhile, I would use my Army time, my work with death, to prepare for the future: for work with life, with Reich, with "orgastic potency" and "orgone energy," no matter what the "armored" people thought or however much they scorned these most important truths.

I have not yet made clear why Reich meant so much to me. Let me do so, first, by giving some of the relevant events from my background, then making explicit their connection to my interest in Reich.

It all began with my mother. In 1931, when she was twenty-six and I was five, my mother had a psychotic breakdown. She never fully recovered, although when not under stress she could function fairly well. In any case, children cannot comprehend madness in a parent. For me she was an extremely perceptive, erratic, and magnetic person. As a child I worshipped her, was dependent on her, and enjoyed making her happy. Retrospectively, I know that somewhere I also felt exploited by her, as she dragged me into one or another of her obsessions while I often yearned for a more normal life.

Let me speak of her obsessions. The first and most enduring one concerned her "dream," as she called it. The dream occurred during her psychiatric hospitalization, which lasted two years. The main themes of her psychosis involved an apocalyptic destruction of the "present order" (capitalism) through a big war, from the ashes of which a "new order" would emerge that was economically Communist and psychologically "free."

Certain aspects of my mother's dream were elastic. She would incorporate current political events to give more up-to-date, factual body to the drama of the dream. But one never-changing detail concerned the mechanism through which immortality was achieved. Immortal life resulted from scientific study of the orgasm. More precisely, it resulted from an "experiment" on sexual intercourse (masturbation would also suffice), in which a "chemical in the blood" was "isolated" during the "acme of orgastic experience."

I put my mother's phrases in quotes because she used them, or ones similar, in the letters she wrote to people like A. A. Brill (the first English translator of Freud) and Alfred Kinsey. Sometimes she managed to have interviews with these people, who were intrigued by her letters. I remember her vividly imitating Brill, then in his seventies, as he humorously made clear that he was "too old" to participate directly in any experiment.

My father disliked hearing my mother relate her dream at almost every social occasion; I also did, since children dislike being different. It violated his sense of propriety, which was as strong as my mother's zeal to bate the bourgeoisie. Born around the turn of the century into a poor immigrant family, my father sold newspapers as a child, worked hard, and by the age of twenty-seven, the time of his marriage, was well launched on what would become a successful business career. Seven years older than my mother, he had been attracted to her greater emotional freedom, she to his sense of responsibility.

As I entered adolescence, my problems vis-à-vis my mother's dream were compounded. What was confusing to me was that she entwined within its eccentricity many ideas that were genuinely innovative and that I liked. For example, education in her new world was based on A. S. Neill's books. Few people in Brookline (the suburb of Boston where we lived) were reading Neill in those days. My mother had most of Freud's writings as well as many books on psychosomatic medicine. Everything that seemed to combine radical political change with psychologically oriented programs was exciting to her and she would track it down.

One part of my mother's dream that disturbed me was that under the "new order," she would be in charge of things. In a phrase she liked, she would be the world's "benevolent dictator." She would have a scientist as her right-hand man, who would take care of the orgasm "experiment" and other detailed work. I dimly felt that the role of benevolent dictator would give her on a global scale the kind of power she exercised, not so benevolently, in our home, where my father would usually defer to her wishes in order to avoid "scenes." (Nonetheless, there was always a bond of warmth and support between my father and me, a bond I feared to develop lest I anger my mother.)

When my mother obtained a copy of *The Function of the Orgasm* in 1943 (I was then seventeen), she was certain she had found her scientist, and she met Reich in person shortly thereafter. While he was not particularly impressed by her "experiment," he enjoyed talking with her. Later, he told me she had the kind of schizoid mind he liked; in fact, my mother exemplified several of Reich's concepts. Thus he wrote a good deal about how the schizophrenic perceived a deeper reality than most neurotics, but lacked the capacity to develop his or her insights. Similarly, persons with the kind of mystical attitude my mother had toward his work could easily become "freedom-peddlers"—his term for those who irresponsibly advocated his ideas without implementing them effectively.

In her turn, my mother was impressed by Reich but also put him down. He was a "peasant," she said. She felt he was not happily married and that he himself suffered from "sexual stasis," a condition he wrote a good deal about. She clearly thought he would be much happier with her, that he desired her but was "afraid" of her. Still, it was with a significant look that she gave me *The Function* to read, as though it provided the ultimate confirmation of her dream.

I read it with great enthusiasm for a different reason. Reich seemed to be talking about the same terrain—the orgasm—as my mother, but in a far more realistic way. I had always tried to bridge the gap between my mother's imagination and my father's practicality, tried to give a sounder cast to her wilder notions. In my mind, at first quite dimly, the idea began to form that in Reich I had a valuable mentor in this task, that he represented the synthesis between my mother's penchant for the new and daring and my father's feeling for reality and genuine achievement. Also, it was not just Reich's work, it was

Reich himself—his example, his heroism, his manliness as I somehow gleaned it from his writings—that was important to me.

In the fall of 1944 I attended the University of Chicago. There I fell in love, unhappily as it turned out. I studied Reich's writings all the more intently in an effort to understand my own experience. I spent the Christmas vacation at home, prior to entering the U.S. Air Corps; it was then that my first interview with Reich took place. I remember looking over family albums at the time and being struck by pictures of myself around four or five, how serious I looked but how genuinely happy when I smiled. I noticed that my expression later became harder, more remote and vague. I did not then connect this awareness with something Reich emphasized a great deal: how after the kind of sorrow ("heartbreak," to use one of his favorite words) I experienced when my mother was hospitalized, one numbs oneself and ceases to feel strongly. Nor did I have any idea of the pain Reich himself experienced in childhood in connection with his mother's suffering.

I noticed something else from the snapshots. Just as I looked better before she entered the hospital, so too did my mother—slimmer, kinder, more beautiful, less embittered. However, only later could I dare to face just how radically her behavior changed after hospitalization, how alternately seductive and brutal she could be. With Reich I was to experience a similar kind of alteration between extreme warmth and rage, though in his case the reasons for the change were more rational than any of my mother's.

As a child I took emotional-sexual life very seriously, "falling in love" around age five with another five-year-old. This seriousness diminished in adolescence. Under the impact of entangled feelings toward my mother, I became more evasive, frightened, guilty, and cynical in general and over sexuality in particular. At the same time, I yearned to recapture the lucidity and directness of my early childhood. Both my clarity and my confusion guided me toward Reich. I hoped he would disentangle the former from the latter.

In January 1945, I welcomed the enforced discipline of military life as an opportunity to prepare myself for work with Reich. I also read with an intensity I had never known before or since. What added zest to the reading was that I was beginning to incorporate what I read into a kind of Reichian world view. I felt that through Reich I understood fully what Nietzsche meant when he wrote: "All the regulations of mankind are turned to the end that the intense sensation of life may be lost in continual distractions."

Since 1942, Reich had been publishing his quarterly, *The International Journal of Sex-Economy and Orgone-Research*. Then, in 1945, *The Sexual Revolution* and *Character Analysis* both appeared in English. I waited breathlessly for these publications, and my reading of Reich was now more systemic and intense. Above all, working hard and living simply in the Army, I felt that I was practicing what Reich wrote about and was less caught up with my mother's fantasies. Still, I experienced great gratitude toward her for putting me in touch with this "new world."

The war ended in August 1945, but I was not discharged for another year. On a furlough I saw Reich a second time. My plan was to move to New York as soon as I was discharged, work for him, and go to school at night. He advised me to get my college degree first. I said there was so little time, thinking of the social revolution I believed to be imminent. I would help to bring about radical change, a kind of Lenin to his Marx. (Later, when I related this to him, he asked ironically: "And who will be Stalin?") So I was surprised when he leisurely waved his arm; he did not seem to share my urgency. Around this time I applied to Harvard and was accepted.

During the same furlough I began to make contact with others who were interested in "the work." I met a woman I shall call Jane Gordon, Reich's assistant and the young person I had seen during my initial visit. At that time I was keenly interested in having a relationship with a girl who was in "the work." Unfortunately, Jane was married, but she invited me to come and meet her husband, Sam (as I will call him).

When I visited them at their apartment, they were both cordial and we chatted as they waxed their skis. I remember their offering me a drink. I didn't accept—drinking was neurotic, I thought—but they told me that the Southern Comfort had been a Christmas present from Reich. I was surprised that Reich did such mundane things as give presents of whiskey for Christmas.

Jane offered me a cigarette. I explained that I thought "smoking dulled one's senses." She said spiritedly that "Dr. Reich" smoked a great deal and she didn't know of anyone with keener senses than he. I mulled that over. Sam talked about how he and Jane had lived together before getting married, something, he said, that Reich approved of. According to Reich, if the relationship went well, sometimes people liked to have the marriage license to look at on the wall. Here Sam imitated Reich imitating the person who felt proud of his marriage license on the wall.

During the summer of 1946, just before being discharged, I spent another furlough week in Rangeley, Maine. The Gordons, with whom I had by now become friendly, were running a camp for children of parents interested in Reich's work. Reich became angry at Sam, thinking he was exploiting the connection through Jane in order to make money. Jane was very upset. I remember discussions with them in which I talked enthusiastically about Reich's work. Jane would say: "The work is one thing, the man another."

In September, I took a room near Harvard. Originally I enrolled as a pre-med student with the vague idea of becoming an orgone therapist, as Reich called his therapy. However, since I was entirely unsuited to either physics or chemistry, I dropped both subjects after a few weeks. I did learn German with the express wish of reading Reich in the original.

In those days I worked hard on working, on noting what was in the way, what was blocking me. Rainer Maria Rilke's letters about Rodin's mode of work were a constant inspiration. So was Reich, whose picture hung on my wall: he represented a "benevolent presence," to use Erik Erikson's felicitous phrase. When my nerves were shattered through some "wasteful" experience or disagreeable talk with my mother, I would sink into the quietness of my room, review in my mind the life and work of my hero, begin to work myself, and feel at peace again.

While anxious to have therapy with Reich, I also wished to be my own therapist, to do it myself. To this end I had enlisted a fellow student and friend whom I will call Jack, so that we could practice therapy on each other. First, he lay down and I helped him breathe and express emotions. Then he would do the same with me. I would bring back information as to how Reich carried out his therapy and we used it in our sessions. My visits every other month or so to New York to see people connected with the work were extremely important. There I did my "field research" on Reich the man and on his work, especially his therapy.

Each time I arrived at Grand Central Station, I was in a high state of excitement. I stayed with a friend who lived in a cold-water flat on the East Side. A kindly, charming person, he was in therapy with Reich. He kept telling me how hard it was, how Reich kept working on what was phony in his character. But hard as Reich sounded, he also appeared—in this person's account—a quite human therapist. While analyzing the patient's affectations he also acknowledged his own pettiness—for example, how as a lieutenant in the Austrian Army during World War I he had sometimes worn a captain's insignia to impress girls on furlough.

I also liked Reich's exchange with a female patient. He told her: "You have a mask." The patient replied: "You have a mask, too, Dr. Reich." He in turn said: "Yes, but the mask hasn't *me.*" That seemed a vivid way of distinguishing between a rigid, neurotic "character armor" and the more flexible armor of the healthy person, who can open up when he chooses to.

Those were the stories I collected. I sought out people who had contact with Reich and then recorded what they told me, always looking for information that would help me and my friend in our self-therapy. And I tried to find out how Reich lived, apart from how he practiced therapy. I kept regular notes under different headings: "Personal Development," "Armor," "Orgonomic Thinking," "Men and Women." My marks at the university were improving, as were my study habits.

In the late spring of 1947, my mother visited my room in Cambridge. I always felt her presence there as quite alien. The room with its books and papers, its orgone accumulator standing in the corner, represented my defense against her. Her presence meant that she had slipped through the defense. In a matter-of-fact way, she disclosed that she and Jack were having an affair. It had been going on for a few weeks, but they had been waiting for an appropriate time to tell me. I must have looked stunned and hurt—at least that was the way I felt. She asked me why I looked "funny," being quite perceptive. I stifled my resentment. Deeply ingrained within me was the "ideal" that one shouldn't be "jealous" or "against" sexuality. Thus did I rationalize the double betrayal I felt—on her part and on Jack's. The relevance of this incident to my understanding of Reich's life will become apparent in Chapter 3.

In September 1947, an educational conference was being held at the Hamilton School in Sheffield, Massachusetts, a school run by Eleanor and Alexander Hamilton, two educators who had studied with Reich. The star attraction was to be A. S. Neill, a former patient of Reich's and by 1947 his close friend. At this conference I met a woman who at first did not particularly impress me, but as I talked with her more I became quite interested. For one thing—and no small thing to my mind then—Grethe Hoff had been in therapy with Reich. She talked a lot, and I asked her a great deal, about her therapy with Reich. She gave the impression—an accurate one, as it later turned out—that Reich liked her very much. He thought she was quite healthy, she said. She stressed how he could empathize with her deepest sadnesses and longings. She said that when she exhaled in breathing, she could feel the streamings of energy in her genitals and legs. This was something Reich mentioned a good deal in connection with his therapy, but many patients I talked with never seemed to have experienced it. That she had done so impressed me considerably.

I was aware—though I tried to fight off the awareness—that I was way over my head in the relationship. I was twenty-one, Grethe twenty-four. I had barely had one relationship with a woman, she had had many relationships before me. I had never been in therapy, she had been in therapy with Reich. Apart from what I associated with her, I was not at all sure that I wanted *her*. And it became clear after a short while that she not only wanted me but a long-term relationship, something that deep down I knew I wasn't ready for with anyone. Yet at this point I was extremely vulnerable to anything posed as a "Reichian" challenge. One final factor that I was not at all conscious of at the time was that I was coming to Grethe Hoff on the "rebound" from my mother's relationship with Jack.

During the fall of 1947, Grethe continued her social work study in New York while I studied at Harvard, but by January 1948 she and I had begun living together in Boston. She had some concern that living with me unmarried would jeopardize her position legally since she was not a citizen of this country, and a lawyer we consulted heightened our fears. Grethe was very much for marriage whereas I was lukewarm outwardly but in fact dead set against it inwardly. However, my mother strongly opposed it, so in demonstrating my freedom from her, I agreed to get married almost immediately. I did not know then, or admit to myself, that transferring tyrannies is no sign of freedom.

Right around this time, Reich asked if I would translate a German manuscript of his. The manuscript consisted of material that was later published as a series entitled "Orgonomic Functionalism" in a quarterly Reich began bringing out in 1949.*

---

*All of these publications were subsequently burned by the FDA and to this date have not been reissued.

I was very excited by the material and worked hard on the translation, but my relationship with Reich had shifted now. Earlier, I never thought of getting anything directly from him, except his approval. I really *wanted* to help the work, to be part of it. Yet now here I was, in one of Reich's favorite phrases, "giving in order to get," which was not in his eyes or mine a very satisfactory way of giving. I wanted to "get" orgastic potency from him, or what he described as complete surrender in the sexual act. I did not know then that—again using his concepts—one does not "get" a full surrender, one gives it.

In the summer of 1948, I arranged with Reich to work at Orgonon, his research center. Now there was ample opportunity for regular meetings about problems of translation. It was a pleasure to work with him. He was appreciative, generally willing to yield to a better word or phrase when I suggested it, though he could be very adamant at times when he definitely preferred another choice. Always he emphasized sharpness and simplicity of expression; he wanted to "clean" (his word) his writing of all German academic phrases.

I had another motive in translating for him—one that inspired me to work but also to rush the work. I wanted to impress him so that he would take me into therapy. On this issue, he kept me at some distance. He warned that it was not a good idea for me to be in therapy with him at the same time that I was working for him. He suggested that I see another orgone therapist, but I strongly rejected the idea: I wanted therapy from *him.*

About a month after I began working at Orgonon and after repeated requests, Reich agreed to see me in therapy. I was extremely pleased but also apprehensive. I no longer recall the exact procedure around this therapy, although one certainly existed. I would undress completely and lie down on the couch, then Reich would come in from an adjoining room. There was something very definite, marked off, about his entrances and exists.

In the beginning the therapy went quite well. I was extremely impressed by the way Reich worked with my body. He would have me breathe and then keep pointing out the way I avoided letting the breath expire naturally. Sometimes, he would press certain parts of my body, particularly my chest. A few times this was followed by very deep sobbing, crying in a way I could not remember ever having cried before. He would encourage me in an empathic way: "Don't be ashamed of it. I have heard it by the millions. That sorrow is the best thing in you."

He also kept calling attention to my "urgency," my straining after things. He mentioned that it came up in the laboratory often. It wasn't "obnoxious," he said, but it was in the way. He advised me not to have so many "ideals" that I struggled after, but to "let 'it' do it"—by "it" meaning the energy within my body.

The comments on my urgency were linked with the bodily work: "Let your air out. . . . Open your throat. . . . Don't try to 'get' anything or have anything. That is the worst thing in you—your urgency, your wanting."

I found it hard to understand intellectually what he meant by "letting 'it' do itself," but on another level, I knew what he meant. I would shiver to recall how in my lonely Army days and first year at Harvard I could get into the swing of my work if I stayed with it long enough so that it was flowing and coming "by itself." Now I was away from this mood, and desperately eager to solve my sexual problems.

I didn't really tell Reich just how unhappy my marriage was, nor did he explore my growing negative feelings. When I complained that marriage and work didn't go together, he would answer that one didn't have to be ascetic. And when I nostalgically told him how I used to imagine him watching me as I studied intently in my room, he replied in a kindly way: "You were in love with me. Give your genitality to your wife and your work to the Orgone Institute." Once again, I felt the "mandate" to solve my difficult problem, that it was my fault. And, indeed, I would put it that way to Reich. I rarely complained about my wife: making her sound quite attractive, I said I only wanted to be healthier with her.

What really staggered me in therapy was experiencing what Reich called at various times the "vegetative currents," "bio-electric current," and—by 1949—"orgonotic streamings." These currents were often particularly strong after intense sobbing. I would lie there, breathing more easily, and would feel this beautiful sweet, warm sensation of pleasure in my genitals and legs. It was glorious, I had never felt anything like it. I had never read anything about it; with the exception of Grethe and a few other people, I had never heard anyone describe it. I knew there was much about Reich's work that I didn't understand. There was a lot about the man that puzzled and disturbed me, but one thing I was never to doubt again: the sensation of those "currents." If the scientific world had paid so little attention to this phenomenon, perhaps the same held true for yet another. The same energy functioned in the atmosphere, according to Reich, registering on his laboratory instruments, which I had observed but knew virtually nothing about.

One of the problems was that the sensation of vegetative currents did not last long. From today's perspective, I understand more fully what prevents their permanence. I can understand why Reich grew impatient with therapy —it was so difficult, people led such complicated lives. Indeed, during one of my first meetings with him, he had advised me not to become a therapist: "You get caught up with people, you get involved in their lives. When a tree has grown crooked, it will never be straight again. Prevention is what counts."

Reich himself was much less helpful in working with my psychological problems than with my bodily armor. He seemed not to be especially interested in examining my relations with people (Grethe Hoff, or my parents) in great detail except where these linked up with a specific bodily issue, some way I had of blocking the sensations. If things weren't too bad, he was often content to leave them alone, seeming to prefer that life and therapy not be more complicated than necessary. For example, I told him in those early sessions about my mother's affair with Jack. He smiled in an almost embarrassed way, saying: "She shouldn't have done that." But there was something in his manner that did not encourage my continuing. Only much later did I recognize his reluctance to deal with this subject.

Other conversations were bothering me. His explanation of the Sam incident was not fully satisfying. By the time I was in therapy with Reich, the situation with the Gordons had deteriorated further. Sam had gone into therapy with one of Reich's therapists, who after a while had been advised to terminate treatment. When I asked Reich for an explanation of this, his reply was: "He was discharged because he took part in an action against the Hamilton School when he was told not to. We didn't want him and that is our privilege."

Such an explanation was hardly satisfying. Discharging a person from treatment seemed to me a very cruel thing to do, yet I was afraid to argue with Reich lest he kick me out for defending such a person. There was the clear sense that certain subjects were not to be brought up, and Sam was one of them. Wanting to express some of my negative feelings, I made the infelicitous choice of Sam as my mouthpiece. Sam had reported, I said, that Reich had done such-and-such a thing wrongly. I shall never forget Reich's towering rage. His voice boomed out, his skin reddened, he was all harshness. He denied the truth of the accusation and was quite furious at me for reporting it. "If there is one thing I cannot stand, it is hearing that 'so-and-so said.' Don't tell *me* what 'so-and-so' said!"

Still, during that summer, the pace of events was more benign, even though I would occasionally witness Reich's rages in the laboratory.

Much as I deplored Reich's behavior toward Sam Gordon, I did admire his capacity to take strong stands. Sometimes what I regarded as his naïveté was extremely deliberate and self-conscious behavior. For example, that summer he applied for research funds to the National Science Foundation. When they asked for further information, he detailed in a letter how much money he actually put into research while most people just talked, and went on in this vein. He seemed to catch from my undertone that I thought the letter would be ill-received, for his comment was sharp: "We don't care what people think. We are not writing for anybody. That is a very important thing. We are supposed to be different. How are we going to make others different if we become like them? If they can't take it, then it is their problem. It does no good to hide."

In many ways, being with Reich on an almost daily basis led to no disillusionment. Up close he was even more remarkable in the range of his capabilities. Socially he kept a distance, but he was very open about what he felt, and he was very much himself with his small son. I remained intrigued and puzzled by the man. Occasionally, in therapy, I asked questions about his personal life and sometimes he would volunteer information. He was both worried and impressed that I was "terribly young" (that summer I turned twenty-two), but then he was quick to point out that he had been even younger when he first came into contact with Freud. He could be contemptuous too about what he regarded as weakness or timidity. He asked me when I started my sexual life and as I mentioned the (from his viewpoint) rather advanced age of nineteen, he looked a little disgusted. I once asked how he managed to remain "healthy," and he replied that he had had a "remarkable mother," but did not elaborate.

On another occasion, I wanted to find out what had led Reich to discover the muscular armor. Had he been armored himself? "No, no," he answered. "I went out to people. I was open, then I met this *wall*—and I wanted to smash it." Generally, Reich would not talk about his own problems except in what might be described as an excess of virtue; for example, he had been too loyal to Freud and Marx. Yet one sensed problems in his background, one had the feeling that his life had been stormy.

Much fascinated me about Reich, in particular that mixture of a very simple human being prepared to do the simplest of tasks, and a grand, remote, lonely person acutely aware of his destiny, of who he was—or at least thought he was. I recall his saying once, more to himself than anyone else, "A person like me comes along once every thousand years."

One further paradox connected with Reich was that the people around him were just ordinary people; they were not "unarmored," "orgastically potent," or anything else special. By and large, as loyal workers they tried to do their best. Often they parroted Reich and were afraid to stand up to him. He in turn "used" them as much as they, in a different way, "used" him, to bask in his reflected glory, to have some sense of being part of great, expanding themes. People would work for him for nothing or for very little recompense. He claimed they were learning a lot, and so they were. He accepted, indeed asked for, considerable financial help from his followers. When people dropped out of his close circle, it hurt him but he went on relentlessly, replacing defectors with new adherents.

So there was Reich, this problematical person, and I was trying hard to understand him, keeping notes on everything, including therapy. One night, late, I remember sitting in the laboratory translating while he was working with his instruments. Half to me, half into the night, he remarked: "When it is late and quiet and lonesome, then it is *good.*" Sometimes on such nights, he would wear a revolver strapped to his waist. The combination of the gun and a bandana tied around his neck made him look like a guerrilla chieftain. He said: "Don't think I am peculiar because I wear a gun on my hip. You will learn about these things after a while."

In the fall of 1948, Grethe and I returned to Boston, Reich to Forest Hills. I continued working part time for him and also remained in therapy, commuting to New York once a week. In January 1949 I was graduated from Harvard, and Grethe from her social work school, so we moved to New York to facilitate my work and therapy with Reich. During the summer I again worked for Reich at Orgonon, though I took a break from therapy.

Throughout this period the various strains with Reich increased. Soon after I resumed therapy with him in the fall of 1949, my treatment, my work with him, and my marriage collapsed. I became acutely aware of many neurotic aspects to all three. I was also furious at Reich for not having seen through my subconscious games of always presenting Grethe Hoff in a favorable light, myself in an unfavorable one. I was furious at his fury as a therapist toward me over the Gordon imbroglio. Now at last my "negative transference," a concept Reich heavily emphasized, fully erupted. Still, I was angry that I had to reach a state of collapse before he could fully accept my hostile feelings.

There were in addition depressed feelings about what I regarded as my failures both as a patient and a worker. I was angry at Grethe, particularly for the pressure she had exerted for our legal marriage. The dream that I had clung to so ardently from my Army days of working with Reich and being with a woman "in the work" had turned, to use Conrad Aiken's description, "to darkness and darkness took my heart."

Separated from Grethe, terminating therapy, and resigning my position, I went home for several months. Slowly my spirits revived. The revival was largely due to a letter from Reich assuring me that the door was always open for my return to orgonomy. He believed, he wrote, that I was "running away" not from him or the work but from myself. His letter filled me with hope for the future. I had handed over to him all my previous work, including my "mistakes," and he still wanted me to return: I had a second chance.

In late May 1950, after a six-month hiatus, I returned to Orgonon, now simply to work with Reich without thought of being in therapy with him. I had the kind of appreciation of life that only a convalescent after a long illness can feel. I remember the summer as golden. Reich was in a very good mood —active, expansive, human. I found it exhilarating to be franker with him than I had ever been, and he appreciated my openness.

During this period I started to keep more systematic notes about Reich and events at Orgonon. Carefully, I recorded much of what he said in the laboratory about science, social events, individuals. He had an unusually vivid and perceptive way of speaking, with far more humor and irony than emerges from most of his writings. I was enchanted by the range and speed of his insights. I did not limit myself simply to recording what he said or what happened, but interpolated my own analysis and connections with insights of others. Reich deeply appreciated my writing and began to refer to me as the "historian" of orgonomy, a role that fitted my own conception of myself.

However, he insisted that *he* should keep my writings, and didn't want me to have a copy. "That's *mine,*" he said, as he touched a pile of my pages. True, a lot of it was what he had said. True, I could understand his concern that some of his latest, unpublished findings, recorded in the notes, would somehow be taken by others. (He always had a "passion for priority.") Still, the notes were my work, and I should have insisted at least on keeping a copy. I should have made it an issue of staying or leaving. But I couldn't—in part because I wanted to be near him, I wanted to understand him. Now, like the rest of the sealed Reich Archives, my notes are not available to anyone except the current executrix of the estate until the year 2007. Thus, I was deprived of the opportunity Reich always said was mine: to work on the notes at Orgonon.

By December 1950, I had achieved a position quite close to Reich. In addition to my historical work, I had a variety of other responsibilities, such as editing the *Orgone Energy Bulletin,* Reich's quarterly publication of the period. I did various kinds of public relations work. I also took on some duties that I should have refused since I was not good at them. As Ilse Ollendorff has noted, Reich was fierce when it came to financial matters. He wanted every bill checked and often felt he was being cheated. I took on some shared responsibility with Ilse for the financial accounts and came to dread the monthly discussion of bills with Reich. In this realm there was a dangerous renewal of my old fear and evasiveness toward him.

Another, more ominous development also occurred that December: Grethe Hoff moved to Rangeley and we resumed our marriage. Once again the triangular, competitive aspects of my relationship with Reich were ignited, though admittedly in less acute form than when I had been in treatment. I gradually became more hidden and "poker-faced," as Reich termed it. The open, free-wheeling exchanges of the summer and fall of 1950 became rarer. Reich in turn reacted to my evasiveness with outbursts of bitter anger, thereby creating a vicious circle.

In May 1952, Grethe and I left Orgonon. My explanation at the time for leaving was that I wanted to continue graduate work in psychology and that my lack of scientific training hindered my usefulness now that the Oranur experiment (involving Reich's work on the poisoning of the atmosphere, to be discussed in detail in Chapter 27) was so much the center of the work at Orgonon. These reasons obtained, but of far greater importance was the deterioration of my relationship with Reich. I felt self-critical about this, but with much less of the anguish experienced when I left in 1949. Also Reich's rages, not only toward me but toward others, were now far more severe. All these factors taken together led me to become emotionally "numb." I left with relief.

But only part of me left. Although I had given up a close working relationship with Reich, I still viewed myself as historian of orgonomy. An essential part of me kept wondering about this phenomenon: How had he become what he was, how much of what he did touched on the truth?

After leaving, I continued finding out about Reich, studying his work and interviewing people about him. And I remained on sufficiently amicable terms that I could attend conferences at Orgonon, correspond with him, and be consulted by him about one thing or another.

However, orgonomy was no longer the sole focus in my life. In 1953 I enrolled in an interdisciplinary Ph.D. program at Harvard University, specializing in psychology and education. My most important experience during this period was working with Daniel J. Levinson on a research project at a small teaching psychiatric hospital affiliated with Harvard, the Massachusetts Mental Health Center. My research was on the personal and professional development of psychiatric residents and, for my doctoral dissertation, the factors leading to "psychological-mindedness" as a personality attribute.[1]

In the course of this work I had the opportunity to study "adult development," in other words, the biographies of young psychiatrists, in a way that utilized both qualitative and quantitative assessments. Like Reich, Levinson also focused on social and intrapsychic determinants of human functioning. My work during those years was to provide a valuable background for the task of writing Reich's biography. However, since the core themes of Reich's work —vegetative currents, orgastic potency, orgone energy—were in ill repute in the academia of the 1950s, I tended to devalue what I was learning in the "establishment." My passion was reserved for my extracurricular life—pursuing the role of orgonomic historian. Nor did I appreciate that I was treated by such mentors as Levinson and the research director of the hospital, Milton Greenblatt, with far more respect for my autonomy and creativity than I had often been by Reich.

In 1953, my wife and I had a son, Peter. In the summer of 1954, we attended a conference at Orgonon. At this time, unbeknown to me, Hoff and Reich expressed what I had long fantasized: a romantic interest in each other. That fall Grethe visited Rangeley, ostensibly to consult Reich about a medical problem, actually to begin a relationship with him. It was not long before she told me about it. Reich also phoned me. He emphasized the independence of my marriage and his relationship with Grethe. The marriage was not good and should end, regardless of what happened between the two of them. Still, our marriage would not have ended at this point had it not been for Reich's reckless action. Our son had become an important bond between us. Whatever the problems, we had consoled ourselves that our marriage was better than many; above all, I did not want to lose our infant son.

At the same time, long dissatisfied with my marriage, I saw in the new development an opportunity to begin my personal life anew. This prospect did not mitigate my sense of hurt and betrayal at the hands of Grethe and, especially, of Reich.

Grethe, too, was experiencing conflict about actually ending the marriage and joining Reich, a step he urged with his usual importunity. Finally, in December, she joined him, taking Peter with her. The subsequent evolution of the relationship between Reich and Hoff is described in a later context. Here, to complete my personal involvement in the long-standing triangle, two further incidents are significant.

In June 1955, Grethe wanted to resume our marriage but I did not. By this time I had entered a new, more satisfying relationship. Still, I felt flattered and somehow "victorious" over Reich that she wanted to return.

At a conscious level at least, Reich and Hoff's relationship had in no way lessened my motivation to be an orgonomic historian. Indeed, in the late spring of that year I had begun working for Reich once more, now on a part-time basis from Boston with occasional visits to Rangeley. Yet the personal events had their impact on the relationship. In August, during a work discussion, Reich brought up his concern that Hoff was "running" from him. ("Running" was one of Reich's favorite words—one "ran" from the depths, from strong feeling, from truth.) He asked me in a quite open, human way whether she also "ran" when she was with me. I replied: "No, she had what she wanted." Consciously, I meant that she had a lifestyle with me she had liked, that she feared the challenge Reich represented. However, there was also undoubtedly an element of superiority to Reich in the remark: she preferred *me*.

In any case, Reich took it that way. I recall his looking very hurt and angry. For a period of a month or so, he attacked me as he never had before —bitterly, relentlessly, often unfairly. Under this barrage I resigned my position. But it did not take long for our relationship to be sufficiently cordial that I once again began attending various meetings, now centered on his legal battles with the Food and Drug Administration.

I was still plagued by an intense sense of disparity between my commitment to orgonomy and my desire to pursue academic training. There was difficulty in completing my Ph.D. dissertation, so in 1956 I went into psychoanalysis. I learned a great deal from analysis about my neurotic bondage to Reich. I learned far more than Reich had ever taught me about what my parents had meant to me. I was able to complete my dissertation and involve myself more actively in the "non-Reichian" world.

However, whereas my analyst had a keen eye for all of Reich's problems with me and mine with him, he seemed blind to Reich's unique contributions and my appreciation of them. He behaved as though I were temporarily hallucinating when I talked about "the streamings" of "orgone energy." His lack of understanding in these matters added to my sense of disloyalty to Reich in being in analysis at all: analysts almost to a person believed the "late Reich" was insane. My guilt was enhanced when in 1957 Reich died in prison while I was on the couch analyzing my conflicts with him. But in another sense I did feel "loyal" to Reich (it has remained a continuous problem to be fundamentally loyal to myself) because I intended to make use of the analysis to fulfill my aim of understanding him and our relationship.

Between 1964 and 1975, I was on the faculty of Tufts Medical School, and engaged in research and education at Boston State Hospital, where Greenblatt was now superintendent. Here I had the opportunity to study closely different styles of leadership, a subject relevant to my later examination of Reich as a leader.[2] I also had the opportunity to learn more about the practice of psychoanalytically oriented psychotherapy, the verbal side of therapy, which Reich underemphasized.

The movement toward healing my split between "Reich" and "the world" was further accelerated by social and therapeutic developments of the 1960s. The cultural revolution of those years—more affirmative attitudes toward sexuality, the "new left," and the rise of "body therapies"—led to a more positive appraisal of Reich. True, many of the essentials of his thought were still ignored, but he was no longer so readily dismissed as psychotic. Universities and hospitals as well as "counter-cultural" groups now invited me to give talks on his work.

I did not identify myself as a "Reichian" therapist because I had never been trained to be one, though it was clear that my therapeutic work was heavily influenced by Reich. Thus, with the growing interest in Reich, my practice evolved and became deeply satisfying to me as a way of making "real" at least some of what I had learned from Reich and as a way of integrating into his concepts more insight-oriented techniques I had learned since leaving Reich. By 1975, I was in full-time private practice.

Full-time except for one major commitment: in 1971, a publisher had asked me to write a biography of Reich. I accepted with enthusiasm. I had no idea at the time that the task would take me ten years. Part of that period was devoted to the actual task of research and writing. A more considerable part was devoted to sifting out once again my own attitudes toward Reich's work and person. Not only did I have to struggle to evaluate the scientific evidence, I had also to deal with what I had noted so often in myself and others, the tendency Reich described as "running" from deep emotions. Just as in treatment with him, the "streamings" could be the clearest reality one day and a distant memory the next, so in writing about his work, periods of appreciating the significance of his efforts alternated with their appearing as "unreal" as my mother's "dream" of sex and immortality.

As for Reich the man, in writing the book it took me a long time to begin to appreciate the magnitude of his duality across the span of his life—the extraordinary mixture of greatness, pettiness, and vindictiveness—just as earlier it had been hard for me to comprehend its expression in his relationship with me. I could not seriously confront him without understanding my own duality. Conversely, without studying his work and personality, I doubt that I could have begun to see the full extent of my own complexity. The problem has been well expressed by Leon Edel, the great biographer of Henry James:

> I am sure that if someone were to attempt to study the psychology of biographers, he would discover that they are usually impelled by deeply personal reasons to the writing of a given life. . . . Another way of putting it might be to say that the biographer must try to know himself before he seeks to know the life of another; and this leads into a very pretty impasse, since there seems to be considerable evidence

that he is seeking to know the life of another in order better to understand himself.[3]

As Edel suggests, there is no complete way around this dilemma. A starting point is to make the impasse as explicit as one can; this I have tried to do. I have also followed Reich's advice to me for historical work, "Don't leave yourself out," meaning that I should make clear my own values, biases, emotions, and the like. But Reich, who could be profoundly dialectic in his thought, gave me another, only seemingly contradictory bit of advice, "Be a fly on the wall," meaning that I should leave my own ego out. To this end I have placed my emotional-subjective involvement in Reich's work and person here in this chapter, so that I can turn now to a more systematic biography and do my best to be that "fly on the wall."

PART II

The Development of the Mission: 1897-1920

3

Reich's Childhood and Youth: 1897–1917

Wilhelm Reich, son of Leon Reich and Cecilia (née Roniger), was born on March 24, 1897, in the part of Galicia that then belonged to the Austro-Hungarian Empire. He was undoubtedly born at home, the custom at that time and place. He once mentioned with some pleasure to his daughter that his head had been massaged and molded after birth, in the course of which there had been some sutures.[1]

Soon after Reich's birth his family moved to the small town of Jujinetz in northern Bukovina, a province of the Austro-Hungarian Empire named after the rich beech trees dominating the forested terrain. Reich's father, Leon, had decided to become a partner of his wife's uncle, Josef Blum, who owned an estate of two thousand acres. Leon gradually took over sole control of the cattle farm on the land, while Blum went on to become a multi-millionaire in other enterprises.[2] A second son, Robert, was born to Leon and Cecilia in 1900.

We know a good deal less about Reich's mother than we do about his father. Only nineteen at the time of Wilhelm's birth, Cecilia appears from photographs to have been considerably younger than the father, though I could not determine his birth date. One family member estimates that Leon was ten years older than his wife.[3] Reich always described his mother as "very beautiful," though this is not apparent from the extant photo. It was clear that he preferred her to his father, a much sterner, more authoritarian person. When the young analyst described his complex family dynamics in a disguised self-history, he wrote of his parents:

He [Reich] was brought up very strictly by his father and always had to accomplish more than other children in order to satisfy his father's ambition. From his earliest childhood, he had tenderly clung to his mother who protected him from the daily outbursts of the father. The parental marriage was not happy for the mother suffered horribly from the father's jealousy. Even as a five- and six-year-old he had witnessed hateful scenes of jealousy on the father's part, scenes which even culminated in the father's violence toward the mother. He took the mother's side which is readily understandable since he himself felt under the same whip as the mother and he deeply loved her.[4]

Later in the same article, he reported that Leon in his jealous rages would accuse his wife of being a "whore."

With a few exceptions, Reich spoke positively about his mother throughout his life. Indeed, according to his third wife, Ilse Ollendorff, Reich idealized his mother, always citing her cooking as a model that Ilse could not reach.[5]

Reich's view of his father, however, seems to have changed considerably over the years. As a young man, he was quite critical of him. In several places in his writings he indirectly alluded to the father's authoritarian ways, and used to speak bitterly about him to friends. But toward the end of his life, Reich's attitude softened, and without even mentioning the more somber aspects, he highlighted Leon's positive attributes. Reich took great satisfaction in the fact that his father was not religious, aside from some ritual Jewish observances to appease more orthodox relatives; that Leon was cosmopolitan in orientation and modern-minded in his farming practices; that he was a working property owner, not a "parasite." In later years Reich stressed that his mother, too, was very active on the family estate, a leader who helped organize the women's work on the farm just as the father directed the men.[6]

Reich's feelings toward his father—both the critical ones of his youth and the more positive later ones—are supported by his sister-in-law, Ottilie Reich Heifetz, whom I had the good fortune to interview at length in 1971. In her seventies then, Ottilie had known Reich's brother Robert since 1915, and was his wife from 1922 until his death from tuberculosis in 1926. She had met Wilhelm, or Willy, as he was always called in those days, when he was in Vienna in 1917 on a furlough from the Army, and until 1930, they were good friends as well as in-laws. In addition, Ottilie knew Reich's maternal grandmother, another source of information about Reich's family origin.

Robert was as reluctant as Willy to speak much about his early family life, referring to it on several occasions as "unhappy." But what he and the grandmother told Ottilie generally confirms Reich's account. Ottilie pictured the father as extremely clever, a vigorous, fascinating, and very dominating man, given to outbursts of temper. He appears to have had a highly possessive attitude toward his young wife that today would be termed male-chauvinist. Ottilie recalls Robert relating how his father once hit Cecilia for not having the dinner ready on time. His possessiveness is perhaps intimated at the time of the engagement to Cecilia: her mother had wanted to give Cecilia a family diamond on the occasion of her wedding, but Leon insisted on giving her his own jewelry.

This incident may reflect Leon's concern over the possible influence of Cecilia's mother on her. Ottilie described Willy's grandmother as a very intelligent, snobbish, dramatic, and meddlesome woman. She seems regularly to have been at odds with Leon, and her visits to the Reich home were a constant source of tension and trouble, since she appears to have been quite capable of standing up to Leon and frequently did so, particularly when Leon and Cecilia quarreled. In one of his few reported criticisms of his mother, Willy was later to describe her as a "silly goose" because she allowed her mother to influence her so much; he, too, disliked his meddling grandmother.

However much the grandmother may have contributed to the family tension, there appears to have been a good deal without her. In a telling anecdote, Robert mentioned to Ottilie at the time of the birth of their own daughter that he wanted her to feel free as a child to speak up, indicating he had never had such freedom. And whatever Leon's oppressiveness toward Robert, it was worse toward Willy, since Robert believed he as the second son was spared some of his father's strictures.

Another story of Ottilie's is revealing. Both brothers were prone to temper outbursts and when one of them became very furious, the other would shake a finger at him and say: "Just like Father."

Relations between the brothers themselves seem also to have been complex. Reich rarely spoke of his brother. Indeed, some of his old friends did not even know that he had a brother. On the other hand, Ottilie feels that in the period she knew them both there was a good deal of affection between them, even if it was mingled with competitive elements. She describes Robert as a gentler, more reasonable person than Willy. In another story that says something about their relationship as well as their feelings toward Leon, Ottilie recalls Willy bitterly criticizing their father: "Father always had to have his own way on the farm." Robert corrected the "always," recalling a time when a foreman had sharply disagreed with Leon. Robert had expected his father to punish the man severely for such independence but, to his surprise, Leon replied quietly: "He has a point." In later years, Reich was to value certain co-workers who possessed this capacity to see "both sides," though he could tease the same people as mercilessly as he must have teased Robert. Once, when a valued associate bristled under such teasing, Reich caught himself up short and said: "I am always the older brother," implying he was aware of his bullying tendencies.[7]

In the family legends, Willy was the more reckless and mischievous son whose misdeeds got him into trouble with his father. Once, Reich either rode a horse before it was broken in or prematurely put his younger brother on a horse. In any case, his father was furious and Robert tried to protect Willy from the paternal spanking.

So far, most of these anecdotes have painted the father in a negative, oppressive light. However, judging from the extent that Reich identified with his father, he must have loved as well as feared and hated him. I have already mentioned Reich's pride in his father's progressive thinking on cultural and business matters. Reich also seems to have very much taken after his father in his excellence at "running things." Indeed, at Orgonon he took pleasure in managing all kinds of practical matters from construction to the selling of timber.

If Leon was oppressive, he was also busy, and Reich appears to have had many opportunities for unsupervised play. He enjoyed farm life—the animals, nature, and his peasant nursemaids. In his later, somewhat idealized memories of his childhood, he referred with a good deal of positive feeling to the Austrian country life—hunting, fishing, riding, and all kinds of interesting visitors to the family estate.

Socially, the long arm of their father was often felt. Reich was not allowed to play with peasant children nor with Yiddish-speaking Jewish children. The father appears to have been socially very ambitious, consorting with government officials and other high-level persons, but Willy's opportunities for playing with peers were scarce. The feudal quality of the life is further revealed by a story Reich told his second wife, Elsa Lindenberg. As a child he was not permitted to take part in village dances. But one night, while he was watching the dance, a peasant boy threw a stone at him. Willy told his father and Leon hit the boy's father. So, quite early, Reich was exposed to the brute power not only of the father in the home but of the property owner in the community, and he experienced both in ways that would mark him.[8]

Given Reich's later interests, it is not surprising that he paid a good deal of attention to his own sexual history. In this area he seems to have had a good deal of freedom, something not uncommon for children who were much in the care of peasant help. He remembered as a boy of four sleeping in the servants' room when his parents were away. On several occasions, he overheard or witnessed intercourse between a maid and her boyfriend. In the course of these experiences, he asked the maid if he could "play" the lover. He stressed to one informant that she permitted him to do so in a very helpful way. Without stimulating him actively, she allowed him to move on top of her.[9] Whether this happened once or often is uncertain. But Reich clearly attributed great importance to his relationship with this peasant girl. He once said that by the time he was four there were no secrets for him about sex, and he related this clarity in part to his sexual play with his nursemaid.

He also related it to his general interest in farm life and to particular experiences he had with a tutor. Thus, Reich wrote sometime around 1948:

> WR's interest in biology and natural science was created early by
> his life on the farm, close to agriculture, cattle-breeding, etc., in which
> he took part every summer and during the harvest. Between his eighth
> and twelfth years, he had his own collection and breeding laboratory

of butterflies, insects, plants, etc. under the guidance of a private teacher. The natural life functions, including the sexual function, were familiar to him as far back as he can remember. That may very well have determined his later strong inclination, as a biopsychiatrist, toward the biological foundation of the emotional life of man, and also his biophysical discoveries in the fields of medicine and biology, as well as education.[10]

The social status of Reich's family combined with the isolation of farm life may have helped Reich educationally, since it permitted him private tutors during his elementary school years rather than having to attend a more rigid school. Judging from Reich's recollection of his "breeding laboratory," at least one of his tutors was an imaginative teacher. (Just how many tutors there were is unclear.) Robert remembered particularly a Dr. Sachter as a remarkable, creative teacher. Ottilie quotes Robert as saying that Dr. Sachter stimulated a "ferocious hunger for knowledge" in the two brothers.

How long Reich was taught at home is not clear. He has written that he was privately educated between the ages of six and ten, and that he attended a gymnasium in Czernowitz between the ages of ten and eighteen. However, since the gymnasium was located several hundred miles from Reich's home, it is possible that he continued to be tutored for several years past the age of ten, going to the gymnasium once a year to take exams. At least Ottilie recalled hearing that something like this may have happened.

The Tragedy, the Curse, and the Origin of the Mission

It is hard to say how unusual Reich's childhood was until the age of about twelve. An authoritarian father and a younger doting mother would not have been so remarkable for that era. However, there seems to have been a degree of family tension beyond the "normal" range, stemming from the father's jealous rages and his high expectations for his children.

The combination of a creative tutor, the young Reich's own zest for learning, and the opportunities afforded by farm life may well have stimulated Reich's intellectual curiosity to an unusual degree. In any case, it is worth noting that his interests as a child seem to have been more scientific than literary. He was not especially shy and bookish, as one might expect from a "mama's boy." Indeed, his extroverted interests appear to have had a good deal in common with those of his father.

At about the age of twelve an event—or a series of events—happened that would radically influence Reich's future. Before describing the crisis, something should be said about how Reich disclosed it. First, he told several people. The ones I talked with were all women; but there were many others, men as well as women, who knew Reich very well, to whom he never mentioned these events. Those he did tell, he pledged to secrecy.

Secondly, the dramatic means of disclosure was also shrouded in secrecy. In late 1919 or early 1920, when he was about twenty-two or twenty-three and already a practicing analyst, Reich wrote his first published article, "Ueber einen Fall von Durchbruch der Inzestschranke Pubertät" ("The Breakthrough of the Incest Taboo in Puberty").

In this article, Reich wrote as though he were treating a patient who illustrated certain psychological mechanisms. However, there can be little doubt that the "patient" is Reich himself, especially since many years later Reich told his elder daughter that the article was a self-analysis.[11] The crucial details coincide so exactly with what Reich told others that one cannot doubt its essential autobiographical authenticity.

Reich's disguise worked. With the exception of his daughter, no one I have talked with knew this article to be autobiographical. Indeed, most people did not know of its existence, since it was published in a rather obscure sexological journal whereas Reich's other early articles appeared in psychoanalytic periodicals. Finally, while Reich faithfully listed the article in his bibliography, he never referred to it in his later writings, nor did he mention it orally to my knowledge. His attitude toward this publication was clearly different from his attitude toward other early writings that he would frequently cite or mention.

To turn to the article itself, Reich declares he is presenting the case because it illustrates in an unusually clear way the breakthrough of incestuous wishes into consciousness in puberty. He describes the patient as a twenty-year-old man, a student at a technical school. This is one of two disguises, aside from the format used in the article, for he himself was a medical student at the time. The other is that he describes the patient as having "four sisters," whereas Reich had only one brother. Interestingly enough, at one point in the narrative he slips in a reference to the patient's "younger brother."

The patient had sought analysis because he suffered from states of depression and a tendency to ruminate, in which he would make a "huge case" out of "little insignificant things." In the report, Reich as analyst writes that the patient broke off treatment after exactly four weeks at the point where it was necessary for him to verbalize certain painful events that had occurred in puberty.

Reich then has the patient send the analyst a lengthy letter describing on paper what he could not say in person. Because of the importance of the incidents, I shall quote from this "letter" in some detail. The analyst opens with an introductory paragraph:

> "The point" at which the analysis broke off after so short a time because of the patient's conscious inhibitions, concerns a relationship which developed between the patient's tutor and his mother, and

which the son observed from its beginnings. Following a lengthy description [in the letter] of the mother's beauty, he [the patient] writes about this relationship.

He then goes on to describe the entire incident in letter form:

N (name of tutor) began to court her, stimulated by walks they took together. He apparently became ever bolder as he recognized how things were going—the jealous scenes, etc. between my parents, and the fact that mother liked him. At the beginning I was not completely clear about the developing relationship. But I began to follow them when I noticed mother going into his room when father napped after lunch. In part I was erotically curious, in part I was filled with fearful thoughts that father would wake up. And from then on I played *spy* and *pursuer,* but at the same time also *defender* (italicized by me—the analyst) against any surprises from father. I cannot clarify further the reasons for my behavior. Either it was unconscious hatred against my father or sexual titillation to be aware of such stunning secrets about which my father remained ignorant. I believe that both factors were equally responsible for my behavior.

The relationship between my mother and tutor grew ever deeper; not a day passed in which they did not seek and find the opportunity to be alone.

This state of affairs lasted about three months. Their meeting always took place after lunch and was limited to a few minutes. I did not think of the possibility of a sexual relationship. But one day I also became certain about that. Father had gone away at about six o'clock. Mother had again gone to N and remained there a very long time. I waited the whole time outside the room, struggling with the decision whether to intrude or to tell father. A vague something held me back. When mother emerged from the room, with flushed cheeks and an erratic, unsteady look, then I knew that it had happened, whether for the first time I naturally could not decide. Crying to myself as I stood in the corner, shielded by a screen, I waited to surprise my mother, but that did not happen, to the unhappiness of all of us. For I am convinced that my surprising her right after the deed would have brought my mother to her senses and even at that late date, would have saved the marriage of mother and father. That was the only possible hope.

What held me back at the time, I am not able to say, but at the same moment there arose in me both sympathy with my father and the desire to leave with my lips sealed. (I was about twelve years of age.)

Shortly after Christmas father went away for three weeks and I experienced the most horrible, the most upsetting events, which burned themselves deeply into my feelings and thoughts.

Mother slept, as always during father's absence, in the last bedroom on the corridor. After that came our room, then the dining room, and then his [N's] room. Right on the first night (I was so tense I had not closed my eyes) I heard my mother get up and—the horror grabs me by the throat!—heard her slippered walk and saw her, clad only in a nightgown, pass through our room. Soon I heard the door of his room open and not completely shut. And then quiet.

I sprang up from my bed and followed, shivering, my teeth chattering from anxiety, horror and cold; I moved right up to the door, which was only partly closed, and listened. Oh horrible memory, which tears my remembrance of my mother to dust, her memory always besmirched anew with dirt and muck! Must I then say everything? The pen bristles, no, my ego, my whole being is against it, and yet I will and must write on.

I heard kisses, whispers, the frightening noise of the bed, and on it lay my mother. And a few yards away stood your son and heard your shame. Suddenly quiet. I had evidently made a noise in my excitement, for I heard calming words from him and then, then again, oh! (The last sentence, especially the last words, written apparently in the highest excitement, with heavy strokes of the pen.)

Only quiet, quiet toward this nerve-shattering tragedy, in order to accomplish the superhuman! To judge objectively! What a mockery! What a resolution!

From that catastrophic night I remember only that my wish at first was to plunge into the room but I was held back by the thought: they will kill you!

I had read somewhere that lovers get rid of any intruder, so with wild fantasies in my brain I slipped back to my bed, my joy of life shattered, torn apart in my inmost being for my whole life!

So it went, night after night; always I slipped back and waited till morning. Gradually I became used to it! The horror disappeared and erotic feelings won the upper hand. And then *the thought came to me to plunge into the room, and to have intercourse with my mother with the threat that if she didn't I would tell my father.*

For my part, I went regularly to the chambermaid.[12]

In giving the patient's sexual history, Reich had earlier commented that the patient had had sexual intercourse for the first time with a household maid at the age of eleven and a half, shortly before he began observing his mother's affair.

Reich next summarizes the "patient's" report of the aftermath of the affair: *"The father apparently discovered it, and the mother committed suicide by taking poison."* Reich does not go into the immediate effect on the patient of the mother's suicide, save to say that "after the death of the mother his relationship with his father improved." The analyst quotes the patient as writing that he became his "father's best friend and adviser."

Reich told other people some crucial details that were left out of the published case history. The most significant concerns how the father found out about his wife's adultery. Reich explained to several persons close to him that *he* himself had told his father.

The version that seems most authentic is that Reich first hinted of the affair to his father.[13] Sternly interrogating his twelve-year-old son, the father was able to force the full story out of him. Leon then took the boy to confront the mother.

How long elapsed between Leon's discovery of the affair and Cecilia's suicide is unclear.[14] Leon appears to have treated Reich's mother very badly after he had found proof of what for years had been his accusation. At one point afterward, Cecilia's mother urged her daughter to take the two grandsons, leave Leon, now even more brutal, and live with her. But this Cecilia could not or would not do. Divorce was not common in her social circle, although it did occur; indeed, the wife of Cecilia's uncle, the wealthy Josef Blum, had divorced him in order to marry another. Later, Robert was struck by the fact that his mother drank a cheap household cleanser, something like Lysol, when there were more efficient agents available. He wondered whether the attempt had not been motivated by the desire to frighten Leon and induce him to stop tormenting her.[15]

If the choice of method was not meant to frighten, it may have been intended to horrify. Cecilia lingered on in great pain for several days. Her mother once again visited the home.[16] What Willy was experiencing we do not know, though we can guess. In the case history, he described how "the patient" had struggled with two impulses: the desire to tell his father, thereby striking back at the mother and the tutor, on the one hand; and, on the other, the desire to protect his mother from his father's revenge. In the kind of compromise Reich was later to study so carefully, he chose to "hint" about what had happened. The results were devastating, and the guilt and remorse he must have felt as a child and a young man can only be imagined. Even into his thirties, Reich would sometimes wake in the night overwhelmed by the thought that he had "killed" his mother.[17]

Following the father's discovery of the affair, the tutor was banished from the home. (What else Leon did we do not know.) Reich tells us little about who the tutor was. From the narrative it appears that he had been in the household only a short time prior to the affair. However, this could be a disguise or a literary condensation. One wonders: Was this the tutor whom the boys found to be such a creative teacher? The same tutor who guided Reich's education in the breeding laboratory between his eighth and twelfth years? (Reich mentioned a private tutor directing his studies in the laboratory, but does not say whether there was one or several tutors.) If so, it was an extraordinary concatenation of intellectual and emotional events: the young Reich is studying the sexual function with a man who has an affair with his mother. In reporting the affair, the child plays a crucial role in the loss of two extremely important people in his life—his mother through suicide, his tutor through banishment. The scientific study of sexuality with the tutor ceases, to be resumed by Reich some years later and never abandoned thereafter.

It is clear that Reich himself felt that the events surrounding his mother's death influenced his later life crucially.[18] The starkly tragic episode could well comprise the stimulus for the development of what Erikson termed "an account to be settled"—one that remains an "existential debt all the rest of a lifetime."[19] Also Reich, like Erikson, was aware that one event or even a cluster of events did not in itself cause the "curse" but rather condensed and intensified pervasive childhood conflicts. Thus, in his self-analysis, Reich carefully noted earlier childhood themes and their relationship to *the* event. As a child, he had witnessed intercourse between his nursemaid and her lover. He recalled noting that his mother would follow his father when he retired for his afternoon nap, and thinking: "Now they must have intercourse."

Moreover, the parental relationship took place in an atmosphere of great conflict and paradox even before the affair with the tutor. The mother slept with the father, but the father accused her of sleeping with others and called her a whore. The mother had intercourse with the father and yet in many ways must have communicated to Willy that he, not the outrageous father, was truly her beloved.

All these themes reappear in a new and shattering form when the affair occurs. Now the mother prefers another over both the son and the father. And however hard it is for a son to accept the sexual claims of his father upon his mother, it is much harder for him to accept her taking a lover, especially a young lover who is close to the boy. The affair not only stimulated into consciousness Reich's incestuous wishes; it must also have provoked in him a deep sense of sexual rejection. At some level the boy Willy must have asked himself: Why did she prefer N. over me? And the answer at some level must have been: Because I am small and inadequate. Understandably, Reich was to show throughout his life an extraordinary competitiveness and a deep sensitivity to put-downs and being made to look "small."

Since the entire incident as well as the family constellation that preceded it help to illuminate so many of Reich's later interests, I shall reserve the main discussion of their significance until they can be more directly connected with his work.

But a few preliminary points should be noted here. First, recalling his memories even from the vantage point of a twenty-two-year-old, Reich tends to blame his mother even more strongly than himself. She should not have had an affair; she "besmirched" herself. True, Reich should have "saved the marriage" by surprising her, but his mother should not have entered the adulterous relationship in the first place. Such emphasis is quite different from the subsequent analysis Reich made of this kind of social tragedy. The role of the authoritarian father, the irrational condemnation of extramarital sexuality, the victimization and persecution of those who break society's sexual laws—all these themes would come later.

Second, Reich follows traditional analytic theory in discussing his own childhood and adolescent sexuality. He focuses on the disruptive aspects of his early sexual experiences, his heightened Oedipal complex, his witnessing the primal scene, his seeing the father pushed aside by the tutor, which impelled into consciousness his own incestuous fantasies—all factors seen as contributing to Reich's conflicts at the time he started his analysis. Indeed, Reich ends the case history by supporting the necessity of the latency period, which presupposes the child's repressing his incestuous wishes through identification with the father. It would take time before Reich became fully aware of the positive aspects of his sexual development and was able to integrate them within his theoretical formulations.

Indeed—and this is my third point—Reich sees, among other sequels of the mother's affair, a profound weakening of the father's authority. Again in the context of the case report, the consequences for the son were negative, awakening his own incestuous hopes. But, for the course of Reich's later development, his not being unduly awed by seemingly strong authority figures was to have its advantages.

Fourth, whatever interpretations one gives, the crisis must have heightened the sense of discrepancy between what Freud called the manifest and the latent and what Reich was later to distinguish as "surface" and "depth." On the surface, the mother was married and belonged to Leon. At another level, in many ways she may well have indicated to her son Willy that she preferred him to his often brutal father. At still another level, she went to Leon, not Willy, for the intimate, exciting, and frightening act of sexual intercourse. And then, as the greatest discrepancy of all, she had an affair with the tutor, pushing aside both the powerful father and the adoring son. These were heavy emotional and cognitive puzzles for a young boy to ponder.

Finally, I would suggest that the crisis and its tragic aftermath markedly increased Reich's sense of guilt and his tendency to look inward, to ponder the deeper meaning of things, particularly emotional relationships. This introspective tendency was combined with a very extroverted, vigorous, practical orientation. The combination was to play its part in some of Reich's remarkable intellectual achievements.

Reich talked relatively little about his early years. But there are a few childhood anecdotes he shared with others, and there is the highly illuminating self-analysis. He wrote or told friends almost nothing about the years between starting at the Czernowitz gymnasium (or secondary school) shortly after Cecilia's death and his entrance into the Army in 1915. Perhaps he was especially depressed during those years and hence did not like to recall them. We cannot say for certain.

We do know that he attended the all-male gymnasium in Czernowitz, which had a Latin and Greek curriculum. He reports that his best subjects were German, Latin, and Natural Science, and that he graduated in 1915 *mit Stimmeneinhelligkeit* (with unanimous approval) on his exams. Later, he spoke with some pride of having had eight years of Latin and Greek, and at times he would show some disdain for those less rigorously educated.[20] Reich had a real affection for certain "old-fashioned" ways, including his traditional schooling. We shall meet this kind of complexity again and again, to the chagrin of those who would prefer a one- or at most two-dimensional hero or villain.

The gymnasium years must have exposed Reich to a wide range of new stimuli. Czernowitz, where he now boarded, was an active, thriving city, the provincial capital of Bukovina, with a population of 100,000. There were four gymnasiums in the city and an excellent university. About one third of the population was Jewish, with many Jewish doctors and lawyers, but few Jewish professors. Anti-Semitism still ran strong in academic circles.

An anecdote Reich told his daughter Eva and which she related to me is telling. In Czernowitz he occasionally frequented brothels and on at least one instance he saw several of his gymnasium professors also at the establishment. Once again apparently stern and demanding male authorities were not so perfect after all.

A student in Czernowitz had the opportunity to see excellent theater. There were Saturday performances that young people could go to at a reduced rate. Ottilie, who also attended gymnasium in Czernowitz a few years after Reich, recalls particularly the happy vacations when she returned to the family's country home, with holiday parties, and sleighing in the winter. Robert commented that such gaiety was not to be found in his home.

During vacations and summers, Reich returned to Jujinetz and helped his father run the farm. Reich mentions his improved relationship with his father in the case history, but we know little of what it was like for him to work with Leon, who was now "completely broken" after the mother's suicide.[21] We do know that Leon placed high expectations on his elder son, but with these expectations went a sense of great privilege. If Leon was the king of the estate, Willy was the "crown prince." Perhaps in Leon's last years he was also preparing Willy to become the real leader. Yet we should remember Willy's recollection of his father as "*always* having to make the decisions."

One incident that reflects the father's concern for his son, but which had unhappy consequences, has to do with Willy's bad skin condition. Exactly when this developed or when it was treated is unclear. When Willy was either a child or an adolescent, his father took him to Vienna for consultation and therapy.[22] Willy stayed at a hospital there for six weeks, but the treatment was of little avail, for he suffered from a skin condition all his life. At some point, perhaps on the Vienna visit, Reich's skin condition was diagnosed as psoriasis.

Sometime during his adolescence Willy received medication that contained arsenic for his skin disease. This kind of treatment is of dubious value, for there are generally side effects such as nausea, bloating, and vertigo; a further side effect is an intensification of the psoriasis. It is possible that this happened to Willy, for in later years he spoke with deep resentment of the treatments, feeling that the medicine had aggravated rather than relieved the illness. Probably his lifelong suspicion of most medications stemmed in part from his experiences with psoriasis. By the time he was twenty-one, those who knew him in Vienna commented on his "acne."

Reich's skin condition may have developed around the time of his mother's death. If so, it would certainly fit psychoanalytic theories of the origin of the illness. These theories posit that psoriasis is psychosomatic in origin— a partial and punitive self-mutilation for some guilt over a real or imagined crime, and also an expression of anger.

Reich's next known trip with his father was under still more unhappy conditions. Sometime during or before Reich's seventeenth year, his father contracted pneumonia. According to both Robert and Willy, he did this deliberately. He took out a large insurance policy, then stood for hours in cold weather in a pond, ostensibly fishing. To die from contracting an illness in this fashion would protect the sons' insurance claim, whereas direct suicide would not.

Leon's illness worsened, developing into TB. Apparently Willy took him either to an Austrian mountain resort several hours from Vienna or to the Swiss Alps for treatment. The father died in 1914 as a result of his illness. (For some reason the boys did not receive any insurance money, and for the rest of his life Reich had a profound distrust of insurance policies, refusing to take out any. He used to say that something in the fine print would always rule out the company's responsibility in an actual claim.)

In the second decade of this century, it was not unusual for a person of seventeen to have lost both parents. However, to have lost both parents in the way Reich did was most unusual. A tragic sequence of events, in which the young man plays an active role, heats to flashpoint the tensions already existent between the parents and their older son. Both parents die by suicide in the aftermath, the mother directly and apparently quite soon, the father indirectly and some years later.

Out of this background, with its parallels to the experience of Dostoevski and Eugene O'Neill, Reich came into young manhood. According to his own account, after his father's death in 1914 he directed the farm himself, without interrupting his studies, until his entrance into the Army in 1915.[23]

It tells us something about Reich's inner resources that he was able to keep functioning effectively, whatever his depression and guilt, after the death of both his mother and his father. Indeed, we can hypothesize that one dominant mode of handling loss for Reich was to throw himself into work, to "keep moving," in a favorite phrase of his. One may also hypothesize that his own guilt and rage connected with the dark tragedies that ended his relationship with his mother, father, and tutor made later enduring relationships, as well as their loss, hard for Reich. A host of other factors connected with Reich's work and the personalities of those he was close to played their part in the painfully disrupted human relationships he was to experience again and again. But from his early traumas he brought a vulnerability—a tendency to repeat his childhood crises in one or another form. In his own mind there was always a question of whom to blame when he and another person or he and an organization quarreled and parted ways. We know that Reich blamed himself heavily, too heavily, for the death of his mother. Afterward, at least in his publications, he was to assign most of the blame to others when things soured, although he would occasionally give glimpses of a dark awareness of his own contribution.

My emphasis at this point, however, is on Reich's capacity to stand on his own after his father's death. From the age of seventeen, he essentially had to manage for himself. The capacity to be independent—an ability Reich was to see as an important attribute of psychological health—was something that he himself gained at a relatively early age. Later in his life, he had the marked characteristic of having to do things himself, of not wanting to be dependent on others. How much this had to do with his identification with his father's mode of functioning, how much with his fear of being dependent after the losses in his life, is an open question.

Even with scant knowledge of the school years, we do know that Reich did other things besides work. In the part of the self-analytic article that deals with his sexual history, Reich mentions that "between fourteen and eighteen, masturbation alternated with sexual intercourse." Incidentally, this sentence immediately follows his description of his first sexual intercourse, supposedly at eleven and a half. The gap in the sexual history between the ages of eleven and a half and fourteen suggests that Reich used the semi-literary form of the article to lower the age for the start of his sexual life. Indeed, he told others that his first intercourse occurred at thirteen. That he should have made this eleven and a half in the self-analysis may be due to several factors. It makes a more dramatic story that he should have had his first sexual relationship at the same time his mother had an affair with his tutor. Then, too, Reich took some pride in the fact that his sex life started early, and the temptation to make it even earlier may have been irresistible. According to Ottilie, Willy in his twenties used to tease Robert for his late start sexually—at fourteen.

Aside from the brothel visits, we know next to nothing of Reich's adolescent heterosexual relationships. One girl almost makes it into reality, but we cannot be sure. Ottilie has a somewhat hazy recollection that when Reich took his sick father away for treatment, he became involved with a cousin, the daughter of Leon's brother, who lived in Vienna. Apparently, the father took with him some jewelry that had belonged to Cecilia. After Leon's death Reich inherited the jewelry and, again according to Ottilie, he disbursed these possessions in a capricious way, giving some of them to his cousin in a vain attempt to win her.

True or not, the story is consistent with the impulsive way Reich in later years could give gifts. There is also a kind of justice that there should have been no lasting material legacy from the tragedy-haunted home. First no insurance, then no jewelry. And, in 1915, the Russian invasion of Bukovina devastated the family estate. If after the mother's affair with the tutor circa 1909 Reich was caught up in one personal tragedy after another, from 1915 on he was caught up in social ones. He had lost his parents; now he lost the estate of which, briefly, he had been the ruler. From being a rich young man, he had become poor. Moreover, before the war's end the whole Austro-Hungarian Empire was to collapse, and the entire way of life that he had known in his formative years—the large farm, the many servants—became a thing of the past.

Reich once told his daughter Eva how war enveloped the family farm.[24] Suddenly in the summer of 1915 the Russians were all around them and the fields were aflame. Reich dashed into the house and saw one of the servants calmly combing her hair. "The Russians are here," he shouted, and they fled. In later years Reich was to keep in mind this image of himself notifying others of dangers they did not know about.

What happened next is obscure. Ottilie believes that both brothers went to Vienna and stayed with Grandmother Roniger. At least she is sure that Robert, only fifteen at the time, was cared for by his grandmother during this period. Perhaps she also helped Willy for a brief time in Vienna before he was mobilized into the Army.

Reich's military years are not well documented. There is no evidence that he experienced them with any particular distaste, at least not until close to the end.

Ilse Ollendorff has gathered together most of the known facts about Reich's Army years:

> There are a few photographs in the archives which Reich some-
> times would look through with us, showing him as a dashing young
> officer in the Austrian Army. He wore a small mustache, and was a
> very handsome young man, indeed. I think on the whole he enjoyed
> his military life. He was not a pacifist by nature, and the responsibility
> for a group of people was very much to his liking. He saw active duty
> on the Italian front, and sometimes told how they were shelled for
> days at a time, dashing out of a shelter one by one at certain counts
> to get food and supplies. He remembered the very cooperative Italian
> girls who taught him a smattering of Italian, and he blamed one
> unhappy episode, when he was stuck for three days in a swampy ditch,
> for a renewed outbreak of his skin condition that was never to be
> completely cured.
>
> He must have liked wearing an officer's uniform. He told us that
> even though he was in the infantry, he always wore spurs, and that
> on his rare furloughs he loved to go riding at the Vienna Reitschule.

I have a feeling that at that time his social conscience was not very developed, and that he took the war in stride without bothering much about the rights and wrongs. He was, up to that time, certainly no rebel.[25]

There are a few important additions that can be made to Ollendorff's account. Reich was more affected by the suffering than her summary conveys. He recalled being horrified at seeing a fellow soldier shot before his eyes on the way to get food.

The Reich of this period is most clearly described by Ottilie, who saw him when he visited Vienna on a furlough. She found him "open, lost, hungry for affection as well as food," and very responsive to the warmth of Ottilie's family. By then, Reich was thoroughly disillusioned with the war; he found it senseless and wondered what the fighting was all about.

Reich had a strong sense of World War I as the watershed between an old world and a new one struggling to be born. Politically, although he could not articulate the position, he was ready to leap into the Socialist youth movement of postwar Vienna.

There is a certain similarity in the way Reich experienced his childhood and the way he experienced the Army. At first, in each case, we seem to be watching a vigorous, extroverted person. Then tragedy hits—or rather, the tragic aspects intensify and bear in upon him. In the first instance, he felt partly responsible. The second was so vast he could feel himself only as victim rather than executioner. Indeed, one can hypothesize that the outer drama and conflict of the war provided some relief from his own inner turmoil. His answers to both were to change over the years. What was the cause of that family tragedy? What was the cause of that devastation, which swept Europe and in which he participated for so long so blindly?

I have assumed a need on Reich's part to work off inner tension through an extremely vigorous, committed life—through the sense of a mission. He made something like this idea explicit when in the mid-1930s he discussed his reaction to the end of World War I. He was relieved, he said, that now he could lift his head above the trench without worrying. He looked forward to resuming his studies. But he also felt sad, and it was some time before he understood why. It was because during the war—for all its misery—he at least had the feeling that he was living under a *heroic destiny*. He was afraid that with the war ended, he would be caught up in the usual trivialities of existence.[26]

This story is important because it points to Reich's strong need to live a heroic life before he had anything specific to be heroic about. In a life of danger, he could feel some relief from the inner pressure, some surcease from the guilt of the past. In time, he would channel this "heroic" effort into a task that made sense, into a mission not of simply staying alive but repairing the conditions that had produced the early tragedies.

One other wartime story rounds out the recapitulation of past themes and at the same time points to the future. Reich recalled to Ottilie the experience of a sexual embrace with a young woman in the Italian village where he was stationed in 1916. Reich went on to comment that he had been having sexual intercourse for some years before this relationship and that he had enjoyed it, but that this woman was different from any he had known before. For the first time he experienced the full meaning of love. Also for the first time he was to experience what he would later name and describe in detail—and for which he was to fight so hard—"orgastic potency." But in 1916 he found the experience very hard to put into words.

To explain Reich's meaning of the term is to anticipate the story. Yet this Army memory serves to underscore one point:

As a nineteen-year-old, Reich noted a kind of sexual embrace that was new and different for him, an event that was to play its part in shaping his future work. He first encountered it experientially, without any clear cognitive understanding. Thus, to the family tragedy surrounding his mother's death and to the social upheaval of the war was added the issue of his own heterosexual life as a momentous question that Reich was dimly struggling to understand.

4

Becoming a Psychoanalyst: 1918–1920

Soon after his discharge from the Army in the fall of 1918, Reich went to Vienna to begin his professional education. Here he entered a milieu of new, provocative ideas and social movements. Vienna was home to Freud and most of his early disciples. Although still isolated from and pilloried by the medical establishment, psychoanalysis was beginning to gain some influence on the larger social scene. Vienna was also home to the composer Arnold Schönberg, the painter Oskar Kokoschka, and the satirist Karl Kraus. These and other artists fought hard against the cultural sentimentality and artificiality of prewar Austria. The new, more trenchant and psychologically profound literature of James Joyce, Marcel Proust, D. H. Lawrence, and Thomas Mann; the candid social criticism of G. B. Shaw, Bertrand Russell, and Havelock Ellis; the cubist vision of Picasso and Braque; the physics of Albert Einstein, Max Planck, and Niels Bohr—these were but a few of the revolutionary trends sweeping intellectual circles throughout Europe. It was a time of breakthroughs. One of the leitmotifs of the period was the urge to look beneath the surface and to see hitherto concealed or unknown forces in man's psyche and social relationships as well as in nature.

In Austria, the Social Democratic Party had recently come to power, eager to initiate a vast program of economic, social, and educational reforms in an impoverished, war-torn country, its people cold, hungry, and embittered in the wake of a disastrous war. Many Austrians gravitated toward the urban-, socialist-, and secular-minded Social Democrats. An almost equal number harked back to the dynastic days of Franz Josef and supported the Christian Socialist Party, which was heavily Catholic in religion, conservative in economics, and rural in constituency. But whether one was on the political left or right, one was likely to be deeply engaged.

Before Reich could fully enter this scientific, artistic and political ferment, he first had to establish himself economically, for he was penniless. His first benefactor was his younger brother, Robert. Although eighteen to Willy's twenty-one in 1918, Robert felt a responsibility to help him continue his education. There seems to have been an understanding between the two that Willy was the especially gifted one and that his education came first. The idea was that Robert would help Willy get his education, and then Willy would help Robert. The second half of this plan never materialized; Robert joined a business enterprise, an international transportation firm in which he rapidly gained an executive position.[1]

Reich's initial plans were uncertain. In the fall of 1918, he enrolled in the Faculty of Law at the University of Vienna. It is not clear why he was attracted to the law. Perhaps the issue of responsibility connected with his family tragedy motivated him; the close connection of the law with politics also may have appealed to him. For if Reich had been apolitical at the start of World War I, he was radicalized by its end. Once a student in Vienna, he became deeply immersed in the Social Democratic "youth movement." Even within the generally socialist ideology of these young people, Reich became known as one who took a quite radical position and argued vociferously against his more moderate friends.[2]

Reich's reasons for leaving the law are clearer than his attraction to it: he found legal studies dull and remote. Before the end of the fall semester, he had switched to the Faculty of Medicine. But on a deeper level, legal versus medical or scientific orientations were to play a part in his thinking throughout his life. Later he was to search for the "exploiters" who caused and benefited from sexual suppression among the masses; and still later, for "conspirators" who "masterminded" the attacks against his work. The quest for underlying emotional-social forces that transcended issues of blame or legal judgment meant that deeper moral issues would often be simultaneously involved.

At medical school Reich was off and running intellectually, never to stop again until his death. Unlike many students who later became psychoanalysts and who found the physician's training a largely tedious route to their desired goal, Reich began medical school with no specific specialty in mind. He was deeply immersed in almost all his courses, particularly anatomy and the clinical rotations. Only pharmacology and forensic medicine left him cold.[3] I have noted his distrust of medication as a result of his treatment for psoriasis. Reich's dislike of forensic medicine may have reflected a continuing recoil from the study of law.

In medical school, Reich encountered a dichotomy in science and philosophy that was relevant to his ultimate choice of psychoanalysis. On the one hand, there was the experimental, mechanistic tradition stemming from Hermann Helmholtz, the German physicist and physician. In this tradition, the laws of physics and chemistry were applied to the study of the human organism. It strongly opposed the assumption of any special forces governing living substances that were not susceptible to laboratory study. Such concepts smacked of the mysticism that thoroughgoing empiricism must always oppose.

An earlier tradition, termed *Naturphilosophie,* included Goethe among its supporters and represented a form of pantheistic monism. If Helmholtz's school saw man as only an especially complicated kind of chemical machine, one capable of preserving and reproducing itself, *Naturphilosophie* saw both man and the universe as organisms, "ultimately consisting of forces, of activities, of creations, of emergings—organized in eternal basic conflicts, in polarity."[4]

Reich first experienced the conflict between the two traditions in terms of the current debate between a "mechanistic" and a "vitalistic" explanation of life. Years later, looking back on this period, he posed the problem in the following way:

> The question, "What is Life?" lay behind everything I learned.
> . . . It became clear that the mechanistic concept of life, which dominated our study of medicine at that time, was unsatisfactory. . . . There was no denying the principle of a creative power governing life; only it was not satisfactory as long as it was not tangible, as long as it could not be described or practically handled. For, rightly, this was considered the supreme goal of natural science.[5]

The vitalists, men like Henri Bergson, who postulated a special force, an *élan vital,* governing living things, greatly appealed to Reich, for "they seemed to come closer to an understanding of the life principle than the mechanists who dissected life before trying to understand it."[6] But as always, he was fascinated by the concrete—in neurology the complexity of the nerve tracts, for example, and the ingenious arrangement of the ganglia.

Reich did very well in his courses. By his second year he was tutoring first-year students, which eliminated the need for any help from his brother, and afforded him considerable pride in his early and complete financial independence.

The most important event during Reich's years at medical school was his encounter with psychoanalysis. How this came about is an interesting story in itself. Grete Bibring (née Lehner), a woman in her seventies when I interviewed her, with a distinguished career in psychoanalysis, recalled the setting in which Reich first heard in detail about psychoanalysis. A first-year medical student in 1919, she was sitting next to Reich and to Edward Bibring, her future husband, at an anatomy lecture. The room was ill-heated because of the fuel shortage, and Willy and Edward wore their Army overcoats, both being too poor to purchase civilian winter clothes. During the lecture, Otto Fenichel, a fellow student (later to become an analyst of renown), passed around a note urging an extracurricular seminar on subjects not covered by the regular medical curriculum, to be run by the students themselves. Willy, Grete, Edward, and several others who have not been identified responded and joined Fenichel in initiating and planning the seminar.[7]

In his published account (1942) of the start of this seminar, Reich omitted to cite Fenichel as the originator, which is not surprising since the two men were to quarrel bitterly in 1934 and so break off a close friendship that had lasted for sixteen years. Further, Reich described the seminar as being specifically devoted to sexology, whereas Grete Bibring stated that it was devoted to "new" topics. However that may be, there is no doubt that sex was one of the main topics not covered by the regular medical curriculum.

Early in the new seminar, the students invited a psychoanalyst to give several talks. Later Reich recalled that while he learned a great deal from these lectures, he objected to the way the analyst, as well as other guest lecturers, discussed sexuality. "Sexuality, in my experience, was something different from the thing they discussed. Those first lectures [by the analyst and others] I attended made sexuality seem bizarre and strange."[8]

Reich had already arrived at his own views about the importance of sexuality. A diary entry for March 1, 1919, reads: "Perhaps my own morality objects to it. However, from my own experience, and from observation of myself and others, I have become convinced that sexuality is the center around which revolves the whole of social life as well as the inner life of the individual."[9]

Reich's initial discomfort with the discussions did not keep him from being very active in the group. By the fall of 1919, according to his own account, he was elected leader of the seminar, and helped organize further groups for the study of various branches of sexology: endocrinology, biology, physiology, and, especially, psychoanalysis. Grete Bibring said that the chairmanship of the seminar rotated among the members and that it was a somewhat less complex organization than Reich claimed. Reich always had a tendency to expand on the organizational depth of undertakings he was currently associated with. In later years he might, for example, have one or two biologists working with him and describe them as practically a department of biology.

The seminar led Reich directly to Freud's writings. Immediately he was enthralled, and especially drawn to Freud's concept of infantile sexuality, which made sex a much larger force than simply adult genitality. One could trace its developmental aspects and see in adult perversions and neurotic conflicts a fixation on or regression to earlier modes of sexual functioning. This viewpoint was syntonic with Reich's own experience of the powerful childhood drama that Freud so emphasized: the boy's sexual love for his mother, and his rivalrous hatred toward his father.

In a wider sense, Freud's method of thought greatly appealed to Reich because it tended to combine the two strands of vitalism and mechanistic science that Reich had already encountered in his own medical training. Freud was not afraid, for example, to address major problems of human emotional life even if they could not be studied in the laboratory. He was prepared to postulate a force—libido, or the energy of the sexual instinct—even though it could not be investigated experimentally or measured quantitatively. At the same time, Freud the empiricist studied the transformations of this postulated energy as carefully as possible. Wherever he could, he used the models and language of physics, speaking, for example, of "cathexes" and "displacements" of energy, of the "quantitative" strength of an idea, of emotion as a phenomenon of "energy discharge." Moreover, he hoped that one day the concept of libido would be more than a metaphor or an analogy, that it would be rooted in a biochemical matrix.

It was not surprising that in Freud's young science Reich found that fusion of soft, amorphous feeling and hard, empirical fact which he was searching for so assiduously in his medical studies. On a more personal level, psychoanalysis in part represented for him a combination of his parents and his dual identifications with them: his mother, who represented feeling, and, in a sense, died for feeling; and his father, who represented the vigorous, practical, tangible world of reality.

The impact of Freud's personality on Reich matched the impact of his work. Many years later, Reich was to describe his visit in 1919 to Freud and others in order to obtain literature for the extracurricular seminar:

> Freud's personality made the strongest and most lasting impression. [Wilhelm] Stekel tried to please. [Alfred] Adler was disappointing. He scolded at Freud. . . . Freud was different. To begin with, he was simple and straightforward in his attitude. Each one of the others expressed in his attitude some role: that of the professor, of the great *Menschenkenner,* or the distinguished scientist. Freud spoke to me like an ordinary human being. He had piercingly intelligent eyes; they did not try to penetrate the listener's eyes in a visionary pose; they simply looked into the world, straight and honest. . . . His manner of speaking was quick, to the point and lively. The movements of his hands were natural. Everything he did and said was shot through with tints of irony. I had come there in a state of trepidation and left with a feeling of pleasure and friendliness. That was the starting point of fourteen years of intensive work in and for psychoanalysis. At the end, I experienced a bitter disappointment in Freud, a disappointment which, I am happy to say, did not lead to hatred or rejection. On the contrary, today I have a better and higher estimation of Freud's achievement than in those days when I was his worshipful disciple. I am happy to have been his pupil for such a long time without premature criticism, and with a full devotion to his cause.[10]

I quote in some detail because Reich's intense admiration for Freud as a man was to be an important part of what psychoanalysis as a whole meant to him. When Reich actually met Freud in 1919, he was quite on his own and proudly so. However, as he expressed it in 1948, he had never been really close to his own father, and Freud represented the kind of mentor and father substitute he so badly needed during this period.[11] And what better exemplar could he have found? Freud's interests corresponded closely to his own, not only in terms of science and psychology but also sociologically, for Freud's work was fraught with educational and group implications. In addition, the example of Freud's lonely struggles must have inspired the young Reich, seeking a heroic destiny, who strove to avoid the "triviality of the everyday." For though Freud's work revolved around his office, he had met more than his due of hate-filled abuse. Indeed, Freud saw himself primarily as a "conquistador," and his letters to his colleagues about outright hostility to analysis on one front, covert resistance on another, and genuine victory on still another often sound like communiqués between a commander-in-chief and his battlefield generals. As a man and a teacher, then, Freud had many attributes that could supply for the young Reich the inspiring but steadying, soaring but disciplined "benevolent presence" (to use Erik Erikson's felicitous phrase again) he longed for.

On his side, Freud must have been quite impressed by Reich. Freud permitted the young medical student to start seeing analytic patients in early 1920 (possibly even late in 1919) and referred several cases to him. Reich was not unique in starting psychoanalytic practice at so young an age (twenty-two or twenty-three) and without formal training, but there were not many in this category. In the summer of 1920, Reich was admitted as a guest member of the Vienna Psychoanalytic Society; in the fall of that year, he presented a paper on Ibsen's *Peer Gynt* to the Society, after which he became a regular member.[12]

The speed with which Reich became an analyst was not solely a function of his own intelligence, energy, and commitment, but also of the milieu. For psychoanalysis did not then have the formidable organizational structure it was to develop some years later, with the requirements of psychiatric residency, training analysis, analytic seminars, and case supervision. In 1920, if one had Freud's blessing—an important "if," since Freud controlled most of the referrals that came to the new specialty of psychoanalysis—one could begin analytic practice with virtually no formal training. One was expected to steep oneself in the analytic literature and required to present an acceptable paper in order to become a member of the Society, but little else. Ironically, Reich himself was to make a significant contribution—not least through the elaboration of "character analysis"—to lengthening the apprenticeship required of analytic candidates.

The significance of Freud and psychoanalysis to Reich becomes even more apparent if we take a closer look at Reich's personality and private life during this period.

Those who knew Reich as a young medical student around 1919–20 focus on his vitality and brilliance. For some, it was not only his forceful nature but also a kind of rudeness that impressed them. Grete Bibring, musing about the young Reich, spoke with a mixture of fondness, admiration, and disdain. She commented on his intelligence, his eagerness to learn, and his capacity to "soak up everything." At the same time she found him less sophisticated and less knowledgeable in terms of general culture than many of her fellow students. She also felt he was quite impressionable and cited an example from around the year 1920. Reich had a patient in analysis who was a Communist. One day Willy excitedly came to Grete and Edward, exclaiming that Communists weren't necessarily fools. Since this was hardly news to the young couple, they did not share Willy's sense of great discovery. A strain on the relationship was Reich's competitiveness with Edward Bibring, for Willy, too, was drawn to the attractive, spirited, and intellectual Grete—a romantic interest she did not reciprocate.[13]

Willy's colleagues also criticized, initially with good humor, later with more acerbity, his tendency to dominate groups. In the student seminar, for example, a story tells how Reich, as leader or temporary leader, was outlining a series of presentations for the coming weeks. He meant to say that after he had presented a certain topic, another member would speak on something else. Instead, he made the slip: *"Nach mir, ich komme"* (After me, I come). The group burst out laughing and someone said: "That's the trouble with you, Willy—'After me, *I* come.' "[14]

Some of the same personal qualities, as well as others, are revealed in Reich's relationship with Lia Laszky. Laszky recalled meeting Reich when both were lab partners in a first-year anatomy course. Reich was taking an accelerated program that permitted him to complete the regular six-year curriculum in four years. He repeatedly urged Laszky to do the same so that they could continue working together. "So like a fool I did. I wasn't as smart as he was, I wasn't as determined. It was all too much for me." Later she was to drop out of medical school altogether.[15]

Lia Laszky felt that Reich at that time was both "fascinating and abhorrent": fascinating because of his vitality, his radiant interests, and his personal charm during good moods; abhorrent because he could apply such pressure to induce her to do what he wanted and because, in his bad moods, he could be so touchy and easily angered. In spite of her mixed feelings, for a period she was very much under his influence. If he failed in persuading her to finish medical school, he succeeded in arousing her lasting interest in psychoanalysis.

During Reich's first year of medical school, Laszky had been helpful to him in a very practical way. He had little money and was often hungry. Through her father, who was a doctor, her family had access to food, so she shared with Reich the daily lunch she brought from home. But Reich also needed supper. Lia persuaded her mother to give her bigger and bigger lunches, ostensibly to assuage her ever more ravenous hunger. Finally her parents began to worry about her health and arranged for her to have a medical exam.

Lia then told them the truth. Her father invited Reich to call and gave him a small allowance. Not long afterward, Lia's interest in psychoanalysis developed under Reich's influence. Her father, a bitter opponent of Freud's work, was outraged and blamed Reich. The allowance was cut off and he was no longer welcomed in the Laszky home.

This incident is very illustrative of the way Reich dealt with help from others. Reich is assisted by someone. He takes it more or less for granted, at least if the person does not seem to be making any great sacrifice. As Laszky says: "He wasn't worried that he often ate my whole lunch." He undoubtedly felt that she didn't have to worry about her next meal, he did. And he also appears to have been quite prepared to take an allowance from Lia's father without any obligation to defer to her father in a major way. Reich was interested in psychoanalysis, Lia should be, and to hell with what her father thought. Conversely, Reich himself was often very generous to people in need so long as he could give freely. If he was expected to give, it could be quite a different story, as we shall see in later contexts.

In spite of the family opposition, or perhaps in part because of it, the friendship between Willy and Lia continued to develop. Whether Reich was in love with her we do not know, though it appears that at one point he wanted to marry her. For all his fascination, Lia Laszky was not in love with him—"I was a virgin and he was a steamroller." She felt that for him the conquest was more the issue than love: conquering this attractive, vivacious, intelligent young girl, this virgin, this daughter of a physician, this in many ways reluctant woman. In fact, they did not have intercourse at that time. According to Laszky, "I was too frightened, too inhibited." Her refusal angered Reich, but it did not stop his pursuit of her.[16]

Another characteristic element of Reich's personality was revealed in his relationship with Lia: his intense jealousy. These feelings were quite realistically aroused by a strong competitor, the conductor Hans Swarowski, whom Lia had met during her first year of medical school. Swarowski wanted to marry her, and over time it became clear that she preferred him to Willy. Her fiancé asked her to give up medical school so she would be free to travel with him. Willy did not surrender easily, but kept pursuing her, once even surprising her by appearing unannounced on a train when she was on her way to visit Swarowski. Willy kept telling her that she was made to be a psychiatrist and that she couldn't leave him. This dual appeal to the woman he cared for was to recur throughout Reich's life: Be with me and do what I am doing!

However close Reich may have been to Lia, he was also close to other women. One important friendship was with a young nursery-school teacher, described by those who knew her as soft, pretty, not especially intellectual, and —unlike Lia—very much in love with Reich. The girl died suddenly of an illegal abortion.[17]

If Reich was the man involved—and the evidence suggests that he was —the event must have had an enormous impact on him. We know that he felt implicated in his mother's death. Now his relationship with the nursery-school teacher repeated the disastrous consequences of sex outside marriage, and he was once again deeply involved. Moreover, if his mother's fate helped determine the broad background of his later efforts to free genitality, so this experience would seem to have been closely related to his later strong interest in a particular sex reform: the legalization of abortion.

The relationships with Lia Laszky and the nursery-school teacher were serious ones. There were also lighter, more casual affairs. Judging from the reports of women who knew him at that time, Reich appears to have had some need to prove his masculinity, to be something of a womanizer. The atmosphere among his friends was quite permissive. Psychoanalysis was used as a rationale (some would say a rationalization) justifying a nonmonogamous way of life. However, Reich and many of his friends were old-fashioned in the sense that they were intensely serious about their studies and careers. They might have casual affairs, but they also worked hard from early morning until late at night. Reich and Otto Fenichel, especially, were regarded as intellectual leaders among the analytically oriented students; Otto was admired for his encyclopedic knowledge and Reich for his capacity to cite just the telling case or concept from the writings of Freud and other analysts.

Along with many of his friends, Reich was involved with the Social Democratic youth movement. Its student wing was a loose association of young, largely middle-class men and women who were devoted to leftist politics, the new in the arts and psychology, the right of the young to determine their own lives, and freedom from "dull, bourgeois" cultural standards in general and conventional mores in particular. (One of the worst curses among this group was to label someone "Victorian.") The youth movement was important on a personal level for Reich because it provided the peer-group support and activities so lacking in his early life. It appears to have been Reich's first major political involvement—not in any very organized or highly theoretical way, but as part of the total social milieu. He would have been exposed, for example, to the Kinderfreunde, a Social Democratic organization devoted to the education of homeless pre-adolescents. In addition to the youth movement, there was also a workers' youth group to which Reich lectured on psychoanalysis in the early twenties. The leaders in the Social Democratic Party had a large vision and did not confine themselves to narrow economic and political questions. They wanted to wrest education from Catholic hands and influence the minds of the young. The idea was to develop the whole person; the aim, to build a "socialist man."

Later, in about 1927 or so, Reich's political interests were to become intense, theoretically informed, and organizationally engaged—women's rights, the rights of youth, communal facilities for homeless young people, connections between political and educational change, anti-religious orientations. By 1919 or 1920, the seeds of these interests had been planted, partly through the youth movement.

A final point concerning the Social Democratic group. If Reich found in Freud the role model par excellence of intellectual daring, he found in the youth movement support for his own emotional and social adventurousness. These young people of the right as well as the left were permeated with a Nietzschean scorn for well-trod, narrow paths of existence, with a love of nature, with a yearning for "something more" than the lives of their parents. On the political right, such yearnings were to degenerate into the fierce nationalism that characterized Nazism. But even in this extreme distortion Reich discerned a genuine, surging feeling, the kind of primary emotion he would always honor even when he condemned its corrupt expressions.

Studies, love, and politics were not Reich's sole concerns during this period. He remained interested in physical activity, joining an Alpine club not long after his arrival in Vienna. He also joined the Schönberg music association, following up on a childhood interest when he had studied the piano. For a brief period in Vienna, he appears to have begun to play the cello, stimulated by Lia, herself a talented cellist. Throughout his life he loved music. Not surprisingly, the tempestuous, struggling, innovative, and many-faceted Beethoven was his favorite composer.[18]

It was also typical of Reich's life, and the lives of many of his friends, that there were no sharp distinctions between work and leisure time or among various interests. One celebrated a political event at a party, one's medical school and extracurricular pursuits interlaced, and love itself was an arena where some of the home truths of the new psychological knowledge were most fully revealed.

In hearing people talk about the young, social Reich, one senses a sparkling person at the center of the groups in which he was involved. However, in play as in work Reich had to be at the center. For example, after animatedly discussing how fascinating and lively Reich could be, Gisela Stein, a friend of Reich's and wife of the internist Paul Stein, reported that he frequently was "unbearably intolerant" when confronted with disagreement: "He had to do everything best—when he went skiing, he had to be the best and everybody had to ski his way."

For all his capacity to be at the center of things, Reich often felt like an outsider. His choice of *Peer Gynt,* the quintessential outsider, as the subject for his first analytic paper was no accident. What contributed to this feeling of alienation on Reich's part at the very time when things seemed to be going so well, when, unlike Peer Gynt, his own bursting strength did not consist simply of dreams and longings but was being channeled into productive outlets?

I have already commented that his experience of sexuality was quite different from the way many of his teachers and peers such as Lia Laszky felt about it. It seems apparent that Reich's intensity and creativity also served to separate him from most people he was to know then and later. At the same time, in spite of professional and personal successes, his self-confidence remained shaky. His country background may have contributed to the outsider feeling, for many Viennese wished that the refugees from the former Eastern provinces would go home. His unusual social situation as a child—the "crown prince" of a feudal estate, not permitted to play with most of his peers—may have contributed to his difficulties with the easy give-and-take of normal friendship even while he yearned for it so much. His psoriasis undoubtedly undermined his physical self-confidence: some of the women who knew him during this period said that while others found him attractive, they themselves were put off by his "acne."

There were obviously deeper factors involved in his feelings of alienation. It is not difficult to trace them to his childhood family conflicts. His intense rivalrous feelings toward his powerful, domineering father were stimulated by his mother's doting love and her and his own abuse at the hands of the father. Inflamed through his (and his father's) defeat by the tutor, there arose an extraordinary sensitivity to being defeated, put down, or otherwise made to look small. One way to avoid such a repetition was to take the dominant position. Subordinacy was only tolerable when, as in the case of his relationship with Freud, he could idolize a somewhat distant, much older mentor who treated him well, indeed, as a kind of favorite. His mother's "betrayal" of her loving son illumined the intense jealousy he experienced toward women and his need to prove himself—his attractiveness, his worth—by winning many women. And while his self-perception of being "different" had many positive bases—energy, creativity, and health—it also had a foundation in feelings of guilt from his role in his mother's death, feelings that led him to believe he was a "marked" man, who must live an extraordinary life to redeem the suffering he had witnessed (and perhaps caused) at such close quarters. Finally, it is worth noting that these painful feelings about his family background are further revealed by the fact that during this period Reich did not discuss his family even with those, such as Lia, he was closest to.

Whatever his personal conflicts, Reich generally was able to maintain his capacity to work effectively. There appears to have been only one brief period when the weight of the past severely interfered with his capacity to function. In the same article (published in 1920) in which he presented his childhood trauma in disguised form, Reich also outlined some of the conflicts he felt around 1919. He described the "patient" (himself) as suffering from states of depression and rumination that led him to lose all interest in his studies. He feared speaking in public lest he make a fool of himself, become all "choked up." He tended to want to be alone and to dwell on small, everyday errors, which he magnified into a "huge case."

Reich also reported that the onset of these feelings of depression occurred in connection with a relationship to a girl who was "intellectually very much below him" (the nursery-school teacher?) and whom he suspected of being unfaithful to him at one point. There the "analyst" (Reich) interjected to say that, in his opinion, the "patient's" suspicion was without objective foundation. Also, the "patient" suffered from a restless quest for an ideal sexual partner, with feelings of disappointment following any actual experience. (The "analyst" later related this quest to the patient's unconscious search for the "perfect" mate, i.e., his mother.)

This personal crisis around 1919 undoubtedly further fixed Reich's intense interest in psychoanalysis. Together with other evidence, the "case history" indicates that he did in fact have some brief analytic therapy around this time. His first analyst was Isidor Sadger,[19] one of Freud's earliest Viennese associates. In the early 1920s, Reich underwent a second analysis, this time with Paul Federn, which also did not last long.[20] Federn was a prominent early disciple of Freud's.

Reich may also have undergone analysis for training purposes. Although a personal analysis did not become a prerequisite for practice until 1926, Freud urged "very young candidates who came to him for advice . . . that they be analyzed themselves."[21] It is reasonable to conjecture that he also gave Reich this advice. I would further assume that Reich's first choice of analyst was Freud, but that the latter's relatively high fees and his reluctance to take Viennese students into therapy with him would have made this outcome unlikely. There is definite evidence that some years later Reich very much wanted to be in treatment with Freud.

In later years Reich never, to my knowledge, talked about his experiences as an analytic patient. We do not know why his analyses were so brief. Perhaps Reich, like the "patient" he described, broke off treatment because of difficulties in even discussing his childhood trauma. Perhaps there were conflicts about technique or personality clashes. Both Sadger and Federn came to dislike Reich bitterly.

In any case, the intensity of the problems that appear to have led Reich into his first analysis could not have lasted long, judging from his extremely rapid progress during those early Vienna years. By the end of 1920 he was already a practicing analyst, with two more years of medical school to complete. He no longer had to scrounge for the means to live since now he could support himself through his practice. In 1920 his living quarters, which also served as an office, were on Berggasse, the same street where Freud resided. He had found the beginning lines of his life work, and in Sigmund Freud the most significant role model of his career. Whatever his conflicts, Reich had demonstrated that he could make it in the world. And he had at least taken some first steps in understanding, and redeeming, the tragedies of his early life.

PART III

Reich as Insider — Building a Career and Marriage: 1920-1926

5

Reich's Work on the Impulsive Character: 1922–1924

In later years, Reich used to speak of his work as existing outside the framework of present-day scientific disciplines. And, indeed, Reich's concepts of genitality and orgastic potency were, as we shall see, rejected even by Freud, to whom Reich was first attracted precisely because of the way he addressed issues of sexuality.

This latent "outsideness" was to become apparent only over time. During the early and mid-1920s, Reich saw himself—and was regarded by others—as functioning very much within the psychoanalytic movement.

Following Reich's graduation from medical school in 1922, he kept up the varied but unified effort that had characterized his earlier student years. In addition to his private practice of analysis, he undertook in 1922 postgraduate study in neuropsychiatry at the University of Vienna Clinic, headed by the neuropsychiatrist Professor Wagner von Jauregg, who later won the Nobel Prize for the malarial treatment of general paresis. Reich's work at this clinic gave him the opportunity to study various kinds of psychotic illnesses and stimulated what would become a lifelong interest in schizophrenia. He also appreciated working under the famed von Jauregg, although the latter was not sympathetic to psychoanalysis and missed no opportunity to poke fun at it. It is worth noting here that as a student Reich had the good fortune to work with the most eminent, organically oriented psychiatrist of the period as well as the leading psychoanalyst.

Reich's thorough professional training is notable on another count. Young people today have picked up the anti-establishment aspects of his work, its "outsideness," as an excuse for not acquiring traditional education or formal training. Reich cannot be used as a model for this kind of rebellion. Despite his defiance of taboos, throughout his life he was intent on learning all he could from others.

Moreover, Reich valued what he sometimes called a "good old-fashioned education." As a young man he was ambitious for public validation. He wanted proper credentials as he wanted the respect of his peers and superiors. And for all his outspokenness on matters of principle, he could exercise discretion in order not to alienate unnecessarily those important to him. For example, at von Jauregg's clinic he would sometimes omit from his patient charts mention of sexual symbolism, since to include analytic interpretations would only invite the ridicule of his chief.

During this period, Reich also began working in the newly established Vienna Psychoanalytic Polyclinic. He was to work part time there for eight years, initially as a first assistant, later as assistant chief, with the senior analyst Eduard Hitschmann serving as chief throughout. Reich's work was extremely important in furthering his social interests since the clinic served laborers, farmers, students, and others with low earnings who could ill afford private treatment. Not only did he have the opportunity to deal with the emotional problems of the poor; he could note how economic conditions contributed to and exacerbated their suffering—social implications that were later significant to him. As was so characteristic of Reich, a given opportunity was useful in several directions at the same time. From a more narrowly psychiatric and psychoanalytic viewpoint, the clinic population was rich in patients not usually seen by analysts—persons whose diagnosis was "impulsive character" (a term coined by Franz Alexander) or what today would more likely be termed "character disorder" or "borderline" patients.

Until this polyclinic opened, psychoanalysis had been available mainly to middle-class patients suffering from the so-called symptom neuroses, for example, patients with obsessive-compulsive complaints such as endless hand-washing, or hysterical complaints such as a paralysis of a part of the body without any organic basis. Reich's study of the impulsive character provided a nice transition to a broader study of the personality, for this malady was typified not by specific symptoms so much as by a chaotically disorganized style of life. These patients, who had frequently been diagnosed as "psychopaths," were often regarded as more "bad" than "sick." They were frequently anti-social and showed self-destructive tendencies in the form of criminality, addictions, outbursts of uncontrollable rage, or suicide attempts. Even today exceedingly difficult to treat, such people are generally considered "troublemakers" and are tossed back and forth among the courts, prisons, and mental health centers.

In 1925 Reich published his first book, a monograph entitled *Der Triebhafte Charakter (The Impulsive Character)*.[1] As he was later to do so frequently, Reich began with some broad theoretical issues. Following Freud's direction in the 1920s, which gave more emphasis to the ego, the character, in contrast to the earlier period of psychoanalysis, which had focused heavily on unconscious impulses and wishes, Reich argued for a "single, systematic theory of character . . . a psychic embryology." Put more simply, he stressed that we do not understand how the variation in human personality comes about. True, fragments of a psychoanalytic embryology existed. Freud, Ernest Jones, and Karl Abraham had posited that persons fixated at the anal stage of development often showed specific character traits such as frugality, orderliness, and stubbornness. But why one person with such a fixation developed a symptom, such as compulsive hand-washing, while another showed only the character trait of cleanliness, was not clear.

Reich then went on to define the impulsive character and to differentiate it diagnostically from the symptom neuroses, on the one hand, and the psychoses, on the other. He saw the impulsive character as a transitional stage from neuroses to psychoses (well conveyed by the current term "borderline" case). The further details of his differentiations need not concern us here save to note that Reich placed a heavy emphasis on the fact that the impulsive character, unlike the symptom neurotic, often rationalized his illness. He would, for example, blame others for his unbridled excesses and not perceive himself as emotionally disturbed. Also, we might note that Reich's fine distinctions regarding these various illnesses make clear why in the early 1920s Paul Federn called Reich the best diagnostician among the younger analysts.[2]

A substantial section of the monograph is devoted to an elucidation of early childhood development of the impulsive character. Reich posited that impulsive persons often, as small children, initially experienced considerable permissiveness. Then, suddenly, impulse gratification was followed by a belated but "ruthless" and "traumatic" frustration.

The childhood sexual history of the impulsive character contained strong stimulation, severe conflicts, and the development of weak or unstable ego defenses. According to psychoanalytic theory, almost all patients have experienced castration threats and the witnessing or overhearing of the primal scene. Reich argued that the impulsive character suffered these events in an especially blatant form:

> Impulsive characters have lived out their sexuality not only very early, but also with fully conscious incest wishes. . . . Owing to a lack of supervision, such patients see and grasp far more of adult sexual life than do the simple neurotics. The latency period is activated minimally or not at all. . . . Puberty is ushered in with extreme breakthroughs of the sexual drive. Neither masturbation nor intercourse, which are taken up at a very early age, can afford relief, for the whole libidinal organization is torn apart by disappointment and guilt feelings.[3]

We might consider here the significance of the similarities between Reich's description of childhood factors in the development of the impulsive character and his own personal history: the combination of stimulation and indulgence, on the one hand, and harsh punishment, on the other; the exposure to striking "primal scene" experiences; the absence of a latency period; and the conscious awareness of incest wishes in puberty.

These factors lead one to think there may have been strong inner reasons for Reich's choice of the impulsive character as subject of his first detailed psychoanalytic investigation. Reich could certainly act very impulsively and, on occasion, was given to unbridled rages. To give but a few examples: Gisela Stein recalls him storming out of the Steins' apartment following a political argument in the early 1920s; Reich's third wife, Ilse Ollendorff, remembers his towering rages in the 1940s and 1950s when confronted with bills he considered excessive or insufficiently controlled by Ilse in terms of the quantity or quality of work done; and I myself remember during therapy in 1948 his fury when I told him of certain criticisms made by a person he detested.

These outbursts were often provoked by various hurts and insults, but they were often disproportionate to the cause. And whatever the justification in terms of external provocation, it was also clear that at times Reich used such justification to rationalize his outburst much as he described the impulsive character explaining away his excesses. On other occasions, he would be genuinely mortified after such an outburst and would immediately apologize to the person he had abused.

One further point should be made about the development of Reich's impulsive characteristics—a point that is in accordance with his general theoretical approach to the development of character traits. In the first section of the monograph, Reich, following Freud, emphasizes the role of identification in the development of the ego: "The process of identification holds the key to the characterological interpretation of personality." In Reich's case, his impulsive tendencies can be seen as the result of childhood stimulation and repression; but they can also be viewed in the light of his identification with his father. For Leon, too, was given to fits of unbridled and rationalized rage, especially when his jealousy was aroused. Throughout his life, Reich was aware of the problematic aspects of his personality that stemmed from his identification with Leon.

I hypothesize, then, that during the early 1920s Reich was involved in his own psychoanalysis, partly with the help of Isidor Sadger and Paul Federn, but largely (I conjecture) on his own. As his first autobiographical sketch informs us, Reich was acutely aware of—and sometimes very troubled by— many aspects of his own life history. It seems likely that this awareness of his own conflicts and the environmental matrix within which they developed alerted him to similar constellations in patients. Clearly, his self-awareness was further heightened by the work with impulsive characters in particular.

It would be erroneous to use the preceding linkage of themes in his life with his work on the impulsive character to substantiate the accusation that some have made against Reich: that he was a psychopath. Those who thought of him in this fashion had their own reasons and problems. The complexity of Reich's personality could provide a field day for the diagnostician. My own aim is something different: to trace his development and to show how creatively—and sometimes destructively—he used what was within him.

In the monograph, Reich's tone is in fact cool and objective, showing considerable distance between himself and his subject matter. These pages reveal him primarily as a sharp, up-and-coming young analyst whose primary goal, along good Freudian lines, is to understand rather than to cure. Indeed, compared with Reich's later clinical works, it is striking how relatively free the monograph is of any suggestions for treatment. Although he makes passing reference to the poor economic conditions surrounding the impulsive characters, there is none of the zeal for social reform that suffuses later publications.

The monograph is furthermore instructive because it shows how slowly Reich arrived at the concepts most closely associated with his name. In the late 1920s, he was essentially to redefine Karl Abraham's notion of the "genital character." He would also formulate pedagogical notions describing the possibility of an upbringing different from either "normal" repressiveness or the exotic mixture of indulgence and punishment that impulsive persons experienced in childhood.

However, he first had to sort out the more conflict-ridden aspects of his own childhood experiences and the experiences of impulsive characters. For *that* kind of sexual permissiveness led to all kinds of problems. And so in 1925, as in 1920, we find Reich still closely identified with many traditional analytic notions. He believed in the desirability of strong ego defenses against sexual wishes and impulses. He also emphasized the cultural value of the latency period—an absence or strong diminution of sexual feelings between the ages of around six and the onset of puberty. Before Reich could transcend psychoanalytic formulations on these matters, he had to comprehend more fully the strengths as well as the weaknesses in his own background and personality.

As I have indicated, Reich's main interests in the monograph per se were diagnostic and etiological rather than therapeutic. His chief suggestion for treatment was to uncover the unconscious of impulsive patients very carefully and particularly slowly.

At the end of the monograph, Reich argued for more research on how to treat the impulsive character. Such study would require an institutional setting to protect the patient from his or her uncontrollable impulses at the same time as it offered treatment. Few such settings existed. Impulsive patients were initially hospitalized because of a destructive or self-destructive act; they would then be discharged, only to be readmitted after another, usually more dangerous outburst. Finally, they often succeeded in killing themselves or they were given custodial care. What Reich wrote of this deplorable course for the patient of the 1920s could be repeated, with slight modifications, to describe current treatment today.

The Impulsive Character won Reich considerable recognition from his mentors and colleagues. Freud congratulated Reich directly, and in a letter to Paul Federn described the monograph as "full of valuable content."[4] Indeed, he thought so highly of it that he urged Federn, then vice-chairman of the Vienna Psychoanalytic Society and Freud's right-hand man in organizational matters, to see that Reich was appointed to the Society's executive committee. More recently, an authority has called it a classic that does for the impulsive character what Freud's case history of Dora does for the hysteric.[5]

The monograph would undoubtedly have received much wider acclaim were it more readily available. The German edition has been out of print for many years, and the piece was not available in English until 1970, when it appeared in the *Journal of Orgonomy*. At least one competent observer, with no ax to grind, believes that it would have been translated much earlier were it not for the quarrels that subsequently developed between Reich and the psychoanalytic establishment.[6]

6

Reich's Early Work on
Character Analysis:
1920-1926

By the early 1920s, Reich had acquired considerable exposure to neurotic patients, the psychotically ill, and impulsive or borderline characters—all good experience for any young psychiatrist. If Reich's most careful diagnostic work was done with impulsive persons, his concern with treatment began with the neurotic patients, whom he saw in private analytic practice.

There were few guidelines as to how an analysis should be conducted, but this lack of requirements and guidelines had its advantages for the young Reich. He could plunge into the practice of analysis directly; he could learn to think for himself; and he was not required to absorb a good deal from others that he would later have to unlearn. He was spared the endless seminars, supervised cases, and so on that today are required of analytic candidates, with the result that they often are unable to abandon the student role, with all its infantilizing features, until about forty. Yet another paradox is that Reich was one of the main contributors to expanding the analytic curriculum for students.

In his own writings, Reich stressed the deficiencies rather than the advantages of his early years as an analyst:

> There was hardly any discussion of psychoanalytic technique, a lack which I felt very keenly in my work with patients. There was

neither a training institute nor an organized curriculum. The counsel to be had from older colleagues was meager. "Just go on analyzing patiently," they would say, "it'll come." What would come, and how, one did not quite know. One of the most difficult points was the handling of patients who were severely inhibited or even remained silent. Later analysts have never experienced this desolate being at sea in matters of technique. When a patient failed to produce associations, if he did not "want to have" dreams or did not produce associations, one would sit there, helpless, for hours. The technique of analysis of resistances, although theoretically formulated, was not practiced. . . . If one told the patient, "You have a resistance," he would look at one uncomprehendingly. If one told him that he "defended himself against his unconscious," one was not any better off. Trying to convince him that his silence or resistance was senseless, that it really was distrust or fear, was somewhat more intelligent, but no more fruitful. Yet, the older colleagues kept saying: "Just keep on analyzing."[1]

In later years Reich spoke even more contemptuously of the "older colleagues," Freud excepted. In an interview with Kurt Eissler, Secretary of the Freud Archives, Reich described the atmosphere of the Vienna Psychoanalytic Society as very boring, and stated that I acted "like a shark in a pond of carps."[2]

When Reich had questions, he tended to go directly to Freud for help. However, Reich felt that while Freud had a marvelous capacity for solving complicated situations theoretically, he was not of great technical assistance.[3] Freud, too, advised Reich to be patient. He warned against "therapeutic ambitiousness." Reich later wrote that it took some years before he understood Freud's point that "premature therapeutic ambitiousness is not conducive to the discovery of new facts."[4]

With Freud's approval, Reich took his first practical step toward systematizing the therapeutic technique. In 1922 he suggested the establishment of a technical seminar, to be led by a senior analyst but designed to meet the explicit needs of young analysts. The main method of the seminar would be the systematic study of individual cases in analytic treatment. Eduard Hitschmann was the first leader of the seminar, Hermann Nunberg the second. In 1924, at the age of twenty-seven, Reich took over the leadership, which he maintained until 1930, when he left for Berlin.

To establish an atmosphere of candor and productivity within the seminar, Reich took several steps. From the first, he proposed that, with the exception of the leader, the seminar should be confined strictly to younger members of the Psychoanalytic Society. In this way the more inexperienced analysts could vent their doubts and troubles without worrying about the opinion of the more senior members. When Reich became leader, he established the requirement that participants present only treatment *failures*, so that there would be no glib smoothing over of difficulties to impress one's colleagues with successes. Reich also set an example by initially presenting some of his own treatment failures.

Reich was dissatisfied with the way cases were presented during the first two years of the technical seminar. The procedure had been for the presenter to fill most of the allotted time with the patient's life history; then, in the ensuing discussion, some rather hit-or-miss suggestions for future treatment would be made. As leader, Reich developed the procedure of having the presenter give only as much of the case history as was necessary for clarification of the technical problems.

Here we see Reich as teacher and organizer, insisting on a system in the rather inchoate field of psychoanalysis. He focused directly on the problem of the choice points for the therapist, his options at any given moment. It is interesting that Reich's method of running the seminar was very similar to the case method of teaching favored today by the Harvard Business School. Their approach is sharply focused on the question: Given such and such a situation, what decision do you make and why? Anyone who has tried to use this approach quickly realizes how much effort is needed by the leader to keep the discussion on the question at hand.

During his first year as seminar leader, Reich focused on "resistances." Freud had already stressed the importance of analyzing resistances after he moved beyond hypnosis, and after he found that direct interpretation of the unconscious (as it emerged in derivatives such as dreams) was often not fruitful. He gave up direct interpretation and tried, instead, to make the unconscious conscious by the elimination of the resistances put up against the repressed material.

Reich directed attention not only to the then familiar forms of resistance that directly impeded the flow of the patient's associations, such as his or her skipping over thoughts as irrelevant or too embarrassing, going "blank," being late for sessions, and the like. He stressed the resistances which, in his opinion, were all the more insidious because they did *not* stop the flow of material. What they did do, Reich was to argue vehemently and in great detail, was to prevent fantasies, memories, and impulses from emerging with strong emotion. Using examples taken from his own treatment failures as well as those of his colleagues, Reich showed that a great number of analyses, as currently carried out, degenerated into "chaotic situations." A welter of memories, dreams, and unconscious ideas was unearthed in helter-skelter fashion, but no strong feelings were released, and the patient showed little improvement.

The first of the resistances on which Reich focused was "latent negative transference," not in itself a new concept. Freud had pointed out that the patient transferred hostile as well as positive feelings to the analyst, feelings originally directed toward parents and other significant figures in the patient's childhood. And it was known that both negative and positive feelings were often concealed. What was new was Reich's emphasis on negative transferences and the technical implications he drew from these.

Reich noted that analysts tended to focus on the patient's positive transference and to overlook subtle signs that the patients were angry or afraid of them. As he put it some years later: "Analysts shied away from bringing out, listening to, confirming or denying opposing opinions and embarrassing criticism from the patient. In short, one felt personally insecure. . . ."[5]

Reich also called attention to another, still more pervasive kind of resistance. He noted that certain characteristic modes of being of the patient—what Reich termed "defensive character traits"—could also block the affective impact of analysis. In Reich's view, such traits as rigid politeness, evasiveness, apprehensiveness, and arrogance had originally developed in childhood as a way of warding off strong emotional stimuli from within or without, stimuli once associated with pain, frustration, and guilt. In analysis, they continued to function as a way of blocking strong emotional experiences, now provoked by the unsettling process of analysis itself. The defensive character traits, which in their totality Reich termed "character armor," served to protect the individual against pain, but also served to restrict severely the capacity for pleasure.

It should be emphasized that Reich's contribution did not lie in the formulation of "character traits" that opposed the process of analysis. For example, Karl Abraham had noted that some patients showed "pathological deformities of character" that interfered with the process of free association, and he had called for the development of a "character analysis" to treat these patients.[6]

Reich argued that *all* patients had defensive character traits, and that there was no sharp distinction between symptom neuroses and character neuroses:

> The difference between character neuroses and symptom neuroses is simply that in the latter the neurotic character has produced symptoms as well—the neurotic symptoms are, so to speak, a concentrate of the neurotic character. . . . The more deeply we penetrate into its [the symptom's] determinants, the further we get from the field of symptomatology proper and the more does the characterological substratum come to the fore.*[7]

How did Reich actually deal with defensive character traits in therapy? Here a distinction he made in *The Impulsive Character* is significant: namely, that a patient often feels his symptom (e.g., a tic, a phobia) as alien, but he tends to rationalize a neurotic character trait as an integral part of himself. Some of the analytic task consists of helping the patient to become aware of

---

*Reich developed these concepts in the 1920s but did not give a detailed presentation of them until he published *Charakteranalyse* in 1933.

his character defenses and to feel them as painful. Reich stressed that the analyst does not urge the patient *not* to be polite or evasive or arrogant. Rather,

> In . . . character analysis, we ask ourself *why* the patient deceives, talks in a confused manner, why he is affect-blocked, etc.; we try to arouse the patient's interest in his character traits in order to be able, with his help, to explore analytically their origin and meaning. All we do is to lift the character trait which presents the cardinal resistance out of the level of the personality and to show the patient, if possible, the superficial connection between character and symptoms; it is left to him whether or not he will utilize his knowledge for an alteration of his character. . . . We confront . . . the patient with it repeatedly until he begins to look at it objectively and to experience it like a painful symptom; thus, the character trait begins to be experienced as a foreign body which the patient wants to get rid of.[8]

Needless to say, a repeated pointing out of the patient's defensive character traits does not endear the analyst to the patient. On the contrary, it usually arouses considerable anger. However, the expression of the anger thus aroused helps undo the need for the particular defense. If a patient is rigidly polite in part because he fears to express his anger, the analyst's provocation by comments can help the patient learn that the consequences of anger need not be so terrible; the patient need not hold on to his controlled politeness.

Reich also stressed the importance of analyzing character resistances in a logical order; that is, to proceed from the more superficial to deeper levels of personality. To continue with the previous example, the defensively polite patient may also be communicating dreams with clearly incestuous wishes. For Reich it would be a very damaging mistake to deal with those wishes before first working through the politeness and the rage. Otherwise, the infantile sexual longings would be discussed, but not deeply experienced.

It is clear from all this that Reich's approach was quite active. It was not active, however, in the didactic sense of advising or exhorting the patient. Nor was it active in Sandor Ferenczi's sense of becoming a direct "good" mother or father surrogate for the patient. The activity lay in the relentless analysis of resistances and in the careful selection of material from the patient's communications.

Some analysts objected that "resistance analysis"—or "character analysis," as Reich later called it, using Abraham's term—violated the principle that one should let oneself be guided by the patient. Selection ran the danger of permitting one's personal biases and interests to override the patient's needs at any given time. Reich replied that the analyst always selected from the patient's associations, for he did not necessarily interpret a dream in sequence but chose this or that detail for interpretation. What really mattered was whether or not one selected correctly within the analytic situation.

A related criticism was that Reich's approach might artificially exaggerate the resistance if the patient's material did not contain clear-cut signs of defensive character traits. Here Reich, along with others such as Ferenczi and Fenichel, replied that the concept of material should be enlarged to include not only the content but also the form of the patient's communications. Case presentations in the seminar convinced Reich that the *nonverbal behavior* of the patient—his look, facial expression, dress, bodily attitude—was not only underestimated but often completely overlooked by many analysts.

The form of behavior was to assume much importance in Reich's development of therapy over the years. By the mid-1930s he was far more interested in the nonverbal emotional expression of the patient than in his or her words. However, as early as 1924 or so, he became convinced that, in Nietzsche's words, "one can lie with the mouth, but with the accompanying grimace one nevertheless tells the truth." And the nonverbal expression often contained the resistive element that had to be dealt with before the words could carry a full emotional charge. That is, a patient might be relating the most dramatic infantile memories, but in a monotonous, low voice. For Reich, it was important to deal with the blocked emotions contained in the vocal expression before getting into the lively content of the communications.

I have gone into some technical detail to give an idea of the problems Reich encountered at the time and the analytic context within which they occurred. The underlying issues can be summarized in a fairly simple fashion.

Reich was trying to understand the conditions under which patients could make use of painful truths, the factors at work in determining when interpretations of the unconscious actually helped the patient in his or her total functioning and when analysis became a mere mental exercise, or "game." Analytic truths are painful because the process perforce stirs up old longings, angers, griefs. These emotions, punished or at least not validated in childhood, are in turn pervaded by anxiety and guilt. Defensive character traits develop as a way of automatically warding off such feelings. Now the analyst disturbs this "neurotic equilibrium." Not only because the patient transfers angry and fearful feelings toward him from earlier figures but because he threatens the patient's precarious peace, the patient comes to dislike the analyst. True, this peace is unsatisfying, otherwise there would be no need for therapy. But that does not mean the patient will not "resist" in all kinds of ways the re-experiencing of tangled emotions painfully endured during childhood.

A way of dealing and at the same time not dealing with this situation is to discuss all kinds of things without really feeling them. What Reich did was to begin to focus intensively on these "inner reservations." However they might be expressed, they all served the function of preventing one from experiencing the whole truth. To shift images, Reich tried to separate out from the muddied palette of the patient's feelings the stronger, purer, more primary colors.

In his stress on strong emotional experience, Reich emphasized an early concept of Freud's. When Freud first studied hysterical patients with Josef Breuer in the 1880s, he used hypnosis. He found that unless a traumatic event was re-experienced, not simply remembered, under hypnosis in all its emotional vividness, there was no alleviation of symptoms.

Freud came to place less emphasis on the particular issue of remembering with affect. Yet while Reich returned to this stress on the emotional re-experiencing of infantile events, he also retained the later Freudian focus on analyzing resistances to the welling up of infantile memories and feelings. He did not attempt to by-pass the defensive process through hypnosis, drugs, and the like.

Indeed, in the face of criticism from different analysts during this period, Reich steadily argued that his own contributions were nothing but a consistent application and extension of Freud's concepts. Only later was he to claim (in my opinion, correctly) that from the very beginning his approach contained some radical differences from that of Freud.

Some of Reich's own personality characteristics may have influenced his choosing to emphasize and develop certain lines of Freud's thought rather than others.

One possible connection between Reich's personality and his theoretical concerns was raised by Richard Sterba, a student of Reich's in the 1920s and currently a well-known analyst in Detroit. Writing some twenty-five years afterward, Sterba acknowledged that "having lived through the era of his [Reich's] impact on the therapeutic thinking of his time and having struggled out of it, I am not altogether in a position to make a completely objective appraisal of their significance for present-day analysis." But he spoke of Reich's brilliance as a clinician, of how impressed he and other students of the technical seminar were, and of how the seminar "led to considerable clarification and provided for me the first orientation in the difficult field of psychoanalysis." Sterba criticized, however, what he believed to be Reich's undue emphasis on latent negative transference, an emphasis which he attributed to Reich's "own suspicious character and the belligerent attitude that stems from it."[9]

There is some truth to this statement, but it is one-sided. In my view, Reich was not initially inclined to emphasize negative transference. It was clinical experience that impressed upon him the importance of latent negative transference. A case in his *Character Analysis*, not published until 1933 but already formulated as a result of his new approach, is worth quoting: "Not until a patient who had, in good positive transference, produced a wealth of recollections and yet had failed to get well, told me many months after breaking off the analysis that he had never trusted me, did I really know the danger of a negative transference which is allowed to remain latent. This made me, successfully, seek for the means of always getting the negative transference out of its hiding places."[10]

The fact that the patient told him of his distrust only many months later may have allowed Reich, with some distance from the heat of the analysis, to ponder quietly its full meaning. Once the significance of latent negative transference did register, it fused with more personal themes in his own life, giving an extra charge to the shock of recognition. More or less hidden negative feelings had played so crucial a role in his own life: his mother's negative feelings toward his father, which led her to take a lover; Willy's own hostility toward Leon, which led him to wish to conceal the affair; and his jealous rage toward his mother and tutor, which impelled him to hint at the affair to Leon. And if there was ever a role model for somebody digging out the truth from its "hiding places," it was his father once Willy had fired his suspicions. In periods of stress, Reich himself sometimes unearthed concealed negative feelings in precisely the belligerent and suspicious way Sterba mentions.

But Reich's emphasis on negative transference was also connected with a more positive aspect of his personality. He liked to make full contact with people. He usually much preferred any disagreements to be aired openly rather than remain concealed. As a teacher, for example, he disliked it when students stared off into space or otherwise indicated preoccupation or boredom with the subject.

Reich's own vitality and emotional directness must have played their part in leading him to elicit the same qualities in his patients. Most of those who knew Reich at different periods of his life comment first of all on the energy, intensity, and directness of his emotional reactions. He in turn welcomed openness on the part of others and experienced unresponsiveness as frustrating and painful.

Thus, Reich brought to psychoanalysis a disposition to understand and break through the armor he often felt in others. This tendency makes clearer his intense interest in Freudian concepts such as resistance. Put differently, Reich did not proceed entirely without preconceptions, as his own writings often make it sound. It in no way minimizes his achievements to see the personal longings and frustrations that played their role in shaping his search. Too often the scientific researcher is described in an objective, unemotional way that overlooks the personal passions, conflicts, yearnings that may also motivate his or her work.

Reich's emphasis on the form of personal communication and on stratified layers of character structure also relate to his preferred modes of investigation. As I have suggested, Reich always preferred to make matters as concrete as possible. Nonverbal resistances—a contemptuous look, an embarrassed smile, a mumbling voice, a highly controlled demeanor—are more tangible than a particular memory or fantasy.

In Reich's keen sense for the form of things, one can detect his country background and the "peasant" quality about him which so many of his colleagues commented on, sometimes with admiration, sometimes with disdain. For a farmer, the form and color of animals, plants, soil, clouds are of practical importance. I was often struck by the similarities between the way Reich would look at a patient and the way he would look at an animal or the atmosphere, noting slight shifts in color, sparkle, or movement.

One particular concept of Reich's vividly illustrates his penchant for physical analogies: his notion of "character armor," which formed the basis of *Character Analysis*. Resistances could now be described in terms of a basic metaphor that allowed for many variations on a central theme. Thus, in the case of the compulsive character, "everything bounces back from his smooth hard surface. The querulous character . . . has an armor which, though mobile, is always bristling. . . . The passive-feminine character seems soft and yielding, but in the analysis that proves to be a kind of armoring which is very difficult to resolve."[11]

If in concentrating on resistances, especially in their nonverbal form, Reich was leading from certain personal strengths, he was also avoiding certain weaknesses. His emphasis on resistances to some extent downplayed the importance of working through infantile experiences. Put more exactly, Reich argued that only a consistent analysis of resistances would bring up early memories in their full affective vividness. However, he was somewhat impatient—and would grow more so over the years—with the slow working through of childhood events, the repeated review of infantile fantasies, and the family constellations within which they occurred. George Gerö quotes Reich as saying in the early 1930s that the psychological reconstruction of childhood events was not his strong point.[12] To some extent this may have been connected with his own difficult childhood traumas.

Character analysis permits—indeed, demands—considerable activity on the part of the analyst. He must make a very careful selection of material: he can be active when the patient is silent by pointing out the latter's nonverbal communications. The traditional, more passive stance of the psychoanalyst was not Reich's preferred approach. He was much more comfortable in the role of vital, active therapist.

A possible danger in this approach was noted by Otto Fenichel. In one of the few careful criticisms of character analysis, Fenichel states his general agreement with and enthusiasm for Reich's concepts. His main caveat concerns not the principles in themselves but the way they may be applied. He warns against an overly aggressive attack on the armor. For we "are familiar with the resistance of some patients, who long for a 'trauma' and expect cure not from a difficult analysis, but from the magic effect of a sudden explosion. There is an analogous longing for a trauma on the part of the analyst also. Let us beware of it."[13]

Fenichel's remarks here are extremely sensitive. Certainly nothing in the essence of character-analytic principles justified harshly aggressive or contemptuous attacks on the patient's armor. I would suggest, however, that Reich may have had some need, inside and outside therapy, to master his own early trauma, which he endured helplessly, by repeating dramatic, emotion-charged events with himself now in the active, trauma-inducing rather than trauma-experiencing role.

Frequently the followers of a pioneer take over the possible misuses of his approach rather than the virtues, which are always harder to achieve. More recent therapeutic approaches, such as the encounter movement, that have been influenced by Reich often err in the direction of sadistic attacks on the armor of patients and of raising false hopes about the beneficial effects of releasing stormy emotions. They spend less time studying and practicing character analysis in its true sense: the careful working through of resistances, with precise attention to where the patient is at any given moment.

Just as Reich's personality influenced his psychoanalytic orientation, so the reactions to his character-analytic work gave him support for his endeavors and at the same time introduced new stresses. The reactions also reveal some destructive organizational processes within psychoanalysis which Reich encountered as his work became more controversial.

Many of the young analysts, like Sterba and Fenichel, welcomed Reich's contributions. In addition, Sandor Ferenczi, one of Freud's closest associates and a renowned Hungarian analyst in the early 1920s, thought highly of Reich. On his trips to the United States, he recommended Reich as an analyst to Americans planning to study psychoanalysis in Vienna. As a result, a number of analytic candidates from the United States, including Walter Briehl, M. Ralph Kaufman, O. Spurgeon English, and John Murray, were analyzed by Reich or supervised by him during the 1920s.

This kind of recognition must have supported Reich's feeling that his work was of value and that he was on to something important. At the same time, many of the older Viennese analysts became quite unhappy with Reich's character-analytic efforts. Theodore Reik, for example, felt that Reich's "schematic" approach to resistance analysis interfered with the free play of the analyst's intuition. The analytic "art" could not be confined to such rules as "no interpretation of content without first interpreting the resistance."

Other senior analysts reacted by saying that Reich's proposals were "nothing new" since Freud had already laid down the principle of analyzing resistances. Reich's reply that the principle was not new but the consistent application of it was rare constituted an implicit indictment of many older analysts' practice. Reich spoke ominously of the frequency of "chaotic situations" in analysis, of therapy shipwrecked because the analyst made all kinds of deep interpretations without first dealing with the resistances in the way of the patient's meaningful use of such insights.

Not only the content of Reich's criticism was provocative but also its form. To judge from his own metaphor of himself as a shark in a pond of carps, he did not mince words in stating his disagreements with others, and indeed at times he may have sounded quite arrogant. In a letter to Paul Federn, dated February 12, 1926, but not in fact sent, he wrote that his active participation in the Society had its drawbacks: at times he was too aggressive, a trait he regretted, and tried to correct.

Reich went on to say that he never intended any personal offense but only said what he felt to be true without regard "for the age or position of the criticized person."[14]

It is interesting that Reich brings up the issue of age; at the time he began making his criticisms of psychoanalysis he was around twenty-seven, while Federn, Hitschmann, and Nunberg were, respectively, fifty-three, fifty-two, and forty-one. Moreover, these men had been with Freud for many years, Reich for only a few.

Some of Reich's analytic peers attributed the hostility shown by senior analysts to their jealousy over the regard that Freud felt for Reich. Freud had permitted Reich to start his analytic practice while still a medical student. He had steadily supported Reich's activities, making warm comments about his articles in the early 1920s and encouraging Reich's efforts in first starting, then leading the technical seminar. One analyst quoted Freud as saying that Reich had "the best head" *(der beste Kopf)* in the Vienna Society.[15] With our knowledge from many sources of Freud's enormous emotional significance as "father figure" to almost all his Viennese colleagues and students, we can imagine how galling it must have been to older "siblings" to see the young Reich so favored by Freud.

The degree of controversy Reich generated among the older analysts can be better understood if we look more closely at the relationship between Reich and the man to whom he addressed the letter cited above—Paul Federn. Federn had been one of Reich's main analytic sponsors during the medical school years and his early period as an analyst. Reich had been to his home for dinner and had been his patient for a brief period. And Federn had called Reich the best diagnostician among the younger analysts.

Sometime around 1924, Federn's attitude appears to have changed. In his letter to Federn, Reich complained bitterly that his efforts had met with "blind criticism or scorn" from Federn and other senior analysts. He went on to say that he was upset that he was the only analyst who discussed his treatment failures in courses and in publications.[16]

In the same letter Reich also complained that he was never appointed to the executive committee of the Vienna Psychoanalytic Society, though this appointment was promised him and he felt he had earned it through his teaching, writing, and administrative activities. He had not complained, he added, when in 1923 he was rejected for committee membership because it was necessary to have one lay analyst (Siegfried Bernfeld) hold office. He also accepted Federn's explanation for the 1924 elections, when a Dr. Robert Jokl was chosen rather than Reich for the position of second secretary because certain differences with Jokl had to be smoothed over. However, in 1925, one of the two secretariat positions was simply abolished. Reich interpreted the administrative move as a "boycott of my person and a completely undeserved wrong."

To understand why the appointment was so important to Reich and why he addressed his complaint to Federn, two facts about the Society at that time should be stressed.

Freud was now ill with cancer of the jaw. Indeed, he did not believe—nor did others—that he had long to live. (In fact, Freud did not die until September 23, 1939, at the age of eighty-three.) He had cut down on his activities and no longer attended the regular meetings of the Society, although he did meet with the executive committee. And, as Reich acknowledged in his letter to Federn, one reason he wanted to be on the executive committee was that it would provide more of an opportunity to see and listen to "the Professor," a motive that was perhaps "infantile, but neither ambitious nor criminal."

Secondly, in 1924 Freud was still chairman of the Society (and the executive committee), but Federn had replaced Otto Rank as vice-chairman. Clearly, the vice-chairman now had considerable organizational power, particularly if, as in Federn's case, he had long been loyal to Freud.

The facts suggest that Reich was not paranoid in thinking that Federn was blocking his advancement to the executive committee. In 1924, Reich was at first chosen by a vote of the committee as second secretary. But apparently Federn, in a private conversation with Freud, persuaded the latter to go against the committee choice and to appoint Jokl as second secretary instead.

However, close upon the heels of this decision Freud received Reich's monograph on the impulsive character. In a letter dated December 14, Freud wrote Federn:

> Shortly after you left I read a manuscript by Dr. Reich which he sent me this morning. I found it so full of valuable content that I very much regretted that we had renounced the recognition of his endeavors. In this mood it occurred to me that for us to propose Dr. Jokl as second secretary is improper because we had no right to change arbitrarily a decision made by the [Executive] Committee. In the light of this fact, what you told me about private animosities against Dr. Reich is not significant. Satisfied with this position, I ask you to abide by the original decision of the Executive Committee and to drop the substitution of Dr. Jokl. I regret that I have to contradict myself so quickly but I hope you will agree this is the only correct decision.[17]

After reading the letter, Federn must have once more communicated with Freud, still urging Jokl over Reich, but now on the grounds that he would be embarrassed vis-à-vis Jokl. For on December 15, Freud wrote Federn again:

> I am very sorry that I cannot rescue you from the embarrassment which you have brought upon yourself. You should have raised your objections against Dr. Reich in the Committee Meeting, not afterward. To try now to get an affirmative vote from individual members

[in favor of Jokl] . . . with the implication that I am motivated to turn against Reich is clearly inadmissible. What would you do if a member refused such an affirmation [of Jokl]? I can therefore only insist that you represent the decision made by the Committee with your cooperation.[18]

But somehow or other Federn managed to arrange that Jokl, not Reich, was appointed. Not until 1927 was Reich appointed a member of the executive committee, on the grounds that he was the leader of the technical seminar, although the same justification could have been found as early as 1924. Reich never did hold a formal office within the committee.

I have gone in some detail into what might be regarded as minor backroom politics in the psychoanalytic movement because it illustrates the growing complexities of Reich's relationships with his colleagues, especially the senior figures. It also provides further evidence of the support Reich received from Freud. Considering the frequent allegations of Reich's paranoid tendencies, it is worth emphasizing that Reich initially underestimated the degree to which Federn was working against him.

Why was Federn so opposed to Reich? Reich's character-analytic concepts, his organization of the technical seminar, the regard Freud felt for Reich, all help clarify some of the reasons for Federn's opposition, but do not fully explain it. To anticipate the story briefly, Federn was also angered by Reich's emphasis on sexuality. For during the years under discussion Reich was also arguing in a series of articles that the capacity for full expression of genitality, or what he termed "orgastic potency," was *the* goal of psychoanalytic treatment.

Furthermore, as Federn undoubtedly knew, Reich, who had married in 1922, was having extramarital relationships. For his part, Paul Federn has been described by his son, Ernst, as a Victorian—an enlightened one, to be sure, but Victorian nonetheless.[19] This outlook (to continue Ernst Federn's description) was shared by many of the older analysts. While psychoanalysis boldly investigated the details of patients' sexual lives, fantasies, and early experiences, Freud's own views on freer sexual expression versus restraint or sublimation were so complex that one could select diverse aspects of his orientation to justify a variety of lifestyles. However, the popular image of the older group of analysts as storming pioneers or radicals in the way they lived sexually is a myth. For Federn and many others, marital infidelity, like homosexuality, was "immoral." And to be "moral" was extremely important.

Thus Reich, initially grateful to Federn, had by 1926 become furious with him. Their hostility was to intensify still further—Federn being one of the prime movers in Reich's expulsion from the psychoanalytic organization in 1934. In the 1940s, when Federn was living in the United States, he would reply to questions about Reich with a sad "Mea culpa, mea *maxima* culpa," referring to the recognition he had given the young medical student and analyst in the days before Reich "went astray."[20] Perhaps he was also intimating that he had done a poor job of analyzing Reich. On his side, Reich was to reserve some of his choicest epithets for Federn, a man he saw as steadily "digging" against him and undermining his good relationship with Freud.

If history is the final arbiter of these psychoanalytic conflicts of the 1920s, Freud was the immediate judge. Freud usually did not express himself on analytic controversies unless he deemed the divergencies from "classical analysis" important enough (e.g., in the cases of Adler, Jung, and Rank) to require a firm stand. Yet Reich was *not* presenting his character-analytic concepts as a revision of psychoanalysis, but rather as a consistent elaboration of cardinal Freudian principles. But the vigor and adamant tone with which he presented his "analysis of resistances" was sufficient to draw Freud himself into the debate.

Freud's view of these quarrels was characteristically complex. In December 1926, ten months after Reich's angry letter to Federn, Reich gave a talk on his character-analytic concepts before a small group of analysts at Freud's home. Reich presented the central problem of whether, in the presence of a latent negative attitude, one should interpret the patient's incestuous desires or wait until the patient's distrust was eliminated. Freud interrupted Reich: "Why would you *not* interpret the material in the order in which it appears? *Of course* one has to analyze and interpret incest dreams as soon as they appear."[21] Reich relates that he kept trying to substantiate his point but could not persuade Freud. It was a special disappointment to Reich because in private conversations about technique he had the impression that Freud supported his approach. Freud's position at the meeting further strengthened the hand of Reich's opponents, who "gloated over and pitied" Reich. Finally, Reich was getting into trouble not only with senior analysts but with Freud himself.

Freud's lack of support for character analysis presaged still more severe disagreements that were to follow over Reich's concepts of genitality and orgastic potency.

7

Reich's Work on Orgastic
Potency: 1922-1926

Reich's contributions to the study of characterology were crucial to establishing his reputation. His originality lay in how he expanded and combined existing psychoanalytic ideas in the development of a systematic character-analytic technique.

Overlapping in time with his characterological work, Reich published a series of papers on orgastic potency that were without precedent in the psychoanalytic literature. Whereas the character-analytic work initially met with considerable approval, Reich's work on orgastic potency was from the first unpopular. Indeed, he has been ridiculed inside and outside psychoanalytic circles from the 1920s to the present as the "prophet of the better orgasm" and the "founder of a genital utopia." Yet Reich regarded his elucidation of orgastic potency as the keystone to all his later work. "It represented the coastal stretch from which everything else has developed," he was to write later.[1]

Reich's path to the study of the function of the orgasm was preceded by a study of genitality. Unlike orgastic potency, the concept of genitality had clear connections with existing psychoanalytic literature. While Freud had enlarged the concept of sexuality to include more than genital experience, for example, in his elucidation of oral and anal impulses and fantasies, he had also posited a genital stage in childhood around the age of four or five. During this period, masturbation, exhibitionism, and genital feelings toward the parent of the opposite sex began to develop. In addition, Karl Abraham had formulated the concept of a "genital character" to describe the kind of person who had successfully resolved the Oedipal conflicts characteristic of this stage.

Freud clearly saw genital union between man and woman as the "normal" adult expression of the sexual instinct. He paid attention to a wide variety of "deviations" from this norm, whether expressed as object choice (e.g., homosexuality) or in the kind of preferred sexual activity (e.g., voyeurism).

For all his stress on "deviation" from "normal" sexuality, Freud did not provide any clear guidelines as to what constituted healthy adult genital functioning. Psychoanalysis could explain—and sometimes treat—gross genital disturbances such as impotence, extreme frigidity, and perversion. If no such clear-cut disturbances existed, if the male was erectively and ejaculatively potent, if the female experienced a predominance of vaginal over clitoral excitation,* then psychoanalysts by and large were prepared to accept the patient's sexual functioning as "normal." True, there might still be various psychological conflicts disturbing the individual's love relations. But the *physiological* sexual functioning itself need not be in question.

It was into this undefined area of healthy adult genitality that the young Reich chose to move both clinically and theoretically. True to the psychoanalytic tradition of studying pathology, he confined himself at first to a more detailed exposition of genital conflicts. Thus in his first paper on the genital experiences of patients, "Über Spezifität der Onanieformen" ("The Specificity of Forms of Masturbation"), written in 1922, when Reich was twenty-five, he noted that "in not a single patient was the act of masturbation accompanied by the fantasy of experiencing pleasure in the sexual act."[2]

Reich also noted that the masturbation fantasies of his male patients could be divided into two major groups: in the first group, the penis functioned, it was erect and active, but it was conceived as a murderous weapon or as a way of "proving" potency. In the second, the penis remained flaccid and there were masochistic fantasies of being beaten, bound, or tortured.

Reich's approach to the study of his patients' masturbation is noteworthy. First, he was clearly not satisfied with the simple report from the patient that "I masturbated." He wanted to know, in detail, *how* and with *what kind* of fantasy. He also assumed that healthy masturbation included the fantasy of heterosexual intercourse, an assumption that—to my knowledge—was not previously present in the psychoanalytic literature. Finally, he was concerned with how closely masturbation had a genital orientation, not only in fantasy but also in physiological functioning (e.g., in the male, erection and thrusting motions).

The following year, 1923, Reich published the first outline of what was to

---

*Psychoanalytic theory posited a shift in normal female development from an active, predominantly clitoral excitation in childhood to a more receptive, vaginal orientation in adolescence and adulthood. This notion, which has come under critical fire in recent years, will be examined in more detail later.

become his major thesis concerning genitality. The article, "Über Genitalität" ("On Genitality"), dealt with the prognostic significance of the patient's having attained "genital primacy" in childhood.[3] Reich also contended that an evaluation of the patient's genital functioning during analysis provided an important, if not the most important, therapeutic criterion.

On the importance of "genital primacy," Reich argued that patients who had reached the genital stage in childhood had a better prognosis than those who, having reached it, later regressed to an earlier mode of psychosexual functioning. The latter in turn had a better prognosis than those who as children had never reached the genital stage but had remained fixated at the oral or anal level.

Had Reich confined himself to these observations, backed by case material, he would have made a valuable but modest contribution to the psychoanalytic literature. The crux of these findings on psychosexual development was not original with him. However, Reich then went on to make statements that were both original and highly controversial.

He argued that *all* patients were genitally disturbed: that is, they did not achieve full satisfaction in sexual intercourse. Reich's discussion of incomplete sexual gratification had explicit connections with some of Freud's early formulations. In 1905, Freud had remarked that "no neurosis is possible with a normal *vita sexualis.*"[4] The classical psychoneuroses studied by Freud—hysteria and obsessional neuroses—were rooted in infantile sexual conflicts.

Freud posited another set of neuroses, and applied the term "actual neuroses" to those that resulted from present-day (*aktuelle* in German) disturbances of adult sexual life. Thus, the two forms of "actual neuroses"— anxiety neurosis and neurasthenia—were disturbances that were the immediate result of damned-up sexuality. Anxiety neurosis was caused by sexual abstinence or coitus interruptus. It had to be distinguished from neurasthenia, which was caused by "sexual abuse," such as "excessive masturbation," and characterized by back pains, headaches, inability to concentrate, and feelings of fatigue.

Actual neuroses, unlike the psychoneuroses, were not amenable to classical analytic treatment. They were treated by eliminating the harmful sexual practices that led to the "damming up" of sexual energy. However, exactly why a patient engaged in such harmful sexual practices in the first place was not clear in Freud's formulation.

If Freud distinguished clearly between psychoneuroses and actual neuroses, Reich came to believe in a strong relationship between the two sets of neuroses. He argued that without some kind of psychic inhibition, there would be no "actual neuroses," for why else would a person abstain from or abuse sex? (Later, Reich would also emphasize social factors such as the unavailability of contraceptives that could contribute to the development of actual neuroses.) At the same time, Reich argued that the actual neuroses provided the driving energetic core of the psychoneuroses. "Where did they (the compulsions and hysterias) derive their energy from? Undoubtedly, from the actual neurotic core of the dammed-up sexual energy."[5]

In the relationship between actual neuroses and psychoneuroses, Reich detected a reciprocal interaction, the kind of interaction he was later to emphasize in diverse realms. He saw the reactivated infantile conflicts, in the form of a psychoneurosis, as further impeding adult genital function, thereby intensifying the actual neuroses, and so on in an endless vicious circle. However, there was also the possibility of a beneficent circle. A fulfilled sexual life with no actual neurosis could lead to a withdrawal of energy from early childhood conflicts. The reduction in infantile inhibitions in turn facilitated ever more gratifying adult love relations. Indeed, in his first article on genitality, Reich claimed that this was happening in his successful cases. He argued that those patients who improved were able, with help from analysis, to maintain the kind of love life that drained off energy from the infantile conflicts. The unconscious material was not so much worked through in detail as it was deprived of the "water" that had previously stimulated its malignant growth.

We can note here two parallel lines, the convergence of which Reich did not initially emphasize. In the technical seminar, Reich was concerned with describing the conditions under which the interpretation of repressed material was effective. It was important for the patient to remember with *affect*, by means of the systematic analysis of resistances. Initially, however, in the technical seminar Reich did not place great emphasis on the genital functioning of patients. By contrast, in his first papers on genitality, he emphasized the deleterious consequences of blocked libidinal discharge, but did not deal with the analysis of resistances. In both contexts, Reich was concerned with the liberation of emotion. In one setting, he was focusing on the characterological obstacles to liberation. In the other, he was stressing the emotional—or more specifically the genital—wave of excitation and its discharge.

In the interrelation between actual neuroses and psychoneuroses, Reich believed he had found some way of short-cutting the long, involved process of resistance analysis he had elaborated in the technical seminar. This particular direction would lead him later into very active social efforts, counseling of the young, birth control clinics, and mass meetings dealing with the connections between politics and sexual suppression. But in the early 1920s, this particular angle of his work had not yet crystalized. What we see during this period is his movement in two theoretical directions: through character analysis into an ever deeper elucidation of *inner* obstacles to psychological health; and through his development of the concept of actual neuroses into an emphasis on more superficial conflicts and reality frustrations, the elimination of which might reverse the neurotic process.

Over the years, Freud himself paid less and less attention to actual neuroses, although he never abandoned this separate category of emotional illness, while most other analysts had little use for it. Among major analytic theorists, Reich alone maintained a strong interest in actual neuroses and the related concept of anxiety as transformed sexuality. In a study generally critical of Reich, Charles Rycroft has commented:

> [Reich's] view of the relationship between actual and psychoneuroses has not been absorbed into psychoanalytic thinking but it has two great merits. It retains a connection between psychopathology and physiology—in the last resort the neuroses are not purely mental formations but arise from and affect the body—and it provides an explanation of why neuroses do not disappear spontaneously. So far as I know Reich is the only analyst to offer any sort of explanation as to why the childhood pathogenic experiences that according to psychoanalysis cause neuroses do not gradually lose their impact when neurotics move away from their childhood environment.[6]

What Reich did not do in this first paper on genitality was to define what in fact he meant by *effective* genital satisfaction. He still accepted the prevailing psychoanalytic definitions—erective and ejaculative potency in men, a vaginal orgasm in women. Reich's scanty description of genital health left him open to criticism that was quick in coming. He himself described the reception to his first paper on genitality, which he presented at a meeting of the Vienna Psychoanalytic Association in November 1923, as follows:

> While I was talking, I became increasingly aware of a chilling of the atmosphere. I used to speak well, and thus far had always found my audience attentive. When I was finished, there was an icy stillness in the room. After a pause, the discussion began. My assertion that the genital disturbance was perhaps the most important symptom of the neurosis, was erroneous. Even worse . . . was my contention that an evaluation of genitality provided prognostic and therapeutic criteria. Two analysts bluntly asserted that they knew any number of female patients with a completely healthy sex life. They seemed to me more excited than their usual scientific reserve would have led one to expect.
> In this controversy I started out by being at a disadvantage. I had had to admit to myself that among the male patients there were many with an apparently undisturbed genitality, though the case was not true of the female patients.[7]

It is interesting that Reich later acknowledged having to "admit to myself" in 1923 that there were male patients who appeared genitally healthy in spite of neurotic symptoms. The paper itself holds no hint of such an awareness. Characteristically, Reich expressed himself at the time as more certain than in fact he was.

The criticisms Reich encountered sent him back to the drawing board, intent on defining more precisely what he meant by a satisfactory genital life, and the ways his neurotic patients failed to show this kind of gratification. This seems to be the first of many instances where Reich fruitfully used opposition to his work in a creative way to define more carefully what he meant: that, in this instance, there were genitally well-functioning patients who nonetheless suffered from neurotic symptoms. Stimulated to further study, he would demonstrate that he was more right than his critics thought, though in a different way from the one originally argued.

In addition to the details of his own patients' sexual functioning, Reich proceeded to examine, through interviews and case records, the love life of over two hundred patients seen at the Vienna Psychoanalytic Polyclinic. He was testing several hypotheses here:

(1)   That genital disturbance was present in all neuroses;
(2)   That the severity of neuroses was positively correlated with the degree of genital disturbance; and
(3)   That patients who improved in therapy and remained symptom-free achieved a gratifying sex life.

Again, Reich was impressed by the frequency and depth of genital disturbances he found. He became very suspicious of the superficial reports about sexual experience, whether supplied by clinic patients themselves or by the psychiatrists who evaluated them. For example, a patient whose sex life was reported to be normal, on closer interviewing by Reich revealed that she experienced pleasurable sensations during intercourse but no climax. Moreover, she was consumed by thoughts of murdering her partner following the act.

Reich's research efforts were a far cry from current standards, though for psychoanalysts in the 1920s they were better than most. In this instance he at least studied more than a few cases before giving his conclusions. Ideally, however, one would like to have had much more specific definitions of what Reich meant by freedom from symptoms in nonsexual areas.

Reich's second paper directly concerned with genitality, published in 1924, "Die therapeutische Bedeutung des Genitallibidos" ("The Therapeutic Significance of Genital Libido"), is significant because in it he first noted that while some patients were potent in the usual sense of the term, they lacked what he called "orgastic potency." Orgastic potency included, among other attributes, the fusion of tender and sensuous strivings toward one's partner, rhythmic frictional movements during intercourse, a slight lapse of consciousness at the acme of sexual excitation, "vibrations of the total musculature" during the discharge phase, and feelings of gratified fatigue following intercourse.[8]

Reich was not unique in his emphasis on the capacity for uniting tender and sensuous feelings in a healthy love relationship. As early as 1912, Freud had noted that many male patients would not unite both tender and sensuous feelings, but would concentrate the former on an idealized mother figure toward whom they could not feel erotic, and their sexual feelings on prostitutes.[9] What *was* original was Reich's emphasis on the involuntary physical aspects of full genital discharge.

In his next paper, "Die Rolle der Genitalität in der Neurosentherapie" ("The Role of Genitality in the Therapy of the Neuroses"), published in 1925, Reich expanded on the "involuntary surrender" and the total bodily involvement of healthy genitality. He also argued that adequate discharge of sexual energy can *only* come about through the genitals: "The pregenital erogenous zones . . . can only serve to increase the level of excitation."[10]

It became clear that the patients Reich—and others—had previously regarded as sexually normal failed to meet these more refined requirements. On the psychological level, Reich noted that seemingly potent male patients who could not completely surrender during intercourse also used very active heterosexual strivings as a defense against other (e.g., homosexual) impulses.

Earlier psychoanalytic literature had documented the variety of motives and wishes at work in love relationships. But they also posited that a patient's sexual act itself could be "normal" in the physiological sense even if his relations with his partners were chaotic or otherwise highly disturbed. What was new in Reich's formulation was that the *physical act* was disrupted when unconscious conflicts were operative.

I have tried to show how Reich's concept of orgastic potency did not emerge suddenly and in full-blown form. On the contrary, since it was intimately related to his clinical and theoretical concerns, it took time to coalesce. Indeed, not until 1926 could Reich present a highly detailed description of what in fact he meant by "orgastic potency." It was contained in his book *Die Funktion des Orgasmus*, written in 1926 and published in 1927.

By this time, Reich's grip on the subject had increased to the point where he could offer a description that, essentially, would satisfy him to the end of his life. When in 1942 Reich published another volume, also entitled *The Function of the Orgasm*, he took almost unchanged the elucidation of orgastic potency from the 1927 German volume, whereas the rest of the later work was radically different.[11]

Because of its pivotal significance, I shall present Reich's description of orgastic potency in considerable detail, quoting parts of it.

Conceptually, Reich divided the orgastically satisfying sexual experience into two main phases: the voluntary control of the excitation, and the involuntary contractions.

In the first phase, for the man, erection is pleasurable and the genital not overexcited. An important criterion of orgastic potency in the male is the urge to penetrate, an urge not found in many erectively potent men with narcissistic characters. The man is also spontaneously gentle, without having to cover up sadistic impulses by a forced kind of tenderness. The genital of the woman becomes hyperemic and moist. Reich also asserts that the "activity of the woman normally differs in no way from that of the man. The widely prevalent passivity of the woman is pathological. . . ."

Reich goes on to describe a rise in excitation in both the man and the woman following penetration of the penis. "The man's sensation of 'being sucked in' corresponds to the woman's sensation that she is 'sucking the penis in.'" As a result of mutual, slow, and spontaneous effortless frictions the excitation is concentrated on the surface and glans of the penis, and the posterior parts of the vaginal mucous membrane. Reich's emphasis on *slow* and *spontaneous* frictional movements in contrast to rapid, forced ones provided yet another key distinguishing mark of orgastic potency: "According to the consensus of potent men and women, the pleasure sensations are all the more intense the slower and more gentle the frictions are, and the better they harmonize with each other. This presupposes a considerable ability to identify oneself with one's partner."

With continued friction, the excitation spreads more and more to the whole body, while the excitation of the genital remains more or less at the same level. Finally, as a result of another, usually sudden increase of genital excitation, there sets in the second phase.

In this second phase, the increase of excitation can no longer be controlled voluntarily; rather, it takes hold of the whole physical being and produces rapid heartbeat and deep expirations.

Bodily excitation becomes concentrated more upon the genital, a "melting" sensation sets in, which may best be described as a radiation of excitation from the genital to other parts of the body.

This excitation results first in involuntary contractions—similar to waves —in the total musculature of the genital and of the pelvic floor. In this stage, interruption of the sexual act is absolutely unpleasurable, for both man and woman; instead of occurring rhythmically, the muscular contractions, which lead to the orgasm as well as to the ejaculation, would occur in the form of spasms. This results in intensely unpleasant sensations and occasionally leads to pain in the pelvic floor and the lower back; in addition, as a result of the spasm, ejaculation occurs earlier than in the case of an undisturbed rhythm.

With an increase in the frequency of the involuntary muscular contractions, the excitation increases rapidly and steeply up to the acme. Now occurs a more or less intense clouding of consciousness. The frictions become *spontaneously more intensive,* after having subsided momentarily at the point of the acme; the urge to "penetrate completely" increases with each ejaculatory muscle contraction. In the woman, the muscle contractions take the same course as in the man. Experientially, the difference is only that during and immediately after the acme the healthy womans wants to "receive completely."

The orgastic excitation takes hold of the entire body and results in *lively contractions of the whole body musculature.* Self-observations of healthy individuals of both sexes show that what is called the release of tension is predominantly the result of a *flowing back of the excitation from the genital to the body.* This flowing back is experienced as a *sudden decrease* of the tension. The complete flowing back of the excitation toward the whole body is what constitutes *gratification.* Gratification means two things: shift of the direction of flow of excitation in the body, and unburdening of the genital apparatus.

Then the excitation tapers off and is immediately replaced by a pleasant bodily and psychic relaxation; usually, there is a strong desire for sleep. The sensual relations have subsided. What continues is a grateful, tender attitude toward the partner.

Reich contrasts this kind of sensation with those found in the orgastically impotent: leaden exhaustion, disgust, repulsion, or indifference, and occasionally hatred toward the partner. In other instances, such as satyriasis and nymphomania, the sexual excitation does not subside. Often in these instances insomnia and restlessness follow.

In reviewing orgastic potency, Reich sounded his dominant chords:

> *The involuntary contractions of the organism and the complete discharge of the excitation* are the most important criteria of orgastic potency. . . . There are partial releases of tension which are *similar* to an orgasm; they used to be taken for the actual release of tension. Clinical experience shows that man—as a result of general sexual repression—has lost the capacity for *ultimate vegetatively involuntary surrender.* What I mean by "orgastic potency" is exactly this ultimate, hitherto unrecognized portion of the capacity for excitation and release of tension.

It has often been said of Reich that he emphasizes orgastic potency, but does not speak of love. In fact, he is quite aware of the psychological aspects of the experience:

> . . . In both sexes, the orgasm is more intense if the peaks of genital excitation coincide. This occurs frequently in individuals who are able to concentrate their tender as well as their sensual feelings on a partner; it is the rule when the relationship is undisturbed by either internal or external factors. In such cases, at least *conscious* fantasies are completely absent; the ego is undividedly absorbed in the perception of pleasure. *The ability to concentrate oneself with one's whole personality on the orgastic experience, in spite of possible conflicts, is a further criterion of orgastic potency.*

With Reich's description of orgastic potency we enter the specific Reichian domain. The very silence of this world—a world of slow, frictional movement, of lapse of consciousness, of involuntary contractions—sets it apart from the usual analytic concern with verbalization and cognitive mastery of the emotive and irrational. Indeed, there is irony in the fact that Reich chooses as his criterion of mental health the individual's capacity to go beyond mental phenomena, to have no thought, no consciousness even, but to surrender completely to the involuntary and to sensations of pleasure.

In this emphasis on the wordless, the ineffable, Reich revealed himself as closer to the truths of certain philosophers and poets than to his fellow psychoanalysts. Nietzsche had written: "All the regulations of mankind are tuned to the end that the intense sensation of life is lost in continual distractions."[12] Wittgenstein asserted that the most important matters of life were essentially not discussable; they were beyond words. And Conrad Aiken has described how most of us reveal only little glimpses of our lives:

> . . . All the while
> Withholding what's most precious to ourselves,—
> Some sinister depth of lust or fear or hatred,
> The somber note that gives the chord its power;
> Or a white loveliness—if such we know—
> Too much like fire to speak of without shame.[13]

Reich's emphasis on the involuntary and nonverbal in orgastic experience later earned him the criticism that he was anti-intellectual, a celebrater of the Lawrentian "pulling of the blood" at the expense of the ego, or of man's cognitive mode of functioning. The charge is unwarranted. Reich was in no way opposed to clear, rational thinking. *Character Analysis,* for example, represents a very high order of sustained, original, intricate conceptualization. Indeed, Reich argued that nothing interfered with productive thinking more than "sexual stasis," since with it often went a nagging preoccupation with sexual fantasies and a heavy investment of energy in quelling the inner turmoil.

Reich's claims for the importance of orgastic potency left him open to more specific criticisms than the accusation of romanticism. The charge has been made that Reich's evidence for his claims was slim. But as Charles Rycroft has commented: "Whereas the typical civilized man with his inhibiting character armor only experiences partial releases of tension which are similar to orgasm, the genital character experiences an ultimate vegetatively involuntary surrender of which lesser mortals have no inkling. . . . One is . . . left wondering how Reich knew, from what experiences of his own or his patients he derived this insight."[14]

Since an important source for Reich's concept of orgastic experience was in fact his own life, let us turn again to the relationship between his ideas and his personality in private life.

It is clear from the vicissitudes of Reich's relationships with women that his sex life varied considerably. When he was nineteen years old, Reich for the first time experienced "orgastic potency" in his relationship with an Italian woman. This was different from his previous sexual affairs; it was also different from many of his subsequent relationships. For example, in his disguised case history, Reich wrote of a period during medical school when he "experienced a restless quest for an ideal sexual partner, with feelings of disappointment following any actual experience."

In the next chapter, we shall see how his marriage deteriorated in the mid-1920s, leading him to resume his relationship with Lia Laszky on a fuller basis than when they were medical students. Throughout his life, Reich was acutely aware of the inner and outer obstacles in his own sexual relations. Psychological and physical compatibility, the degree of trust, social conditions, outbreaks of jealousy—all these could and did affect his sexual experience.

Many factors were at work, it is clear, in Reich's formulation of and emphasis on orgastic potency. They included his personal problems in the usual sense; the wide range in his functioning, which posed a challenge for him to understand; and the opposition to his own intense feelings.

The same combination of factors emerges if we turn to the earlier determinants of Reich's interest in genitality. His later emphasis allowed his family tragedy to been seen in a new light. In his first paper, Reich had focused on the disruptive aspects of his mother's affair on his own psychic development. A few years later, he was able to look at his mother's actions from her point of view. Although his social criticism was still not highly developed in the early 1920s, he did comment on the "plight of the unhappily married woman who is economically chained to her husband under irreconcilable, desolate circumstances."[15] No longer is his mother's affair with the tutor to be denounced.

The concept of orgastic potency provided Reich with a solution to a general problem as well as to some of his own specific concerns. If genitality had been understood and affirmed, his mother need not have died, his own development would have been less riven by conflict, and his strengths might have received a more nourishing response from the world.

Related concepts that Reich emphasized also seem to have been connected with his own experiences, for example, the notion of "actual neuroses" or "stasis neuroses." Reich himself, especially as a young man, may have suffered a good many somatic symptoms under conditions of sexual abstinence. He once told Richard Sterba that he experienced sharp feelings of physical discomfort when deprived of sexual intercourse for any length of time.[16] During medical school his relationship with Lia, which stopped short of intercourse, may well have led to actual-neurotic symptoms.

Reich's discomfort with abstinence could also have been related to his distaste for the concept of sublimation. In his early papers on genitality, Reich maintained, in contrast to Freud and most analysts, that the capacity for sublimation was insufficient as a criterion for therapeutic cure. "Clinical experience [shows] that the psyche cannot discharge the total libidinous excitation in the form of work for any length of time." Reich went on to say that the majority of patients were not scholars or artists whose work could, at least for limited periods of time, absorb enormous amounts of energy. "They needed direct and effective genital gratification."[17]

Reich was right, I believe, in his assertion that the best basis for solid, pleasurable work was a fulfilled love life. However, I also believe that he underestimated the capacity of many people to use work as an effective way of binding sexual energy in the absence of direct genital gratification. His adamant position on this issue stemmed in part from the fact that work, in the absence of love, was difficult for *him*.

Reich's sexual concepts also related to his preferred mode of investigation. Reich was fascinated by the concrete and the tangible. The phenomena described by Freud in connection with actual neuroses, such as anxiety attacks, palpitations, and the like, had a direct physiological quality that greatly appealed to him. As he put it some years later: "It is not surprising that [Freud's] theory of the actual neuroses, struck me as more in keeping with natural science than the 'interpretation' of the meaning of 'symptoms' in the psychoneuroses."[18]

Again and again, Reich picks up on early Freudian notions that strike some special resonance in him. Drawn to Freud's early work on "catharsis," he made it a central part of his character-analytic endeavors. He was drawn also to actual neuroses, which, in the form of stasis neuroses, were to become linchpins in his theory building and clinical work.

It is interesting that the concept of "sexual stasis," like the concept of resistance, facilitated a very direct clinical approach. In analytic sessions, Reich could note the rapid alternation between feelings of anxiety and genital excitation:

> It happens frequently that a patient becomes excited during the analytic therapy session because of unconscious sexual fantasies regarding the transference situation. If the sexual repression has not as yet been dissolved, one finds that they complain about fatigue, weakness, faintness of the extremities, feelings of heat or cold, palpitations of the heart, anxiety, etc. The symptoms of anxiety disappear and genital pleasure sensations appear in their place, if one succeeds in liberating the patient's genital sensations, after the repressed fantasies have been made conscious. . . . It is an analytic triumph if the therapy succeeds in helping the patient to stop repressing the perception of the newly emerging sexual excitement which causes powerful, growing sexual feelings which often are extremely hard to tolerate.[19]

Reich was unusual, if not unique, among analysts in working so directly with the patient's genital sensations. Undoubtedly, the directness of his therapeutic approach (even before he moved to touching the patient's body) strengthened the conviction of some older analysts that Reich was an "immoral" therapist as well as an "immoral" man.

Indeed, Reich's penchant for the concrete, the physical, the tangible is no more evident than in his description of orgastic potency. Reich, of course, did not directly *see* orgastic potency in his patients. He had to rely on verbal reports from his patients of their own sex lives. However, during analysis he made a point of eliciting and observing bodily phenomena that were close to the experience of "real-life" sexuality.

Which brings us back to the original question: On what evidence did Reich base his concepts concerning orgastic potency? I have made clear my belief that Reich started from his own sexual experiences. He then went on to find corroborating and amplifying evidence from his clinical work and from general social-cultural observations. Gradually, he wove an interlocking network of evidence to support his sweeping hypotheses.

Freud utilized the same procedure when, on the basis of his own self-analysis, limited clinical experience, and wide reading in anthropology and literature, he proclaimed the universality of the Oedipus complex. That this complex was not as universal as he assumed does not detract from the magnificence of the discovery. Nor do the possible qualifications regarding Reich's concept of orgastic potency substantially detract from its magnificence. Even though the evidence for the degree of correctness of Reich's sexual concepts is far from conclusive, orgastic potency remains an immensely fruitful concept.

It takes an unusual kind of mind, an unusual courage, indeed, an unusual narcissism, to say: What is true of me is true of all men. Emerson once wrote: "In great writers we meet our own rejected thoughts." This kind of approach can lead to huge errors, if uncontrolled by objective research. But it can also be the path to great discoveries. Throughout his life, an important ingredient of Reich's work method was to begin with feeling, with subjective experience, and then move on to more controlled observation. I have emphasized here his commitment to the first part of this method, a commitment that distinguishes him from most contemporary scientists.

Reich was criticized for the content of his concepts, but equally for his manner of presenting them. For example, Helena Deutsch, looking back to the 1920s, speaks with distaste of Reich's "aggressiveness" and "fanaticism" in advancing his ideas on sexuality.[20]

A closer look at Reich's presentation of his views on genitality yields a more complex picture. If there is a note of fanaticism in the early papers on genitality, Reich was also capable of going back to clinical issues and reviewing them more carefully in response to criticism. Furthermore, there was a tentativeness that revealed itself less in his manner of presentation than in the absence of any presentation at all. In the technical seminar, for instance, Reich wrote that "the actual goal of therapy, that of making the patient capable of orgasm, was not mentioned in the first years of the seminar. I avoided the subject instinctively. It was not liked and aroused animosity. Furthermore, I was not too sure about it myself."[21]

In certain instances the opposition clearly stung Reich, perhaps even inspired him, to pursue his efforts all the more vigorously, to state his conclusions all the more sweepingly. But he could also complain about specific ill treatment. For example, in the unsent letter to Paul Federn of February 12, 1926, Reich spoke of the "irrelevant personal criticism" Theodore Reik had made of one of his papers. He also mentioned the "personal insults of Drs. Hitschmann, Nunberg, and Hoffer." He went on to write that he would not even itemize all the instances of "needling" lest he appear foolish.[22]

Reich was perhaps needled for other aspects of his work besides his formulations on genitality, although these seem to have been the main target. And he appears to have been especially sensitive to any allusion that he advocated promiscuity or lived a promiscuous life. An anecdote from around 1920 illustrates this sensitivity.

During his medical school days, Lia Laszky and Reich attended a party given by Paul and Gisela Stein. Paul, it seems, had a sarcastic wit and was not hesitant to use it even against friends. At the party, a game was played, a kind of charade, in which one person would leave the room and an object would be selected to represent the missing person. The person then returned, and he or she would have to determine why the particular representation was chosen. When Lia, who was Reich's girlfriend at the time, left the room, Paul chose a fruit bowl to represent her.[23]

The point of Stein's little joke lies in the double meaning of the word "fruit" in German, its second, slang meaning being "sexual philanderer." Lia was the "bowl" in whom the "fruit" Reich lay. Reich did not get the joke at first, but when he did, he was furious—so furious he almost left the party. Laszky commented ironically that he wasn't angry because their relationship had been joked about in so public a fashion. He was angry because *he* had been called a philanderer. Perhaps his chagrin was all the greater because, in fact, his "philandering" with Laszky was quite limited at that time.

Whatever Reich's sensitivities to the criticism from his analytic peers, they were as nothing compared with his concern over Freud's reactions. For Reich kept arguing that just as his character-analytic concepts were the "logical" extension of Freud's resistance analysis, so his concept of orgastic potency was the "logical" amplification of Freud's emphasis on freeing libido from its pregenital fixations.

It mattered a great deal to Reich that Freud should endorse the legitimacy of this view. Reich felt a strong sense of loyalty to Freud and certainly a strong desire for his approval. Given the attacks from older analysts, Reich's concepts would have been utterly intolerable if he had not linked them so closely with Freud's.

Freud's initial reaction to Reich's work in the sphere of sexuality was positive. In reply to the 1925 paper Reich wrote on "actual neuroses," Freud commented in a letter to him:

> I have known for a long time that my formulation of *Aktual-neurosen* was superficial and in need of thorough-going correction. . . . Clarification was to be expected from further, intelligent investigation. Your efforts seem to point a new and helpful way. Whether your assumption really solves the problem I do not know. I still have certain doubts. . . . However, I trust you will keep the problem in mind and will arrive at a satisfactory solution.[24]

Given this encouraging response, Reich was quite upset when Freud responded less warmly to a more systematic presentation of Reich's views on actual neuroses and the function of the orgasm. This elucidation occurred in his book *Die Funktion des Orgasmus,* which Reich presented in manuscript form to Freud on the occasion of the latter's seventieth birthday on May 6, 1926. The manuscript was dedicated: "To my teacher, Professor Sigmund Freud, with deep veneration." When Freud saw it, he hesitated a moment, then said, as if disturbed, "That thick?" Reich felt uneasy and thought that Freud would not have made such a cutting remark without a basis.[25]

Worse still, Freud took more than two months to respond to the manuscript, whereas his usual habit was to give a written opinion within a few days. When he did respond, Freud wrote:

> Dear Dr. Reich:
> I took plenty of time, but finally I did read the manuscript which you dedicated to me for my anniversary. I find the book valuable, rich in observation and thought. As you know, I am in no way opposed to your attempt to solve the problem of neurasthenia by explaining it on the basis of the absence of genital primacy.[26]

Why Reich read this letter as a rejection is not clear since, on the surface, it does not seem so. Perhaps it was its brevity. Probably Reich was also reacting to the whole sequence of events. At any rate, Freud's reaction was sufficient for Reich to postpone sending the book to the publisher until January 1927.

Exactly what Freud thought about Reich's orgasm theory is not clear on the basis of evidence from those years. However, there are documented reactions from a slightly later date that give some clues to what may have been in Freud's mind when he responded to the manuscript of *Die Funktion des Orgasmus.*

In a letter dated May 9, 1928, to Lou Andreas-Salomé, friend of Nietzsche, Rilke, and Freud, and a practicing psychoanalyst in the later years of her life, Freud wrote: "We have here a Dr. Reich, a worthy but impetuous young man, passionately devoted to his hobby horse, who now salutes in the genital orgasm the antidote to every neurosis. Perhaps he might learn from your analysis of K. to feel some respect for the complicated nature of the psyche."[27]

Freud was responding to a description by Andreas-Salomé of a woman (K.) who suffered from hysteria "with the typical father tie" but who nonetheless had sexual experiences that revealed a "capacity for enjoyment, a spontaneity and an inner psychical surrender such as in this combination of happiness and seriousness is not often to be met with."[28] It is clear from Freud's response that he shared the attitude of many analysts that there *are* sexually healthy neurotics.

Freud's emphasis on pregenital factors in the development of neuroses was made even more explicit at an evening meeting held in his home in 1928 or 1929. When Reich presented his views on orgastic potency, Freud replied that "complete orgasm" was not the answer. There were still pregenital drives that could not be satisfied even with orgasm. "There is no single cause for the neuroses" was his verdict.[29]

Thus, Reich was probably correct in sensing some coldness in Freud's response to his manuscript. The growing divergence between the two men abounds in ironies. While Freud certainly stressed pregenital factors, initially he had also been impressed by genital ones in the development of the neuroses. In 1914, he wrote about the "bad reception accorded even among intimate friends to my contention of a sexual etiology in the neuroses."[30] However, he then recalled earlier conversations with the analysts Breuer, Charcot, and Chrobak. Each had related rather casually anecdotes involving the sexual— in the sense of the genital—causation of neuroses. Charcot's example is the most vivid, as related by Freud:

> . . . At one of Charcot's evening receptions, I happened to be standing near the great teacher at a moment when he appeared to be telling . . . [a friend] some very interesting story from the day's work. . . . A young married couple from the Far East: the woman a confirmed invalid; the man either impotent or exceedingly awkward. . . . [His friend] must have expressed his astonishment that symptoms such as the wife's could have been produced in such circumstances. For Charcot suddenly broke in with great animation, "*Mais, dans des cas pareils c'est toujours la chose genitale, toujours . . . toujours . . . toujours*"; and he crossed his arms over his stomach, hugging himself and jumping up and down. . . . I know that for one second I was almost paralyzed with amazement and said to myself: "Well, but if he knows that, why does he never say so?"[31]

Now Reich was expanding on the role of *les choses genitales,* yet Freud was rejecting it. Whatever comfort Reich may have taken from the thought that he, too, would have to endure the "splendid isolation" that Freud had experienced in his fight for the "sexual etiology in the neuroses," Freud's coolness in 1926 was a severe blow. Although Freud's overall attitude to Reich remained positive, his lack of support for Reich's most controversial contributions at this time made the latter's position increasingly perilous within the psychoanalytic organization.

Over the years, the most common criticism of Reich's orgasm theory has remained the argument that there are neurotic, even psychotic persons who are orgastically potent. In 1960, the novelist James Baldwin expressed this criticism quite succinctly: "There are no formulas for the improvement of the private, or any other, life—certainly not the formula of more and better orgasms. (Who decides?) The people I had been raised among had orgasms all the time and still chopped each other up with razors on Saturday nights."[32]

Considering how incisively Baldwin has written about sex on other occasions, one would think he would know better than to speak so glibly about having orgasms. However, Baldwin is answering Reich the same way analysts in the 1920s (and many still today) answered him: people can "have orgasms" and still be terribly disturbed. This may or may not be true, but in fairness to Reich's argument one should at least take into account his description of orgasmic functioning, and demonstrate its presence in cases of neuroses.

The concept of orgastic potency met with some serious consideration, starting around 1945. In that year, Otto Fenichel, Reich's old friend but by that time quite separated from him, wrote his celebrated book *The Psychoanalytic Theory of the Neuroses*. In it, he commented: "Persons in whom the genital primacy is lacking, that is, orgastically impotent persons, are also incapable of love. Warded-off pregenitality has resisted this primacy; after it is freed from entanglements in the defense struggle, its forces are included into the genital organization. It is primarily the experiences of satisfaction now made possible that once and for all abolish the pathogenic damming-up."[33]

Although Fenichel's language is more Reichian than Freudian, this quote is a good example of how Reich's equation of orgastic satisfaction and emotional health crept into some of the analytic literature, minus—indeed ignoring —the stormy debates of the 1920s.

Another example is evident in Erik Erikson's highly influential book *Childhood and Society*. Without citing Reich, Erikson gives a key emphasis to orgastic potency: "Genitality, then, consists in the unobstructed capacity to develop an orgastic potency so free of pregenital interferences that the genital libido (not just the sex products discharged in Kinsey's outlets) is expressed in heterosexual mutuality, with full sensitivity of both penis and vagina, and with a convulsion-like discharge of tension from the whole body."[34]

It has to be stressed that there are still no systematic studies, from Reich or anyone else, comparing a large number of orgastically potent persons with orgastically impotent ones. All we have are some studies relating aspects of sexual responsiveness and overall psychological functioning. In a careful review of the research literature correlating women's reports of their degree of sexual responsiveness with their general psychological well-being, Seymour Fisher concluded that no clear relationship could be established.[35]

Such research studies do not speak directly to Reich's work. In my view, the connection Reich made between sexual and emotional health is not especially valuable when presented as a question of degree—that the "better" the sex life, the "better" the mental health. This is clearly simplistic. Far more fundamental but much less testable is his assumption that orgastic potency goes hand in hand with a kind of psychological functioning that is radically different not only from neurotic or psychotic behavior, but also from much that passes for "normal."

As recent arguments over the "vaginal orgasm" make clear, it is easy to be sidetracked from the significance of Reich's central thesis. In discussing female sexuality, Reich followed to a certain extent traditional psychoanalytic thinking in giving favored status to vaginal over clitoral sensation. Indeed, in agreement with Karen Horney, he stated that vaginal sensation existed in childhood, and disputed the Freudian notion that the girl makes a transition from a predominantly clitoral sensation in childhood to vaginal excitation after puberty. However, for Reich the key point was not clitoral versus vaginal orgasm. For him, orgasm could not be considered complete if it was only felt in the genitals (vagina, clitoris, or both). Involuntary participation of the whole organism was its indispensable attribute.

A related argument against Reich's concept has been advanced by Herbert Marcuse and Norman O. Brown. They claim, essentially, that Reich espoused the "tyranny of genitality." Thus, Brown writes:

> If the repression of sexuality is the cause of neuroses, what alternative to neuroses does mankind possess? Psychoanalytic therapy is supposed to undo repressions and bring the hitherto repressed sexual energy under the control of the patient's ego. But what is the patient's ego going to do with his own sexuality, now brought under his conscious control?
> ... The crux of the problem is not the repression of normal adult genital sexuality but what to do with infantile perverse pregenital sexuality. For Reich ... the pregenital stages would simply disappear if full genitality were established. . . .[36]

Brown is incorrect. Reich emphasized that society represses pregenital as well as genital sexuality, leading to the failure of some persons to reach the genital level at all and the vulnerability of others to regress to pregenital levels. And, according to Reich, given full genital expression, pregenital impulses and conflicts do not "disappear"; they simply lose their significance and their power to disrupt healthy genitality. Unlike Brown and Marcuse, Reich *did* see healthy psychosexual development culminating in genitality, just as walking becomes the preferred mode of human locomotion.

One final reaction is not so much to Reich's work in particular as it is to an entire cultural trend that he influenced—the increasing emphasis today on sexual happiness in general and orgastic satisfaction in particular. Critics have argued that to talk so much about *"the* orgasm" and to make qualitative distinctions about orgasm renders people dissatisfied with what they do enjoy and contributes to an endless quest for more intense and ecstatic experience; it entails jumping from therapist to therapist, partner to partner, sex manual to sex manual.

There is definite merit to this argument. Undoubtedly, many people today have made an "ideal" of the orgasm. Reich was very cognizant and very critical of this trend, even if his polemics against "armored man" and "orgastic impotence" contributed to the cult of the orgasm. But the concept of orgastic potency itself can no more be blamed for such distortions than Freud's concept of the unconscious can be blamed for empty party-talk about "motives" and "complexes," or Sartre's existentialism for one or another mindless binge. As Goethe said long ago: "The people must make a sport of the sublime. If they saw it as it really is, they could not bear its aspect."

Where does this review of both the skepticism and the enthusiasm greeting Reich's theories lead us? I do not believe there is any clear verdict. Reich's concepts and findings concerning the orgasm are testable, but they are not easily verified or disproved.

There are three lines of evidence, however, that do seem to suggest Reich was largely right. The first was the fruitfulness of the concept in terms of his own work—clinically, socially, and experimentally. The second is the response to the concept. In spite of all the ridicule, it did not die; on the contrary, it has influenced a good deal of current thought and contemporary therapeutic endeavors. This argument is not conclusive: wrong ideas have often been quite influential. Nonetheless, it says something about the viability of Reich's work. Indeed, a good case can be made that much of the current sexual monomania and obsession reflects a widespread and deep yearning for what Reich described as orgastic potency.

The third factor is unabashedly personal. After all the arguments pro and con, one comes back to one's own experience. From my own, Reich's argument is convincing, though not in all details. When I experienced or believed I experienced what Reich termed "orgastic potency," the emotions and sensations were sufficiently different from other forms of eroticism that I can never refer to the latter as "normal," even though for me the orgastic experience occurs quite rarely.

At the same time I believe that until his last years, Reich was overly optimistic about people achieving orgastic potency through Reichian therapy or through more sex-affirming social attitudes.

I also believe that Reich underemphasized the wide range of functioning possible within what he termed the state of orgastic impotence. One can be more or less productive, happy, loving under such conditions. To use an analogy, it was as though Reich had discovered that the overwhelming majority of people were blind. He argued first for a treatment that would address the blindness, then in later years for its prevention. He was not especially concerned about the wide variation among blind people in their capacity to work, be loving, hear, or taste. More, he saw in the general emphasis on this variation an evasion of the issue of blindness.

8

Personal Life: 1920–1926

Reich's initially successful psychoanalytic career was paralleled by several developments in his personal life. Sometime in the early part of 1920, Reich met Annie Pink, a seventeen-year-old girl who was about to enter medical school at the University of Vienna. Reich knew her from the youth movement and as a fellow medical student. However, he got to know Annie well when she came to him for analytic treatment. She was referred by Otto Fenichel, a good friend of Annie's oldest brother, Fritz, who was killed in World War I.

Annie was an attractive, highly intelligent young woman. She was the daughter of Alfred Pink, a successful Viennese exporter-importer, who was well educated and cultured, a man who provided the best for his children. His first wife, Annie's mother, had died of influenza during World War I. Not long afterward, Alfred married a woman named Malva, whom Annie and others regarded as warm and kindly but very Victorian in outlook.[1]

Details of the relationship between Willy and Annie during their courtship and the early years of their marriage remain unclear. In later years, Reich rarely talked about those days, and what remarks he did make about Annie were embittered by the subsequent experiences and divorce. Those who knew the couple during the first years of their romance made a good deal of the fact that the relationship started in the context of Annie's being a patient of Reich's. A mutual friend, the child analyst Edith Buxbaum, described the Annie of that period as "spellbound" by Reich— "It would turn any patient's head to have her analyst fall in love with her."[2]

When Reich became aware of the strong feelings between them, he suggested that they should discontinue the analysis and that Annie should see someone else for treatment. Reich was certainly aware of the transference and counter-transference feelings involved in a love relationship between patient and analyst. He advised a "cooling-off" period and a change in therapist to see to what extent transference factors were determining the relationship. However, he also believed that there were "real" feelings possible between patient and therapist, and that these could not be entirely ascribed to transference.

Annie went to another, older analyst, Hermann Nunberg, but Edith Buxbaum believes that she was still so under Reich's spell that this second analysis could not proceed properly. Some years later, Annie entered analysis with Anna Freud.

Thus, Reich's relationship with Annie started under something of a cloud concerning analytic practices, just as it was to end in part over disputes between Reich and other analysts about the future direction of psychoanalysis.

It is probable that an element of defying taboos entered Reich's relationship with Annie. His first paper on "The Breakthrough of the Incest Taboo in Puberty" had dealt with his mother's violation of the taboo against extramarital sexuality and his own conscious incestuous wishes. In his behavior toward Annie, Reich acted analogously to his mother, and also lived out his own dangerous, unfulfilled adolescent wishes: he took the taboo object, defying the father (the analytic community and its standards). It is not my intention to reduce Reich's attraction to Annie to her significance as a taboo object but, rather, to call attention to his willingness, for rational and irrational reasons, to violate taboos in his personal as well as his scientific life.

All sorts of complexities arise when personal analyses are combined with professional relationships. Nunberg saw Annie as a patient at the same time that he and Reich were professional colleagues. Disputes arose between them, with Nunberg siding against the kind of resistance analysis Reich advocated. How much the relationship between the two men was clouded by the fact that Nunberg treated Annie, we cannot say. But it is worth noting that almost all the younger analysts were in treatment with the relatively few senior analysts then available in Vienna. These senior men treated not only the young candidates but also often their mates, lovers, and friends. Undoubtedly, in discussions among themselves and with Freud, the older men could preserve confidentiality yet still transmit a nonverbal opinion derived from the analytic situation by a shrug, an enthusiastic nod, a pained look. At least Paul Federn's son, Ernst, suggests that this subtle interplay between judgments from personal analyses and evaluations of professional work often occurred.[3]

In Reich's case, Federn, Sadger, and Nunberg—all older analysts—were familiar not only with his clinical work but with the most intimate details of his life.

An anecdote related by Lia Laszky further illustrates the complexities of such interactions. During his analysis with Isidor Sadger around 1919, Reich had talked about Lia and, it seems, had urged Sadger to take her free of charge when Reich relinquished treatment. Sadger agreed. However, around the time that Laszky began her analysis, Sadger grew jealous of Freud's approval of Reich—a much younger man and a relative newcomer to the psychoanalytic scene. Sadger would become irritated when Laszky talked positively about Reich, thereby giving her a sure way to provoke her analyst's anger.

On her side, Laszky was irritated by the fact that Sadger used the analytic setting to fit her with a diaphragm. This step arose ostensibly through his concern with "actual neurosis": when Sadger heard that Lia practiced coitus interruptus, he urged her to use a diaphragm and proceeded to fit her for one.[4]

In the context of defending his own behavior, Reich spoke critically of Sadger and others. He said that under the guise of doing a medical examination they would touch their patients genitally. On the other hand, when he was strongly attracted to a patient he would stop the treatment and allow time for the patient and himself to decide what they were going to do.[5]

Although it was certainly not uncommon for an analyst to marry a former patient (Bernfeld and Fernchel, for example), the psychoanalytic community disapproved Reich's step in marrying his former patient.

One other aspect of Annie may have contributed to Reich's sense of conquest. Like Grete Bibring and Lia Laszky, Annie certainly belonged to the educated, upper middle class of Vienna. Reich's own social background was impressive, but nevertheless he was raised in an outlying former province, and in Vienna that was a stigma. Reich may well have wanted to win a woman from the upper middle class; the same kind of ambition he showed in the professional world for the proper credentials could also at this time have affected his choice of a partner. He had "lost" with Grete and Lia; now he won with Annie. His choice was to cause problems later when Reich's more radical sides emerged fully, clashing with Annie's more conventional, indeed, somewhat snobbish characteristics.[6]

Not especially interested in psychoanalysis, Mr. Pink knew enough to be suspicious about "transference"; but although he was hardly enthusiastic about his daughter's relationship with Reich, he posed no objections. However, there was pressure from both Annie's father and her stepmother against premarital intercourse. In the early 1940s Reich with some bitterness told his daughter Eva that Annie's stepmother, Malva, had inadvertently run into Annie and Willy while they were walking arm in arm. When they returned to Annie's house, she congratulated them on being engaged, a step they had no intention of taking at that time. More seriously, on another occasion late at night Malva opened the door of Annie's room and found Annie and Willy in a sexually compromising position. She told her husband, Annie's father, about her "discovery" and he in turn demanded that Willy marry Annie. The young couple were very angry about his decree.[7]

How much the marriage was determined by the attitudes of Annie's father and stepmother is hard to say. Whatever Reich's motives, he married Annie on March 17, 1922, one week before his twenty-fifth birthday. If the act of legal marriage reflected some capitulation to Victorian standards, the form of it did not. It was a simple secular service with only two other people in attendance: Edith Buxbaum, Annie's closest friend; and Otto Fenichel, Reich's closest friend and colleague.[8]

We must pause a moment here to see in Malva's "discovery" one of the emblematic events in Reich's life. First, her behavior was strikingly similar to that of the young Willy spying on his mother and tutor. Both Malva and Willy report the "crime" to the father, who then imposes "law and order." If the effect of the early family tragedy was to weave its way into many of Reich's concepts, the result of Malva's and Alfred's intervention was to be apparent in Reich's later slashing critique of the social taboo against premarital intercourse.

Although Reich was near the end of his medical studies when they married, Annie still had several years to go. Briefly, she and Willy lived with her parents, which indicates that the relationship with the Pinks could not have been so bad at that time. Moreover, Annie's father paid some of her medical school expenses and was to be financially helpful throughout the marriage.[9]

Annie and Willy moved into their own small apartment shortly after their marriage. On April, 27, 1924, their first child, Eva, was born. When Annie also became a practicing analyst, the young family moved into a larger apartment where both had their offices as well as their living quarters. Throughout his life, Reich's living and work settings were always closely connected.

In most ways the couple's way of life was not so different from that of many of their colleagues. It was quite common for analysts to have mates who were also in the profession. It was also common to avoid a stereotypic division of their roles with the husband as breadwinner and wife as homemaker. However, the Reichs seemed to have carried the equal partnership further than most, even though Reich was surely the dominant partner. For example, each had a separate bank account, just as each had an independent career. Fairly early in their marriage there seems to have been the understanding that extramarital relationships were not proscribed, although this particular alternative would have been more attractive to Reich than to Annie. Reich's jealousy in relationships does not seem to have been a factor with Annie, who described herself as being the jealous one.[10]

In setting up the apartment, Reich made a point of obtaining good furniture and other household items. An interesting contradiction should be noted here, one that Ilse Ollendorff, his third wife and co-worker during the 1940s and early 1950s, also observed. Reich could be very generous to others and very generous to himself. He usually wore good clothes, ate good food, and, in general, enjoyed many of the conveniences and pleasures of fine possessions. At the same time, he could often resent daily living expenses. Moreover, when consumed by some cause that required a large financial investment, he could at times skimp on all personal expenses in order to dedicate most of his resources to his work. His fear of the "trivial" existence sometimes manifested itself as a dislike of domestic demands that drained one's energy and money.

Around 1926 or so, this financial conflict seems to have arisen in his relationship with Annie. At that time, the "cause" that began to consume him was political. Exactly when Reich's strong social involvement originated is not clear. My conjecture is that sometime in the mid-1920s Reich began to donate money toward supporting the left-wing faction of the Social Democratic Party. Then his commitment to social concerns and Annie's focus on household needs began to clash.

Intense as Reich was about his work, his early years as an analyst included considerable socializing with his colleagues. There are photographs of Annie and Willy from this period playing ball at the beach with friends, at parties, on ski trips. Never again will we see photos of Reich so entirely at play. One photograph shows Annie and Willy caught mid-air; another captures Willy and some of his colleagues making teasing faces for the camera. These photos of Reich contrast sharply with formal portraits taken during the same period. One from 1921, when Reich was only twenty-four, reveals an extremely serious, determined man, with a deep, penetrating, and somewhat hurt-angry look around the eyes.

In the first half of the 1920s, too, Reich's sense of personal mission was somewhat subdued by his intellectual and organizational subordination to Freud. He saw himself as working *for* psychoanalysis. He was to continue this personal vision for several more years; only after 1927 would he fight the psychoanalytic organization—and the older Freud—in the name of the younger Freud. Until this time, he interacted with his young colleagues as one of Freud's children. Never again was Reich to enjoy the kind of social belonging to a professional world that he experienced between 1921 and 1926.

Reich at this period could be a warm and generous friend. Richard Sterba, then an analytic candidate, recalls how helpful Reich was to him around 1924. He referred private patients to Sterba and also helped him to obtain his first position at the psychoanalytic polyclinic. As good friends, the Reichs and the Sterbas enjoyed skiing and summer outings together. The relationship was not without friction—few relationships with Reich were. Sterba remembers how competitive Reich could be, a competitiveness revealed once by Reich's dismay that, when skiing downhill, Sterba fell only three times whereas Reich took six spills.

The relative harmony of those years also characterized Reich's relationship with his first daughter, Eva. Both he and Annie, very absorbed in her upbringing, kept careful records of her development. Eva was not initially brought up in accord with Reich's later concepts of self-regulation. In the early 1920s, Reich was imbued with many traditional psychoanalytic notions of child rearing. He shared particularly the concern of many analysts about fixation at a pregenital level of development, a fixation that presumably could result from deprivation but also from overindulgence. Thus, as an infant Eva was raised on a fairly strict feeding schedule, with both Willy and Annie paying a good deal of attention to the exact details.[11]

Although the couple were very much concerned in principle with Eva's upbringing, they delegated many of the daily tasks to nursemaids. They led busy professional lives and did not have a great deal of time for their children. (A second daughter, Lore, was born in 1928.) Nor was it a "child-oriented" home in the American sense of the term. For example, the children ate separately in European fashion; and Reich always expected them to behave properly when eating out or on public occasions.

The most traumatic personal event in Reich's life at this time concerned his brother, Robert. Robert had risen rapidly in the transportation firm he joined after World War I, and in 1920 he was sent to Rumania to handle shipping traffic on the Danube. In 1921 he married Ottilie, who, as noted earlier, had been a friend of his and Willy's for several years. Two years later the young couple had a daughter, Sigrid. Then, in 1924, tragedy struck: Robert contracted tuberculosis and the family returned to Vienna for expert diagnosis and treatment.[12]

Willy was at the station to meet them. He also arranged for Robert to be checked by the best specialists in Vienna. The diagnosis of severe tuberculosis was confirmed and a sanatarium in northern Italy was recommended for treatment.

The family moved to Italy. Contrary to Ilse Ollendorff's later report,[13] Ottilie informed me that the move posed no special financial problem for Robert and his family. Robert's firm thought so much of him that they kept him on the payroll during his illness. In addition, help was available from Ottilie's fairly affluent family. They therefore had no need to turn to Willy for financial assistance, but he was helpful in terms of sending medicine, especially morphine, to relieve the pain Robert suffered. He also sent detailed information about a medical procedure to help with breathing—an interesting sidelight in view of Reich's later work on the relation between respiration and emotional blocking.

The issues that arose between Willy, on the one hand, and Robert and Ottilie, on the other, concerned more personal matters. The first quarrel occurred when Reich wrote his sister-in-law's parents urging them to persuade Ottilie to take her daughter from the sanatarium lest they also become infected with tuberculosis. Ottilie was outraged that Reich should have worried her already anxious family. At the sanatarium she and her daughter lived in separate quarters from Robert and took other precautions against infection. In any case, she felt it was no business of his to interfere in this fashion, especially without even notifying her.[14]

One can only speculate as to why Reich behaved thus. As a result of his experiences with his own parents, he always had fears that one marital partner could negatively affect the other. For example, in later years he would sometimes be concerned that a co-worker's mate, if not interested in or even hostile to his work, would turn the partner against Reich. He spoke of the hostile person's attitudes "infecting" or changing the position of a sympathetic person. In the case of his brother and sister-in-law, the danger of infection was more literal.

Even more upsetting to both Ottilie and Robert was the fact that Willy did not visit his brother during the many months of his terminal illness in Italy. Reich wrote, he sent medicine, but he never came himself. Robert was deeply hurt. Once he received a long, warm letter from Willy. He shook his head and said something to the effect that his brother had a split personality. Ottilie asked why he said such a thing and Robert replied: "Because he can write a letter like that and still not visit me."[15]

When Ottilie later asked Reich directly why he had not come to Italy, Reich replied that he had been busy, and besides he had not felt like it. Undoubtedly, Reich *was* busy and he was a careful custodian of his talent. Often he took the stance that his dedication to work prevented his participation in a host of activities others deemed essential. He was not a man who attended weddings, funerals, and the like. But equally clearly the roots of the explanation lay much deeper. He may have felt guilt because Robert had helped him during the difficult postwar years, perhaps at some sacrifice to Robert's own well-being. As Robert went on to a successful business career, Reich had no occasion to repay this help. Yet other stories Ottilie tells suggest a greater concern on Robert's part about being fair to Willy in money matters than Willy reciprocated.

One has to allow for the possibility tht Ottilie would like to paint Robert, her first husband, in a more favorable light than her more famous brother-in-law. Nonetheless, the hypothesis of guilt on Reich's part seems reasonable. Robert died in the sanatarium in April 1926. One can often infer Reich's experience of guilt from noting what he blames others for. In the case of Robert's death, he blamed his well-to-do relatives for not being more helpful to Robert during the impoverished postwar years.[16]

Robert represented Reich's last tie with his family of origin. Reich had witnessed firsthand the painful deaths of his mother and father under conditions where he felt some responsibility. Perhaps he was not up to witnessing directly the fatal illness of his brother, to experiencing again the terrible helplessness, for there was now nothing to be done to reverse the coming of death. Perhaps, too, he feared that he would be infected by his diseased brother —the last heir but one of a tragedy-ridden family.

Yet when all is explained or guessed at, the incident reflects the kind of callousness Reich could sometimes show toward people once very close to him, who had helped him, but who for one reason or another were no longer relevant or for whom nothing could be done. This was particularly the case when someone died. I recall his reaction to the death of a promising young psychiatrist who had been in training with him and whom he had liked very much. When Reich heard the news, he simply said grimly, "The best die young," and went on about his business.

If Reich personally distanced himself from Robert during the illness, he was close to Ottilie after Robert's death. Ottilie was now in difficult straits: she had no career, and there was a young child to care for. In the fall of 1926, she moved in with the Reichs in order to pursue a professional training in Vienna. At the time Ottilie was interested in becoming a nursery-school teacher, and Reich helped her not only to obtain a formal education but also with various extras that he was in a position to arrange, such as a psychoanalytic seminar on adolescence given by August Aichorn. Ottilie was as grateful to him for this attentive help as she had earlier been disappointed by his behavior.[17]

At the close of 1926, Reich's personal life revealed a similar mixture of success and storm clouds on the horizon as his professional life did. By 1926, he had won considerable attention through his writings, his seminar, and his clinical skills. At the same time, several influential analysts now disliked him intensely and Freud himself was giving less than full support to the more controversial aspects of Reich's contributions. As far as the marriage was concerned, Annie felt that until 1927 it was a happy one and their mutual life together a satisfying existence. But for Reich, things were more complex. He undoubtedly felt some dissatisfaction with his marriage. Annie was less than enthusiastic about the direction his work was taking in emphasizing the function of the orgasm, though there is no evidence that she opposed it at that time. And what ancient scars and griefs his brother's death triggered can only be imagined.

PART IV

The Radicalization of Reich: 1926–1930

Reich's Illness and Sanatarium Stay in Davos, Switzerland: Winter 1927

The year 1926 had been a difficult one for Reich. It included Freud's coolness toward his orgasm theory and character-analytic technique, the death of his brother, and incipient problems in his marriage. How much his emotional state contributed to the tuberculosis that sent Reich for several months' rest during the winter of 1927 to a Swiss sanatarium we cannot say. There is evidence to suggest that Reich thought it did, especially his depression over Freud's reaction to his work.[1] Whatever the role of Freud in precipitating the illness, Reich's relationship with his mentor was clearly much on his mind during his sanatarium stay. A photo of Reich taken at the sanatarium in Davos in February 1927 bears the inscription in Reich's handwriting: "Conflict with Freud."

Reich's sense of being rejected by Freud may not have been limited to scientific disagreements. Ilse Ollendorff has reported that Annie Reich stated Reich sought a personal analysis from Freud and was refused.[2] The implication in this account is that Reich sought the analysis prior to his TB attack, but Annie Reich is not quoted as specifically stating the time of the request. Rather, she emphasized the heavy impact on Reich of Freud's refusal.

My own conjecture is that both request and refusal occurred before the illness, and that they were among the precipitants of the "conflict with Freud," together with the theoretical differences between the two men. This view is based in part upon the severity of Reich's depressive reaction at the time of his illness. Reich himself never mentioned his request to be analyzed by Freud and Freud's refusal to anyone that I knew. He much preferred to concentrate on his scientific disagreements with Freud; it would be entirely characteristic of him to keep silent about such a personal rejection.

Freud's stated reason for refusing Reich's request was his reluctance to take Viennese colleagues into treatment, on the grounds that to do so would complicate their work relationship. However, Freud was never hesitant to break a rule when it suited him. He had analyzed Helena Deutsch and Heinz Hartmann, for example, both of Reich's generation and both resident in Vienna. In short, we do not know Freud's real reason for denying Reich's request.

One can infer the degree of rejection Reich suffered in 1926–27 from his later remarks about his relationship with Freud. In the late 1930s, Ola Raknes, a Norwegian psychoanalyst, was in treatment with Reich, well after Reich had left the psychoanalytic movement. At one point Reich said to his patient that when Raknes was through with his treatment, Reich would perhaps have some sessions with him in order to deal with Reich's own dependency on Freud.[3] It speaks to the weight of pain Reich carried about the separation from Freud, the seeds of which began around the Davos time, that he could consider Raknes as his own future therapist. I know of no other occasion when he mentioned the possibility of going into therapy with a former student.

Some ten years later, Reich would often refer to Freud and how much Freud still meant to him. In 1948, when I knew Reich, he recalled Freud's pleasure in the early 1920s when Reich vigorously collected "dues" from his fellow analysts in order to help defray the costs of the psychoanalytic poly-clinic. More ruefully, Reich also recalled the time when, as a medical student undergoing analysis, he had impetuously hidden a fellow student under the couch so that he could learn what analysis was all about by overhearing a session. "Freud was very angry when he heard about it," Reich commented with an embarrassed smile.

Significantly, Reich often compared his own work and life with Freud's. "Breuer first had the energy principle and he ran from it," he said in 1948. "Then Freud had it and he ran from it. Now I have it and I haven't run yet." He was intent on avoiding the mistakes he thought Freud had made. He often spoke of how Freud's organization had "killed him"—meaning pushed him in a more conservative direction. But, as he saw it, Freud had permitted it to happen. "Freud was interested in fame, I am not—that is the difference be-tween us." Reich could defend Freud and compete with him in the same sentence. I once commented that Freud seemed to have been a very reserved person. Reich denied it: "No, he was very sparkling—not as sparkling as me, though."[4]

Judging from how much Reich still thought of Freud in 1950, one has some idea of how painful the conflict must have been in 1927 when Reich was thirty, even if one is surprised by his strong feelings to Freud's reaction to the orgasm theory. For the entire thrust of Freud's thought at that time—for example, his emphasis on the intricate balance between instinctual gratification and repression necessary for psychological health, on the one hand, and "civilization," on the other—was moving in a direction quite different from Reich's work. Reich tried to solve this problem by returning to the early Freud, the Freud who had emphasized the role of genital frustration in the development of the neuroses, in particular, Freud's paper "On the Most Prevalent Form of Degradation in Erotic Life."

However, I would suggest that Reich practiced a kind of self-deception in not realizing the full extent to which he was challenging much that was dear to Freud, at least to the Freud of the 1920s. Such self-deception seemed necessary to preserve his image of himself as the "loyal son" of Freud, on the one hand, and the fighter for genitality, on the other.

Nor is it hard to understand why this composite picture was so important. For we recall what grief had befallen Reich the boy over the issue of genitality.

Now the issue between his mentor, Freud, and himself also concerned genitality. Aside from this issue—and it is a big aside—the relationship between Freud and Reich could have continued very positively. It is true that Freud had also been critical of Reich's oral presentation of some character-analytic principles. In general, however, he had responded very favorably to those publications of Reich where the orgasm function and its affirmation were not central; he had been especially positive about Reich's monograph on *The Impulsive Character,* where the few references to genitality were very much in accord with psychoanalytic tradition.

Still, Reich could not be the "good son" at the price of forgoing orgastic potency. Nor was he prepared yet to stop being any kind of son and go his own way. He wished to "undo" the bad relationship with his father and the trauma of their joint complicity in the mother's death. This time the good father and the good son would unite together in support of their shared undertaking— genitality. But Freud would not have it that way.

One must also pay attention to what Reich does not stress. Singularly absent in Reich's remarks to various people about this period was any mention of the impact of his brother's death. We cannot say for certain what that impact was, but we can speculate that to his growing sense of his "differentness" within the psychoanalytic movement was also added his familial sense of separateness. He alone was destined to survive the tragic family experiences that had killed his mother, father, and brother. What "survivor guilt," to use Robert Lifton's phrase, Reich experienced we do not know. Some of that guilt was reflected in his conviction, expressed at various times, that he himself would not die a "normal" death—that he would be killed or at least "die alone like a dog."[5] Certainly, Robert's fate increased his loneliness and his need to repair the "wounds" to family and self by working all the more intensely and without regard to costs, by being all the more willing to bear whatever insults might come his way because of his discoveries.

The time at the Davos sanatarium provided Reich with an enforced rest, a kind of moratorium in which he could sort out his relationship with Freud, regroup his energies, and plan for the future. This sabbatical followed eight years of intense activity centered on psychoanalysis. Reich had taken vacations before in Austria and Switzerland, but usually very active, social ones—skiing in the winters, going to the lakes in the summer, and being with family and friends. Now he was away from the normal work routine, family, and familiar surroundings.

The Davos crisis came when Reich was turning thirty, a phase of life Daniel J. Levinson has termed "the age thirty transition"—the time when a man is likely to question and reappraise the previous years of establishing himself in the world.[6] Reich had spent most of his twenties building a career. Were it not for his "fanaticism" about his "hobby horse," many associates said, there was no telling how far he might go in contributing to psychoanalysis— clinically, theoretically, and administratively. At this juncture, Reich had to consider what would happen to his relationship with the psychoanalytic organization, his "second home," as he once put it, if he persisted in following the direction he believed his work was taking him.

His marriage was also running into trouble. Like his career, it was in many respects quite successful; but Annie did not share Reich's emphasis on genitality, and it was characteristic of Reich to want those close to him to be fully involved in whatever occupied him. Several years later, Reich was bitterly critical of the institution of "lifelong, compulsive monogamy," partly on the grounds that a partner chosen in one's twenties may be incompatible with one's psychic development at thirty.[7] It is clear that when he formulated this criticism, he had his own experiences much in mind.

The weight of all these varied concerns is reflected in photos of Reich from the time. The photo carrying the inscription "Conflict with Freud" shows a brooding man—the depth of the hurt is striking. Another picture from Davos shows him standing on the snowy steps in front of the sanatarium, his legs in a wide stance, hands on hips, the look still hurt and angry but also determined, as if to say: I will be my own man, no matter what.

It was during the sanatarium stay that Reich began a custom he was to continue throughout his life—that of sending pictures of himself to absent friends. In Vienna, Grete Bibring received one from Davos that bore the inscription: "So that you will recognize me." Reflecting on Reich many years later, she saw a biblical reference in that inscription and cited it as evidence of Reich's incipient psychotic megalomania. A more benign interpretation might regard it as a half-ironic reference to his literal absence and to their drifting apart as friends, something that was indeed happening during this period.

There is no doubt that at Davos Reich was taking himself more seriously than ever. From that time on, he saw himself as living or wanting to live a heroic destiny. And from that time on, he had a sense of his remarkable powers. He recorded his life in voluminous detail, keeping careful notes and diaries of his intellectual and personal development. To a high degree he had that "fierce love of one's own personality" that Isak Dinesen noted as a hallmark of the creative individual.

The sense of himself as a remarkable person, perhaps a historic figure, was heightened—I am suggesting—during Reich's stay at Davos. His daughter, Eva, thought that this was the time he "found out who he was."[8] Even those who deplored the kind of person he found himself to be and the kind of person he became saw the sanatarium period as critical. Annie Reich believed that before Davos, Reich had been an essentially "normal" person, whatever difficulties there may have been. After it, she felt he became a much angrier, more suspicious individual, and, indeed, that a psychotic process dated from that time.[9] Which of these two opinions—that of his daughter or his first wife—one prefers, or which blend of the two, depends on how one views his later development.

Reich rested at Davos, but he also worked. One task was going over the proofs of *Die Funktion des Orgasmus*. The last chapter of the manuscript was entitled "The Social Significance of Genital Strivings"—Reich's last chapters in books or last paragraphs in articles very often signaled upcoming concerns.[10] Here he argued that much sadistic destructiveness, as well as the anxiety states of "actual neuroses," stemmed from dammed-up sexual excitation. Here, too, he began his critique of negative social attitudes toward genitality. In particular, he stressed the ways these attitudes destroyed erotic happiness. The split between tender and sensual feelings in the male, the deep suppression and repression of genital strivings in the female, made marriage a sexual misery. The dogma of premarital chastity (with the proviso that men could sow their oats with prostitutes and other "bad" women) ruined what it was alleged to protect, happiness in marriage.

Reich's social criticism was still embryonic at this stage. Lacking any explicit social viewpoint, he made references to connections between sexual suppression and "capitalist bourgeois morality," but did not provide any details. Still, after Davos he would never again limit himself to the study of the individual without regard for social factors as he had largely done earlier.

The social criticism of the book's last chapter is undeveloped and strongly mixed with more traditional Freudian notions that Reich would later abandon. For example, Reich kept to certain Freudian concepts such as the death instinct in part because he half-believed them, in part because he did not want to step too far out of line from psychoanalytic doctrine as enunciated by Freud. Reich himself was not clear in early 1927 as to what should be the stance of the parent and educator toward the child's pregenital impulses. For he shared the prevailing analytic concern that undue gratification of these impulses would prevent the development of "genital primacy." And he also shared the view that "sublimations" of pregenital impulses were important for both the individual and society. His focus at this time was on the kind of genital fulfillment in early adulthood that would withdraw energy from the inevitable conflicts between the pregenital and Oedipal phases of development.

In *Die Funktion des Orgasmus* he had said nothing about affirming childhood or adolescent heterosexuality, so this view represented a step toward a rather different viewpoint.

In contrast, Reich appears to have been more outspoken in public lectures. In the early 1920s, Ernst Papanek, who directed the Social Democratic Party's educational efforts for young workers and teachers, had invited Reich as well as Otto Fenichel and Siegfried Bernfeld to speak on psychoanalytic themes to young worker groups. Reich spoke weekly on "sex education" for several years; then Papanek was forced to stop inviting him. Reich, he said, was an extremely effective speaker: "He was too good to let him continue. If he had been more mediocre, we would have carried him—he would not have attracted so much attention."[11] What concerned Papanek was that Reich's positive attitude toward premarital sexuality appealed to many young people but made some quite anxious. In particular, he was concerned that Reich's lectures would alienate the parents of the young people. The Social Democratic Party wished to increase its strength among Catholic voters and Reich's positions were likely to frighten rather than attract them.

Sometime in the late spring of 1927, Reich left Davos cured of tuberculosis. I believe he also left Davos more intent than ever on finding a way to make genitality a matter of public concern, on changing the public attitudes toward contraception, abortion, and premarital and extramarital love life. But further influences and opportunities were necessary to convert this readiness into practical endeavor, and to facilitate the development of his social position.

July 15, 1927, and Its Aftermath: 1927–1928

When Reich returned to Vienna from Davos in the late spring of 1927, there were no radical changes in his routine. As in most people's lives, these important turns were gradual developments rather than rapid shifts in design or structure. The significant points only become clear in retrospect.

Reich resumed his flourishing psychoanalytic practice, his position as assistant chief of the Vienna Psychoanalytic Polyclinic, and his leadership of the technical seminar for analytic candidates. Starting around this time, he appears to have been one of the analysts most sought after by American students visiting Vienna eager to learn the new discipline of analysis. During the late 1920s, several future luminaries of American psychiatry became patients or students of Reich. Finally, whatever Reich's inner conflicts with Freud, Freud continued to endorse his work with the technical seminar and to welcome his contributions to psychoanalytic theory and technique. Indeed, it was in 1927 that Reich gained what he had long sought—a place on the executive committee of the Vienna Psychoanalytic Society, now granted on the basis of his leadership of the technical seminar.

Reich was also determined to continue his marriage. Soon after his return from Davos, Annie and he decided to have another child, partly in an effort to improve their relationship. Lore, born on March 13, 1928, was the fruit of this decision. It is interesting that in his later clinical work Reich paid close attention to the reasons why people have children. He specifically looked for the desire to give fruit to sexual love through offspring, and was sharply critical of the kind of motivation he may well have experienced himself in 1927, the desire to "make things better" in a marriage by having a child.

External events as well as Reich's own inner disposition were, however, to lead him in a different direction from that of the prominent analyst with a growing family. Some years later, Reich was to review these political events in an unusual book entitled *People in Trouble*.[1] A few words about this work are in order first.

People in Trouble is a remarkable volume, not least because it is so highly personal. It describes events that occurred largely between 1927 and 1934 when Reich became an active participant in the impassioned, sometimes frenetic political wars of Vienna and Berlin. More than in any other of his writings, Reich gives a detailed description of his *feelings* about these experiences. But historically, it is difficult to date what feelings occurred when. For example, he described many events of 1927, but one cannot always be sure whether his reflections and emotions about these events actually occurred in 1927 or later, when he transmitted the narrative to paper.

People in Trouble was not in fact published until 1953, when Reich was living in the relative social isolation of Rangeley, Maine, and long after his radical political phase had ended. In his introduction, Reich wrote that "the book is composed of different writings from the years between 1927 and 1945."[2] However, a careful examination of the text suggests that most of it was written between 1936 and 1940, although Reich drew heavily on notes written earlier. It is hard to date different sections because Reich had the disconcerting habit of adding material to suit his purposes. The bulk of a section might have been written in 1936, but put aside. If Reich found a newspaper clipping in 1942 that fitted his theme, he would then insert it into the text without necessarily indicating that this material was added some years after the rest of the chapter was written.

By 1927 the conservative Christian Socialist Party had gained national leadership, although "Red Vienna" remained in the hands of the Social Democrats. The bitter political polarization between the Christian Socialists with their rural Catholic constituency, many still devoted to the monarchy, and the urban, secularly oriented Social Democrats was more intense than ever. Like Germany with its paramilitary factions, the Christian Socialist Party in Austria was linked to an independent military group, the Heimwehr, which received financial support from the Fascist Italian government. The Social Democrats had their armed unit, the Schutzbund, which, unlike the Heimwehr, was clearly under civilian control. Individuals on both the right and left, inside and outside the armed factions, participated in sporadic violence, though rightists were the more frequent perpetrators. Moreover, conservative judges often gave right-wing perpetrators light jail sentences, a policy that further inflamed the Social Democrats and contributed to severe tension throughout the country, but especially in Vienna.[3]

One terrorist attack that particularly enraged the political left occurred on January 30, 1927, in Schattendorf, a small Austrian town near the Hungarian border. A group of World War I veterans, all members of the Heimwehr, wantonly shot into a crowd of Social Democrats, killing a man and a young child. The accused were brought to trial but acquitted on July 14.

Whatever the fairness or unfairness of the verdict—and historians to this day debate what actually happened at Schattendorf—it enraged the workers of Vienna. On July 15, a physician who had come to Reich for an analytic session told him that there was a protest strike of Viennese workers, the police were armed, workers were occupying the inner city, and several people had been killed. Reich interrupted the session to join the crowd out in the streets.

The direct confrontation between police and crowd was limited to the area in front of a courthouse, which the protestors had set fire to as a symbol of fraudulent justice. Then they tried to block the firemen. With quick strokes Reich paints a vivid word picture in the subsequent *People in Trouble:* the excitement, the impulsive movements of the crowd, the mounted police riding into the demonstrators, the ambulances with red flags coming to collect the wounded.

Reich continued to mill about with the large crowd. He was struck by the difference between Marxist descriptions of such clashes and what he witnessed. The rhetoric had the "capitalists" fighting the "workers." For Reich, on the other hand, there were only workers in uniforms shooting at workers without uniforms.[4]

Reich was exaggerating a little. Marxist theory did not say that capitalists fought workers; rather, the *agents* of capitalists, e.g., the police, fought workers. Reich's very naïveté allowed him to be impressed by simple facts without the distortion of a highly refined theoretical lens. Before July 15, Reich was a man of the political left, although he had not carefully studied social theory in general or Marxism in particular. His intense scrutiny of Marx and Engels came after these events.

When Reich arrived home to tell his wife what was happening, she went with him to see the events for herself. So Reich and Annie joined the crowd still watching the courthouse fire. A police cordon started to move toward them. When they were a short distance from the crowd, an officer gave the command to fire. Reich jumped behind a tree and pulled his wife after him.

The shooting lasted three hours, and left eighty-nine people dead and over a thousand wounded. Vienna had not seen such carnage in the streets since the days of the 1848 revolution.

Reich then describes how it felt to be a demonstrator and how the various factions looked to an involved and extremely curious participant. Most striking to Reich was his impression of the police. He emphasized not their brutality but their mechanicalness. Reich suddenly saw them as rigid automatons. He, too, he realized, had been just such a robot when he fired on the enemy in World War I.[5]

Even though Reich felt a strong desire to throw himself upon the police, he restrained it. At the time he believed that he had held back out of cowardice. Reich's attitudes toward the various political factions were charged with feeling. He was indignant at the vacillation of the Social Democratic leadership, particularly its failure to have the Schutzbund participate in the demonstration. He was enraged by the Christian Socialist Party, which he saw as triggering the events through the orders to the police. At the time he was quite sympathetic to the Communist Party, then a minuscule group with only several thousand members throughout Austria. He expected the leaders of the party to take an active role in "leading and organizing" the spontaneous demonstrations of July 15; he excused their absence from events on the grounds that they were "still preparing themselves." And on the same day, Reich enrolled in a medical group affiliated with the Communist Party.[6]

Reich came to recognize that the Communists were far too few to be an effective lever for change, and placed his more realistic hopes on the "left opposition" group within the Social Democratic Party, which shared Reich's views of its weak and vacillating party leaders. But he did not allow this Social Democratic commitment to stop him from participating in the Communist Party, even though such action could be grounds for censure, and possibly expulsion, by the Social Democrats. So, too, could the stringent criticisms Reich began to make of the party leadership. However much he may have regretted or downplayed it later, his strongest political sympathies in the late 1920s lay with the Communist Party's ideology. One must bear in mind that being a Communist in Vienna at that time did not signify a commitment to violent revolution, as communism had in czarist Russia in 1917. On the other hand, Reich and the Communists believed in principle that violence from the right should be met with equal force.

We have seen Reich's impressions of July 15. Now the significance of that day as he experienced it at the time and from his later insights should be dealt with.

The reader of *People in Trouble,* written nearly ten years after the event, cannot but be impressed simply by how important that day was for Reich. Throughout his life there were benchmark experiences in which the broodings of earlier days, months, and years coalesced and sharpened. These crucial happenings in turn led to new experiences, to new "life structures" (in Daniel J. Levinson's phrase), and to the selection of still different experiences. The events surrounding his mother's death were one such set of experiences; his meeting with Freud another.

Now he had partaken in an experience not just crucial to himself but to an entire nation, for the events of July 15 seared the Austrian consciousness. The Vienna uprising presaged many later political events of the 1930s in Europe: initial sporadic violence by extreme right-wing individuals or groups, supported by the silent sympathy and protection of a conservative government or party; hesitancy and striving to avoid civil war by the Socialist government or party; the growing strength of increasingly repressive right-wing forces;

dissension on the left (especially between Socialists and Communists); and the final victory of a reactionary regime.

The events of July 15 drastically increased Reich's sense of political urgency. He sought a way to stem the conservative tide, a tide he felt the Social Democrats should have vigorously and courageously opposed.

Just as character analysis could free the individual from inner oppression and release the flow of natural energies, so—Reich hoped—radical Socialists and Communists would rescue the masses from external oppression and release a natural social harmony, a "classless" society. Put somewhat differently, Reich's desire for strong action on the political left paralleled his clinical search for measures that would bring about rapid individual change. Thus, genital breakthroughs might liberate the patient, in spite of unresolved psychic conflicts and without prolonged analysis. Social revolution led by decisive leaders might lead to social breakthroughs in spite of all the fears and contradictions among the citizens. Reich's attempt to integrate his clinical and social hopes would form the crux of his endeavors between 1927 and 1934.

The next point concerns the interaction between his more established clinical work and his embryonic social endeavors. In his clinical work, Reich had been increasingly impressed by "character armor"—the automaton-like quality of patients, their lack of spontaneous feeling. Undoubtedly, his clinical observations alerted Reich to the same kind of armored, affect-lame behavior on the public scene. At the same time, his immersion in the political arena broadened his approach to his patients. Prior to 1927, Reich's analytic writings had not dealt with social issues, with the exception of his criticism of conventional sexual standards. Like most analysts, Reich emphasized the patient's inner difficulties in coping with reality. But the Vienna demonstrations made Reich more aware of the way destructive social factors interfered with the treatment of emotional disturbances as well as the way they contributed to their development.

Finally, what about our own reactions to Reich's account of the events of July 15? How contemporary it all sounds! Just as Reich's case histories in *Character Analysis* make us feel that we know these people, that they are not merely relics from the 1920s, so his description of July 15 reminds us of what the United States experienced in the 1960s and early 1970s. Reich's method of social investigation, his deep immersion in the day-by-day happenings, and his method of reporting—including his own feelings and reactions—all remind us of the "new journalism." He was not the cold, objective historian; he was the man, he was there, he suffered.

As the political situation steadily deteriorated from the viewpoint of the left, Reich worked with both the radical left of the Social Democrats and the Communist Party. On one level, he was involved in immediate political issues, the tactics and strategy of social struggle. On another, he was asking deeper questions about the psychological receptivity of the average individual to one or another political outlook. He termed this focus "mass psychology." In 1927 his insights were only dimly formulated, if at all; but over the next ten years they would far exceed in significance his immediate concern with political tactics.

From this perspective, Reich gradually came to realize that the main problem lay in the character structure of the masses themselves, especially their fear of freedom and responsibility.[7] However, in 1927, as I have suggested, this view did not dominate his thinking. Reich began to take part in demonstrations of the unemployed. He shared the communist illusion that the working class would soon overthrow the yoke of capitalism and build a new socialist order.[8]

He was to experience keenly the futility of such demonstrations. The police cooperated to the extent of permitting small gatherings. If the meeting looked as though it might become troublesome, they would quietly disperse the "illegal" demonstrators. Even more significantly, workers with jobs did not take part in the demonstrations for fear of losing their employment. Nor did marches of the unemployed impress the onlookers. Reich's hope that the unemployed would move the people on the street into action did not materialize. Occasionally, the marchers would shout "Down with Capitalism!" or "Freedom and bread!", but the people on the sidewalk were soon used to that and hardly paid any attention.

Dismal as these demonstrations were, Reich continued to take part in them, first because of his concern for the unemployed and his political conviction at that time that somehow, some way, radical change could develop, but also because he learned so much from the demonstrations. Once again we can note Reich's love of the concrete and the practical. He immersed himself in these first sociological endeavors much as he had earlier thrown himself into psychoanalytic practice—with some guiding theoretical formulations, but with a hunger for direct experience.

Reich's political commitments as well as his eagerness to learn are well illustrated by his involvement in one demonstration that had farcical overtones.

In the midst of the growing civil unrest, the leaders of the Heimwehr scheduled a large march for October 7, 1928, in Wiener-Neustadt. The leaders of the Social Democratic Party felt that they, too, had to act lest their restive membership become even more embittered. So they scheduled a countermarch in the same city and on the same date.

The small Communist group had decided that it should participate in the demonstration with the express purpose of disrupting the marches of the other groups. As Reich put it: "They 'mobilized' their workers' defense for October 7 . . . with all the earnestness of revolutionary courage—I do not say this mockingly—an organization of about two hundred and fifty unarmed men undertook to fight armed and organized groups of a combined force of about forty thousand men; that is 'to *prevent* their march.' I can bear witness, for I was among those two hundred and fifty men."[9]

Reich's capacity for humor and self-irony is evident in the descriptions of his adventures in Wiener-Neustadt. Along with two other physicians, he was supposed to carry knapsacks containing bandages; this little band formed the "medical wing" of the Communists' "fighting troops." Proceeding "inconspicuously," the Communist phalanx was to form the "spearhead" of a revolutionary movement to disrupt the proceedings—exactly how, no one knew. To increase its camouflage, the 250-man army got off the train one stop before Wiener-Neustadt. At the nearby village they were greeted by a party functionary also trying to look "inconspicuous," and taken to the local inn, owned by the Social Democratic mayor of the village.

Early the next morning, the little band was betrayed by the mayor: they awoke to find the inn surrounded by police. Thereupon the "phalanx" divided into two factions—one in favor of immediately fighting the police, the other in favor of withdrawing to fight another day. Reich, disliking surrender but fearing some senseless bloodshed, was chosen as moderator for the militants. The majority voted to withdraw. So, flanked by the police, they all marched back to the village station and Reich noticed the indifferent faces peering from the windows of working-class homes. " 'They are only taking away some Communists,' we could almost hear them say."

The band of Communists managed to get off the train before it arrived in Vienna's Central Station, so they walked home without police escort. But that was small consolation, especially for Reich, who would long wonder how he could ever have participated in such a crazy venture. At the time one of his explanations for his actions that day was that if the Communists were "right" and "set an example," others would "have to recognize it."[10] To a marked degree Reich's expectation that people would recognize what he recognized was based on his conviction that what should happen *would* happen. Again and again this characteristic was to emerge, in spite of his deep awareness of why people could not recognize what he did.

One also has to be aware of Reich's tendency, as he recalled the late 1920s, to mix his insights and awareness of a later period with his contemporary attitudes. Immediately after the fiasco of October 7, it seems likely that the perfidy of the Social Democratic mayor and of the Social Democratic leadership in general was more on his mind than the "indifferent faces" he met on his way home, though the latter image had planted itself in Reich's thought, to grow in significance just as the significance of the mayor's actions would wane. But in the context of 1928, Reich's own injured pride required a more tangible target than the "indifference" of the masses.

Reich's involvement in the events of 1927–28 highlights his steadily increasing commitment to radical politics. However, he was to shape his own contribution to fit his unique gifts.

The Application of Sex-economic Concepts on the Social Scene—The Sex-pol: 1927-1930

In addition to joining political demonstrations, Reich felt he could serve a specific function within the revolutionary social movement—a function determined by his psychoanalytic orientation.

From the early 1920s, Reich had given talks on psychoanalytic subjects to various lay groups. By 1927, however, he felt dissatisfied with this effort. People did not understand complex psychological issues, such as the castration complex.

If working people did not respond to psychoanalysis as usually presented, they were also turned off by the purely economic analyses presented by the leftist political parties. To capture their interest, Reich sought a perspective that would stimulate them to look at what was relevant to their own emotional needs.

One way he did this was to shift the subject matter of his talks from the more theoretical aspects of psychoanalysis to the concrete problems of people's sex lives. Here Reich began what he was to call the "sex-pol" movement: a complex theoretical and practical effort—first, to help the masses with their sexual problems; and second, to render the sexual needs of normal love life relevant political issues within the framework of the larger revolutionary movement.[1] Questions of sexual life and child upbringing aroused burning interest among the public.

Reich wished to take other steps, besides public speaking, to reach the public. He drew considerable support from his friendship with working men, especially a man named Zadniker. On the basis of his experiences with Zadniker and others like him, Reich evolved the idea, later to be abandoned, that industrial workers were sexually healthier than middle-class persons. Clearly Reich felt Zadniker to be an open, genuine person, with an objective, natural attitude toward sexuality. Indeed, Zadniker must have struck Reich as more like himself than many of his professional colleagues, with their emotional reserve and subtle moralisms.

Parenthetically, we should note Reich's gift for finding the kinds of intellectual and emotional support that he most needed. In the early 1920s there had been Freud, the youth movement, and his analytic colleagues, who gave direction to his burgeoning interest in psychology, especially the psychology of sex. In the late 1920s, when Reich's elucidation of the orgasm function, combined with the general political unrest, was leading him toward a wider social orientation, he discovered the social sweep and revolutionary hopes of Marxism. Emotionally and socially, he found in many working people an openness and simplicity he sorely missed among his more "cultivated" friends and colleagues.

Zadniker strongly supported Reich's view that he should work as a physician rather than as a politician within the leftist movement. Reich should help the people medically and educationally. Accordingly, during the spring and summer of both 1928 and 1929, Reich engaged in a kind of "community psychiatry," or at least his version of it. Reich, together with a pediatrician, a gynecologist, and his friend Lia Laszky (who had become a nursery-school teacher), would go out several days a week into the suburbs and rural areas around Vienna. They would drive in a van, announcing their visits in advance. Interested persons gathered at a local park and Reich's group spoke to them about sexual matters. Reich would talk with the adolescents and men, the gynecologist with the women, and Lia with the children. Upon request, the gynecologist would also prescribe and fit contraceptive devices.[2]

Sometimes the group would go door to door distributing pamphlets with sexual information. Most of these activities were of course illegal. More than once the group was chased away by the police, and on a few occasions members of the "team" were arrested on spurious charges. One of these was that the children, who enjoyed exploring the van, were "corrupted" by contact with sex information and devices. However, charges against the group were usually dismissed. They were just "nuisances."

In addition to the sex counseling, Reich would also give political talks in the evening. He began with questions or problems people had raised in smaller discussions with the team during the day. For example, young men and women complained about how the lack of money forced them to live at home, hampering their sexual freedom. Others spoke of their fear of unwanted pregnancies. Reich would deal with some of the personal aspects of these problems. However, at some point he would invariably connect them with larger political issues. People could not have a satisfying sexual life without adequate housing for all; hence this kind of public policy required a truly Socialist society. The problem of unwanted pregnancies could only be met by progressive sex legislation, in other words, the legalization of birth control and abortion, the kind of legislation the Christian Socialists always opposed. In their turn, the Social Democratic leaders avoided these issues; the public should pressure them to take a strong positive stand.

Reich had an unusual ability to start with a concrete example and then find the larger concepts and implications contained in that example. This ability was important in all his teaching, but it especially facilitated his contact with nonprofessional audiences. While he was frank in answering questions, he had considerable sensitivity to the "touchy" issues for any given audience or individual questioner, and he would approach them with care. In simple language he could appeal to people's longing for a richer sexual-emotional life, while recognizing the fears and guilts they experienced at the idea of such an existence. This was true of the audiences that attended sex-political meetings. With professionals, Reich could use the same kind of sensitivity to highlight the differences between his position and that of others in a way that often was abrasive.

Reich had a superb speaking style. Dr. Kurt Eissler, a prominent psychoanalyst and Freudian scholar, heard Reich give a few political talks in Vienna in the late 1920s. He found him to be a "marvelous" speaker, eloquent and forceful.[3] A Danish newspaper reporter who heard Reich speak in 1934 wrote: "He is a phenomenon. . . . The moment he starts to speak, not at the lectern, but walking around it on cat's paws, he is simply enchanting. In the Middle Ages, this man would have been sent into exile. He is not only eloquent, he also keeps his listeners spellbound by his sparkling personality, reflected in his small, dark eyes."*[4]

Reich's political speech always concluded the evening. Before it, there would be various kinds of entertainments studded with "messages." For example, the team wrote new lyrics, with sex-political themes, set to the music of Marlene Dietrich's popular song from *The Blue Angel*, "Falling in Love Again," which Lia Laszky was called upon to sing. And the audience participated in group singing to guitar accompaniment.[5]

---

*The same characteristics were apparent when I heard him speak before small professional groups in the 1940s and 1950s. He usually spoke from a very few notes, which permitted him to look directly at his audience, and spoke very fluently. He had a way of emphasizing key points through added vocal force, which, combined with his wit and directness, kept audience interest high. The repetitions and variations, combined with the inflections and cadences of his voice, gave a musical quality to his speech. He was the most charismatic speaker I have ever heard.

Once again, one has the uncanny sense of Reich's anticipation of later political developments on the left. He was well aware that the average citizen was bored to death by the usual approaches of the left—the long speeches on economic policy, foreign affairs, and the like. In his practical sex-political work, everything he did was geared to *involving* people.

In 1928, Reich dreamed that within a short time many teams would be going out with vans and offering the people sexual information and counseling, together with a more socialist political orientation. But this plan never materialized, partly because others did not share his commitment, partly because his own modus operandi changed. Reich was providing most of the driving force behind the enterprise and almost all the finances (the van, the cost of printing pamphlets and announcements, etc.). He threw himself into the sex-pol work with all his usual gusto. As Laszky remarked: "He loved it—it was meat and potatoes to him."

A further characteristic of Reich's style was that while he was the recognized leader of the enterprise, the team atmosphere was open, frank, and collegial. In all the sex-political work, as in the technical seminar, Reich encouraged the open acknowledgment of mistakes, taking the lead himself in describing his errors; each day's activities would be scrutinized afterward.

Laszky did not continue to be so enthusiastic about the sex-political work. After the initial excitement, she was disappointed. In her view, the expected movement of people toward a more radical political stance did not occur. Some were very interested in the sexual information and in obtaining contraception; others were quiet and just listened. But few made the connection between the issues of personal sexual life and larger political concerns.

Such a connection was essential to Reich. The concepts he was formulating during these years and was to detail in *The Mass Psychology of Fascism* some years later may be briefly summarized:

Sexual suppression and repression made the masses of people cowed and uncritical. The energies congealed in the character defenses, the "armor," were unavailable for rational social criticism. Preoccupation with emotional problems in general and sexual conflicts in particular led to political apathy. Lack of clarity about sexual issues and, worse, lies and deceit regarding human love life undermined the capacity of people to see through political chicanery.

Conversely, if people were more in touch with their sexual desires, their way would be paved for closer contact with larger social issues. As the women's movement in the United States was to emphasize many years later, it was necessary to begin with the personal, to politicize the personal. The political right—especially Nazism, as we shall see—was well aware of this. Its leaders constantly used sex-political propaganda, but of a negative kind. They played on people's fear of their own impulses and their fear of chaos by calling upon the need for moralistic defenses, for "law and order," for protection against the "Bolshevik menace" to the family. In this sense, Reich wrote, the

Catholic Church was the most powerful sex-political organization in the world.[6]

Reich was not so naive as to believe that simply informing people about their sexual needs would necessarily lead to changes either in their capacity for sexual fulfillment or in their political ideology. From his character-analytic work he knew too well the strength of the defenses, the anxieties and guilts that surround man's impulsive life. In this period of his work, Reich dealt with sexual need in a way similar to the Marxists' handling of economic want. That is, one heightened awareness, one "raised consciousness" about the problem. It could only be out of a concern with the problem that solutions would follow. To the criticism that his sex-politics merely heightened the awareness of sexual need without heightening the capacity for gratification, thereby rendering the suffering more acute, Reich answered:

> . . . The same objection holds with regard to hunger. . . .
> We admit: consistent [sex-political] work brings silent sufferings to the surface, it accentuates existing conflicts and creates new ones, it makes people incapable of tolerating their situation any longer. But at the same time it provides liberation: the possibility of fighting against the social causes of the suffering. True, sex-political work touches upon the most difficult, most exciting and most personal aspects of human living. *But does not the mystical infestation of the masses do the same thing?* What matters is, to what purpose one or the other is being done. He who has seen light in the eyes of the people in [sex-political] meetings; he who has listened to and had to answer thousands of questions of a most personal nature, knows that here is social dynamite which can make this world of self-destruction stop and think.[7]

Everywhere he went, Reich was impressed with the people's need for emotional help. And he strove to find some solution between the very brief contact of van missions and the long-term psychoanalysis of the individual, a socially useless endeavor because of the time it took and the small number of available therapists.

In January 1929, Vienna newspapers carried notices about new sexual hygiene clinics for workers and employees, opened by the Socialist Association for Sex Hygiene and Sexological Research, which Reich had founded. Four psychoanalytic colleagues and three obstetricians joined Reich in starting the organization.[8]

The sex hygiene clinics were opened in different districts of Vienna, each one directed by a physician. As the clinics were extremely busy, the lack of time on the part of the staff became a painful reality. Each case required about half an hour to be diagnosed conscientiously, and many persons who came needed considerable help. What exactly Reich and his associates did in these consultations is not clear. His sex-political writings are not as rich in case examples as are his psychoanalytic papers. However, we know that he gave prominence in his early clinical experiences to the problems of abortion, contraception, and adolescent sexuality.

Abortion was the most immediate problem because the first patients tended to be women wishing to terminate unwanted pregnancies. Reich's approach to this issue was amazingly advanced. He was impatient with, indeed outraged by, current debates about restricting or enlarging the categories of "medical indications" that would permit the interruption of pregnancy. For him the outstanding fact was that the women didn't want children and that they were incapable of bringing them up in a healthy way. Reich also stressed the terrible economic and social conditions under which many of these expectant mothers lived.

Using emotional and economic factors as legitimations for abortion did not satisfy Reich at all. The essential point was that women should have the right to terminate their pregnancies, regardless of their medical condition or social-economic situation. Nor should this position be justified on the grounds that, with this right, women would have just as many children as before, but "under joyful conditions." Reich was not concerned whether or not the population declined because of legalized abortion. In his own work he did everything he could to arrange illegal abortions, where necessary, for women who sought to end their pregnancies but who did not have the "proper" indications. In so doing, he often took grave legal risks.

Reich met with little success in seeking any political support for the legalization of abortion. Social Democratic leaders who privately were in favor of legalized abortion refused to take a public position for fear of alienating the Catholic vote. The Communist Party avoided the issue, in part because Marx had rejected the Malthusian position that the number of births should be restricted if social misery was to be eliminated. Marx argued that this stance diverted people from the "real" problem of radically changing the social order.

Thus, the whole issue of abortion languished in terms of direct political action. If the masses were unwilling to politicize the personal, the parties were unwilling to personalize the political.

The liberal position in Europe on contraception in the late 1920s was primarily to fight for it within the context of marriage. A more radical position was to advocate the right of unmarried adults to obtain contraceptive devices.

Yet by 1929 Reich was affirming the right of adolescents to learn about and to obtain contraceptives. His path to this position was somewhat more gradual than his advocacy of abortion and contraception for adults. For, of course, the issue of contraception for adolescents was inextricably linked to adolescent sexuality.

The question posed itself in practical terms when young people came to the sex hygiene clinics and asked not only for help with sexual problems per se but for advice about contraception. Since these young people ranged in age from fourteen to twenty, Reich found himself wondering: Should one give contraceptives to young people fourteen or fifteen years old?

Reich was not to answer this question in print with a clear-cut affirmation until 1929, but he was grappling with the answer from at least 1927 on. His advocacy of adolescent sexuality was a more radical and also a lonelier position than, say, his support for "abortion on demand." Since it was also extremely controversial, it was not something he embarked upon lightly.

That he could not evade the issue seemed clear to him, "if one wished to stick to the problem of the prevention of the neuroses."[9] Reich began to study adolescents more closely, in terms of their psychodynamics and in their social milieu. He got to know those who came to the clinics as well as those he met in various leftist youth meetings—his conclusions about adolescent problems were not based simply on a subsample of youth who might be termed "disturbed" because they attended the clinics.

Reich noted that some young people had sexual partners, while others wished to find one. In both instances, problems occurred: internal ones such as premature ejaculation, frigidity, shyness, depression, and nervousness; social ones such as the lack of contraception, inadequate space to be with a partner, and parental disapproval. Stressing the interaction between internal and external factors, Reich would say, for example, that premature ejaculation was based on Oedipal conflicts but it was also more likely to occur when genital intercourse was carried out in one's clothes and hastily.[10]

In his counseling work in clinics and youth organizations, Reich felt the need for a practical position. He had to reject the choice of abstinence, if for no other reason than that it was totally unrealistic. Most adolescents (especially males) masturbated. Even among those who did not, sexual daydreaming was common, a form of psychic masturbation that is stimulating though not gratifying. Reich also rejected masturbation, that "pale substitute of love," in D. H. Lawrence's phrase. He held that guilt feelings with masturbation are much more intense than with sexual intercourse because it is more heavily burdened with incest fantasies (conscious or unconscious). Incidentally, the prevalence of masturbation rendered suspect one psychoanalytic argument against adolescent intercourse, namely, that intercourse would decrease the cultural achievements of youth by weakening "sublimation."[11] Why should one assume that sexual intercourse interferes with achievement while masturbation does not?

Reich was initially optimistic about the number of adolescents who could be helped if they were exposed to sexual enlightenment, given some counseling, and provided with contraceptive aids. As he put it, "The younger the boy or girl concerned was, the more quickly and more fully they swung around after listening to only a few clarifying sentences."[12]

This implies a change in functioning as well as intellectual orientation. Yet Reich was also aware that deep-rooted adolescent problems would not be altered simply by intellectual change. Some years later, reporting on a successful, brief consultation with an adolescent couple, Reich noted that such successes of simple counseling were unusual, due to the depth of the neuroses in most of the young people who came to the clinics.

The truth probably lies somewhere between the two quotations. Edith Jacobson, a prominent psychoanalyst when I interviewed her in the 1970s, worked with Reich in a sex-political clinic in the early 1930s. I asked how much such counseling could accomplish with adolescents. She replied succinctly: "Surprisingly much."[13]

Two further central interests in sex-political work developed for Reich in this period: the issue of childhood sexuality and the problem of marriage.

The depth and extent of sexual problems in adults and adolescents led Reich to stress prevention rather than treatment. By 1929, he was referring to sexual disturbances as an epidemic among the masses, and counseling as being only of very limited value.

In 1930, in a speech before the World League for Sexual Reform (WLSR), Reich reported that over a period of eighteen months his centers for sexual counseling had seen seven hundred cases.[14] Of those seeking help, approximately 30 percent could be successfully advised, while the remaining 70 percent had problems of such severity that they could not be treated by short-term counseling. Nor were there other available resources to help them. Most existing public health programs either totally ignored neuroses or prescribed bromides. While a few public programs offered psychotherapeutic treatment, the permitted length of treatment was entirely inadequate.

Such figures strengthened Reich's conviction that the neuroses could only be attacked prophylactically. In his WLSR speech he vehemently insisted on certain social measures: adequate housing and nourishment; availability of contraceptives and abortion; social support for the care and education of children; and a change in the marriage and divorce laws. These changes could only be implemented, Reich believed, in a socialist economy. But even if they were realized, a large number of adults and adolescents would still remain sexually crippled because of irreversible pathology generated during childhood —irreversible, that is, without long-term individual treatment.

The logic of this reasoning led to an exploration of childhood factors that contributed to neuroses. In keeping with the Freudian tradition, which emphasized the Oedipal period of development (ages four to about six), Reich began by analyzing social attitudes toward the child's genital impulses. Punishment and threats of punishment by parents and educators toward the child's masturbation were still common (as, indeed, they still are in many circles). However, the more progressive attitude, especially among the psychoanalytically oriented, consisted in ignoring masturbation or gently distracting the child from it.

Reich opposed both attitudes. In counseling parents, he stressed the need for affirming childhood masturbation. Throughout his life, Reich put considerable emphasis on the distinction between affirming childhood sexuality and *tolerating* it. Toleration was insufficient to counteract a generally sex-negative culture. Moreover, if sexual behavior is distracted, the child cannot help but feel that he or she is doing something wrong in masturbating.[15]

Toleration also contributed to the mystification of sex—surrounding it with silence, the mysterious distractions when the child touches its genital. For Reich this was in some ways more dangerous than direct suppression. Authoritarian education was at least clear: Sex outside marriage was sinful. In much permissive education, sex simply did not exist; the child had to deal not with thunderbolts of punishment but with a secretive fog.

Reich distinguished between two kinds of childhood masturbation. One type expressed the natural urge for genital pleasure. The second was connected with anxiety and anger: the child used auto-eroticism not primarily for genital pleasure but as a way of discharging fear and rage. Reich affirmed the first kind of masturbation; the second already indicated some degree of emotional disturbance in the child.

Reich took the same basically affirmative stance toward heterosexual play in children. Indeed, over the years he came to stress the importance of this activity even more than he did masturbation.

Reich's daring in affirming heterosexual play in the 1920s is highlighted if we compare his position on the subject to that of Dr. Benjamin Spock in the 1950s. Spock is rightly considered permissive toward the emotional expressions of the infant and child. However, of sexual play, he wrote:

> If you discover your small child in some sort of sex play alone or with others, you'll probably be at least a little bit surprised and shocked. In expressing your disapproval it's better to be firmly matter-of-fact rather than very shocked or angry. You want him to know that you don't want him to feel that he's a criminal. You can say, for instance, "Mother doesn't want you to do that again," or "That isn't polite," and shoo the children off to some other activity. That's usually enough to stop sex play for a long time in normal children.[16]

In discussing masturbation, Spock warns against making threats or dispensing severe punishment. He goes on to say that even if we magically could rid ourselves of our discomfort at masturbation, he doubts that it would be in the best interests of the child: "There is lots of evidence that all children feel guilty about masturbation whether or not their parents have found out about it or said anything about it."[17]

I do not know the evidence that Spock is drawing upon. But one line of theorizing, forcefully advanced by Anna Freud, posits that "there is in human nature a disposition to repudiate certain instincts, in particular the sexual instincts, indiscriminately and independently of individual experience. This disposition appears to be a phylogenetic inheritance, a kind of deposit accumulated from acts of repression practiced by many generations, and merely continued, not initiated, by individuals."[18]

This kind of genetic speculation concerning an "archaic unconscious" stands in sharp contrast to Reich's emphasis on social factors determining the anxiety and guilt that so often surround genital impulses.

Reich emphasized that one benefit of masturbation and particularly of heterosexual play was to mitigate the intensity of the Oedipal configuration— the child's passionate love for the parent of the opposite sex and his equally strong hatred and fear of the parent of the same sex. He argued that the complex would be less charged if the child had a sensual outlet with peers.

It would also be less intense if there were considerable communal involvement in the care and education of children. And it would be less intense if the parents, particularly the father, were generally less authoritarian, if they interacted with their children in a more human, fallible way.

All of these conditions Reich found in Bronislaw Malinowski's report on the sexual life of the Trobriand Islanders,[19] which he first read in 1930. Indeed, Malinowski argued that the presumed "universal" Oedipus complex was absent among this people, an absence he attributed to the matrilineal organization of the family. Yet the findings permitted Reich to make somewhat different emphases, namely, on the affirmation of both childhood and adolescent sexuality among the Trobrianders. It further fitted Reich's theoretical framework that Malinowski found the Trobrianders to be a warm, open people, relatively free of the neuroses, perversions, and sadism so common in the "civilized" world. Malinowski became one of the few authors Reich would cite frequently.

Further stressing the demystification of sexuality during childhood, Reich argued that nakedness among children and between adults and children should be accepted as matter-of-fact. His rationale was as follows:

> Among the infantile sexual impulses, those aiming at the observation and the display of the genitals are particularly well known. Under present educational conditions, these impulses are usually repressed at a very early time. As a result of this repression, children develop two different feelings: first, they develop guilt feelings because they know that they are doing something strictly forbidden if they give in to their impulses. Second, the fact that the genitals are covered up and "taboo" gives a mystical air to everything sexual. Consequently, the natural impulse to look at things changes into lascivious curiosity.[20]

Reich's main point was that educators and pupils, parents and children, when bathing and swimming, should feel free to appear naked before each other when it was natural to do so.

Not surprisingly, Reich felt that the child's questions about sex should be answered frankly. But even to this he added a novel provocative twist: How should we answer a child who asks if he or she can witness parental intercourse? Reich dismissed the argument that watching parental intercourse was harmful. After all, analytic experience showed that practically every child listened anyway, and many children observed intercourse between animals. Reich concluded that the only valid argument against the child's witnessing parental intercourse did not concern the child but the parents: it would interfere with *their* pleasure.[21]

Reich's position on this issue was distorted by his opponents, including many analysts. He was accused of advocating that children should watch intercourse and that his children did. Neither accusation was true. His point about the right argument—the argument for adult privacy—against such observation was lost.

Reich's emphasis on nudity and the question of the child's observation of parental intercourse diminished over the years. Indeed, it is interesting to speculate why he had emphasized these as much as he did. In *The Impulsive Character,* published in 1925, Reich after all had stressed the dangers of overstimulation to the child. He noted how often impulsive patients expressed "precocious sexuality" in childhood, witnessed the "primal scene" in a blatant form, and so on. From his disguised self-history, we know Reich himself felt he had suffered severely from having overheard sexual intercourse between his mother and tutor.

By the late 1920s, I believe that Reich was reviewing his own sexual history and coming to rather different conclusions from those of the early 1920s. Some of his early experiences *were* certainly provocative and overstimulating. But Reich saw the problem as stemming less from his "precocious sexuality" than from its context, the repressive and sex-negative atmosphere of his father's house.

If his desire as a child to witness forbidden things had led to such devastating consequences, it also led to a characteristic that became one of his chief virtues in adult life: his ability to see beneath the surface or "clothing" of things, to explore what the general consensus deemed "off limits."

By the late 1920s, Reich was struggling to maintain his own line of thought and investigation against considerable criticism. As we shall see in the next chapter, many of his analytic colleagues became hostile to his sex-political work. Characteristically, Reich reacted strongly. If his colleagues disliked the affirmation of adolescent and childhood heterosexuality, let them think about nudity between parents and children; let them consider the rational arguments for preventing children from witnessing parental intercourse. After the heat of battle, Reich was better placed emotionally to qualify his views and to take into account some of the criticisms of his opponents. Thus, after 1935 or so, Reich stressed once again that adults could be destructively provocative as well as suppressive in dealing with children.

Persons critical of permissive attitudes toward the sexual life of children and adolescents often charged that such attitudes would undermine marriage and the family. The reaction of many liberal sex reformers was to attempt to reassure these critics. Even today, the American organization SIECUS (Sex Information and Educational Council of the United States) argues that sexual enlightenment will improve marriage. Dr. Mary Calderone, the leading spokesperson for the organization, makes a point of not advocating premarital intercourse.[22]

Reich, of course, was scornful of such evasion. He agreed in part with his conservative critics: the affirmation of childhood and adolescent sexuality would indeed undermine the institution of marriage—in the sense of the traditional concept of marriage or what he termed "life-long, compulsive monogamy."[23] Conversely, the denial of sexuality in childhood and adolescence prepared the way for this kind of marriage precisely because it helped to flatten the emotional vitality of people, thereby making them more resigned to a dull relationship. At the same time, Reich emphasized—as his critics did not—that such an upbringing also destroyed marriage, robbing it of its joys and contributing to myriad marital problems.

What did Reich foresee as replacing the institution of "life-long, compulsive monogamy"? He disagreed with many conservative critics of sex reform who claimed that promiscuity in adulthood resulted from the relaxation of "proper" sexual standards in childhood and adolescence. In his view, traditional marriage would be replaced by something like what in fact seems to be happening today—serial monogamy. Reich termed this kind of marriage "the lasting love relationship," and saw the capacity for it as the hallmark of the healthy adult.[24] The "lasting love relationship" also had a strong component of tenderness, based in part on gratitude for sexual pleasure in the past and anticipation of pleasure in the future. Reich sharply distinguished this kind of tenderness from the sticky, clinging affection often shown between spouses in compulsive monogamy. In the latter instance, frequent "honeys" or "dears" cannot conceal an underlying sense of frustration and rage.

Why did the ties that make the healthy love relationship lasting not also make it permanent and exclusive? For several reasons: first, the interests of the two partners might diverge over time. The couple who entered a relationship in their twenties might be quite different people in their thirties. More importantly, Reich coined the term "sexual dulling" to describe what happened over time between even the most passionate couple. He viewed "sexual dulling" as the inevitable result of close physical proximity to one partner, and the simultaneous exposure to new sexual stimuli emanating from others. When the relationship between two people is at its height, the desire for others has little effect. The healthier the individual, the more conscious is the attraction to others and hence the easier to control, so long as the original relationship is basically satisfying and the desire for others not too strong.

Several factors ensue from this "sexual dulling," which make it extremely difficult to deal with. The dulling may occur in one partner and not the other.

If the partner whose interest has flagged enters another relationship, the still attached partner may experience acute jealousy. Reich did not agree with some extreme radicals who dismissed all jealousy as a sign of neurosis, but he did distinguish between normal jealousy and possessiveness. In the presence of the former, the painful feelings created by one's partner having an affair with another can be worked through and mastered.

Reich made a point of characterizing the "love relationship" in terms of its quality rather than its length. It might last for months, a few years, or many years; but the qualities of sharing, tenderness, and development over time distinguished it from a more purely sensual temporary relationship. It was not monogamous in the sense that there might be experimental affairs, especially during periods of sexual dulling with the original partner.

Reich stressed that this kind of solution to the problem of dulling—the experimental affair, the openness of the ultimate solution—required personality structures and social conditions that applied only to a minuscule minority of the population. Social-economic factors also militated against the kind of solutions he proposed. The economic dependence prevalent for so long often made it difficult for a woman to leave a relationship. Throughout his adult life, Reich adamantly opposed such economic dependence for women. He strongly believed that women should have their own careers and manage their own finances. In this way, the link between love and economic need could be broken: people could stay together because they chose to, not because they were forced to do so. If they separated and there were children from the relationship, each should contribute to child support.

During the late 1920s, Reich was as concerned with the economic dependence of women as he was with a variety of other "patriarchal" attitudes. In particular, he inveighed against the sexual double standard that permitted male youth to sow wild oats yet punished "bad girls" who did the same; against the notion that women were "naturally" passive sexually; against "machismo" attitudes that regarded male infidelity as something the woman should tolerate but female infidelity a terrible blow to the man's pride; and against education for the supremacy of man which makes fully mutual mental companionship with the woman impossible.[25]

Reich also called attention to the way in which traditional marriage, while providing support and protection for women and children, also exploited the woman. She was not only the sexual object of the man but her unpaid work in the household indirectly increased the profit of the employer. The man could work at low wages because women did work in the home without pay. If the wife was also employed, she had to work overtime, without pay, to keep her home in order.

Reich's position on the raising of children varied. In the late 1920s and early 1930s, he stressed the importance of social care and communal upbringing for children, though he never went into detail as to how this should be arranged or its combination with parental involvement. He sometimes called for increased but limited state participation in child rearing, through laws concerning maternity leave, child support, and the provision of day-care facilities. At other times he called for something like the abolition of the family:

> The prevention of neuroses is inconceivable as long as there continues to be family upbringing and, with it, Oedipal conflicts. We regret, of course, the complexity of this problem, but it cannot be helped: the prevention of neuroses begins by excluding from the education of the child his or her own parents, who have proven themselves to be the most unqualified educators. The sexual education of the small child will be put instead into the hands of specially trained personnel who will be less biased. This, however, presupposes the education of *society* in general.[26]

By 1935 or so, Reich was no longer speaking of "excluding" the parents from their children's education. He continued to emphasize the need for social support and an involvement in their upbringing far beyond the existing structure. But over the years he made much more of the contrast between the "natural family" and the "compulsive family" than he did of the contrast between the family as educator and the state as educator. The "natural family" was nothing more (or less) than the "lasting love relationship," where the partners had children and were responsible for them in some not too clear combination with social facilities such as day-care centers.

However, the fate of the children, if the relationship between the parents dissolved, was a question Reich never discussed in detail. And, as we shall see subsequently, his relationship with his own children after his marriage with Annie dissolved was a source of great anguish to him.

It is interesting to speculate why Reich maintained for a period so extreme, so dubious a view as the exclusion of parents from the education of their own children. It would seem, again, as if the pressures from his own unhappy childhood and from his increasingly unhappy marriage in the late 1920s contributed to his bold formulation: abolition of the family.

The question arises: How original were Reich's concepts concerning the affirmation of genital love life for adults, adolescents, and children? Certainly many aspects of his criticism of Babbitt-like marriage, of attitudes toward women, of repressive laws concerning marriage, divorce, contraception, abortion, premarital and extramarital sexuality, were very much "in the air" and part of the intellectual climate in progressive European circles. Havelock Ellis, Bertrand Russell, Max Hodann, Ellen Key, Fritz Brupbacher, Helena Stocker, and a host of others were fighting for a revision of conventional sexual mores at the time.

Reich was clearly influenced by the liberal policy of the Soviet Union toward sexual issues. He had read much about what was going on in the "first socialist society." Then, in the summer of 1929, he and Annie visited Russia for a few weeks, where Reich gave some lectures. He came back more convinced than ever that sexual misery and economic exploitation were inextricably linked and that a solution to the sexual question could not take place without a social revolution. His trip also convinced him that certain measures then being taken in the Soviet Union—simple divorce, legalized abortion, attempts to break down the economic dependence of women, and some sexually permissive "children's collectives" (especially the one run by the psychoanalytically oriented educator Vera Schmidt)—were only possible in a Communist society. He noted the signs indicating that by 1929 the Soviet Union was already beginning to retreat from this kind of revolutionary policy, although formal reactionary measures would not fully emerge until the 1930s.

Even more important was the influence of Marx on Reich's thinking. From Freud, Reich had received the beginnings of a truly dynamic psychology of individual development within one particular form of family life—the nuclear, patriarchal family. For Marx, family form was itself dependent upon socioeconomic conditions, which were in a process of continuous change based on the class struggle. Marx and Engels at times had spoken of the "abolition of the family" under communism, but they had no clear sexual theory. Still, their prediction of "unalienated" Communist men and women fulfilling all their potentialities without economic or sexist exploitation was undoubtedly an important influence on Reich's own social vision.

I would like to note here that my method of presenting different aspects of Reich's work in separate chapters has the disadvantage of obscuring just how much Reich was involved with at any given time. Thus, from 1927 until 1934, Reich was pursuing his character-analytic studies with even greater vigor than in preceding years (Chapter 14). He also devoted considerable time and energy to his practical sex-politics (this chapter and Chapter 13). Finally, he was making a major conceptual effort to integrate Freud and Marx, to bring social theory to Freud's work on the individual and a dynamic psychology to Marxist theory and practice.[27] In recalling her association with Reich, Grete Bibring shook her head and said that Reich's evening technical seminar would often last until one in the morning. Frequently she was tired and would have liked to stop earlier, "but no work was too much for Willy."

Reich was more original in his clear-cut affirmation of adolescent and child genitality. However, what really distinguished his position was not the advocacy of one or another specific viewpoint: it was the way he formulated a syndrome of concepts. In this sense, Reich's contribution in the social field was similar to his clinical contribution. In his character-analytic work he wove together existing concepts such as latent negative transference, defensive character traits, nonverbal communication, and "actual neuroses." These linkages of existing clinical concepts were made in the service of a new therapeutic goal —the establishment of orgastic potency.

Similarly, in his social concepts Reich interwove a series of affirmations of genital life, connecting them with a psychiatric theory that provided distinctions many libertarians were unable to perceive. That is, it made all the difference in the world not just whether the child masturbated, but whether the masturbation was motivated by genital pleasure or as a means of discharging anger and anxiety. It made all the difference in the world whether a person, in rejecting compulsive monogamy, moved on to a "lasting love relationship" or, incapable of that kind of closeness, was promiscuous. Without such precise distinctions, conservatives could cite (as they still do) the unhappily masturbating child or the compulsively driven Don Juan as proof that the "living out" of sexual impulses led to misery and chaos.

As usual, Reich sought support for his social concepts just as he had for his clinical ones. Yet his sex-political work aroused considerable opposition, especially among psychoanalytic colleagues. And it contributed to the deterioration of his marriage to Annie.

Personal Life and Relations
with Colleagues: 1927-1930

When Reich was reunited with his family after his stay in Davos, he was intent upon saving his marriage. Yet new strains appeared in his complex relationship with Annie. For one thing, after the incidents of July 15, 1927, direct contact with the poor and unemployed heightened his sense of guilt about his own economically privileged position, a guilt he partially assuaged by contributing money to the Communist Party, to the "left opposition" within the Social Democratic Party, and to his sex-political efforts.[1] In addition, he gave money directly to fund-raising efforts for the unemployed.

These heavy financial commitments led to friction with Annie, who, while not hostile, was by no means passionately devoted to his political causes. She participated by working as a psychoanalyst at his counseling centers, but without the genuine enthusiasm she brought to her private practice. There were quarrels between the two of them about household expenses. From the beginning of their marriage, Reich was determined that each would be economically independent. However, according to Annie, Reich was often insufficiently aware of or concerned about the difficulties in the way of her contributing financially, especially when she was pregnant or had a small baby to care for.

Then, after the Vienna uprising, Reich's relentless concern for raising money clashed with Annie's interest in continuing their comfortable life together. There were quarrels as to whether money should be spent for new curtains or pamphlets on sex information. Annie's father, Alfred Pink, seems to have helped out financially. Most of the time, Annie herself was earning a good income so that, to some extent at least, both curtains and pamphlets were feasible.

From his side, by 1927, Reich was determined more than ever to live that heroic existence he had envisioned in the Army and feared would be undermined in the trivialities of peacetime. Money and its disposition was always one of the chief battlegrounds on which Reich fought out his war against the quotidian.

But, I believe, the financial arguments were symptoms of a deeper disturbance on Reich's part. So long as he was involved with more traditional aspects of psychoanalysis, such as the impulsive character, the relationship with Annie seems to have been fairly stable. However, the more his own direction became manifest, as in his clinical work on the function of the orgasm and in his sex-politics, the worse the relationship between them became. Reich expected a full response to and affirmation of his work from his mates; he had done so with Lia in the medical school days and would do so again later in other relationships. When that support was lacking, he became angry and embittered.

A further complicating factor was the entanglement of analytic relationships. Around 1928, Annie went into analysis with Anna Freud, at that time a young analyst. Miss Freud attended Reich's technical seminar and had a high regard for his contributions to analytic theory and technique. However, she had a much more conservative sexual orientation than Reich, and he feared that she might influence Annie against his work. There is no evidence that he ever opposed the analysis, but he was not happy about it.[2]

Another source of friction was the fact that in 1927 Reich again began to see a good deal of Lia Laszky, who was now divorced. Laszky was very much involved in the study of psychoanalysis, but, unlike Annie, she had an intense commitment to radical politics. Indeed, she had joined the Communist Party earlier than Reich. Her life crossed his at still another point: she taught at the Montessori nursery school attended by the three-year-old Eva.

Reich found the vivacious Laszky a stimulating companion with whom to share his sex-political work as well as his clinical writings. In addition, Lia Laszky had become a beautiful, mature woman with considerable piquancy. Given his marital difficulties, including Annie's ambivalence and attitude toward his work, he was very receptive to Lia's sexual charms. On her side, Lia found the vibrant thirty-year-old Willy a much more secure person than the volatile youth she had known in medical school. His stature as an analyst, combined with his political radicalism, exerted a strong appeal. Finally, she was much less the reluctant virgin she had been in medical school, although Reich remained the pursuer in the developing relationship.

Their affair seems to have been more than casual but less than deeply involved. Each was very busy and their times spent together, aside from work, were sporadic. There was no talk of marriage. As Laszky's interest in Reich's social work waned during 1929, so did their sexual relationship. It ended cleanly, and they remained good friends for years after. Unlike so many others, Lia Laszky never blamed Reich for either their personal or professional involvements. For a time she had been excited by him and by sex-politics; and that was that. She also tended to look back on both the affair and her work participation as somewhat illicit: the first violated her feelings for Annie Reich, the second her lifelong commitment to psychoanalysis.[3]

On Reich's side, the feelings may well have run deeper. Reich slept with many women, but Lia was one of the few he would mention frequently and warmly long after the liaison had ended. It says a good deal that when he was isolated in Rangeley, Maine, in the 1950s, (see Chapter 30), under attack from all sides and seeing only those who were "in the work," he permitted Laszky to visit and give him some frank advice "out of our old friendship," in her own words. For a period in the 1920s, Lia Laszky, with her interests, her verve, and her candor, had been able to embody a sexual-emotional-intellectual excitement for Reich that complemented his enthusiasm for Marxism, sex-politics, and "the function of the orgasm"—the book of that title published in the same year his affair with Lia began.

Exactly how Annie felt about the affair we do not know. Ottilie, Robert's widow, who lived with the Reichs from September 1926 to June 1927, felt that Annie "shut her eyes" to the relationship.[4] However, it cannot have been easy for her to know that Reich was involved with a woman who was also her friend. Annie appears to have had the habit of blunting her own anger, but presenting her situation in a way that stirred up the anger of others on her behalf.[5]

Reich was also having trouble with analytic colleagues. Many had regarded him as intense and "fanatical" even before his radical political involvement. After it, the number who took this view sharply increased. Richard Sterba, Reich's friend during the early and mid-twenties, found that after 1927 Reich was far more "belligerent" than he had been earlier. The two men argued about Reich's professional direction until an increasing coldness set in between them and there was little further contact.[6]

Reich had always shown a tendency to meet opposition with indignation and belligerence. This disposition undoubtedly contributed to the growing conviction on the part of many analysts that from 1927 on, Reich exhibited "paranoid" trends. At least, Sterba, Grete Bibring, and—in retrospect—Annie Reich felt that this was the period when Reich "changed."

Other observers felt differently. Lia did not perceive the Reich of the late 1920s as "paranoid"; on the contrary, she described a much less "touchy" person than the youth she knew at medical school. Yet her description has one element in common with those more antagonistic to Reich. When criticized, she said, Reich in certain moods "could take anything" with equanimity. But in other moods he could take nothing without flaring up.

If some of his colleagues found Reich belligerent, he found many of them infuriatingly remote from the turmoil of the times. If they found him fanatical, he saw them as lacking either conviction or the capacity to apply their psychoanalytic knowledge to the social scene.

Reich could still be a delightful companion, participating in a variety of social gatherings. Ottilie has described how sparkling and winning he could be at parties: "I never knew anyone who could be so seductive—not sexually seductive, but charming. That smile!" However, increasingly the social evenings were mixed with work discussions. As Grete Bibring put it, "One could not be around Reich long without the discussion turning to work." Bibring interpreted it as another sign of Reich's taking himself too seriously when in 1928 he sent her a photo of himself at his desk with an inscription on the back: "The researcher at work."

Reich experienced the same mixed attitudes from his colleagues that he had experienced earlier, only now in more intensified form. Most of his associates liked his work on character defenses but disliked his views on genitality. By 1927, his sex-political work combined with his ardent Marxism added to the widespread criticism that he was advocating a "genital utopia." It should also be stressed that in the 1920s psychoanalysis as a profession was entering a more respectable and settled phase. With his affirmation—among other things—of adolescent and childhood sexuality, Reich threatened to provoke anew the anger of society.

If Reich found many of his colleagues turning against him, he received a warmer response from the poor, who had to deal with the harsh economic reality of post-imperial Vienna of the late 1920s, and he felt more at home among them. There is a fascinating picture taken of Reich in 1927 or 1928 that highlights his increasing identification with the working class. The photo shows him standing with a group of twenty or so other people in front of a building with signs posted up saying: "Mit den Kommunisten gegen die Faschisten" (With the Communists against the Fascists) and "Wählt Kommunisten!" (Vote Communist!). Reich stands at the edge of the group, wearing a tie but also a leather jacket, a frequent part of his dress during this period. The picture is in sharp contrast to photos taken of Reich with his analytic colleagues. The latter, in other photos, are clearly middle class and professional, and dressed accordingly. In the political photo Reich is with simple people, some of the working class, all very nonacademic in appearance. There is a man in some kind of uniform standing in the front of the group, straddling a bicycle. A boy in a knit cap watches the scene. The photo is haunting, bringing to mind the Depression years, the rise of fascism, and the searing political struggles of the late 1920s and early 1930s.

In these years Reich was still trying to combine different milieus—the world of the poor and the world of his professional colleagues, the world of marriage and the world of his political relationships. Ottilie, for example, recalled Reich reading to her one night from something he had just written: "He was so warm, so full of compassion for people that I loved him at that moment. And then the next day he could be cold and callous to the people around him." She also contrasted the different ways he could look—his dark brown eyes sparkling with that "wonderful smile" when he was happy, then the angry look, when his eyes became smaller, his mouth tightened, and the redness of his skin was accentuated.

Ottilie also described a trait of Reich's that was a characteristic throughout his life. At times he could exert a heavy-handed pressure on people around him, not only to follow his work but also to be guided by him in personal matters. For example, after Robert's death Ottilie was not interested in other men for some time. Reich frequently urged her to have a sexual relationship, to overcome her "genital anxiety." He also diagnosed her as having a "martyr complex." He combined these two notions into an informal "character analysis," which Ottilie sometimes found helpful, at other times very annoying. When she expressed her irritation, Reich apologized and stopped.

Reich's diagnosing of Ottilie is a good example of how he interwove professional and personal concerns. The same kind of interlacing was apparent in his relations with his children. Both in his writings and in his rearing of Lore, Reich began to emphasize "self-regulation" for anal as well as genital life. He no longer feared that an absence of strictness would lead to a fixation through over-indulgence. Rather, there was a maturational progress toward the genital stage, just as there was a natural progression from sitting to walking. However, it was not until some years later that Reich would stress the negative consequences of a strict feeding schedule during the oral phase of development.

Reich's upbringing of his daughters was most influenced by his concepts concerning genitality. Eva was early told the "facts of life," and as a youngster of four or five (in 1928 or 1929) she took some pride in the fact that older children would come to her for sex information. Probably under Reich's influence, Annie kept a diary of Eva's sex education. The parents seem to have shared a concern about finding ways to enlighten their children without being "seductive."

It should not be construed that the children's sexual education occurred in a cold, intellectual atmosphere. On the contrary, Reich was sometimes criticized for being overly affectionate with Eva. (Eva seems always to have been his favorite. Lore's birth in 1928 took place as the relationship between Reich and Annie was deteriorating.) Lia Laszky recalls leaving her son Tony, then three or four, with the Reichs for a week or so while she took a vacation. Visiting briefly at the Reichs' summer home, she commented to Reich that he cuddled with Eva too much; it would prevent her from having a good relationship later with a man. Reich became annoyed. Laszky reminded him that she was his expert on children so he should listen to her. He replied that she wasn't the expert on raising *his* children.

On a theoretical level, Reich believed in the affirmation of genital play among peers during childhood. And he was curious as to what such play was like in the "natural" situation. Just how curious is well illustrated by a story Ottilie relates. Tony had come over to play with Eva. At nap time, Eva and Tony undressed and lay down to rest. Ottilie reports that Reich watched them through the keyhole. He told Ottilie that he was interested in noting who took the initiative for sexual play—the boy or the girl. Although he invited her to observe, Ottilie was not interested. She was amused at Reich's disappointment when the children just giggled and then fell asleep.

Ottilie related this story in a way which suggested that, in her opinion, Reich behaved quite foolishly. From one viewpoint, he did. One can also read into the incident, I think justly, an obsessive curiosity about his children's sex lives, a theme to be repeated many years later with his only son, Peter, born in 1944. One might see in it, too, the same voyeuristic trait that had led Reich to observe his mother and tutor.

Over and beyond Reich's psychodynamics, the incident is a nice illustration of Reich's commitment to the study of genitality, his interweaving of the personal with the scientific, and his method of naturalistic "field research." As a researcher, he preferred to observe phenomena *in vivo*. If the observation of childhood genitality without altering the phenomena required looking through a keyhole, so be it.

Whatever Ottilie's impatience with Reich's insistence on genitality, it did not impair their good relationship. What did lead to its disruption had to do with money.

Ottilie left the Reich home in 1927, after completing her training as a nursery-school teacher. She was now in a position to support herself and her child, and was also eager to leave because she disliked Reich's affairs, his periodic coldness toward Annie, and his occasional cuttingly critical remarks, which could demolish Annie or any other target around him.

In 1929, Ottilie turned to Reich for help, this time for his maternal grandmother. Grandmother Roniger was a person Reich never liked: he considered her vain and meddlesome.[7] However, both she and her wealthy brother Josef Blum, for whom she kept house, had been bankrupted in the severe Depression of 1929. Josef was accepted into one of the B'nai Brith homes for the elderly, but Josephine had no such recourse. Ottilie asked Reich for a contribution to the relatives' fund so that his grandmother would not have to depend on public charity. Ottilie became incensed when Reich not only refused help but couched his refusal in callous terms. He said his grandmother could live in a poorhouse as far as he was concerned. He would have been happy to help support the old family cook, a working woman, but he would not give a penny to help such a "meddlesome parasite" as Josephine. Ottilie appealed again on the grounds of his contributing in memory of his mother, but to no avail.

Immensely upset, Ottilie vowed never to see him again. Four years later, Reich had to flee Berlin when Hitler came to power in March 1933. While passing through Vienna, he got in touch with Ottilie. She agreed to see him and they had a generally cordial meeting. She told him his grandmother had died in the intervening years, and that she had not had to live out the remainder of her life in a poorhouse. Ottilie's relatives had managed to support her without her ever knowing that she was dependent on the generosity of others. When Reich heard the story, he shook his head and said: "Sentimental fools!" Ottilie replied: "We may have been sentimental fools but you are a pig so it's a good combination." Not long after this meeting, Reich gave her a copy of his new book, *The Mass Psychology of Fascism*, with the inscription: "To my beloved sister-in-law."[8]

Why did Ottilie remain angry with Reich over a period of years? There seems to have been something more at work in the intensity of her reactions than the particular incidents she cites. Yet Reich was to be accused many times of breaking off relations with people he knew well. The completeness of their rupture was also so characteristic of Reich's personal relations that I shall postpone a fuller analysis until later; but two aspects deserve some discussion here.

The first concerns the way Reich insisted on making a principle out of what others considered a "failing." To have an affair was one thing; to make a principle of it another. Not to help out a relative was one thing; to assert that it would be wrong to help a "parasite," that one's money was better spent elsewhere, was different. Then there was Reich's anger toward the target of his disapproval. Not only did the grandmother not deserve his support; she merited the "poorhouse."

The second factor, associated with the first, concerns the lack of empathy most of Reich's friends felt for his principles, or what he called the "red line" of his life and work. Even when, like Ottilie, they did not actively oppose his interests, they often felt he made too much of them. This, in turn, made them less sympathetic to the ways he implemented his "mission" and the people he hurt along the route.

Reich himself was not always aware of just how limited was the support he received for his concepts. In his polarizing way, he tended to regard his associates as either against his work or for it. He was usually right about those he labeled against it. Analysts like Paul Federn, in fact, thoroughly opposed him. However, his friends often liked him and even parts of his work, without fully sharing in what he regarded as his central concerns.

Lia Laszky, for example, participated closely in Reich's sex-political work. Yet, in addition to doubting how much sex education and counseling would influence the masses politically, she was far from committed to the affirmation of childhood and adolescent genitality. Undoubtedly, Reich's personal influence, his charisma, and the desire of those close to him to win his approval pushed some of them to go along with his work more than they actually believed in it. Edith Buxbaum, one of Annie's university friends, participated in Reich's sex-counseling centers; she also tried to "enlighten" the students at the high school where she taught, an effort not appreciated by the school officials.

In looking back on her relationship with Reich, Buxbaum underscored his personal influence on her and her admiration of him as a brilliant young analyst and as first the lover, then the husband, of her closest friend. She also stressed how much she learned by attending his technical seminar and being supervised by him. However, she looked back on her sex-political activity as foolishness done under Reich's influence.[9]

Even the "younger generation" of analysts and analytic candidates, whom Reich viewed as sympathetic in contrast to the older, more hostile analysts, went only a part of the way with him and seldom on the aspects he valued most: his clinical concept of orgastic potency and his social, mass-psychological work. Richard Sterba and Grete Bibring, both very positive members of the technical seminar, were after 1927 joining those like Helena Deutsch who had early regarded Reich as a "fanatic," although they still considered him an excellent analyst and teacher.

Many of the personal characteristics mentioned—Reich's principles that violated the general consensus, his passionate determination to live by those principles, his tendency to badger others into following his beliefs, his polarization of colleagues, his blindness to friends' criticism unless such criticism was clearly stated—remind us of intellectual adolescents. So, too, does Reich's desire to work in a variety of fields and not "settle down" to one thing.

Goethe has said that the genius periodically re-experiences all the expansion of adolescence, the excitement of new intense emotions, concepts, and creations. What the adolescent—or genius—discovers seems so self-evident, so important, and so enchanting that he or she cannot believe others will not share the excitement once they are exposed to it.

The difference between the truly creative adult and the adolescent is that the former is repeatedly able to channel his or her excitement into enduring accomplishments, however many realms of creation are involved. However, it often takes time for the creator's discoveries to be seen in their fullness. Meanwhile it is the adolescent aspects of the personality—the storms and demands rather than the achievements—that most impress and depress his or her family and friends.

In September 1930, Reich decided to move from Vienna to Berlin. Despite his marital difficulties and the worsening of his collegial relationships, it is my guess that Reich might well have remained in Vienna had it not been for two factors: Freud's attitude toward his sex-political work and his own conflict with the Social Democratic Party.

When Reich began his sex-political counseling, he felt he had Freud's support. Freud was generally encouraging toward diverse enterprises along analytic lines even when he was not fully in agreement with them. And, to some extent, he was in sympathy with Reich's direction. Freud had long been concerned with finding ways to bring psychoanalytic knowledge to a broader public than could be reached through individual treatment. Furthermore, Reich's sex-politics reflected Freud's early interest in the treatment of the actual neuroses.

In addition, Reich's critique of conventional sexual morality was not without resonances in Freud's work. To give but one example, Freud had commented early on the prevalence of sexual unhappiness in marriage: "The uninitiated can hardly believe how rarely normal sexual potency is to be found in the man, and how often frigidity in the woman, among those married couples living under the sway of our civilized sexual morality: what a degree of renunciation is associated often for both partners with marriage, and of how little the marriage comes to consist of bringing the happiness that was so ardently desired."[10]

Freud also shared with Reich the hope that the Soviet Union's experiment in relaxing divorce laws and other measures of sexual liberation would be successful.[11] Still, even here Freud was hesitant, fearing that too great a liberalization would lead to social chaos. For he held the belief that considerable frustration of the sexual impulse was necessary for civilization.

In short, whatever support Freud gave to Reich was always qualified. As Reich continued to insist on drawing social consequences from psychoanalytic findings, Freud's coolness increased. In a private conversation in 1929, when Reich discussed the problem of compulsive monogamy, Freud remarked that if Reich pursued this line, he would be provoking a good deal of trouble.[12]

The most extensive information on Freud's reaction to Reich's social views comes from an evening meeting on December 12, 1929, held at Freud's home. This particular session was one of a series of regular monthly meetings attended by the inner circle of Viennese analysts, including such persons as Paul Federn, Hermann Nunberg, Felix and Helena Deutsch, Heinz Hartmann, and Ludwig Jekels, in addition to Freud and Reich. Guest members also came to particular meetings.

In his presentation that evening, Reich outlined his views (summarized in Chapter 11) on the need for sweeping changes in man's sexual and economic life in order to prevent an "epidemic" of neuroses. In the ensuing discussion and at subsequent meetings, Freud answered with the arguments later to be published in his *Civilization and Its Discontents:*

> There can be no doubt about its purpose [the purpose of the pleasure principle], and yet its program is in conflict with the whole world, with the macrocosm as with the microcosm. It simply cannot be put into execution: the whole constitution of things runs counter to it. One might say that the intention that man should be "happy" is not included in the "scheme of Creation." What is called happiness in its narrowest sense comes from the gratification—most often instantaneous—of highly pent-up needs, and by its very nature can only be a transitory experience. . . . Civilization is built on renunciation of instinctual gratifications. . . . This "cultural" privation dominates the whole field of social relations between human beings. . . . Civilized society is perpetually menaced with disintegration through this primary hostility of men toward one another. . . . Hence its system of

methods by which mankind is to be driven to identification and aim-inhibited love relationships; hence the restrictions on sexual life.[13]

In commenting upon the meeting of December 12, Reich mentioned that the atmosphere was "very cold." Here he was referring to the other analysts present. As for Freud, he was strict with Reich but it was a kind of strictness Reich could take without his usual sensitivity.[14]

The most specific example of this hardness was reported not by Reich but by Richard Sterba, a guest at the meeting. I have already referred to his quote in connection with Reich's clinical concept of orgastic potency; the particular context was Freud's criticism of Reich's social concepts (see page 100). According to Sterba, Freud commented that "complete orgasm" was not the total answer. There was no single cause for the neuroses. When Reich kept arguing for his own viewpoint, Freud replied sharply: "He who wants to have the floor again and again shows that he wants to be right at any price."[15]

According to Reich, his most acrimonious discussion with Freud occurred in September 1930 just before his move to Berlin. Reich visited Freud at Grundlsee, the Austrian village where Freud spent his summer vacations. They continued their debate about the family problem. Reich had argued that one had to make a distinction between the genuinely loving family and the family bound together by guilt or obligation.[16]

This account, of course, reflects Reich's memory of the conversation twenty-three years after it occurred. Given the context of 1930, it is quite possible that Reich stated his position in a more extreme fashion. It was around this time, in his talk before the World League for Sexual Reform, that he had spoken of the need to remove children from the family setting, if the Oedipus complex and neuroses were to be prevented (see page 136).

In any case, whether he stated his views in their more moderate or in extreme form, Freud did not agree. He had replied that Reich's viewpoint had little to do with the moderate stance of psychoanalysis. Reich had answered that he regretted the disagreement but he had to maintain his position.[17]

Reich clearly remembered Freud's final comment to the effect that it was not Freud's intention or the intention of psychoanalysis to cure the world of its ills, in which Freud was referring indirectly to Reich's social ambitiousness, his need to "rescue" the world.

Reich remembered clearly his last impression of Freud. As he left, he gazed back at Freud's house and saw Freud in his room pacing to and fro. The image of Freud as a "caged animal" lingered in his mind.[18]

In spite of the sharpness of the exchanges between the two men, there was justification for Reich's view that Freud still thought well of him while others were pressuring Freud to take a more negative stance. For example, in 1928, Reich's old enemy Paul Federn wanted to have Reich removed as director of the technical seminar, ostensibly on the grounds that Reich was so busy. On November 22, 1928, Freud wrote Federn:

When you spoke to me the day before yesterday about relieving Dr. Reich of the leadership of the seminar, I thought it would probably be desirable to him, too, since he is so busy with other activities. I hoped in this way to meet both your wishes. It seems, however, I erred [about Reich's feelings]; and so you will have to relinquish your wish because I do not want to give the impression of a punitive dismissal of Reich without his consent and through an order I do not desire to issue and for which there is no reason. The criticisms which you and other colleagues raised about him are balanced by his great merits to the intellectual life of the Association. He is really quite good.

I have to ask you to maintain a collegial relationship with him. If he wants to keep the seminar leadership, we have to grant him this.[19]

It also appears that when Reich decided to leave for Berlin, he was not certain how permanent the move would be; yet Federn used the opportunity to remove Reich from leadership of the technical seminar and from membership in the Vienna Psychoanalytic Society. In some distress, Reich wrote to Freud about this. Freud in turn wrote to Federn on October 10, 1930. He reported that he had answered Reich's complaint by saying, ". . . we promised him that he could keep his positions [should he decide to return] and that we wished to hold to that agreement, but we did not have any understanding about the way a temporary leave would be handled." After making the point, Freud added a qualification: "Of course, you could have done it differently. First, Dr. Reich could have been elected, and then he could have asked for a temporary leave." Freud then went on to repeat that they intended to reinstate Reich should he return to Vienna, followed by another qualification—"if he has not become impossible." By "impossible," Freud was undoubtedly referring to the degree of aggressiveness Reich might bring to his presentation of the proper clinical and social goals of psychoanalysis.

One final point about the connection between Reich's relationship with Freud and the move to Berlin should be made. At their last meeting in the country, Reich had suggested that as a check on any irrational element in his social position he might consult with some analyst in Berlin. Freud had replied that it would be hard for so eminent an analyst as Reich to find a suitable therapist. Nonetheless, Freud suggested Sandor Rado or Siegfried Bernfeld.[20]

It would not have been easy for Reich to consider having more analysis, given his feelings of rejection about Freud's earlier refusal to accept him as a patient. However, it would have been far more difficult for him to see a Viennese analyst than someone in Berlin. In Vienna the relationships had become so entwined over the years, the various competitions and dissensions so great as to preclude Reich's establishing a viable therapeutic alliance with any analyst other than Freud.

Reich's political difficulties proved even greater than his psychoanalytic ones. Austria was undergoing a severe depression and by the fall of 1929 the political situation in Vienna had deteriorated sharply. The Heimwehr was showing increased recklessness, attacking Social Democratic workers' homes and meetings. The Christian Socialists were demanding emergency powers for the national leadership, powers that would curtail civil liberties and require constitutional changes. Fearful of even worse consequences, the Social Democratic leadership was negotiating compromises with the Christian Socialists.

The Communists and the left wing of the Social Democratic Party were outraged by such compromises. Reich organized the Komitee Revolutionär Sozialdemokraten (Committee of Revolutionary Social Democrats) to oppose the party on the constitutional issue.[21] This committee had a small core of ten members, some of whom Reich had met through his clinics. He financed the group's activities, which included the brief publication of a newspaper.

The first public meeting sponsored by the committee took place on the night of December 13, 1929. (It is striking that this meeting occurred only one day after the discussion at Freud's home on the prevention of the neuroses.) Reich gave the main speech, sharply criticizing the Social Democratic leaders for making militant press statements and simultaneously behaving so cautiously toward the Christian Socialist government. Worse, they had tried to gag party members who opposed this vacillating policy. Reich concluded by calling for the mobilization of the working class, for their taking the offensive against the Heimwehr and the Christian Socialists. Anson Rabinbach summarizes: "By openly confronting the leadership with almost no support in the party except among certain discontented elements among the youth and the Schutzbund, Reich clearly put himself in a position that courted expulsion."

Reich was, in fact, expelled from the party on January 16, 1930. He was accused of violating party discipline by attacking the leadership and by working closely with the Communists. The main witnesses against Reich were two associates from the committee. They claimed they did not know that Communists were going to attend the December 13 rally. One of them said that he had visited Reich's clinic after years of unemployment and was vulnerable to Reich's "seductive influences." The two men were permitted to remain in the party because of their testimony against Reich and for having seen the error of their ways.

Reich's account of the period in *People in Trouble* in no way contradicts Rabinbach but is far less complete. He emphasizes his empathy with some young Schutzbund members who at the clinic discussed their political desperation as well as their sexual problems.[22] But he says nothing about the committee or his expulsion from the party; Reich could at times omit incidents unfavorable to himself. In later years, Reich liked to highlight his participation as a physician in the radical political parties. In the committee he had functioned as a politician leading a quixotic venture.

These then were the cumulative factors at work in Reich's decision to move to Berlin: his strained relations with his Viennese colleagues and the opportunity to work in Berlin with more analysts who shared his social concerns; the political weakness of the Austrian radical left versus the strong German Communist Party (with over 4 million members); and a better opportunity to pursue his personal analysis in Berlin. What is also interesting is that no matter how constrained Reich felt within the psychoanalytic organization, no matter how great the frictions in his marriage, and no matter how weary he could become of political struggles, he left for Berlin without intending any major break in his life. He planned to join the Berlin Psychoanalytic Society, to have Annie and the children follow him once he was settled, and to become a member of the German Communist Party. He wanted to enlarge his existence while still maintaining the basic contours of its professional and personal design.

PART V

Liberation and Rejection—Reich's Breaks with the Communist Party and the Psychoanalytic Association: 1930-1934

13

The Sex-political Furor:
1930-1934

The years between 1930 and 1934 witnessed Reich's continuing involvement with psychoanalysis and politics. Initially, Berlin met his expectation that it would provide a more hospitable environment for his work than Vienna had. Many of the younger Berlin analysts—Otto Fenichel (who had moved to Berlin several years before), Erich Fromm, Edith Jacobson, and Karen Horney —were sympathetic to Reich's efforts to link psychoanalysis and Marxism, though none was as actively engaged in politics as he was.[1] The younger analysts were also interested in Reich's contributions to character analysis. So, shortly after his arrival in the German capital, Reich established a technical seminar similar to the one he had conducted in Vienna.

Reich also joined the Communist Party, then the third largest party in Germany. As in Vienna, he worked within a variety of political organizations and concentrated on sex-political themes. One of his first talks in Berlin, given before the Association for Socialist Physicians, concerned the prevention of emotional disturbances; and early in 1931, he addressed a student group on "The Fiasco of Bourgeois Morality."

The ensuing discussion among the youth went on until five A.M.[2] For Reich, such meetings held an air of excitement that arose again when he reminisced about this period. He loved contact with people, especially the young. After 1934, when he was devoting himself more to research, he kept recalling this period. I remember the note of sadness in his voice when in 1948 I told him I was going to speak before an anarchist group. He replied, "I envy you. I used to love to give talks but I can't any more."[3] Even as late as 1952, when Reich had long since detached himself from politics, he told Dr. Kurt Eissler about the Berlin period and the tremendous excitement generated at the sex-political meetings. "I still thrive on that experience."

Along with his public speaking, Reich soon developed sex-counseling clinics similar to those he had organized in Vienna. The work included sex education discussions, contraceptive information, and individual short-term counseling. Annie Reich—who, with the children, joined Reich in Berlin in the late autumn of 1930—Fenichel, Jacobson, and Käthe Misch, all at the time members of the Berlin Psychoanalytic Society, were among those who worked with Reich in the clinics. Yet, as in Vienna, Reich was the driving force behind the enterprise intellectually, emotionally, and financially.

If Reich anticipated today's emphasis on dealing directly with sexual problems, he was also ahead of his time in going directly to people rather than waiting for them to come to his clinics. In this respect, he anticipated current community mental health practice, which advocates professional participation within the context of people's daily lives—in schools, courts, industry, and the like. Reich still worked actively within the youth organizations of the Communist Party. He related an incident that had moved him deeply. A fourteen-year-old girl came from the Hitler Youth to one of the Communist youth groups Reich counseled. She was pregnant and had heard that "the Reds" had doctors who would be helpful. Reich made sure that the birth of the child occurred under good conditions. "I will never forget the burning expression in the eyes of this girl."[4]

In addition to all his own work, Reich was also trying to influence the many fledgling organizations in Germany that were devoted to sex reform. These organizations were part of the general atmosphere of innovation and sexual permissiveness that flourished during the Weimar years.[5]

Despite their activity and their diversity, however, such organizations had little influence on legislation. Because they sought Catholic support, the leftist political parties were loath to affirm progressive sex legislation. The state thus continued as the stern guardian of private morals. This puritanical policy angered many left-wing intellectuals who perceived it as a strong weapon of the bourgeoisie; the middle class, after all, could afford certain means not available to the proletariat, such as illegal abortions.

Even though these organizations proved ineffective in changing legislation, they represented a considerable force in German life. Reich estimated that in 1930 there were around 80 such groups, with a total membership of about 350,000 persons. He himself supported many of their efforts, such as trying to provide legal and moral support to persons indicted for giving abortions, since their efforts were congruent with his own mass-psychological work.

At the same time, Reich had his differences with the sex organizations. He urged them to take a bolder stance on basic sexual matters, especially adolescent intercourse, rather than limiting themselves to a cautious endorsement of premarital relations for engaged couples. He also pushed them to make clearer distinctions between healthy and sick sexuality. According to Reich, the illustrated newspapers put out by many organizations were not sharply distinguished from pornography. Dealers in contraceptives moved around at the public meetings, selling contraceptives at high prices.

Within the reform movement, one of Reich's main opponents was Magnus Hirschfeld, a leader of the World League for Sexual Reform. Reich strongly opposed Hirschfeld's concern that the various forms of sexual repression should not be punished, and were moreover equally valid. What Reich advocated was a person's right to live as he or she wished sexually so long as it did not harm others. However, he did oppose a kind of "democracy of sexuality," in which all sexual expressions were "equal." Thus, he differed radically from Hirschfeld, from the decadent atmosphere of the Weimar Republic, and, indeed, from many current lifestyles.

At that time the leaders of the World League for Sexual Reform wanted to avoid political alignments, to represent their own cause independent of any particular party. But one of Reich's aims during the early 1930s was to unite the sex reform organizations with a Marxist political program. He proposed that the separate sexual organizations should form a united front with cultural representatives from the German Communist Party. The Communist leadership agreed to the setting up of such an organization; it was called the German Association for Proletarian Sex-Politics (GAPSP), and Reich became one of its directors.

The executive body of the World League for Sexual Reform rejected Reich's proposal as "too communistic." But many of the individual organizations found his sex-political program very attractive. Representatives of eight organizations representing some 20,000 people attended the first Congress of the GAPSP, which was held in Düsseldorf in the fall of 1931. There Reich presented a seven-point program, proposing:[6]

1. Free distribution of contraceptives to those who could not obtain them through normal channels; massive propaganda for birth control.
2. Abolition of laws against abortion. Provision for free abortions at public clinics; financial and medical safeguards for pregnant and nursing mothers.
3. Abolition of any legal distinctions between the married and the unmarried. Freedom of divorce. Elimination of prostitution through economic and sex-economic changes to eradicate its causes.
4. Elimination of venereal diseases by full sexual education.
5. Avoidance of neuroses and sexual problems by a life-affirmative

education. Study of principles of sexual pedagogy. Establishment
of therapeutic clinics.

6. Training of doctors, teachers, social workers, and so on, in all
relevant matters of sexual hygiene.

7. Treatment rather than punishment for sexual offenses. Protection
of children and adolescents against adult seduction.

Reich noted that the Soviet Union had made considerable strides in implementing such a program, although he did not express his uneasiness about
certain unwelcome changes in their progressive position. Rather, he concentrated on the incompatibility, in his view, of progressive sexual legislation and
capitalism.

Representatives of the organizations at the Congress joined Reich's Association, and many members of other sex reform organizations were enthusiastic about his efforts. Branches of GAPSP were formed in Stettin, Dresden,
Leipzig, and Charlottenburg; within a short time, 40,000 members were affiliated. Reich was soon traveling extensively throughout the country, meeting
with groups and helping to set up clinics.

Reich's furious activity was in part stimulated by the growing threat of
Nazism. It was already late in 1931; he was appalled that so many on the left
still tended to underestimate the appeal of Hitler and the Nazis and to dismiss
Nazism as a passing aberration. Few studied carefully what Hitler was saying
or why so many Germans were taken in by his propaganda. Reich took Hitler
very seriously as a mass psychologist.

Reich's analysis of Hitler's propaganda and why the average German was
receptive to it was formulated during the early 1930s, and published in 1933 as
Massenpsychologie des Faschismus (The Mass Psychology of Fascism). [7] Reich
began with the question that had haunted him almost from the day he arrived
in Berlin: Why did the masses turn to the Nazis instead of the Communists?
According to Marxist theory, the "objective conditions" for a socialist economy were present: a large industrial proletariat; economic impoverishment of
the working class; a strong Communist Party to provide the "vanguard" of the
proletariat. Yet no swing to the left occurred.

The explanations offered by the left for the rise of Nazism struck Reich
as incredibly superficial. Each time the working classes behaved in a manner
that belied their social interests, the Communists asserted that the workers had
been deceived, that they lacked "class consciousness," or had a "false consciousness." Or they denied the significance of Hitler's success by claiming that
things would soon change for the better.

Here we can note a similarity between Reich's critique of psychoanalysis
and his critique of the Marxist parties. In each case he begins with a "negative
finding," a finding that he, no more than others in his camp, initially expected.
In the case of psychoanalysis, the negative finding was that patients did not

necessarily improve after "the unconscious was made conscious." In the case of Marxism, the workers did not necessarily become more revolutionary in the face of economic misery.

Reich argued that a *social psychology* was necessary to explain the contradiction between the economic frustrations endured by the proletariat and their lack of revolutionary assertion against social conditions. He went on to argue that the character structure of the worker reflected his current socioeconomic position; it also reflected earlier social experiences, particularly his familial ones. The worker-as-child had learned obedience to his parents in particular and to authority figures in general; moreover, he had been taught to suppress his sexual impulses. Hence in the adult, rebellious and sexual impulses were accompanied by anxiety, since both had been indiscriminately suppressed by the child's educators. Fear of revolt, as well as fear of sexuality, were thus "anchored" in the character structures of the masses. This "anchoring" in personality provided a key to the irrationality of the working class—an irrationality that was often inadequately explained by such abstractions as "the force of tradition."

What Reich did so well in his social analysis was to apply his clinical findings on character armor to his analysis of the average person's political or apolitical behavior. Just as character armor prevented the patient from arriving at true "emotional" insight, so it prevented the citizen from taking an aggressive stance toward social problems. As Reich put it:

> Suppression of the natural sexuality in the child, particularly of its genital sexuality, makes the child apprehensive, shy, obedient, afraid of authority, good and adjusted in the authoritarian sense; it paralyzes the rebellious forces because any rebellion is laden with anxiety; it produces, by inhibiting sexual curiosity and sexual thinking in the child, a general inhibition of thinking and of critical faculties. In brief, the goal of sexual suppression is that of producing an individual who is adjusted to the authoritarian order and who will submit to it in spite of all misery and degradation. At first the child has to submit to the structure of the authoritarian miniature state, the family; this makes it capable of later subordination to the general authoritarian system. The formation of the authoritarian structure takes place through the anchoring of sexual inhibition and sexual anxiety.[8]

Today, through the efforts of such social analysts as Erich Fromm, Theodor Adorno, and Richard Hofstadter, we have become very familiar with the notion that to understand political movements one must grasp the psychological structure of the people connected with them. But when Reich wrote *The Mass Psychology of Fascism* in 1933 (almost ten years before Fromm's *Escape from Freedom,*[9] almost twenty years before *The Authoritarian Personality*[10]), his ideas were exceedingly original.

But how did Reich's ideas apply specifically to the rise of Nazism? Reich's stress on the submissiveness of the average person might lead one to expect that the German voter would support a conservative, authoritarian government, but not necessarily the emotional frenzy Hitler represented. However, in Reich's analysis, the average German was not simply "armored." In addition to the economic misery that mobilized the workers, there were also strong emotional desires, longings that emerged in distorted form. These impulses were intensified by the increased permissiveness of the 1920s.

The Germans, then, were caught—to follow Reich's analysis—by their simultaneous desire for freedom and their fear of it. Calls for a more exciting life *as well as* appeals to "law and order" struck deep resonances. And it was precisely here that Hitler demonstrated his genius as a mass psychologist. His opponents criticized him for his contradictions; but as the historian Konrad Heiden remarked, it was Hitler's "art of contradiction which made him the greatest and most successful propagandist of his time."[11]

In no other sphere did Hitler play so skillfully on the contradictions within the average German as with his family ideology. Hitler idealized the German family, calling for its preservation against "cultural Bolshevism." (The Soviet and German Communists were identified with the break-up of the family and "free love," a position the Russians had already retreated from and one the German Communists never endorsed.) Hitler promised the subjugation of woman to man, the enforcement of her economic dependence, and strong measures against both the birth control movement and abortion.

As Reich noted, however, at the same time that Hitler supported traditional family life he also endorsed many of the demands of the young against the old. He attracted youths in large numbers from parental homes and collectivized their existence. Indeed, "Aryan" youths were encouraged to have children, inside or outside marriage, if they believed that they were begetting them to improve the race. And the Nazi emphasis on "Mother Germany" and "Father Hitler" permitted many Germans to transfer familial feelings to the mystique of the super-nation—the Fatherland.

Hitler's racial policies at once mobilized the average person's sexual fears and provided him with a convenient scapegoat. Again and again, Hitler harped on the Jew and the Negro as polluters of the "Aryan" blood. This paranoic concept, with its emphasis on the "poisoning of the national body," had a wide appeal. The Jew especially, in Hitler's mythology, provided a target for the projection of sexual, anti-sexual, and anti-capitalist sentiments, since the Jew was pictured simultaneously as seducer, castrator, and Shylock.

The left erred badly when it tried to refute Nazi propaganda by asserting that Hitler was a reactionary, used by big business to serve its interests. While objectively true, this missed the essential point of how Hitler was uniting the contradictions in the people. Much of his propaganda called into play revolutionary sentiments in the form of diffuse protests against the capitalist "bosses" who ran things. At the same time, the fear of international revolutionary change—the sense of chaos it invoked, the threat to nationalist pride—was mobilized by attacks on "swinish" Bolsheviks who would subvert the German nation. The very term "national socialism" expressed this unity of contradictions, appealing to nationalistic feelings *and* to the yearning for socialism. For Hitler did not require people to think through the facts seriously; he would take care of everything for them.

Reich had a keen eye—and ear—for Hitler's use of sexual imagery and feeling in his propaganda techniques. The emphasis on soldiers marching, on uniforms, on mass candlelight meetings, the sexually toned imagery of Hitler's speeches, his rhythmic, hypnotic oratory—all helped to whip people into an emotional frenzy. One has only to see the faces of people listening to Hitler (conveyed so vividly in the documentary films of Leni Riefenstahl) to realize the kind of orgiastic satisfaction the Germans could allow themselves in their devotion to the Führer. This intense libidinal excitation, combined with a sense of moral righteousness, was strikingly similar to the atmosphere at religious revival meetings.

As part of his analysis of Hitler's mass-psychological appeal, Reich devoted a short chapter to the symbolism of the swastika. Studying the design itself and the history of the symbol, Reich concluded that the swastika was a schematic but unmistakable representation of two intertwined bodies.[12]

Faced with the cleverness of Hitler's appeal to the emotions, Reich was all the more appalled at the ineffectiveness of Communist propaganda. He recalled with horror one particular Communist meeting, attended by about 20,000 industrial and white-collar workers. Shortly before, there had been some fatalities in clashes with the Nazis, so the crowd's mood had risen to the boiling point. Everyone waited tensely for the main speech. Then the Communist leader, Ernst Thälmann, killed the mood totally by devoting his talk to a complex analysis of the government's budget.

Reich believed that the only political answer to the distorted "sex-politics" of Hitler was his own positive sex-politics. One did not answer Hitler's use of the Jews as scapegoats by pointing out the intellectual fallacies of his argument or its function as a diversion from other issues. One countered by directly dealing with the people's sexual longings. Reich's position was based on his conviction that "the average individual will affirm the sex-economic regulation of sexual life if he is made to understand it. . . . Sex-economy gives the political answer to the chaos which was created by the conflict between compulsive morality and sexual libertinism."[13]

Reich coined the term "sex-economy" around 1930. By it he meant "that body of knowledge which deals with the economy of the biological energy in the organism, with its energy household."[14] The use of the word "economy" also reflects a Marxist influence: The safeguarding of the distribution of goods requires a rational economic policy. A rational sexual policy is not different if the same obvious principles are applied to sexual instead of economic needs.

In his sex-political work, Reich soon met with difficulties that he blamed on everyone else but the "average individual." Work seemed to go poorly when he was not present. The Communist functionaries complained that nothing but sexual questions were discussed. Emphasis on the class struggle receded. There was also a falling off of commitment from the allied sex reform groups, for which Reich blamed the party functionaries.[15]

In later years, Reich was critical not only of the Communists but also of his own approach. In his interview with Kurt Eissler, he commented that he moved too rapidly and stirred up more interest among the people than he had the resources to deal with effectively. By the time of the interview, he believed that one should not approach sexual questions politically. However, one should change antisexual laws.

Reich's aversion to politics after about 1936 is a subject for future chapters. I will simply note here an apparent contradiction: the injunction against "doing it politically" combined with the injunction to "change the laws," which cannot be done except politically.

In the context of the Berlin period, however, we return to the question of why Reich "did it politically." He was quite aware of the argument advanced by one psychoanalyst against sex-politics: "How is it possible to overcome sexual repression in the masses if one does not have a mass technique corresponding to the individual analytic technique?"[16]

Reich's answer was that perhaps a technique would emerge from the practice of sex-politics. He was working with two hypotheses: that without positive sex-politics, Hitler's diabolical manipulation of distorted sexuality would triumph; and that his own sex-politics could win, if the leadership was right. Although he never abandoned the first conviction, in later years he realized that the second hypothesis overlooked the depth of sexual anxiety in people; that any leadership would have failed with the people responding to Hitler's "unity of contradictions."

The very naïveté of his optimism provided learning experiences a more cautious person would have missed. Thus, Reich noted that while he did not have a technique for mass therapy, there were certain advantages to group meetings over individual therapy:

> She [the patient] does not feel alone. She feels that all the others also listen to these "prohibited" things. Her individual moral inhibition is countered by a collective atmosphere of sexual affirmation, by a new, sex-economic morality. . . . It is a matter of making the suppression conscious, of setting the fight between sexuality and mysticism into the focus of consciousness, or arousing it . . . and of channeling it into social action.[17]

Even later he never disavowed this mass therapy approach entirely, although he did reject its political connection as he became more aware of the pitfalls that surrounded it. It is ironic that in the same year Reich published *The Mass Psychology of Fascism,* 1933, he was also to publish *Character Analysis,* which focused on the intricate problems in the way of removing the defenses against sexuality. The Reich of *Character Analysis* lives on through therapists who practice individual treatment—largely with upper- and middle-class patients. The Reich of *Mass Psychology* is reflected in various kinds of group approaches that make use of nonprofessionals, for example, the use of discussion groups in the women's movement. These approaches attempt to reach a large number of people. Their aim is often more to "raise consciousness" than to give immediate help. The establishment therapists and the socially engaged group leaders may fight each other's views; yet each quotes the parts of Reich that fit their argument best. Few move as restlessly, as tormentedly, back and forth between the positions as Reich himself did.

In the early 1930s, however, Reich was primarily the mass psychologist bent on defeating Nazism. He felt at least as thwarted by his political friends as by his enemies. In particular, the Communist Party leadership was increasingly disturbed by his activities. In 1932, he was involved with several publications dealing with sex-political issues for the average working person. The first, which Reich himself wrote, was entitled *Der Sexuelle Kampf der Jugend (The Sexual Struggle of Youth).* [18] Aimed at a youthful audience, the pamphlet described simply and clearly the sexual issues of adolescents, relating these to the political struggle. At Reich's suggestion, Annie Reich wrote a pamphlet on sex education for mothers, *Wenn Dein Kind Dich Fragt (When Your Child Asks You).* [19] Again at Reich's suggestion, and with his collaboration, several teachers composed a small booklet for children entitled *Das Kreidedreieck (The Chalk Triangle).* [20]

The last publication deserves a few words, for I believe *The Chalk Triangle* was unique in its time for the frankness with which it dealt with sex education to be read to or by children between the ages of eight and twelve. In very simple language and with an absorbing story line, it tells how a group of children debate among themselves where babies come from. Stork myths, babies from kissing, and so on prevail. One girl suggests her parents will explain the true facts. The parents, clearly modeled on the Reichs, answer some of the children's questions about reproduction. The children talk over what they have heard. They seek and have a second talk with the parents because they still do not understand how the baby gets inside the mother's stomach. In true analytic fashion, the father tries to elicit their ideas, and they come close—"Is it like what happens between animals?" But many of their notions are confused, even frightening—"the man pierces a hole in the woman and it hurts terribly."

The father explains the process of intercourse, emphasizing its pleasurable aspects. The content of intercourse is not confined to legal marriage nor its goal to reproduction. Contraception is explained. The children leave enlightened. Then one of the boys is severely punished by his parents when he tells them what he has learned. The other children help the boy hide from his parents, who out of alarm become repentant. The story is interlaced with heavy-handed political messages: children told lies about sex will later believe capitalist political lies; the unity of the oppressed (the children) overcomes the oppressors (the boys' parents); and so forth.

All three publications were extremely popular in working-class circles. *The Chalk Triangle* was used by Communist discussion leaders for children's groups. But *The Sexual Struggle of Youth* was to evoke a controversy so intense that it culminated in Reich's exclusion from the Communist Party.

There were intimations of the controversy in the pre-publication period. Reich wanted the Communist Party to publish the work, so he submitted the final manuscript to the committee for youth in the German Communist Party. The latter accepted it but sent it along to the central committee for youth in Moscow. The Moscow committee approved the book but felt it would be wiser if the party were not to publish it. They recommended its publication by a "front" organization, a workers' cultural association close to the party but not part of it. Reich gave this association the manuscript during the summer of 1931; by March 1932 it still had not appeared. Reich believed the organization was sabotaging publication, but exactly why was not clear to him.[21]

Ever impatient and ever the analyst, Reich always observed resistance and hostility, or at least ambivalence, in such postponements, and he could work himself into a fury about such stumbling blocks. Finally, exasperated with the delays, convinced that publication of the pamphlet was essential to counteract the Nazis' appeal to youth, Reich established in the summer of 1932 his own publishing house, Verlag für Sexualpolitik. The same year it brought out *The Sexual Struggle of Youth* as well as *When Your Child Asks You* and *The Chalk Triangle.*

Reich's decision to establish his own press was wise, since by 1932 he was beginning to have difficulties in publishing his clinical papers in the *International Journal of Psychoanalysis.* Before that, he had always published his papers and books through analytic media or in Marxist journals. After 1932, no publishing house other than his own would accept his manuscripts during his lifetime.*

For some months the German Communist Party helped to circulate the sex educational works, which initially received positive reviews in the various party newspapers. But trouble was already brewing. New difficulties arose when Reich attended a youth conference in Dresden on October 16, 1932. At its conclusion a resolution was issued strongly endorsing adolescent sexuality within the framework of the revolutionary movement.

The adult Communist leaders were aghast. Afraid that opponents would make political capital out of this bold statement, they quickly disowned it,

---

*Four years after his death, in 1961, Farrar, Straus & Giroux began the publication of much of his work in the English language.

claiming that the resolution dragged political tasks "down to the level of the gutter." They also asserted that the "instigator of the resolution should be excluded from the Party immediately."[22]

When it was learned that Reich was the instigator, there was considerable embarrassment. Not only had the party distributed his writings; he himself was prominent in leftist circles. Something clearly had to be done to put a distance between the party and Reich. This the party did with the following notice in the December 5 issue of the German newspaper *Roter Sport (Red Sport),* stating that Reich's pamphlets would no longer be circulated because they were contrary to the true Marxist education of youth.[23]

Following the edict, bitter disputes arose between youth groups strongly in favor of the sex-political publications and the party hierarchy that opposed them. The party brought in its big guns to crush the opposition. Its leaders declared that Reich was "counter-revolutionary," that "Reich wishes to make fornication organizations out of our associations," that his publications "discredited Marxism," that "there were no orgasm disturbances among the proletariat, only among the bourgeoisie," and that Reich was replacing the "class struggle" with the conflict between the young and the adults.

Under such pressure, a woman representative who had previously been enthusiastic about sex-political meetings now took the position that "anatomic details" and "unaesthetic irrelevancies" should not be discussed.[24] Reich was impressed that people could change their opinions so rapidly, moving with the tide and particularly with the leaders' shifts in sentiment. Later on he made a point of not fully trusting students and associates until "I first see how you are in a crisis."

He received considerable personal support, even though he did not actively wage a campaign against his opponents. In one meeting of GAPSP, he gained 32 votes, the Communist Party representatives 39. But the force of party leadership eventually swung sentiment fully in its favor—and against Reich.

Reich's defeat within the Communist Party coincided with the left's defeat at the hands of the Nazis. On January 30, 1933, General Hindenburg appointed Hitler Chancellor of Germany, the first step toward his total dictatorship a few weeks later. On February 27, the Reichstag fire broke out, an incident the Nazis used as a pretext to arrest 1,500 left-wing officials and intellectuals. Many of Reich's Marxist friends had gone underground or been arrested. On March 2, an attack on Reich's youth book appeared in the Nazi newspaper *Völkischer Beobachter.* Reich felt he had to flee quickly, so about March 3 he left for Vienna. His children had left shortly before to stay with their grandparents in Vienna. Soon afterward, Annie Reich would also leave for Vienna. However, by this time the marriage was over, as we shall see in Chapter 15.

On March 5, Hitler received 44 percent of the vote in a national election, enough of a plurality to assure him dictatorship. There was now no question of Reich's returning to Berlin.

In retrospect, it is clear that Reich never had a chance of organizing a major sex-political effort against the Nazis. A few years later, in *People in Trouble,* he compared his effort to that of a physician who faced the facts while the party continued to believe "in the healing power of useless medication." He realized that he was dealing with a "moribund patient" who could not be helped.[25]

Yet part of Reich still could not believe that the patient was moribund, and felt that his approach *could* win. Such optimism is puzzling in someone like Reich who realized the inner obstacles to healthy adult sexuality. His crucial error during this period lay in the belief that the "average individual will affirm the sex-economic regulation of sexual life if he is made to understand it." This statement is nonsense unless all kinds of qualifications are contained in the subordinate clause. And as we have seen, Reich reacted as though the main obstacle to getting his message over to the average person were some of the party leaders.

In his excessive optimism, Reich was also an extremely poor political tactician. He said as much about himself in claiming, "I am not a politician." But something more was involved. Whenever he was engaged in a battle— whether with the Social Democrats in 1929, the Communists in 1932, or the Food and Drug Administration in the 1950s—he could not make a realistic assessment of who was for him and who against him. Such over-optimism would ultimately cost him dearly.

Reich remained in Vienna for less than two months. It soon became apparent that his position there was untenable, for Freud's objections to both Reich's sex-political work and his ardent communism had grown in the intervening years. Ironically, while the Communists escalated their attacks on Reich as a "Freudian," the psychoanalytic establishment was eager to distance itself from the way Reich drew social conclusions from clinical research.

The parallels were reflected in the matter of his publications. In January 1933, Reich had signed a contract with the International Psychoanalytic Publishers (of which Freud was the editorial director) to publish his book *Character Analysis.* On March 17, Freud advised Reich—whether by letter, phone, or in person is not clear—that the contract was canceled.[26] According to Reich, Freud gave as his reason the deteriorating political situation in Vienna. For on March 4 the right-wing government of Engelbert Dollfuss had utilized "emergency laws" to restrict all civil liberties.

Undoubtedly, Freud's decision was not due simply to political caution— as Reich implies—but to his distaste for Reich's sex-political activities. Reich protested the decision, yet there was little he could do about it. The book was already in galleys, the psychoanalytic publishing house would help distribute it, but printing costs had to be paid for by Reich, and the official publisher was to be his own Verlag für Sexualpolitik.

Unhappy with the situation in Vienna, Reich decided to move to Copenhagen, arriving on May 1. Several people in Denmark had expressed interest in studying with him, and very shortly he had a practice going. One of his first concerns there was to complete his manuscript *The Mass Psychology of Fascism*. But he had to develop his analytic practice in the new city before he could afford to publish the book in the fall of 1933.

No sooner had he left the psychoanalytic conflicts in Vienna than Reich was back amid controversies with the Communists in Copenhagen. Despite all his difficulties in Berlin, he still considered himself a Communist; accordingly, he turned to the Danish Communist Party to help out many needy German refugees now settled in Copenhagen. But when the party representative started asking to see the emigration permits, including Reich's own, Reich exploded with frustration. This incident, he believed, further aggravated the wrath of the Communists against him.[27]

Two other incidents occurred. A Danish Communist journal, *Plan*, had published an article by Reich, "Where Does Nudist Education Lead To?" which had originally been published in 1928 in the *Journal for Psychoanalytic Pedagogy*. A zealous Minister of Justice in Denmark had brought a suit against *Plan*'s editor, charging him with pornography. At least part of the alleged offense turned on a translation of the German word *Wipfi*, a children's term for the genitals. Questioned by a Danish journalist, Reich commented that the translation of *Wipfi* and a few other terms was careless, but there was no question of pornography. When the editor of *Plan* received a jail sentence of forty days, the Danish Communist Party accused Reich of betraying the editor with his slight qualification.[28]

The other charge against Reich concerned *The Mass Psychology of Fascism*. Its first sentence read: "The German working class has suffered a severe defeat" (i.e., the victory of Hitler). But according to the party line, the working class had only suffered "a temporary setback in the revolutionary surge," so when the book appeared, the party journals characterized it as an attack on revolutionary politics.[29]

On November 21, 1933, a notice appeared in large print in the Danish Communist newspaper *Arbeiderblatt*, announcing that Reich had been expelled from the party. The bases for the expulsion were Reich's "party-inimical and uncommunistic" behavior and his publishing a book with "counter-revolutionary" content. Writing in 1952, Reich made much of the point that he could not have been expelled from the Danish Communist Party because he never belonged to it. Nor could he have been excluded from the German Communist Party because it had ceased to exist in March 1933. This was not his view at the time. Even after his exclusion he continued to consider himself a member of the Communist movement, if not of the party: "My position was that of a badly mistreated and misunderstood opposition."[30]

Why did Reich stay so long in the party, and why did he refrain from attacking it for some time after his expulsion? Why did he put up with party officials "criticizing" his manuscript? He once said admiringly to his friend Lia Laszky with regard to her membership in the Communist Party: "You were the smartest of us—the first to join and the first to leave."

Part of the reason for Reich's lengthy, if partial, acceptance of Communist leaders he considered to be blockheads was his overall commitment to Marxism as a socioeconomic philosophy. More immediately, for Reich the Communists seemed to provide the only political answer to the threat of Nazism. And even as late as 1933 he regarded the Soviet Union, the Marxist experiment, as the most progressive society in the world.

Perhaps, too, some of his reasons were more personal. Reich alluded to these factors in *People in Trouble* (about 1936) when he stated that he remained in the party despite misgivings because it had become a "second home."[31]

"A second home"—Reich had used a similar phrase to define how he perceived the psychoanalytic movement, which he also had a very hard time leaving. Reich's early home life had been unhappy. In many ways his marriage with Annie had been unhappy. Not surprisingly, he felt a strong need for family, not just his own private family but a family of fellow fighters, scientists, revolutionaries. And a part of him still wanted a *pater familias* and a *mater familias*.

Metaphorically, Reich had described his scientific origins when he wrote: "Psychoanalysis is the father and sociology [Marxism] the mother of sex-economy."[32] On a more personal level, as we have seen, Reich sought the paternal in Freud and Freud brought out the paternal in Reich, for learning analytic skills involved a master-apprentice relationship.

Marxism, too, was scientific and systematic, but its practical application was far more fluid than the translation of analytic theory into practice. The most expert theoreticians could prove to be the biggest fools in actual events, while the poor and untrained could have the keenest sense of what was really happening. And while Marxism claimed to be unsentimental, simply clarifying the class struggle, there could be no doubt that it stimulated infinite hopes for a better life. And not simply a better life, but a fulfilled and "unalienated" one. For Reich, this kind of yearning may well have represented his mother's influence.

Reich was deeply hurt by his exclusion from the Communist Party. It meant not just the end of three years' work with the German Party, but the end of his formal affiliation with the political left, an affiliation he had maintained in one form or another ever since he joined the youth movement in Vienna after World War I. One way Reich softened the blow of his exclusion was to permit the full implications of leaving radical politics to sink in only little by little. In 1934, he was still "loyal" to the Communist movement but critical of the party apparatus. In his optimism, he was searching for a new revolutionary social organization that would be willing to learn from the lessons of the catastrophe. But the one such possible party available to him, Trotsky's Fourth International, proved unsatisfactory. Several leading Trotskyites visited him around this time. In the course of the discussion Reich realized that his visitors, while sympathetic, did not take sex-politics seriously.[33]

The year 1934, then, was one of political uncertainty for Reich as he struggled to reorient himself. He wrote a pamphlet, *Was ist Klassenbewusstsein? (What Is Class Consciousness?)*, in which he clarified the progressive and conservative aspects of "class consciousness" in women, working-class men, adolescents, and children. Again, his social endeavors paralleled his clinical concepts: in both realms he sought to dissolve the defenses, anxieties, guilts, and to strengthen the genuine, progressive, vital forces.

In the same pamphlet, Reich clearly stated his organizational position as of late 1934. The sex-political movement, he wrote, had the choice of starting its own organization and recruiting members based on its declared program; or it could be allowed more time to develop informally. Reich concluded that the second alternative would avoid premature bureaucracy and the dangers of sectarianism; it would also permit greater influence within other organizations.

The decision was an important one since it anticipated much of Reich's later social thought and practice. It was still a political decision, in that he believed his ideology would in time permeate the masses to such an extent that the organization of a political party would be feasible. Basically, Reich was to maintain this model, with one significant alteration—he dropped the idea of ever organizing a party. What would permeate the masses would be work skills and orientations; people with such skills would join together to perform practical tasks in education, medicine, sociology. Once again we can note a crucial transition in 1934, a transition that contained elements of the old as it moved toward the new.

Leon Reich, Reich's father.

Cecilie Roniger Reich,
Reich's mother.

Wilhelm Reich, aged 3.

Above right: **Reich, relaxing at Millstadt, 192**

Above left: **Wilhelm Reich on furlough, *c.* 191**

Reich as a student, *c.* 1919.

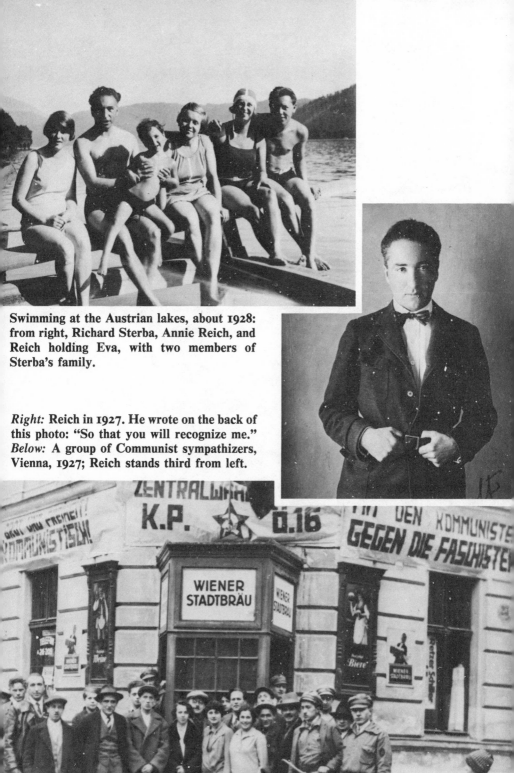

Swimming at the Austrian lakes, about 1928: from right, Richard Sterba, Annie Reich, and Reich holding Eva, with two members of Sterba's family.

Right: Reich in 1927. He wrote on the back of this photo: "So that you will recognize me." *Below:* A group of Communist sympathizers, Vienna, 1927; Reich stands third from left.

Reich at the Davos sanatarium, Winter 1927.

eich at children's collective near Berlin,
31.

Lia Laszky, *c.* **1929.**

group of young analysts, late 1920s:
anding, from left to right, Grete Bib-
g, Reich, Otto Fenichel, Edward
bring, unidentified woman; sitting
right, Annie Reich.

Reich, Berlin, 1932.

Elsa Lindenberg, Berlin, 1932.

Reich and Elsa Lindenberg
skiing in Norway.

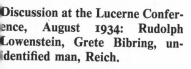

Discussion at the Lucerne Conference, August 1934: Rudolph
Lowenstein, Grete Bibring, unidentified man, Reich.

Reich, c. 1933

Reich, Ilse Ollendorff,
and Peter, Orgonon, Summe
1944.

Reich with Peter, Orgonon, 194:

Left: Reich in Forest Hills, N.Y., 1946 (photo copyright, Anton Swarowsky).
Right: Eva Reich, *c.* 1948.

View of the Observatory, Orgonon.

Theodore Wolfe, June 1953,
a year before he died in Arizona
(photo: Kari Berggrav).

Below left: Dr. Simeon Tropp.
Below right: Ola Raknes.

Reich's last conference at Orgonon, on the medical DOR-buster,
August 1955. Aurora Karrer is the woman in the white smock; Chester
Raphael is second from Reich's left; James A. Willie is second from
Reich's right (photo: Kari Berggrav).

Opposite top: Wolfe (left) and Reich during the First Orgonomic
Conference, Orgonon, August 1948. William Washington is directly
at Reich's right. The author is standing behind the antenna (photo:
Kari Berggrav). *Opposite right:* Grethe Hoff sitting in an orgone
energy accumulator. *Opposite left:* Cloudbuster at Orgonon.

A. S. Neill with Peter Reich, near the Observatory, Orgonon, 1948 (Photo-chrome, Montreal).

Walter Hoppe and Gladys Meyer, with her daughter Erica, on lake shore, August 1948 (photo: Kari Berggrav).

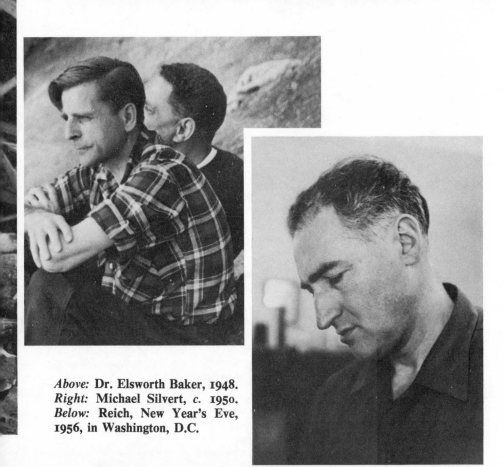

Above: Dr. Elsworth Baker, 1948.
Right: Michael Silvert, *c.* 1950.
Below: Reich, New Year's Eve,
1956, in Washington, D.C.

Reich escorted to prison
by Deputy Marshall William Doherty, March 1957.

14

The Psychoanalytic Furor
and Reich's Break with the
Psychoanalytic Association:
1930-1934

Reich once said: "There has always been a conflict in me between the urge to participate in the social battle, on the one hand, and my scientific work, on the other. In social struggles, you have to be here, there, and everywhere; in scientific work you stay in your study with books, patients, and instruments."[1]

While we have seen Reich struggling "in the social battle" during the 1930s, the other side of him was quietly developing his theory of character analysis. Many of the analytic students in training with him at that time were only in touch with this side of his work and personality. One American student, Dr. O. Spurgeon English, who was in analysis with Reich between September 1929 and April 1932, has given a good account of the clinical Reich in the Berlin years. He opens with: "I recall Dr. Reich utilizing his interest in other than verbal presentations of the personality. For instance, he would frequently call attention to my position on the couch. . . ."[2]

One issue concerned Reich's training standards and the discipline he imposed. Reich had reminded English that he would need a letter from Reich in order to become a member of the International Psychoanalytic Association. He said that English took many psychoanalytic concepts too lightly and that if Reich "continued to hear the still present sounds of ridicule about analysis," the letter of recommendation would not be written.

English, jolted by this edict, was nonetheless grateful for the hard and fruitful work it stimulated. "Somehow or other I had landed in the hands of a no-nonsense, hard-working, meticulous analyst who had a keen ear for the various forms of resistance and a good ability to tolerate the aggression which almost inevitably follows necessary confrontation of subtly concealed . . . resistance."

In connection with Reich's handling of negative feelings, English related the following incident:

One day Reich telephoned to ask if he could change English's appointment from morning to afternoon. English said he already had a social engagement. Reich retorted, was the social engagement more important than the analysis? Irritated, English replied that it was. After hanging up, he became incensed that Reich should question his right to enjoy himself socially: the longer he thought about it, the angrier he got. During the next session English told Reich he had always kept to the analyst's schedule, and that having made an appointment Reich should keep it. English went on to rail against Reich's busy life, which now necessitated requesting the change. Reich listened patiently until English wound down, then merely said: "You are perfectly right." English was amazed. "I had the first and perhaps greatest lesson in my life of the fact that a human being may be self-assertive and be given the right to an opinion and not be criticized for it or have acknowledgment given grudgingly."

English's account of his treatment with Reich contains no new information about Reich's theory or techniques. Yet the period was extremely important in the evolution of Reich's therapy. Until the late 1920s, Reich had concentrated on three main concepts in his character-analytic work: latent negative transference, defensive character traits, and nonverbal forms of expression. During the late 1920s and up to 1934, his focus fell on three other subjects: the development of a typology of neurotic character structures and their childhood etiology; the distinction between the genital character and the neurotic character; and the problem of masochism.

In his development of neurotic character structures, Reich brought a sharp focus to the way character attitudes are shaped in childhood and the particular form they take because of particular experiences, especially familial ones. A good example of Reich's work in this realm is his presentation of the "aristocratic character." This example illustrates why the psychiatric scholar Leston Havens has called Reich perhaps the only equal of the famed nineteenth-century diagnostician Emil Kraepelin in "psychiatric portraiture."[3]

A thirty-three-year-old man came to analysis because of marital difficulties and work problems. The connections Reich made between the patient's difficulties and his early childhood experiences were—at a content level—not especially striking. What is more impressive, and what Reich focused upon, was the patient's manner and attitudes:

The patient is good-looking, of medium height; his facial expression is reserved, serious, somewhat arrogant. His gait is measured, refined. . . . It takes him quite some time to get from the door to the couch. His speech is measured. . . . He lies on the couch in a composed manner with his legs crossed. His dignified composure hardly ever changes at all, even with the discussion of . . . painful subjects. When after a while . . . he discussed his relationship with his mother whom he loved very much, it was easy to see how he intensified his dignified attitude in order to master his excitation. In spite of my repeated admonitions to give his feelings free reign he maintained his attitude.
. . . This much had become clear: his behavior, no matter what was its origin, protected him against violent emotions. . . . [His character] had already become a resistance.[4]

One day, Reich went on, "I told him he was play-acting an English lord, and that this must have a connection with his youth."[5]

Reich's remark triggered the patient's comment that he had never believed he was really the son of his father, a small Jewish merchant; he thought that he was in fact of English origin. He had heard rumors that his maternal grandmother had had an affair with a real English lord and that his mother was half-English.

Reich continued: "Consistent analysis of the 'lordly' behavior showed that it was connected with . . . his tendency to deride everybody. . . . The sadistic fantasies . . . were gratified in the derision and warded off in the lordliness. . . . The arrogant behavior . . . served the purpose of warding off a drive as well as its satisfaction."[6]

Reich connected the development of the lordliness trait with the man's specific childhood experiences. For one thing, it was a counter-identification with his father, who was anything but lordly; in fights between the parents, the boy took the mother's side and vowed to be as unlike his father as possible. There was also a specificity to the timing of its origin. Between the ages of three and six, the patient had suffered from an intense phobia about mice. The lord fantasy provided a way of binding the phobic anxiety. Indeed, after its development the fear of mice disappeared.

Reich summarizes: "The development of a phobia indicates that the ego was too weak to master certain libidinal strivings. The development of a character trait or typical attitude at the expense of a phobia means a strengthening of the ego in the form of chronic armoring against the id and the outer world. . . ."[7]

The notion of character traits as a way of *binding emotions,* especially anxiety, is a key to Reich's characterological work. The kind of detailed description Reich provided for his "aristocratic" patient he also gave for more general types, for example, the hysterical character, the compulsive character, and the phallic-narcissistic character. Although his descriptions as well as his theory continued the investigations made by other analysts, notably Freud and Karl Abraham, Reich added a wealth of detail, an elaborated conceptual framework, and suggestions for therapy that surpassed previous work. His characterological typology has been quoted more than any other aspect of his work.

Yet Reich's original contribution lay not so much in the distinctions among various neurotic character types as in what distinguished all of them from another type—the genital character.

In a paper published in 1929 and later incorporated in expanded form into *Character Analysis,* Reich distinguished between character structures in a fundamentally new way: on the basis of the presence or absence of orgastic potency. Here, he linked his character-analytic work with his work on genitality. Orgastic potency, or the unimpeded expression of genitality, became the explicit goal of character analysis.

Reich described the genital character as one that has fully reached the post-ambivalent genital stage; the wish for incest and the wish to eliminate the parent of the same sex have been relinquished. Up to this point, Reich essentially followed Abraham. But now he sounds a unique note: the genital character is capable of orgastic potency, which prevents the damming up of libido and the pathogenic outbreak of pregenital impulses.

The neurotic character, on the other hand, is completely under the sway of infantile impulses and wishes. "If there is any sexual life at all, its infantile nature can be readily seen: the woman represents the mother or the sister and the love relationship carries the stamp of all the anxieties . . . and [inhibitions and] neurotic peculiarities of the infantile incest relationship."[8]

For the genital character, achievement does not represent a proof of potency as in the neurotic person but provides a natural gratification. The neurotic character experiences a more or less conscious feeling of impotence; social achievement becomes primarily a compensating proof of potency. Still, no matter how hard he works, the neurotic character never gets rid of an inner emptiness and feeling of incapacity.

Reich defends himself against the charge that the genital character lives in a kind of paradise. He or she is in fact accessible to a high degree of unpleasure as well as pleasure: "The capacity for tolerating unpleasure and pain without fleeing disillusioned into a state of rigidity goes hand in hand with the capacity to take happiness and to give love. To use Nietzsche's words: he who wants to learn to 'jubilate to high heaven' must be prepared to be 'dejected unto death.' "[9]

The genital character has an armor, but that armor is pliable enough to allow adaptation to various situations. Reich vividly describes the emotional range of his "genital character": "[He] can be very gay but also intensely angry; he reacts to an object-loss with depression but does not get lost in it; he is capable of intense love but also of intense hatred; he can be . . . childlike but he will never appear infantile; his seriousness is natural and not stiff in a compensatory way because he has no tendency to show himself grown-up at all cost. . . ."[10]

In contrast, the neurotic character "would like to be gay or angry but cannot. He cannot love intensely because his sexuality is essentially repressed."[11] Nor can he hate appropriately because his hatred has grown violent due to libido stasis, and therefore he has to repress it.

I would stress the paucity of data Reich had on which to base his concept of health. It seems clear that he studied himself as a source of data for the genital and neurotic character and for what he meant by "healthy" functioning. When he first described orgastic potency, he drew upon his own experiences and the experiences of relatively few patients. By 1929, he could add some experience with industrial workers whom he considered "healthy" and Malinowski's ethnographic reports on the Trobrianders (see Chapter 11). But above all he appears to have continued to draw on his self-observations. His distinctions between genital and neurotic characters hinge heavily on the greater vitality of the former. And vitality was what everybody—friend and foe alike —noted in Reich.

Although Reich often wrote about the "genital character" as though it were a "real" thing, he was well aware that it was a construct or an "ideal type." As he put it:

Since the distinction [between the neurotic character and the genital character] is based on a quantitative criterion—the extent of either direct sexual gratification or libido stasis—there are all kinds of transitions between the two ideal types. In spite of this, a typological investigation is not only justified but imperative because of its heuristic values and of the help it provides in practical work.[12]

In connection with the third subject—masochism—Reich often wrote about his technique of character analysis with considerable optimism, at the same time that he was aware of the depth of the therapeutic obstacles. This awareness was also stimulated by others' formulations of the problems in ways that he opposed. The case in point is Freud's later concept of masochism.

In his early work, Freud had viewed masochism as the expression of destructive impulses toward the world that turned against the self out of frustration and fear of punishment. In this view, the basic initial conflict was between self and the world; it followed the pleasure principle. To torment the self, physically or psychologically, was less painful than to lose the love of parents or parental surrogates, less painful than the feared punishment for expressing the anger outward.

Around 1920, Freud believed he had to move "beyond the pleasure principle." On the basis of that principle alone, he felt unable to explain certain repetitive phenomena such as the fondness of children for repeating games, even painful ones; the recurrent dreams of war-neurotics in which the original trauma is revived again and again; the pattern of self-injury that can be traced through the lives of many people; and the tendency of a number of patients to reenact during psychoanalysis (despite ample self-awareness) unpleasant experiences of their childhood.

Freud now explained these and related phenomena on the basis of a "death instinct" that led to a *primary* masochism. The same instinct could also be directed toward the world in the form of sadistic urges and actions.

This concept of the death instinct clashed with Reich's more positive view of clinical theory. Prior to the early 1930s, Reich avoided any direct confrontation with a concept that carried Freud's full authority, though he had talked about the "sublimation" of sadistic impulses and their decrease with sexual gratification. But by 1932, Reich felt prepared to publish a case history of a masochistic patient in an article that directly challenged "death instinct" theory. The case history presented was that of a young man who had been in treatment for four years.

Reich's introductory description of typical masochistic character traits is brief: "Subjectively, a chronic sense of suffering, which appears objectively as a *tendency to complain;* chronic tendencies to *self-damage* and *self-deprecia-tion* (moral masochism) and a compulsion *to torture others* which makes the patient suffer no less than the object."[13]

Right from the start he focused on the patient's sexual behavior. The young man, who was incapable of working and had no social interests, would masturbate every night for hours. He would roll around on his stomach with the fantasy that a man or woman was beating him with a whip. When the excitement mounted, he would hold back the ejaculation, let the excitation subside, and then begin all over again.

After Reich did some work on the patient's defenses, the patient entered a spiteful phase. In answer to any request from Reich, he would cry: "I won't, I won't." This kind of stubbornness was what he had shown his parents as a young child, when he would kick and yell, rendering his parents helpless and furious.

At one point the patient reacted suddenly with involuntary kicking. This was the first time Reich reported large bodily movements in the course of an analysis. He was confronted with a choice: to ask the patient to render his feeling into words or to encourage the kicking. Reich described what he did: "I seized the opportunity and asked him to let himself go completely. At first he could not understand how anybody could ask him to do anything like that. But . . . he began to thrash around on the couch, which behavior turned into highly emotional yelling and inarticulate animal sounds. His actions began to assume an almost frightening character. . . ."[14]

However, Reich reasoned that this was the only avenue of approach to the patient's deep emotions. Only in this way was he able to relieve his infantile neurosis affectively, and not just in the form of recollections.

The meaning of all the kicking and screaming eventually became clearer to Reich. The patient was trying to provoke his parents and—through transfer-ence—Reich. When the patient found out that in analysis he would not be punished for his tantrum-like behavior, he continued his uproar out of enjoyment. Reich recognized that emotional behavior could itself become a resistance, a stereotyped way of acting out rather than remembering and reaching still deeper affective layers. Unlike much of modern expressive therapy, Reich was keenly aware of the *defensive* functions emotional outbursts could often serve.

The patient continued complaining about the "morass"—and indirectly about Reich for not freeing him from the bog. Reich used the technique of imitation or "mirroring." When the patient entered the office, Reich would stand there in utter dejection. He began to use the patient's childish language. Sometimes he would lie on the floor and scream the way the patient did. Initially, the patient was dumbfounded, but one day he laughed in an absolutely unneurotic fashion.

Why did Reich imitate the patient? The neurotic person generally does not perceive defensive character traits such as spitefulness as painful, the way he perceives a symptom such as a tic or phobia as debilitating and embarrassing. One way to facilitate his self-perception is to show him his behavior, or to imitate him. If this mirroring is done punitively, it can be humiliating. If it is done with some humor and warmth, it can be very illuminating, as it was on the occasion reported above.*

Reich now analyzed the patient's complaints as an expression of his demand for love. Through his misery, he would force Reich to love him. Why is the masochistic character's demand for love so excessive? Reich suggested that the masochistic patient has an intense fear of being left alone, something he experienced with great pain in early childhood. This fear of being left alone is, in turn, related to the anxiety the masochistic character feels when contact with the skin of the beloved person is lost. Here Reich connects his own findings with previous observations on the role of skin eroticism. The masochist frequently fantasizes or acts out some kind of skin abrasion, being pinched, for example, or making the skin bleed. However, these wishes do not basically reflect a desire for pain. The patient wants to feel the *warmth of the skin—* "the pain is taken into the bargain."[15]

"The pain is taken into the bargain"—here is a key phrase in Reich's formulation of masochism. Earlier in the case history, he reported how the patient developed fantasies of being beaten on the buttocks. This was not primarily from desire for pain but out of relief that he was not being beaten on the genitals. The patient's choice of the lesser pain is quite consistent with original psychoanalytic theory.

The importance of skin excitation is an interesting emphasis of Reich's. During this period, Reich was especially concerned with events from the Oedipal and anal psychosexual stages; yet, with his emphasis on skin warmth, he was anticipating his later investigations of mother-infant interactions.

---

*I still remember vividly the exactness, subtlety, and wit of Reich's mimicry.

Another key mechanism soon became apparent during the analysis. When the patient developed strong genital desires, his masochistic attitude sharply diminished. However, during his first sexual intercourse, he felt pain instead of pleasure. This experience threw him back into his "morass."

Here Reich called attention to a specific sexual mechanism: a rigidity not only in the patient's psyche but also *in the musculature of his pelvis.* This blocked any strong pleasurable excitation and turned it into pain. This spasm was connected with childhood anal inhibitions and conflicts, since the father had severely beaten the patient when he soiled his pants.

In this short passage we note one of Reich's major transition points. He is moving from character-analytic rigidities to bodily ones, from the character armor to the muscular armor. Within a few years, Reich's main therapeutic attention would be devoted to these bodily spasms or "armor segments" not only in the pelvis but throughout the body.

While Reich was developing his concepts on masochism, his sex-political work was bringing him into contact with many ardent Christians. He noted how many religious philosophies fitted the masochistic pattern: "The religious individual expects from God, an omnipotent figure, the relief from an inner sin, that is, an inner sexual tension: a relief which the individual is unable to bring about himself. Someone else has to do it—in the form of a punishment, an absolution, a deliverance."[16] As John Donne put it in his well-known sonnet: "Bend your force, to breake, blowe, burn, and make me new."

What was so significant to the overall development of his work was Reich's observation of the feeling of tension, of tautness ("my penis would boil") resulting in the desire for, and simultaneous fear of, bursting. This phenomenon became central to his thinking about masochism per se and also to his entire therapeutic work. He came to believe that this mixed attitude toward bursting could be found to a greater or lesser degree in all patients.

Reich's strong opposition to death instinct theory did not please Freud or most of the older analysts. Moreover, while the paper on masochism was not political, other writings by Reich during the same period clearly were. It is therefore more than probable that Reich's sex-political activity and his clinical direction combined to provoke Freud.

What also distressed Freud and other analysts was the degree of incandescent fierceness Reich brought to collegial relations concerning his work. He would insist that his associates link psychoanalytic with political (as well as social) concepts the way he did. Since Reich's politics changed, in writing about the course of his conflicts with Freud and the Psychoanalytic Association he could retrospectively distort and minimize the political intensity of his message in the early 1930s. Here he followed Nietzsche's sequence: "Memory says I did it. Pride says I couldn't have. Memory yields."

I also believe that Reich would have seriously considered criticism of his Communist politics and their relation to psychoanalysis if such criticism contained a genuine comprehension of his insistence on the *social* affirmation of genitality. However, his opponents did not make these kinds of distinctions. The entangled mass of their polemics struck at his enduring concepts as well as at their time-bound appendages.

In any case, in January 1932, Freud as editor of the *International Journal of Psychoanalysis* planned to add a prefatory note to accompany Reich's article on masochism. The note warned readers of the *Journal* that Reich was a member of the Communist Party and that its members were not permitted to deviate from its doctrine.[17]

According to Reich, some German Socialist physicians prevented the publication of this note. According to Ernest Jones, "the theme of . . . [Reich's] paper was the 'amalgamation of Marxism and psychoanalysis' "[18]; a summary wildly wrong since the paper does not mention anything political. It is amazing how many writers have picked up on the implications of what Freud and Jones thought about the article. Some have even gone so far as to say that Reich believed the death instinct was a "product of capitalism." He believed nothing so idiotic. In his sex-political writings, what he did hope was that the sex-affirmative direction of the Soviet Union in the 1920s would eventually lead to the prevention of the neuroses and, with it, of a primary masochism and sadism (the death instinct). And at that time (ca. 1932) Reich believed that a consistent sexual affirmation was incompatible with capitalism or, for that matter, with feudalism.

In the article on masochism, Reich's argument was presented on strictly theoretical and clinical grounds and should have been answered in the same way. However, if Freud's tendentious use of a political argument (Reich's membership in the "Bolshevik Party") was remarkable, equally remarkable was the fact that he permitted publication of the paper at all. In view of the many attacks on Freud as an intolerant dictator, it is striking evidence to the contrary that he could publish a paper directly challenging a concept quite dear to him.

Freud's critical attitude toward Reich stimulated or permitted others to take a harsh view of him as unorthodox not only in his social but also in his clinical views. Thus, during October 1932, in the midst of the German Communist Party's attacks on Reich's book on youth, Max Eitingon, director of the Berlin Psychoanalytic Society, asked Reich to limit his seminar to practicing analysts and not permit candidates to attend.[19]

Aware that this limitation undermined his status as a senior analyst, Reich refused to obey the request. But this trouble was only part of the gathering storm. When Reich returned to Vienna in March 1933, Freud informed him, as we have seen, that the psychoanalytic publishing house would not bring out his book on character analysis. After Reich gave a lecture before the Socialist students in Vienna, Federn wrote him in April asking that he not lecture any more before Socialist or Communist groups. Federn was undoubtedly reflecting Freud's concern about Reich's radical politics. A few weeks earlier the Christian Socialist, authoritarian, yet anti-Nazi regime of Engelbert Dollfuss, which Freud supported, had suspended parliamentary government, prohibited demonstrations, and curtailed freedom of the press. A number of Freud's students and patients were dismayed by his endorsement of a party so opposed to much of what psychoanalysis represented. However, Freud, almost eighty and very ill, had become increasingly conservative in his social outlook.

Reich refused Federn's request, though he did agree to consult with the executive committee of the Vienna Psychoanalytic Association before accepting further speaking invitations. But this concession was not good enough: Federn wanted a binding promise. Reich refused and asked for a written communication on the matter. (Reich always had an eye on the written record.) Federn told Reich he could no longer attend the meetings of the Vienna Psychoanalytic Association. Federn also said to Annie Reich that were he, Federn, in Reich's position, he would have long since resigned.[20]

In order to settle the issue, Reich proposed a discussion before the executive committee. A meeting took place on April 21, 1933. According to his own account, Reich offered to refrain from publishing and lecturing on political matters provided that the Vienna Association took an official position on his views. Reich asked that the Association either explicitly dissociate itself from his social concepts or give him the same freedom it gave to other trends divergent from those of Freud. Reich did not want to be quietly silenced or forced to resign.

The April 21 meeting was inconclusive. According to Reich, the secretary of the Association, Anna Freud, remarked that the "powers that be" were against Reich; she, as secretary, would be sending him further information. That information never came.[21]

His professional situation in Vienna was clearly untenable. A young Danish physician, Tage Philipson, visited Reich in Vienna with the idea of going into analytic training with him even though he was warned this might not be acceptable to the International Psychoanalytic Association. Philipson told Reich that others in Denmark would like to study with him and urged him to emigrate to that country.

So Reich left Vienna in late April 1933, without his family. His marriage with Annie was over, though they were not divorced. He traveled to Copenhagen by freighter, arriving on May 1. On May 2 a number of people were already visiting Reich's hotel to seek therapy with him or to talk about mutual concerns. The social life was so intense that Reich moved into a small apartment.

Enmity as well as enthusiastic support was not long in coming. In addition to Reich's difficulties with the Danish Communists, he was soon under attack from government officials, who had only given him a six-month visitor's permit.

One of the first people to seek treatment from Reich in Copenhagen was a hysterical patient who had previously made several suicide attempts. Reich told her that he would see her for a few diagnostic sessions; at the end of this period, he referred her to one of his Danish students. Several days later, he heard that she was in a psychiatric hospital because of attempted suicide. The hospital psychiatrists declared the attempt "the result of treatment," and turned the case over to the Danish police. They also recommended that Reich's visa not be extended.

As a result of the hospital psychiatrists' opposition, a Danish newspaper on October 29 called for Reich's expulsion from the country, in order "to prevent one of these German so-called sexologists from fooling around with our young men and women and converting them to this perverse pseudo-science."[22]

Meanwhile, an analytic student of Reich's, Erik Carstens, had written Freud seeking to enlist the master's aid on behalf of Reich. In his reply of November 13, Freud acknowledged Reich's stature as an analyst but stated that his political ideology interfered with his scientific work. He refused to join Carstens' appeal to the Minister of Justice.[23]

So, on December 1, Reich had to leave Copenhagen. He decided to settle temporarily in Malmö, Sweden. His Danish students planned to hire a boat and commute across the three-mile strait, and students also were to come from Oslo. Reich's library and press remained in Copenhagen.

Soon after he arrived in Malmö, early in January 1934, the Swedish authorities became suspicious of Reich. The police watched the boardinghouse where he resided. His commuting students were intercepted and taken to police headquarters for questioning. Police in Denmark and in Sweden synchronized their activities. Thus, on the same day in April, Philipson's home in Copenhagen was searched while he was in Malmö and Reich's rooms were scrutinized by the Swedish police.

No charges of any kind were raised against Reich or his students. Friends of Reich organized a letter campaign protesting his harassment in Malmö. The anthropologist Bronislaw Malinowski, who was now living in London, wrote a warm letter supporting Reich. Again Freud maintained his negative position, writing: "I cannot join your protest in the affair of Dr. Wilhelm Reich."[24]

In late May, Reich's visitor's visa expired and he returned, illegally this time, to Denmark for the summer.

Two aspects of Reich's hectic movements between Denmark and Sweden should be underscored. The Danish campaign was the first state attack against him. Hitherto, the attacks had come from certain groups: the Social Democrats, the Communists, and—with growing momentum—the psychoanalysts. But starting with Denmark, each government of the country where he resided became embroiled in legal moves against him.

Secondly, we should note Reich's striking ability to gather around him immediately a stimulating and capable group of people. R. L. Leunbach, a leader of the World League for Sexual Reform, Tage Philipson, and several other Danish followers helped Reich move to Copenhagen. Then an aristocratic Danish woman, Ellen Siersted, joined his cause and would later help him publish his *Journal for Political Psychology and Sex-economy* in 1934.[25]

In 1932 a Norwegian psychoanalyst, Nic Hoel, had studied in Berlin and become fascinated by Reich's work. When she returned to Oslo, she stimulated the interest of her husband, Sigurd Hoel, who was a novelist, and several other analysts. Harold Schjelderup, a professor at the University of Oslo, and Hoel, who both went into therapy with Reich while he was in Denmark, were instrumental in helping Reich move to Oslo. Thus, as so often with Reich, while old ties were being disrupted, new ones were already forming.

Throughout this period, Reich continued to be immensely concerned with his perilous position within the psychoanalytic organization. He entertained hopes that a substantial group of younger, Marxist-oriented analysts (such as Otto Fenichel, George Gerö, then an analytic candidate training with Reich, Karen Horney, and Edith Jacobson) would support his work and do battle for him and with him. Reich was aware, of course, of the difficulties of organizing an "opposition movement." If one espoused the cause clearly, one risked a break with the existing organization. If one organized a new home too early, one faced the danger of premature structuralization of still nascent concepts and techniques.

Reich made use of his own struggles to understand those around him. He, too, feared "homelessness." By 1934, however, he felt much less "organizationally bound" and much more prepared to accept loneliness.[26] He also recognized that he had put more of his work within the psychoanalytic and Marxist organizations than properly belonged there. Unfortunately, he would find that other Marxist-oriented analysts did not share this awareness.

In the months before the annual International Psychoanalytic Congress, to be held in Lucerne that August, Reich was preoccupied with the role of the opposition movement. On August 1, he received a letter from Carl Müller-Braunschweig, secretary of the Berlin Psychoanalytic Society. Reich was informed that because of the political situation, his name would not be included on the list of German members. But, the secretary added, this was only a formality. The Norwegian Society was going to be recognized at the Congress and the listing of Reich's name in that affiliate at a future time would suffice to keep his association membership.[27]

Reich was not especially upset by what seemed to be a diplomatic maneuver, even though he doubted that the downplaying of a controversial analyst would spare noncontroversial ones from Hitler's wrath (as indeed it did not). At first nothing seemed out of order. But during the evening reception, an embarrassed Müller-Braunschweig took Reich aside to say that the German executive committee had excluded him from membership altogether; hence he was not entitled to attend the business meeting. Later, Reich was to discover that he had been excluded from the Berlin Society a whole year earlier.

Reich informed his sympathizers of what had happened; some were upset, others minimized the incident since Reich would soon be accepted by the Norwegian group. Reich wanted his friends to refer to the controversial theoretical issues in their lectures to the Congress. However, although people such as Fenichel and George Gerö dealt with subjects that involved Reich's theories, all the controversy surrounding his work was ignored. Reich's hopes were dashed that a group of people would sharply and dramatically confront the old guard. If anyone was to show the flag of the opposition, he would have to do it alone.

Reich could only expect enmity from most senior analysts. The one distinguished older analyst who had steadily endorsed him, Sandor Ferenczi, had died in 1933. Another old benefactor, now a bitter enemy, Paul Federn, was reported to have said: "Either Reich goes or I go."[28] Now Ernest Jones, president of the International Psychoanalytic Association, revealed that he had every intention of excluding Reich, contrary to what he had said some eight months earlier. Indeed, unbeknown to Reich, Jones had been campaigning against him well before the Lucerne Congress. In May 1933, he wrote Anna Freud that Reich would have to choose between psychoanalysis and politics. That June, he wrote A. A. Brill, the early translator of Freud, stating that Reich was one of the troublemaking "madmen" in psychoanalysis.[29]

At the Congress, Reich asked Jones whether he could still deliver his scheduled lecture and take part in the business meeting. Jones answered that he could give his lecture as a guest but not take part in the business meeting. (The bureaucratic mills grind slowly, yet they grind exceedingly fine.)

It finally became clear to Reich that the leadership of the International Association fully sided with the German executive committee in excluding him. He fumed against Jones's duplicity. Talking with Heinz Hartmann, the famed analytic theorist on the adaptive mechanisms of the ego, and several other analysts, Reich wondered whether he should punch Jones. His associates patiently advised restraint and Reich reassured them.[30] But in the early 1950's, or almost twenty years after Lucerne, Reich could still rage against Federn and Jones.

The executive committee appointed a high-level subcommittee, which met with Reich the day before the business meeting. The committee hoped to obtain Reich's resignation and thereby avoid any public unpleasantness. At the subcommittee session, Reich stated that he understood his exclusion if opposition to the death instinct concept and Freud's theory of culture were incompatible with membership. At the same time, he considered himself the legitimate developer of natural-scientific psychoanalysis and, from that viewpoint, could not concur with the exclusion.

Jones took Reich's recognition of the distance between his concepts and those of psychoanalysis in 1934 as an act of resignation. In his biography of Freud, Jones wrote: "It was on this occasion [the Lucerne Congress] that Wilhelm Reich resigned from the Association. Freud had thought highly of him in his early days, but Reich's political fanaticism had led to both personal and scientific estrangement."[31]

Whatever Jones thought, Reich never in fact resigned. At the time, he stressed that he was excluded from the Association. In later years, out of his hurt, he would sometimes play down the rejection and focus on the fact that he was offered membership in the Norwegian affiliate. But, more basically, in the psychoanalytic rupture, as earlier in the Communist one, Reich felt he could not be excluded scientifically because he himself represented the true tradition. For him, the psychoanalysts, like the Communists, had removed themselves from the living core of their heritage. He remained at the center.

But for all his arguments and consoling insights, the events at Lucerne cut extremely deep. What hurt Reich the most he talked least about—that Freud must have approved the action, if he did not actively seek it. Several persons who spoke with Reich at Lucerne commented years later that he looked quite depressed. And pictures from this time show the same hurt-brooding look revealed in the Davos photos.

Depressed or not, Reich delivered one of his best papers at the Congress on August 30. It was published in expanded form in May 1935 by Reich's press as "Psychischer Kontakt und Vegetative Strömung" ("Psychic Contact and Vegetative Current"),[32] and later included in the 1945 edition of *Character Analysis*. Reich opened with the words: "After fourteen years as a member, I speak for the first time as a guest of the Congress." As he put it, "attention was paid to me as never before. . . . I had the feeling that the [Psychoanalytic Association] had excluded the theory of sexuality which formed its very core. . . . And now [it] spoke as a guest in the homeland. . . ."[33]

Reich began his paper with a review of an older psychoanalytic concept that formed his starting point, the social origin of neuroses. He went on to challenge death instinct theory directly, and then linked what appeared to be "primary masochism" in analysis to the patient's unresolved negative transference.

So far nothing new, though Reich in a supercharged atmosphere had publicly thrown down the gauntlet. He went on to say that "it becomes less important whether, early in the analysis, one obtained much or little material, whether one learned much or little about the patient's past. The decisive question came to be whether one obtained, in a correct fashion, those experiences which represented *concentrations of vegetative energy*. . . . The accent shifted from experiential content to the economy of vegetative energy."[34]

This is the first occasion on which, in a character-analytic context, Reich speaks of "vegetative energy," although he had developed this theme in another paper from 1934, "Der Urgegensatz des vegetativen Lebens" ("The Basic Antithesis of Vegetative Life").[35] Characteristically, since he expected his Lucerne audience to have read this article, he felt he could use the term "vegetative energy" without further amplification.*

Reich then cited as a clinical example a patient who showed strong resistances against the uncovering of his passive-homosexual fantasies. After analysis of the resistances, the fantasies emerged; so, too, did signs of acute anxiety. The color of his face kept changing from white to yellow or blue; the skin was mottled and of various tints; he had severe pains in the neck and occiput; the heartbeat was rapid; the patient had diarrhea. Once again we witness Reich in one of his favorite realms: the direct observation of very tangible, clinical reactions, which express themselves in changes of color and other vivid forms.

In the same paper Reich introduced another important new term, "contactlessness." His awareness of this phenomenon grew out of some discontent with his therapeutic results. As he put it: "Gradually it became clear that although a thorough dissolution of the modes of behavior led to deep-reaching breakthroughs of vegetative energy, nevertheless it was incomplete in a way difficult to define. One had the feeling that the patient did not relinquish some outposts of his 'narcissistic position.' "[36]

Reich gave several common subjective perceptions of contactlessness. One was the frequent feeling many people have of "inner loneliness" in spite of the presence of others. There was also the feeling of "inner deadness" that appears in spite of a seemingly active and interesting existence. The phenomenon of "inner deadness" especially concerned Reich. It is not an unfamiliar one to patients and to "normal" people. (More recently, the movies of Antonioni, Fellini, and Bergman, the plays of Harold Pinter and Samuel Beckett have focused on this state of nonbeing or "contactlessness.")

Certain phenomena of contactlessness appeared most vividly near the end of therapy. Reich distinguished here between elimination of "individual layers" of the armor and the final breakdown of the total armor. The latter phase is often characterized by an alternation of what he called "streaming" *(Strömung)* and emotional contactlessness. By "streaming," Reich was referring to the subjective perception of a feeling of aliveness, of a current flowing through the body, although he does not elaborate at this point. He went on to state as a goal of therapy "the reestablishment of vegetative streaming. . . . The transition from the streaming condition to the frozen condition is one of the most important therapeutic and theoretical problems."[37]

---

*We should note briefly that the Berlin internist Friedrich Kraus had introduced the phrase "vegetative current" some seven years earlier in reference to fluid convection processes in the body. Around 1933, Reich had been studying the physiology of bodily changes during specific emotions, such as pleasure and anxiety. Reich was often unwilling to explain a concept or term previously defined. I recall once suggesting that he give a brief review about some issue in a book to make it easier for the reader; he criticized me for the "socialist fallacy." "Let them study my previous writings—we don't write *for people,* we write *about things.*"

Reich illustrated the combination of feelings of "contactlessness" and the "frozen condition" through a case example. We meet a man who is "exaggeratedly polite and reserved and somewhat dignified," but who has a secret wish to "feel the world," to be able to "stream" freely with it. The patient suffered from an intense fear of object loss. He would react with acute disappointment if he did not immediately have an erection when he kissed a woman. The slightest disappointment would lead him to retreat from heterosexuality.

With this patient, Reich used for the first time the phrase "penis anesthesia." By this he meant that touching the penis resulted only in tactile but not pleasurable sensations. "Penis anesthesia" can and often does occur in the presence of erective potency. It is a vivid bodily counterpart to the psychological feeling of "contactlessness." Reich speculates that "genital anesthesia is not merely a psychic process but a disturbance of the electrophysiological function at the penis surface."[38]*

In this paper, Reich was more concerned with how the contactlessness and deadness came about than with how to overcome them. As he came to grips with the subject, he was more able to acknowledge his uncertainty:

How is it possible that a withdrawal of sexual excitation and outgoingness is immediately experienced as a "going cold" or "freezing up"? . . . In brief, we do not know. . . . The transition from full living experiencing to inner deadness is usually caused by severe disappointments in love. However, this still does not explain the mechanism of this inner freezing up.[39]

Fifteen years later Reich was to start an "infant research center" where the "freezing" process could be studied from the first day of life.

Reich followed the discussion of contactlessness with an analysis of a sister concept, "substitute contact." If contactlessness represents the state of inner emptiness, substitute contact represents the effort to connect with other people despite all the inner obstacles. Substitute contact is a compromise solution. Reich gives an example: "The sadistic attitude of the compulsive woman toward the man has not only the function of warding off her genitality but also that of compensating for the . . . contactlessness and of maintaining the contact with the original love object, although in a different form."[40]

Reich's emphasis on contactlessness and substitute contact permitted a quantum advance in his social critique. With Marx, he could indict the history of civilization. If Marx said that there can be no civilization until exploitation is abolished, until man's alienation from his own labor is removed, Reich could

---

*Around this time Reich was planning experimental work on measuring sensations of pleasure and anxiety. A description of this work follows in Chapter 16. I note it here to stress once again the interactions between Reich's clinical work and his other concerns.

join that critique and add his own: No true civilization until man is in contact with his feelings and can "stream" in the world, until his contactlessness and his pathetic efforts at "substitute contact" are no longer necessary. In the Lucerne paper, Reich was moving toward the physiological and biological, but he was also moving outward to the social world, to what remained one of his deepest commitments.

At the Lucerne Congress the Norwegian analysts were told that if they made Reich a member, they would not be accepted as an affiliate. The Norwegians refused to accept this condition. However, given all the controversies and the direction of his own work, Reich was uncertain about joining an affiliate of the International Association. And, much as he wanted the Norwegians to offer him membership, he did not wish his membership to jeopardize their analytic standing. He left Lucerne in the fall of 1934 and headed for Oslo, ready to begin a new phase of his career yet significantly no longer a member of any formal organization.

Personal Life: 1930-1934

The Berlin years proved unhappy ones for Reich's family life. The marriage between Annie and Willy, already deteriorating in Vienna, became worse in Berlin. Eva remembers "big, noisy fights" between her parents.[1] Even in good times the parents were very busy and the children always had to be quiet in the apartment while the Reichs saw patients. (The combination of living and office quarters, begun in Vienna, was carried on in Berlin.)

Annie continued to participate in many of Reich's endeavors, if without any great enthusiasm. The income from her private practice enabled Reich to spend more time in writing and political activity than might otherwise have been possible.

Reich involved not only his wife but also his children in his concerns. His older daughter Eva, who was between six and nine during the Berlin years, recalls how her father used to urge her to join in the Communist marches, something she was reluctant to do. Once when she was marching with a children's group, shouting in unison: "Hunger! hunger! Give us bread," a passer-by noticed her and pinched her plump cheeks, saying, *"You* are not hungry!" And it was true, she thought, I am not hungry, I am lying.[2] As often happened with Reich, he tried but failed to impose on others the enthusiasm he felt for a cause. In this instance, his enthusiasm backfired completely, leaving Eva with a lasting distaste for politics.

A more serious family dispute concerned the children's education. At one point during the Berlin years, Reich felt strongly that they should be brought up in a Communist children's collective. He may also have felt this was important because Eva was suffering from certain symptoms—night terrors, temper tantrums, and obsessive ideas. A collective education would ameliorate the intensity of the Oedipus complex, he believed. Annie opposed the idea but eventually gave in to pressure. So the children went to live at the collective; for how long is not clear, but at least one summer and for some months during the regular school year.[3]

Eva recalls her father visiting the center. All the children were very excited about his new car. Time was limited and he could not take all of them for a ride in it, so he divided the group in half and flipped a coin to see which children would be given a ride. Eva was not in the half that won, and she naturally felt very badly. As an adult she understands her father's thinking—he loved all children, it was a collective, fair was fair; but at the time it was hard.

Both children disliked the residential center—the poor food, the dirty living conditions. Lore, who was only around four at the time, left earlier than Eva. But Eva did not stay long. On a visit to her parents she walked around the apartment and argued that there was plenty of room for her there; there was no reason for her to return to the dreadful collective. As a clincher, she said: "Anyway, *you* are the Communist. You go live at the center. *I'm* staying here."[4]

One of Reich's stated reasons for moving to Berlin was to have analytic sessions with Sandor Rado to determine whether there were any neurotic motives behind his scientific conflict with Freud.

There are several versions of what happened in the Reich-Rado relationship. According to Annie Reich, Rado mistreated Reich by permitting him to enter therapy knowing that he, Rado, would be moving to America six months or so after the start of treatment. However, from Rado's account, he did *not* know that he was going to stay in America when he planned an extended vacation in 1931.[5] It was only after his arrival in the United States that the deteriorating German political situation led him to turn the trip into a permanent change of residence.

By Rado's account again, after Reich heard of Rado's vacation plans, he wrote that he was stopping analysis because his sex-political responsibilities were so time-consuming. In other words, Reich would leave Rado before Rado left Reich.

Reich had his own version of what happened. In his interview with Dr. Eissler, he stated: "I saw Rado several times. Nothing came of that. Rado was jealous, awfully jealous. . . . Emmy, his wife, and I had very strong genital contact with each other. Never anything like full embrace happened between us, but we danced a lot together and we had very strong contact. And Rado was jealous."[6]

More importantly, according to Edith Jacobson, Rado told Annie that Reich was suffering from an "insidious psychotic process," and advised her not to continue living with him.[7] Annie rejected the diagnosis and the advice, at least for a few more years. We do not know the context in which Rado communicated his opinion about Reich to Annie, but on the face of it for an analyst to vouchsafe such opinions to a patient's mate seems thoroughly unprofessional. We do know from one other source that Rado bandied damaging diagnoses of Reich, basing his opinion by inference on his analytic experience with the man.[8]

Reich cannot have known what Rado told Annie, for as late as 1933 he was writing Rado a friendly letter from Denmark, seeking his advice about emigration to the United States. He described Rado as "among the few colleagues with good judgment."[9]

Rado's diagnosis of an "insidious psychotic process" completed the fateful picture of Reich from around 1934 on: his concepts on genitality, his social views, and his personality were seen singly as dangerous, combined as deadly. Prior to the 1930s, some analysts, especially Federn, had called Reich a "psychopath." However, as far as I can determine, it was not until Rado that the diagnosis of a "psychosis" was made.

According to Reich, Rado's diagnosis was also circulated, starting around 1935, by both Annie Reich and Otto Fenichel. Thus Reich's former therapist, his former wife, and former best friend were to launch—with some authority —a very damaging view of his personality. These evaluations of his personality and his work mutually reinforced each other: his "psychosis" would underlie his "erroneous" work, and his "crackpot" ideas would prove his "psychosis."

In May 1932, Reich began a serious relationship with Elsa Lindenberg—a relationship that led to the final dénouement of his marriage to Annie.

Born in Germany in 1906, Elsa was the youngest of five children. Her father was a book printer, an active Social Democrat, and a man who loved music. He died when Elsa was six, so the family suffered great financial difficulties. Her mother, a sensitive person who often read poetry to the children, had to take a job in a factory. From an early age Elsa was interested in dancing and was to make that her career. In 1919, when she was thirteen, an older brother was killed in the Spartacus (Communist) uprising in Berlin. Some years later, Elsa felt committed to carrying on her brother's work and became a Communist herself.[10]

At the time she met Reich, Elsa was a dancer with the City Opera of Berlin as well as a political activist. In her mid-twenties she was a strikingly attractive woman, to judge from various dance photographs in her Oslo apartment when I interviewed her in the 1970s. She had already heard about Reich, who was then thirty-five, from a friend who was a member of the same Communist cell as Reich.[11] Her friend had told her that she should meet Reich —he brought new ideas to politics. But, he also laughingly warned, she should watch out; he was very "seductive."

Reich and Elsa first noticed each other on a train taking them to the May Day demonstration in Berlin. She had been struck by his giving her (a total stranger) his coat to hold while he temporarily went to another carriage. Then, during the demonstration march, Elsa was looking for someone to walk with who would be good company and could also serve as a protector. Noticing two sympathetic-looking men, one of whom was Reich, she began walking with them.

Elsa observed that Reich exerted a strong influence on people. When he stepped out of the row of marchers, a group would follow him. She also noticed his fury when Nazi hecklers made threatening gestures. It was all he could do to restrain himself from fighting back.

Elsa and Reich were strongly attracted to each other from the start. Elsa remembers that they put their arms around one another, more preoccupied with their growing infatuation than with the boring speech by a Communist leader that ended the demonstration. Afterward they began to see each other frequently. When Elsa learned of his marriage, she wanted to break off the relationship. Reich made it clear to her that he no longer loved his wife, but he was deeply upset by the prospect of separating from the children.

The relationship continued to grow in intensity. It was far more serious than Reich's previous affairs. Reich has described Elsa as one of the few women in his life whom he truly loved. Finally, when the break-up with Annie was becoming more and more of a reality, Elsa urgently suggested a meeting with them both to discuss the situation. (Reich had made no effort to keep the affair secret; in fact, the word "affair" hardly describes his relationship with Elsa.) During part of the meeting Annie and Elsa talked alone, as Willy had stepped outside. Later, Annie wrote a note that contained the sentence: "Your [Elsa's] happiness will be built on my tears." However, when Elsa offered to withdraw because of the children, Annie said bitterly that this would be of little help since if it were not Elsa there would be another woman.[12]

Reich and Annie did not actually live apart until they left Berlin singly for Vienna early in March 1933. Annie stayed on in Vienna a few months, then moved to Prague, where she reestablished her analytic practice. Eva and Lore had left Berlin a few days before their parents and returned to Vienna to live for almost a year with their grandparents, Alfred and Malva Pink.

As with many of Reich's separations, there was some question of who finally left whom. Annie's version was that she found life with Reich intolerable, not because of his affairs per se but because of the way he treated her— his domineering insistence that she completely follow *his* work and *his* ways, his explosive rages, his alternating coldness and tenderness, the quarrels about money.[13] Reich's version is simple: "She was sick. I just had to leave her."[14] However, when Reich was quarreling with someone, he could use the word "sick" with a meaning of his own—Annie was not a "genital character." For some time before the separation and in the many years after it, she symbolized for him all that enraged him in the analytic community, the intellectual "smugness," the "mustiness," the fear of the "juices of life," and with that fear, the fear and hatred, however politely wrapped up, of his own work.[15]

Lia Laszky, who visited Berlin in 1932, conveys some of the tensions between Willy and Annie in the last years of their marriage. Willy, Annie, Fenichel, and the two children were taking a trip through the German countryside, and Willy invited Lia along. But he became furious when his car kept on stalling en route. Eva was getting very upset and the atmosphere was tense and charged. During a stop, Fenichel took Lia aside to say that he had gone along in order to testify about Reich's behavior at a possible divorce proceeding Annie planned. "And you want me to testify, too?" Lia asked. Fenichel nodded. Lia decided immediately to leave the group. She told Reich of her intention without giving the reason for it. Even more upset, he begged her not to leave, saying that it would turn out to be a good trip. When she insisted, he became angry. Then, at the next train stop—not the one she would have chosen—he let her out. Characteristically, if someone was planning to leave Reich, he would reverse the situation so that he determined the parting.

Reich's separation from Annie opened the way for living with Elsa. However, much as Elsa was in love with Reich, she was hesitant about leaving Germany. For one thing, she was active in the movement against Hitler. For another, her professional independence was important to her: she had a good career in Germany, and was uncertain of her opportunities outside the country. Reich partly supported her aspirations, but typically also wanted her to center her life around him.

Between March and May 1933, Reich bombarded Elsa with letters urging her to join him in Vienna. He also persuaded their mutual friends to encourage Elsa to take the step. Eventually, she joined him in Copenhagen in late May.

In spite of all his difficulties with the Communists, the International Association, and the state authorities in Denmark, in spite of his pain over separation from his children, once they were together, Reich was very happy with Elsa. Elsa has given a vivid description of him:

> I realized how strong his love for humanity was and how he could suffer for and with others. But he could also be happy as I have never known anyone to be—his sensitivity, his sensuousness, his ability to register the feelings of others.
>
> He was aware of his gifts and he knew he had an outstanding contribution to make. But he was also afraid for himself, afraid of where his development might take him. At times he believed that he would achieve fame and recognition in his life time; in other moods he feared that he would go "kaput," that his life would end tragically in one way or another.
>
> Sometimes at night when he couldn't sleep he would speak to me about his fears, including the fear he might go mad. He also spoke to me about his guilt over feeling responsible for his mother's death.

Just as Reich could share his hopes and fears with Elsa, he could also share joy and simple fun. They loved to dance together. In Elsa, he found a woman who could participate enthusiastically in his growing interest in the emotional expression of the body and in the phenomenon of muscular armor. She also shared his intense political commitments, which remained strong during this time. As Elsa put it, "We were devoted Communists, very disciplined." She added ruefully, "What idiots we were!"

Those close to Reich, and especially the woman he lived with, had to share his interests. Annie had been an enthusiastic student and practitioner of analysis in the years when this was at the center of Reich's life; but she had barely gone along with his sex-political concerns and his development of the orgasm theory. Lia Laszky was more involved in the political arena, but she was not prepared to leave the psychoanalytic framework or professional milieu. For both Annie and Lia, Freud was the last word, and anything Reich (or others) had to add were but refinements to a basic text. Both women came from upper-middle-class Viennese families and were highly educated.

Elsa was different. Coming from a working-class background, she had known poverty, and, like Reich, had been on her own from an early age. She had never studied psychoanalysis, although she was interested in—and a quick learner of—those aspects of analysis that especially appealed to Reich. Her education had been in the dance, not academic. She was a freer spirit and a warmer person than either Annie or Lia. Finally, she spoke of Reich with more love than any other woman who knew him that I interviewed.*

One anecdote illustrates how, in Elsa's company, Reich continued to combine his scientific and private interests. In Copenhagen, he and Elsa liked to visit the Tivoli Gardens amusement park. There they would observe people's reactions to the roller coaster ride: their anxiety, terror, pleasure. Around this time in his therapeutic work, Reich was concentrating on his patients' "fear of falling," a fear that often became prominent during the final stages of therapy when orgasm anxiety was strong. He connected the fear of falling with the fear "of the typical sensations in the diaphramatic region which are experienced on a roller coaster or in a suddenly descending elevator."[16]

After the clash with Danish officialdom in the fall of 1933, Reich decided to take a four-week vacation in early December. He wanted to visit London, which he was considering as a possible permanent residence; to see his children in Austria; and to visit friends in other European cities. This month's sojourn was the only time Reich traveled widely not out of necessity but choice.

In London, he met Bronislaw Malinowski for the first time. A friendship begun through letters was now enhanced by personal contact. In his book *Der Einbruch der Sexualmoral (The Invasion of Compulsory Sex-morality)*, published in 1932,[17] Reich had made use of Malinowski's findings about the Trobrianders to postulate that patriarchy, sex negation, and a class division had long ago "invaded" the natural state of matriarchy, sex affirmation, and primi-

---

*I never met Annie Reich, who died in 1971, so my views of her are based on accounts from others.

tive communism. At that time Malinowski was one of the few academic scholars who thought highly of Reich's writings.

Reich's visit with Ernest Jones was less successful. Among other factors contributing to Jones's dislike of Reich was the latter's personal and intellectual closeness to Malinowski. Jones and the anthropologist were then engaged in divisive polemics about the universality of the Oedipus complex.

The ever correct Jones invited Reich to present his views at a meeting of English analysts. According to Reich, the atmosphere of the meeting held in Jones's home was one of rigid formality. Reich stressed the social origin of the neuroses, a view that met with vague agreement qualified by Jones's insistence on a strict separation between science and politics. Nonetheless, Jones privately told Reich that he would strongly oppose any move to expel Reich from the Psychoanalytic Association. However, after meeting with Jones, Reich relinquished any idea of a move to London.[18]

In Paris, Reich met with several officials of Leon Trotsky's Fourth International, the militant but tiny Marxist organization in opposition to Stalin's "state capitalism" as well as to private capitalism. Yet the officials could see no practical place for Reich's concepts in their political work.[19]

Reich also attended meetings of German radical refugees in Paris. He found these radicals still happily talking about "categories of class consciousness," without seriously considering the implications of Hitler's victory for their concepts and activities. Irritated and spurred by the scholastic discussion, he returned to his hotel room and outlined what later became his masterful article, "What Is Class Consciousness?" (see page 174).

Reich next went to Zurich, where he saw an old friend, the sexologist and political radical Fritz Brupbacher, author of 40 Jahre Ketzer (Forty Years a Heretic), which Reich considered to be a "brilliant account of Philistinism in the workers' movement."[20] Brupbacher's deep concern for people and decades of involvement with social struggles "fascinated" Reich—and Reich did not report being fascinated by many people. At this meeting, Brupbacher was profoundly discouraged about the present and future of humanity. Reich shared his diagnosis but not his prognosis.

From Zurich, Reich went to the Tyrol in the Austrian Alps to see his children at Christmas time. Eva and Lore were now attending a Viennese private school directed by Margaret Fried, a friend of Annie's. Mrs. Fried and her husband had a home in the Tyrol where pupils could, if they wished, spend summers and Christmas vacations.

Some thirty-five years later, Mrs. Fried remembered the Reich of the Tyrol visit well as being "friendly and liberal."[21] She noted that he was an excellent skier, with a mobile body more like a man of twenty-five than thirty-five. He had good contact with the schoolchildren and some vacationing adolescents. Lore, then almost six, tended to cling to her father. Eva, almost ten, was concerned whether people liked "Willy," as she called him. Her disquiet here undoubtedly reflected the growing bitter schism, to be described in Chapter 19, between her father and his world and Annie, her grandfather, and the analytic community.

Annie also came to the Frieds' for Christmas. According to Reich, there was no hint of the acrimony that "later devastated our lives."[22] However, Reich could overlook signs of trouble when he preferred not to see them. In Mrs. Fried's view, Annie was embarrassed and displeased by Reich's presence —something of a surprise—on her turf. Mrs. Fried did criticize Reich for being "too outspoken" on sexual matters. A few of the adolescents present had read his book *The Sexual Struggle of Youth,* and they seized the opportunity to discuss it with the author in person. His answers to their questions were frank and the discussion spirited. Mrs. Fried and her husband were disturbed because some of the pupils were from conservative, Catholic homes. At one point Mrs. Fried took Reich aside and said that the students' parents would be very upset if they should hear about this kind of conversation. Reich said he hadn't realized the difficulties and subsequently desisted from such exchanges.

After Christmas Reich went on to Vienna, where he stayed with friends. Some six weeks later the Dollfuss government would raid the Socialist headquarters there and the Socialist leaders would be forced to flee or be arrested. Reich, who predicted this outcome, heard friends and colleagues still mouth their old positions: the Communists were prepared for the revolution and the Social Democrats believed that compromises would avert disaster. What had happened in Germany could not happen in Austria. Later, visiting friends in Prague, he noted the same kind of illusions—in this case, about Hitler's overthrow by the Church, the Western powers, the German Army, and, "of course, the increasingly mature workers in the factories."[23]

To avoid a long trip back to Sweden through Poland, Reich traveled by way of Germany after ascertaining that no lists of names were kept at the border. He made a stopover in Berlin: "Soldiers everywhere. Depression, sluggish movements, anxious peering." He thought he recognized a former Communist comrade but was uncertain whether to greet him. Many Communists had become Nazis now. Reich wondered about the worth of convictions: How did it happen that a person could be passionately for one doctrine and then suddenly just as fervently support a radically different ideology?[24]

Reich's journey through Europe gives another vivid example of how he lived without any strict separation between work and leisure. Always he was observing and making connections between these observations and the themes of his work. Then, too, the itinerant Reich reveals—like the Reich of the 1927 Vienna demonstrations—his sensitive barometer for group moods. His weathervane registered clearly the subdued, appeasing mood in Europe, gripped by hopeful illusions, after Hitler's rise to power and the Stalinization of Russia, and before the Holocaust and World War II.

During the stopover Reich met Elsa, who had been visiting family and friends in Berlin while he traveled. Not well known as a Communist, she could still move freely in Germany. Together, they returned to Sweden. On arriving in Malmö in January 1934 they took rooms in a boardinghouse, the atmosphere of which Reich described as frigid and stuffy, with people staring intrusively at Elsa and himself.[25] Both of them spoke German, and, in addition, word may have gotten around that this unusual couple were not married. Still, Reich thought, it was better than being in a concentration camp.

With the help of Reich's students, Elsa commuted to Copenhagen, where she spent several days a week continuing her dance work. Reich had ample leisure for study and writing in addition to seeing patients. He also had the opportunity to observe life in a relatively small city, a new experience for him. He found Malmö to be a quite unpretentious place, where "civilization could sleep in 'law and order.'" At night adolescents walked to and fro in the streets, separated by sex, and giggling at each other.

With his Swedish visa due to expire in late May and the authorities suspicious and unwilling to renew it, Reich and Elsa decided to spend the summer of 1934 illegally in Sletten, Denmark, where Reich lived under the pseudonym Peter Stein. They planned to settle in Oslo in the fall.

Eva and Lore, who visited Reich and Elsa that summer, both recalled that Reich was much happier in Denmark than he had been in Berlin. Eva, too, contrasted the gray, tight atmosphere of her life in Vienna with the joyous summer in Denmark: "It was light, fun, jolly. There were trips, eating out, people dancing, people coming and going—fat Fenichel and others. It was alive."[26]

In Denmark, Reich brought Eva more into his work than he had done in the past. She happily recalled his discussing his current interests with her and permitting her to attend informal seminars at a small congress he was organizing. Lore described this kind of behavior on Reich's part more negatively: he made no distinction between children and adults. Eva, in particular, he treated in a way that was beyond her years, a criticism later vehemently repeated by Annie and her friends.

Eva remembered a journey by car from Denmark to the Lucerne Congress in Switzerland in August 1934. They camped out along the way through Germany, for Reich loved camping. There were memories of dancing with Elsa, the smell of honeysuckle all around them; of free bodies exercising, and of bathing in the nude; of Reich being tender to Elsa in a way Eva rarely remembered his being with her mother. All these evocations of what must have been a golden summer for Eva created antagonism in others. One person mentioned with strong distaste that Reich sent his daughters a photo taken during the trip to Lucerne showing Elsa and Eva dancing, both nude to the waist.[27]

At Lucerne the "family" continued to camp out, now by the lake near where the Congress was held. This, too, led to stories. In discussing those days with Dr. Eissler, Reich mentioned that he didn't like hotels, and, besides, it would have been difficult for him to live in one with Elsa since they were not married. Reich went on to say that he lived with Elsa in a tent at Lake Lucerne. He also had a camping knife with him. Out of these facts the highly distorted rumor later circulated that he had been psychotic, wore a dagger, and lived in a tent in the lobby of a hotel.[28]

People interpreted the story as further evidence of how far Reich had gone astray. Grete Bibring, his student friend, saw it as another sign of his sinking into psychosis. Eissler, who assigned the diagnosis of psychopathic rather than psychotic to Reich, used the story to show how wantonly provocative Reich could be, considering how conservative the Swiss were at that time.[29] And various interviewees referred to Elsa as "Reich's concubine" or "Reich's dancer," much as one might speak of a kind of prostitute.

Whatever the interpretation, Reich's relationship with Elsa in general and his appearance with her at Lucerne in particular fanned the outrage against him. There were scientific and political differences between Reich and many analysts, but there were also intensely personal reasons for other analysts to resent him. For him to appear with Elsa, when Annie was also attending the Congress, exacerbated the family quarrel aspect of the whole imbroglio. Many analysts who were Annie's good friends as well as Reich's took her side in the dispute. By all accounts, they regarded her as a very kind, gentle, intelligent person, much abused by Reich. She advanced no controversial theories, she was not an embarrassment to them, and, as they saw it, she was the injured party.

All of this was conveyed rather than explicitly stated in interviews. Most participants intellectually held an "enlightened viewpoint": one did not blame a husband or wife for having affairs, or for leaving a marriage. Analysts did have affairs and did divorce, without a *cause célèbre*. But somehow Reich was different. From his viewpoint, he was more open; from theirs, he was provocative and indiscreet. Everything Reich did had a quality of being underlined, a kind of glamour and dash if one liked it, a note of wanton provocation if one didn't. He was not just a Communist, he was a militant one; he was not just a psychoanalyst, he claimed to be *the* continuer of the vital tradition within psychoanalysis; he did not discreetly have an affair, he openly avowed his love. Nor would he curb his freedom even if the Swiss—or the analysts—did not like his living with a woman not his legal wife in a tent by the lake.

From today's viewpoint it is easy to forget how conservative the average middle class was in the 1930s in Europe—and America. Even in Denmark, supposedly one of the centers of sexual permissiveness, the atmosphere then was quite puritanical. Sexual relations were fully appropriate only within marriage; maybe, it was not so terrible if an engaged couple had intercourse. But the taboos against open discussion of sexuality and open relationships outside marriage were very strong. And it is worth underscoring that the analytic community *as a group* was not so different in its outlook from society generally.

In the previous chapter Reich's break with the psychoanalytic organization was discussed largely in terms of the scientific disagreements and the "opposition movement." Here it is important to emphasize how bitter was Reich's personal disappointment that so few colleagues and friends supported him at the Lucerne showdown. Once *the* analyst recommended to many American students, he had plummeted to one with hardly any backing as he faced exclusion.

The older analysts were either for his exclusion or quite willing to go along with those who sought this step. However, next to the rejection by Freud, the worst blow for Reich was the passivity on the part of the younger group of analysts, many of them his friends. Grete Bibring felt that she should remove herself from the dispute precisely on the grounds that, as a friend of Reich, she was insufficiently neutral.[30] Edith Jacobson, who shared so much with Reich in Berlin, felt that she was too young an analyst to carry any weight in the proceedings.[31] I have little information about what Fenichel's precise actions at Lucerne were. According to Reich, Fenichel submitted a "lame resolution" at the business meeting, most probably on behalf of Reich since it was quickly tabled.[32] Only Nic Hoel made a spirited speech in Reich's defense.

After Reich's exclusion, Anna Freud reportedly said: "A great injustice has been done here."[33] But she herself took no steps to prevent its passage. (A few years later, when someone asked for her opinion of Reich, she was to say: "A genius or . . . ," her pause indicating that the concluding word was "madman.")*[34]

With the exception of the Scandinavian group—and all the members of this group were new friends, not old ones—there was no one who came to Reich's aid when he most needed it, after the many years of comradeship and recognition in Vienna and Berlin. It is not surprising that he later spoke of this lack of support as "the hardest blow of my scientific career" (and this was said in 1945 when, from other perspectives, far more dangerous events had occurred).[35]

After the Congress, Reich and Elsa left for Oslo. The children returned to their grandparents in Vienna. Annie went back to Prague, where she lived with Thomas Rubinstein, a former official in Alexander Kerensky's short-lived 1917 Russian government, whom she would later marry. A dour, compulsive man, he was disliked by Eva and Lore, in part because he worked at home on research and insisted on quiet and perfect order. Willy and he loathed one another, Thomas referring to Reich as "the skunk."[36] Annie appears to have chosen a second husband who was the opposite of Reich save in his capacity to hate.

It is difficult to tell how Annie felt about Reich's exclusion from the analytic organization at the time. There were fights and tensions between them at Lucerne. Not long after the Congress, Annie would say that Willy could

---

*Reich may well have been especially disappointed over Anna Freud's lack of support for him at Lucerne. I recall his pleasure when he mentioned several times in the 1950s that during the twenties she had once sent him a postcard in which she described him as a *spiritus rector* ("inspiring teacher").

only tolerate close relations with people who were in thrall to him *(hörig),* as she felt she had been for many years.[37] Judging from her later career as a totally orthodox Freudian analyst, one can only imagine that part of her was very glad to be done with him, not to mention those concepts of his she had followed more out of submissiveness than genuine conviction. Now that Reich had been rejected by—and in many ways had rejected—his "second home," the psychoanalytic organization, the only remaining objective tie between them was their children. However, Annie had deeply cared for Reich, and subjectively the repercussions of the relationship would continue for a long time, as we shall see.

In the course of a year and a half, then, Reich had endured significant partings from the Communist Party, the International Psychoanalytic Association, and Annie Reich. In each case, the ruptures were many years in the making. In each case, there was some question as to how much Reich was cast out and how much he himself determined the finale.

Later, Reich sometimes spoke of the suffering the familial separation had caused him not only because of the children but also because of the loss of Annie. At other times, he could speak of her with great bitterness. For him, as for Annie, the process of separation involved much more than leaving, and it took its toll. However, Reich's greatest emphasis was on how crucial it had been for his work that he *did* leave, that he did not "get stuck" as so many people did—stuck in outdated concepts, stuck in organizations needed for security, stuck in neurotic patterns, and stuck in marriages they were unable to leave. He especially cited Freud and Federn as men in this position.[38] For Reich, to leave a no longer viable relationship was as important as any step he took to preserve the integrity of his life and work.

The costs, however, were great. Reich always tended to underestimate his own contribution to the unhappiness connected with his disrupted relationships. Two sad children, feeling abandoned by both parents, were part of that cost. And no amount of later anger and blame toward Annie could completely assuage Reich's guilt over the pain and suffering of his children. In 1934, two paths diverged. Reich chose the less traveled one—both in his work and in his personal life.

PART VI

First Steps on the Road to Life—Reich's Experimental Work in Scandinavia: 1934-1939

16

The Bio-electrical
Experiments: 1934-1935

In 1934, Reich began his natural-scientific experiments. Before dealing with this quite controversial subject, I should make clear that my own competence for evaluating his scientific work is not as advanced as it is for dealing with his psychiatric and sociological work. In addition, there is very little to draw on in making critical assessments of this work that is not either fulsomely positive, hence inadequate, or contemptuously negative, many writers having dismissed Reich's experiments as absurd *prima facie*.

I shall limit myself then to a brief account of Reich's scientific experiments, presenting the major arguments, pro and con, which have been advanced by others. More importantly, my aim is to show the overall theoretical framework within which his scientific work developed and how this research influenced his psychiatric and social endeavors.

No longer a member of the psychoanalytic organization or the Communist Party, Reich was now freer to pursue his research without having to look over his shoulder to see what Freud or the party leaders thought about it. His social interests remained strong and vigorously expressed in his quarterly, established this year, the *Journal for Political Psychology and Sex-economy*. However, his sex-political efforts were not welcome in any political organization.

By 1934, the physiological emphasis of Reich's therapeutic work was becoming increasingly important: the investigation of the streamings of energy (libido) in pleasure; the reverse movement of that energy in anxiety; and the muscular spasms which, along with the character armor, prevented the free emotional expression of the organism. But Reich was not content simply to progress further in his therapeutic technique. He also wished to prove his own concepts and, with them, Freud's early hypothesis of the libido, in a demonstrable, quantitative way.[1] He wanted to provide the biological foundation for psychoanalysis that Freud had predicted, even though Freud himself had abandoned his early efforts to link analysis with physiology.

Crises had a way of stimulating Reich to further advances. As in the late 1920s, when he had combined various concepts and findings from Freud, Marx, and Malinowski to create his sex-politics and to oppose the more conservative social directions of Freud and psychoanalysis, so now, in another *furor intellectualis,* Reich drew upon findings by Freud, and by the physiologist L. R. Müller, the internist Friedrich Kraus, and the biologist Max Hartmann, in a synthesizing effort that cut across different fields and paved the way for subsequent experimentation.[2]

From analysis, Reich turned once again to Freud's early notion of "actual neuroses." In his clinical and social work, Reich had been concerned with the relationship between actual neuroses and psychoneuroses. In 1934, his attention moved to a basic research question: the nature of pleasure and of anxiety. Interestingly enough, in 1926 Freud had said that the physiological "stuff" of which anxiety was made had lost its interest for him. Characteristically, Reich picked up a question Freud had dropped. And he did so in an effort to affirm the younger Freud against the older Freud and the analytic establishment that had just expelled Reich.

In 1931, L. R. Müller had published the third edition of *Die Lebensnerven (The Nervous System),* in which he summarized the functions of the two major divisions of the autonomic nervous system: the sympathetic and the parasympathetic.[3] The autonomic system operates outside consciousness, unlike the central nervous system, which includes the brain and the spinal cord. The autonomic nervous system activates the cardiovascular, digestive, sexual, and respiratory organs. The sympathetic division responds to dangerous or threatening situations by preparing a person through anxiety for "flight or fight" reactions; the parasympathetic division controls the same life-sustaining organs of the body under danger-free, relaxed conditions.

Some examples of how particular organs respond to sympathetic or parasympathetic activation are: sympathetic—accelerated heartbeat, increased blood pressure, constricted blood vessels, increased inspiration in breathing, and reduced blood supply to the genitals; parasympathetic—slow and full heart action, decreased blood pressure, dilated blood vessels, stimulation of expiration, and increased blood supply to the genitals.

Reich was so impressed by Müller's organization of autonomic nerve responses that he began to see the task of therapy as one of reversing the "general sympatheticotonic contraction of the organism." In other words, he wanted to combat not the acute emergency reaction of fear but the chronic anxiety (and the defense against it) that continued long after the stimulus had vanished. Thus, for example, the child once held his breath to inhibit genital excitations that got him into trouble with his parents. As an adult he continued, through early conditioning, to hold his breath, even though this response crippled his capacity for pleasurable functioning.

To my knowledge, Reich was the first psychoanalyst to emphasize the role of sympathetic response in neurotic illness. It is interesting to note that current bio-feedback techniques often involve the replacement of anxiety states with calmer ones by conditioning the patient to relaxing (parasympathetic) thoughts and feelings. The puzzling successes of faith healing and the "placebo effect" may work on the same principle, stimulating hope (parasympathetic innervation) and reducing anxiety (sympathetic response).

It should be stressed that Reich's therapy, unlike bio-feedback techniques, did not aim at the avoidance of anxiety states. On the contrary, the *binding of anxiety* in the armor was more of a problem than free-floating anxiety itself. Intense anxiety was often aroused in the course of therapy as the armor loosened. The patient was helped to work through his anxiety states, not avoid them. The cardinal therapeutic problem became the fear of intense emotions and, in particular, the fear of strong pleasurable sensations (what Reich termed "pleasure anxiety").

Through the work of two Germans, the biologist Max Hartmann and a zoologist, Ludwig Rhumbler, Reich was able to relate his two basic directions of energy flow—"toward the world" in pleasure and "away from the world" in anxiety—to the movements of the amoeba. In a series of experiments, Hartmann and Rhumbler exposed amoebae to a variety of stimuli (chemical, mechanical, thermical, electrical, and optical). Depending upon the quantity and quality of these stimuli, the amoebae reacted in one of two ways: either they sought these stimuli (moved toward them), or they avoided them and assumed a spherical shape ("played dead").

The two researchers had also found *internal* movements in the form of fluid currents within the amoeba. Plasma currents toward the surface of the amoeba were accompanied by the active approach of the amoeba toward the object (corresponding to what in the human would be called a parasympathetic response). Conversely, the movements away from the world were accompanied by plasma currents from the surface toward the center (analogously, a sympathetic response).

Finally, when the amoeba was at rest, the investigators noted pulsating movements in the form of a rhythmic alternation of expansion and contraction. The movement of expansion was accompanied by plasma currents from the center to the surface; those of contraction by currents from the surface to the center.

Hartmann and Rhumbler's research permitted Reich to add a further polarity to those of pleasure and anxiety, parasympathetic and sympathetic innervation: the polarity of plasma currents from the center to the surface in "outgoing" amoeba responses, from the surface to the center in "withdrawing" reactions.

Another major influence on Reich during the same period was Friedrich Kraus. His book *Allgemeine und Spezielle Pathologie der Person (General and Special Pathology of the Person)*, published in 1926, presented data showing that living substances consisted essentially of colloids and mineral salts, both of which when dissolved in body fluids were electrolytes; this meant that bio-electricity was present.[4] Kraus considered the biosystem to be a relay-like switch mechanism of electrical charge (storing of energy) and discharge (performance of work).

For our purposes it is sufficient to emphasize that Reich drew especially upon Kraus's focus on the movement of electrical charges within the organism. Reich also made use of some studies of plant physiology, which revealed a significant connection between fluid movements and electrical discharge processes.

The most important antecedent to Reich's experimental work was his own study of the function of the orgasm.[5] Clinically, as we have noted, he had long been impressed by the fact that mechanical sexual processes (such as erection and ejaculation in the male) could occur without strong sensations of pleasure. Clinically, too, he had been concerned with alleviation of this condition. Now he wanted to move toward laboratory investigation: What had to move, what had to be present beyond known processes, for pleasure to be experienced?

Several lines of thought influenced Reich to hypothesize that bio-electrical processes were involved in the flow of sexual pleasure. As we have noted, he had been impressed with Kraus's bio-electrical model of the organism. Secondly, he noted the popular idea of a kind of "electricity" between a man and a woman who are attracted to each other. (Reich tended to take quite seriously everyday expressions for energetic or emotional processes within or between people.) Third, he had commented that moisture, a conductor of electricity, played an important role in sexuality: "There is an almost irresistible urge for complete contact between the two organ surfaces when the erect male organ touches the moist mucous membrane of the vagina. . . ."[6]

Reich now returned to two old observations, but from a new angle: slow, gentle frictional movements during intercourse produced much stronger sensations than harsh, rapid movements; and after orgasm, the genital became refractory to any further excitations. From these observations, Reich hypothesized that the orgasm represented a form of electrical discharge. Then he went on to make one of his bold leaps: he described a four-part process which, in his view, characterized not only the orgasm but also cell division (mitosis). This process, which he termed the "orgasm formula" or the "life formula," consisted of four steps:

(1) *Mechanical tension* (filling of the organs with fluid; tumescence, with increased turgor of tissues generally).

(2)   The mechanical tension associated with an increase of *bio-electrical charge.*

(3)   *Discharge* of the accumulated bio-electrical charge through spontaneous muscular contractions.

(4)   Flowing back of the body fluids: detumescence *(mechanical relaxation).*

I have intentionally lingered on Reich's preparations for experimentation, for several reasons. First, this period around 1934 is a nice example of the gradual evolution of his work, an evolution that is in contrast to the popular image of his sudden leap from psychoanalysis and libido theory into grandiose notions about orgone energy. On the contrary, between libido theory and his orgone energy concepts lay six years when his thought and experimentation were based on an electrical model of sexual functioning.

Second, the period I have discussed illustrates well the synthesizing qualities of Reich's mind and his particular attraction to the convergence of independent work from different fields for his own goals. He was now drawing on the work of Freud and other researchers for his own ends, just as in the early 1920s he had used the work of Freud, Ferenczi, and Abraham to develop character analysis. In reviewing the work of others, Reich did not provide a critique, unless circumstances compelled him to do so as in the case of Freud. He was, for example, impatient with the controversies surrounding Kraus's concepts, so much so that he does not tell us what they were. What Maxim Gorki wrote of Tolstoy was also true of Reich: "When you speak to Tolstoy of things which he can put to no use, he listens with indifference and incredulity. . . . Like a collector of valuable curios, he only collects things which are in keeping with the rest of his collection."[7]

Finally, Reich's reactions to crises are significant here. The period around 1934 produced more numerous, if not more dangerous, ones than any other comparable span of his life. There were hurts and scars from these experiences, not to mention the energy lost in all the physical upheavals. But there were liberations, too—from an unhappy marriage to a far more gratifying love relationship; from controversies and endless explanations with the powers-that-were in the organizations to which he belonged; and, most significantly, from subordinating his own thinking to the basic guidelines of others, in particular, Freud and Marx.

It would not be accurate to say that Reich deliberately chose opposition, enmity, and crises. But it is true that his views were clearly sharpened by controversy, that he enjoyed defining himself against opposition, and, indeed, that, like Freud, he could find in enmity an index of the subversive, revolutionary thrust of his work. Above all, the repeated crises of his life—and especially those around 1934—helped him to find the strength to stand alone. After many years in various "second homes," he was learning to follow Schiller's dictum: "The strong man is at his most powerful alone" *(Der Starke ist am mächtigsten allein).* He was learning, in his own words, "never to yield to the pressure of wrong public opinion."[8]

One of Reich's principal reasons for moving to Oslo in the fall of 1934 was that Harold Schjelderup, an analyst and professor of psychology at the University of Oslo, had offered him the use of laboratory facilities at the Psychological Research Institute connected with the university. While in Sweden, Schjelderup had begun treatment with Reich; now he wanted to continue, partly in order to learn his technique. Schjelderup was not especially interested in Reich's experimental work; indeed, he later became quite critical of it. It was the kind of trade-off typical for Reich: people wanted therapy from him and to learn about his technique; in return he received diverse help from them.

What Reich had in mind was to investigate whether there were differences in electrical activity of the skin in states of pleasure and anxiety, and, in particular, whether there were differences of the erogenous zones.[9] Once in Oslo, Reich sought the help of an assistant to decide on the appropriate kind of apparatus to test his hypotheses. The apparatus, an oscillograph and an amplifier, which they decided to build, cost around 3,000 Norwegian kroner or about 500 dollars at the time. Reich raised this money through his clinical and teaching activities. From 1927 to 1933, a large part of Reich's earnings from private practice had gone to support his sex-political activities; after 1934, the bulk of his earnings as a therapist—and he earned well, charging around $15 a session in 1934—would be devoted to his experimental work.

Characteristically, Reich proceeded by combining elements from other people's research but at the same time giving them a novel twist. When he reviewed the relatively new field of skin electrophysiology, for example, he found techniques had been developed that might test his hypotheses, but that no one had ever considered using these techniques to study pleasure. The two available quantitative techniques, both discovered about 1890, were those still in use today: skin resistance and skin potential measurements.[10] Most work, in Reich's time as today, used patterns of skin resistance response as an indicator of emotional response. Reich was not interested in this line of research because it could not distinguish between pleasurable and unpleasurable reactions. He was drawn instead to skin potential, because here one was measuring a spontaneous, sustained charge within the body—a charge that showed variations in two directions, negative and positive.[11] He particularly noted previous research that showed an increase in charge (more positive) after delicate touching of the skin. Further, it had been shown that there was often a substantial potential (or charge) between an electrode placed on intact skin and an electrode placed over a scratched or injured site, the latter site reflecting a charge beneath the skin surface toward the "interior" of the body in which Reich was interested.

He seems to have absorbed the available literature rather easily, including the evidence that the sweat glands played a role in at least some of the skin's electrical behavior, moisture being a conductor of electricity. Reich responded characteristically to this evidence by writing that the emphasis on finding a local mechanism (e.g., sweat-gland activity) "errs by confusing the means of fulfilling a function with the function itself." He argued that this reasoning set the local mechanism "apart from the functional unity of the organism as a whole," in other words, the pleasure-anxiety function.

Reich set out to clarify the role of the electrical charging of the skin as "the expression of a unitary function related to the bio-electric totality of the organism." He saw the skin as a "special kind of membrane," with the capacity to hold or give up electrical charge as a function of the "vegetative antithesis" he had already described qualitatively and which he now sought to quantify. He reasoned that the antithesis of "moving toward the world" or "moving away from the world" must also involve two directions in the flow of bio-electric charge. Pleasurable sensation should accompany charging of the periphery (toward the world), while sensations of fear, anxiety, and disgust should parallel a decrease in peripheral charge (toward the interior).

Sophisticated skin potential measurements had only been possible for a few years, since the development of the triode vacuum tube. Reich describes his measurement apparatus in some detail. It was a substantial apparatus for the times, involving the use of a vacuum amplifier tube connected to an oscillograph whose moving light beam was filmed continuously.

His basic approach was to place the "experimental" electrode on an intact skin site, and the "reference" electrode on a site that had been scratched so that the charge beneath the skin surface would be measured. (The same principle is used in traditional research today.) First, he established that in a state of rest, nonerogenous zones have a potential of 10–40 millivolts more negative than the "interior" (injured) site—a finding that was in keeping with the earlier research of others. The potential was relatively steady, varying little over time for any one individual. Next, he studied subjects' erogenous zones —"penis, vaginal mucosa, tongue, inner surface of the lips, anal mucosa, nipple." These zones were found to be much more variable and were capable of a much greater charge, either positive or negative.

The central experiments consisted of attempts to measure potential changes in the erogenous zones during pleasurable or unpleasurable stimulation: tickling (pleasurable) and sudden pressure or sound (unpleasurable). His data showed that

(1) When the subject felt pleasurable streaming sensations, the skin potential increased in a positive direction.

(2) When the subject felt pain, pressure, or any unpleasant sensation or emotion (except for anger), the potential became more negative.

(3) The subjective intensity of the sensation reported by the subject correlated well with the quantitative positive or negative change.

(4)   The same subject responded differently on different occasions in accordance with his or her general mood.

(5)   There was a "disappointment" reaction. After a response to fright, positive changes are much more difficult to obtain. It is as if the organism had become "cautious."

(6)   Reich also noted a "dulling" effect. If the same pleasurable stimulus was given repeatedly, the initial positive tracings flattened out.

These findings depended upon one critical condition: the appropriate subject had to be emotionally healthy enough to feel pleasure, and particularly pleasurable streamings, in his or her body, and to be able to report these sensations accurately. Here we encounter one of the problems of evaluating Reich's research: most subjects are unable to feel or report these sensations reliably, and no other researcher has ever taken such variables into account. Reich found that an erect penis with no pleasure sensations had no increase in positive potential. These observations supported Reich's orgasm theory: mechanical tension (such as erection) had to be followed by energetic charge (more positive potential) before adequate pleasurable discharge and relaxation could take place.

In a "critical control," Reich drove home his assertion that sensation and charge are identical. He had his subjects sit in a separate room from the experimenters, connected to the amplifier by long wires. They would tickle or stimulate themselves according to instructions, and then, based on their *qualitative* sensations and emotions, they predicted the kind of *quantitative* tracing. Their guesses matched the tracings. For example, a subject reported two strong sensations of pleasure while tickling her nipple near the electrode, corresponding with the two sharpest positive deflections of the tracing. Reich could now offer evidence that subjects only showed significant positive potential changes at erogenous zones when they subjectively felt pleasure, and that they did not feel pleasure without an increasing positive potential: the two processes appeared to be identical.

Reich also described some measurements of breathing taken over the abdomen, showing more negative potentials with inspiration and more positive potentials with expiration. He was not surprised when subjects with more inhibited respiration and less capacity to exhale completely showed less positive potential change during expiration than healthier subjects. This supported his clinical belief (to be described in Chapter 18) that inhibited respiration is a central mechanism of a disturbed bio-energetic economy, suppressing the development of bio-energetic impulses from the solar plexus "toward the world."

The measurement in which he was most interested—potential changes during sexual intercourse—proved technically impossible to set up without interfering with the experience because of the problem of electrode placement and stability. Reich had to settle for tracings made during masturbation and measurements of two subjects kissing or caressing.

In his conclusions, Reich emphasized the functional identity of somatic and psychic processes, as expressed in the correspondence of skin potential measurements and subjectively felt sensations and emotions; and the antithetical directions toward the periphery (increased skin charge) and away from the periphery (decreased skin charge), corresponding with pleasure and unpleasure sensations and emotions. Anticipating later work, he asserted that organic diseases might result from disturbances of the bio-electrical equilibrium of the organism. And he moved closer to a unitary theory of biological energy:

> Since only pleasurable vegetative sensations give rise to an increased surface charge . . . we must assume that pleasurable excitation is the specific process of all living organisms. Other biological processes show this also—for example, cell division, in which the cell shows an increase in [electrical] surface charge coinciding with the biologically productive process of mitosis (cell division). Hence the sexual process would simply be the biologically productive energy process. . . . The orgasm formula of tension–charge–discharge–relaxation must represent the *general formula for all biological functions.* [12]

What can we say in evaluation of these experiments? When one shows Reich's methodology and measurements to modern electrophysiologists, they raise a number of technical questions. For one thing, Reich did not always use the kind of firm electrode attachment, with an electrolyte paste interface between electrode and skin to maintain electrical stability, that is accepted procedure today. But this defect does not explain the striking difference between erogenous and nonerogenous zones, nor the consistent correlation of positive charge with pleasure and negative with unpleasure.

Modern researchers also question Reich's way of reporting his results in narrative style and giving selected illustrative examples rather than supplying the details of number of subjects and complete data. However, such an approach was common in the mid-1930s.

The fact is that the unique features of Reich's experimental approach have never been replicated, either by Reich's own students or by traditional researchers. None of his followers has been able to achieve the necessary combination of technical expertise, access to subjects, and sufficient time to make multiple observations with a variety of subjects. Reich himself spent a good part of several years mastering both the technical and clinical problems of achieving consistent results. On the other hand, traditional electrodermal researchers have never approached these phenomena from anything resembling Reich's vantage point. In a 1971 review of studies of sexual arousal, Marvin Zuckerman notes that Reich was the first to study skin potential changes during sexual excitement.[13] It was not until 1968 that others made electrical measurements of erogenous areas. The studies cited by Zuckerman measured primarily skin resistance, with no distinction between positive and negative charge. More basically, no other researcher has ever approached electrodermal functions as Reich did—as aspects of a *unitary pleasure function* in the body.

I could find but one detailed criticism of Reich's bio-electrical research by another scientist, and for this we must return to Reich's stay in Norway. The critique was by Wilhelm Hoffmann, a man well trained in physiology at the Kaiser Wilhelm Institute in Berlin. His critique was reported in newspaper articles about the controversy over Reich's bion research (to be described in the next chapter). Sometime in 1935, Hoffmann collaborated with Reich. He was especially interested in testing Reich's hypothesis that withdrawn schizophrenics would show a lower skin potential than normal persons. He found that the patients' skin potentials were not in fact lower. Nor did Hoffmann find any differences in skin potential between erogenous and nonerogenous zones of the patients.[14]

Reich in turn criticized Hoffmann's procedures. Hoffmann, he said, had used electrodes attached to glass cups that were then fastened over the subjects' nipples with adhesive tape. "From a mechanical viewpoint," Reich commented, "everything was perfect. Hoffmann only overlooked one point and that was the crucial one. A pleasure reaction doesn't occur if one attaches glass with adhesive tape to a living organ."[15]

The controversy between Reich and Hoffmann neatly illustrates a problem inherent in Reich's research and others' response to it. Theoretically there was merit on both sides, paralleling the differences between Reich's and current traditional skin research. Hoffmann argued that Reich's technique did not exclude spurious results, and he altered the technique in a way that matches modern practice. Reich argued that Hoffmann had taken insufficient care not to interfere with the subjects' experience of pleasure, a criticism that would apply equally well to virtually all modern research. And the difficulty was exacerbated by the events that followed, which is also typical of Reich's career. After their initial friendly collaboration, Hoffmann became extremely embittered toward Reich and denounced him as totally unequipped for laboratory work in electrophysiology. He went so far as to suggest that Reich be expelled from Norway as an undesirable immigrant. Reich, in turn, dismissed all of Hoffmann's criticisms as stemming from his irrationally hostile or "mechanistic" attitude.

Given the furor that surrounded Masters and Johnson's work some twenty-five years later, one would have expected considerable criticism of Reich for undertaking laboratory studies of sexuality at all, whether well or badly. There was some criticism along these lines, but its severity was diminished for several reasons. First, by the time Reich published his findings in 1937, they were soon overshadowed by the storm of controversy surrounding his work on the bions, to be discussed next. Second, during the first years of his Norwegian residence, Reich successfully kept a low profile. He had many colleagues and students, but he made no effort, as he had done earlier, to disseminate his work widely among the public. His articles appeared in German in his own journal, which had a small circulation, and he gave few public talks.

But when the storm did erupt late in 1937, the bio-electric experiments were one of the targets. Various rumors circulated in the press, the most pernicious of which was that Reich wanted to use mental patients as subjects in studies of sexual intercourse. A particular kind of condensation was at work here. Reich *did* want to study mental patients and, as noted, Hoffmann carried out some studies with such patients. Reich also wanted to investigate bio-electrical changes during sexual intercourse with normal subjects, but the technical difficulties we have noted precluded this experiment. (There may well have been social obstacles, too. Studies of masturbation and of a nude couple kissing were bold enough steps for the 1930s!)

Hoffmann's experiments and Reich's plan were telescoped into the oft-repeated story that Reich did study, or planned to study, sexual intercourse between mental patients. The conception of Reich's experiments involving "crazy" sex orgies would pursue him to the end of his days, as would the dual criticism that he entered fields where he lacked knowledge and that he failed to design his experiments properly or in replicable form.

The Bions: 1936–1939

The first few years in Norway provided a peaceful period for Reich. Once again he had a lively, talented group of people around him—psychotherapists, social scientists, and writers. He was evolving new techniques in therapy based on muscular armor. He was busy with the bio-electrical experiments in the laboratory. He was working on his manuscript *People in Trouble,* in which he was beginning to chart his work-democratic concepts. And his relationship with Elsa was a relatively happy one.

At this juncture Reich chose to begin research on the bions—vesicles which, Reich asserted, represented transitional stages between nonliving and living substance. This research was to seal the diagnosis of his psychosis for many contemporaries. Until now, Reich had worked in psychoanalysis, sociology, and electrophysiology, all fields devoted to the study of human beings. Still more specifically, his work had centered on human sexuality and its various manifestations, clinically, socially, electrodermally. Even the bio-electric experiments might have been charitably interpreted by his critics as a misguided effort on the part of a zealous amateur who took Freud's "metaphor" of the libido too seriously and tried to measure it.

The bion research, however, was to take Reich outside the human realm —to the study, he was to assert, of the development of pulsating minute particles from nonliving matter, and of the development of protozoa (unicellular microorganisms, the most primitive forms of animal life) from nonliving matter—to the problem, in short, of biogenesis. Reich frankly acknowledged that he was not well trained in this particular domain.[1]

I would like to anticipate, briefly, a question that is bound to surface: Why did Reich choose to tackle a problem for which, according to his own admission, he was not "sufficiently" prepared? And why at a time when he was still engrossed with another problem—the bio-electric experiments—for which he was also insufficiently prepared? Two alternative answers are possible.

The first, offered by many of his critics, was that Reich was in the grip of a megalomanic passion that required ever greater achievements. Since there was no substance to his fooling around in the laboratory, he had to move on from one "discovery" to the next. No slow, careful, fruitful development could issue from any of his fantasies.

The second, offered by Reich and his students, was that he was following the logic of his research. Like Thoreau, but for different ends, Reich wanted "to drive life into a corner and reduce it to its lowest terms." In his therapeutic work, Reich had shifted from an analytic focus on complex psychological processes to his own stress on relatively simple streamings of energy-emotion and their blockage by the character-muscular armor. However, only at times could he directly glimpse these streamings and their culmination in the "orgasm reflex," the goal of his treatment. Microscopic observation of the primitive protozoa was one key path Reich traveled to the discovery of the bions. By studying protozoa he could move much closer to his own domain—the question from medical school days: What is life?—with far fewer extraneous processes than was the case with patients. He could directly observe the streamings of vesicles and reproduction through cell division.

If Reich's path was logical, one can still question its wisdom. There is something brave and foolhardy, effective and self-defeating, about Reich's working in such diverse fields. Brave and effective because if he was on to something in each research realm, he was undoubtedly right that the initial breakthrough was harder than the subsequent details. Foolhardy and self-defeating because others were more likely to join any such effort only if a solid, well-controlled set of studies was available for scrutiny.

Reich would argue the last point by stating that even where he had provided considerable detail (in his clinical studies of orgastic impotence and orgastic potency, for example), few saw fit to collaborate with him on studying the particular issue of involuntary body convulsions during sexual intercourse. Only those aspects of his work that could be subsumed within existing conceptual schemes, his character-analytic and his mass-psychological studies, received wide acclaim.

In order to observe protozoa, Reich went to the Botanical Institute in Oslo to obtain cultures of amoebae, the most common form of protozoa. An assistant at the Institute told him that all he had to do was put blades of grass in water and examine them after ten to fourteen days. Reich reported that he asked the assistant—"at the time naively and without any special reason in mind"—how the protozoa came into the infusion. "From the air, naturally," the assistant replied, with an astonished look at Reich. "And how do they come into the air?" Reich asked further. "That we do not know," the assistant answered.[2]

Reich may have asked his questions "naively" at the particular moment, but the question of the origin of living organisms from nonliving matter was very much on his mind. As we shall see, right around this time he was starting another series of experiments on biogenesis. Reich was always put off by vague explanations that were difficult to test. Finally, the reaction of "astonished" looks to his questions led him to believe that his questions were important.

Reich had recently obtained an excellent Leitz microscope, which he proceeded to use to examine the grass infusion. As he had been told, protozoa did appear after some days. He was able to observe various types of amoebae and paramecia (another form of protozoa). He observed both the place-to-place serpentine movements of the protozoa and the internal plasmatic streaming that had been noted by Ludwig Rhumbler and Max Hartmann.

However, Reich was also interested in the *developmental* processes he noticed at the edge of the grass blade. He was struck by the following phenomenon: If the plant tissue was kept under continuous observation from when it was first put in to soak, the cells at the edge gradually disintegrated into vesicles, which eventually broke off from the main structure and floated freely in the water. (Vesicles are here defined as "small bladders, cavities, sacs, cysts, bubbles or hollow structures.") Often the vesicles would collect together and float around in clumps, initially without any clearly defined borders or membranes.

Reich also described the process in which a clear border or margin developed:

> I observed the change taking place in both the vesicular structure and the formation of a border in *one* object over a period of four hours. An irregularly structured, boundaryless, vesicular object had formed at the margin of a piece of plant. The object gradually swelled and detached itself from the section of plant. Double refracting margins appeared on the edges. The vesicular structure became more regular and homogeneous and the vesicles refracted light with greater contrast. In its structure the object was almost indistinguishable from a passing amoeba. It assumed a long oval shape and became increasingly taut as the margin became more complete and distinct.[3]

In another instance, Reich saw a formation that showed both the vesicular structure and the well-defined margin. It adhered to a stalk on the grass infusion. Occasionally, the cluster of vesicles would try to jerk away, only to be pulled back by the stalk.

Since Reich wanted to observe developments within the grass continuously, he utilized time-lapse photography, a procedure now quite common, but rarely used in the 1930s. He had to solve a series of technical problems, one of them being the requirement of a completely still preparation for the purposes of photography versus the need for oxygen to prevent the dying off of any germinating forms.

One cannot overstress the significance of his continuous observation. Around the middle of the nineteenth century, Louis Pasteur had demonstrated that the kinds of living forms the upholders of spontaneous generation affirmed did not occur when the nonliving matter, the water in which it was immersed, and the surrounding air were all sterilized. Since Pasteur, biologists have been in total agreement that protozoa develop from spores in the air that settle in the grass. Over time, in interaction with the grass infusion, these spores or germ cysts become protozoa. Whether this explanation is valid or whether Reich's conceptual scheme is correct (namely, that the protozoa develop not from spores but from the disintegrating grass infusion alone), the initial point is that no one since Pasteur had carefully described developments within the grass infusion from which protozoa eventually emerged. To quote Reich: "They say nothing about *what takes place* in the grass or moss. They simply state that after a few days the protozoa are 'there.' "[4]

The study of grass infusions revealed various kinds of motility, which he first observed, then photographed. In particular, Reich distinguished four separate types:[5]

ROLLING—Individual vesicles within the clump of particles rolled rhythmically toward and away from each other, as though showing attraction and repulsion.

ROTATION—Circular movements of vesicles within the heap were observed, and if these movements were strong enough, the whole heap including the membrane would rotate. This movement might continue for hours.

CONFLUENCE OF THE ENERGY VESICLES—In many kinds of developing protozoa, the boundaries between the individual vesicles disappeared and the plasma formed a homogeneous mass. In others, the vesicular structure remained until fully developed.

PULSATION—At a magnification of about 3000x, one could see very fine movements of expansion and contraction within individual vesicles in the heap and in the heap as a whole.

He also observed that at the edges of the disintegrating grass, one could find, in addition to "finished" protozoa, every stage in their development and form.

When individual vesicles or particles showed the kinds of spontaneous, inner movement described above, Reich called them "bions," transitional forms between the nonliving and the living. In his view, protozoa developed from the heaps or clusters of bions, which in turn emerged from the disintegrating grass.

Apart from the question of where the "life" of the protozoa originated, Reich's fascination with, his persistent attention to, transitional states between the nonmotile and the motile is evident here once more. The same trait was manifested in his careful attention to the loosening of "nonmobile" rigid character traits, followed by the emergence of the "life" of strong affects; to the loosening of chronic, inflexible muscular spasms, again followed by the emergence of "spontaneous" sensations and emotions; and to the breakdown of fixed social patterns, with the emergence of freer and sometimes also more chaotic ways of life.

There is one technical objection to Reich's microscopic work that should be dealt with immediately. This concerns the very high magnification—up to 4000x—he used. The standard criticism was that clear definition of structure is not possible above a certain power of magnification, around 2000x. However, in many instances Reich was not primarily concerned with the fine details of structure but rather with motility within the vesicles and heaps of vesicles. Although he made this point over and over again, critics still claimed that he did not understand microscopy, since he did not know there was a limit on magnification using light.[6] The electron microscope, devised after the period under discussion, would not have solved Reich's problem. While it permits much higher magnification, it can only be used with stained tissue.

The study of protozoal development in grass infusions was not Reich's only path to the investigation of transitional forms between the nonliving and the living. About the same time as he began his protozoal studies, Reich was curious about the transformation of food into energy. For his first "experiment," he "threw meat, potatoes, vegetables of all kinds, milk and eggs into a pot which he filled with water; he cooked the mixture for half an hour, took a sample and hurried with it to the microscope."[7]

Reich had the wit and distance from himself to note that anyone who observed him playing with food would only have dismissed him as "crazy." But at the same time he makes an argument for exactly that kind of childlike "playing" at the beginning of a research endeavor, comparing it with the great "discoveries" of a young child.[8]

When Reich put his mixture under the microscope, he thought he would be able to distinguish the different foods that comprised the brew. However, the preparation contained nothing but vesicles, of different sizes but the same basic type. More significantly, when he observed the vesicles using higher magnifications (over 2000x), he noted a motility within them, an *inner* expansion and contraction. He believed that these vesicles from foodstuffs were functionally identical with the vesicles observed in the grass infusions. And he called them both bions.

Reich now made infusions of many different types of substances, organic and inorganic. Sometimes he would simply allow the substances to disintegrate in water, sometimes he would heat them. Sometimes the bionous development was slower or faster; but disintegration was never absent, no matter what the original material.

The vesicular heaps of bions showed other lifelike characteristics besides pulsation. They moved about. They ingested unattached vesicles—that is, they appeared to eat. At times they divided into smaller heaps, which expanded as they took up fluid or unattached vesicles, thus simulating reproduction and growth.

Reich's critics would later claim that Reich believed he had "created life." This version suggests that Reich alleged he had developed some kind of artificial life, like Dr. Frankenstein. Reich's position was not that he had created artificial life, but rather that he had succeeded in revealing experimentally the developmental living process that was continually occurring in nature. In geology, this kind of perspective has recently become dominant under the name "uniformitarianism," the theory that "the present is the key to the past, that if you want to understand how a rock is formed you go watch it forming now."[9] For Reich, life was like a rock in this respect: you could go watch it forming now. This orientation contrasts sharply with the orthodox biological notion that life was created once in the far distant past and since then "all life has come from life."

Three explanations have been offered for the presence of motile forms in Reich's preparations—the first two by his critics, the third by Reich himself.

The first is that Reich's preparations were not completely sterile and there had been accidental infection by "spores" or "germs" from the air. What Reich was observing and culturing were known forms of bacteria or protozoal organisms, which came "from outside." Alternatively, his materials contained spores in a dormant state, which were liberated in solution.

To meet this objection, Reich sterilized the substance to be placed in the infusion as well as the solution itself. The result of the sterilization procedure was surprising: not only did the vesicular behavior still occur, but it appeared more rapidly, and gave rise to more vigorous movements.

Moreover, Reich heated coal particles to incandescence (1500°C) before immersing them in solution. It should be noted that classical biology claimed no germs could survive above a temperature of 180°C. Still, Reich was able to observe mobile forms from the coal particles immediately after their sterilization.

Reich's final answer to the argument of air-germ infection was a series of control experiments devised by an associate, Roger du Teil, who set up a hermetically sealed system. This, too, had no effect on the development of the bions.[10]

The second interpretation was that the movements Reich observed were not biological at all but physico-chemical. Physics was familiar with the fact that small particles oscillate slightly, due to the phenomenon known as Brownian movement, believed to be caused by the bombardment of the particles with molecules.

Reich gave several answers to this interpretation. Brown was concerned with the place-to-place movement of particles. Brownian movement could not explain the *inner* motility, the pulsation of the bions, which Reich emphasized.

Moreover, particles of coke or earth had other life properties besides movement, such as ingestion of particles and division, which Brownian movement was obviously unable to account for.

Reich's own interpretation was that the preparations contained forms with some life properties. Some kind of transitional organization between the nonliving and the living had been discovered. Reich had succeeded in the laboratory in reproducing some of the conditions for the "natural organization" of living forms from nonliving matter.

Reich's bion research yielded in turn the first inkling of a new form of energy —an energy he was later to name "orgone energy." Briefly, the initial path was as follows:

In some of his preparations, Reich noted two kinds of bions: the more common, packet-shaped, blue amoeboid vesicles, and much smaller, lancet-shaped red forms. Reich termed the first type "PA-bions," and the smaller type "T-bacilli," for reasons that will be described in connection with his work on cancer (in Chapter 22).

He soon discovered that the two types had an antithetical effect on each other. The PA-bions immobilized the T-bacilli. In his own words: "T-bacilli which are in the neighborhood of the blue bions show a restless activity, they turn round and round, then remain, with trembling movements, in one and the same spot and finally become immobile. As time goes on, more and more T-bacilli conglomerate around the blue bions; they agglutinate. The 'dead' T-bacilli seem to attract and kill the still living ones."[11]

Reich here made several observations, the full significance of which would only become apparent later:

The blue color of the PA-bions would be found to be characteristic of many orgone energy phenomena.

In his observation of the PA-bions, Reich was noting an *action at a distance.* Some force within the PA-bions was not simply providing the source of inner motility but was affecting another organism. He noticed the same effect even more dramatically in a laboratory accident.

In January 1939, one of his assistants took the wrong container from the sterilizer and, instead of earth, heated ocean sand. After two days there was a growth in the solution which, inoculated on egg medium and agar, resulted in a yellow growth. This new kind of culture consisted microscopically of large, slightly mobile, blue vesicles. Examination at 2000–4000x showed forms that refracted light strongly and consisted of heaps of six to ten vesicles. It appeared that the effect of these bions—which Reich called "SAPA-bions"—on bacteria in general and T-bacilli in particular was much stronger than that of other bions.

In the course of studying these bions, Reich's eyes began to hurt when he looked into the microscope for a long time. As a control experiment, he used a monocular tube; he noticed that, regularly, only the eye with which he looked at these cultures began to hurt. Finally, he developed a violent conjunctivitis and the ophthalmologist prohibited microscopic work for a few weeks. His eyes improved, but now Reich more definitely suspected the existence of a radiation.

Reich proceeded to test the sand culture for radiation by holding the test tubes of SAPA-bions against his palm. Each time he thought he felt a fine prickling, but he was not sure of the sensation. To test the objectivity of the phenomenon, he placed a quartz slide on his skin, put some SAPA-cultures on the slide, and left the preparation there for about ten minutes. On the spot where the culture had been (separated from the skin by the slide), an anemic spot with a red margin developed.

Reich was also surprised by certain visual phenomena observable in a dark basement room where the SAPA-bions were kept. When he tried to study these phenomena more carefully, he noted:

> The . . . observations in the dark were somehow 'weird.' After the eyes had become adapted to the darkness, the room did not appear black, but *grey-blue*. There were fog-like formations and bluish dots and lines of light. Violet light phenomena seemed to emanate from the walls as well as from various objects in the room. When I held a magnifying glass before my eyes, these light impressions, all of them blue or grey-blue, *became more intense, the individual lines and dots became larger. . . .* When I closed my eyes, the blue light impressions continued, nonetheless.[12]

By 1939, the bion research was becoming expensive. With funds from his own earnings together with gifts from students, colleagues, and friends, Reich managed to raise about $9,000 to pay for a good microscope, microfilm equipment, and other laboratory instruments he needed. In addition, Reich and his associates raised about $300 weekly to pay for his laboratory assistants.

David Boadella has written that "it says much for the loyalty of the group that had formed around him, and of his friends and even patients that those who could help with donations responded magnificently."[13] Unfortunately, matters were more complicated than that. Most of the people who helped Reich were in therapy with him and, often, in a kind of "training analysis" in order to learn his technique. With justification, Otto Fenichel has criticized Reich for abusing the transference situation—the patient's dependence upon and devotion to his therapist—by getting such people to help him through working or giving money or both. The fact that many were also students, eager for his stamp of approval, for referrals from him, heightened this situation. Often when for one reason or another they became disappointed in Reich, and when he was under attack from more scientifically trained professionals, they could regret their earlier enthusiasm. Sometimes they would ask for their money back, which led to ugly scenes. Reich's reminder that he had expressly warned them before they gave money or other help seems somewhat self-serving in the face of the blinding power of transference. The rage Reich felt toward those who went back on their original loyalty was the kind of rage one may feel when one also has guilt feelings.

Reich faced a predicament. He had appealed to the Rockefeller Foundation in Paris to support the bion project, but his request was turned down. Ever since his medical school days, Reich had been convinced that his life and work were a heroic mission and that they therefore "deserved" support. Given the world's opposition, he could not afford to be fastidious about where that help came from. Once when he was analyzing certain dishonest mechanisms in a patient who was also working for him, he said: "I can see the scoundrel in you because there is a scoundrel in me. I recognized that many of your motives for working had nothing to do with the work itself but stemmed from a desire to please me. And still I used you because I needed your help."[14]

A further complication of this period—and one that was to continue through the rest of Reich's life—was that most of his colleagues were trained in medicine, clinical psychology, literature, sociology, or philosophy. To my knowledge, not one was a trained natural scientist. Nor were they able or willing to make the long investment to become one. Among his close associates in Oslo were Odd Havrevold, a psychiatrist; Ola Raknes, who had received his Ph.D. in linguistics and then trained as a psychoanalyst in the early 1930s; Harold Schjelderup, who was academically the most prominent of Reich's associates but still not a trained scientist; and Nic Hoel, the psychiatrist whose husband Sigurd, the well-known novelist, served as editor of Reich's *Journal.*

These people took a variety of stances toward Reich's experimental work. Schjelderup, who was skeptical even of his sociological endeavors, was distinctly cool, claiming that he lacked the competence to judge the experiments but was nonetheless dubious. Indeed, when the public attacks started against the bion research, Schjelderup severed Reich's connection with the Psychological Institute because it had become an embarrassment to him.[15] At the time, Nic Hoel criticized the attitude of those who waited for the verdict of others as intellectual laziness and cowardice. Later she, too, withdrew her support from Reich's experimental work, arguing that before she could intelligently respond to it, she would have to undergo a completely new training in physics and biology; after seven years of training in medicine, seven in psychiatry, and four in child psychiatry, she was not prepared for a whole new education.[16] Only Raknes felt prepared to defend Reich's work quite fully, in Norway as later in America, on the basis of his own laboratory observations and the theoretical persuasiveness of Reich's approach.

One supporter of Reich during this period not at all involved in therapy was Roger du Teil, whom Reich had met on a visit to France in February 1936. At the time, du Teil was a professor of philosophy at the Centre Universitaire Méditerranée in Nice. A man of broad interests and great personal charm, he had published a book of poetry as well as psychological and philosophical works. Du Teil had a theoretical interest in problems of biogenesis but apparently had done no experimental work prior to his association with Reich. Reich attended one of du Teil's lectures and saw in him a potential supporter, one well situated in French intellectual circles.

For his part, du Teil was interested in Reich, "whom I knew by name for he had written a book, *Character Analysis,* which immediately interested me since my research in psychoanalysis was along the same lines." Du Teil describes how, "After a long conversation which continued late into the night, Reich asked me if I would be willing to control his experiments . . . on biogenesis. . . . He was near forty then, and I fifty-one, which explains his request. . . . To him I was an influential person. He counted on me to make his discoveries 'official,' so to speak, and get them accepted in high scientific circles."[17]

When Reich returned to Oslo, he sent some bion specimens to du Teil. During the summer of 1937, du Teil came to work with Reich in the laboratory in Oslo. "Upon my return to France I carried out some other experiments on the same subject [bions] not without first having conceived and devised an adequate apparatus for the purpose of avoiding all possible contamination from air germs."

One of the criticisms later directed against Reich's work was that du Teil was no more a scientist than he was. In response, du Teil declared that it was "unnecessary to be a director of research or a Nobel Prize winner to know how to work correctly and under sterile conditions in a laboratory." In any case Reich valued du Teil's work, and, in an unusual gesture, included his report on several bion experiments in his new book *Die Bione (The Bion),* which was published by his Sexpol Verlag in 1938.

Du Teil's role became somewhat problematic, however, when he began to speak of the discovery of the bions as a joint achievement. Reich had no intention of sharing the discovery with anyone. Whatever his annoyance with du Teil, it never affected the respect he felt for the man. And du Teil never questioned the originality and value of Reich's work on the bions, although he did not entirely agree that bions represented living forms. In 1973, when du Teil was eighty-seven, he still wrote of Reich with affection and respect, if also with the somewhat patronizing tone of an older man assessing an extremely gifted but impulsive younger colleague.[18]

In 1936, du Teil was also responsible for initiating contact between Reich and the Académie des Sciences in Paris. Reich sent the Academy a preparation of charcoal bions. In January 1938, Louis Lapicque of the Academy sent a reply:

> Dear Dr. Reich:
> Charged by the Academy to study your communication of January 8, 1937, I waited for the film which you wrote you were going to send. When it did not come I examined microscopically the prepara-

tions you sent with your first report. I have, indeed, found the lifelike movements which you describe. There is something surprising here, in view of the long time that has elapsed since the preparations were made.

I would like to suggest to the Academy a brief publication of your findings, followed by a short note by myself confirming the facts and containing a physico-chemical interpretation for which I alone would be responsible. Leaving aside your electrical theory which has nothing to do with the experiment, would it be agreeable for you to have your communication published simply in the form of the enclosed extract, which, in fact, is a summary of the important part? It seems to me that in this way your wish to see your findings published in our *Bulletin* would be satisfied.[19]

Reich characteristically refused consent to publication under the conditions proposed by Lapicque. If he was willing to accept help for dubious motivations, he was unwilling to take support wherever strings were attached. Although he badly needed even the partial confirmation of an august body like the French Academy, he would not make a bargain that vitiated what he believed to be the most significant part of his findings.

Whatever professional support Reich received was as nothing compared to the avalanche of attacks his experiments evoked publicly. The criticisms were precipitated by a preliminary report on the bion experiments in Reich's *Journal* in the summer of 1937. On September 22, the Norwegian newspaper *Aftenposten* published a brief summary of the article, followed by comments from a Norwegian biologist, Klaus Hansen. Hansen took a cautious, let's-wait-for-the-full-report position, but offered the opinion that it was extremely unlikely that Reich had succeeded in developing living substance. He further opined that Reich had confused life signs with Brownian movement.

Hansen's comment about Brownian movement was typical of the frustrating quality of the dialogue between Reich and his critics. Reich would present a finding with a given interpretation (particles or bions with an inner pulsation), and the critics would then make another interpretation (Brownian, place-to-place movement) rendering the initial finding totally insignificant. Reich would reply along lines already discussed, but the critics would ignore the answer or repeat the original criticism, attributing stupidity or grandiosity to Reich for failing to have understood them the first time.

The newspaper criticism might have stopped with Hansen's relatively cautious remarks. However, right around that time Reich sought the assistance of Leiv Kreyberg, Norway's foremost cancer specialist, since Reich had come to believe that his bion research might be relevant to the cancer problem. Kreyberg and Reich had met in 1936. They shared an interest in photomicrographs; Kreyberg, who never had anything else good to say about Reich, commented that Reich's film equipment and technique were excellent.[20]

Reich spent two hours in the fall of 1937 showing Kreyberg various bion demonstrations. Kreyberg took a sample home, studied the specimen, and identified the forms as simple bacteria resulting from air infection. Nonetheless, Reich and Havrevold continued to seek further research materials from Kreyberg. According to Kreyberg, he met the two men in the hospital where he worked in order to test Reich's expertise to see if some kind of collaboration was possible. Again according to Kreyberg, Reich failed the test, being ignorant of basic bacteriological and anatomical facts.[21]

Reich's version of the same meeting is that he refused to permit Kreyberg to test him. Indeed, Reich claimed that when Kreyberg had visited his laboratory, the famous cancer specialist had not recognized live cancer cells under high magnification.[22] Thus an opportunity for a scientific exchange degenerated into mere name-calling.

A similar kind of encounter occurred between Reich and Professor Thjötta, a well-known Norwegian biologist. Reich had sent a preparation to the Oslo Bacteriological Institute where Thjötta worked, with a request for an identification of certain forms. Thjötta used the occasion to issue a statement that he had controlled Reich's experiments and that Reich had again discovered nothing more than bacteria resulting from air infection.[23]

The fact that Reich had turned to Kreyberg and Thjötta undoubtedly gave them—along with their acknowledged scientific prestige—a kind of authority over his work in the eyes of the press and the public. Their opinions were published in the *Aftenposten* on April 19 and 21, 1938, some six months after the first criticism by Hansen. Kreyberg's tone was especially cutting, referring throughout to "Mr. Reich" and claiming that "Mr. Reich" knew less anatomy and bacteriology than a first-year medical student. When Reich and his supporters requested that detailed control studies be done, Kreyberg replied that Reich's research did not merit such expense. He had already seen enough to render a negative opinion of the studies themselves and of Reich's competence as a scientist.

In response to the reports of Kreyberg and Thjötta, Reich issued a statement on April 27, contending that his opponents had not conducted "an extensive and accurate control of my experiments. It would be advantageous if there could be an end to the futile discussions, interpretations and comparisons which have appeared in the press lately."[24]

Reich suggested that independent experts should carry out control studies —studies that would require two to three hours of daily work for two to three weeks. Reich set two further conditions: his set of instruments must be used, and "I myself must be in charge of the experiments."

Here Reich went to extremes as much as his critics. They had quickly explained away his findings and refused to replicate his experimental procedures. He in turn was asking for a degree of control over replications of his work that was quite beyond any accepted scientific procedure. Replications of original experiments have to follow the original protocol, no matter how laborious or complex that protocol may be. But the very idea of independent verification of a finding precludes the original experimenter's being "in charge of" the control studies. Reich's proposal was never taken up. Essentially, his critics did not deem his studies worth the effort of repeating.

Had Reich's experiments been the only target of his opponents' wrath, the newspaper uproar might have waned after the critiques of Kreyberg and Thjötta. However, his experimental work was but the most ludicrous part of his endeavors; many other delectable items remained for public perusal. Indeed, even before the interviews with Kreyberg and Thjötta, Ingjald Nissen, an Adlerian psychologist who some years earlier had praised Reich's character-analytic work, now declared in the Norwegian daily, *Arbeiderbladet,* for December 28, 1937: "Psychoanalysis in this country has become sort of a weedy garden, where all kinds of parasites and climbers strike root and almost choke what is of value." He complained about the quackery of "psychoanalytic sectarians" who "do not even call themselves psychoanalysts any longer," and who practice "some sort of quasi-medicinal relaxation analysis" which "only leads to sexual relations." Nissen felt that something should be done about the situation. He suggested that Norwegian physicians and recognized psychologists should band together to decide who should be allowed to practice psychoanalysis.

An ominous note had entered the controversy. One was no longer dealing with alternative explanations for the movement of minute particles, something beyond the ken of the average reader, but with psychiatric "quackery" that led to "sexual relations." The debate was beginning to involve Reich's professional practice. Nissen was correct that Reich no longer called himself a psychoanalyst. Later, I shall detail Reich's therapeutic developments during these years; suffice it here to say his technique involved more direct work on the muscular armor. He was now seeing patients clad in shorts (men) or bra and shorts (women) so that he could observe fluctuations in body movement, expressions, and temperature more closely. Semi-nude patients, bio-electric experiments with a naked couple kissing, pulsating vesicles—it was a volatile mixture indeed for the popular press and for the quiet city of Oslo.

The person who channeled the diverse criticism into a barrage of newspaper articles during the spring and summer of 1938 was Johann Scharffenberg, M.D. Scharffenberg, then in his seventies, was the grand old man of Norwegian psychiatry. He had little sympathy for psychoanalysis of any kind and held moralistic views on sexual matters, although politically he was no reactionary.

Whatever his reasons, Scharffenberg was relentless toward Reich. He used every argument, fair or foul, he could find. These included that Reich's experiments were nonsense; that Reich might never have received an M.D. degree; that Reich wished to arrange sexual intercourse between mental patients for experimental purposes; that his psychiatric treatment aroused lascivious excitement; that his "sex propaganda among the young should be investigated," for if the young followed his teaching, "they would very soon end up in conflict with the Norwegian Criminal Code"; and that Reich was violating the conditions of his Norwegian visa by treating patients rather than simply limiting himself to teaching and research.[25]

Only the last point needs any elaboration at this stage. Scharffenberg based his accusation on a case history Reich published about an "alcoholic engineer." Reich's adherents replied that Scharffenberg must be unaware of the policy of disguising case histories, and that in fact all of Reich's "patients" were professional persons who were also undergoing training with him. This last argument was somewhat stretched to include the writer Sigurd Hoel, whose therapy undoubtedly contributed to his editing Reich's *Journal,* but who was not in fact being trained as a therapist.

Another related point was made by Wilhelm Hoffmann, the replicator in 1935 of the bio-electrical experiments but now one of Reich's bitterest opponents. Hoffmann wrote, correctly, that "Mr. Reich" had not taken any examinations in Norway to practice medicine, a requirement made of émigrés. Reich had by-passed this regulation on the grounds that he was not practicing medicine but engaging solely in teaching and research.[26]

By February 1938, Reich's visa had expired and the authorities were confronted with his request for an extension. The opposition, led by Scharffenberg and Kreyberg, argued vehemently against any extension. As Kreyberg put it:

> If it is a question of handing Dr. Reich over to the Gestapo, then I will fight that, but if one could get rid of him in a decent manner, that would be the best. More than one million miserable refugees are knocking at our door and there is reason for us to show mercy. It seems sad to me, however, that a man of Dr. Reich's nature is admitted. . . . Dr. Reich's visa is a blow to those of us who would like to see a more open door policy to refugees. It is people like him who have partly created the refugee problem . . . by their irresponsibility.[27]

Reich's supporters received equal space in the Norwegian press. Their defense and their appeal for an extension of his visa varied depending upon the individual, ranging from Nic Hoel's and Ola Raknes's spirited rejoinders to all the criticisms to Schjelderup's more qualified position. Most dubious now about Reich's experimental work, Schjelderup nonetheless believed the visa should be extended because of Reich's past and present contributions to psychotherapy:

> There can hardly be any doubt that Reich has provided such rewarding methodological contributions, and, with them, such significant new clinical experiences that his work must be regarded as pioneering. . . . I recommend a visa and work permit for Reich in Norway because of his merits in the field of character analysis. . . . It is all wrong that

the "bion" affair . . . has become a central matter in the visa question. . . . Dr. Reich's strength lies in his intuition which has made it possible for him to make a number of important empirical discoveries and to provide *directions* of the greatest significance to other researchers.[28]

Sigurd Hoel provided a satirical defense. He viewed the criticism of Reich's experimental work as a side issue, but also saw the public's position: "We, the big public . . . think it real fun when scientists attack one another and divest each other of honor and dignity. Moreover, this Reich seems to be a highly dubious person, and it is a good thing that we have people like Scharffenberg . . . who can put down this slim customer."

Then Hoel went on to add that there were a "few very odd things about the controversy. All of a sudden it is claimed that Dr. Reich must be expelled from the country. When did it become a crime to perform some biological experiments, even if they should prove to be amateurish? When did it become a reason for deportation that one looked in a microscope when one was not a trained biologist?" Hoel argued that the real reason for the intense outcry was not Reich's experiments but his revolutionary work on human sexuality. After all, psychoanalysis had met the same kind of opposition Reich was now encountering.[29]

In addition to his Norwegian colleagues, Reich received professional support from two persons outside the country who had independent reputations. The first was Bronislaw Malinowski, whose work Reich had drawn on so heavily a few years earlier. Malinowski wrote to the Norwegian press on March 12, 1938:

> Both through the works he [Reich] has published and through personal meetings he has impressed me as an original and sound thinker, a true personality, and a man with an open character and courageous views. I consider his sociological works to be a distinct and valuable contribution toward science. In my opinion it would be a very great loss if Dr. Reich should in any way be prevented from obtaining a full opportunity to work out his ideas and scientific discoveries.
>
> . . . My statement is perhaps further strengthened by the fact that it comes from a man who does not share Dr. Reich's radical opinions, nor his sympathies with Marxist philosophy. I usually consider myself to be an old-fashioned, almost conservative liberal.[30]

The second foreign supporter was A. S. Neill, founder and director of the pioneering progressive school Summerhill in England. Neill had independently evolved and practiced at Summerhill many of the same principles of self-regulation Reich had elucidated. Neill's controversial books had made Summerhill known throughout the world. In 1936, Reich attended a lecture Neill gave in Oslo. Neill, who had just read *The Mass Psychology of Fascism* with considerable excitement, later phoned Reich, who invited the educator to dinner. In Neill's words about that first encounter: "We sat till far into the morning. If I remember aright his English was just as bad as my German, so that he spoke his language and I mine. On departing I said, 'Reich, you are the man I've been looking for for years, the man who joins up the somatic with the psychological. Can I come to you as a student?' "[31] Reich agreed, and Neill, fourteen years Reich's senior, became not only Reich's patient over the next two years but also his good friend until Reich's death.

On June 25, Neill published a letter in the Norwegian press:

> To me the campaign against Reich seems largely ignorant and uncivilized, more like fascism than democracy. . . . The question is not: Is Reich a bad person, a scoundrel destroying morale? The question is: Is Reich a useful person who is bringing new knowledge to the world? For my part I feel that he is, and I say so as a Scotsman, who would not waste time travelling to Oslo [to see Reich] if I did not know that I would get my money's worth.[32]

The "Reich affair" put the Norwegian visa authorities on the spot. On the one hand, such leading scientific personages as Kreyberg, Thjötta, and Scharffenberg had denounced him and argued against any extension. In addition, Reich was working at least on the border of medical practice without proper certification. The opinion of the university's Faculty of Medicine had been sought regarding Reich's residence permit. A committee limited itself to stating that his continued presence in Norway was not essential in terms of his medical contribution.[33]

On the other hand, Reich was defended by a number of prominent persons, including reputable psychiatrists and psychologists who insisted on Reich's significance as a psychoanalytic pioneer, a well-documented fact. The whole affair had taken on a "civil liberties" dimension—and Norway prided itself on its intellectual tolerance. Only a year or so earlier the authorities had violated this tradition when, under Soviet pressure, they had expelled Trotsky.* They wanted no repetition of the protests connected with that decision.

A compromise was found. Reich was permitted to stay, but suddenly a royal decree went into effect that anybody who practiced psychoanalysis or psychotherapy had to have a special government license. (Current Norwegian therapists are still bedeviled by this monarchic requirement.) It was generally understood that such a license would be refused to Reich.

Reich took the position that his psychiatric work had advanced to the

---

*Reich and Trotsky met briefly while the latter was still in Oslo, but I do not know any details of this meeting.

point where it could no longer be considered psychoanalysis or psychotherapy. Hence he never requested a license and the authorities had no chance to refuse him one. Nor did the authorities act against his continuing to carry out therapy because by early 1939 Reich had decided to emigrate to the United States. He felt that the constant publicity combined with the continuing practical difficulties made Norway no longer the hospitable environment it had been until late in 1937.

I have given only a scant picture of how bitter the press campaign in Norway became. Between September 1937 and the fall of 1938, over a hundred articles denouncing Reich appeared in the leading Oslo newspapers. His supporters got their share of space, but they were usually on the defensive, responding to one or another charge of the critics. Moreover, with a few exceptions his supporters came from *avant-garde* circles. The weight of established scientific opinion ran against Reich.

Throughout the outcry Reich himself issued only one public statement, the request for a commission to replicate his experiments. He continued working productively throughout the period. But the pressures markedly affected his personality and his relationships with Elsa and colleagues. He felt enraged and humiliated by the notoriety he had acquired; he was no longer comfortable in public. As I have suggested, he saw in such onslaughts one kind of index of the power of his work. But they also shook his self-confidence and reinforced his sense, acquired from the childhood tragedies, of being a "marked man."

If Reich refrained from denouncing his opponents in public, he did not remain quiet in private. To the growing roll of his enemies were now added the "Scharffenbergs, Kreybergs, and Hoffmanns," whom he would bitterly denounce as late as the 1950s. In quieter moments he might recall their activities, shake his head slowly, and remark: "What a way to go into the history books—as my enemies!"

Psychiatric Developments: 1934–1939

When Reich presented his paper on "Psychic Contact and Vegetative Current" at the 1934 Lucerne Congress, he focused, as we have seen, on various somatic manifestations in his patients. Thus, in one patient he noted the phenomenon of "penis anesthesia," the experience of tactile but not pleasurable sensations when the penis was touched.

During the Norwegian years, Reich's observations of and direct work with the patient's body increased markedly. His clinical work had been taking him in that direction since at least 1930. Now his bio-electrical experiments focused on the flow of electricity as well as body fluids in pleasure and anxiety. In addition, his highly sensuous relationship with Elsa, their shared common interest in bodily expression and movement heightened his sensitivity to variations in emotional changes as they manifested themselves in differing color, temperature, and expression. Finally, he felt freer to break two strong psychoanalytic taboos—the taboo against touching the patient and the taboo against seeing the patient undressed.

According to analytic theory, the patient should not be touched because touch provided gratification. The point of analysis was to establish and analyze the transference neurosis—the repetition of old loves and hates for significant persons in the past, especially the patient's parents. The analyst was to be neutral, a "blank screen," to which the patient could "transfer" the complex relationship he or she experienced with parents. Touching would violate the principle of analytic neutrality.

The taboo against the patient being undressed had a similar basis. The nudity or semi-nudity of the patient would heighten the erotic meanings of the present analytic situation, thereby confusing the working through of the past with all its unconscious infantile sexual conflicts. Freud had worked hard to separate psychoanalysis from the usual medical procedures, procedures of examining and treating patients who, indeed, were often undressed for better observation and palpation.

Finally, apart from any theoretical concerns, psychoanalysts had reason to be upset by any touching of the patient or seeing him or her in the nude. For long they had defended themselves against the accusation that they advocated a wild acting out of sexuality, inside or outside the analytic situation. It had taken concerted efforts to convince professional and public opinion that their goal was to analyze sexual conflicts, not conduct or condone orgies.

Reich moved slowly in breaking away from these rules. In the early years of his focus on the body, he limited himself largely to commenting on various muscular spasms. Then gradually, in the late 1930s, he began making more intensive use of touch to attack the body armor directly and elicit emotions bound up in muscular spasms. He would press hard with his thumb or the palm of his hand on a particular segment of body armor, the jaw, neck, chest, back, or thigh. Such pressure often stimulated an outburst of crying or rage. His kind of touch should not be confused with any massage technique. It was generally directed toward the release of emotion but was itself usually affectively neutral and somewhat medical. I would note here that in devising the method of psychoanalysis, Freud had sharply moved away from his earlier use of hypnosis, which at times included massage of the patient. This "laying on of hands" had unsavory connections with the methods of Franz Mesmer, an eighteenth-century physician and therapeutic innovator whose techniques were criticized for, among other dangers, arousing female patients sexually. In my view, it was a remnant of Reich's psychoanalytic superego and reflected his fear of association with pornography that he only occasionally used physical contact in a supportive, comforting way. In the 1940s, Alexander Lowen, then a young therapist in training with Reich, mentioned that he had inadvertently left his hand resting on the patient's back, and the patient had commented on how good it felt. Reich reflected, then commented without committing himself: "The analysts would call that seductive."[1]

Reich also moved gradually and incompletely with regard to the patient's nudity during therapy. He saw Raknes in shorts and nude by 1938.[2] He always saw female patients clothed in bra and panties. Reich drew some lines out of social concern: rumors were rife that he was seducing his female patients.

Touching the patient and seeing the patient either in the nude or semi-nude remain two of the most controversial aspects of Reichian technique, especially in established circles. The focus on touching and nudity has tended to obscure Reich's central therapeutic endeavor: the dissolution of characterological and muscular rigidities, the eliciting of strong emotions and energy "streamings," the working through of the anxiety connected with pleasurable sensations, and the establishment of orgastic potency. Reich summarized his therapeutic advances of the mid-1930s in a monograph entitled *Orgasmus-reflex, Muskelhaltung, und Körperausdruck (Orgasm Reflex, Muscular Attitude, and Bodily Expression)*, which was published in 1937.[3] One of his new and important emphases was on respiration:

> The respiratory disturbances in neurotics are the result of abdominal tensions. . . .
> What is the function of this attitude of shallow respiration? If we look at the position of the inner organs and their relation to the solar plexus, we see immediately what we are dealing with. In fright, one involuntarily breathes in; as for instance in drowning, where this very inspiration leads to death; the diaphragm contracts and compresses the solar plexus from above. A full understanding of this muscular action is provided by the results of the character-analytic investigation of early infantile mechanisms. Children fight lasting and painful anxiety states, which are accompanied by typical sensations in the belly by holding their breath. They do the same thing when they have pleasurable sensations in the abdomen or in the genitals and are afraid of them.[4]

Respiration came to play a role in Reich's therapy, which he now termed "character-analytic vegetotherapy,"* comparable to the role of free association in psychoanalysis. In psychoanalysis, one is told to "say everything that comes into one's mind," with the analyst pointing out the ways that one "resists" this "fundamental rule." Correspondingly, in Reich's therapy, the patient is asked to lie down and to breathe. Then attention is called to a variety of ways in which he or she "resists" natural inspiration and expiration. He may be told that he breathes in fully, but lets little air out; or that the chest does not move; or that he huffs and puffs unnaturally.

When the patient's breathing was shallow or forced, Reich would make use of touch to stimulate an emotional flow and, with it, fuller respiration. After deep sobbing, especially, the patient would breathe more freely. During the Norwegian period, the patient was also urged to talk a good deal about

---

*The "character-analytic" part of this term denotes the continuity of Reich's evolving treatment with psychoanalysis and his contributions to it. "Vegetotherapy" stems from "vegetative nervous system," a commonly used term for the "autonomic nervous system." As we saw in Chapter 16, Reich was ever more impressed with the role of sympathetic innervation in neuroses and the importance of parasympathetic activation during therapy. Overall, the term "vegetotherapeutic" reflected his increasing interest in the *bodily* expression of emotions and energetic changes in the patient. In America, however, he abandoned the term because of its unfortunate associations with "vegetables" and "vegetate."

his current problems, his feelings toward Reich, and his childhood experiences. Just as Reich had always noted whether the patient spoke with appropriate emotion, now he noted, too, changes in respiration with particular topics.

While Reich was dealing with blocked respiration, he was noting—and helping the patient to experience—a variety of other distorted emotional expressions. Thus in his 1937 monograph, Reich mentioned a female patient whose face had a striking expression of "indifference." Reich called this expression to her attention; the patient experienced it more keenly and connected it with other aspects of her personality. Then another expression in the lower part of her face emerged. "It became clear that the mouth and chin were 'angry' while the eyes and forehead were 'dead.' "[5] With attention called to the mouth and chin, the patient developed strong impulses to bite—impulses she once felt toward her father and now felt toward her husband. After expressing the biting impulses, the mouth and chin softened and the patient experienced a flow of sensation through her body. However, genital excitation was still inhibited.

Reich noted that, with the increase of sensation, the expression in her eyes changed from one of indifference to an angry, critical gaze. In their investigation, Reich and the patient detected that her eyes and forehead "watched closely what the genital was doing." Moreover, exploration of the patient's past yielded the finding that

> the severe expression of eyes and forehead derived from an identification with her father who was a very ascetic person. . . . He had again and again impressed on her the danger of giving in to sexual desires. Thus, the attitude of the forehead had taken the place of the father in guarding against sexual temptation. . . . To the same extent to which the "dead" expression was replaced by the "critical" expression, the defense against genitality became accentuated. . . . With the final disappearance of the critical attitude of the forehead and its replacement by the cheerful attitude, the inhibition of genital excitation disappeared also.[6]

Reich's vignette provides a good example of the interweaving of his observations of the patient's bodily expression, her characterological attitudes, and her early history. Yet it was a great oversimplification of what happened in the typical course of therapy.

What has this to do with respiration, the starting point of Reich's therapy? The connection is in fact straightforward: the release of blocked feeling, through the expression of rage or sorrow, was usually accompanied by freer, fuller, easier breathing. Reich would carefully note ways the patient would "shut down" a particular feeling, both mentally, by being ashamed of sobbing, considering it self-indulgent; and physically, by constricting the throat, tightening the mouth and chin, raising the chest and—above all—by stopping full exhalation. (He once described deep sobbing as the "great softener" of the whole musculature.)

During the 1930s, Reich developed a keen eye for the ways the muscular armor was expressed in different segments of the body—how it looked to the observer, how it was subjectively experienced, the signs of its incipient dissolution, and the anxieties that accompanied freer feeling, particularly genital excitation, when the armor was more fully dissolved. Thus, the forehead might *look* tense, with eyebrows raised and a haughty expression of the eyes; the patient might *feel* a "band around the forehead" or complain of headaches. Patients might have a masklike expression around the mouth, chin, and neck; or their voice might be low, monotonous, "thin." "One only has to imagine that one is trying to suppress an impulse to cry; one will find that the muscles of the floor of the mouth become very tense, the muscles of the whole head become tense, the chin is pushed forward and the mouth becomes small."[7]

Characteristic expressions of other "armor segments" are a tight, forward-jutting chest, especially pronounced in the "he man"; a hunch of the shoulders, as though one is perpetually carrying a big burden; contracting the diaphragm with a resultant feeling of "pressure" or a "tight band" just above the stomach; an arched back with a retracted pelvis and a protrusion of the upper abdomen and chest; and a dead, heavy, lifeless expression in the legs.

From the very beginning of his work on bodily expression, Reich focused on starting the armor dissolution farthest from the genitals. Characteristically, he would begin with facial expressions, the expressions which strike the observer first and which the patient is more likely to be aware of than other armor segments.

Reich's vegetotherapeutic work during the 1930s influenced his thinking about the goal of treatment. In the broadest sense, the goal remained the same —the establishment of orgastic potency. However, direct work on the body permitted Reich to see a kind of miniature model of orgastic potency within the therapeutic session. If the therapist worked correctly, he could observe, after the dissolution of the armor segments, that not only was the respiration felt all through the body, with sensations of pleasure following expiration, but a wave of spontaneous, involuntary movements went through the body from the throat downward and upward. If the patient lay on his back with his knees raised to an angle of about forty-five degrees, breathing deeply and freely, his head would tilt slightly backward, his shoulders slightly forward, the chest and the belly would sink and the pelvis raise itself slightly from the couch, all these movements accompanying the exhalation in one wave.

In one of the first patients whom Reich treated with his new armor-dissolving technique, the spontaneous movements became quite reflex-like and so strong that they could be held back only with an effort. Reich termed these movements the "orgasm reflex," because they also appeared during orgasm in orgastically potent persons.

The attainment of the orgasm reflex during therapy, as well as of orgastic potency in sexual intercourse, became the twin goals of Reich's treatment. It should be noted that the orgasm reflex in therapy could be experienced without the sharp rise and discharge of excitation characteristic of orgasm. The *sine qua non* were strong sensations of pleasurable currents throughout the body, particularly in the pelvic area, and spontaneous, convulsive-like free movements of the whole body. As Alexander Lowen noted from his own treatment with Reich, it is possible to experience the orgasm reflex without being orgastically potent in intercourse.[8] The former was simpler. One had the encouragement of the therapist and lacked all the problems involved in relating to a love partner in "real life."

However, in therapy Reich and the patient were able to observe directly many of the phenomena patients had previously only *related* from their sexual experiences. During the end phases of treatment, some patients had reported difficulty in giving up hard, jerky movements during intercourse and replacing them with softer, more gentle ones. The same phenomenon was apparent in therapy: as the orgasm reflex developed, the patient would substitute—as a way of controlling the intensity of the excitation—exaggerated, artificial motions for the involuntary convulsions. Or he or she would suddenly become very still, as in intercourse.

Observing the naked or near-naked body directly, concentrating his focus on bodily changes, Reich was getting to where he had long wanted to be: a therapy that elicited and dealt with the deepest emotions and with the flow of energy, which he now named "bio-electricity." Reich loved the concrete, the tangible. The study of the "end phase" of therapy presented in condensed form the Reichian world—the world of intense sensation, of soft movements culminating in convulsions of the body (the orgasm reflex). This was in sharp contradistinction to the enemy within—tightenings of the throat, the pelvis, and the legs; restriction of breathing, dulling of the eyes; expressions of intense anxiety; and the reemergence of defensive character traits. These phenomena intensified in the face of increasingly free, pleasurable sensations, sensations that in turn increased "orgasm anxiety" or the fear of full surrender. Now Reich's talent for observing transitions could most fully be employed, as he observed a vague look in the patient's eye, a sly smile, a restriction in breathing right at the moment of genital excitation or the beginning of a "shutdown" of excitation.

There were of course difficulties involved for the patient, such as very strong bodily reactions, which could sometimes even be dangerous. This was one of the factors that led Reich to believe his therapy should only be practiced by physicians. He was willing to make exceptions—Ola Raknes, for example —but in general he held to the medical practice of his therapy.

These difficulties, together with the kind of rigor Reich advocated for the total treatment, made him uneasy about the popularization of such therapy. He feared that untrained persons might pick up his techniques and then commit irresponsible blunders with patients or simply dilute them and so render them "superficial." As he wrote in the preface to his 1937 monograph, he had not solved an old dilemma. His social self, his Marxist self, demanded the popularization of scientific knowledge. But at the same time, "I would like to prevent the expression 'vegetotherapy' from becoming a fashionable slogan among other fashionable causes. . . . The more generally a scientific formulation is valid, the stricter one must be in the demand for serious and deep-going popularization."[9]

Reich never found the means to achieve a "serious and deep-going popularization" of his therapeutic work. Indeed, in Norway and even more when he got to America, he moved in the opposite direction. He tried to keep a tight rein on those who utilized his techniques, for he was terribly afraid that his concepts and techniques would be misused to the detriment not only of patients but of his own work and his person.

In today's climate, it is easy to forget how radical Reich's approaches were for the 1930s and 1940s. At that time, traditional psychiatry used organic treatments such as electroshock therapy. Psychoanalysts—Freudians, Adlerians, or Jungians—limited themselves strictly to talking with patients. Now the already controversial Reich was seeing patients nude or semi-nude, touching them, reporting about all kinds of sexual excitations, including the orgasm reflex, during therapy. It was a volatile atmosphere, and Reich did not want a spark lit by the suicide or mistreatment of a patient allegedly treated by a "Reichian" therapist whose work he himself had not approved.

There were also other, less rational, motives behind the control Reich attempted to keep on his therapy (as well as on other aspects of his work), behind his avoidance of superficial "popularization." In the late 1920s and early 1930s, he had moved toward the widest possible distribution of his sex-political concepts. He had printed brochures in simple, clear language and distributed them by the thousands to the Communist Party and other organizations. He had worked also to train nonprofessional "youth leaders" on sexual issues. Now he was limiting himself to writing in his small, obscure Journal. Moreover, he never described his therapeutic techniques in great detail, partly out of the fear that the untrained might use such a "cookbook" to conduct "wild" therapy.

I would suggest that in his early deep concern for helping humanity, Reich was not motivated solely by his genuine compassion for "people in trouble." In Freudian terms, he also had a rescue fantasy, a desire to save the world, with a concomitant overestimation of the world's desire and capacity to be saved. With this went his often quite unrealistically optimistic view of people's readiness for rapid change, whether individually or socially.

A different set of motives, related to his family tragedy, was operative in the late 1930s and 1940s. As Reich's sense of his own work developed, as it became clear that he was not simply continuing psychoanalysis or Marxism, that he was no longer the "son" but now the "father" of new disciplines, he became quite concerned with the priority of *his* therapy, *his* sex-economy, *his* bio-electrical and bion experiments. Others might somehow run off with his discoveries, and "wear them in the world's eyes as though they'd wrought them," to borrow from Yeats. Not only would they steal his discoveries. They might dilute them, and, in diluting them, defile them. They would steal and defile, but not suffer, truly suffer for them, as he had suffered.

In the 1930s and after, his accusations became ever harsher against those he believed were stealing his work. However much someone like Fenichel may have deserved reprimand, Reich's ferocity was undoubtedly excessive. His accusations were clearly directed to someone else, another person who had been close to Reich—in other words, the tutor who slept with his mother, who had "stolen" the mother from Willy and his father, who had (in Willy's mind) defiled his mother. The tutor had also gotten off easily, compared to the suffering of Willy and his father.

As Reich became a father, the father of a new therapy and a new science, he became more like his own father, especially under stress. And, in particular, the negative aspects of his father—the jealousy, possessiveness, demandingness, the high expectations of "sons" and the difficulty in accepting their independence—now came to the fore.

How much of psychoanalysis was in fact retained in what Reich termed "character-analytic vegetotherapy"?

In the 1930s, at least, Reich still paid attention to one cardinal goal of psychoanalysis—the resurrection and making conscious of unconscious memories. As with character analysis, he claimed that vegetotherapy brought back these memories with more vividness than classical analysis. To quote from his 1937 monograph again:

> The dissolution of a muscular rigidity not only liberates vegetative energy, but, in addition, also brings back into memory the very infantile situation in which the repression had taken place. . . . We can say: every muscular rigidity contains the history and the meaning of its origin. It is thus not necessary to deduce from dreams or associations [patient productions Reich was never especially interested in] the way in which the muscular armor developed; rather, the armor itself is the form in which the infantile experience continues to exist as a harmful agent.[10]

Reich claimed even more. Work on the muscular armor brought up memories with more affect and immediate significant insight by the patient than was the case in psychoanalysis. In the same monograph he cites a patient who suffered a severe anxiety attack during a session. The man suddenly sat up with a painfully distorted mouth, his forehead covered with perspiration, his whole musculature tense. He hallucinated an ape and emitted sounds that seemed to come from the depth of his chest. This intense experience was immediately connected with frightening childhood memories of his father, a figure he as a small child had perceived as a terrible "gorilla" interfering with the little boy's relation with his mother.[11]

Again and again, Reich stresses the vivid reenactment of early memories through work on the musculature. At the same time, his thinking was moving away from ideational memories and toward total concentration on the play of forces between the flow of energy and emotion, on the one hand, and the muscular rigidities and fear of pleasure, on the other.

Several technical points also reflect the continuity with psychoanalysis, as well as the growing divergencies. During the Norwegian period, Reich saw patients at least several times a week. (Typical analysis involved five sessions each week.) Later, in America, he would see many patients once a week, though he felt that two or three weekly sessions were optimal.

Reich also always saw the patient lying down. Just as psychoanalysis assumed that the supine position increased regression and the "relaxation" of controlled thought processes, so Reich thought this position heightened the flow of emotion.*

Reich maintained a very professional relationship with his patients; there was no doubt who was the therapist, who the patient. However, he always believed in behaving as humanly as possible:

> Many psychoanalytic rules had the definite character of taboos, and thus only reinforced the neurotic taboos of the patient. Thus, for example, the rule that the analyst should not be seen, that he should be a blank screen, as it were, upon which the patient would project his transferences. This, instead of eliminating, confirmed in the patient the feeling of dealing with an invisible, unapproachable, superhuman, that is, according to infantile thinking, a sexless being. How could the patient overcome his fear of sex which made him ill? Treated thus, sexuality remained forever something diabolical and forbidden, something which under all circumstances was to be "condemned" or "sublimated" . . . I attempted in every possible way to free them of their characterological rigidity. They should look at me in an unauthoritative, *human* way.[12]

In line with letting the patient see the therapist, and also permitting the therapist to observe the patient, Reich sat next to him rather than behind him (the customary analytic position). Sometimes, too, Reich would answer questions the patient asked about him, rather than using the more standard analytic technique of querying: "Why do you ask?"

---

*Of those working directly in the Reichian tradition, Alexander Lowen was the first (in the late 1950s) to make use of other patient positions, especially standing.

In contrast to the usual analytic mode, then, Reich could be revealing of himself. He could also demonstrate the negative sides of the human therapist —the sides the analysts so rightly warn against. For all his theoretical commitment to the patient's "overcoming any fear of criticizing me," he could become extremely angry at patients both in Norway and later in America. This was particularly likely to occur when he was being criticized indirectly.

Thus Reich sometimes violated the good part of the analyst's neutrality, his basic accepting and nonjudgmental stance, his refusal to repeat old sado-masochistic struggles with the patient. In therapy, as in most of his other endeavors, Reich was a man of extremes. At his best, he played in a league all his own. At his worst, he made mistakes a first-year psychiatric resident (or physicist or biologist) wouldn't make.

What are the connections between Reich's psychiatric treatment and his experimental work—in this period, his bio-electrical and bion research?

I have already suggested some mutual interaction. Thus around 1933 Reich had noted "dead spots" in the organism, for example, penis anesthesia. The bio-electric experiments in 1935 objectively confirmed for Reich the lack of flow or charge when pleasure was not experienced. Conversely, the experiments heightened his confidence that he was observing a flow of measurable energy in his patients.

The study of microorganisms, particularly cell division, renewed Reich's conviction during this period that in the case of orgasm reflex and orgastic potency, he was dealing with basic life processes, processes that transcended purely psychological phenomena. He began to look at the patient not—or not only—in terms of his or her various conflicts and particular life experiences, but, in words he once used, as "a sack of fluids and energy."[13] The issue was what prevented that "sack" from pulsating freely and from discharging excess energy through the orgasm. The softening in the laboratory of the rigid structure of matter leading to pulsating bions became analogous to the softening of the patient's armor, which led to the eliciting of strong, involuntary emotions.

Reich was getting a largely negative response from the world for his experimental work, and no more than lukewarm tolerance from his friends, as we have seen. But he was able to derive positive "feedback" indirectly. His students and patients *were* enormously enthusiastic about his therapeutic work. The gratitude they expressed when their rigidities softened, when energy flowed freely, could not help but give him greater confidence in the validity of the "pulsations" he observed.

For a time Reich considered calling his treatment "orgasmotherapy," but decided that this frank nomenclature would be too overwhelming for his students.[14] His treatment was not a "direct sex therapy" in the current sense of that term. Rather, he contended that blocks in the function of the orgasm were connected with blocks in the total character and musculature. These had to be worked through before the total orgastic convulsions—not simply local genital release such as Masters and Johnson would later describe—could occur. The person who could not cry deeply or express his or her rage freely could also not, according to Reich, convulse orgastically. His treatment thus concerned the whole organism, not just the patient's sexuality.

Finally, what is the relation between Reich's vegetotherapy and current forms of treatment such as primal scream therapy, Gestalt therapy, bio-energetics, and encounter groups? Bio-energetics should be separated from this grouping because it essentially represents, as Lowen has pointed out, a popularization and amplification of Reich's work and hence is a direct descendant of it. The other schools make use of various Reichian techniques. Primal scream, for example, works with direct touch of the body and is oriented around deep emotional expression. Gestalt therapy involves considerable emphasis on awareness of body feelings but does not directly use touch. Encounter groups employ a variety of methods to get people "out of their heads" and "into their feelings."

None of these techniques involves a systematic working through of layered character defenses and segments of muscular armor. None postulates the release of an energy from these blocked defenses. None has the treatment goal of orgastic potency or orgasm reflex. In a later chapter I will consider the question of how effective Reich was in achieving his goal with patients and why he believed it was so important to maintain the *principle* of orgastic potency as the criterion of health quite distinct from the therapist's success in reaching this goal. It is enough here to emphasize Reich's extraordinary pioneering contributions of the 1930s to classical theory and practice—contributions that were guided by his own relentless quest to comprehend the nature of life energy and what, in man, might block its spontaneous flow.

Personal Life and Relations with Colleagues: 1934-1939

The three years between the fall of 1934 and the fall of 1937 were among the happiest in Reich's life. His relationship with Elsa Lindenberg continued to be a very satisfying one. Reich was supportive of Elsa's work, acting on his belief in marital partners' exercising their independence. Elsa, whose political interests were stronger than Reich's at this particular time, was an occasional choreographer for a "Red Review" put on by a young workers' group. Once when Reich came to a rehearsal and helped with the drilling of a Prussian goose-step routine, Elsa recalled the warm, direct way he had with these young workers, and how everybody enjoyed a big party afterward.[1]

Reich and Annie were divorced in late 1934. Reich had considered Elsa to be his wife in all but the legal sense for some time, at least since she joined him in Copenhagen in May 1933. He was reluctant to take the step of marriage with Elsa, in part because of the potential for bitter harassment in the case of a subsequent divorce, in part because he wanted to be very certain that their personal relationship harmonized with his rapidly developing work.

In the early Oslo years at least, there was less reluctance on Elsa's part. When she became pregnant in 1935, she was overjoyed to have a child with Willy. Initially, he too was thrilled by the prospect and bought clothes and furniture for the coming infant. But then doubts set in. He felt that the future of his work was too unsettled to provide the right kind of environment for a child. To Elsa's great sorrow, he insisted on an abortion.[2] They decided to have the abortion in Berlin, where Edith Jacobson, still practicing analysis and now also in the German resistance movement against Hitler, helped arrange the illegal operation.

During this period, Reich's relations with his colleagues were also harmonious. The Norwegian group was an exceptionally lively one. Both Sigurd and Nic Hoel, and people like Arnulf Overland, poet laureate of Norway, and August Lange, a well-known sociologist, were friends as well as colleagues. There were parties, skiing vacations, and informal meetings, together with courses and the diverse work collaborations Reich usually had with his associates. In the summer of 1935 a kind of summer school developed, with seminars and lectures; mostly friends, students, and assistants gathered informally in the Norwegian countryside. As Ilse Ollendorff has noted:

> The atmosphere was casual, in great contrast to the much more formal climate that was to prevail in the American organization later on. . . . In my request for information in Scandinavia, I was struck again and again by the way people referred to Reich as Willy. No one in America, except his closest family, and some of his old friends from Austria, ever referred to him as Willy. He was always Reich to a few, and Dr. Reich to most.[3]

Early in the Oslo period, the controversy with Otto Fenichel erupted again. Fenichel had migrated to Oslo before Reich. Nic Hoel and Ola Raknes started psychoanalytic treatment with Fenichel, although their first choice was Reich. Later, both transferred from Fenichel to Reich, exacerbating the friction between the two men. Hoel and Raknes, along with Schjelderup, very much wanted Reich to join the Scandinavian Psychoanalytic Institute and thereby be reinstated within the International Association. Moreover, they were prepared to take the risk, threatened by the International executive committee, of the exclusion of their Institute should Reich become a member. Fenichel, however, was opposed. He was not prepared to face exclusion, believing the best way he could serve the cause of psychoanalysis was to remain a member of the Association fighting for those scientific directions he supported.[4]

As we saw earlier, Reich was quite ambivalent about rejoining the International Association. On the one hand, he felt his work was so different from the dominant trends within the psychoanalytic establishment that he did not belong there. On the other hand, he felt that any continuer of the true analytic tradition did belong. In any case, he deeply resented Fenichel's opposition, which whetted his appetite for readmission.

A meeting was held in Oslo on December 14, 1935, attended by Reich, Fenichel, Nic Hoel, Raknes, and other members of the "opposition group" of analysts, to discuss, among other things, the question of Reich's relationship to the Scandinavian Institute. Fenichel clearly had the better of the argument on several points raised. For example, even after the events of Lucerne, Reich still continued to believe that he could count on considerable endorsement among the rank-and-file members of the International Association, an opinion fueled by hope rather than realistic assessment. In a paroxysm of blame, Reich accused Fenichel at the December 14 meeting of not explaining to potentially supportive analysts just where Reich's concepts and late Freudian views differed. On his side, Fenichel had no such illusions about the degree of effective allegiance his adversary could rally. Reich also still believed that the psychoanalytic organization had to take a political stance, now not with the Communist Party per se, but in "the camp of the political left." Understandably, Fenichel saw this demand as unnecessary provocation to the more conservative analysts.[5]

Equally, Reich was right about the originality of his orgasm theory. Fenichel believed that Reich's genitality concepts substantially stemmed from Freud. Reich argued that a consistent and radically new elucidation of the psychological, sociological, and physiological aspects of the orgasm was a quite different matter from Freud's early but scattered references. Yet for a long time Reich himself had not been entirely clear about the precise differences between himself and Freud. His expectation of clarity on Fenichel's part led to a comical interlude at the December meeting when Reich said: "I myself have only realized over the last three months why and how the orgasm theory so absolutely contradicts death instinct theory." Fenichel interjected the ironic comment: "And during the preceding years, *I* never explained to *you* why and how you differed from Freud?" Reich angrily: "No, you did not!" which was followed by an outburst of laughter from those present, the point of which escaped him. Reich's ludicrous moments—and he had many—often helped to obscure from his contemporaries the magnitude of his accomplishments.

A difference of opinion had fused with a personal rivalry. Fenichel, a man of formidable intellectual gifts, was about the same age as Reich and had introduced his friend to psychoanalysis back in medical school days. It could not have been easy for him to be in Reich's shadow. Such a position was tolerable if painful when Reich led an "opposition" group within psychoanalysis. Then they were both the intellectual children of Freud; in fact, Fenichel was much better versed than Reich in the details of Freud's writings and those of other analytic theorists. (To use Isaiah Berlin's classification, Fenichel was a fox, Reich a hedgehog: "The fox knows many things, but the hedgehog knows one big thing.") It was quite a different, indeed an intolerable thing for Fenichel to do what Reich now demanded of him: to join the grandchildren such as Hoel and Raknes in sharp, passionate commitment to *Reich's* concepts, to risk being cut down in the volley of shots aimed at Reich by the psychoanalytic establishment.

The controversy between Reich and Fenichel was further fanned by Reich's students. Some attended Reich's seminars, which were held separately from the Norwegian Psychoanalytic Institute; a few were in analysis with Fenichel, and Nic Hoel reported on this situation: "When I said positive things about Reich, Fenichel's movements became nervous and his voice shrill, even if he only said 'yes' and 'no.' " When she broke off treatment with Fenichel after a year to join Reich, she sensed that Fenichel was furious.[6] Raknes maintained that while Fenichel never said outright that Reich was psychotic, he implied as much.[7] Further, Fenichel resented those students of Reich who came to the analytic meetings and in the discussions made issues of the differences between himself and Reich. Whether oppressed by antagonisms between the two groups, or fearful that he was losing patients to Reich, Fenichel decided to leave Oslo at the end of 1935 to settle in Prague.

The long relationship between Fenichel and Reich was now over, leaving only bitter enmity between the two. Neither man ever expressed in writing the sorrow he felt at the rupture. Fenichel, according to his former wife, was very depressed by the controversy.[8] And Elsa Lindenberg has reported that Reich could not understand why Fenichel was so angry toward him. More typically, his hurt over Fenichel's behavior was expressed in rage. The "Fenichels" now joined the "Scharffenbergs" and "Kreybergs" in Reich's roll call of enemies, people who were frightened by his work and who, unable to follow, had resorted to slandering him.

With Fenichel gone, Reich was clearly dominant among Norwegian analysts, even though he was no longer an analyst himself. Some of his students —Schjelderup and Hoel, for example—remained members of the Psychoanalytic Institute; others, such as Ola Raknes, dropped their membership as Reich's work evolved away from psychoanalysis and as his emotional stand hardened against his former analytic colleagues.

Reich may have left the analytic establishment, but his feelings for Freud remained as intense and conflicted as ever. According to Elsa Lindenberg, he debated for a long time whether to send a congratulatory telegram on the occasion of Freud's eightieth birthday on May 6, 1936. He finally decided to do so. Reich also published an article entitled "Our Congratulations to Freud on His Birthday," which detailed what he believed to be the fruitful parts of Freud's work, continued in sex-economy, and the more sterile tendencies that increasingly dominated psychoanalysis. The conclusion of the article stated: "No matter how difficult or hurtful the conflicts between psychoanalysis and sex-economy may have been, they will never cause us to forget what we owe to the life work of Freud. For nobody knows better than we, nobody experiences more painfully than we, why the world used to damn Freud and today removes him from a fighting reality."[9]

More painful than the break with Fenichel and Reich's continuing disappointment in Freud was Reich's relationship with his children, especially Eva. When Reich moved to Oslo, Eva and Lore were living in Vienna with Annie's parents, Malva and Alfred Pink, while Annie was establishing her practice in Prague. Sometime in 1934 Eva went into child analysis with Berta Bornstein, a well-known Vienna child analyst trained by Anna Freud. Both Annie and

Willy agreed that Eva needed analysis and that Bornstein was a good choice. Eva's analysis with Bornstein was one of the reasons the children remained in Vienna. As agreed, Eva spent summers with her father.[10]

Prior to the Reichs' move to Berlin in 1930, Bornstein had been a good friend of the family. She had cared for Eva and Lore when the Reichs visited Russia in 1929. (She never married, but for a period in the 1920s she and Otto Fenichel were lovers.)[11] Following the Reichs' separation, she sided strongly with Annie. In the 1930s her involvement with the family was not considered a counter-indication to her being Eva's analyst. Today, such a practice would be strictly disadvised.

Annie, Bornstein, and Alfred Pink had strongly objected to Reich's "encouraging" the precocious Eva to attend his seminars and to read Malinowski's *The Sexual Life of Savages.* Pink clearly disapproved of his granddaughter's "premature" sexual interests, a definite attitude Reich preferred to the tolerating stance of Annie and Bornstein, which allowed Eva to make her own decisions rather than "imposing" a *Weltanschauung* the way they claimed Reich did.[12]

Reich countered that he had not encouraged Eva but neither had he discouraged her spontaneous interest in these activities nor concealed his pleasure over her curiosity. In his view, to have done so would have contributed to the mystification of sexuality that resulted from the vague disapproval or unspoken toleration of sexual curiosity.

The same issue erupted again over an exchange of letters between Eva and Willy. On January 12, 1935, she wrote Reich about a matter that "I tell Berta only rarely." Now almost eleven, Eva had met a thirteen-year-old boy, K. They liked each other, kissed, and engaged in sex play. But he also liked and went out with other girls. And that for Eva was a problem: "I thought to myself, I won't let anyone play around with me, and now I don't know what to do. To be mad or to be friends? I am disappointed but am I not right? I think sometimes: 'Go back, retreat, you have no rights to him.' But when he takes my hand I think the opposite. . . . I am sick of the whole affair. . . . It sounds like a love novel. . . ."[13]

According to Eva, Reich was concerned that she hadn't told Berta about K. Eva was impressed with how seriously Reich took her feelings for K. and the clear, simple way he had advised her. He had said that perhaps she could overcome her jealousy and let K. see others as well as herself. On the other hand, her desire to have K. for herself might be so important that she could not share him. He also told her to look at her feelings of vanity. And even if she did lose K., she should remember she was a fine person and would soon have another boyfriend.

Bornstein believed that Eva was in part acting out her transference to Bornstein through her relationship with K. Also, Eva was trying to play her father off against her therapist, a maneuver Reich had fallen for. Bornstein, Annie, and Alfred believed that Reich's letter illustrated once again how he foisted his own views on her, views Eva parroted in order to keep his love. Indeed, in their view, her relationship with K. was an effort to impress her father with her interest in sexuality.[14]

Caught between the very different lifestyles and orientations of her quarreling parents, Eva suffered considerable anguish. At the end of her visit to Willy in August 1935, she very much wanted to spend the following year with him in Oslo. She found the impending separation extremely hard to bear: it reminded her of the pain she had experienced after the previous year's summer visit with Reich.

Initially, Reich agreed to Eva's wish. However, he wanted to consult with Annie, since their divorce agreement specified that the children remain with their mother until they reached the age of fourteen, at which time they could make their own decision. Together Eva and Willy went to Grundlsee, in Austria, where Annie, her husband Thomas Rubinstein, and Bornstein were vacationing. Annie adamantly refused to agree to Eva's wish. Bornstein and she felt that Eva should complete her analysis, which would not need much more time. According to Reich, Berta Bornstein stated that in all likelihood Eva could move to Oslo in the spring of 1936 if she still wished to do so. Mollified, still partly convinced of the importance of Eva's analysis, and uncertain of his legal status as a controversial refugee in Oslo, Reich persuaded a very unhappy Eva to remain in Vienna until the following spring. Later, Reich believed that the ensuing events were partly due to his not taking a stronger stand in Eva's behalf that fall.[15]

After Reich returned to Oslo, Eva grew more fearful with her mother and Bornstein and became much more distant toward her father. Indeed, she entirely relinquished the idea of living with him and became very ambivalent even about visits. She chose not to see him at Christmas 1935 or during the summer of 1936.

When Eva refused to come for the summer visit, Reich became thoroughly convinced that Annie and Bornstein had unfairly alienated his daughter from him. A very angry Reich visited his former wife and children, quite uninvited, at Marienbad where they were vacationing during August 1936. There were furious arguments between Reich and Annie (aided and abetted by Thomas and Berta). Reich repeated a request he had made many times to Eva: that she come and live with him as she had wished to do a year earlier. Eva quoted Bornstein as saying Reich was financially unreliable. At one point Annie bitterly declared she wanted full custody of the children. She would forbid Eva from living with Reich even if she wished to do so. Reich became more enraged than ever. Finally, Eva told Willy to leave—he was upsetting everyone.

Once back in Oslo in September, Reich took retaliatory steps. According to Eva, Reich now took the position that he would no longer give child support to Annie but would instead put the money in escrow until the children visited and maintained a decent relationship with him. Around this time, Reich also began preparing an eighty-page document entitled "How I Lost Eva," in which he detailed his anguish and tumult in letters, reports of phone calls, and other recollections (plus his own interpretations) of events.

There was no further communication between Eva and Reich until August 1938. Hitler had annexed Austria that March, and Annie made plans to emigrate from endangered Prague to America. Reich was angry that he was not consulted and that the children did not visit him before leaving. The move itself he thoroughly approved, being convinced that Hitler intended to conquer Europe and that the democracies were ill-prepared to meet this threat.

Annie and the children arrived in the United States on July 21, 1938. Working on a farm during her first American summer, Eva, now fourteen years old, wrote her father on August 28: "It is the first time that I do something [writing Reich] which perhaps is not good for Annie, but I had this feeling, now or never, that I simply write it, throw it in the mail box, and then will be sorry afterward."

Eva went on to speak of her love for both her mother and her father. About her father: "Be proud that your daughter tells you that you have such charm that if one comes into your vicinity one simply must be fond of you." However, Eva was worried that she had "lost" Reich because she had been unwilling to visit him before leaving Europe. She still found it difficult "for me to be quite honest with you." Hoping he would reply, she concluded her letter by imagining Reich's reaction to it: "You are a little confused and read the letter again and again."[16]

According to Eva, Reich replied with a brief letter. He was concerned that whatever he said might only serve to drive Eva back into her fear of him. He was extremely touched that for the first time in three years she had reached out to him, but he was worried that in so doing she felt guilty toward Annie. In fact, she was not harming her mother by writing to him.

Some years later, Reich told Eva how hurt he was that she had been so concerned about her mother's feelings should Eva approach him and so little concerned about his feelings should she not. The whole conflict, Reich said, arose because he represented the great forbidden.

Today, Eva Reich, who is a physician, travels around the world lecturing on her father's work. In interviews with me in the early 1970s, she saw Annie, and especially Berta Bornstein, as essentially responsible for the almost four years of fear-filled separation from her father. They "brainwashed" her into believing her father was seductive and sick, his influence on her largely destructive. Eva's view of what happened received corroboration from Edith Jacobson, no friend of Reich's by 1935–36 and certainly not by 1971, when I interviewed her. Jacobson entirely agreed with Bornstein's diagnosis of Reich as very sick, but felt that Berta's insistence on convincing Eva of this truth boomeranged, eventually driving Eva closer to her father.

For all her commitment to Reich's work today and for all her indignation toward Bornstein and Annie for their role during her early adolescence, Eva still harbors resentment that Reich left the family. She also feels she was always undertaking things before she was ready—a sentiment that surely includes her following some of Reich's passions that he endeavored so hard to get others to share. In later years, Reich recognized his contribution to Eva's childhood tragedy. He said he would not try to influence his son Peter, born in America in 1944, to enter his work the way he had tried to influence Eva.[17]

If the situation was never black and white, neither was there equal responsibility for the events. Reich's central commitments were at stake in the battle over Eva. He believed in the affirmation of genitality in a world that condemned it, and he was not prepared to surrender this affirmation toward Eva in order "to keep peace in the family." Only when his gentle, understanding approach, as in his letter to Eva about her relationship with K., met condemnation from Annie and Bornstein did he become harsher, more insistent in his dealings with Eva and her Viennese world, thereby exacerbating the parental division rather than attempting to heal it.

Moreover, Reich was open about his convictions. When he had questions about Eva's analysis, particularly her inability to speak freely to her therapist, he wanted Bornstein as well as Eva to be fully informed of his concern. For her part, Annie prior to 1936 and Bornstein throughout never fully revealed the extent of their radical disagreement with Reich and their intense dislike of Eva's relationship with him. They only kept repeating the partial truth that they wanted Eva "to make up her own mind."

Finally, whatever his mistakes (and he made many with Eva), in his affirmation of Eva's childhood genitality Reich was on the side of the future, whereas Annie Reich and Berta Bornstein represented the past, even if they belonged to the most enlightened wing of a dying world.

Hearing Eva discuss the extent of Reich's concern about her between 1935 and the fall of 1936, it is easy to forget that at the same time he was doing an immense amount of work completing his bio-electrical experiments, discovering the bions, and developing his psychiatric therapy.

In his relations with Oslo colleagues, students, and assistants, Reich was becoming very much the leader. His *Journal* provided ready publication of his own papers and those of his colleagues on a wide variety of subjects—his theoretical and experimental papers and clinical articles, reports by colleagues on therapy, education, and political psychology. Reich retained a generally leftist orientation and still considered himself a dialectical materialist. Indeed, he used dialectical concepts in his research, stressing the role of antithetical forces, the emergence of living substances from "material" conditions, quantitative shifts yielding qualitative differences.

Reich's movement away from the more political aspects of Marxism was heightened by experiences with his colleagues during these years. Difficulties emerged especially around the issues of publication. Several of his young socialist assistants wanted "equal" rights in determining the content of the *Journal.* Reich felt that since he was primarily responsible for most of the ideas and for paying publication costs, he was "more equal" than the others.[18] This led to charges that he was "dictatorial," a criticism not without some justification then and one that was to be repeated throughout his life.

Reich's closest male friendship during this period seems to have been with Sigurd Hoel, the novelist. In 1957 I met Hoel and found him to be an extremely engaging, witty, reflective person, still full of warm memories if also criticisms of Reich. He liked Reich as a therapist: "He was a very good therapist with me. I saw him four times a week. The only thing that interfered was the fact that I was also seeing him socially. I saw him almost every day for five years."

As noted, Hoel for a period served as editor of Reich's *Journal,* so that he met Reich as patient, friend, and co-worker. Yet Hoel felt that Reich wanted even more from him: "There was nothing of the liberal man about Reich. . . . He was a tyrant. . . . He wanted your whole life. . . . He knew he couldn't have mine—I had my writing, my loves."[19]

It was a mark of the two men's intimacy that Hoel felt comfortable going unannounced to Reich's apartment on the night of Hitler's invasion of Austria in March 1938. He thought Reich should not be alone. "I never saw Reich cry, but he was close to tears that night. He said he had wondered if any of his friends were thinking of him."

Hoel's reference to Reich as a "tyrant" applied especially after the start of the Norwegian newspaper campaign in late 1937. Then Elsa Lindenberg and most of his colleagues discerned a change in him. Hoel commented that after the campaign Reich ceased to be such a good therapist: "He began to take out his anger on his patients. He never did that with me, but he did it with others. I saw him crush several people. That was unforgivable because he was the strongest one in the group. *Unforgivable!"*

Hoel also told me the one well-documented example of Reich's sexual indiscretion with a patient:

"Shortly after the Norwegian campaign started, Reich took on a female patient, the ex-wife of a close colleague. She was a very beautiful actress. She had gone into therapy with the explicit purpose of seducing Reich. In the beginning Reich told her that that of course was out of the question. But in time she succeeded. The analysis stopped, the relationship began: then the relationship would stop and the analysis resume. How long this went on I don't know, but at some point both the relationship and the analysis ended, the relationship at least at Reich's instigation. The patient was furious and was determined to tell the press about the incident. Reich suggested that I speak to her, which I did. She poured out her hatred. I confined myself to listening and to pointing out how much she would hurt herself—not only Reich— through newspaper stories about the affair. She finally decided not to go to the newspapers."[20]

When Hoel asked Reich why he had behaved thus, his reply was succinct: "A man must do foolish things sometimes." The last thing Reich needed at the time was a well-documented newspaper story concerning his seduction of a patient.

Such sexual impulsiveness with a patient was one of the minor examples of his neurotic behavior during this period when he was undoubtedly under stress. Elsa Lindenberg told me that after Reich's discovery of the bions, and especially after the start of the newspaper campaign, his behavior changed. He became more suspicious, defensive, and jealous. Before the bion research, she had felt familiar with the broad outlines of his work. She could raise questions, criticize in a way that Reich found helpful. But she had no background at all in natural-scientific work nor any particular disposition to learn it. Nor did Reich make it easy for her to familiarize herself with his research, being so defensive that he interpreted all questions as criticism.

As the press campaign intensified, Reich withdrew socially. He and Elsa saw much less of friends like the Hoels. They, too, found him more domineering and suspicious. His enemies attacked him and his friends did not understand. He felt relatively alone in his bion work. He was especially hurt when Schjelderup, as much as anyone his original sponsor in Norway, severed Reich's connection with the Psychological Research Institute and dissociated himself from Reich's experimental work.

Reich's most striking symptom during this time was his jealousy toward Elsa. Until 1937, he had been supportive of her career; now he wanted her closer to him, sharing his work and life entirely, without other distractions. Here he was behaving like his own authoritarian father, not the champion of women's independence he was in his writings and, for the most part, in his life.

The quarrels about Elsa's independence reached a high point at some time during 1938 when Elsa was offered the opportunity to choreograph and dance in a work jointly planned with a composer. Elsa accepted the assignment in the face of Reich's intense opposition. Shortly before opening night, Elsa and the composer had to meet late in the evening at the composer's apartment to plan some last-minute production details. They were working when they heard a knock at the door. It was Reich. He entered and sat silently for a while. Then he launched into a tirade: What Elsa was doing in the theater was trivial compared to what she might be doing with him! Suddenly he started punching the composer. Elsa considered calling the police but wanted to avoid a scandal in the papers. Fortunately, Reich's rage soon subsided. The composer agreed not to speak of the incident and he kept his word, even though questions were raised when he arrived at the theater the next day with a black eye.[21]

Following this outburst, Elsa refused to return home with Reich but went to stay with a friend. Reich followed her there and, at first, continued his jealous accusations. Somehow or other, they finally made up and went home together. But for Elsa the relationship was scarred. This kind of incident made Elsa less committed to Reich. Shortly after the tumultuous evening, Reich asked her if she would emigrate to America with him. She replied: "No," although she admitted: "It was the hardest 'no' I ever had to say." She felt she had to get back to herself, to protect her independence against Reich's demands, and to consider calmly whether she really wanted to continue their relationship.

Reich's jealousy must have been all the more painful to Elsa because he himself had been having an affair quite recently with a young Norwegian textile designer named Gerd Bergersen. This relationship, more serious than the one with the actress-patient, came to light in the late 1970s, when Gerd sent tapes describing her involvement with Reich to Colin Wilson, who was working on *The Quest for Wilhelm Reich*.[22]

In Wilson's account, the relationship appears to have lasted several years and to have been of considerable significance to Reich. However, in one letter to me, Gerd described it as lasting a "short year," and, in another, she mentions the "very short period" she was close to Reich. She adds: "Emotionally, I do not think I got under his skin."[23]

Briefly, summarizing Wilson's account, Reich and Gerd met in 1936, when she was twenty-five, he thirty-nine. Reich was taken by her from the moment he met her, saying: "You interest me. I want to know you." Gerd had had some disappointing experiences with men and was not eager to enter a new relationship, but Reich pursued her. His interest was not primarily sexual— he was attracted to her vibrant spirit, her quest for a creative, independent life. He wanted to be a mentor to her and he succeeded, for Gerd has described their relationship as "perhaps the most fruitful of her life." A well-known, older, brilliant man was taking her seriously even when she challenged his basic views. "Reich was unoffended," Wilson writes, "when she told him that she rejected Freud's view that sex was the most basic human drive." In Gerd's words: "He accepted me as a rational human being."[24]

There is no suggestion that any effort was made to conceal their relationship from Elsa even when it became a sexual one. Reich and Gerd met with Oslo intellectuals where Gerd participated eagerly in discussions. At one point Elsa became hurt and disturbed by their growing intimacy. She was now in the same position—that of the injured wife—to Gerd as Annie had once been to her.

When the Norwegian newspaper campaign erupted in 1937, Gerd saw another side of Reich. It was not the rageful side Elsa experienced; rather, it was a "hunted and tormented" Reich. After some particularly bitter attack had appeared, he would go to her apartment with the newspaper under his arm to talk until the early hours of the morning. He spoke of the coming Nazi invasion of Norway, something few people in Oslo envisioned at that time. At some point during the newspaper campaign Reich half-proposed marriage and Gerd refused him.

There is some question of just how deeply involved Reich was, how much he was spinning out a fantasy to escape from reality, a fantasy he knew she would not accept. More, he may have wanted to end the relationship by getting her to reject him. At any rate, it appears to have ended soon after Gerd's rejection. Gerd felt relief as well as pain at the termination, for she had been startled by her physical responses—"The passion of the body was taking charge, and there was something frightening about this. It was destructive."[25]

On Reich's side, the relationship with Gerd is revealing in that it shows once more one of his patterns with women. When his work was under fire, he turned to his mate for support. He felt insufficiently understood—first with Annie, now with Elsa. With Annie, Lia for a while proved a more sympathetic ally, then Elsa. In time Elsa, too, became embroiled in his demand for total understanding and support. He turned to Gerd, seeking a "safety valve," respecting her independence more because she was not so close. And, with a blind self-righteousness, he justified these affairs on the basis of his mates' shortcomings, whereas their affairs, even flirtations, were evidence of utter perfidy.

In his commotion with women, Reich may well have been displacing the rage he felt toward his real opponents. There was no way of getting at his critics or stopping them save through continued work. He did not want to stoop to the level of the "Kreybergs and Scharffenbergs"—the level of personal mudslinging. As Ilse Ollendorff has well noted, his rage was lived out against his wife, his friends, his colleagues, even his patients. The fiercer the hostility and lack of comprehension in the press, the more he wanted enveloping warmth, understanding, and support from those around him, and the less he felt he got it.

Most colleagues could not share Reich's awareness of the significance of the bions. They were awed by his earlier discoveries, but that was not enough for Reich. It was always the latest "child" who was most beautiful, but who was somewhat alien to his followers since they had been drawn to the Reich of former findings. More and more he urged them to look, to see, to appreciate. More and more, under his pressure, with their awareness of their scientific inadequacies and in the face of frightening criticisms from noted specialists, they pleaded: "I am ignorant, I will defend you against unfair harassment, but I cannot give you the intellectual support, the loving criticism, the shared collaboration in further research you ask of me." And, more and more, he felt alone and misunderstood by those closest to him.

Even Odd Havrevold, who of all Reich's associates (with the possible exception of Roger du Teil) had the clearest idea of what Reich was doing, was full of uncertainties. According to Reich, it was Havrevold who had urged him to consult the noted bacteriologist, Thjötta, about the identification of certain biological forms—a step that Reich felt turned out disastrously.[26]

Havrevold's concerns about winning others over in support of the work —always a sign, according to Reich, of inner skepticism—is better revealed in one of Fenichel's "Rundbriefe" from Prague in March 1937. Havrevold had urged an analyst visiting Oslo to look at Reich's work. Later, the analyst reported to Fenichel how he went to the laboratory, where

Reich was very amiable, and demonstrated a lot for two and a half hours. What I saw: particles moved in soot which glowed and floated in bouillon. I asked how one distinguished these movements from

Brownian movement. Reich replied: "It is a question of the growth of these forms in a culture," and he showed me colonies. I didn't have the factual knowledge to evaluate what I was seeing. Schjelderup . . . feared that if Reich's work underwent a scientific critique and a mistake was found which overthrew the whole thing, that would be a catastrophe—not only for Reich personally, but the whole of Norwegian psychoanalysis would be compromised publicly and scientifically.[27]

Reich could appreciate, indeed at times he shared, the attitude of Havrevold, who sought advice from others. He could also appreciate Schjelderup's position that he could not evaluate the bion research. Yet he felt an intense aversion to hesitation, to standing aside. As Charles Péguy has written: "Woe to the lukewarm. Shame on him who is ashamed. Woe to and shame on him who is ashamed. The question here is not so much to believe or not to believe. Shame on the man who would deny his faith to avoid ridicule, to avoid being laughed at, to avoid being branded a fool. The question here concerns the man who does not trouble to find out whether he believes or does not believe."[28]

The enduring problem for Reich's students remained: how to take the trouble to find out whether they believed or did not believe; it was no small task for persons not trained in the natural sciences.

A related problem between Reich and his colleagues was that he felt he had burned his bridges for the sake of his work. It was he, not most of his followers, who had left the Psychoanalytic Association; he, not his followers, who bore the full brunt of the accumulating newspaper campaign. He resented the fact that someone like Schjelderup could have the best of both worlds, learning from Reich, but not endangering his secure position within the psychoanalytic movement or academia. Reich discerned a certain small-mindedness in his supporters' *not* finding out whether or not they believed, say, in the bions. If they found his findings convincing, as persons of integrity they would have to defend them and be subject to similar hostility. So there was immediate safety in ignorance. And there was historical safety. If Reich were later proved correct, they could say they had always been sympathetic to his work; if proved wrong, they had always been skeptical and scientifically unable to judge.

Confronted by the opposition of his enemies, the license requirement to practice therapy, and the uneasiness of his friends, Reich no longer found Norway a viable home for his work. A possible solution emerged when, late in 1938, a psychiatrist came from the United States to study with Reich. Theodore P. Wolfe, then thirty-seven years old, had been born in Switzerland, and had acquired most of his medical and psychiatric training in that country before moving to America. At the time he met Reich, he was a member of the Department of Psychiatry at Columbia Medical School, and had done research for the pioneering psychosomatic text *Emotions and Bodily Changes,* written by his former wife, H. Flanders Dunbar. Reich's writings and his whole approach deeply impressed Wolfe, so he resolved to visit Norway, to undergo therapy with Reich, and to study his work firsthand.

For Wolfe, as for many others, meeting Reich and his work represented the turning point in his life. As Gladys Meyer, Wolfe's last wife, wrote in an obituary:

> "Real" life began for Dr. Wolfe with his work with Dr. Reich. He would describe how everything he read, saw, heard, and felt changed in quality; and the vague, impatient emptiness [he had previously experienced] began, with great anxiety to be filled up. A bond of gratefulness to Reich stemmed from that deepest core of himself which Reich had made accessible to him. And he loved Reich, as Neill and Raknes and other old associates loved him.[29]

In the course of his visit, Wolfe suggested that Reich move to America, where he could find a more congenial atmosphere. Exhausted by the Oslo situation, fearing the outbreak of a disastrous war in Europe, attracted to settling in America ever since 1933, Reich leaped at the idea. Furthermore, Wolfe now offered to help facilitate the move.

Like others who at least in the early stages of their relationship with Reich were grateful for the contact with their "core," Wolfe was prepared to expend endless energy to aid Reich and to further his own association with him. On Wolfe's return to the United States, he managed to obtain an official request from an academic institution for Reich to teach in the States, an invitation that was necessary for a residence visa. The New School for Social Research was prepared to make such an offer, after Wolfe and Walter Briehl, another American and an old student of Reich's, put up several thousand dollars guaranteeing Reich's salary.[30] However, the immigration question was so complicated at that time with the influx of refugees from Nazi Germany that Wolfe had to pull strings through Adolph Berle, a high official in the U.S. State Department, for Reich actually to get the visa.[31]

Reich meanwhile was waiting impatiently in Norway. He had sent his secretary and laboratory assistant, Gertrud Gaasland, ahead to New York in May 1939 to find a new home and to set up the laboratory. Reich expected to follow in a matter of weeks, but the bureaucratic entanglements entailed a longer delay.

The months of waiting proved difficult. In anticipation of an early departure, Reich had stopped his research, teaching, and therapeutic activity. He had sold his car to Ola Raknes and dismantled his apartment, staying with friends. He and Elsa still saw each other but she had definitely decided not to accompany him to the States then, although she did not exclude the possibility at a later time.

His letters to Gertrud Gaasland during this time reflect his mood about the visa, the difficulties of waiting, almost elegiac thoughts about his Oslo life and friends, and—most of all—hope for the future of his work in America. The relative isolation of this time as well as the sense of the "end of a period" contribute to the unusually introspective mood of these letters. Reich generally revealed himself more in dealing with women than with men.

Above all, there was the steady drumbeat of his work. He could not wait until the bureaucracy decided to let him live. With his talent for finding the good news in the bad, he had the feeling that the move to America, uprooting as it was, might help the work to go forward. He also told Raknes that without his work he simply could not live. The experience of yet another exile reinforced Reich's sense of his heroic mission.[32]

Not even Reich with his occasional sense of doom could have predicted the near-total break with his Norwegian colleagues that was to ensue. Only Ola Raknes, by no means the person closest to Reich then, would maintain an intermittent relationship. Sigurd Hoel was never to see Reich again, claiming that he felt Reich had abandoned him. Schjelderup would bitterly complain that Reich abused the therapeutic relationship with him. Havrevold denounced Raknes for his close ties with Reich, a man of questionable scientific practices. For most of them, it was a relief to see Reich leave.

In August 1939, Reich finally received his visa. On August 19, he set sail on the *Stavenger Fjord*, the last boat to leave Norway for the States before World War II broke out on September 3. While Reich was en route to America, the Soviet Union and Nazi Germany signed a non-aggression pact, thoroughly revealing what Reich had been saying for some years: the revolution's promise for the Russians had been betrayed.

Elsa Lindenberg received a letter from him, written in his cabin, saying that he had cried a good deal on the trip, that he missed her, and wanted her to join him.[33]

On His Own in America—Total Immersion in Studies of "Life Energy" (Orgone Energy): 1940-1950

Getting Settled in America: 1939–1941

When Reich arrived in the United States in late August 1939, Theodore Wolfe was at the dock to meet him. Wolfe's arduous efforts had prevailed—for Reich had just made it out of Norway.

Along with Wolfe on the dockside stood Walter Briehl, the American psychiatrist. Briehl had studied with Reich in Vienna in the 1920s and in the early 1930s in Berlin. During the intervening years, he had established his American practice and had enrolled for further training at the New York Psychoanalytic Institute. Although greatly influenced by Reich, Briehl had not followed the later Norwegian developments. When Wolfe got in touch with him about the visa problem, Briehl had lent part of the money needed to guarantee Reich's salary at the New School for Social Research in New York.

Watching Reich as he descended the gangplank, Briehl felt immediately that his teacher had aged considerably. He also thought Reich looked depressed. Briehl made some effort to entertain Reich during his first days in America, taking him to a Harlem nightclub to show him something of the city, and inviting him to a relative's farm in New Jersey for a weekend.[1]

It was undoubtedly not easy for Reich, a proud man, to accept the hospitality of Briehl during this lonely and difficult period. Reich found it hard to spend time with people with whom he could not share his deepest concerns, and with Briehl he did not have this kind of intimate relationship.

With Lillian Bye, he did. An attractive, very intelligent Norwegian, Bye later became an outstanding social worker in this country and in Norway. She had met Reich in Norway and moved to the United States about the same time

Reich did. They had a brief sexual relationship. During the fall of 1939, he told Bye not only of his intense longing for Elsa and the unresolved problems between them, but also of his first impressions of America.[2] He told her how very beautiful it was to see Broadway, the huge neon signs that almost turned night into day, the many cinemas and theaters. Most of his contrasts with European cities favored New York, with its mix of ethnic groups and races. The supple Negroes (as they were called in those days) appealed to him, but not the many white males who impressed him as rather rough. American women were pretty—and not his type. He liked the fact that so many Americans were childlike and not disillusioned. On the other hand, he noted that strikers picketed but their protest was not linked to larger social-political concerns.

Reich recognized that it would not be easy to establish himself in America; one could get lost in the millions of people. It would be years before he could achieve the same kind of influence in America that he had had in Scandinavia. Still, once again he found the good news in the bad: "I will have time to work in peace."

Seen through Bye's remarks, Reich's early American weeks convey a kind of "moratorium," some respite before his work momentum was reestablished, which allowed him time to reflect upon his past, present, and future. The first weeks in America were similar to his experience at Davos in the winter of 1927. Once again there were scars to heal, this time from his Norwegian scientific upheavals and his conflicts with Elsa. He took long walks in what was then the countryside around Forest Hills, where shortly after his arrival, with the help of Wolfe and the trusty Gertrud Gaasland, he rented a house on Kessel Street. Once settled in, Reich would be able to pursue his myriad activities within one setting.

Ilse Ollendorff has described the house:

> It had a small basement which was used for animal experiments, and a large room on the first floor which served mainly as Reich's office but also had to function as dining room, living room and as accommodation for the seminar [with his American students] every other week. The regular dining room adjoining the kitchen was made into a laboratory with microscopes, oscillograph, electroscopes, and other instruments. The maid's room on the other side of the kitchen was used both as office and as preparation room for the laboratory cultures and media. The two bedrooms on the top floor were shared by Gertrud and the maid, and of the three small rooms on the second floor one was used as Reich's bedroom and the others for psychotherapy.[3]

The setup of Reich's home reflected his increasing commitment to laboratory experimental work. His natural-scientific research, begun in Norway, was to shape the basic design of his life in America.

It also shaped his new relationship with Ilse Ollendorff. In the beginning of October that year, Reich met Ilse through their mutual friend, Gertrud Gaasland. In Germany in the early 1930s Ilse had been involved in the small Socialist Workers Party; then she had emigrated to Paris, where she met Gertrud and Gertrud's lover of that time, Willi Brandt.* All three were members of the leftist party in exile.[4]

When Gertrud and Ilse renewed their friendship in the United States, their common interest soon became Reich and his work. Gertrud in her enthusiasm about both urged Ilse to meet Reich. In Ilse's words: "I met Reich briefly and was very impressed by him, even a bit awed. He was a striking figure with his grey hair, ruddy complexion, and white coat."[5]

At the time of their meeting, Ilse was divorced and not deeply involved with any man. In France she had held a position of considerable responsibility, working with a Jewish organization helping refugees. However, in America the clerical work she was doing bored her. Clearly, she was ripe for a major experience, personal or professional. Reich, too, was needy. In a historical account written some years later, Reich described the state of affairs when Ilse appeared on the scene—the tremendous amount of work that needed attention.[6]

Ilse soon began her fourteen-year involvement in "attending" to that "tremendous amount of work." In December 1939, he asked her if she would be interested in working for him, since Gertrud could no longer handle everything herself. The original plan was for Ilse to take over the secretarial and bookkeeping tasks, while she learned laboratory techniques from Gertrud.

When Reich first met Ilse, he told her of his strong attachment to Elsa but claimed the relationship was over. As we shall see, this description was far from complete. However, Ilse had the great advantage of proximity. She was also extremely hardworking, intelligent, and resourceful. She was open to new ideas and a person of broad culture. An attractive, youthful woman, twenty-nine to Reich's forty-two at the time they met, Reich was undoubtedly drawn to her sexually. On Christmas Day, they started living together in Forest Hills, though they were not legally married until 1946. Ilse began working for him on January 2, 1940.

In one way, Reich was relieved to be with someone less passionate and emotional than Elsa. Joyous as that relationship had often been, it had also taxed Reich. Elsa had refused to stay in place. Elsa (like Annie before her) had

---

*Brandt, whose major residence after Hitler's coming to power was in Norway, had some contact with Reich in the late 1930s, when he was a volunteer subject in one of Reich's bio-electrical experiments. From Spain, Brandt wrote Reich a letter about the political situation, including some comments regarding the poor status of women in the Loyalist Army, but their relationship was never a close one, personally or intellectually. Shortly before Reich left Norway, he wrote Gertrud that he had recently seen Brandt. The two men had good contact. However, Reich felt that Brandt did not grasp the biological essence of his work.

not only a career but a vocation apart from Reich; neither Annie nor Elsa was willing to make Reich's work the center of their professional lives. Ilse was. Moreover, Ilse was the only woman of Reich's not at all interested in therapy —either practicing or receiving it. Annie was an analyst and Elsa underwent psychotherapy several times, and, reflecting Reich's influence, became a dance therapist who utilized many concepts pertaining to body armor. By the time Reich came to America, therapy was less than ever at the center of his professional concern. Biology, physics, and education were what preoccupied him now. In Ilse he had found a woman who would mold herself to help him to the utmost in fulfilling his daily scientific routine. Whether it was setting up appointments with patients, preparing biological experiments, keeping the books, or carrying out household tasks in an efficient, economical way, Ilse did it all and did it well.

With a mate in place by Christmas, Reich also had his chief co-worker at his side from the first few weeks. Theodore Wolfe knew English and German well, was a clear writer and translator, and, in addition, had a remarkable aptitude for editing and publishing. In the early years, he was full of enthusiasm for the work. He was able to follow Reich in his current research on orgone energy, unlike others who had joined Reich at an earlier phase. Moreover, he felt enormously grateful to Reich for his therapeutic help.

How much therapy Wolfe had with Reich once he was in the United States is uncertain, but Wolfe would undoubtedly see him for sessions when difficulties arose.[7] Reich often had this kind of therapeutic relationship with American trainees: a period of intense work, averaging around a year and a half, then more sporadic sessions as need dictated. However, when Reich had a close working relationship with someone—especially as close, extensive, and intensive a one as he had with Wolfe—he preferred to see the person, literally and figuratively, as a co-worker rather than patient as soon as possible. The period of intensive therapeutic work was often shortened.

Wolfe worked like a demon. His advice to Reich on all kinds of matters was always frank and incisive; his attitude was as uncompromising as his mentor's. But he was not afraid to disagree with Reich, as were so many of Reich's students. All the people closest to him during this period—Wolfe, Ilse, and A. S. Neill (through correspondence)—spoke their minds. These were not yes-men or -women.

A third essential ingredient for Reich in establishing his new life was to form a circle of people around him. He needed patients, he needed assistants, he needed a response from the world. One resource was his course at the New School for Social Research, which was entitled "Biological Aspects of Character Formation" and given in the spring of 1940 and again in the spring of 1941. Of the several dozen persons who attended, about eight to ten pursued a more serious interest in Reich's work, seeking therapy with him and attending a biweekly seminar in his home. Among them was Alexander Lowen, at that time a teacher. By 1944, he was practicing Reichian therapy with young people and would be very active in the totality of Reich's work.*

More pertinent to establishing himself was Reich's need to provide the American public with access to his publications. Here Wolfe as translator, editor, and publishing adviser was crucial. Reich and Wolfe made the decision not to translate one of the earlier works for the initial American publication. Each of his earlier major books—*Character Analysis, The Mass Psychology of Fascism, The Sexual Revolution, The Bion*—dealt with one or another aspect of his work, but none showed clearly the development of his thought or the interlacing of the different facets. In addition, all of these books were fast becoming out of date in one way or another, lagging behind the surge of his current work.

Reich solved this problem by writing a new book and giving it an old title, *The Function of the Orgasm.* [8] The choice of title reflected his commitment to that function, or to what he called the "red thread" running through his protean labors. It was also confusing because in 1927 he had published a quite different book with the same title. But Reich rarely cared about such confusions. As he once put it: "We don't write *for* people, we write *about* things."[9] If the same title fitted a new work as well as an old one better than any other title, then use it and let the public wend its way through any subsequent confusion!

There was a further source of confusion. Reich mixed a provocative but clear title with an unclear one. On the title page, *The Function of the Orgasm* is listed as Volume I of a series named *The Discovery of the Orgone.* Nothing about this new term had been previously published; moreover, although *The Function of the Orgasm* surveyed his work in detail until 1940, the definition of and evidence for "orgone energy" was only briefly indicated. No matter. If "the function of the orgasm" was the retroactive red thread running through his work, "orgone energy" was a prospective red thread, as we shall discover. What was new was Reich's conviction that he now was able to study this energy practically and to measure it inside and outside the organism.

These qualifications aside, *The Function of the Orgasm* is not a difficult book and it *does* keep the reader in mind. Stylistically, Reich was in a felicitous phase. He had broken away from his earlier, more academic, Germanic style without getting into the angry outbursts that disfigure some of his later publications. The book presents a fine mixture of personal and scientific work, beginning with Reich's medical school days and his interests of that time; it follows him through the early devoted discipleship to Freud, the development of character analysis, the controversies with Freud and the other analysts over orgastic potency, and his sex-political endeavors (he downplayed here his

---

*In 1948, partly due to Reich's insistence that practitioners of his therapy be MDs, Lowen went to medical school in Switzerland. On his return to America in the early 1950s he launched his career in bio-energetics, an offshoot and popularization of Reich's therapy.

earlier commitment to communism). It finishes with his bio-electrical experiments, the development of vegetotherapy, and a few preliminary remarks about orgone energy.

According to one source, the original German manuscript contained material about Reich's early life, including the childhood tragedy involving his mother and tutor. However, Wolfe persuaded him that so autobiographical a section would not be appropriate for Reich's first American publication.[10] Perhaps Wolfe was right in his advice, but for biographers the decision was unfortunate.

Reich wrote most of *The Function of the Orgasm* in 1940, in his native German. It is remarkable that he could have written so clear, well-organized, and comprehensive a work under the many stresses of his first year in America. Extremely disciplined about writing, Reich would work a few hours on writing every day save Sunday. (He practiced—and urged others to follow—the policy of taking one day a week completely off from work.) Sigurd Hoel once ruefully compared himself to Reich: "He was very disciplined, he wrote every day. I took the days as they came."[11]

The book was revised, translated into English, and sent to the printer in 1941. It appeared early in 1942. To publish it, Reich and Wolfe had to set up their own publishing house, the Orgone Institute Press, for no existing publishing house would have accepted *The Function of the Orgasm* in those days.

As director of the Press, Wolfe with an assistant supervised all technical aspects of publication and distribution. A meticulous man, Wolfe took considerable pride in the excellence of his work—not only the translations themselves but the format of the publications. Around the time *The Function* was published, Reich and Wolfe also established a quarterly periodical, the *International Journal for Sex-Economy and Orgone-Research,* with Wolfe as editor and Reich as director of the Institute for which the *Journal* was the official organ. The new *Journal* represented a continuation of Reich's Norwegian periodical, the *Journal for Political Psychology and Sex-economy.*

Neither the *Function* nor the *Journal* became best-sellers. Sales figures from the early years are not available; however, we know that in 1950 about 450 copies of *The Function* were sold and the sales had been fairly steady.[12] Reich and Wolfe were not disposed toward any big promotional efforts. As Reich put it in a tribute to Wolfe, published in 1950: "We did not wish to join those one-day celebrities who make up in publicity for what they lack in deep-going search."[13] Reich has said of him that Wolfe respected Reich's way of expressing himself and Reich respected Wolfe's way of rendering it in English.[14] In fact, matters were somewhat more complicated. In later years, Reich complained that Wolfe smoothed out the "climaxes" that Reich liked in writing.[15] Early in his translation work, Wolfe once bristled when Reich tried to control his translation style. Reich backed off and from then on made no complaints directly to Wolfe.[16] It was a considerable relief to him when around 1948 his command of English was sufficient for him to write in that tongue, independently of translators.

There were few reviews of *The Function of the Orgasm* when it first appeared. In 1942 a lukewarm, anonymous review was published in the *Journal of the American Medical Association*. [17] The reviewer's main emphasis was on Reich's "rehashing" his disappointment with Freud, the irrelevance of Reich's political work, and his neglect of the contributions of others to psychoanalysis. *The American Journal of Psychiatry* published a review by Abraham Myerson, an eclectic psychiatrist of some repute. Myerson was largely caustic, focusing on Reich's tone of "absolute certainty" and his "monoideology" (i.e., orgastic potency). [18] Writing in *Psychosomatic Medicine,* Martin Grotjahn was entirely hostile. The book was "nuttier than a fruitcake . . . a surrealistic creation," yet it aroused "the same fascinating interest with which an analyst listens to the strange associations of a patient." [19]

It was not until 1945, after *The Sexual Revolution* and *Character Analysis* had been translated and published by Wolfe, that more serious critical attention began to be paid. In 1946, the most laudatory and insightful review was published by Paul Goodman in Dwight MacDonald's periodical *Politics,* which reached a small but very influential audience. [20] Goodman contrasted Reich's radical approach to political issues, combined with his depth-psychological, sex-affirmative orientation to the individual, with Erich Fromm's reformist and sexually diluted approach. A talented anarchist writer, Marie-Louise Berneri, wrote one of the first appreciations of Reich in England in the same year. [21]

As well as establishing new relationships that fitted his current interests, Reich was concerned to deal with past relationships that might or might not be compatible with his new work. One such relationship was with Walter Briehl, who, interested in further therapeutic work with Reich, had some sessions with him. Reich charged him $20 an hour, a sum to be deducted from the money Reich owed Briehl for subsidizing Reich's teaching contract. Briehl rather resented Reich's fee: "It was a lot of money in those days." Nor did he find Reich's new bodily techniques especially effective. [22]

Briehl's wife, Marie, a psychiatrist, and her sister, Rosetta Hurwitz, a psychologist, also knew Reich from the Vienna days when he had been one of their analytic teachers. They, too, resumed contact with Reich in New York. In his usual way, Reich was eager to show the Briehls and Rosetta Hurwitz the new orgone energy phenomena which so engaged his interest and enthusiasm. Walter wasn't able to see certain things (orgone energy in the dark room); Rosetta could, which convinced Reich of her greater aliveness and Briehl of her greater suggestibility.

There was still another issue between Briehl and Reich. Briehl had urged Reich to take the examinations for his medical license in New York. As he had recently taken them himself, he offered to help Reich study for them. Reich was indignant at Briehl's repeated admonitions, believing that on the basis of his contributions to psychiatry, he should be granted the license without taking exams. According to Briehl, Reich became "paranoid" and began telling Briehl that he didn't appreciate who Reich was. Hearing Briehl's account some thirty years later, it was easy to see how Reich had felt patronized and Briehl felt rejected for his concern.

Whatever the motivations on Briehl's side—Reich's fee, Briehl's dissatisfaction with therapy, Reich's headlong plunge into research on orgone energy, or his refusal to get a license—Briehl decided to break off treatment. After his last session, he folded up his sheet (Reich would ask patients to bring their own sheet, which was kept in a separate bag), shook hands, and said goodbye, never to see Reich again. One final issue remained, a familiar one when people ended their relationship with Reich: money. Briehl wanted back the difference between the money he had advanced Reich and the cost of his sessions. Reich suggested that the New School pay the difference. Eventually, Briehl received the money but only after Alvin Johnson, then director of the New School, put pressure on Reich.

None of the efforts to resume earlier relationships resulted in much better outcomes than the one with Briehl. Characteristically, Reich himself took the initiative with a woman, Edith Jacobson, the German-born psychoanalyst whom he had deeply respected during the Berlin years. After fighting against Hitler in the underground, she had been arrested and spent two years in prison, where she became sick with diabetes and a hormonal disturbance that had not been successfully diagnosed. Through the efforts of the International Psychoanalytic Association she was released from prison, went to Prague, and then came to the United States in 1938.

Not long after Reich arrived in the States he heard of Edith's continuing illness, which involved some difficulty in breathing. He visited her in her New York apartment and, after a talk, said that he believed his new therapeutic techniques might help her. So without really getting her permission, he tried to mobilize her respiration by pressing on her chest.

Edith didn't want his therapeutic aid. She told him it was impossible for him to help without her cooperation. Feeling hurt and offended, he left, though she thanked him for his good intentions.[23]

There is real poignancy to this meeting. Reich thought he had a chance to help Edith and to show her firsthand the efficacy of his therapeutic developments. She permitted neither. Indeed, for all her respect for Reich's character-analytic and mass-psychological work, Edith thought he had gone too far in his research on the bions and orgone energy. She believed that Reich's latest scientific work was delusional and that she should say so plainly.

There was another factor at work in the tension between Reich and Edith. Edith remained close to Annie Reich, who had already emigrated to the United States with the children. The continuing strain, indeed enmity, between Reich and Annie affected his relationship in the new country with Edith and also with his sister-in-law Ottilie.

The wave of immigration from Hitler's Europe brought yet another old friend to America, Lia Laszky, Reich's lover from medical school and Vienna years. She had remarried, recently emigrated, and felt somewhat stranded in the United States without a job. When she visited Reich, he was delighted to see her and "took beautiful pictures" of her. Characteristically, he was not especially interested in her European ordeals since leaving Germany in 1933, but full of enthusiasm for his own work, which he wanted to share with her.[24]

Reich told Lia about the bions and orgone energy. He had her put her hand over the bions and asked her what she felt. She said she felt a hot, prickling reaction—"He could have kissed me." In his enthusiasm over her response, Reich said she should come and work with him. Lia asked about her husband, but Reich replied that he would not fit in. Reich and Lia's husband had known each other slightly in Vienna but had taken a mutual dislike to each other then. Nothing came of the idea of Lia's working with Reich, but they remained on friendly terms and, indeed, were to have one more important meeting.

Reich also had some social meetings with his old medical school friends Paul and Gisela Stein. Paul was now an internist in Manhattan. Once again Reich wanted to focus the contact around his recent discoveries, but Paul did not wish to get involved in Reich's work and withdrew from the relationship.[25]

If Reich could not have contacts with his old European friends on the basis of his current interests, he wanted no contact at all. The same "all or nothing" aspect of his character arose with Gertrud Gaasland. Here the major differences between them seem to have been political. Even before coming to the United States, Reich was moving away from his more doctrinaire Socialist views. Shortly before leaving Norway, he had published an article entitled "Die Natürliche Organisation der Arbeit" ("The Natural Organization of Work in Work Democracy"); significantly, instead of signing it, he described the author as a "laboratory worker."[26] Perhaps he did so because the paper represented a sharp break with his more traditional Marxist views, a break he was not yet prepared to identify with publicly.

This paper also contained his growing disillusionment with all political parties, indeed, with politics itself. He had become more and more committed to the notion of work determining interpersonal relationships. Only those who had factual knowledge about a particular work process should participate in making decisions about that work. Here he was clearly influenced by his own experiences. Sometime after his discovery of the bions, he called in various associates to discuss with them its implications. He was dismayed to find many of them giving opinions and advice beyond their knowledge of what the bions were all about.

From a short-term viewpoint, Reich had by no means abandoned his political concerns. Right at the start of his American experience he expressed great admiration for Franklin Delano Roosevelt. On November 7, 1940, in his still clumsy English, he wrote A. S. Neill the day after Roosevelt's third-term election about his great pleasure in Roosevelt's victory. He also expressed his disgust when he encountered Socialists and Communists who denounced Roosevelt.[27]

Gertrud was undoubtedly one of those European Socialists who disliked Roosevelt. According to Ilse Ollendorff, Reich's stress on work democracy rather than political parties led to a sudden break with his assistant, following a violent discussion one evening early in 1941. Gertrud left his employ the next day and eventually returned to Norway. It was one of the less admirable sides of Reich's personality that he forbade Ilse to keep in touch with her old friend. The two women did not resume their friendship until the 1960s.[28]

But the most complex relationships of all were undoubtedly with his children. Reich resumed seeing them after his arrival in New York, under strained conditions. Eva recalls Reich's visiting her mother's apartment in New York sometime in 1941 on the occasion of her (Eva's) graduation from high school at seventeen. There was a huge quarrel between Reich and Annie and Thomas.[29]

Annie permitted the children to visit their father but remained uneasy about the contact. Ilse did everything she could to facilitate such visits and to serve as an intermediary between Reich and the Rubinsteins. On one occasion, Annie was reluctant about Lore's staying overnight with Reich and Ilse. Ilse was conducting the negotiations when Reich took the phone and asked bitterly: "What's the matter—are you afraid I'll seduce her?" to which Annie replied with equal bitterness: "I wouldn't put it past you."[30] (The old accusation that Reich was seductive and "hypnotizing," especially with Eva, continued to be made by Annie and her circle.)

Despite reaching out warmly to her father by letter after her arrival in New York, Eva remained highly ambivalent toward him during her high-school and college years. She was no longer in analysis with Bornstein but continued to be divided by the conflict between her parents and her internalization of Annie's judgments concerning Reich's sanity.

Reich connected Annie's animosity toward him with a dangerous incident that occurred shortly after Pearl Harbor. On December 12, 1941, Reich was picked up at his home at 2:00 A.M. by the FBI on the grounds that he was an "enemy alien" and taken to Ellis Island, where he was detained for over three weeks. Since his credentials as an anti-Nazi and anti-Stalinist were impeccable, it was hard to understand why he was being held. It may have had something to do with his earlier Communist Party affiliations, or with his views on sexuality (a factor that gains weight in the light of J. Edgar Hoover's obsession with that subject), or his generally "subversive" ideas.[31]

In any case, for Reich to be arrested by agents of a country he was coming to admire and love was intolerable. As always, he preferred to blame persons who were or had been close to him. In the case of the FBI arrest, he blamed Annie and her friends. His evidence was extremely tenuous, based as it was on some ambiguous statements made by his children when they were angry at him. There is no solid evidence that Annie ever took any specific action against Reich, or that she reported him to the FBI or any other agency. She and her friends had little use for him. They badmouthed him among themselves; they thought his work delusional and his influence on the children destructive. But there was never a question of taking retaliatory action of the kind Reich suspected.

The Ellis Island arrest left other scars on Reich. His skin condition erupted. The doctor agreed that he needed special care and had him transferred to the hospital ward, where Ilse was permitted to visit him twice a week. Wolfe and a lawyer tried their utmost to find out what the charge was against Reich. Wolfe went to Washington several times and the lawyer insisted on an immediate hearing, but despite all efforts the hearing did not take place until December 26. Eventually, after Reich had threatened to go on a hunger strike, he was conditionally released on January 5, 1942.[32]

In the edgy atmosphere right after Pearl Harbor, the authorities may have been concerned about certain books the FBI seized when they searched Reich's home a few days after his arrest: Hitler's *Mein Kampf,* Trotsky's *My Life,* and a Russian alphabet for children Reich had bought in 1929. At the hearing, Reich was questioned about his possession of these books. Once again he had to point out that in order to understand mass behavior, one had to study such books—to understand Hitler was not the same as supporting him.

The stress of being arrested not only aroused Reich's suspicions about who had instigated it but also about what went on during his absence. Here again his suspicions fell on those closest to him. During his detention on Ellis Island, he nursed the idea that Wolfe and Ilse might be having an affair.[33] Not much was made of this suspicion at the time, but a great deal was to be made later when his relations with both had deteriorated markedly.

Once again in this early American period it is important to stress the familiar mix whenever Reich entered a new phase of his life and work: the break-up of old professional and personal relationships; the establishment of new ones; changes in both his scientific and his social outlook. However, there was a special quality to his American reorientation. The change of continents was accompanied by a shift in his identity comparable only to that of the Davos period, when he had committed himself, with or without Freud's approval, to the study of the function of the orgasm.

We can see the background of this shift most clearly in the way he resolved his relationship with Elsa Lindenberg. During the fall of 1939, he missed her intensely. Elsa told me he wrote once that even though a particular day had brought him a scientific success, by night the success meant nothing compared to his anguish over her absence; he had cried like a baby. For her part, Elsa missed him acutely and saw the relationship in a far more positive light; the time for reflection had led her to realize her contribution to their problems. Still she feared submergence in his work and personality—"I did not want to be just a wife."[34] And, to her dismay, he kept pounding at her to reveal fully "the secret" of her affair.

When Elsa finally but vaguely acknowledged that some sort of liaison had occurred, she added that she had been secretive because she did not want to provoke his jealous rage, intensified by his "childhood drama." Reich replied that precisely the opposite was true: secrecy reawakened childhood traumas much more powerfully than an acknowledged affair. The latter he could "forgive."*

In December, Elsa was prepared to join Reich. But by this time Reich was very much involved with Ilse. He did not love Ilse as he loved Elsa, but she was *there,* she was kind, helpful, loyal—and he had learned to love her.

In Oslo, Elsa had complained about their social isolation. Now Reich saw even less of people. He was no longer prepared to give endlessly and to receive so little in return. He also realized that precisely those he had been closest to —Fenichel, Annie, Berta—were the ones he believed had slandered him the most. He would keep apart. He told Bye he was going to follow the "remarkable law": Be distant, even a little haughty, withhold love, and then people will respect you. One can perceive how carefully thought through was his creation of the "Dr. Reich" his American students would come to know: the man who very rarely took part in social occasions and whom no colleague, not even Neill, called by his first name.

This stern persona was accompanied by an equally strict resolve to carry out his own work. No longer would he speak in the name of Freud and Marx. He had to conquer in himself the feeling that he was a difficult, inaccessible, guilt-ridden person. He had to be himself.[35] It was not easy to become one's own man, especially when the stakes were as high as they were for Reich.† Reich's deep sense of guilt played a role in his various renunciations of these months, culminating in the ending of his relationship with Elsa. "Elsa must be sacrificed!" he told Bye around this time. If he punished himself, if he proved himself worthy, he could go on to make the large assertions he believed were implicit in his work.

---

*It is of course risible for Reich to speak of "forgiving" Elsa for what was at most a brief liaison when he had had a more enduring affair with Gerd Bergersen, an affair for which, as far as the record shows, he never sought "forgiveness." In view of his writings against the double standard, his male chauvinist behavior brings to mind W. H. Auden's lines from "At the Grave of Henry James":

> Master of scruple and nuance,
> Pray for me and for all writers living or dead,
> Because there are many whose works
> Are in better taste than their lives,
> because there is no end
> To the vanity of our calling. . . .

†In their important study of adult life development, *The Seasons of a Man's Life,* Daniel J. Levinson and his associates have conceptualized the problematic issue of "becoming one's own man" as occurring around age forty. Reich was forty-two at this juncture.

However, early in January 1940 his assertions were less on his mind than his pain. Elsa told me that he wrote her a letter around this time that revealed his sense of personal despair and hopelessness more fully than she had ever seen before. He no longer blamed Elsa but himself for the failure of their relationship. He wanted Elsa to be happy and he believed that he brought knowledge to the world but not happiness. He did not believe in his personal future but in his downfall—he would die alone like a dog. He would not experience any rest or peace. He did not want Elsa to share this fate. Elsa belonged to another world of which Reich had dreamed all his life—a world of peace, joy, sunshine, and companionship. Reich could not give her this in return. It hurt him terribly, for Elsa was among the very few people who understood him.[36]

Reich worried that his social reserve and his renunciation of Elsa would hinder his creativity even while they protected it. They did not hurt his productiveness, but they hurt him personally, and others. During the American years his anger at the cost of his decision would grow, erupting in furies even more incandescent and destructive than those reported by the Europeans. His plight has been aptly described by Nietzsche:

> Such lonely men need love, and friends to whom they can be as open and sincere as to themselves and in whose presence the deadening silence and hypocrisy may cease. Take their friends away and there is left an increasing peril; Heinrich von Kleist was broken by the lack of love, and the most terrible weapon against unusual men is to drive them into themselves; and then their issuing forth again is a terrible eruption. Yet there are always some demi-gods who can bear life under these fearful conditions and can be their conquerors and if you would hear their lonely chant, listen to the music of Beethoven.[37]

During periods with Elsa, Reich was able to unite work and love in an integrated design for life. For a decade after this separation he put aside hopes for his own emotional and sexual fulfillment. At the end of 1939, Reich saw "the clever hopes expire of a low dishonest decade," to quote W. H. Auden, recognizing that he was alone personally as well as scientifically. Whatever his despair, he would continue to show a "life-affirming flame," but the flame he affirmed was no longer to be found in adults, individually or collectively. He would find it instead in infants and in orgone energy.

Elsa herself was hurt and angered when Reich wrote to her breaking off their romantic relationship; she fought hard to win him back. His desire to reunite would well up from time to time and he would invite her to come to America to "see" in person how things were after all the inner changes that had occurred. Then, in April 1940, Hitler invaded Norway. Though Reich was prepared to do everything he could to get Elsa a visa, the chances were now very slim. Moreover, Elsa had little heart for coming to America not as Reich's mate. She preferred to stay in Oslo, despite the suffering she faced from the German occupation. She was never arrested but on several occasions had to flee to Sweden; the war years were also a time of severe financial and emotional stress for her.[38]

When I interviewed Elsa Lindenberg in Oslo during the late 1970s, she was seventy years old, strikingly attractive and vivacious. She could still show great emotion when she recalled Reich's jealous rages, his affairs, and above all what she believed to be his abrupt termination of their relationship after his passionate letters during the fall of 1939. She spoke of Reich with a mixture of tenderness, passion, humor, and criticalness that revealed a deep, genuine, and unsentimental love. No other woman whom I interviewed talked about Reich with that same kind of love—not Lia with her affectionate sarcasm, Ottilie with her marked ambivalence, or Ilse with her detachment. After Reich, Elsa never had another serious relationship with a man, although she was only in her early thirties when they parted.

Although Elsa truly loved Reich, she did not especially love his work and could not follow the natural-scientific research. For a few years after World War II, she taught a form of dance therapy that was much influenced by his psychiatric concepts. Today, she is a respected teacher of the Gindler method in Oslo.*

Yet another irony emerges in Reich's life. For all his efforts to get his mates to appreciate and follow his work, none did so after he and they parted, not even the woman who understood him best and loved him most.

---

*Elsa Gindler was a German woman who taught body techniques similar to the Alexander method and radically different from Reich's.

The Discovery of Orgone Energy: 1940

It is difficult to pinpoint the exact date for Reich's formulation of orgone energy, a term that he was first to use in publications after his arrival in America. However, a gradual flow of observations and new concepts was emerging from his research during the last six months in Norway and during the first year in the United States. In a letter written from Norway to Gertrud Gaasland on June 12, 1939, Reich referred to "orgone radiation." This, to my knowledge, is his first mention of the term "orgone."* In order to clarify the process of Reich's discovery, it is necessary to review briefly his experiences with the SAPA-bions in his last months in Norway.[1]

As noted in Chapter 17, bions developed from heating ocean sand (what Reich termed SAPA-bions) were much more effective in killing bacteria and at a greater distance than other bion forms. In addition, Reich had noted certain visual phenomena observable in the dark basement room where the SAPA-bions were kept, for example, bluish light emanating from the walls and from various objects. However, he was unable to exclude clearly subjective impressions with regard to the light phenomena.

Soon after he was established in Forest Hills, Reich addressed himself to further investigation of the hypothesized SAPA radiation. For our analytic purposes, his research on this energy—which, with increasing conviction, he would assert was orgone energy—will be divided into three sections: visual

*The neologism is derived from the words "orgasm" and "organism."

observations, thermal measurements, and the electroscopic effect. The medical studies of orgone energy will be discussed in the next chapter.

Visual Observations of Orgone Energy

Reich's next step in the study of energy radiation from the SAPA-bions was to attempt to build an apparatus that would contain the radiation.

To accomplish this, a closed space had to be constructed for the radiation to prevent its rapid diffusion into the surrounding air. According to Reich's observations, metal reflected the energy whereas organic material absorbed it. However, metal alone would deflect the energy on all sides. In order to avoid or minimize this external loss of radiation, Reich designed a boxlike apparatus that had metal walls on the inside backed with organic material on the outside. He reasoned that the radiation from the cultures would be reflected back by the inner metal walls; the outer deflection would be reduced by the external layer of organic material. One panel of the apparatus had an opening with a lens through which possible manifestations of the presumed energy could be observed by the researcher from the outside.[2]

In effect, Reich had designed the essential features of what he would later call an orgone energy accumulator. Few people realize that initially this apparatus was not devised to treat illness but to study visually the SAPA-bion radiation. Reich often began, as his critics alleged, with very strongly held hypotheses, indeed so strongly held that they sounded like proven convictions. In the present instance, his conviction concerned the existence of a radiation from SAPA-bions and a determination to study it. But his belief that he had devised an apparatus that would isolate the radiation soon proved wrong.

When Reich began to observe through the lens the enclosed dark space containing the SAPA-bions, at first he noted what he expected: the same kind of visual phenomena but in an even more intense form than he had previously seen. Now it was possible to distinguish two kinds of light phenomena: bluish, moving vapors, and sharper, yellowish points and lines that flickered. Reich expected that when he removed the SAPA-bions and ventilated the apparatus, the light phenomena would disappear. However, he found exactly the same light phenomena, though not as strong, in the empty box, *in the absence of SAPA cultures.* He first assumed that the organic part of the enclosure had absorbed energy radiating from the cultures, and this was what showed. Then he took the box apart, dipped the metal plates into water, put in new cotton, and ventilated everything for several days. But when he tried once more, he still found some visual phenomena. He also had another box built, with a glass front wall but without organic material outside. This box he kept carefully away from rooms in which SAPA cultures were stored. However, no matter what he did, he could not eliminate the radiation from the empty box. The light phenomena were not as intense as when the box contained cultures, but they were undoubtedly present.

Confronted with the ever present visual phenomena, Reich groped to the conclusion that the energy he was studying was "everywhere." In his account, he did not arrive at this belief easily:

> During the first two years . . . I doubted every one of my observations. Such impressions as "the energy is present everywhere" . . . carried little conviction; on the contrary they were apt to raise serious doubts. In addition, the continuous doubts, objections and negative findings on the part of physicists and bacteriologists tended to make me take my observations less seriously than they deserved to be taken. My self-confidence at that time was not particularly strong. Not strong enough to withstand the impact of all the new insights which followed from the discovery of the orgone.[3]

Reich often wrote—and acted—like a person with supreme self-confidence, even arrogance. In this instance he was struggling with a continual problem: how to trust himself in the face of great discoveries, and not yield to self-doubts accentuated by the external criticism of his method and his findings. Over and over again he was haunted by the question: If what I see exists, why wasn't it discovered before? And the corollary: Am I badly off track?

With the problem of a seemingly ubiquitous energy in mind, Reich, with Ilse, took his first American vacation in the summer of 1940—a camping trip through New England. After a week in New Hampshire, their tent leaked. They then drove into Maine, to the northwest part of the state, where they rented a cabin on Mooselookmeguntic Lake, near the small town of Rangeley. The lake was large, the cabin simple and quiet. The air was clear and dry, not hot and humid as summer was in Forest Hills. Reich loved the region immediately. It was to have a deep significance in his life. Here he would spend longer and longer summer periods, then establish his main research center, which he called Orgonon; finally, after 1950, he would live year round in the area.

It may have been a "vacation," but once located on Mooselookmeguntic, Reich wasted no time in getting down to work. Again, he proceeded in his naive way. One night he was watching the sky above the lake. He noted stars flickering, stronger in the east than the west, though the moon was low on the western horizon. Reich reasoned that if the theory that the flickering of the stars was due to diffuse light was correct, the flickering would have to be the same everywhere or even more intense near the moonlight. But exactly the opposite was the case.

Just as earlier Reich had looked at the emotional expression of the body in a new fashion, so now he began to watch the sky above the lake in a manner radically different from that of current observation with its panoply of instruments. In relying initially on his own organism as his main research tool, Reich returned to the earlier investigative emphasis of Goethe: "Man himself, inasmuch as he makes use of his healthy senses, is the greatest and most exact physical apparatus; and that is just the greatest evil of modern physics—that one has, as it were, detached the experiment from man and wishes to gain knowledge of nature merely through that which artificial instruments show."[4]

In Reich's view, to have limited his study of nature only to what he could measure through instruments would be equivalent to having studied the emotions of man only by means of quantitative indices. He would have had to rule out his *subjective* impression that the patient had, for example, a soft or hard or "aristocratic" character armor. However, unlike the artist or the philosopher, Reich was as interested in arriving finally at objective data in his study as he was in obtaining the same kind of evidence concerning the emotional life of man.

In Maine, Reich began to look at individual stars through a wooden tube. Accidentally, he focused the tube on a dark blue patch between the stars. To his surprise, he saw a vivid flickering, then flashes of fine rays of light. The more he turned in the direction of the moon, the less intense these phenomena appeared. They were most pronounced in the darkest spots of the sky, *between* the stars. It was the same flickering and flashing he had observed so many times in his box. A magnifying glass used as an eyepiece in the tube magnified the rays. All of a sudden, Reich's box with its flickering lost its mysterious quality. The explanation was simple: the energy in the box, in the absence of cultures, came from the atmosphere. Hence the atmosphere contained an unknown energy.

Reich went on to make a series of visual observations of this energy, including magnifying the phenomena in order to rule out the possibility of their being only subjective sensations. However, these efforts were never decisive in the sense of permitting a critical test. David Boadella has summed up this controversial subject succinctly:

> If such phenomena as Reich described in the sky in fact exist, why is it, one may reasonably ask, that other people have not commented on them? Let us consider a related phenomenon that can be observed in the daytime, which Reich also described. If one looks into the daytime sky on a clear day, relaxes the eyes, and looks into empty space, a number of brilliant points of light become visible. They appear to dance about in whirling motions.
>
> Anyone who looks at the sky in this way can observe these points of light, yet few people are in fact aware of them until their attention is specifically directed. One does not find in the annals of science a description of these points of light. . . . Whether they are phenomena associated with the human eye (endoptic) or phenomena that are properties of the atmosphere (exoptic) as Reich believed, one will find

an account of them neither in textbooks of vision, nor in textbooks of meteorology or atmospherics. The phenomenon is one that was never studied because scientists did not give up valuable time to looking at darkness, or into empty boxes, or at a blue sky.[5]

It is characteristic of Reich's method that in reporting his path to orgone energy, he interrupted the account of various experiments to deal more broadly with "subjective impressions of light." He recalled children's fascination in closing their eyes and playing games with afterimages. Reich was doing something interesting in this little exegesis. The very process of turning away from inner childhood sensations, including the delight in "seeing things with our eyes closed," contributed to the adult fear of direct observation. Reich always kept central his awareness of how much our attitudes toward our own sensations could affect reactions to his "orgonomic"* findings—from orgastic potency to the bions to orgone energy in the atmosphere. Afraid of the energy within us, we cannot see the same energy outside ourselves. As Goethe put it in a favorite quote of Reich's: "Is it then so great a secret, what God and mankind and the world are? No! But none like to hear it, so it rests concealed."

Initially, Reich was puzzled by the nature of the bion radiation, then further perplexed by his inability to isolate the radiation. We leave him in the summer of 1940 finding victory in his failure: he could not isolate the radiation because it was "everywhere."

As far as Reich's formulation of orgone energy was concerned, in one sense he had been working with it throughout his long focus on bodily energy. He was certainly working on it more concretely in the bio-electrical experiments, the spontaneous motility of the bions, and the radiation from the SAPA cultures. But he himself dated the discovery to his visual observations over a lake in Maine.

The observations at Mooselookmeguntic Lake represent a moment of epiphany for Reich. For the first time he allowed himself fully to believe that he was observing a radiation apart from the SAPA cultures, and, although he could not prove it, distinct from subjective light phenomena. It was not until he felt he was dealing with an energy outside the body, outside matter itself, that he could break away from more conventional terminology—libido, bio-electricity—for the energy within the body, and refer to his discovery as "orgone energy."

Over and beyond that, the Mooselookmeguntic experience represented the sharpest possible contrast with the science of Reich's day. Just ten months earlier, on October 11, 1939, President Roosevelt had received Einstein's letter urging the development of an atomic bomb in the face of Hitler's likely push toward the same goal. That letter was to inaugurate the Los Alamos project.

---

*All phenomena pertaining to the spontaneous movement of orgone energy Reich came to subsume under the name he gave his science, orgonomy.

Meantime, Reich was making his lonely foray with the most primitive equipment and "foolish" observations in dark basements and over a lake. He was often to contrast the technical magnificence devoted to the "death rays" with the simple unsupported efforts that led to the discovery of the "life rays."

The contrast should not obscure the similarities between Reich's approach and that of traditional science, however. Reich yielded to no scientist in his concern for objective measurement. Although his visual observations had not led to any "crucial experiment," he was soon to turn to verifiable hypotheses and replicable experiments.

Thermal Measurements of Orgone Energy

The device Reich had constructed to observe visual phenomena from SAPA-bions became the orgone energy accumulator. In other words, the apparatus for enclosing the radiation from the bions also attracted (and accumulated) the energy he saw "everywhere." His reasons for this were several. For one thing, the visual phenomena of orgone energy were stronger within this kind of enclosure, in the absence of SAPA cultures, than they were in the free air or in a simple Faraday cage (an enclosure with walls of copper wire mesh to block electromagnetic radiation). For another, Reich noted a sensation of heat or a fine prickling, if the hand or skin surface was held at a short distance (about four inches) from the walls of the accumulator. These subjective sensations were the same as he had experienced when working with the SAPA-bions.

Reich's scientific explanation for the capacity of his apparatus to concentrate orgone energy from the atmosphere was as follows:

Organic material attracts and absorbs orgone energy. When our hair or a nylon slip or a rug crackles with "static electricity," this is a similar phenomenon. Such crackling is likely to occur more vigorously on a dry, clear day than on a humid one. For Reich, static electricity was one manifestation of orgone energy.

Metallic material also attracts orgone energy but repels it again rapidly. The metal radiates energy to the outside into the organic material and to the inside into the space of the accumulator. The movement of energy inward is free, while toward the outside it is being stopped. Thus, it can oscillate freely on the inside, but not to the outside. In addition, part of the energy radiated outward is absorbed by the organic material and given back to the metal.

Reich cited an unexplained aspect about the accumulator: "In which manner the energy penetrates the metal we do not know. All we know is that it *does* penetrate it, for the subjective and objective phenomena are far more intensive within the apparatus than on the outside."[6]

Here Reich was stating a genuine puzzle. But the admission was seized upon by his critics to ridicule him. Reich said he didn't know how the energy penetrates the metal, but somehow it did; the critics acted as if the admission itself removed his work from serious consideration. Whatever his uncertainties, Reich then proceeded toward more objective criteria. He designed a small accumulator so that the scale of a decimal thermometer, once inserted, could be read through a glass-covered aperture. An identical thermometer was suspended at the same height outside to measure the room temperature. Reich found a constant temperature difference between the two thermometers, ranging between 0.2°C and 1.8°C with a mean of 0.5°C. The accumulator was constantly warmer than the surrounding air. As a control, Reich repeated the experiment, but this time using a box of the same size built of wood or cardboard only. The temperature in both the room and in the wooden box equalized quickly. A temperature difference appeared only when the box was lined with metal on the inside.

During 1940 and 1941, Reich made observations of the temperature difference in the accumulator and outside it—a difference that he labeled "To-T." The "To" stood for the temperature inside the accumulator, with "T" representing the temperature in the control box. On many days he measured the temperatures every two hours. In addition to indoor measurements he also measured To-T outdoors, both above ground and with boxes buried in the soil. The differences were more marked outdoors than indoors, and stronger in good, clear weather. During rainy weather, the temperature differences were minimal or altogether absent. Reich also noted that visual observations of orgone energy were stronger in good weather than in humid or rainy weather.[7]

I shall postpone a more detailed critique of these temperature findings until later. But Reich believed he had taken an enormous step forward. He had gone beyond the troublesome issue of "subjective light" phenomena that had complicated the visual observations. Moreover, he had found an experimental setup that did not depend on the "vegetative liveliness" of the experimenter, for the recordings were entirely objective. Indeed, with modern equipment, the measurements could be made without a human observer. The hypothesis of a higher temperature in the accumulator could be readily replicated all over the world.

The Orgone Accumulator
and the Electroscopic Effect

In the growing fervor of his conviction that he was on the track of a universal energy, Reich began to measure orgone energy by means of an electroscope about the same time as he was recording To-T.

The electroscope itself consisted of a vertical metal pole to which a fine gold or aluminum leaf was attached, the whole being enclosed in a glass and metal case. When a source of voltage or electrostatic charge (e.g., from rubbing one's hair with a comb) was brought near to, or into contact with, the metal pole, a movement of the leaf away from the pole could be observed; this represented a "deflection" of the leaf measured in degrees of angle. This device has been used since the eighteenth century to measure voltage and monitor "atmospheric electricity."[8]

Several factors influence the rate of fall or discharge of the deflected leaf. According to electrostatic theory, essentially it discharges because of humidity in the air, since moisture acts as a conductor. Also, other things being equal, the greater the radiation from such sources as X-rays, ultraviolet rays, cosmic rays, the faster the discharge. Thus, electroscopes discharge more rapidly at higher altitudes due, presumably, to the stronger effect of cosmic rays.

Reich reasoned that since other manifestations of orgone energy, such as the temperature difference and the visual phenomena, were stronger in less humid or more orgonotically charged weather, the electroscope should discharge more slowly in an accumulator than in free air. (Whereas classical electrostatic theory had no problem in explaining a more rapid discharge of the electroscopic leaf in humid or rainy weather, it would not predict *any* difference in discharge rate within the kind of box Reich termed an accumulator.)

Reich's experiments confirmed in fact that the speed of discharge was slower on the inside of the accumulator than on the outside. On the average, the electroscope discharged twice as slowly in the accumulator as in the free air. The difference between the inside rate and outside was less in humid and rainy weather, just as the visual phenomena and To-T were less marked during those periods.[9]

As a control against the objection that the difference might be due to better air circulation outside the electroscope, Reich introduced a fan into the accumulator to circulate the enclosed air. This had no effect on the rate of natural leak.

The electroscopic findings combined with the temperature difference gave Reich increased confidence about the objective significance of his research on orgone energy. Initially, heat and a fine prickling were felt in the accumulator. The thermometer registered a higher temperature in the accumulator than outside it or in a control box. The electroscope had a slower rate of discharge inside the accumulator. Moreover, all of these differences were more pronounced on drier days than on humid ones. Subjectively, as Reich said, we also feel better with low humidity, when there is more "orgone energy" in the atmosphere.

Given the potential significance of these findings, why did Reich not immediately seek confirmation from the scientific community? In his own way Reich did just that. First, as noted, Wolfe and he were making every effort to publish a journal with the results of Reich's experimental work. Second, and more immediately, on December 30, 1940, he wrote to Albert Einstein, requesting a meeting to discuss orgone energy research.[10] On January 13, 1941, a five-hour meeting between Reich and Einstein took place in Princeton, New Jersey.[11]

It was highly characteristic of Reich to go right to the top of the scientific community. As a young analyst he had wanted to deal directly with Freud as much as possible rather than Freud's lieutenants. Later, as we shall see, when he believed his work had great significance for national public policy, he tried to deal directly with the White House and the Atomic Energy Commission.

Why exactly did Reich seek a meeting with Einstein? After his experiences with the Norwegian scientific authorities, Reich was determined not to turn again to presumed experts for support or validation of his work. He would quietly publish his findings and let the world react as it would. Yet when A. S. Neill sent Reich's books and journals during the 1940s to people like H. G. Wells, Reich was at first appreciative. Then, when Wells and others dismissed the work as rubbish, Reich became angry at Neill's seeking approval from upholders of established modes of thought. As Reich once commented, Neill would have been indignant if his books on Summerhill were sent to the New York Department of Education for approval.

Now Reich was turning to Einstein. As we have seen, Reich felt armed with the important objective evidence of the discovery of the temperature differential and the slower electroscopic discharge. Certain positive medical effects of the accumulator (to be discussed in detail later) also made him hope that his work in general, and the accumulator in particular, might play an important part in the war effort.

Although he was quite aware of the revolutionary quality of his work and the consequent need to proceed slowly (or organically, as he would say), he continued paradoxically to think that his work could be rapidly accepted in times of social crises. This led him to hope that the crisis of World War II, with America's involvement imminent, might provide the stimulus, the emergency, to propel his work to its rightful place. In addition, Einstein might help supply the badly needed resources he lacked to push a concerted effort on orgone research.

But probably the most important reason for going to Einstein was Reich's professional loneliness. In a letter to Neill around this period, he wrote that only Wolfe and Ilse understood what he was doing. Here he was being optimistic. Wolfe did not work in the laboratory, despite considerable pressure to do so. Ilse participated in laboratory work; with extraordinary conscientiousness, she shared an existence, as she later described it, dominated by the stopwatch measuring the electroscopic discharge rate. However, she lacked the scientific training to understand truly the nature of Reich's investigations. A. S. Neill, the person with whom Reich corresponded most during the early forties, was very supportive of Reich's educational and psychiatric work but took the position that he knew nothing of science and hence had no opinion on "orgones" (as he and others were wont to call orgone energy, to Reich's considerable irritation). It took Reich quite a while to persuade Neill to build and use an accumulator. Thus Reich had a strong desire for scientific "company."

Finally, there was Reich's personal need for Einstein's understanding and support. Since his break with Freud, Reich had not had a close relationship with an older man who could be a source of strength and guidance. We know how difficult that rupture was. It was not until 1946 that Reich told Raknes he was at last free of his dependency on Freud.

Reich had been defying authorities for some time—Freud, the Marxists, the electrophysiologists, the bacteriologists, and now the physicists. This willingness to see things for himself, not to take the authorities' word for it, had some roots in his early familial conflicts. He had disliked his father's authoritarianism and he had also seen that the "old man" was not so powerful or right as he seemed to be. He—and other supposed "last words"—could be defeated where it counted, for all their seeming strength, power, even arrogance. The truth was not necessarily as it was perceived.

In spite of his other responsibilities, Einstein must have been intrigued by the brief description Reich gave in his letter, for a few days later he replied, asking Reich to arrange an appointment.

Ilse Ollendorff has described Reich's mood:

> Reich was very excited and had his approach to Einstein carefully prepared when he left for Princeton on January 13 around noontime. He returned very late that evening, close to midnight. I had waited up for him, and he was so full of excitement and impressions that we talked far into the early morning hours. He told me that the conversation with Einstein had been extremely friendly and cordial, that Einstein was easy to talk to, that their conversation lasted almost five hours. Einstein was willing to investigate the phenomena that Reich had described to him, and a special little accumulator had to be built and taken to him. . . . Reich spoke of how exciting it was to talk to someone who knew the background of these physical phenomena, who had an immediate grasp of the implications. He started to daydream of possibilities for working with Einstein at the Institute for Advanced Studies, where he would be in a community of scientists on a level where he, Reich, would not always be the giving one, with everybody else taking, as it was in his own Institute, but where he could find a give and take on his own level. He had wanted for a long time to be done with the world of the neurotic, to devote himself solely to the biophysical aspects of the discovery. . . . He spoke that night of such possibilities, and hung onto this daydream for the next few weeks.[12]

In his own account, Reich stuck to the factual and scientific issues. In a conversation that began at 3:30 and ended at 8:30 in the evening, he explained to Einstein about the bionous disintegration of matter, the discovery of orgone energy in the SAPA-bions and then in the atmosphere. Einstein became increasingly interested and excited. Reich had brought with him a device through which the flickering phenomena could be observed and, in a darkened room, they made their observations. Einstein was amazed at what he saw, but then queried: "But I see the flickering all the time. Could it not be subjective?"[13]

Reich then moved on to measurable findings. He told Einstein about the temperature difference in the accumulator. Einstein replied that that was impossible, but if true it would be a "great bombshell."[14] He also promised to support Reich's discovery if the findings were verified. Before leaving, Reich suggested that Einstein could now understand the rumor that he was insane. Einstein replied that he certainly could.

Reich built a small accumulator, which he took to Einstein about two weeks later. The accumulator was put on a small table with a thermometer above it and another suspended a few feet away. Together, the two scientists observed that the temperature above the accumulator was about one degree warmer than the temperature away from the accumulator. Einstein wanted to observe the phenomenon over a period of time.

Subsequently, he wrote Reich that he had limited his efforts to the temperature difference because of his inability to exclude subjective impressions regarding the light manifestations of orgone energy. Initially, he found the accumulator temperature regularly higher than that registered at the second thermometer. However, an assistant had offered the explanation that this difference was due to convection currents between the air over the table and the air of the room as a whole.

Einstein then took the trouble to note a temperature difference of 0.68° C between the air above the table top (with the accumulator removed) and the air below, due to warm air convection from the ceiling and cooler air currents below the table. He suggested that this process was entirely sufficient to explain the temperature difference that Reich had observed and that Einstein had confirmed.[15]

Reich reacted strongly to Einstein's letter.[16] First, he outlined several experiments which he had conducted to control the interpretation of Einstein's assistant. Most decisively, he stressed that the temperature difference was even stronger out of doors, removing the issue of "convection currents" from the ceiling.

In his twenty-five-page response to Einstein, Reich did much more than describe his further experiments. He also expressed a deep concern, a poignant anxiety, that Einstein might withdraw from the whole affair. "Convection currents from the ceiling" would now join "air germs" and "Brownian movement" as convenient explanations for new findings, without the critics' having to take pains to deal with Reich's answers to these explanations. The new findings could be neatly categorized. To Einstein's credit, he thought seriously for a while and he experimented. But once satisfied with his own explanation, he believed the matter "completely solved," and showed no wish to pursue Reich's further experiments.

In an effort to enlist Einstein's sympathy, Reich made common cause with him—for the first time, to my knowledge. His letter noted that it was Einstein's concepts about the relation of energy to matter that had led Reich to "smash matter" through heat and soaking, thereby releasing bionous particles. He tried to convince Einstein of the urgency of his discoveries, which could help in the treatment of cancer and with the victims of war. Working alone, it would take Reich decades; with Einstein's support, a major breakthrough could occur much sooner to the benefit of mankind. He could understand if Einstein, preoccupied with other matters, did not wish to invest time and energy in Reich's work. But there was the added danger that word might get around that Einstein had "controlled" Reich's work and come up with a negative conclusion. The world, scientific and lay, would accept that as the final judgment. Reich still was very grateful to Einstein for taking the pains that he had, no matter what his future decisions.

Reich's near-desperate efforts to keep Einstein's support—his anxiety that Einstein would withdraw, or worse, that his negative interpretation would irreparably damage Reich's work in the eyes of the world—all remind us of similar feelings when Freud refused to support Reich's orgasm theory long before. Freud's course of support and rejection had spanned fourteen years, Einstein's a matter of months. Once again, Reich had turned to an older man whose work had stimulated him, both as a student and teacher, turned with the idea of "continuing" Einstein's work on energy and matter.

Not exactly bashful, Reich now pressed Einstein as he had pressed Freud. If far more had been at stake personally with Freud, far more was at stake scientifically with Einstein. It was a question of basic laws of nature, of a concrete energy concentrated in a simple device that had healing potential. Reich was prepared to appear "pushy," for, in one of his favorite phrases, "we are not playing for peanuts." There was nothing apologetic in his stance toward Einstein; Einstein *should* follow through on his initial enthusiasm, at least to the extent of replicating Reich's additional experiments. Although he left Einstein the excuse of pleading other preoccupations, Reich was determined that the famed scientist not be quoted as "refuting" Reich's work. For Einstein had everything in terms of credibility in the scientific and popular community, while Reich had next to nothing.

Einstein never answered Reich's long letter or the several subsequent ones. When rumors began to circulate about Einstein's refuting Reich's work, Wolfe wrote Einstein directly, saying that it would be necessary to publish the full correspondence between the two scientists in order to set Einstein's "negative finding" in proper context.[17] Einstein responded angrily about having his name used for advertising purposes.[18] Reich in turn reacted angrily, citing the damage done by incomplete stories about the encounter.[19] Einstein replied that he had not been the source of these stories, that he had treated with discretion their written and oral communications, and that he hoped Reich would do the same.[20]

Reich's final reply, never mailed, stated that he had requested Wolfe not to publish anything on the subject.[21] He was still puzzled by Einstein's silence in response to his own long letter about the additional experiments. Then Reich used a characteristic defense after disappointment. He maintained that he himself had no interest in official confirmation of his findings, but many of his colleagues wanted to have the discovery of orgone energy generally accepted. It was they who were pressing for publication.[22]

The correspondence was published, but only in 1953 when Reich and his work were in great peril.*

I have described the encounter with Einstein from Reich's viewpoint only. We do not have Einstein's version. His sympathetic biographer, Ronald W. Clark, has written off the matter as quite insignificant. In a few amused paragraphs, he describes how Einstein, "the most amiable of men," kindly granted that "eccentric" figure Reich an audience, succumbing to "the bait" of Reich's suggestion that orgone energy might be useful in the fight against the Nazis. Einstein later found a "commonplace explanation" of the phenomena Reich had shown him. That was that.[23]

Clark's tone is remarkably similar to the one employed by Ernest Jones in his official description of the Reich-Freud conflict. In both instances, the Reich "affair" was treated as quite inconsequential in the careers of two great men.

There have been about twenty positive replications of varying quality of Reich's thermal and electroscopic findings, starting in the 1950s and continuing into the 1980s. The best-controlled replication of the temperature difference was conducted by Dr. Courtney Baker, son and student of Elsworth F. Baker, the man Reich subsequently placed in charge of training orgonomic psychiatrists, as we shall see later.

Courtney, a psychiatrist with graduate training in physics, added to Reich's experimental design a very carefully constructed control box with precisely similar insulating properties as the accumulator. This "balanced" control box then showed the same sensitivity to fluctuations in room temperature as did the accumulator. On the basis of 204 readings over 15 days, he found a positive temperature difference 51 percent of the time, a negative temperature difference 25 percent of the time, and no temperature difference in 24 percent of the readings.[24] On only one occasion—just before a severe storm in 1950— had Reich observed a *negative* temperature difference.

Baker hypothesized that the considerable number of negative temperature differences in his study was due to changes in the atmosphere, especially the

---

*There is no evidence that Reich ever sought permission to publish these letters from Einstein who was still alive in 1953, nor is there any evidence that Einstein ever commented on them. The Einstein pamphlet had, in any case, a very limited publication of about 1,000 copies.

effects of pollution that had occurred since Reich's original work. What is significant in this context, however, is the large number of positive temperature differences. Also significant is that from the vantage point of traditional physics there should be *no* temperature difference, positive or negative.

The one available negative replication was conducted in the course of the Food and Drug Administration (FDA) investigation of the accumulator during the late 1940s and early 1950s. This investigation belongs in detail to a later chapter, but one point deserves mention here. The FDA contracted with Dr. Kurt Lion of the Massachusetts Institute of Technology to replicate Reich's findings. He found no positive temperature difference within the accumulator, but he did find a number of negative temperature differences.[25] Although Dr. Lion did not balance the accumulator and the control box so that they fluctuated equally with changes in room temperature, he did place the accumulator and the control in a fairly constant room temperature and took a great number of readings over a two-week period.

However, Dr. Lion did not describe in his protocol *how* he achieved a fairly even room temperature. If this was done by air conditioning, particularly in a closed air system, it could affect the orgone energy properties of the atmosphere.* This is another example of the subtle problems involved in replication of orgonomic experiments. In a legitimate effort to control an extraneous variable, such as fluctuations in room temperature, one may obliterate the very thing under study. These issues place a responsibility on the experimenter to meet Reich's conditions and at the same time achieve an objective test of the hyothesis.

Before considering the significance of these temperature difference replications, positive and negative, let us look briefly at the control studies of the electroscopic findings. Here again the best positive replication was done by Dr. Courtney Baker. Like Reich, he found a slower rate of discharge for the electroscope in the accumulator than in free air.[26] The main negative replication was contained in a brief report to the FDA by another physicist, Dr. Noel C. Little of Bowdoin College. His report states that "Identical quantitative measurements were obtained both inside and outside the accumulator. . . . Results were exactly what would have been expected."[27] There is no supporting description of such factors as atmospheric conditions in the experimental room or the weather.

Dr. Lion also presented for the FDA a theoretical refutation of Reich's

---

*In this connection, Ernest Hemingway has made an interesting comparison of several "bad" atmospheres similar to Reich's analysis: "I can be depressed by [the weather] when it is rainy, muggy, and with constant barometric changes. . . . So I'm working in an airconditioned room which is as false a way to work as to try to write in the pressurized cabin of a plane. . . . When mornings are alive again I can use the skeleton of what I've written and fill it in."—Ernest Hemingway, "The Private Hemingway: From this Unpublished Letters," ed. James Atlas, *The New York Times Magazine,* Feb. 15, 1981, 98–99.

electroscopic findings. Unlike Dr. Little, Dr. Lion believed that one would not expect identical readings on the electroscope inside and outside the accumulator. On the basis of electrostatic theory, one would expect the results Reich obtained—a slower discharge in the accumulator—since metal acts as a shield against ionizing radiation in the air.[28] So Dr. Lion did not carry out any replication. For him, Reich's findings were completely predictable—and banal. Thus, two reputable physicists derived from the same theory very different predictions concerning the accumulator's effect on the discharge rate of the electroscope.

There are several further problems with the replications. First, all the positive studies have been conducted by persons enthusiastic about much, if not all, of Reich's work. Could not experimental bias have been the chief reason for the positive results? When asked to comment on this, Dr. Baker replied:

> It is true that I am "sympathetic" to Reich's work in the sense that I believe in its value and validity, and that it should be supported. Does this make me unreliable when it comes to an objective experiment? The implication from the statement "Baker wished a favorable outcome" is that my work and that of other supporters of Reich is biased and skewed. This is a subtle catch-22: those who take the trouble to demonstrate the validity of his work become tainted as "sympathetic" and thus excluded. . . . I would have been personally happier had [Reich's] pendulum experiment come out exactly as Reich states, but it did not and that is what I reported.[29]

The negative replications of Drs. Lion and Little contain the possibility of a reverse bias. The FDA chose both men as expert scientists in part because they indicated an eagerness to be helpful in what they thought was a worthwhile effort to stop an obvious fraud. This kind of attitude does not suggest "objectivity" any more than the enthusiasm of the positive replicators.

A second, more important point concerns the paucity of these replications. It is now over forty years since Reich asserted a temperature difference in the accumulator. Why has so little been done when so much is at stake? And, especially, why has so little been done by highly qualified scientists?

These questions presuppose a disinterested scientific community that will look calmly at any new concept or finding, if it has even a remote possibility of adding to our knowledge. However, as the scientific historian Thomas Kuhn brilliantly argues, upholders of an established conceptual scheme (or "paradigm," in his language) are not likely to be kindly disposed toward any new paradigm or "revolutionary science."[30] This resistance is not due simply to prejudice or pigheadedness, though both may be factors in any given instance. Representatives of a particular scientific discipline may accomplish a great deal by pursuing an agreed-upon paradigm and applying it to an increasing number of problems—in short, to pursuing "normal science." Scientists are reluctant to abandon their established concepts unless through their investigations they uncover such significant "anomalies" or divergent findings as to constitute a "crisis" in the field. "The reason is clear," Kuhn states. "As in manufacture, so in science—retooling is an extravagance to be reserved for the occasion that demands it."[31]

It is much easier to try to find some means of explaining new findings through the old theory or adumbrations to it. An example of using the old theory to explain orgonomy is to posit that Reich's bions developed not from disintegrating matter but from highly heat-resistant air germs. An example of adumbration is to explain the effect of the accumulator in terms of negative ions, obviating any need for a new orgonomic paradigm.

The proponents of the new paradigm have the responsibility to advance their case with sufficient persuasiveness to win over a young generation of scientists not yet totally immersed in the existing conceptual scheme. In the grim words of the renowned German physicist Max Planck: "A new scientific truth does not triumph by convincing its opponents and making them see the light, but rather because its opponents eventually die, and a new generation grows up that is familiar with it."[32]

In this connection it is useful to recall that it was not until a hundred years after Copernicus's death that there was a sizable number of supporters of the heliocentric theory. One might expect that so long a delay in the acceptance of a better scientific paradigm belongs to the past, when religious dogma ruled more powerfully than today. However, there is an analogous example from our own century which also makes the point.

In 1912, a meteorologist named Alfred Wegener suggested that the continents had moved. To quote John McPhee: "He was making an assertion for which his name would live in mockery for about fifty years."[33] Not until the 1960s did Wegener's original theory of "continental drift," now in the more sophisticated form of "plate tectonics," win the paradigmatic debate in geology. The earth's "plates" had more than moved, they were still moving, albeit only a few inches a year.

These two long-resisted new paradigms concern the movement of what established thought claimed to be immobile. All of Reich's basic findings or his various new paradigms concerned spontaneous movement where it was not supposed to occur, for example, in the total bodily convulsions of the orgasm, the expansion and contraction of the bions, and the pulsation and movement of atmospheric orgone energy.

That Reich could find an explanation for the world's hostility to his findings in its fear of spontaneous movement; that there are many examples, long past and recent, of eventually triumphant paradigms which have been ridiculed for generations—these arguments in themselves do not make his work convincing. Ultimately, the test of his work lies in replicating his experiments and developing new ones. Ultimately, a broad-based research program must determine whether his paradigms fit the findings better than competing paradigms.

This kind of research is precisely what most orgonomic adherents have failed to do over the last forty years. Too often such adherents have been content to rail against the establishment for not taking orgonomy seriously. Many enthusiasts have claimed lack of scientific training as their excuse for not repeating and developing orgonomic findings. Others with more solid scientific backgrounds (who have repeated some experiments) take refuge from further inquiry in their lack of financial support, insufficient time, and the cloud of scandal that has hung over orgonomy, especially since the FDA's injunction in 1954.

Granted that the social and scientific atmosphere has not been conducive to serious orgonomic investigation, none of these arguments is sufficient to explain the neglect of a potential scientific gold mine by persons who have good reason to believe a successful strike was possible. Reich explained this neglect as due to the deep fear of spontaneous movement in orgonomic friend as well as foe. Again, such an explanation does not make orgonomy any more "right." However, it does help to make more comprehensible why few have tried to pursue the paradigm, so that we can see how fruitful or sterile it may be.

I have underscored the vast silence surrounding the orgonomic findings outlined in this chapter. There is another side. The steady trickle of experimental reports continues, just as there continues to be a steady sale of Reich's books. Not surprisingly, many of these reports come from people outside the scientific establishment. Kuhn has made an analogous point:

> Almost always the men who have achieved these fundamental inventions of a new paradigm have been either very young or very new to the field whose paradigm they change. . . . They are the men who, being little committed by prior practice to the traditional rules of normal science, are particularly likely to see that these rules no longer define a playable game and to conceive another set that can replace them.[34]

Similarly, those attracted to a new paradigm are often "outsiders": the first Copernicans were largely not astronomers, the first psychoanalysts not psychiatrists, the first nutritionists not physicians.

Even within the scientific establishment, the ambiance toward orgonomy is changing. We can expect that a serious debate over Reich's revolutionary paradigms in biology and physics will soon begin. Accompanying this ferment will be considerable controversy over his medical concepts and findings.

22

The Medical Effects of the
Accumulator: 1940-1948

We have seen how Einstein's rejection deeply disappointed Reich. However, he did not dwell on his hurt and anger but reacted in his usual way to rebuff, by pursuing his research all the more vigorously, as if to say, my work will yet prevail. And he gave special attention to the medical effects of the accumulator, effects which, he had advised Einstein, could be useful in the war effort.

To understand the use of the accumulator in the treatment of illness, we have to return first to the Oslo days. During 1937, Reich had observed that PA-bions immobilized various kinds of bacilli. They also immobilized T-bacilli —one kind of bacteria resulting from the disintegration of animal tissue. The paralyzing effect of the PA-bions led Reich to hypothesize an antithetical relationship between these two organisms, with healthy properties attributed to the PA-bions and noxious ones to the T-bacilli. Between 1937 and 1939, Reich ran a series of experiments injecting 178 healthy mice: some with T-bacilli alone, some with PA-bions alone, some with PA-bions and then with T-bacilli, some with T-bacilli followed by PA-bions.

The results largely supported his hypothesis. They showed that the T-bacilli–injected group had significantly more deaths within the experimental period than the PA–injected group. The results also suggested that PA-bions had an inoculatory effect against T-bacilli, but could not reverse the damage done if T-bacilli were injected first.[1]

When Reich investigated the cause of death in the thirty mice injected with T-bacilli alone, he found that thirteen showed cancerous cell formations and another seven showed ripe cancer cells in various tissues.[2]

Reich thus came to America with the finding that T-bacilli apparently effected the development of cancer in mice and with preliminary evidence that PA-bions played some role in combating this effect.

Reich's initial findings concerning the role of T-bacilli in the development of cancer led to his spending much of the next four years, until about 1944, studying the etiology and treatment of cancer.

Reich's investigation of cancer represents one of the most lucid examples of the interlacing of his psychiatric, sociological, biological, and physical research. It also became the most attacked part of his work. Because of his later assertion that the accumulator could *help* (not cure) in the treatment of cancer, he was dismissed by practically everyone as a sincere but psychotic "former psychoanalyst" or as a swindler.

In describing Reich's work on cancer, I shall follow three main areas: his studies of the origin of the cancer cell; the clinical account of the cancer process, suggesting a bio-emotional disposition toward the illness; and his actual experimental treatment, first with mice and later with patients.

The Origin of the Cancer Cell

The first opinion Reich formed from his experimental production of cancer tumors in mice was that the T-bacilli he injected were specific tumor agents. Thus, his initial thinking ran along traditional lines: a specific agent or virus for a specific illness. However, the T-bacilli did not prove to be specific for cancer. Reich examined samples of blood and of secretions, and found that T-bacilli could be obtained from persons who were perfectly healthy. For example, he found T-bacilli in a small erosion of his own tongue.

This negative finding led him to shift the focus from the agent of the disease to the host organism, in other words, to the question of "resistance to disease." As Reich put it: "It is always reassuring to find the 'specific cause' of a disease. This enables us to delineate the disease from healthy organisms in which this specific cause is absent. But this concept is erroneous and blocks the approach to the nature of *immunity,* that is, the natural defense reactions of the organism. . . ."[3]

It should be stressed that when in the early 1940s Reich asked these questions, "holistic medicine" and intensive immunological research had not yet become part of the cultural-scientific climate. Mann and Hoffmann have rightly asserted that Reich was one of the pioneers, if generally unacknowledged, in the shift from concern with the disease agent to the defenses of the host.[4]

Reich had observed that while healthy blood and secretions also showed T-bacilli, in the case of cancer patients the T-bacilli developed easily and rapidly; the blood and excretions of healthy individuals, however, had to be subjected to a process of degeneration, sometimes lasting for weeks, in order to obtain T-bacilli. Reich reasoned that in a healthy organism the T-bacilli were destroyed by the white blood cells. But if the organism was flooded by T-bacilli, then a secondary, pathological defense against the T-bacilli developed. The tissue and blood, weakened by the struggle against T-bacilli, began to decay prematurely into vesicles, both PA-bions and further T-bacilli.

Very early in his American work, Reich's concepts about the energetic processes in the organism changed. After his discovery of atmospheric orgone energy, in 1940, he began to think of the energetic charge of the tissues no longer as a "bio-electrical" but as an "orgonotic" charge. The energy he was observing in the atmosphere he believed to be the same as the energy in the organism.

Reich noted that in the blood of healthy individuals, one saw the PA-bions surrounded by dead T-bacilli: the PA-bions had combated them successfully. He assumed that the struggle between PA-bions and T-bacilli took place all the time and everywhere in the healthy organism. He further reasoned that the weaker the energetic charge of the PA-bions, the more would form in order to get rid of the T-bacilli present. So, as Reich put it, "The cancer cell is in reality a product of the many PA-bions which were formed from blood or tissue cells, as a defense against the local auto-infection with T-bacilli."[5]

Reich was struck by a parallel here between the development of cancer cells in animal tissue and the development of protozoa in disintegrating grass. He had already noticed that it was extremely difficult or altogether impossible to obtain protozoa from infusions of fresh spring grass, while autumnal grass gave an abundance of numerous protozoa. In the same fashion, cancer cells developed in deader, less vital blood and tissue. The essential point for Reich was that there was a functional identity between the development of protozoa in the grass infusion and of the cancer cells in the organism. Each developed from PA-bions in matter that had disintegrated. Neither developed in a young, flourishing organism, but both did so readily in a biologically damaged, "autumnal" host.

Reich then followed the development of bions into bion heaps that aggregated into club-shaped cancer cells moving with a slow, jerky action, visible at a magnification of 3000x. He was able to distinguish five stages in the growth of cancer cells that eventually formed tumors. In the first stage, all that was apparent were changes in the shape of the normal cells and the presence of T-bacilli within the cell and around its periphery in the adjacent fluid.

As a result of studying the blood in healthy and diseased mice, and later in healthy and sick people, Reich devised three tests for assessing the biological vitality of the blood. These tests have elsewhere been described in detail;[6] I shall limit myself here to a brief summary of the main findings.

Healthy red blood cells disintegrated much more slowly than blood from cancerous patients or mice. When it did disintegrate, healthy blood broke up into large uniform granules, whereas unhealthy blood disintegrated into shrunken granules. In another test procedure healthy blood, inoculated into a culture medium, left the culture clear after a day or two had passed. Unhealthy blood yielded T-bacilli that caused the broth to turn putrid.

The immediate significance of these tests was that they provided a crucial diagnostic tool. Unhealthy blood as defined by the above tests could be observed in stage one of the cancer process or well before the appearance of a tumor. A blood test showing abundant T-bacilli meant that the patient was a "high risk" candidate for tumor development. Preventive measures such as the regular use of the orgone accumulator were strongly indicated (see below).

The blood tests illustrate well both the conceptual unity and the practicality of Reich's work. Just as in psychiatry he had worked directly with the vitality or emotional-energetic flow of the organism, so in his biological work he focused on a similar kind of energetic expression. Biologically vigorous, strongly pulsating red blood cells show microscopically a wide margin (or "energy field") of an intense blue color, in contrast to sick cells, which show a reduced pulsation and a very narrow margin with a weak blue color. As with patients, so in examining blood, Reich paid close attention to color, form, and movement. As with patients, he moved from broad theoretical formulations to concrete techniques and findings, which in turn sharpened his conceptual lens.

Reich also examined the sputum, excreta, and vaginal secretion of patients. His description both of what he saw and why others had not seen these relatively simple observations in the past is worth quoting in some depth:

> Let us examine the sputum of a patient with lung cancer at magnifications above 2000x. . . . We find a wealth of very small lancet-shaped bodies which we did not see below 2000x. They have the same shape and motility as the T-bacilli which we can cultivate from degenerating tissue or blood, or from putrescent protein.
>
> Since T-bacilli are the result of tissue degeneration and putrid disintegration, the conclusion is inevitable that a process of disintegration and putrefaction is taking place in the lung tissue. . . .
>
> In healthy living tissue and in healthy blood, examined at 2000x, we find exclusively such cells as are described in the literature as the normal constituents of the organism. Now let us examine blood, excreta, and tissues of a cancer patient with carcinoma of the lung. We find formed cells and unformed shapes such as we never see in healthy experimental animals or healthy humans. In particular, we find *striated* or *vesicular* structures with a strong *blue glimmer* which look neither like cells nor like bacteria. . . .
>
> In no comprehensive work on cancer is there as much as a mention of the existence, let alone the form or variety of *living,* mobile

cancer cells in living tissues or in excretions. It is almost inconceivable that several generations of cancer researchers can have so grievously erred.[7]

On various occasions Reich would offer diverse explanations of why cancer cells in blood and excreta were overlooked. Traditional cancer researchers did not work with unstained specimens; they concerned themselves with substances and structures, but avoided the primitive movements and energetic processes of the living. Indeed, the concern with structure over movement also barred the use of higher-power magnification in cancer research, since at such magnification some details of structure are lost although finer movements can be observed. In addition, the high degree of specialization in modern science inhibited connections between different realms. Protozoa in grass were one thing, cancer cells in the human organism quite another; neuroses were one thing, cancer quite another.

Significantly, if orgonomic and traditional cancer research proceeded under quite different assumptions and often used very different methods, some concordance in cancer findings has emerged since the early 1940s. Over the past two decades classical research has been studying minute bodies called mycoplasmas, which have a number of properties in common with Reich's T-bacilli. Whether T-bacilli are identical with the mycoplasmas has not been established. But very similar forms, first obtained directly from cancer tumors in 1964, have been found to have a close association with cancer.[8]

Reich's ability to diagnose cancer by examination of cells in the body secretions anticipated the PAP cervical smear test by at least fifteen years. The discovery that cancer cells could be detected in the sputum of cancer patients before tumors developed was not made by classical cancer pathology until 1955.

Reich himself quoted the research of a number of cancer specialists who observed amoeboid forms in the tissues of cancer patients and paid no attention to them, believing they were amoeboid parasites stemming from infection outside. Then in 1950, Enterline and Coman published a paper in which they concluded that the amoeboid cells were not parasites but were endogenous (arising from within) or derivatives of the cancer itself.[9]

There is considerable conceptual overlap between Reich's approach and current immunological research on cancer. Both focus on what goes wrong with the natural defenses of the organism, or the individual's "resistance to illness," rather than on the toxic agent. The differences between the two approaches are also striking. Immunology stresses the failure of the white blood cell system to combat "foreign bodies" properly; Reich emphasized the struggle between energetically weakened red blood cells and T-bacilli, with the resulting disintegration of the cells into PA-bions and especially into further T-bacilli.

The Bio-emotional Disposition to Cancer

Between 1941 and 1943, Reich saw fifteen cases of cancer diagnosed at hospitals and previously treated with X-rays. All were in advanced stages of the disease. Reich was not initially drawn to the idea of seeing these patients psychiatrically. When he became immersed in the biology of the cancer cell, he confessed to a secret relief that he had gotten away from the "cursed sex problem" and could concentrate on organic pathology.[10] Yet when he came to study the lifestyles of his patients, Reich found that he was again confronted, albeit on a much deeper level, with the problem of sexuality.

In his cancer patients, Reich early noted that the cancer tumor was no more than one symptom of the disease. Indeed, the Reich blood tests had indicated that a cancer process was at work well before the appearance of the tumor. Reich coined the term "cancer biopathy" to convey the underlying process of cancer. And he used this term "biopathy" to cover a series of illnesses such as cancer, heart disease, and schizophrenia. He felt that the basic cause of such degenerative diseases was a chronic malfunction of the organism's biological energy. These diseases were to be distinguished from infectious or bacterially caused illnesses, for the development of biopathies was largely dependent upon the patient's emotional make-up. Whereas modern medicine has been extremely successful in comprehending and preventing infectious disease, it has been unsuccessful in dealing with the biopathies in any basic way.

In Reich's work with cancer patients we see once more his powers of acute observation. He paid the same strict attention to the way their bodies and characters expressed or concealed emotions as he had in his long study of neurotics. Here is Reich's description of one case—that of a woman whose hospital diagnosis was carcinoma of the left breast with bone metastases, pronounced hopeless:

> The chin was immobile; the patient talked through her teeth, as if hissing. The jaw muscles were rigid. . . . The patient held her head somewhat pulled in and thrust forward, as if she were afraid that something would happen to her neck if she were to move her head. . . . *Respiration* was severely disturbed. The lips were drawn in and the nostrils somewhat distended, as if she had to draw in air through the nose. . . . When asked to breathe out deeply, the patient was unable to do so; more than that, she did not seem to understand what she was asked to do. The attempt to get the thorax into the expiratory position, that is, to push it down, met with a vivid active muscular resistance. It was found that head, neck and shoulders formed a rigid unit, as if any movement in the respective joints was impossible. . . .[11]

Reich was also concerned about her sexual life.

> She had been married unhappily for two years when her husband died. She initially suffered from her sexual frustration caused by her husband's impotence, but later "got used to it." After her husband's death, she refused any contact with men. Gradually her sexual excitation subsided. In its place, she developed anxiety states; these she combated by way of various phobic mechanisms. At the time when I first saw her, she no longer suffered from anxiety states; she appeared emotionally balanced and somehow reconciled to her sexual abstinence and her personal fate in general.[12]

Far from abandoning his psychiatric lens, Reich was looking at his patients from a great diversity of analytic viewpoints.

Reich came to certain clinical generalizations about the "cancer biopathy" or the underlying illness behind the tumor, which were later to be presented in *The Cancer Biopathy* (1948).

Characterologically, cancer patients showed predominantly *mild emotions* and *resignation.* In this respect they could be distinguished from patients suffering from cardiovascular biopathy, who were more emotionally labile, anxious, explosive. Both groups suffered from sexual stasis, but in the cardiovascular cases the sexual excitation remained alive—biologically, physiologically, and psychologically. Cancer patients seemed to be affected in the core of the organism. "Chronic emotional calm . . . must correspond to a depletion of energy in the cell and plasma system."[13]

Reich made the following comparison:

> In a running brook, the water changes constantly. This makes possible the so-called self-purification of the water. . . . In stagnant water, on the other hand, processes of putrefaction are not only not eliminated, but furthered. Amoebae and other protozoa grow poorly or not at all in running water but copiously in stagnant water. We still do not know what this suffocation in stagnant water, or in the stagnant energy of the organism, consists in; but we have every reason to assume the existence of such a process.[14]

The characterological resignation led to a biopathic shrinking of cell functioning. Here Reich used a "core" model:

> Let us think of the biological, physiological and psychological functions in terms of a wide circle with a center (core). The shrinking of the circle periphery would then correspond to the characterological and emotional resignation. The center, the core, is as yet untouched. But the process progresses toward the center, the biological core. This

biological core is nothing but the sum total of all plasmatic cell functions. When the shrinking process reaches this core, then the plasma itself begins to shrink.[15]

He carefully noted that "these processes in cancer can only be deduced but not directly observed microscopically." He could however observe the resignation of cancer patients as well as the rapid disintegration of red blood cells or the presence of cancer cells in sputum and excreta. And he postulated the intervening variable of a shrinking within the organism's core that led to the diminution of excitation and affect, to what he called "stagnancy."

Muscularly, Reich found spasms in various body segments of cancer patients. Many of these, especially in sexual areas such as the chest and pelvis, proved to be sites for tumor development. The muscular rigidities were part and parcel of the deadening process conducive to tumors.

Respiration in cancer patients proved chronically deficient. Here Reich connected with an earlier observation of Otto Warburg, who in 1924 had related oxygen deficiency to cancer.

Recent research has noted several personality variables characteristic of cancer—resignation, loss of hope, an almost "painful acquiescence," and emotional blockage. The studies have not yet conclusively demonstrated that these personality traits *preceded* the onset of cancer. However, it has been found that cancer patients who can more freely express their emotions have a better prognosis than those who do not.[16]

Perhaps the most striking convergence between Reich's approach and current psychosomatic research lies in the new field of psychoimmunology. This discipline has found that individuals who have undergone severe stress, such as loss of a loved one, are more likely than a control group to suffer disturbances in the immune system and reduced resistance to diverse illnesses.[17]

I cite these studies to suggest that Reich was years ahead of his time in connecting emotional states with the cancer process. His explanation provides physiological links (e.g., reduced respiration) between the psychic attitude of resignation, on the one hand, and the cancerous tissue disintegration, on the other.

Boadella has summarized this perceptively:

Reich was far ahead of traditional cancer research, which only recently, in a cautious and fragmentary way, has begun to understand some of the psychiatric implications of cancer. . . . It was almost uncanny the way each phase of his earlier work had equipped him with the special skills needed to understand different aspects of the cancer process. His work on the orgasm problem linked him with those researchers who found aversion to sex linked with cancer; his studies of the character-resistances linked him to those who found blocked emotions were typical of cancer patients; his work on the ameboid movements in his bion cultures had prepared him for the ameboid cancer cells that Enterline and Coman were to confirm were derived from within and not from parasites. Similarly the studies of the basic antithesis [expansion and contraction] had given Reich just that kind of understanding of the *contraction* process as a total psychosomatic shrinking that was necessary if the cancer disease was to be comprehended.[18]

Experimental Treatment with the Orgone Energy Accumulator

As we noted, in Norway Reich had found that injections of T-bacilli led to cancer in many experimental mice. He had also found that SAPA-bions were the most effective kind of bions in killing T-bacilli. In America, these observations led him to conduct a series of experiments during 1940 involving the injection of cancer mice with SAPA-bions. Treated mice lived significantly longer than control cancer mice. "But finally all of them died; in some the tumors had receded, in others it had first receded or disappeared and then grown larger again."[19]

The Cancer Biopathy explains in detail Reich's partial success with SAPA-bion treatment. Suffice it here to note that blood tests showed that the red blood cells (erythrocytes) of the treated mice were taut and biologically vigorous, while the blood of the untreated mice presented the typical picture of cancer: shrunken membranes of the erythrocytes, T-spikes, and abundant T-bacilli in the blood. Through these and other observations, Reich came to the conclusion that the erythrocytes, charged with energy from the SAPA-bions were the bearers of the therapeutic function, rather than the SAPA-bions themselves, as he had originally thought.

With the treated mice, Reich noted that many died not from tumors or from T-bacilli intoxication but from tumor remains clogging the kidneys. The larger the tumor, the greater was this danger. In other words, they died from the results of the elimination of the cancer.

During the extraordinarily productive year of 1940, Reich worked on a broad front: observing the visual effects of orgone energy, building an accumulator, and taking thermal and electroscopic measurements within it. In his work with the accumulator, he also experienced considerable prickling and heat sensations similar to those he had noted with SAPA-bions. Reich's postulation of a common identity between the SAPA radiation and the atmospheric orgone energy led him to wonder whether the orgone accumulator itself might not be worth exploring as a treatment for cancer. If so, it would be much simpler to use than SAPA injections. So, in 1940, he gave up the arduous and time-consuming injections and instead kept cancer mice in the accumulator for one half hour each day. The results, in Reich's words, were startling:

> The very first tests revealed an astoundingly rapid effect; the mice recuperated rapidly, the fur became smooth and shiny, the eyes lost their dullness, the whole organism became vigorous instead of contracted and bent, and the tumors ceased to grow or they even receded. At first, it seemed [unlikely] that a simple cabinet, consisting of nothing but organic material outside and metal inside, should have such a pronounced biological effect.[20]

It is hard to imagine exactly how Reich felt when he first put cancer mice in a simple wood and metal box. Certainly he must have doubted himself. The rationale for the SAPA-bion treatment at least had a history of several years; the accumulator had only been studied for six months when Reich started using it as a treatment agent. That he dared to use this laughably simple device to treat a terrible illness took rare courage and self-confidence. In retrospect, the most remarkable aspect of all was his resoluteness in the face of ridicule and attacks in pursuing so steadily his concepts, observations, and experiments.

His daring paid off. The average life span of untreated cancer mice was four weeks, of SAPA-injected mice nine weeks, and of mice treated in the accumulator eleven weeks. Also, Reich, his colleagues, and his students began using the accumulator themselves and noted a marked increase in their vitality.

By early 1941, Reich felt prepared to start investigations of the accumulator with sick human beings. By this time his thinking about its therapeutic mechanism had also evolved. Initially, he thought that orgone energy in the accumulator simply penetrated the organism like X-rays. However, this hypothesis did not explain why some persons who used the accumulator reacted to orgone energy immediately whereas others needed a number of irradiations before they showed any reactions. Reich had also noted that the accumulator functioned much better if its walls were about four inches from the organism treated. Ignorance of this fact initially caused a series of failures. The effect of accumulators on mice was poor when they were treated in large accumulators built for humans. A third key observation was that there was a slight rise in body temperature when persons used the accumulator.[21]

These findings led Reich to change his hypothesis about the mechanism behind the accumulator's beneficial effect. He shifted from the more mechanical idea of orgone particles hitting the organism within the accumulator to the notion of a mutual excitation between two energy fields—that of the organism and that of the accumulator. Here his thinking returned to earlier concepts: the attraction between two people with a "field of excitation" and the lumination he had observed between bions. This explanation fit the finding that energetically sluggish persons usually did not react to orgone energy in the accumulator until after a number of sessions.

In May 1941, Reich began using the accumulator in the treatment of cancer patients. The physical orgone therapy involved larger, man-sized accumulators that Reich had constructed in December 1940. They were about two feet six inches square in floor area and about five feet high, so that when a person sat down inside he or she was surrounded closely by the metal walls, without actually touching them. An aperture in the door, about one foot square, provided ventilation. According to the construction, the intensity of the energy accumulation effect could be varied. Thus, walls made of alternating layers of celotex and sheet iron (later, layers of glass wool and steel wool were used for additional concentration) increased the accumulation strength. The early accumulators were built of only a few layers, up to five-fold.*

When Reich's first cancer patient sat inside for her thirty-minute treatments, she experienced the typical subjective reactions already described. She began to perspire, her skin reddened, and the blood pressure decreased. Cancer was a disease of *contraction;* the orgone accumulator provided an *expansive* therapy that stimulated parasympathetic innervation.

However one seeks to explain the action of the accumulator, Reich found evidence for its positive effect on the cancer patient. The hemoglobin content of her blood increased markedly in three weeks. Her pains receded and she was able to sleep well without morphine. She was no longer bedridden and could resume her normal housework. Her breast tumor could not now be palpated, after eight therapy sessions, although the entire treatment included many more irradiations.

In spite of the patient's vast symptomatic relief, the full danger of the cancer biopathy made its appearance only after elimination of the tumor. About four weeks after the start of orgone therapy, the patient became quite anxious and depressed. Though physically better, she

> now found herself in the tragic situation of waking up to new life, only to be confronted by a nothingness. As long as she was ill, the tumor and resulting suffering had absorbed all interest. Indeed, her organism had used up great amounts of biological energy in the fight against the cancer. These energies were now free, and in addition were amplified

---

*Not long after he designed these accumulators for total body irradiation, Reich devised two kinds of smaller, special purpose accumulators: the so-called shooter and the blanket. The "shooter" was a box about one cubic foot in size, built with the same alternation of organic and metallic layers as the large accumulator. It was equipped with a hollow cable, one end of which was inserted through a hole into the box with the other end attached to a funnel. The funnel was then placed close to but not touching an injured part of the body for local irradiation. The flexible blanket was constructed of wire mesh with several layers of rock wool (organic) and steel wool (metallic) covered on the outside with plastic. It was used for bedridden patients and for local application.

by the orgonotic charge. In a phase of particularly intense depression the patient confessed that she felt herself ruined as a woman, that she felt herself to be ugly, and that she did not see how she could suffer this life. She asked me whether the orgone energy could cure her neurosis also. This, of course, I had to deny, and the patient understood the reason.[22]

The patient's subsequent complaints included pain but even more an intense fear of pain, strong fear of falling, and weakness to the extent of being bedridden for weeks again. Reich offered to work with her in psychiatric orgone therapy and saw her for two hours every day. Now he noticed many of the usual reactions in character-analytic vegetotherapy, particularly the intense fear of falling and contractions in the face of pleasurable expansion. Some improvement occurred, but it was followed by an unforeseeable catastrophe: the patient fractured her left leg. In the next four weeks she declined rapidly, and finally died. Reich concluded: "The orgone therapy had prolonged her life for about ten months, and had kept her free of cancer tumors and cancer pains for months and had restored the function of her blood system to normal. The interruption of the orgone treatment . . . interdicts any conjecture as to a possible favorable outcome."[23]

This case deserves further comment since it well illustrates Reich's handling of cancer cases, and, indeed, his overall approach. First, one cannot but be impressed by Reich's synthesis of various data—psychiatric, social, medical, biological—that were apparent in the case history. As different aspects of the case emerged, he was ready with different weapons from his own theoretical and technical arsenal. When the patient improved physically with accumulator treatment, but then succumbed to depression and fear over the state of her life, Reich brought into play the psychiatric treatment he had evolved to deal with just such problems. The oft-made criticism that he jumped from field to field does not so much miss as make the point. It was the very multiplicity of his work that permitted his elucidation of complex underlying aspects of the cancer process.

It is also characteristic that Reich failed to report some of the elementary details of the case. Thus, we do not know the patient's age. We know she had at least ten sessions in the accumulator, followed by marked improvement, but there may have been more than ten, and we do not know if these sessions were daily. Reich speaks of the orgone accumulator as the main treatment, with psychiatric therapy occurring only after her subsequent collapse. Still, he must have spent considerable time talking with her before more intensive psychiatric treatment. As is often the case with his highly condensed writing, the specific sequence of events remains unclear.

Third, in treating the patient described above, as well as other cancer patients who had shown improvement, Reich noted that attending physicians and surgeons were singularly unimpressed by the results with the orgone accumulator. They simply ignored its help. One physician told the patient's relatives that he was not interested in the accumulator until it was "recognized by official medicine."

A frequent criticism of Reich's treatment was that its real harm lay in depriving patients of genuine medical therapy. However, Reich was not opposed to the use of other treatments for cancer in addition to the accumulator. In one particular case, he urged the excision of the tumor even though it had decreased in size. On the other hand, he felt that the illness was being combated by the accumulator with sufficient efficacy to warrant a delimited excision rather than a radical mastectomy. A surgeon at the Leahy Clinic in Boston, who was friendly to Reich's work, agreed to this procedure and to the use of the accumulator post-operatively. The surgeon was later reproved by the hospital administration for cooperating with a "Reichian" physician in pursuing this "unusual" treatment procedure.

Fourth, Reich was often accused of promoting a "cancer cure." Of the fifteen cases he saw between 1941 and 1943, all were in advanced stages of cancer. Three patients died as expected by their physicians' estimates. Six patients lived five to twelve months longer than expected before dying. In all cases, Reich reported that the pain was greatly alleviated and the use of morphine reduced or eliminated. Six patients were still alive at the time Reich published his results (1943), but on none of these did he have a two-year follow-up.[24] As in the case described, Reich was optimistic about the accumulator's effect on the tumor but extremely guarded about its dealing with the underlying biopathy.

When the Food and Drug Administration later attacked his cancer work, Reich downplayed his optimism and highlighted his caution. Yet whatever the demurrals, his report in the above case that the tumor was no longer palpable after eight accumulator sessions can easily be read as an account of the miraculous. I do not know how justified Reich was in stating a causal connection between tumor disappearance and accumulator use. Tumors sometimes—though rarely—disappear without any treatment. I am better able to assess his scientific style in sociology and psychiatry, with a suggested extrapolation to his medical endeavors. In his enthusiasm for sex-politics, Reich was highly unrealistic about the possibilities of rapid and positive social change; throughout his career he could overestimate the effectiveness of his psychiatric therapy.

In my view, his at times impaired scientific skepticism had at least three sources: an intense excitement about his findings, the desire to bury his enemies under a creative avalanche, and his intuition that only by going too far could he find out how far he could go. One has to be a great pioneer to be justified in employing such a risky approach. It remains for further investigation to determine the blend of pioneering discovery and unscientific error in his medical work with the accumulator.

Fifth, one of the constant rumors connected with the accumulator was that it was some kind of "sex box" that promoted orgastic potency. Reich always vigorously denied that the accumulator had anything to do with "orgastic potency." The increase in sexual excitation that this patient—and others —experienced through accumulator treatment occurred naturally because, as they improved, less energy was needed to fight the illness. However, the accumulator could not resolve the patients' *fear* of excitation nor their incapacity to discharge the excitation. Hence, it did not promote orgastic potency.

Even though Reich did not claim a cure for the cancer biopathy, he did assert that he had elucidated important avenues to the prevention of cancer. The route to such prevention was the same as the route to the prevention of neuroses. As he put it:

> These cancer patients brought again to my consciousness, in the sharpest focus, what I had learned to see for the past twenty-eight years: *the pestilence of the sexual disturbances.* No matter how I tried to get away from it, the fact remained: *Cancer is living putrefaction of the tissues due to the pleasure starvation of the organism.* That this extremely simple fact had hitherto been overlooked was not alone due to inadequate research methods or the traditional errors of biology. I had hit upon it only because I had to be consistent as a sex-economist and had to follow the results of the sexual disturbances no matter where the search was going to lead. What has really prevented this discovery from being made long ago is the prevailing concept of life, the moralism, the sexual crippling of our children and adolescents, the moralistic prejudices in medicine and education. . . . We have outlawed the most important life function, have given it the stamp of sin and crime and have denied it any social protection. . . . We have lost confidence in the natural laws of life and now we have to pay the price for it.[25]

Reich saw the key to the prevention of cancer in mastering the sexual biopathies in children and adolescents, that is, in eliminating the unhealthy processes that lead not only to cancer but to any kind of biopathy. But in the case of cancer he had a more limited, simpler apprach: the widespread use of the accumulator as a preventive measure. "The orgone accumulator promises to become an important or even indispensable weapon in the fight for public health. It effects an orgonotic charging of the blood which increases the resistance to disease. . . . The orgone accumulator thus will be an indispensable weapon in the fight against diseases which consist in decreased defense functions of the organism."[26]

It is a mark of Reich's unbounded confidence that he could propose, for research purposes, a plan whereby ten thousand people would regularly use the accumulator. The incidence of cancer in the "accumulator group" would then be compared with a matched sample that had not used the accumulator. Within five years, such studies would yield definite indications as to general cancer prevention.

The plan was the more surprising at a time when, aside from a few score students and followers, Reich's accumulator and his orgone energy aroused no interest whatsoever. But that did not stop him. On April 13, 1945, he founded the Orgone Institute Research Laboratories, which served as the distributing organization for accumulators. Until that time, Reich had refrained from letting patients have the devices in their homes, partly from medical considerations, since he wanted to keep a close watch in the initial period of experimentation.

The one exception was Herman Templeton, the Maine guide who had sold Reich his cabin near Rangeley back in 1940. Reich and Templeton became good friends. In late 1941, Templeton contracted cancer and was given a year to live at most. During the summer of 1942, Reich saw his friend near death and persuaded the independent Templeton to build his own accumulator and use it in his home. Templeton did so and improved markedly; in fact, he took on the job of constructing accumulators in Maine. From his workshop they were then distributed to persons for whom Reich had prescribed them. When he died in 1944, his daughter took over the enterprise.

Templeton's case clearly impressed Reich with the advantages of home usage:

> The patients who came to the laboratory for their orgone treatment were, every day, on their way "to the doctor." Our friend was his own doctor. He could use the accumulator whenever he pleased. When he developed pain, he need not wait for the appointed hour with the physician, he could avail himself of the orgone immediately. . . . He had the leisure to become acquainted with the orgone, to make friends with it, as it were. . . . He was not just the passive object of the treatment but he was active. He learned to think about the energy which so greatly helped him and to do something with it.[27]

It is revealing to see this side of Reich's personality. With the accumulator, he was always prepared to acknowledge his ignorance and to encourage the patient to find out for himself or herself what was best: the amount of time for each sitting, the frequency of sittings, and the like. Once when a patient asked him how long to use the accumulator, he replied: *"We don't know.* We're idiots about this energy. We know we have it but all the details remain to be discovered. *You* find out what's best for *you."* And he replied in a similar fashion to a physician who inquired whether a twenty-fold accumulator should be used in a particular case: "We don't know the simplest things—whether to go fast or slow. We have to find out."[28]

Whereas Reich's physical findings concerning the accumulator had met largely with indifference from authoritative sources, his cancer research touched a raw nerve of mindless opposition. In 1949, Austin Smythe, then secretary of the Council on Pharmacy and Chemistry, published a scathing attack on the orgone accumulator in the *Journal of the American Medical Association*. His concluding paragraph read: "Inquiries received concerning the 'institute' publishing this nonsense indicate that the 'theory' is promoted as a method of curing cancer. There is, of course, no evidence to indicate that this is anything more than another fraud that has been foisted on the public and medical profession."[29]

Although Reich's main medical efforts with the accumulator were directed toward cancer treatment, he also reported that accumulator treatment could dramatically reduce the incidence of colds and was extremely useful in promoting the healing of wounds and burns.

Physicians working with Reich in the 1940s and early 1950s used the accumulator to treat a variety of illnesses: angina, heart disease, hypertensive states, pulmonary tuberculosis, and ichthyosis (a rare disease involving scaly, itching skin).[30] Their case histories suggest positive results from accumulator treatment, but the number of cases seen was too few to permit any conclusive judgment.

In the late 1950s, Dr. Bernard Grad, a biologist at McGill University who had worked with Reich, conducted research on the accumulator treatment of leukemic mice. Treated mice lived no longer than untreated ones but autopsies disclosed that a significantly smaller number died of leukemia.[31] In 1975, Richard Blasband reported that accumulator-treated mice lived significantly longer than nontreated ones.[32]

Then, in the mid-1960s, Dr. Bruno Bizzi, the vice-director of an Italian hospital, introduced orgone accumulators for the treatment of diverse human illnesses, including a few cases diagnosed as cancerous.[32] He also obtained positive confirmations in the reduction of tumors and succeeded in interesting Professor Chiurco, the director of the International Research Center on Pre-Cancer Conditions at Rome University. Professor Chiurco in turn sponsored an international seminar on cancer prevention in Rome in October 1968, at which Dr. Walter Hoppe, an old colleague of Reich's, presented a paper on a successful case with the orgone accumulator.[33]

What can we say in 1982 about the use of the accumulator for the treatment and prevention of cancer and other illnesses? Very little that could not have been said in the early 1950s. There is an even greater paucity of medical replications than physical ones. An important factor here is the force of the injunction decree obtained by the FDA in 1954 against the interstate shipment of the accumulator (to be described in Chapter 29). That injunction, as we shall see, was legally binding only on Reich and the Wilhelm Reich Foundation. But the fact remains that as late as 1963 at least—six years after Reich's death—

FDA investigators were making inquiries to see if any physicians were prescribing the accumulator. In 1981 the FDA still displayed the accumulator in the media as one of the more ludicrous examples of medical quackery stopped by the agency's assiduous efforts,[34] and the Administration continues to exert its "chilling effect" on the medical use of the accumulator. The *Journal of Orgonomy*, edited by Elsworth F. Baker, M.D., has since 1967 published numerous articles on psychiatric and scientific orgonomy but none on the use of the accumulator with human beings. One reason for this omission is fear of disciplinary action by state or professional organizations. Yet the fallout from the FDA injunction fails to explain the paucity of studies in other countries.

The growing shift in medicine from an agent- to a host-oriented perspective is beginning to facilitate a reevaluation of Reich's contribution to the origins of cancer. Let us hope that these changes in the intellectual climate will also encourage serious inquiry regarding Reich's prodigious efforts to develop and utilize the orgone accumulator in the treatment and prevention of cancer and other illnesses. Let us hope that the accumulator will be liberated from the shroud of stale clichés—such as *Time*'s obituary for Reich in 1957, describing a "box" that "could cure common colds, . . . cancer and impotence"—under which it still lies buried.

23

Psychiatric, Sociological, and Educational Developments: 1940–1950

After his arrival in America, all of Reich's work with human beings was influenced by his discovery of orgone energy. Since he had already utilized energy concepts (calling them libido and bio-electricity), his orgone energy findings represented no sharp break with his previous clinical and social endeavors. However, in the 1940s he would make less use of psychoanalysis or Marxism in explaining man's dilemmas; instead, his own views on human health were to be featured more prominently.

Psychiatric Developments

Reich's psychiatric work in the United States, as earlier in Europe, provided the main source of financial support for his research as well as an opportunity for contact with people. Almost all of those who were in close touch with him during the 1940s were initially interested in receiving therapy from him or learning his techniques. Usually both goals were combined, especially after 1945, when Reich started to devote himself entirely to "training therapy," as we shall see later.

It is significant that amid all his activities, Reich was able to maintain a psychiatric practice four to six hours a day. The financial needs of his research dictated this. In the early 1940s, he commanded a fee of $20 per session;

by 1948, he was charging $50. Between 1936 and 1950, Reich spent around $350,000 to support his own research.[1]

Initially, Reich's technique was very similar to the treatment he utilized in Norway. Indeed, his description of this therapy published in his first American book, *The Function of the Orgasm* (1942), was translated directly from a 1937 German monograph.[2] Then during the 1940s, some important therapeutic developments took place, although Reich never wrote them up in the detail with which he presented his natural-scientific findings.

In this period, Reich's major new therapeutic concept concerned the "segmental arrangement of the armor." The 1937 publication had shown him groping for a "law" central to the dissolution of the muscular armor. In America, he now conceived of the armor as consisting of various "segments" or "rings" that were at right angles to the spine. The streamings and bodily excitations—what Reich now perceived as a current of orgone energy—flowed vertically along the body axis. The therapeutic battle lay between the armor rings, on the one hand, and the streamings of energy, on the other. As Reich put it, since "the armorings are in segments at right angles to the movement of the currents, it is clear that the orgasm reflex cannot establish itself until after the dissolution of all the segmental armor rings."[3]

What were the particular segments or armor rings? Reich discussed these in roughly the order he would deal with them in therapy. He started at the top of the body, or the "ocular" ring:

> In the ocular armor segment we find a contraction and immobilization of all or most muscles of the eyeball, the lids, the forehead.
> . . . This is expressed in immobility of the forehead and eyelids, empty expression of the eyes or protruding eyeballs, a masklike expression or immobility on both sides of the nose. The eyes look out as from behind a rigid mask. The patient is unable to open his eyes wide, as if imitating fright. . . . Many patients have been unable to cry for many years. In others the eyes represent a narrow slit.[4]

To illustrate more precisely how Reich worked with a particular segment, when I was in therapy with him, he would have me follow his finger with my eyes as he moved his finger sideways and up and down, now slowly, now rapidly. At the same time he would note whether I was breathing naturally, as well as other aspects of my emotional expression. Sometimes he would make direct eye contact, asking me to open my eyes wide in fright as he made a threatening look or gesture. On a few occasions the wide-eyed, frightened expression brought up childhood memories of my fear of being kidnapped as I lay in bed looking anxiously around me. We then discussed this fear and some of its psychological as well as bodily connections.

It is worth noting once again the continuity in Reich's therapeutic work, in spite of some real differences to be described later. His goals remained the same: the establishment of the orgasm reflex in therapy and of orgastic potency in sexual life. The underlying conceptualization was also similar. We recall that in character analysis he worked from the surface to the depths, from the more superficial character traits (e.g., politeness) through to deeper emotions (rage, love). Now in psychiatric orgone therapy—as he began to call his therapy—he also worked from the top down, but with a difference. He started literally from the top of the body to loosen the horizontal armor rings in the way of the vertical flow of energy. Yet he was never mechanical in therapy. He worked on the *total* bodily expression, emphasizing different segments at different times.

The second armor segment, which Reich termed the "oral," included the musculature of the chin, the throat, and the back of the skull. Once one advanced to the second ring, the functional interplay of the segments became more apparent. Reich stressed that a particular emotional expression, such as crying, would not fully emerge unless several armor rings were released. Working with the armoring of the chin might release the impulse to cry; but if armoring in the ocular segment had not previously been loosened, it would be difficult fully to liberate the crying impulse.

Reich retained an earlier interest from character analysis in the tone of voice. He noted that with armor in the throat, the voice is "usually low, monotonous, 'thin' . . . In this condition, one will try in vain to talk with a loud and resonant voice. Children acquire such conditions at a very early age, when they are forced to suppress violent emotions to cry."[5]

The third segment centered on the deep neck musculature and the upper back. In working with the second and third segments, Reich was confronted with a problem: the therapist cannot put his or her hands on the larynx as he can on the superficial neck muscles. Here Reich used a very simple technique but one that carried great force. He simply asked the patient to put his finger down his throat and gag. This technique was used to combat the patient's tendency, learned in childhood, to "swallow down" feelings of anger and sorrow. With successful gagging, or what Reich called "eliciting the gag reflex," the swallowed emotions were "thrown up," often with literal vomiting. (A bucket became part of Reich's therapeutic equipment.)

Reich was a superb teacher, a kind of conductor, of gagging. He taught his patients not to force the gagging by rapidly sticking their fingers down their throats, all the while holding their breath and bracing against the gag reflex. Rather, he would have them do it slowly, gently tickling the back of the throat; he would urge them not to swallow, to keep breathing, to make a *wha-a-a* sound as they gagged. At such moments he became a kind of exorcist fighting the devil of swallowing and blocking the gag reflex.

The fourth segment is the chest; the fifth comprises essentially the diaphragm, the stomach, the solar plexus, pancreas, liver, and two always plainly evident muscle bundles alongside the lower thoracic vertebrae; the sixth segment includes the spasm of the large abdominal muscles, a specific contraction of the lateral muscles that run from the lower ribs to the upper margin of the pelvis, and, in the back, armoring of the lower sections of the muscles; and the seventh segment is the pelvic segment.

The reader is referred to Chapter XV of *Character Analysis* for a more complete description of the armor segments. Here I shall limit myself to some general comments.

In his discussion of the armor rings, Reich was not concerned with a mechanical softening of the musculature. He constantly sought to correct the false impression that psychiatric orgone therapy consisted of some kind of massage because it involved the "laying on of hands." Again and again he would say that "therapy does not consist of working on 'tensions' or 'muscles' as such, but of working on emotions—on the *expression* of emotions."[6]

In working with each segment, Reich studied the extent to which a patient could experience an emotion throughout his or her body. Thus, working on the throat block might elicit crying. Reich would then be concerned with the depth and extent of the crying. He would pay careful attention to whatever part of the body was not entering the total emotional experience. If the patient was angry, were the eyes, the voice, the arms, the legs expressing anger? If one part held back, Reich would then focus his attention on the nonparticipating segment.

Reich's interest in the function of respiration, sharply evident in Norway, became even stronger in America. His eye was especially tuned to seeing subtle manifestations of blocked respiration. Much of his therapeutic work now centered upon dealing with such blocks. Forced breathing ("No Yoga exercises, please!"), shallow breathing, closing the throat against the breath—all such expressions of inhibited respiration drew his lightning-like attention.

Just as Reich organized the therapeutic process around the orderly dissolution of segments, so he also organized therapy toward the orderly expression of emotions. One of his crucial diagnostic questions was: Which emotion is closest to the surface? Is the patient more afraid of crying than of being angry, or vice versa? It was a cardinal mistake for the therapist to press for crying if anger was in fact closer to the surface. Thus Reich's concern for an orderly therapeutic process sharply distinguishes his work from some of the neo-Reichian, encounter-type methods, which press for "letting feelings out" in a chaotic way.

Some syntactical confusion arose around 1945, when Reich changed the name of his psychiatric treatment from "character-analytic vegetotherapy" to "psychiatric orgone therapy." In the public's mind the latter term became confused with accumulator treatment, which Reich termed "physical orgone therapy." It was extremely characteristic of Reich to make this change in terminology even though he thereby contributed to the common misconception that the accumulator could, like psychiatric orgone therapy, promote "orgastic potency" and the associated misconception that the use of the accumulator was part of "psychiatric orgone therapy." Although Reich had become convinced that he was dealing with one and the same energy whether he was *releasing* organismic orgone energy from armor segments in psychiatric treatment or *confining* atmospheric orgone energy within the accumulator, the commonality and differences between the two treatments were not always clear to the reader. As always, the clarity of concepts and terminology in his rapidly integrating mind meant more to him than carefully fostering clarity in everyone else's mind.

By the mid-1940s, then, we see Reich studying the psychiatric interplay between two forces: streamings of energy, on the one hand, and segmental armor rings, on the other. Reich never failed to pay considerable attention to character traits, but the linking of these with early family history and unconscious memories was often done in a cursory fashion. He was tired of psychoanalysis, even though he once said to me after making a few interpretations: "You see, this work involves more than 'squeezing the muscles.' We are not against good psychoanalysis."[7]

In my view, Reich's impatience with verbal techniques hurt his efficacy as a practicing therapist. Patients need to talk a good deal about their past and present lives as well as work through armor segments. The most harmful aspect of his movement away from analysis was his tendency, at times, to veer too far from the wise aspects of the analytic principle of "neutrality": for example, the therapist should not meet the patient's hate with hate, but rather should help the patient to understand the infantile sources of his or her transferred rage. Reich could at times be blind to the shortcomings of patients who stirred his own infantile positive feelings and he could be unduly angry at others who evoked his old insecurities and rages. This weakness of Reich's was very apparent in Norway (as we saw in Chapter 18), but it was more pronounced than ever in America and it provided ammunition for his opponents, especially psychoanalysts.

However, I would also argue that his downplaying of psychoanalysis facilitated the development of his energy-block paradigm. Reich opened up a new domain through his almost exclusive emphasis on the emotional, the energetic, the wordless. Today, it is time for the "mopping up" phase of "normal science," in Kuhn's words, to make room within Reich's revolutionary paradigm for a more extensive and judicious use of verbal techniques than he was able to employ in his late years.

One of Reich's most substantial contributions to psychiatry occurred in 1941–42, when he had a schizophrenic patient in psychiatric orgone therapy for the first and only time. This young woman, previously hospitalized for many years, came to Reich on the recommendation of her brother, a student of Reich's. The psychiatrist at the state hospital where she had been treated and where she still went on an outpatient basis agreed to her entering therapy with Reich. The encounter between Reich and his schizophrenic patient was extraordinary, as revealed in the case history that was written six years later, in 1948, and published in 1949.[8] (Indeed, it is the only detailed case history Reich ever published.)

There is great gentleness in the way in which Reich treated this patient. With psychotic patients, as with impulsive characters, it was not a question of breaking through defenses to get to deeper feelings. Feelings were out in the open, if distorted—the impulsive character through his acting out, the schizophrenic through his delusions and projections. While he never romanticized the schizophrenic in the fashion of R. D. Laing and others, Reich did appreciate the candor with which the schizophrenic spoke of his or her inner processes:

> Every good psychiatrist knows that the schizophrenic is embarrassingly honest. He is also what is commonly called "deep," i.e., in contact with happenings. When we wish to learn something about human emotions and deep human experiences, we resort as biopsychiatrists to the schizophrenic and not to *homo normalis* [Reich's term for the average character neurotic]. This is so because the schizophrenic tells us frankly what he thinks and how he feels, whereas *homo normalis* tells us nothing at all and keeps us digging for years before he feels ready to show his inner structure.[9]

Reich's new comprehension of orgonotic energy functions was immensely helpful in understanding the patient's symptoms. She felt both protected and persecuted by "forces," the nature of which she did not understand. Reich began to view her "forces" as a projection of her body sensations. In therapy, he did not argue as to whether the forces were real or not. Rather, he kept coming back to her fear of her bodily streamings, especially her genital sensations. In an extremely vivid and dramatic account, the case history described the struggle between Reich and the patient, and within the patient herself, to permit her to accept her body feelings. Nowhere else in Reich's writings does the fear of the streamings, of strong genital sensations, emerge more graphically. He also stressed more carefully than ever the importance of the *gradual* release of emotion and energy flow so that the patient was not overwhelmed.

The most notable advance, however, was the attention Reich paid to the eyes, for he viewed schizophrenia as involving a split between sensation and perception. Whereas the neurotic person shut off his or her deeper sensations completely by means of heavy armor, the less armored schizophrenic was in touch with these sensations but distorted them. The schizophrenic suffered from a specific disturbance in eye contact—contact with his or her own inner processes and with the external world. One expression of this eye block was the typical "far-away" look of schizophrenic patients. As he worked with his patient, Reich found that the eye block intensified whenever she experienced an increase in pleasurable streamings in her body. "I ventured the preliminary assumption," Reich wrote, "that the 'going off' in the eyes was due to a local contraction of the nerve system at the base of the brain. According to this assumption this contraction had the same function as all other biopathic contractions: to prevent too strong bodily streamings and sensations."[10]

The patient made considerable gains during the three months of orgone therapy. However, the treatment was broken off at one phase when her anxiety mounted with the increase in pleasurable feelings and her self-destructive acts reached dangerous proportions. Reich, the patient, and the patient's family believed treatment could continue on an outpatient basis in spite of the dangers involved. The hospital psychiatrist felt differently. After some months in the hospital, the patient was discharged and subsequently maintained the improvement she had achieved with Reich. She was able to work and function, although problems remained in her love life. Her clinical picture was much more neurotic than psychotic at this point. The essential experiment over, Reich referred the patient for continuing treatment to an orgone therapist he himself had trained.

Our immediate concern is not really with the improvement of this patient —for many schizophrenics do improve from diverse treatments and with no treatment at all—but rather with Reich's conceptualization of schizophrenia and with the techniques he formulated for treating it. Let us look at the scientific issues and also what it meant for Reich personally.

First, significantly, he spoke of schizophrenia as a disease of the brain. As a psychoanalyst he had long opposed traditional organic explanations of mental illness, as being due to some genetic defect, for example. Reich opposed such physical explanations partly because schizophrenics had been stored away for so many years in mental hospitals in the belief that they suffered from "brain damage," and no brain pathology was ever found. However, now that an *emotional* factor in the form of armoring emerged as a "local contraction of the brain due to severe anxiety," he was much more disposed to consider schizophrenia a "brain disease."

The significance of this formulation lies in what Reich did with it. The task was not to operate on the brain (or give electric shock treatment, both treatments Reich opposed) but to help the patient tolerate intense sensations without "going off" in the eyes—rolling the eyeballs upward. It also influenced Reich's formulations on early infancy, especially the importance of eye contact between mother and infant, a subject to be discussed in the last section of this chapter. Equally significant was Reich's openness to ideas that permitted old, previously rejected concepts to be reinterpreted. As he once put it: "Everybody is right in some way; it is a question of finding out in *what* way."[11]

The very severity of the schizophrenic illness permitted Reich to be more daring in his therapeutic concepts than hitherto. (The same quantum leap in therapy, we recall, occurred when Reich treated a difficult case of masochism in the late 1920s.) For example, the patient suffered a severe throat block, a block Reich related to her fear of being strangled and her fear of strangling. As Reich put it:

> Our patient had suffered several decades of cruel monstrosities on the part of her nagging mother. She had developed the impulse to choke her mother in order to defend herself. Such impulses are very strong and cannot be fought off in any other way than by armoring against the welling up of the murderous hate in the throat.
>
> Quite spontaneously, the patient asked me *whether I would permit her to choke my throat.* I confess that I felt, not embarrassed, but a bit frightened; however, I told her to go ahead and do it. The patient put her hands *very cautiously* around my throat and exerted a slight pressure; then her face cleared up and she sank back exhausted. Her respiration was full now.[12]

Another important aspect was the human situation between the patient and Reich. In the early 1940s, as we have seen, Reich experienced little empathy not only from the world but also from many of his colleagues. On the other hand, his schizophrenic patient had considerable contact, albeit in a distorted fashion, with energetic processes within her organism. At times she perceived her "forces" as being on the walls of the room; at other times, she felt outside herself. Reich saw these distortions as projections of her own *energy,* not simply as projections of ideas and feelings. At various points the patient made references to the sun as containing the same kind of energy as the forces. Reich was staggered to see how the patient, even if in a confused way, could link up her own energy (the "forces") with external energies (the sun, the aurora borealis).

The poignancy of the encounter is enhanced if we keep in mind that during the period Reich was treating the patient, he himself was frequently being described as schizophrenic. Like his patient, Reich was seeing energy everywhere and describing "currents" in his body. Characteristically, he turned around the whole accusation of being crazy by examining more closely what craziness was, and finding it in many ways superior to so-called normality.

Reich's work on schizophrenia illustrates once again how the different aspects of his research mutually enriched each other. His intensive investigations of physical orgone energy alerted him more than ever to the disturbance in energy flow in patients, to the projections of energy in the schizophrenic, to the concrete reality his patient was referring to—albeit in a distorted way—when she spoke of her "forces."

Reich's energy-block paradigm yielded great therapeutic hope, at least in the case history described above. If the patient had not yet become "orgastically potent," Reich implied that with further therapeutic work she would eventually do so. Yet at the same time, the more Reich was in touch with the power of streamings, of organismic orgone energy, the more he also appreciated the "obstacles in the way"—the armor segments, the intense fear, indeed terror—in the face of surrender to the flow of orgastic excitation. However, Reich was so committed to the principle of orgastic potency that he never made clear publicly, though he sometimes did privately, that very few patients actually achieved orgastic potency. In his own way he contributed to the "cult" of the orgasm through his rather optimistic case history vignettes and this detailed case history of the schizophrenic patient.

Apart from the question of results, Reich continued to deplore the social inadequacy of therapy. Indeed, he resented the fact that the therapists he had trained were, largely, interested only in private practice and devoted little effort to education or to research. Once when an educator contemplated becoming a therapist, Reich said sharply: "No, if you do that, you will just make a lot of money and do no work."[13]

An intensely social animal, Reich never wanted to limit himself to the treatment of a relatively few privileged people. He was genuinely concerned with social and educational change, and with public policy.

Sociological Developments

This same period marked a turning point in Reich's social thought, a period in which we see the idiosyncratic quality of his thought emerge. It was as though his own thinking itself had to emerge from a kind of armor—the armor of wrong, culturally inherited ideas or the armor that reflected his own problems.

Here, too, the social environment played its role. Just as Marxism and apparent progress in the Soviet Union had spurred on his sex-political concepts in the 1920s, so the failure of the Russian Revolution in the 1930s, culminating in the Nazi-Soviet pact of August 1939, led him to revise many of his ideas, such as the readiness of people for a revolution and the capacity of leaders to help them. As with his move away from classical psychoanalysis, the movement of his social thought was gradual. Although he left the Communist Party in 1933, it took the rest of the 1930s before he broke clearly with Marxist political theory.

Reich's movement away from radical politics and Marxism was also encouraged by his American experience. He found in the United States a greater openness compared to Europe, less concern with hierarchy, and more willingness to experiment. The trend toward a more permissive upbringing of children, which Spock both reflected and promoted in his 1946 publication *Baby and Child Care,* was already manifest in the early 1940s. It deeply impressed Reich, especially in its contrast to what was occurring in the Soviet Union. There, even co-education had been abolished. Nothing in Marxist theory could explain the progressive, evolutionary movement toward freedom within capitalist America, while "socialist" Russia witnessed reactionary, anti-sexual developments.

His disappointments in America were not of the kind to lead him back to his Marxist political orientation. Thus, he found the American trade union movement very middle class. He never expressed the fondness for the industrial worker of America that he had felt for the European proletariat. He did have a positive regard for the rural Maine craftsmen, but such workers were not radical or even politically active.

Most important to the evolution of his social concepts was the totality of his work. His investigations of orgone energy permitted him to see more vividly than ever how blocked the flow of this energy was in human beings. His research on cancer and schizophrenia in the 1940s pointed to an early development of such blocks and highlighted how difficult they were to remove once they became chronic. His optimism about the average human being, badly damaged by his disillusionment with the Russian experiment, diminished still further. Political appeals, right or left, seemed ever more like a pandering to the public. The government in power, the Jews, the bosses, the Bolsheviks were all to blame, but never the average citizen with his armoring and his resulting fear of freedom and responsibility. For Reich in the 1940s it was precisely the masses themselves who had become the chief obstacle to human freedom: "As a result of thousands of years of social and educational warping, the masses of the people have become biologically rigid and incapable of freedom. They are no longer capable of organizing a peaceful living-together."[14]

The changes in his social thinking led Reich to ponder a good deal before he brought out *The Mass Psychology of Fascism* in an American edition in 1946. The original text, published in German in 1933, brimmed with Socialist fervor. In going over it in 1943, Reich noted that most of the book had stood the test of time: "I . . . found that every word pertaining to sex-economy was as valid as years previously while every party slogan which had found its way into the book had become meaningless."[15] What Reich did was to make relatively minor but significant changes in the text to reflect his current position, which was becoming evolutionary rather than revolutionary. The words "Communist" and "Socialist" were replaced by "progressive." "Class consciousness" became "work consciousness" or "social responsibility."

The change in Reich's social thought represented more than just a shift from a revolutionary outlook. At one level, he had come to despair of politics itself. As he expressed it: "Put an end to all politics! Turn to the practical tasks of real life!" To replace politics, Reich introduced the concept of "work democracy" (1946). By work democracy he meant the "natural process of love, work, and knowledge which has always governed economy and the social and cultural life of man and always will, as long as there is a human society. Work democracy is the sum total of all naturally developed and developing life functions which organically govern rational human relationships."[16]

As Paul Goodman noted, Reich's formulation of work democracy had much in common with anarchism.[17] The difference between Reich's approach and those of anarchist groups was that Reich did not advance work democracy as a new political goal or organize a new political movement around it. He regarded it as the *natural* form of social organization that existed whenever people cooperated harmoniously in the service of common needs and mutual interests. Just as in individual therapy one did not "acquire" orgastic potency, one removed the obstacles in the way of a naturally given function; so one did not organize or "get " work democracy. Rather, one removed the obstacles in the way of the naturally given work-democratic functions. But this was no easy task. Reich therefore formulated certain maxims:

   (a)   The masses of people are incapable of freedom;
   (b)   The general capacity for freedom can be acquired only in the daily struggle for a free life;
   (c)   It follows that the masses, who are incapable of freedom, must have social power if they are to become capable of freedom and capable of creating and maintaining freedom.

Reich never resolved the dilemma of how sick individuals could take social power and become capable of freedom. At various points in his writing he suggested certain directions, but these indications never amounted to a clear program. For example, in the 1930s he emphasized a long-standing concern for the industrial worker's alienation from the total work product plus the monotony of labor in a highly rationalized, modern industrial society. He saw one of the major tasks of progressive social development as finding ways to permit workers an involvement with the work product and with decisionmaking about work; at the same time, ways had to be found to accomplish these goals without losing the benefits of rationalization and division of labor. In these hopes Reich anticipated certain industrial experiments such as those in various Japanese industries and the work at the Volvo company in Sweden, where teams of workers participate in different aspects of the total production process as well as in decisions concerning work conditions.

Reich was quite aware that work democracy could not replace political struggle in the near future. When he said, "Put an end to all politics!" he was expressing a long-range goal. In the meantime he was all too aware that political forces would contend with one another and that there were "lesser evils." He never took the position, like the anarchists, of saying: a plague on all your parties and governments. He made choices in the real world: for the United States and the Allies over Germany, for the United States over the Soviet Union, for Roosevelt over his Republican opponents, and—in the 1950s, as we shall see—for Eisenhower over his Democratic rival.

From the 1940s on, Reich never lost sight of the fact that there could be no political organization of orgonomic findings. His basic position was that his work would have to penetrate quietly and organically, the way a tree grows, in one of his favorite analogies. It did not need—indeed, it would be killed by

—an organization made up of "believers" who would "vote" for orgonomy. Reich was impressed with the failure not only of Marxism but of other revolutionary ideas such as Christianity. He felt the discrepancy between truth and power. He would have agreed heartily with Thoreau's statement: "Just as when there is a lull in the wind a snowdrift piles up, so when there is a lull in truth an organization springs up."

What orgonomy needed, he felt, was not a political party but people with skills—physicians, nurses, scientists—who could root orgonomic findings in practical endeavors and who would win the respect of people through concrete accomplishments. It could not force its way.

Yet Reich always had problems distinguishing between short-term and long-term realities. At times he wrote as though there could be protection *now* for the truth in general and for his work in particular, even though the masses were armored. Indeed, sometimes he asked not just for freedom for his work but for the suppression of "irrational" opinion: "General formulations such as the 'freedom of the press, of expression, of assembly,' etc., are a matter of course, but far from sufficient. For under these laws, the irrational individual has the same rights as the rational one. As weeds always grow more easily and rampantly than other plants, the Hitlerite will inevitably win out."[18]

There were other signs of Reich's desire for immediate control over "irrationality." For example, he pointed out that one needed a license for such mundane activities as barbering, "but there is still no law for the protection of newborn infants against the parents' inability to bring up children or against the parents' neurotic influences."[19] Reich also believed that "every physician, teacher or social worker who will have to deal with children must show proof that he or she . . . is sex-economically healthy and that he has acquired an exact knowledge of infantile and adolescent sexuality. That is, training in sex-economy must be obligatory for physicians and teachers."[20]

It is so characteristic of Reich that he called for the requirement of sex-economic education at a time when such education was quite taboo. There is the typical defiant assertion that the rightful place of his work in a decent society should be granted right now. But Reich never solved the question of *who decides* which potential parents are neurotic; which teachers are sexually healthy; whose speech is irrational. Reich never intended there to be some kind of vote on these matters. He believed that healthy people should decide— people like himself. They would fail, not least because the masses would never select people who told them what was wrong with them.

In the meantime, in spite of his awareness of the extreme difficulty of real social change, Reich's bitterness and impatience with the masses grew. By the time he wrote *Listen, Little Man!* in 1945 (published in 1948), it was the "average man" who received his thunder and condemnation.[21] *Listen, Little Man!* is about the "average person," but it is also written for him or her as the "ideal reader." The prose is clear and simple. Whereas in his psychiatric writings Reich speaks of "chronic muscular spasms" and the like, now he says the same thing in basic English. Addressing the "Little Man": "You can only ladle in and only take, and cannot create and cannot give, because your basic bodily attitude is that of *holding back* and of spite."

Reich used the term "little man" in various senses. One meaning was the "common man," the "man in the street." At other times, Reich had in mind the "average man" who has gained power—Stalin or Truman (whose use of the atomic bomb at Hiroshima and Nagasaki Reich always excoriated). In the largest sense, *Listen, Little Man!* was addressed to all men and women, for we are all little in some ways and at some times. Reich meant by "little man" something akin to what Flaubert meant by "bourgeois": "I call 'bourgeois' whoever thinks meanly." The great man, Reich writes, was also once a little man, but "he learned to see where he was small in his thinking and action."

Listen, Little Man! served a further function for Reich: he used it to settle old scores. The reader familiar with Reich's life can recognize, though they remain unnamed, old enemies and "betrayers"—Paul Federn, Otto Fenichel, party hacks from his Communist days in Berlin, Leiv Kreyberg and Johann Scharffenberg from the Oslo campaign, Berta Bornstein and Albert Einstein, to name but a few who make cameo appearances in the book.

Still, the main target is the "common man." Reich was like an Old Testament preacher denouncing the stiff-necked, the hard of heart, the withholding, but a preacher informed by knowledge of the armor and of orgastic impotence:

> Your taking, basically, has only *one* meaning: You are forced continuously to gorge yourself with money, with happiness, with knowledge, because you feel yourself to be empty, starved, unhappy, not genuinely knowing nor desirous of knowledge. For the same reason you keep running away from the truth, Little Man: it might release the love reflex in you. It would inevitably show you what I, inadequately, am trying to show you here.

Reich had said the same things in *Character Analysis* and elsewhere, but with detachment and empathy for the neurotic condition. Now he was writing with tremendous force and eloquence, but also with a note of harsh blame, as though the "little man" had chosen to be the way he was. Reich never wrote about cancer patients as though their cancer cells were ugly. But he wrote about the little man's character traits, fully as determined as cancer, as though they were despicable. I once told Reich that I preferred the quiet tone of many of his other publications to *Listen, Little Man!* He agreed but said: "Everybody else has a chance to wipe off their mouth, so why shouldn't I?"[22] The tone of *Listen, Little Man!* was somewhat softened by the illustrations of William Steig, the noted cartoonist and a close follower of Reich's during the 1940s, as we shall see. His illustrations were sharply satiric but etched with a wit and empathy Reich often lacked.

Let us look more closely at these outbursts of rage, which so resembled those of Reich's father. Freud once said of himself that he needed two people in his life, one to love, one to hate. Reich also needed someone to hate. However, in addition to the vengeful quality of his rage, there was another side. It is a side well captured by Alfred Kazin in his description of Flaubert's anger:

> Anger is a great quality, a classic quality, and one rarely evident today, for what most people feel just now is usually resentment and bitterness, the telltale feelings of people who consider themselves imposed on, who know that they are not getting their due, who feel *small.* Flaubert's anger, on the contrary, is that of a powerfully caged beast . . . of a man who, feeling his strength to the uttermost, is continually outraged by the meanness, the self-seeking, the lowness, the vulgarity around him. It is because he feels his strength—unlike most of us today who feel only our weakness—that he is so magnificently angry. . . .[23]

Still, Reich was saddened that the little man could not stay with his moments of depth and intensity. As Saul Bellow has Augie March say: "Intensity is what the feeble humanity of us can't take for very long." Nothing hurt Reich more than the failure of people to take for long his intensity and the intensity of orgonomy.

While Reich's anger was directed at the little man, his even greater fury was directed toward a particular kind of little man whom he termed the "emotional plague character."[24] By "the emotional plague," Reich meant the destructive acting out of neurotic impulses. Whereas the ordinary "little man" limited himself or herself to taking and not giving, to being spiteful, to avoiding conflict, the little man with the emotional plague was actively destructive toward expressions of life. To give Reich's favorite example distinguishing the two types: People who sit quietly on their porch, minding their own business but giving little to others, are character neurotics. People who maliciously gossip about their neighbors, who organize with others to persecute one or another "immoral" person, suffer from the emotional plague.

By the late 1940s, Reich was becoming increasingly concerned with the way certain individuals who suffered severely from the plague interacted with the average individual or the character neurotic. In his own experiences as well as in the case of other innovators, he found very often one or two people (people with the emotional plague) who actively stirred up the average person's hatred. In his own case, he found the average person indifferent, if not initially friendly, toward his work. (As we know, Reich could at times exaggerate the degree of people's receptivity to orgonomy.) Then one or two would begin gossiping viciously about Reichian "orgies" and the like. The average person would not stand up to the rumormongers for a variety of reasons, not least because he feared defamation himself for whatever "indiscretions" he had committed.

No example more beautifully illustrates this process than the late J. Edgar Hoover, who tried to destroy Martin Luther King, Jr., with the threat of publicizing information about King's sex life obtained by concealed tape recorders. Hoover could get away with these tactics because others refrained from opposing him, partly out of fear of what his files may have had on *them*.

Reich was not only condemnatory of the emotional plague. He believed that people thus afflicted were richly endowed with energy and had the potential for considerable emotional and intellectual achievement. However, because their armor was also strong, they were incapable of developing their positive impulses. The resulting severe tension made them especially envious and destructive toward others who could flow more freely. The envy in turn was highly rationalized. Coleridge spoke of the "motiveless malignity" of Iago toward Othello because none of his stated reasons for persecuting Othello held water when examined closely. In Reich's description of the plague's hatred of life, he found a motive for such malignity.

Nor is the emotional plague confined to one special character type, even though some are more inclined to it than others. We all have our emotional plague impulses, as we all have our T-bacilli. There was no point Reich emphasized more adamantly than people's responsibility to recognize these impulses and to take measures to limit their destructive fallout.

Much can be said in criticism of Reich's writings on the little man and on the emotional plague. He was often self-justifying and punitively blamed others. He often used the term "emotional plague" to dismiss behavior he himself did not like, even though he warned against the danger of the term's becoming a cliché or curse word.

However, in my view these writings are among Reich's most profound statements on the human condition. He has moved—as he always wished to do—from diagnosing patients to diagnosing humanity. As I have suggested, his diagnoses of the little man and of the emotional plague are free of his earlier romanticization of "the masses" or his confinement of destructiveness to the capitalist class, the Church, or a given political party. The very sweep of the illness made "treatment" difficult. Reich had hit upon something like "original sin," except that although the sin went deep it was still not original. He lost faith in everything but the eventual triumph of unarmored life. In his descriptions of the little man, the emotional plague, and bio-energetic health, as well as the embryonic delineation of their interactions, Reich left a social legacy we shall be developing for a long time.

Stylistically, even though Reich was at times self-indulgent and given to repetitious verbal tantrums, he was taking an enormous step forward here and in many of his other writings during this late phase. His prose had become very direct, hard-hitting, and clear. He had come to feel as Thoreau did about much scientific writing: "I look over the reports of the doings of a scientific association and am surprised that there is so little life to be reported: I am put off with a parcel of dry technical terms. Anything living is easily and naturally expressed in popular language. . . . These learned professors communicate no fact which rises to the temperature of blood heat. It doesn't all amount to one rhyme."

From about the mid-forties on, Reich was writing at "the temperature of blood heat" or higher. This was no accident, but—again—one of his carefully thought-through decisions. So much writing seemed to him more than ever an evasion of the essential. "Always use the sharper phrase!" he would exhort, when I was translating some of his earlier articles. "Don't remove my climaxes!" was another refrain. His determination "to be himself" was now more manifest than ever, in his work, in his personal relations, and in his prose.

Educational Developments

In addition to the connection between Reich's psychiatric and social thinking, there was a close linkage between his psychiatric and educational work. In his preventive efforts during the late 1920s and early 1930s, Reich had tried to find ways to affirm genitality in children and adolescents, thereby helping to prevent neuroses. As his psychiatric work focused on pregenital issues, so his educational interest was drawn to problems of infancy and early childhood. Just as in therapy Reich was now concentrating on release of emotions and not on ideas, fantasies, or the content of experiences, so in education his attention now became riveted by how the flow of feeling had come to be blocked in the first place and how this blockage might be prevented.

Reich's observations and concepts regarding the infant's emotional life can best be seen through his experiences with his own son, Peter, who was born in 1944. Reich wrote up his observations of Peter's infancy in an article stimulated by an attack of "falling anxiety" Peter experienced at three weeks of age. Before dealing with the specific symptom of falling anxiety, Reich discussed some general characteristics of neonatal life. During Peter's first days, Reich was impressed by how baffling the infant's emotional expression was: "[The infant] possesses only one form of expressing needs, that is, *crying*. This one form covers innumerable small and great needs, from the pressure of a diaper crease to colic."[25]

He noted that in the infant, "the pre-eminent place of contact is the bio-energetically highly charged mouth and throat. If, now, the mother's nipple reacts to the sucking movements in the proper biophysical manner with pleasurable sensations, it becomes vigorously erect, and the orgonotic excitation of the nipple combines into a unit with that of the infant's mouth."[26]

One of the most striking early observations Reich made of Peter was that of his "oral orgasm": "At the age of two weeks, the infant had his first orgastic excitation of the mouth region. This occurred while he was nursing; the eyeballs turned upwards and sideways, the mouth began to tremble as did the tongue; the contractions spread over the whole face; they took about ten seconds, after which the musculature of the face relaxed."[27]

Reich's attention was drawn precisely to the *energetic* features of infancy. The fusion or energetic contact he detected between the erect nipple of the healthy mother and the bio-energetically, highly charged mouth of the infant was the same kind of fusion he had already noted in the adult heterosexual act and in the lumination of two bions between which a "radiating bridge" is formed.

Reich noticed no particular disturbance in Peter until his first oral orgasm. Then the infant began to cry a great deal, and the people around him were unable to understand the crying. "I often had the impression that the child wanted *something definite* but I did not know *what*. Only two weeks later did I understand that what he wanted was *bodily contact.*"[28]

The increased crying of the second week foreshadowed a more specific symptom: an acute "falling anxiety" at the end of the third week. It occurred when the baby was taken out of the bath and put on his back on the table. It was not immediately clear whether the motion of laying him down had been too fast, or whether the cooling of the skin had precipitated the falling anxiety. At any rate, the child began to cry violently, pulled back his arms as if to gain support, tried to bring his head forward, showed intense anxiety in his eyes, and could not be calmed down.

Reich was puzzled as to the source of the falling anxiety in an infant. He had long noted the fear of falling that occurred in adult patients when orgasm anxiety appeared; however, an infant could not be experiencing orgasm anxiety. Nor would it be a rational fear of falling, for an infant lacked any concept of "high" or "low." Nor in the absence of words and ideas could there be a phobia.

Reich reasoned that Peter's falling anxiety represented a "sudden withdrawal of the biological energy to the biophysical center."[29] The withdrawal of energy to the center left a depletion at the extremities; hence the loss of the feeling of equilibrium.

Reich traced the falling anxiety attack to the fact that for a period of about two weeks the orgonotic contact between mother and baby was poor; apparently the baby had strong impulses toward contact which remained ungratified. "Then occurred the orgasm of the mouth region, in other words, a perfectly natural discharge took place of the high-pitched excitation of the head and throat region. This increased the need for contact even further. The lack of contact led to a contraction, to a withdrawal of biological energy as a result of unsuccessful attempts to establish contact."[30]

Reich utilized his skills as a therapist in dealing with Peter's falling anxiety. He noted that the infant's right shoulderblade and the right arm were pulled back and less mobile than the left arm. There was a definite contraction in the musculature of the right shoulder. The connection between this contraction and the falling anxiety was clear: during the anxiety attack, the child had pulled back both shoulders, as if to gain a hold. This muscular attitude persisted even in periods free of anxiety.

The therapeutic steps he took with Peter provided the essential principles upon which his later work with other infants was based. These steps can be briefly summarized:

First, the child was picked up and held when he cried.

Second, the shoulders were brought gently forward out of their backward fixation in order to eliminate the incipient armoring of the shoulders. Playfully, with laughter and sounds which the baby loved, Reich moved both shoulders forward. This was done daily for about two months, always in a playful manner.

And third, Reich had the child "fall" in order to accustom him to the sensation of falling. Reich would lift him by the armpits and then lower him, slowly at first, then increasingly quickly. At first, the child reacted with crying, but soon he began to enjoy it; he would lean against Reich's chest and seemed to want to crawl up on him. On top of Reich's head, he would squeal with pleasure. In the ensuing weeks, the "climbing up" and "falling" became a favorite game.

The falling anxiety disappeared three weeks after Reich began his treatment. Nor did it appear over the next six months, at which time Reich wrote up his experiences with Peter.

Reich noted other aspects of infancy. He began to see that the aliveness of the newborn requires aliveness of the environment:

> I mean aliveness not only in the expressive language of the adult, but movement in the strict sense of the word. The infant prefers alive colors to dull ones, and moving objects to stationary ones. If the infant is placed in a higher position so that the walls of the carriage do not obstruct the view and if one removes the roof, the infant can observe his environment; he will show glowing interest in people who pass by, in trees, shrubs, posts, walls, etc.[31]

Several years later, Reich would also emphasize the importance of the infant's eye contact with its mother. "The eyes, those silent tongues of love (Cervantes) played as important a role between mother and infant as between lovers." However, whereas one could arrange vivid colors for the infant to see, in spite of one's own emotional state, one cannot "arrange" a lively visual contact between mother and child. If the mother has a hostile or dull look, the infant will fail to respond with full contact. It may "turn away" figuratively from such contact altogether, "blanking out" with its eyes, for example. Here was rooted the armoring of the eyes Reich had noted so vividly in the case history of schizophrenia.

Reich's experience with Peter led him to oppose the concept of a "withdrawn" autistic infant, although he emphasized that infants would withdraw if they met false "baby talk" or strict, distant expressions. "It is possible to evoke in an infant of a few weeks vivid pleasure and lively response if one talks to him in *his* guttural sounds, if one makes *his* motions, if one has, above all, a lively contact oneself."[32]

I have summarized Reich's paper on infancy in some detail not only because of what he discovered about infancy per se, but also because it illustrates with unusual clarity his capacity to integrate the strands of his work. Some of his concepts were:

The conceptualization of Peter's falling anxiety was informed by, and in turn enriched, Reich's experiences with adult patients. Both neurotic and cancer patients experienced falling anxiety, accompanied by such symptoms as pallor and shocklike states, following a sharp increase in their capacity for pleasurable excitement. After his experiences with Peter, Reich more fully understood this process from an energetic viewpoint. Falling anxiety resulted from a *sudden* contraction of energy after a strong expansion. The process was sufficiently distinct from the chronic contractions of a rigid armor and sufficiently important to warrant its own name—anorgonia—which clearly expressed Reich's evolving orgonomic framework of thought.

Secondly, the absence of pleasurable excitement in the mother had an impact on the infant. The energetically charged lips that moved out for contact as well as milk often got, at best, only the latter. The infant's pleasurable impulse diminished, the energetic "juiciness" and suppleness of the oral segment was replaced by "deadness," dryness, contraction—in short, the armor. Prior to the study of Peter, Reich had to rely on analytic reconstruction in tracing adult oral symptoms such as "speech disturbances, emptiness of emotional expression, eating disturbances, and fear of kissing" to the infant's experiences with his mother. Now he was able to begin to connect these adult phenomena with the *in vivo* study of the mother-infant relationship, even though he had but one example.

Third, on the negative side, Reich's emphasis on the importance of orgonotic contact between mother and infant contributed to guilt feelings on the part of mothers who subscribed to his concepts but who had difficulties establishing this kind of contact. There is no easy answer to this dilemma. What Reich stressed about the mother-infant relationship is of great significance even if the optimal experience is—like orgastic potency between lovers—quite rare. At the same time, Reich can be faulted for his tendency to picture "orgonotic contact" as an all-or-nothing phenomenon rather than one of degree, and for insufficiently emphasizing that parental guilt feelings often make matters worse.

Fourth, in the oral orgasm Reich delineated once again the orgasm formula: tension–charge–discharge–relaxation. When we combine this observation with Reich's noting, to be described soon, the "orgasm reflex" in children starting with the genital phase, then we can see how he connected one or another form of the orgasm with the entire life cycle. It was Reich's energetic-emotional paradigm which permitted him to assert that the phenomena he observed, such as the turning upward and sideways of the eyes and the trembling of the mouth, did indeed constitute a kind of orgasm. He could so easily have interpreted it as an attack of gas, if not a minor epileptic seizure.*

Fifth, in the handling of Peter's falling anxiety, Reich innovated a kind of "play therapy," one derived from his long work with the bodily and emotional expression of adults and closely related to the energy functions he was studying in many different realms. Moreover, the kind of therapy he evolved was ideally suited for working with infants. Unlike the usual play therapy, it did not even require that the "patient" act out his fantasies in play and activities. It did not require any understanding of interpretations. All that Reich did was work directly with the emotional expression and the flow of energy through contact, body "games," and muscle movement.

The Orgonomic Infant Research Center (OIRC)

Apart from his experiences with Peter, Reich did not work directly with infants and children during most of the 1940s. However, he remained deeply concerned with education and trained many teachers. One of his students, Lucille Denison, ran a nursery school based on Reich's principles for about a year. Various controversies with educational officials and internal difficulties led to its demise. It was the kind of undertaking Reich yearned for, but few of his students were able to carry through on their own as Neill had done.

It was not until December 1949 that Reich developed an organizational plan for studying infants and children. At the time, he was deeply immersed in studying orgone energy in the atmosphere. As he wrote to Neill in January 1950:

> As I pondered over the problem whether to stay in Maine or return to New York, I felt that I would not be able to produce a single orgonometric thought [mathematics of orgone energy] if I were to discontinue my work on the human structure. And I returned to New

---

*Indeed, in 1981 a mother who was interested in Reich's work wrote an article on the upbringing of her children and commented: "I believe both children had oral orgasms. . . . At first, it was startling and we were afraid our son might be ill, but otherwise he didn't seem sick at all. After it had happened a few times, we thought it was probably nothing to worry about"—Mary Vahkup, "Raising Two Children," *Offshoots of Orgonomy*, 2, 1981, 23.

Two mothers interested in Reich's work told me of very similar reactions to oral orgasms in their infants. However, apart from these three communications, I have read or heard nothing about the oral orgasm since Reich's publication in 1945. If this relatively common phenomenon, however interpreted, has been so ignored, and, when noticed, so disquieting even to those familiar with Reich's work, his explanation of the fear-filled avoidance of *all* manifestations of orgonotic pulsation becomes more plausible.

York at the end of November and swiftly chose from a list of about
120 physicians, educators, nurses, social workers, psychologists, etc.,
about 40 people of the best suited and began to establish an Orgonomic Infant Research Center for the study of health and not of
sickness. We must finally get away from pathology and start our work
with the healthy child.[33]

Much as Reich often deplored the distraction from natural-scientific work
which therapy represented, he also felt a strong need to continue therapy to
maintain his scientific zest. The plan to work with infants and children kept
the human connection at the same time that it allowed him to focus on the
study of energy in its natural state.

Most of the observations sketched in Reich's brief but packed comments
on Peter's infancy were contained in the design for the new Orgonomic Infant
Research Center, or OIRC. Special focus was to be put on the prenatal care
of mothers; supervision of the delivery and the first few days of the newborn's
life; and prevention of armoring during the first five or six years of life.[34]

Reich's way of studying infants more systematically was characteristic of
his entire approach to research. He started with very strongly held hypotheses,
hypotheses that were in fact stated as findings. For example, he believed, on
the basis of little evidence, that infants of emotionally healthy mothers had a
better intrauterine environment than infants of less healthy mothers.

When it came to a more detailed study of prenatal and postnatal development, Reich allowed for the possibility that he might be wrong. Thus, he
included in his research design children from two groups of mothers: relatively
healthy mothers (group A) and basically sound but somewhat more problematic mothers (group B). He was interested in noting the differences, if any,
in the children from the two groups.

This scientific procedure created certain unanticipated problems. Some
group A mothers went around boasting that they were "healthy"; some group
B mothers felt that they had been labeled defective. Reich blamed others for
these misperceptions, for making an ideal of the "perfect" mother. But his own
writings, as mentioned earlier, contributed to the very situation he deplored.

With the assistance of a social worker, Grethe Hoff, and several orgonomic physicians, Reich proceeded in a very careful way. The plan was to
follow the research subjects from early in pregnancy and the infants from their
very first moments of life into adolescence. In selecting mothers for the OIRC,
Reich examined them psychiatrically to assess the degree and kind of armoring. He also interviewed the husbands. In the initial discussions with the
prospective parents, he was particularly interested in exploring their ability to
resist familial pressure for circumcision or other destructive practices in child
raising. I would also note that Reich was always very careful to deal with the
issue of what is now called "informed consent" from research subjects. In
general, he would let everyone—from patients undergoing therapy, to assist-

ants in scientific experiments, to parents in the OIRC—know as fully and honestly as the could about the possible risks as well as benefits (both personally and in terms of scientific knowledge) involved in their participation.

Reich also informed the parents about various alternatives for delivery and elicited their own views on these. For physical reasons, he stressed, hospitals were safer than home delivery, but emotionally it was of great importance for the baby to be with the mother right after birth, something most hospitals did not permit at that time. Most parents elected to have the delivery in hospitals where they could—sometimes with great difficulty—modify routine procedures.

Reich was ahead of his time in urging extreme caution about the use of medications during pregnancy since he was concerned about their possible effect on the embryo. The times have caught up with him in this respect, but not with regard to his advice that pregnant mothers use the orgone accumulator.

Reich hypothesized that the very act of carrying the embryo had an energetic effect on the mother. As he once put it: "The fetus acts like a stove; it is another energy system in the mother and it energizes the mother's whole being."[35] In one case, it could enhance the mother's genitality; in another, it could decrease it out of anxiety from the rise in the bio-energetic level.

Reich was extremely critical of various obstetrical practices at the time of birth that were considered routine during the 1940s though many are now being opposed. Some of these practices were drugs to induce birth, particularly when such induction was based on the doctor's convenience; heavy sedation for the mother during labor when the need for it was not clearly indicated; unnecessary use of forceps; and routine episiotomies.

To assist mothers in not requiring heavy medication, the OIRC tried to have an orgone therapist in attendance at birth in order to help the mother breathe and relax. Chester M. Raphael, a physician who worked with Reich, has well described how useful a therapist can be in the delivery room.

The first mother he attended had been in labor for more than forty hours:

Her condition seemed desperate. I found her sitting up supporting herself with her arms held rigidly against the sides of the bed, her face ashen, her lips cyanotic, her pulse thready, her hands cold and clammy, her shoulders hunched up acutely. . . . Between contractions, her eyes rolled up into her head and her distress was extreme with each contraction. . . .

It took considerable effort to make her lower her shoulders. Succeeding in this I asked her to breathe more deeply, to prolong her expiration. . . . She clenched her jaws but I discouraged it immediately and helped her to let her jaw drop. The spasm in her shoulders and intercostal muscles—which were exquisitely tender—was gradually overcome. Her respiration improved. . . . The severity of the pain of uterine contractions began to subside. . . . Despite more than forty hours in labor, a good part of it agonizingly painful, she began to look comfortable and pleased. An important quality of her reaction to pain was a distinct withdrawal in her eyes. When she did this, she appeared to lose all contact. She did not hear me, seemed confused, and it was difficult to bring her back.

The mother herself reported later: "Only when you called me back would I, with a very definite effort, bring my gaze back. It was so easy to go off that I believe you had to call me back quite often. By this time I was tingling all over. I began to feel warm and relaxed, whereas previously I was chilled and tense. . . . I can't quite understand it myself. I only know that it helped me tremendously."[36]

Beyond the elimination of harmful neonatal procedures, Reich very early practiced certain kinds of intervention, or what he came to call "emotional first aid," with infants and children. Thus, one infant, the son of an orgone therapist and a mother very interested in Reich's work, developed an illness soon after birth. For reasons not too clear the infant boy had been circumcised. Reich, who saw the infant soon after birth, described him as rounded like a "bluish balloon." His chest was high and respiration was disturbed. An angry cry broke out as though the organism wanted to get out of itself. The penis was cyanotic. The baby had been crying almost constantly and jumped at the slightest touch. It was like a chain of events where one link pulled the other.

Reich advised stopping all enemas and all chemical treatments. The baby had to be given considerable warmth. Finally, the blown-up chest had to be eliminated. How *does* one work with a baby's chest? One can't go in with the knuckles or tell the baby to breathe. Reich tried to help him breathe by gently tickling and swinging him. Gentle massage was also used. Reich helped the mother to learn the same techniques; she also proceeded to stroke the rest of the child's body. And the parents tried to help the infant gag.

Some months later, the child was much improved and his movements were more gentle.[37]

Reich's intervention here clearly illustrated several of his principles. First, he modified techniques derived from the study of heavily armored adults to handle more acute contractions and armorings in an infant, contractions that in an adult would take longer to release. Second, he brought the mother into the treatment. Once again he was searching for ways to make his endeavors more practical socially. Much as he believed that only a physician should treat severe emotional disorders, he also believed that others could apply "emotional first aid" in less severe disorders. As Reich put it: "Only healthy and right structures can do the right thing. What made it here was the ability of the mother to give love. The mother must have contact with the child before anything else can happen."

Reich distinguished between three kinds of mothers in terms of emotional interventions: those who easily learned first-aid techniques; those who could but who were afraid and who needed support; and those who were too sick to learn them.

Here again we perceive the continuity in all Reich's social efforts. He was most concerned about the second kind of persons—adolescents, mothers, or whoever—who could reach out and function in a much healthier way *if* they received support. This was the swing group, so to speak. There were relatively few in the first or healthy group, and the third required lengthy therapy before they could be useful.

Although Reich's primary aim for the OIRC was the study of health in the prenatal, postnatal, childhood, and adolescent periods, and active intervention, not long-term treatment, in any acute difficulties, he also had a secondary broad social aim. He assessed the potential contributions of persons connected with the OIRC. A sociologist could make a study of legal difficulties and implications regarding the newborn. An orgone therapist who had formerly been an obstetrician could locate hospitals receptive to more flexible procedures and might also be willing to do home deliveries. An orgonomically oriented internist could study the existing hospital conditions as they pertained to the newborn. A mother could observe the oral orgasm in infants and a nursery-school teacher the orgasm reflex in children.

Reich believed that when children entered the genital phase, they were capable not only of genital excitation but also of a convulsive discharge of excitation. The excitation did not reach a sharp peak, followed by a rapid discharge of excitation, as it did in adults; there was no climax. The rise and fall of excitation was more gradual.

It is interesting—and sad—to note that after some thirty-five years we know little more about the orgasm reflex in children than what Reich described.

The OIRC functioned actively for only a few years. All in all, Reich studied closely about twelve mothers and their offspring; in addition, he consulted on about a dozen cases of older children with various problems. At its height an OIRC social worker, Grethe Hoff, worked half-time for Reich, following the mothers during pregnancy and the mothers and infants during the first weeks and months of their lives. In addition, several therapists were very active in consultation.

After early 1952, under the pressure of other events we shall soon discuss, Reich spent little time with the OIRC. Like so many of his undertakings, it had a short, vivid life. Out of it he culled not only important concepts but a number of very specific techniques. When one reads of Reich's achievements in summary form, much of what he says seems so simple and obvious. It is easy to overlook the fact that no one in his time was seeing and doing what he was seeing and doing.

Today, Reich's work with infants and children is not so much represented by any organization that bears his name as it is by a myriad of workers, some of whom are familiar with his research, many of whom are not. His concepts and findings concerning such factors as the oral orgasm, the dissolution of armor blocks in infants and children, and the affirmation of childhood genitality are clearly unique to him and his students. Other of his emphases, for example that on natural childbirth, were and are advanced by many others. However, he provides a unified theoretical framework not available in the work of those who may advance particular approaches identical with or similar to him. It is important that the distinctive quality of his research should be constantly noted, as the *Journal of Orgonomy* does so well. It is equally important that his work should be connected with the broad sweep of our century's progressive educational development, a development he both influenced and reflected.

24

Personal Life and Relations
with Colleagues: 1941-1950

Once established in America, Reich entered a period of quiet work and living dominated by scientific research. He was able to find and purchase his own home in late 1941, for Ilse and he had had trouble with the house they rented in Forest Hills. To quote Ilse:

> They [the neighbors] objected to our letting the hedge around the house grow high; they objected to our having a Negro assistant, a young biology student who studied for a while with Reich and, of course, shared our meals; they objected to the "rats" in our basement and they transmitted these complaints to our landlord. He sent an investigator who could find no reason for the complaints and was very much surprised to find our mice confined to securely closed boxes neatly arranged on shelves. . . . However, we felt our privacy invaded by our particular neighbor who continued to observe our every move, and we did not want to live at the mercy of a landlord's whim.[1]

In the fall of 1941, Reich bought a home at 99-06 69th Avenue, a block from the Forest Hills Tennis Stadium. Here he was to spend eight to ten months a year, the summer period in Maine being expanded as the years progressed. The basic pattern of his life was established, not to be altered until his full-time move to Rangeley in 1950.

Ilse provides a picture of how thoroughly their home life was dominated by work: "The large basement with a separate laundry room was ideal for laboratory purposes and had a separate entrance. The rooms in the house were larger than in the old one. Reich could have his library in his study, out of the way of the laboratory and the various household activities. As before, the dining room was used for electroscopy, and later on for X-ray work. The living room became a combination waiting room, office, and dining room."[2]

The Forest Hills home was the center of Reich's therapeutic and organizational activities from 1942 until 1950, just as the Maine home was the center for his scientific research. However, considerable research also went on at Forest Hills. Here Reich was constantly bothered by having to switch from writing and research to seeing patients. It was not until he moved to Maine year round that this particular problem was resolved.

The period in his life between 1942 and 1945 was outwardly quiet. Many persons came for therapy, including a number of teachers and social workers. But he had few colleagues, Wolfe continuing to be his chief co-worker. His relationship with Ilse centered heavily upon work.

The emotional connection between them during this period is more obscure. In her thirties now, Ilse was eager to have a child. Initially, Reich was not. When Ilse did become pregnant, Reich insisted on an abortion.[3] (We recall that in the mid-1930s he had insisted that Elsa Lindenberg have an abortion.) Much as Reich loved children, he was not one to let accident, or his mate's wishes, dictate his destiny. With Ilse he may have felt continuing uncertainties about the relationship itself. Also, the heavy pressure of his work may have made him feel the time was not ripe for a child.

It is hard to overestimate Reich's commitment to work during these years. With the discovery of orgone energy, a long-held sense of mission was intensified. Even in Scandinavia, there had still been time for fun—skiing, tennis, and parties. In America there was no skiing, no tennis, no parties. Diversions were limited to such activities as a Sunday trip—with Ilse and his daughters —to Jones Beach, or to dinner and a movie with Ilse.

The closest thing Reich had to a friendship during those years was his relationship by mail with A. S. Neill in England.[4] Neill's independence, strong sense of personal identity, and achievements, combined with his deep respect for Reich, permitted the two men a relationship nearer to equality than Reich was to have with anyone else. But even with Neill, Reich's letters are almost totally devoted to work. The frequent references to social problems were part of Reich's work, since he never lost the sense of himself as a socially engaged researcher, with the deep conviction that his ideas had many answers to the turmoil then raging. Reich hardly ever wrote to Neill about his personal life —his relationship with Ilse or his feelings toward co-workers and students other than his evaluation of them as workers. Personal joys and complaints rarely entered the correspondence.

Yet the letters convey more of a sense of the man than some of his communications. And one feels his love for Neill, just as Neill's letters convey his love for Reich. Typically with Reich, his letters are especially directed to themes of concern to the recipient as well as himself. With Neill, the shared concerns were education and social-political developments. Occasionally, he confided in Neill about something quite beyond Neill's ken, such as the encounter with Einstein, simply because there were so few people with whom he could discuss such events.

Despite the relative absence of attacks on his work, memories of old ones could still stir in Reich the kind of rage that provoked his own authoritarian tendencies. This tendency was to reach a crescendo in the 1950s, but it could clearly be seen in a relatively minor incident from the early 1940s.

In 1942 Gunnar Leistikow, a Norwegian journalist, had written an article on the Norwegian newspaper campaign for the *International Journal for Sex-Economy and Orgone-Research.* [5] Leistikow protested certain editorial changes made in his article without his permission, the most important of which was the title Wolfe chose, "The Fascist Newspaper Campaign in Norway." Leistikow's original article did not contain the word "Fascist." After the article appeared, he wrote Wolfe that it was highly misleading to label the campaign "Fascist" when in fact a Socialist newspaper had been in the forefront of the attack. In response, Wolfe wrote that the sex-economic definition of fascism had nothing to do with party membership, nationality, or class. But an author's title had been changed in a drastic way without his permission. It would seem clear that Wolfe made this change at Reich's instigation. Reich, usually so scrupulous in respecting an author's intention, in this instance flagrantly violated his own policy. The trigger was evident: his rage at the newspapers that had slandered his work in Norway.

If particular interactions could stir old resentments, they could also stir old hopes. Alexander Lowen has told me that around 1943 he knew staff members of the Settlement House connected with the Union Theological Seminary in New York City.[6] He arranged for Reich, who he then thought "could change the world," to speak before the staff of the House. Reich proposed a plan whereby he would give talks at the House for the staff and youth on sexual problems and their social connections—in short, an effort along earlier sex-political lines but without the Marxist, revolutionary perspective. As at the earlier sex-counseling centers, Reich, Wolfe, and a few others would also offer sex counseling free of charge for adolescents connected with the House who wished this opportunity.

According to Lowen, Reich spoke superbly and the staff greeted the plan enthusiastically. However, the board of the House vetoed the proposal. Like his scientific overtures to Einstein, Reich's social initiative was dashed after what looked like a promising beginning. Never again would he make this kind of social effort.

By 1943, Reich had changed his mind, and was eager to become a father again. The birth of his son Peter on April 4, 1944, was a tremendously joyful event, which he shared with Neill. Reich's personal delight in having a baby boy blended inextricably with his scientific sense of wonder. For, as noted earlier, the birth of Peter gave a tremendous spur to Reich's long-standing interest in the newborn.

Peter added a new and stabilizing dimension to Reich and Ilse's relationship. For all his dislike of compulsive monogamy and whatever his problems with Ilse, part of Reich was definitely a family man. He enjoyed doing things with his family. And he loved his son. He was undoubtedly eager not to make some of the same mistakes with Peter he had made with Eva and Lore. They had been put on a rigid feeding schedule; with Peter, everything was done in accordance with the principles of self-regulation and of orgonomy.[7]

Reich's interest in Peter does not imply that he was the kind of husband who "shared" child-caring responsibilities with his wife. As Reich once wrote to Neill, he was a great child lover but a poor child caretaker. Ilse has related the anecdote of how Reich very generously told her to take some time off and go fishing, only to call her in a panic when Peter needed to have his diapers changed.

For all Reich's emphasis on the importance of the mother-infant relationship, he was keen for Ilse to have considerable time to work for him. At some point in Peter's first year the Reichs employed a full-time maid, which relieved Ilse of many daily chores with both the home and the child, but enabled her still to have time with Peter. In my dealings with the Reichs I was always impressed by how Peter was fitted into the daily schedule so that he received considerable attention as work continued.

Peter's integration into the busy home life reflected Ilse's ability to handle a great variety of tasks with remarkable "grace under pressure." She exuded a calm, unpretentious serenity that provided a fine grounding for Reich's volatility. At a deeper level, the relationship remained more problematic. As noted, Ilse was never in therapy, although almost everyone else involved in Reich's work had been or was in treatment. Partly, Reich was relieved that Ilse was not preoccupied by her own emotional problems. When students raised the question of why she had not been in therapy—the kind of personal question one could raise with Reich in the context of the relative safety of a treatment session—he would reply impatiently that she did not need it. But Ilse had trouble getting close to people. This kind of psychological distance bothered Reich, and he would frequently erupt over one or another of its manifestations. Reich also continued his practice of acting out on those around him the frustrations he felt from other sources.

Reich and Ilse did not marry legally until April 17, 1945, when Peter was a little over a year old. Reich retained his animus against legal marriage; he decided to take this step on the advice of their lawyer, Arthur Garfield Hays, who warned that they would not be able to pass the naturalization hearings as they planned unless they were married.[8] It was a civil ceremony with strangers as witnesses. The wedding was unadorned because Reich and Ilse initially intended to get a legal divorce as soon as they both became U.S.

citizens. Ilse sailed through her naturalization hearings in November 1945. After a much longer but friendly hearing, Reich became an American citizen on May 28, 1946. For reasons not entirely clear, they relinquished the initial plan to get an immediate divorce.

While Ilse was visiting her mother and brother in England during April–May 1947, Reich had a brief affair.[9] (He may well have had other affairs during the 1940s but there is no record of them, and, indeed, no gossip about this one. Reich successfully kept a very tight lid on his personal life.) Characteristically, he went into a jealous rage when Ilse returned from England, interrogating her mercilessly about her fidelity to him during her vacation. Reich had shown such pathological jealousy once before when he was detained on Ellis Island. Typically, this second outburst occurred after a vicious article against his work —the first of its kind in America—was published in May 1947 in *The New Republic* (to be described in Chapter 25).

Reich's relationship with Eva and Lore remained problematical. While she was a college student in the early 1940s, Eva visited fairly often. At one point, Reich had hoped she might come and live with him; he kept a room available for her, but she was still too much torn between her parents to accept this offer. She moved closer to her father in the second half of the 1940s, when she was attending medical school. Her interest in his work grew steadily but was accompanied by considerable anxiety. Eva recalls being surprised to hear a student of Reich's talk very glowingly about him—she was not used to hearing her father referred to in this way.[10] Reich remained eager to win her over completely as a daughter and a student. When she visited in Maine, I noted with some surprise his being upset that she "did not spend more time with him," a common parental complaint one did not expect from Reich. Reich contributed to Eva's medical education, but only very modestly; there were further scenes between Annie and him on this account.

Lore's visits became rarer as the forties progressed. The long-standing alliance of Lore with her mother deepened. In 1948, Lore paid a surprise visit to Reich in Forest Hills after years of separation. According to Ilse, Reich had just had a series of painful tooth extractions and her visit occurred when his jaw was so swollen he was unable to talk to anyone. He refused to see her, a rejection so total one cannot attribute it solely to his pain, silence, and facial disfigurement. In addition, he had grown to feel that Lore did not belong to his way of life, and once such a decision was made he could be ruthless. Understandably, Lore was deeply hurt and there was practically no further contact between them.

Wolfe was the first co-worker to join Reich in spending summers in Maine. He bought a cabin very near Reich's so they could have easy access to each other and the opportunity to discuss translations and other matters in a far less hectic atmosphere than New York City. At the time Wolfe was living with Jo Jenks, a sensitive, spirited sculptress whose work Reich very much admired. Jo was also a patient of Reich's—and much in awe of him.

Reich's attitude toward the relationship between Theo, as Wolfe was called by those close to him, and Jo vividly illustrates how important Wolfe was to him. In 1942, Wolfe had a recurrence of his tuberculosis and was invalided for some months. After his recovery, Reich told Jo in a therapeutic session that Wolfe was so valuable to orgonomy he must ask her to end the relationship. Jo had three children from a previous marriage, and Wolfe was not prepared for that kind of familial burden, Reich maintained; it would interfere with his work. Jo, stunned, took up the matter with Theo that night over dinner at a restaurant. His silence led her to believe that he concurred with Reich. She left the restaurant abruptly and the relationship broke off. She maintained her contact with Reich, however, and later became friendly again with Theo.[11]

I have heard this incident only from Jo herself; there may have been mitigating circumstances. On the face of it, Reich's self-serving directive violated the true therapeutic spirit. It is another frightening example of the lengths he would go to protect his vital interests or, as he would put it, the vital interests of orgonomy.

In the summer of 1942, it was Jo who discovered the abandoned farm that Reich would later buy and name "Orgonon" and that would become his scientific base. Located a few miles west of Rangeley village and a few miles east of Mooselookmeguntic Lake, the farm was part woodland and part meadow. The hill, which Reich thought would be the ideal site for a future observatory, had a beautiful view of the mountains and lakes. There were a well and a spring on the land, and about half a mile of shoreline on Dodge Pond. In 1942, when Reich bought the land, the 280 acres cost about $4,000.

Orgonon grew over the years. In 1943, Reich built his first cabin on the land, a one-room structure that provided some isolation for his writing while the family remained at the small Mooselookmeguntic cabin. In 1945, he had a laboratory constructed, which could accommodate a large number of students who wished to observe the energy phenomena, to learn the Reich Blood Tests, to study the effects of orgone energy application on cancer in mice, and to study protozoa and bions under the microscope. The Students' Laboratory had a very large main hall for microscopic work, facilities for biological preparations, a mouse room, and a room completely encased with sheet iron, lightproof, and equipped with many special instruments for the observation of orgone energy. It was a very beautiful place to work, with large windows overlooking the mountains and lakes, and it was to be the center of orgonomic conferences, lectures, and courses for many years.

In 1946, Reich developed his world at Orgonon still further by building a winterized family cabin on the property. This enabled him to stay on in Maine well into the fall in the atmosphere he loved so dearly.

Reich's most elaborate structure was built in 1948-49: the Observatory. This was constructed on top of a high hill, with marvelous views. The Observatory reflected Reich's growing interest in astrophysical studies. Since it was intended to carry a heavy telescope, the foundation was laid on solid rock. In *Listen, Little Man!* Reich had used the line: "Build your life on rock!" I recall Reich watching the masons laying rocks for the Observatory building and saying, "You see, I mean what I wrote: Build your life on rock."

Reich was deeply involved in the actual building process. He watched the progress daily and admired the workers' skill. He was especially fascinated by the work of the stonemasons—their almost intuitive knowledge of which stone to place where. The workmen in turn responded to Reich's keen interest. He treated them as equals, without pretense, and they appreciated it. He talked with them about their families and children, and to this day some of them have retained their warmth and loyalty toward him.

A few further words should be said about Reich's relations with the Rangeley workmen. The first important relationship was with Herman Templeton, who had sold him the cabin at Mooselookmeguntic and built the first accumulator. Over and beyond their work relationship, Reich found in the Maine guide a sympathetic and understanding audience:

> We had come close to each other when I told him about the nature of the bions. This simple man disclosed a spontaneously acquired knowledge of the living with which no academic biology or physics can compete. I asked him whether he wanted to see the life energy under the microscope. I was flabbergasted when my friend, even before looking into the microscope, gave me a correct description of the bions. For decades, he had been observing the growth of seeds and the character of the humus with the unerring instinct of somebody who has always lived close to nature. There are, he said, very small vesicles ("bubbles") everywhere. From these, everything develops that is "life." They were so small, he said, that they could not be seen with the naked eye. Yet, the moss on the rocks developed from them: the rock, always exposed to the weather, "softens up" on the surface and forms these life bubbles. He said he had often tried to talk about this with academic tourists, but had only met with a peculiar smile. Nevertheless, he said, he was sure that he was right. I had to admit that he was right, for how could moss "germs" "strike root" in the rock?[12]

Reich later developed a similar kind of relationship, combining the roles of employer, friend, and colleague, with another Rangeley man, Tom Ross. Forty at the time, Ross became caretaker of the Orgonon property in 1948. But the word "caretaker" does scant justice to Ross's role there. Not only did he keep up the property; he also helped Reich in a variety of ways from constructing different kinds of equipment to participating in experiments, and he became a trusted friend. Unlike so many of Reich's students, who brought to their relationship with him all kinds of therapeutic expectations, a thirst for knowledge or love from the marvelous leader, Tom made no such demands. He was doing a job, he liked Reich, he was prepared to learn from him; but if things did not work out, he could go elsewhere without too much sadness, guilt, or anger. Tom was able to perceive many orgonomic phenomena, such as the tingling heat of the accumulator when he put his hand close to it. However, when he did not feel or understand something, "I told the doctor that—I didn't have much education, I only finished the eighth grade."

Just as in the late 1920s and early 1930s Reich had found that his industrial worker friends were more in touch with basic social truths than his sophisticated psychoanalytic colleagues, so in the 1940s he felt that many of his Maine country friends were in touch with natural-scientific truths that eluded the Einsteins and Oppenheimers. Reich spoke often of the need for a response from the environment. He had his own talent for finding it.

Such was Rangeley's charm: the climate, dry and clear; the geography of mountains and lakes; friends like Templeton and Ross who could to some extent follow Reich's work; the relatively simple human work relationships that existed in a small rural town and that closely fitted Reich's model of a work democracy; the opportunity for sustained research, uninterrupted by patients and other involvements of his New York existence—all these made the Maine summers vastly appealing to Reich. He did everything he could to extend the length of the Rangeley phase of his yearly schedule, starting with a month in 1940 and building up to about four months by 1949. In May 1950, he began to live at Orgonon on a year-round basis.

Reich had elaborate plans as to how Orgonon would become a center for orgonomic research and education. Few of his hopes came to pass. Over the years, several courses and conferences were held at Orgonon for physicians and other students. A handful of serious researchers spent considerable time there. But as with so many of Reich's plans for group development of his work, his dreams for Orgonon were barely fulfilled.

The end of World War II marked the end of Reich's relative isolation from the psychiatric world. Prior to 1946, he had only two therapists working with him, Wolfe and William Thorburn. The latter was an osteopath. Reich had a good opinion of this quiet, gentle man's therapeutic skill, but Thorburn was never close or particularly active in the organizational development of orgonomy. Some of the physicians associated with Reich after the war were to be important.

The first was James A. Willie. Willie owned a private psychiatric hospital in Oklahoma at the time he read *The Function of the Orgasm.*[13] He was suffering a depression in late 1945, and after reading the book, he decided to seek treatment from Reich. He moved to New York, initially with the idea of staying only as long as his treatment required. As often happened in people's relationships with Reich, Willie got more than he intended: he became so involved with orgonomy that he never returned to Oklahoma.

A few months after Willie began his treatment, Reich urged him to start seeing patients. Willie did not feel ready to begin, but Reich prevailed upon him. It was characteristic of Reich that he tended to take it as a sign that someone was ready to start if the person felt he was not. Such an attitude indicated a sensitive awareness of the difficulties rather than the cocksureness Reich detested.

Willie was an independent person, never to be Reich's yes-man. Difficulties developed in the early 1950s, but in the first years Reich had a high opinion of him. One saw Reich at his least dictatorial and most accepting in many of his interactions with Willie. To give a single example: Not long after Willie started psychiatric treatment, Reich urged him to use the accumulator. After Willie had used it a few times, Reich asked him what he thought of it. Willie responded that he had felt nothing in it and that he thought the accumulator was "a lot of bullshit." Reich simply laughed and told him to go on using it. Later Willie, a red-faced, hypertensive individual, became so charged by the accumulator that he could not tolerate using it even for a short time.

Another physician to study with Reich, starting in 1946, and one who was to be the most important to him in subsequent years, was Elsworth F. Baker. A quiet, modest man, Baker was chief of the Female Service at Marlboro State Hospital in New Jersey at the time he met Reich. He was also secretary of the New Jersey Medical Society. Like Willie, Baker was depressed at the start of treatment, and he began therapy simply with the idea of being a patient and working on his problems.[14] Again like Willie, Reich urged him to begin seeing patients and cautiously to use Reich's techniques soon after he started treatment. Baker also made a considerable effort to become familiar with the totality of Reich's work, spending time in the laboratory doing microscopic work under the direction of Ilse, and, occasionally, Reich himself. By 1948 or so, Baker was part of the informal inner circle that included Wolfe, Ilse, and Willie.

Initially, Baker saw Reich for six months, three times a week. Reich felt Baker could stop at that point, but the latter insisted on another six months of treatment. At that time Reich wanted to make therapy as short as possible, urging his students to go out on their own, coming back for additional treatment if necessary. In this respect, his treatment philosophy had become similar to Freud's, who also tended to give relatively brief treatment to many analysts-in-training. Freud considered analysis a lifelong process, a process the treatment per se only initiated. Things had come full circle. Now with his concentration on armoring and energy flow, on prevention rather than treatment, on orgone physics and biophysics, Reich was impatient with long-term treatment and used a highly modified form of character analysis in addition to his body techniques.

Since Baker was held in high regard by his colleagues at Marlboro State Hospital, his interest in orgonomy stimulated several other staff members. Drs. A. Allan Cott, Chester Raphael, and Sidney Handelman each entered treatment with Reich not long after Baker started. Of these new recruits Raphael was to become the most important, participating actively in cancer studies, the OIRC, and administrative matters. Boyish in appearance, Raphael was very intelligent and often a man of independent judgment but not inclined to contradict Reich openly.

The Reichian Marlboro cohort (which also came to include some non-medical staff) began to alarm the hospital's medical director, J. B. Gordon. Gordon spread rumors that Baker was schizophrenic and that he masturbated his patients. Such was the noxious effect of Reich, for previously Gordon had considered Baker an outstanding psychiatrist. In 1948, Baker, Raphael, a social worker, and a psychologist were personally reprimanded by Henry Cotten, Deputy Commissioner of Mental Health for the state of New Jersey.[15]

Cotten's interview with Baker, et al., covered such topics as whether Reich was in a mental hospital, whether Baker masturbated patients, whether patients undergoing orgone therapy screamed with pain, and what the "orgone box" was.

Four weeks later, Cotten committed suicide. The reasons for this act or even its connection with Reich are open to doubt. At the time, Reich commented vengefully: "That's a good way to get rid of the emotional plague." Suicide, by friend or foe, always had a particular fascination for him, a reaction undoubtedly connected with the suicide of his mother.

The war against the Reichians at Marlboro State Hospital continued. Several young physicians who had started therapy with Reich were fired. Baker himself had too secure a position to be dismissed, but the unpleasantness generated by the attacks led him to resign in October 1948. By this time his private practice in orgone therapy had grown to a point where he no longer needed or desired a state position.

Another newcomer in 1946 who was to become important to Reich was Simeon J. Tropp. Tropp was a surgeon in New York City at the time he met Reich. During his American years Reich held the policy, one that Wolfe opposed, of accepting physicians for training who had not had prior psychiatric experience. Tropp was among this small group. Reich had hoped that Tropp would be especially active in developing medical orgonomy, for example, the use of the accumulator in the treatment of various physical illnesses and the short-term use of psychiatric techniques for certain acute somatic disturbances that had an emotional component. For a few years Tropp did pursue these interests, but eventually his main concern became the psychiatric treatment of neuroses.

Tropp's special contribution for Reich lay not in any intellectual achievement but in the personal friendship, approbation, and support he gave him. Tropp had a warm, whimsical personality and was financially more affluent and personally freer than many of the other therapists. He made many generous contributions to Reich's work. He was the only therapist who moved with

Reich to Rangeley in 1950 and had frequent contact with him in the remaining years. But much as Reich liked him, Tropp's lack of intellectual discipline led Reich to hold him in distrust as well as affection.

Other therapists to join Reich in the late 1940s were Oscar Tropp (Simeon's brother), Victor Sobey from the Veterans' Hospital, Philip Gold, Charles Oller, Morton Herskowitz (like Thorburn, an osteopath), Emanuel Levine (later killed in an auto accident), and Michael Silvert, a psychiatrist-in-training at the Menninger Clinic in Kansas. All of these physicians would remain committed to orgonomy and helpful to Reich until the end of his life, but only Silvert was to play an important role in later years.

With some exceptions, the American therapists were less outstanding and accomplished far less than his Viennese, Berlin, or Oslo students. Reich's work had grown more controversial; few physicians were prepared to take the ridicule and ostracism that accompanied allegiance to orgonomy. Of those who did, Helena Deutsch's description of Freud's early students is pertinent:

> One might . . . expect these first pupils to have been revolution-
> aries of the spirit . . . a select and courageous advance guard. Such
> an expectation could be realized only in individual instances. . . .
> Many were impelled by their own neuroses . . . or by identification
> of their lack of recognition with Freud's lot. . . . The objective truth
> of Freud's researches was of less importance than the gratification of
> the emotional need to be esteemed and appreciated by him. . . .[16]

It says something about the lack of creativity or the blocks to independent productivity among the physicians who studied with Reich that only a few of them were able to write about and teach orgonomy after Reich's death.

Physicians attracted to orgonomy may not have been especially creative, but at least they could earn a good living. Many people seeking therapy from Reich were referred to his students—another aspect of his power. However, researchers interested in the field of orgonomy lacked any practical means of supporting themselves, for Reich, generally, could not find the funds to pay salaries. Nor was there any hope of grants from the government or support from universities. Three of these researchers had to pursue orgonomy in their spare time: Bernard Grad, Ph.D., a biologist from McGill University; Sol Kramer, Ph.D., an entomologist from the University of Wisconsin; and Helen MacDonald, Ph.D., a biologist from the University of California. These talented and devoted people became acquainted with Reich's work in the late 1940s and studied with him during summers at Orgonon. Other researchers, more tentatively interested, did not follow through, usually because of sharp differences between their traditional outlook and Reich's approach.

For his part, Reich was glad to have well-trained physicians and scientists join his work. He yearned for the scientific and social acceptance of orgonomy;

he also wanted more contact with people who understood what he was doing. However, he would sometimes behave as if such acceptance were of little moment to him. Baker has reported the following exchange during his therapy:

> Reich asked me if I thought he was glad that I had come to him. ... I said yes, I thought he was, because I was a classical physician, a Freudian analyst, and secretary of a medical society. ... I mentioned also that I was responsible for five other physicians becoming interested in his work. Reich let go with a full salvo and gave me to understand that it was unimportant to him whether I had come or not. He said he didn't need me or anyone else.[17]

The Reich who "didn't need me or anyone else" was part of the stern persona adopted soon after arrival in America. However, it was not simply a mask. Reich was convinced that he was orgonomy's main asset and that no one was going to hinder his progress. He was a more overwhelming leader than he had been in Europe. Although he remained a generous and stimulating teacher to the end, his chief interest now lay in a relentless pursuit of his own destiny. Others were secondary, to be sacrificed when they interfered with his creativity. It was no facile warning he gave one student: "Keep away from me. I am overwhelming. I burn through people."[18]

In America, Reich was able to attract a number of intellectuals who did not actually work with him, but who were much influenced by his teachings. The artist closest to him was William Steig, who illustrated *Listen, Little Man!* Steig was one of the few persons who came to Reich with an independent, successful career. His contributions to *The New Yorker* and his books had already made him one of America's most innovative cartoonists. He was also a charming, witty person with a feeling for the nuances of life. A patient of Reich's in the mid-1940s, he was deeply grateful for the help he received, and believed the accumulator had saved his mother's life. He was totally committed to Reich, and in the 1950s he would work hard on Reich's behalf.

Paul Goodman, poet, essayist, philosopher, psychologist, and man of letters, was in therapy with Alexander Lowen around 1945.[19] After Goodman wrote the first positive review of Reich's work to appear in America, Reich telephoned him and asked Goodman to come and speak with him.[20] Excited at the prospect of working with Reich, Goodman was disappointed when at the meeting Reich expressed displeasure over Goodman's linkage of orgonomy with anarchism. He asked Goodman to cease making this connection. In his turn, Goodman pointed out similarities between the concept of work democracy and the ideas of Peter Kropotkin, a noted Russian philosopher of anarchism. Goodman was touched by Reich's frank, embarrassed acknowledgment that he was not familiar with Kropotkin. But he was chagrined by Reich's authoritarianism. His annoyance did not prevent him from continuing to be a persuasive advocate of many of Reich's psychological and social concepts, however, although he was never involved in the natural-scientific side of orgonomy.

Saul Bellow, the distinguished novelist, was in therapy with one of Reich's students in the 1940s and for a period was so devoted to Reich's work that he quarreled bitterly with Alfred Kazin, who was considerably less enthusiastic.[21] Bellow's *The Adventures of Augie March* and *Henderson the Rain King* were especially influenced by Reich. Norman Mailer never met Reich, nor was he ever in Reichian therapy, but he absorbed and utilized many of Reich's concepts.[22]

During the same period, the talented short-story writer and critic Isaac Rosenfeld was deeply involved in Reich's ideas. In a vivid if often acidulous diary, parts of which were published posthumously in *The Partisan Review,* Rosenfeld mockingly commented on Irving Kristol, Nathan Glazer, and Robert Warshaw, all of whom then wrote for *Commentary;* among the things Rosenfeld disliked about them were their put-downs of Reich. Rosenfeld also aimed some of his shafts at "Reichians":

> The form in which orgone theory is handed around is often very funny. Thus, I was talking to Bill Steig, who said: "A new Bulletin [Reich's *Orgone Energy Bulletin,* which began appearing in 1949] has just come out. Very exciting. Reich says that light doesn't come from the sun.
>
> It turns out that this is merely an account of the diffusion of light through the atmosphere, by the excitation of the orgone through solar energy. But the form in which this news comes—"Stop the Press. Light doesn't come from the sun!"—is undeniably fun.
>
> Or must I suppose that to the degree I find such things funny, to that degree I am still resisting and looking for a way out?[23]

The diffusion of Reich's concepts by these and other writers remains a largely untold story. With the exception of Steig, Reich devoted little attention to such persons. Caught up in his scientific and practical tasks, he concentrated his energies on relationships that could be of more immediate help to him. Reich often utilized his physicians to defend himself against attacks. On one occasion in 1948, New York State medical officials were investigating Reich for practicing medicine without an American medical license. Willie, Cott, and Ilse went to see the appropriate officials, stating that Reich was not engaged in the practice of medicine but in research and the teaching of a new discipline. They succeeded in quieting the officials. Some of Reich's supporters, however, shared this official concern. Willie, for example, clearly felt Reich should have gotten a license and that he was inviting trouble by not doing so.[24] He himself went to considerable pains to acquire a Maine license so that he could practice in that state when he spent summers in Rangeley. At the same time, he was eager to help Reich against harassment.

The continuing attacks against orgonomy, especially as reflected in the hospital incident, further reports of an investigation by the American Psychiatric Association, constant rumors about Reich's insanity and malpractice with patients, all were beginning to form a clear and present danger to orgonomy. The danger became more acute when in 1947, as we shall see, the FDA launched its investigation of the accumulator. These various threats, and especially the FDA investigation, led Reich to feel the need to establish a medical organization that could represent his viewpoint accurately, fight the attacks, and spare his energies for research tasks.

Hence, in 1948, Reich encouraged the development of the American Association for Medical Orgonomy (AAMO), and by the end of that year such an organization was formed. The board of directors appointed by Reich consisted of Baker, Cott, and Willie. Twenty-one physicians became members of AAMO, as well as Ola Raknes, the Norwegian psychologist. Nic Hoel (now Waal) of Norway, who had resumed contact with Reich, and Walter Hoppe from Israel were members of the original group.

Willie was elected the first president of the Association. In his own remarks about its founding, Reich struck a chord almost in anticipation of later difficulties:

> We rely on *knowledge* and not on form; on *learning* and not on empty law; *on facts* and not on titles; on the deep-rooted knowledge about the laws of life which are in man, and not on the politician; on *love* and not on the marriage license; on *work* well done and not on opinions about work done by others. . . .[25]

It was not long before controversies erupted between Reich and Willie. A major issue centered on rules and regulations. Willie and some of the other physicians wanted highly formal requirements for admission to AAMO: medical school plus internship plus a few years of psychiatric training. Wolfe remarked that with these requirements he himself would not be acceptable since he went directly from medical school into psychiatric training, skipping an internship. Reich had argued strongly that the chief requirement should be a medical degree *or its equivalent;* in the end, his opinion prevailed. Despite his clear commitment to medical training as an essential prerequisite for the practice of psychiatric orgone therapy, Reich always wanted to leave the door open for persons with "special gifts"—the phrase is Willie's—to be able to practice orgone therapy without medical training. Raknes fell into this category, and Reich maintained this option even though he had had some bad experiences with nonmedical people already.

Willie served as president for one year and was scheduled to serve a second when Reich intervened. According to Willie, "Reich felt that I was trying to take the doctors away from him." I asked Willie if this was true. Willie smiled and said, "Competitiveness is woven into the very warp and woof of my personality." In any case, Willie was removed as president and Baker replaced him, in accordance with Reich's wishes.

A welcome respite from external and internal crises was provided by visits from European colleagues during the postwar period. In September 1946, Ola Raknes came for a four-month visit, the first European co-worker to meet Reich again after the war. He spent September working with Reich in the laboratory at Orgonon. At the end of the month, he and Reich returned to New York, and he continued his studies in Forest Hills.

Raknes was the kind of student Reich liked. Many of Reich's former Scandinavian associates came to the conclusion that he had gone astray in America, basing their judgment on a cursory perusal of his U.S. publications. Raknes took the trouble to devote several months to careful study of the new orgonomic phenomena directly under Reich's and Ilse's supervision. Reich greatly appreciated Raknes' seriousness, independence of mind, and receptivity to new ideas, combined with his determination to test them for himself. Raknes differed with Reich on many matters, but this did not spoil their good friendship. Indeed, the differences enhanced the relationship, since they shared a devotion to the central concepts of orgonomy.

I have already mentioned the importance of Reich's correspondence with A. S. Neill. The first opportunity they had to meet after World War II occurred in the summer of 1947. Neill arranged a visit to America that included a lecture tour and a stay with Reich at Orgonon. Ilse's description of Neill's visit at Orgonon is worth quoting:

> Neill and Reich talked deep into the night over a glass of whiskey and innumerable cigarettes. All their favorite topics were taken up: criticism, recognition, socialism, communism, sex-economy in pedagogy, and especially the newborn child, as Neill had recently become a father of a little girl and found this experience, as did Reich, a marvelous field of study. . . . Neill saw some of the experimental work that was going on at Orgonon but he maintained that he did not fully understand it. . . . One incident that Neill remembers very clearly is that one afternoon, during which we all sat together talking about cars and other mundane matters, Reich told Neill that such drawing-room conversations about nothing were sheer agony for him, they took him out of his sphere of thinking and he could not participate. This was always true for Reich, and was mentioned as a part of his character by many others to whom I talked. He could not and would not participate in chitchat and small talk.[26]

Then Reich planned the First International Orgonomic Conference for late August 1948 to give all the co-workers, American and European, an opportunity to meet with one another, hear papers, and exchange views for a few days. Undoubtedly, Reich had in mind some of the International Psychoanalytic Congresses he had attended in the 1920s and early 1930s. Like them, there was to be a social reception to precede the conference. Neill arrived from England, Raknes from Norway, and Dr. Ferrari Hardoy, a psychiatrist who had earlier studied with Reich, from Argentina.

Walter Hoppe was also scheduled to attend. Hoppe, a German psychiatrist, had emigrated in the thirties to Palestine; had made contact with Reich's writings in the early 1940s. Subsequently, Reich and he corresponded frequently and Hoppe had his first orgone accumulator built while the war was still on. Hoppe experimented with the medical use of the accumulator more extensively than any other physician with the exception of Reich. Reich greatly appreciated his independence, daring, and quick grasp of functional principles. He looked forward to meeting Hoppe in person.

Inexplicably, Hoppe was detained at Ellis Island upon arrival in New York on August 28. Reich was furious at this capricious action by the immigration officials. The anger and hurt from the FDA investigation, the hospital incident, and accusations of insanity that had overwhelmed him during the past year were now unleashed on behalf of Hoppe. In a torrent of activity he sent telegrams to the State Department, the Justice Department, Ellis Island, and his lawyer Arthur Garfield Hays. "This too is research," he commented. "*He* cures their cancers and *they* throw him in jail." He attributed Hoppe's detention to bureaucratic stupidity rather than any animus against his work from the federal government. The reasons for Hoppe's detention never did become clear.

On August 30, Reich succeeded in obtaining Hoppe's release. Wolfe accompanied him from New York in a chartered plane that landed dramatically on Dodge Pond on the evening of August 31, where many of the conference participants were already on the small wharf. I recall Reich rather peremptorily waved the rest of us back as he stood alone to welcome Hoppe.

Hoppe proved to be a delightful, witty man. Short and wiry, his low-keyed ironic approach offered an interesting contrast to Reich's. He had taken his detention philosophically, with much less upset than Reich. Yet his talk showed the same kind of appreciation for orgone energy, and the same awareness of man's tendency in general and of scientific authorities in particular to explain away the results of the accumulator.

A full report on the conference has been presented elsewhere.[27] Here I will limit myself to some highlights, with particular emphasis on the ways the conference illuminated Reich's interactions with his colleagues and his mood and thinking at that time.

On August 31, in a meeting limited to physicians, Simeon Tropp spoke on the short-term, experimental use of psychiatric orgone therapy in the ordinary medical office. Here he was dealing with a wide variety of so-called psychosomatic complaints that might well lend themselves to orgone therapy. Reich was intensely interested in this particular kind of application of orgone therapy. However, he worried about the incautious use of these methods by insufficiently trained physicians.

Hoppe, speaking in German as Wolfe translated, related how he had used a twenty-fold accumulator (as well as regular accumulators) in order to establish the work by showing the rapid and intensive effects of orgone treatment. He also spoke of the ridicule he was receiving from physicians; as with Reich, his positive results were dismissed as "miracle cures," faulty original diagnoses, and the like.

In the discussion period, Reich noted that Hoppe had gone further than American orgone therapists, including himself, in the extent of his use of the twenty-fold accumulator. Here the fear existed that there might be danger in such an intense application of orgone energy, but Hoppe reported no injurious effects. Nevertheless, Reich advised the greatest caution in using the accumulator.

Hoppe's experience with mocking physicians was instructive, Reich stated, in that it showed that the hostile reaction to orgone energy was not caused by Reich's aggressive personality. The mildest of men, Hoppe could not be accused of belligerence. Yet he had met with the same skepticism and ridicule Reich had.

Beside the formal papers given at the conference, there were opportunities in the mornings for demonstrations of orgonomic phenomena such as the bions in the orgone energy dark room.

During these demonstrations Reich moved around, pointing out certain things and answering questions. He gave several informal talks in which he stressed the technique of orgonomic functionalism underlying all experimental results—a technique that was neither mechanical nor mystical, that moved from the complicated to the simple, and that was based on a thorough study of emotional functioning. Reich emphasized that orgone energy could not be understood without a knowledge of the emotions, nor could the energy behind the emotions be fully understood without some knowledge of how the same energy functioned outside the organism.

Ilse Ollendorff showed a film Reich had made in Norway on the bions and the development of protozoa (it is now in the sealed Reich Archives). Another film shown had been made by Reich that summer, with Kari Berggrav serving as photographer under his direction. This film included more of his recent discoveries as well as footage on the Rangeley lakes and mountains. Berggrav, whom Reich had known in Norway, had filmed for him there, too; a spirited woman, she sometimes quarreled with Reich about procedure. Once she remarked that he had given her more latitude in the filming in Norway. Reich responded sharply, "This isn't Norway. I'm the boss here," contrasting his authoritarian leadership with the more egalitarian arrangements earlier.

In making this film, Reich featured his own name in big letters as the discoverer of orgone energy, commenting: "I used to hide under the table. But that didn't do any good." Just as the American Reich was more distant from his students and more evidently the "boss," so he also was more intent on clearly identifying his name with his accomplishment. "I took the beating—now I want the credit." At other times he explained the emphasis on his name in a different way: it was identified with the most uncompromising expression of his concepts and he wanted that quality to come through.

For all the stress on his name, Reich was curiously reluctant to have his face appear in the film. Kari wanted to take some footage of him, so he agreed to walk up and down in front of some instruments. Later, when he looked at the resulting footage, he told Kari to take it out—it looked phony.[28] In the finished film the most one sees of Reich are his hands. For a large man he had surprisingly small hands, thin, quick, and somehow more delicate than one would have expected.

Reich was at his best during the conference. One could see him then as one rarely saw him—thoroughly relaxed, enjoying the companionship and success of his work that this gathering in part reflected, eager to share knowledge, Reich the man who enjoyed people. Yet he kept apart in a definite though not easily definable way. One example was that he did not participate in any of the parties given by the people, like Willie and Wolfe, with summer homes in the Rangeley region. While Reich was warm and expansive at the conference, there was very little small talk from him.

On August 30, Ola Raknes had reported on sex-economy and orgone research in Norway. After his visit to the United States in 1946, Raknes had built an accumulator in his own home, with much opposition from everyone, including Nic Waal and Odd Havrevold.

Then, on September 1, Reich spoke of the "Consequences of Orgone in Vacuum." The preceding winter he had made the discovery that orgone energy existed in the so-called vacuum, and that a vacuum tube, if sufficiently charged with orgone energy in an accumulator for several months, luminated blue when excited by another orgone field or a small electrical charge.[29] Reich demonstrated this phenomenon during his talk. However, on this occasion he was not so much concerned with technical orgonomic problems as he was with the question that had preoccupied him that summer while writing *Ether, God and Devil*, namely, Why had not orgone energy been discovered long before? This question linked the physical and the psychiatric aspects of his work: the same fear that prevented the discovery of orgone energy blocked the discovery of the child's true nature.

Unable to penetrate to the primordial, cosmic energy, man—according to Reich—erected two systems of thought, mysticism and mechanism, which were essentially built around the concepts of "God" and "ether," respectively. God was behind all subjective, spiritual, qualitative phenomena; the ether behind all material, physical processes. Without intending to, Reich said, he had hit upon both the God and ether problem when he discovered the cosmic orgone energy. Orgone energy, like God and ether, was everywhere and permeated everything. It was behind both the physical processes in nature and the perceptual processes in the human organism. But whereas hitherto man had mechanically split up the cosmic energy into spiritual "God" and physical "ether" and then was unable to reach either, functional thinking discovered the cosmic orgone energy and was able to understand and handle the concepts *practically*. And the same factor that throughout the centuries had prevented the discovery of orgone energy, of orgastic potency, of "what it is like to be a child"—man's armoring—now was at the basis of the tremendous fear and hatred of orgonomy.

With great intensity Reich spoke of the painful experience of hearing repeatedly from people to whom he showed orgone experimentation, "Very interesting," and then no more. This armoring against real-life problems, this constant, impotent "Very interesting," had to be overcome before any genuine progress could be made. Reich concluded by saying that there were no authorities in the field of orgonomy. If orgonomy represented a new way of thinking and a new science, then to ask the authorities of the old science to confirm it was—to say the least—naive.

I never heard Reich speak so eloquently. It was as though on that night everything came together. In his scientific thought he had advanced far enough to know exactly what he had discovered. He had attracted a number of colleagues who, with varying degrees of commitment and intelligence, listened attentively, giving him at least some of the response he wanted, even though there were still far too many reactions of "Very interesting." He was surrounded by very good friends that evening: Neill, Raknes, Wolfe, Hoppe, and others. There was no visible attack on the horizon to harass, distract, or infuriate him. It was one of those precious lulls between storms.

There was extraordinarily little bitterness from Reich during the conference. It was as if he were beyond bitterness. He held his own ground adamantly against the attribution of authority to persons who had not earned it, an attribution rampant even among some of his closest co-workers who wondered, covertly if not overtly, what "real" scientists thought of his work. But there was no rancor.

In subsequent years Reich was to go on making discoveries, discoveries that were perhaps even more important than those he demonstrated at the 1948 conference. However, his rage was also to grow as the harassment intensified. Never again was there to be quite the same golden sense of harmony, insight, and understanding. Never again was Reich to seem so receptive, so accepting yet firm where the central themes of his work were in jeopardy. Recalling Reich in the summer of 1948, one cannot help but wish that his environment had provided more of the support and peace that was in evidence during the First International Orgonomic Conference. Although he often said he could work alone, that he needed no recognition, it was equally true that people were important in his lifetime and that their responses buoyed his spirit.

I have commented at some length on Reich's excellent contributions and demeanor during the conference. However, he can be faulted quite severely in one respect: he did not really facilitate a similar quality from others. He invited good questions and comments, and was always generous with praise for contributions. Yet he reacted so sharply to what he considered to be poor questions or comments that participants often censored their valuable as well as their hostile or banal reactions. A discussion led by Reich might consist of a few comments from others, to which Reich would then respond with mini-lectures. He rarely invited a more general discussion. For all his emphasis in therapy on expressing negative feelings, there was little room for doing so in conferences. Reich could not, or perhaps would not, expose himself to the same material outside therapy.

Inevitably, no strong group could be sustained in this atmosphere. And however understandable Reich's position, it also reflected his own need to control events around him. The group atmosphere was authoritarian, in Kurt Lewin's sense of the term. Most of the lines of communication were between Reich and students, little between student and student. Reich further contributed to the intensity by insisting on a high degree of professional secrecy among co-workers. Reich once commented on his failure to build up a viable organization along work-democratic lines, adding: "If that should continue, it would reflect a problem in *me.*"[30] It did continue and it did indeed reflect his own problem.

One of Reich's chief preoccupations during the summer of 1948 was the orgone energy motor.* During the following summer, these fears were heightened when an assistant, William Washington, who had been working on the motor, did not appear at Orgonon as scheduled.

I had met Bill, who was black, in the fall of 1944 at the University of Chicago, where we were both freshmen. He was especially interested in mathematics and physics, but had a wide-ranging knowledge in many realms. Although he talked extremely little, he always followed with slight nonverbal motions very carefully what others said. He seemed to me extremely intelligent and I attributed his taciturnity to his being very short. He appeared to be enthusiastic about Reich's work when I introduced him to it.

In 1947, Reich was looking for an assistant to help him in mathematical

---

*Reich never published the design for the orgone energy motor and I no longer remember the details of the experimental set-up or its operation. I do recall that it involved the use of an accumulator attached to a wheel; concentrated orgone energy was triggered by a small amount of electricity, an amount insufficient to rotate the wheel without the accumulator. I also recall that when the wheel was rotated entirely by electricity, it had a steady grinding motion. When powered by the combination of orgonotic and electrical energy, it ran smoothly and quietly; but its speed varied depending upon the weather—more rapidly on dry, clear days, more slowly when the humidity was high. During this summer, Reich was extremely excited about the motor and envisioned its industrial applications. He also expressed considerable concern that the "secret" of the motor might be stolen, which may have contributed to his reluctance to publish the details.

and experimental work. Bill started working with him in the summer of that year, concentrating on mathematics. The following summer Bill did more laboratory work and had the particular responsibility of helping Reich develop the orgone energy motor. When he left Orgonon in the fall of 1948, he took the motor set-up with him in order to work on further refinements. He was supposed to return to Orgonon in early summer 1949, but he did not appear, nor was there any word from him. By August, Reich was extremely concerned about Bill and the motor.

During this time we checked out various stories Bill had told us about his previous employment, for example, that he had once worked at the National Argonne Laboratories (a division of the Atomic Energy Commission). None of these stories proved true. Nobody ever discovered what happened to Washington or the motor, but Reich was able to speak with him on the telephone late in the summer of 1949. He sounded quite hesitant in his speech—a hesitation Reich construed to mean that he was not free to speak. At one point, Reich asked if he was being coerced. Washington answered, "In a way," but did not elaborate. It was my impression that Washington was happy to grab at any straw to get him off the hook of being, for whatever personal reasons, unable to finish the assigned job. However, Reich did not choose that mundane explanation. He provided Washington with the suggestion that he was being externally coerced—by the Atomic Energy Commission, the Communists, or someone. Washington's answer was just enough to keep Reich's idea alive, although he also entertained the possibility that Bill was simply sick or sociopathic.

Washington was never heard from again. I have lingered on the incident because such episodes made one wonder about Reich and his work. If he could dredge up a possible kidnapping or espionage plot on such slim evidence as existed about Washington, when a simpler explanation was readily available, of what other inventions might he be capable? In retrospect, I see the Washington story as another example of how wrong Reich could be about people and social events when his own wishes and fears were strongly involved. At such times his marvelous capacity for seeing the underlying, objectively fruitful patterns in man and nature degenerated into the wildly oversimplified symbolism of the western movies he so loved, with their good guys, bad guys, and dramatic dénouements. As Lavater once put it: "A daring eye tells downright truths and downright lies."

In short, the Washington incident provides a nice example of the paranoid aspect of Reich's psychic functioning. He had always been capable of such erroneous pattern-finding, but this tendency increased sharply in his last years. His critics use examples like the Washington case to seal their diagnosis of his entire later work as a grandiose paranoid system. Many of his supporters in their turn go to tortuous lengths to find justifications for his view of Washington and for other instances of his bizarre thinking.

In my view, the truth is not so neat. During the same period Reich was capable of the most profound, objective thought and experimentation *and* of the most extreme, paranoid ideas. How do these pieces fit together? In part, there is the aforementioned disposition toward pattern-making which, as Ernest Hartmann has suggested,[31] is common to both creativity and paranoia. But one cannot explain everything. In Donald Hall's words about the dual Ezra Pound—the great poet and most generous mentor to other poets, and the dispenser of the crudest anti-Semitic, pro-Fascist propaganda: "I do not fit these pieces together; they *are* together in the mystery of a man's character and life."[32]

During the fall of 1949, Reich seriously considered staying year round at Orgonon. He was tired of dividing his time between New York and Maine. In late 1949, he made one of his few references to his age (he was fifty-two at the time): "I have only a few productive years left and I must safeguard every moment."[33] He was also eager for the physicians to participate more in the scientific aspects of orgonomy. And most of them were prepared to participate, but only up to a point.

Although not ready to make the move that fall, Reich came to the decision in the spring of 1950. For a period during that winter Reich was very happy. He had returned to New York, and was delighted to start the Orgonomic Infant Research Center. However, in the end he decided that the gains of Orgonon outweighed the losses of leaving the city. As we have seen, for years he had resented the interruptions to his research and writing caused by seeing patients. Now he was extremely tired of clinical work, of becoming "entangled" in people's problems. Reich also recognized that he was no longer such a good clinician in the sense of being accepting and patient.

Some half dozen co-workers made the move to Orgonon with Reich in 1950: Ilse Ollendorff; Eva Reich, who by this time had completed her medical training and whose interest in her father's work had grown considerably; H. Lee Wylie, a young physician who also had some background in physics; Lois Wyvell, the managing director of the Orgone Institute Press; Simeon Tropp, his wife Helen, and his three-year-old son Jimmy; and I. (As we shall discover, Wolfe had largely withdrawn as an active co-worker, though his advice was still valued by Reich.)

In late May 1950, after six months of not working with Reich, I returned to Orgonon, now simply to work with Reich with no thought of being in therapy with him. That summer I remember as golden. There was a glamour surrounding his activities. Reich was in a very good mood—active, expansive, human. I was franker with him than I had ever been and he appreciated it. Among other tasks, I was responsible for the editorial preparation of the *Orgone Energy Bulletin,* a quarterly Reich had begun publishing in 1949 to replace the *International Journal for Sex-Economy and Orgone-Research.*

There were other incidents that suggested some darker currents beneath the apparently smooth surface of Orgonon's relationship with the community. Helen Tropp applied for a teaching position at the local public school (which

Peter Reich now attended) and the principal informed her that no one connected with Orgonon could be employed there.*

Another, more dangerous, incident concerned the investigation of Orgonon by a representative of the state police. The investigator went to a children's camp nearby, which had no connection with the Orgone Institute. There a counselor was interrogated about where the children came from, whether the camp "fed" children for the Orgone Institute, whether it was a nudist camp, and so forth. Another investigated rumor involved my alleged chasing girls at night.

Reich took various actions against these rumors. He continued the policy established earlier of confronting very directly the originators of the rumors, going to some lengths to determine who they were. One particular example was telling. We suspected a local citizen, seemingly friendly toward Orgonon, of saying that Reich and his associates were Communists. At Reich's direction, I wrote the person asking if he had in fact circulated the rumor. There was no reply, but others confirmed his identity as the rumor-spreader. Reich prepared a letter, signed by the Orgonon staff, which was sent to a number of Rangeley citizens. In it, he described the danger of slander and gossip, and the way that slanderers, or people with emotional plague, rely on other people's fear of being slandered themselves. Here Reich was applying concretely—and I think with some success, in this instance—his sociological emphasis on the interaction between emotional plague citizens and the average neurotic.

During this period, however, a far more ominous, if subterranean attack was continuing. I am referring to the Food and Drug Administration's investigation of the orgone energy accumulator.

---

*It is an ironic historical footnote that on July 15, 1981, a symposium was held at Orgonon on "Self-regulation and Learning in Children," honoring the publication of *Record of a Friendship: The Correspondence Between Wilhelm Reich and A. S. Neill.* The chairman of the symposium was the Head Teacher for the Rangeley Head Start Program, and another participant was a high-school teacher in Rangeley. No one was impolite enough to mention that thirty years earlier the Rangeley School system would not hire a teacher connected with Orgonon. "A tragedy enacted secures applause/That tragedy enacting too seldom does"—Emily Dickinson.

PART VIII

The Road to Death— The FDA Campaign and Oranur: 1948-1957

25

The American Campaign Against Orgonomy—The Beginnings: 1947-1948

The American years were for Reich relatively peaceful until 1947. The operative word is "relatively." For only in contrast with the Norwegian press campaign of the late 1930s and what was to come afterward can the period between 1940 and 1947 be viewed as peaceful. It included Reich's detention at Ellis Island in 1941, various snide articles, and, above all, constant rumors concerning Reich's alleged insanity and malpractice with patients. But there were no organized or sustained attacks, jeopardizing his capacity to function.

All this was to change shortly after an article appeared in the May 26, 1947, issue of *The New Republic*. The article, under the byline of Mildred Edie Brady, a free-lance writer, was entitled "The Strange Case of Wilhelm Reich." The subheading, in large type, ran: "The man who blames both neuroses and cancer on unsatisfactory sexual activities has been repudiated by only one scientific journal."

Other attacks had appeared in the American press. However, no one combined truths, half-truths, and lies as skillfully as Ms. Brady. Many future writers on Reich were to rely almost solely on her for their information. One key passage that was picked up by many writers ran as follows: "Orgone, named after the sexual orgasm, is, according to Reich, a cosmic energy. It is, in fact, *the* cosmic energy. Reich has not only discovered it; he has seen it, demonstrated it and named a town—Orgonon, Maine—after it. Here he builds accumulators of it which are rented out to patients, who presumably derive 'orgastic potency' from it."

If one combines the subheading with the quoted passage, Brady's message is clear. The accumulator gives "orgastic potency," the lack of which is responsible for everything from neuroses to cancer. Ergo, the accumulator will cure neuroses and cancer. Moreover, Reich makes a profit by renting cure-all accumulators to the public.

Brady had taken the trouble to read—or misread—Reich's writing, something many of his critics had not done. In addition, although Reich made a practice of refusing press interviews, Brady was able to talk with him by posing as an enthusiast of his work with news from friends on the West Coast. Having bearded the lion in his den, she was able to create a kind of chatty intimacy with the reader about the strange Reich:

> . . . Reich runs a considerable establishment . . . , and he has more patients than he can take care of. As you climb the stairs to his second-floor office, you find pictures of stellar nebullae along the way. You find Reich to be a heavy-set, ruddy, brown-haired man of 50, wearing a long white coat and sitting at a huge desk. Between periods of training students in his theories and putting patients into orgone accumulators, he will tell you how unutterably rotten is the underlying character of the average individual.

In this passage Brady correctly plays Reich's individual notes, but she totally distorts his melody. Her deft insinuation that Reich was a swindler and a megalomaniac would permeate many subsequent articles on orgonomy as well as the FDA investigation.

Brady's main point could be discerned from the insinuations: the psychoanalytic organization should discipline itself, in other words, do something about "the growing Reich cult," or else it will "be disciplined by the state."

The political context of the article is important, not only in itself but for what Reich made of it. At the time of the Brady article, *The New Republic* was under the editorship of Henry A. Wallace. Wallace had resigned from the Truman administration in 1946 in protest of its cold-war policies. In 1948, he was to run for President on the Progressive Party ticket. By even the most charitable accounts he was much influenced by American Communists during this period.[1]

As a sign of *The New Republic*'s Stalinist line under Wallace, the magazine on December 2, 1946, had published a review by Frederic Wertham of Reich's *The Mass Psychology of Fascism*. Wertham accused Reich of "utter contempt for the masses" because he stressed their mysticism and incapacity for freedom. Reich, Wertham said, represented a threat to the left because he confused liberals by leading them away from the political struggle. Reich advocated "psycho-fascism."

Given the all but universal fear of orgonomy, Reich had long worried that a campaign of the magnitude of the Norwegian one would break out in America. The American Psychiatric Association, the American Medical Association, the psychoanalysts, the pharmaceutical industry, one or another political party—all were possible candidates to mobilize the opposition. The appearance of Wertham's and Brady's articles in short succession in a fellow-traveling journal convinced Reich that the Stalinists had won this dubious honor.

If Reich was right in stressing Wertham's and especially Brady's role in spearheading the American campaign, he was wrong in ignoring the contribution of the political right to his difficulties. In the late 1940s, many Americans were shocked to discover both the barbarity of Soviet totalitarianism and the extent of Stalinist penetration of various domestic organizations. These genuine fears merged with an irrational anxiety about "un-American" radicals. Right-wing demagogues such as Joseph McCarthy were quick to exploit and escalate this amalgam of concern over "subversive" individuals.

Brady's article was extremely successful in drawing positive attention to itself and negative attention to Reich. A condensation of it was published in *Everybody's Digest,* a now defunct popular magazine that then had a circulation in the millions.[2] *Collier's* borrowed from it heavily in an article which stated that the "orgone and the accumulator can lick everything from the common cold to cancer, according to Dr. Reich."[3] Excerpts appeared in Scandinavian, French, and Swiss papers. As late as 1954, when Irwin Ross published a long article on Reich in the *New York Post,* he took over Brady's title and much of her content.[4] But the most outrageous use of the article was by a well-regarded psychiatric journal, the *Bulletin of the Menninger Clinic,*[5] which simply reprinted Brady's piece in its entirety as the *Bulletin's* official position on Reich, about whom the editors had had inquiries. This intellectual laziness on the part of a professional journal is a good example of how contemptuously Reich was regarded by the establishment: one did not have to study his writings, one need only republish a hatchet job by a free-lance writer. Brady wove the slander together; others kept repeating it.

The most dangerous result of the article was that it alerted the Food and Drug Administration to the "Reich problem." About two months after the article appeared, on July 23, Dr. J. J. Durrett, director of the Medical Advisory Division of the Federal Trade Commission, sent the following letter to the FDA:

> Attached is a photostatic copy of an article by Mildred Edie Brady which deals with Wilhelm Reich. . . . We have not investigated Reich and his activities. From the article it appears that he has set himself up as a local practitioner of psychiatry. . . . The reason I am sending this to you is that he appears to be supplying his patients with a gadget which will capture the seemingly fantastic substance "orgone" and accumulate it for the benefit of the person who occupies

the space within this device. I thought you might want to look into this.[6]

"Wharton* has been variously described by FDA people who worked with him as 'ruthless' and 'dictatorial' as well as one of the five most powerful men in the agency at that time.[7]† When Wharton eventually obtained an accumulator for study, he kept it in his office and "joked about it as a means of gaining sexual prowess, à la Brady. 'This is a box,' Wharton wrote on August 26, 'in which a man is placed and thereby becomes permeated with orgone, which is a progenitor of orgasm . . .' Charles A. Wood, resident FDA inspector for the state of Maine and the first FDA agent to 'investigate' Reich and his work, said of Wharton many years later: 'He was crazy about that Reich case and didn't think of anything else during the whole time. He built it way out of proportion.' "[8]

Wharton directed Wood to launch a preliminary investigation of Reich and his Maine headquarters. On August 27, Wood went to Orgonon to meet Reich. "Dr. Reich is fifty years old, speaks with a German accent, and was dressed in blue dungarees and a work shirt at the time of the visit," Wood later reported. He added an editorial comment: "He looked anything but professional."[9]

Greenfield has described how Wood "was greeted cordially by Reich, to whom he explained that he had come to find out whether the accumulator might be classified as a device according to FDA law." Reich asked Wood how he had found out about the accumulator. He was angered by Wood's mention of the Brady article as his source. "He admitted that the accumulator was indeed a device, though in an experimental state. . . ."

Reich then arranged for Wood to visit the site where the accumulators were constructed. This visit led to a novelistic twist in the story. At the workshop, Wood met Clista Templeton. Clista had taken over the construction of the accumulators after the death of her father, Herman, in 1944. Some three months after Wood met Clista, they married. Clista was the main informant to Wood about the accumulators. This was a particularly dramatic example of how personal and scientific issues often became enmeshed where Reich was involved.

Wood learned from Clista Templeton that to date some 250 accumulators of varying sizes had been built. Most important, Clista supplied names and addresses of accumulator users to Wood. Her guilt or fear about her role as informer was expressed in her reluctance to become a witness in any trial against Reich; she did not want Reich to know that she had "doublecrossed him," to use Wood's phrase.[10]

Following Wood's report, Wharton replied in September in a letter to the

---

*R. M. Wharton was chief of the Eastern Division of the FDA.
†For this and other material about the investigation in general, I am indebted to Jerome Greenfield's fine study, *Wilhelm Reich Vs. the U.S.A.* (New York: W.W. Norton, 1974).

Boston office out of which Wood worked: "From our review of this material it appears that we have here a fraud of the first magnitude being perpetrated by a very able individual fortified to a considerable degree by men of science. In order to invoke appropriate . . . action, we must lay our foundation well and secure in the beginning considerable data and information."[11]

On September 24, Wood returned to visit Reich at Orgonon. He continued his questions about Reich's teachings, whereupon Reich referred him to his books. Reich became angry when Wood asked about his expulsion from the International Psychoanalytic Association. It must have seemed demeaning to Reich to discuss his important and painful conflict with Freud in answer to a routine question from an FDA agent who knew absolutely nothing about these matters except Brady's statement that "Freud saw fit to take issue with him."

During the course of his visit with Wood (who on both occasions had come to Orgonon without prior notice), Reich was interrupted by someone from Rangeley who had come to discuss his accumulator treatment. (Reich did not usually see patients at Orgonon but made an exception for local citizens, whom he treated free of charge.) To quote Wood in his report:

> According to Dr. Reich, Mr. Brackett was confined to his bed with arthritis three years ago and could not walk or use his hands. Brackett is an old man with hands stiff and out of shape, but he could move his fingers and walked fairly well. He was the real "testimonial" type and Dr. Reich took great delight in bringing out Mr. Brackett's miraculous story of recovery by use of the accumulator. (His case can be investigated if desired.)[12]

For a period, Reich continued to cooperate with the FDA. He told physicians working with him to answer questions about the accumulator but not to supply the names of patients. Patients who had been contacted by the FDA—through Clista's list of users—were advised by Reich to answer questions about their use of the accumulator, but not about their personal or sexual lives.

However, it became clear during the fall of 1947 that the FDA agents were suspicious of, among other things, a sexual racket of some kind. Dr. Simeon Tropp, for example, reported being questioned about women associated with orgonomy and "what was done with them."[13] When Reich became aware of these questions, he was enraged. Nothing angered him more than the accusation that he ran some kind of "sex racket." He had not yet reached the point of breaking off all contact with the FDA but he was close to it.

The evidence also continued to support the idea that the FDA had prejudged the case. Thus, Wood visited Tom Ross at Orgonon later that fall. Tom reported: "Mr. Wood . . . came in while I was working in my workshop and told me spontaneously . . . that the accumulator was a fake . . . and that Dr.

Reich was fooling the public with it. He said the case would break soon and hinted that Dr. Reich would go to jail."[14]

The combination of the pornography accusation and the FDA's blatant prejudgment persuaded Reich to limit his cooperation forthwith. Thus, when the FDA asked for an accumulator for the purpose of testing it, Reich refused to comply unless the FDA permitted an orgonomist to take part in the testing and unless the agency made clear what it was investigating. "I would . . . rejoice . . . if the testing by the administration would be made in a rational manner," Reich wrote. "[But] the one who in the name of the government will undertake the testing will have to prove that he believes in our honesty."[15]

On November 19, Reich's lawyer, Julian Culver from the Hays law office, telephoned Wharton. In a memorandum of the conversation, Wharton denied any preconceptions on the FDA's part. They were still investigating and had not reached any conclusions. Wharton insisted that there could be no cooperative testing, although "we would be perfectly willing to listen to Dr. Reich and let him make any demonstration he cared to make with the device."[16]

Wharton made a favorable impression on Culver. The latter advised Reich to give the FDA an accumulator since they would get one anyway.[17] Reich did not follow his lawyer's advice. He believed it was a mistake to cooperate in the testing of the accumulator under conditions that made a fair test remote. One of his chief concerns was a circumstance he had encountered often in the past: the idea of a box accumulating energy from the air was so ridiculous that the control experiments would be sloppily executed. The insinuation of pornography and the evidence of prejudgment boded ill for a bona fide test.

Reich was also keenly aware, as his lawyer was not, of the depth of hatred against orgonomy. Lawyers, as well as many of Reich's colleagues, were often inclined to discount the emotional significance of irrational statements or actions by the FDA and to overemphasize what appeared to be reasonable behavior, as in Wharton's phone conversation with Culver. Reich took the opposite tack, highlighting the irrational and perceiving a conspiratorial explanation for the FDA's action (the influence of the political left on the investigation). The two orientations were bound to clash.

Reich also refused the FDA's request for the names and addresses of patients on the grounds that this was privileged information. Here he was supported by his lawyer, who stated that since the privilege belonged to the patient alone, it could not be waived by Reich. Unbeknown to Reich or his lawyer, the FDA had its own source of information for the names and addresses of accumulator users.

By the winter of 1947–48, Reich was reaching the end of his tether. A statement he wrote in December and mailed to accumulator users and colleagues conveyed his state of mind. His first written protest was formally entitled "Statement Regarding Competence in Matters of Orgone Energy":

I would like to plead for my right to investigate natural phenomena without having any guns pointed at me. I also ask for the right to be wrong without being hanged for it.

I am angry:

I am angry because there is so much talk of free speech and fair play. True, there is much freedom and fair play in regard to everyday matters. But, to my great surprise, I found that newspapers and magazines were open to smearing attacks on my work and my name; that one writer after another copied Brady's slanderous statements, without first trying to find out the truth in our literature, and that the same newspapers and periodicals seemed unwilling to publish a simple correction of misstatements.

I am angry because a Government agency which is supposed to safeguard human health *did* take affidavits from people who professed *not* to have been helped by the accumulator but *did not* take affidavits from others who told them they *had been* helped.

I am angry because smearing can do anything and truth can do so little to prevail, as it seems at the moment.

I am angry because once again the political plague knifed hardworking people in the back.[18]

Reich was wrong in one regard: the FDA files do not contain any affidavit from any accumulator user indicating dissatisfaction. From time to time the FDA would lament its inability to obtain such affidavits.

The statement also contained a line of attack which, unfortunately, Reich was to elaborate in increasing detail, namely, the idea that he had been knifed by the "political plague." Here Reich was referring only in part to the FDA. More importantly, he meant Mildred Edie Brady. The idea was growing in his mind that Brady was more than a fellow traveler; she was a Stalinist, and may well have been acting on direct instructions from the Communist Party. Brady's Stalinism became a firm conviction. The evidence about Brady was scant—the tone of her article, its appearance in *The New Republic* under Wallace's editorship, and some hearsay about her politics. A friend of Reich's wrote him that in 1936 Brady was "in sympathy" with the Communist Party, but later information was not available.[19] Regrettably I, too, contributed to the loose political characterization of Brady by repeating to Reich a statement heard from Dwight Macdonald. Macdonald had casually mentioned something about the fellow-traveling or Stalinist sympathies of Mildred and her husband, and Reich exaggerated the significance of this vague remark.

His time eaten up by the FDA investigation, Reich was strongly tempted to turn the whole matter over to the physicians working with him. On December 20, he informed Culver that he was transferring all rights to the medical use of the accumulator to the Orgone Institute Research Laboratories, the nonprofit corporation he had formed on April 30, 1945, to further his research.

Dr. Willie, Dr. Tropp, and Ilse Ollendorff would deal with the FDA and related matters in the future. "I have done my part in discovering orgone energy, in elaborating some of its qualities, and in constructing a device to accumulate it which, to my experience, has shown great possibilities in being useful as a medical device," he concluded.[20]

Whenever one reads of Reich's intention to divest himself of responsibility for the accumulator, one can only fervently wish that he had executed this plan. Accumulator rentals were helpful in supporting his research, as we know; yet he could have made more money from his teaching and clinical activities in less time and with less aggravation than from the accumulator and its administrative concerns. But the Reich who discovered orgone energy could not abandon his "device," as the FDA was forever describing the accumulator; he could not abandon its practical implementation or function through others. Nor did he trust his associates to fight for the accumulator in the proper way. They would follow legal advice and give the accumulator to the FDA, which for Reich was tantamount to the Jews digging their own graves in concentration camps. They would answer—they had answered—FDA questions that had nothing to do with the accumulator in order to be "good guys" or out of fear of having their medical licenses revoked. *They* would muddy up his clean discovery.

By the same token, in my view, they would *not* have made some of his mistakes. They would not have referred to Brady as a "communist sniper," as Reich did in a 1947 communication.* Indeed, Reich could not get Wolfe— to Wolfe's credit—to attack Brady for being a Communist, when in 1948 Wolfe wrote a brilliant polemic, *Emotional Plague versus Orgone Biophysics,*[21] in response to her *New Republic* article and its aftermath. Nor would they have become enmeshed in such issues as whether or not the FDA had jurisdiction over the accumulator. In short, they would have been more likely to avoid Reich's characteristic errors when confronted with irrational, unacknowledged rage and contempt—his denial of any common humanity between his opponents and himself, his refusal to try persistently to engage in rational discourse with the opposition, and his belligerent ascription of only the worst motives to his challengers.

These important caveats aside, as one reviews the documents from the fall of 1947 one sees that Reich was right in many of his key assessments—the

---

*In fairness to Reich, it should be noted that in recent years at least one astute observer of left-wing politics has said that in 1947 Brady, whom he had met, parroted the Stalinist line of that time (cf. letter of August 12, 1982 from Jerome Greenfield to the author about this observer). This evidence is far from ironclad and it does not prove that Brady was a member of the Communist Party, but it gives a sounder basis to some of Reich's views that they had in the late 1940s. It should also be noted that we cannot peruse the files of communist parties to see what they may have been planning against Reich and what persons they may have enlisted as hatchet men in the same way that we can study the FDA's file on Reich since the Freedom of Information Act was passed in 1971.

FDA's prejudice, the pornographic misrepresentation of his work, the linkages between the Brady article, psychoanalytic-psychiatric attacks on his work, and the FDA investigation. Above all, he was right in recognizing the scope of his work, the magnitude of the hatred against it, and the necessity for developing and following clean, direct ways of responding to the attacks, for not feeling guilty in dealing with the energy of sexuality.

Reich knew well the temptations of compromise and how simple it was for his students to succumb to those temptations. He might well have stated with Nietzsche: "Now why will [the great man] . . . try to feel life? Because he sees that men will prompt him to betray himself, and there is a kind of agreement to draw him from his den. He will prick up his ears and gather himself together, and say: 'I will remain my own.' He gradually comes to understand what a fearful decision it is."[22]

Under the impact of a persistent attack from the FDA, Reich's co-workers felt frightened and were strongly tempted to go the "pleasant conventional way." His lawyer assured people that Wharton was a very reasonable man, he just wanted an independent test of the accumulator. How easy to succumb, especially if one wonders: Maybe the accumulator is not all that Reich claims for it. One's inner self-doubts are triggered and amplified by these attacks.

By contrast, Reich characteristically fought off his own guilt feelings by attacking his enemies even more than they deserved. Excessive blame of others often masks self-recrimination, and so it was for Reich in many of his personal and professional relationships. But it also served an adaptive function here: it helped to protect him from the enervating effects of guilt and self-doubt at times when almost everyone, through threats or blandishments, was urging him to violate his principles.

There was a lull in the investigation during the spring of 1948. Wharton had sent the information gathered so far to Washington for a decision as to whether a full-scale testing effort should be undertaken in order to secure an injunction against the accumulator. Keen as he was on obtaining such an injunction, Wharton was also aware of certain problems. As he reported on May 18, 1948: "No dissatisfied users were located and all persons interviewed were extremely satisfied with the results which they attributed to the device."[23] The FDA was also interested in linking Reich's literature with the accumulator, claiming the former was promotional material for the latter. However, as the FDA noted, users had often obtained Reich's books and journals long before they ordered the accumulator, so that the written works were not in fact "accompanying literature."

Reich misinterpreted the pause in the investigation, believing it had permanently stopped. Moreover, he also believed that the FDA had been impressed by his frank policy of noncooperation and his refusal to surrender. This kind of misreading of events furthered the tragic and irrational aspect of

Reich's handling of the case. He *wanted* his policy to stop the investigation. He came to believe, quite erroneously, that it *had* stopped it. As we know, Reich was prone to dramatize events, especially under stress. He took the real hatred of orgonomy on the part of many groups, political and scientific, but then gave that hatred a conspiratorial twist it did not possess. Similarly, he overestimated the effects of his own actions in stopping the FDA. He could never fully accept the "banality of evil"—that the bureaucratic action against him, however much inspired by the special venom of a Brady or a Wharton, also proceeded on its own momentum, quite impervious to Reich's blasts or proud refusals to cooperate.

Reich's undue optimism about the course of events was to lead to some major errors. However, it helped him rechannel his energies back to his work. The investigation was finished, he had won, he did not have to worry about the FDA. At the same time, a more realistic side of him *did* continue to worry even if in a less direct form than previously. One way he expressed this concern was to search urgently for still more dramatic, socially needed applications of orgone energy.

26

The Oranur Experiment: 1950–1953

With the permanent move to Orgonon in 1950, Reich became preoccupied with the relationship between orgone energy and nuclear energy. He had been concerned since the first atomic bomb was dropped on Hiroshima in August 1945. In November 1945 he had published the following remarks: "We shall have to learn to counteract the murderous form of the atomic energy with the life-furthering function of the orgone energy and thus render it harmless."[1]

The Korean War, which broke out on June 25, 1950, added to Reich's sense of urgency. He had never ceased to be an intensely political animal in the etymological sense of that word, concerning the citizenry. He believed the accumulator could help in the war effort, especially in the treatment of wounds and burns. There was also a general fear that the Korean War could lead to a global nuclear conflict; Reich had hopes that orgone energy might be helpful as an antidote to nuclear radiation.

These hopes were based on several earlier findings. The most relevant observation was that accumulator treatment increased the bio-energetic vigor of the blood. Hence, it might alleviate the blood system disturbances (e.g., anemia, leukemia) associated with radiation sickness. More specifically, Reich had noted that burns due to X-rays could be healed by orgone treatment. In December 1950, he published a brief report in which he cited his findings and outlined a research project to investigate whether concentrated orgone energy could diminish the harmful effects of nuclear radiation.[2] He named this study *Oranur*, an abbreviation for Orgone Energy (OR) versus Nuclear Energy

(NR). It stated clearly what he wanted to prove: First, a degree of immunity against nuclear radiation could be achieved through prior exposure to concentrated orgone energy. To this end, a group of healthy mice would be charged with orgone energy for several weeks. Then one half of this group would be injected with a half-lethal dose of radioactive material, the other half with a lethal dose. These two groups would be compared against each other and against control groups of healthy mice untreated by the accumulator that received half-lethal and lethal doses of radioactive material. The results would help to establish if and to what extent preventive orgone treatment was useful.

The second proposed experiment involved treatment. A group of healthy mice would be injected with a half-lethal dose of nuclear radiation prior to any exposure of orgone energy. Then one half of the injected mice would be treated with orgone energy, the other injected but untreated half serving as a control. This experiment was designed to represent two groups of people some distance from a nuclear explosion, with both groups suffering a half-lethal dose of nuclear radiation but only one receiving post-injury orgone treatment.

Before proceeding with these experiments, Reich made what was to prove a fateful decision: he decided to run a preliminary experiment to explore the effects of orgone energy on radioactive material itself. So he ordered two one-milligram units of pure radium, one to be exposed to concentrated orgone energy, the other to serve as a control.

Let me comment here on the background of Reich's use of radium in this experiment. First, it is an interesting historical footnote that this step took Reich back very close to the beginning of the atomic age. In 1895, Wilhelm Röntgen discovered artificially induced X-rays, a form of radioactivity. In 1896, Henri Becquerel set out to determine whether a radiation like X-rays was emitted by "fluorescent" bodies through the action of light. To his surprise, he found that uranium salts, without the presence of light, emitted a *spontaneous* radiation that penetrated photographic plates.

In 1898, Marie and Pierre Curie discovered radium, which emitted a much more powerful radioactivity than uranium. Only a few years later, Pierre Curie became the first victim of "radiation sickness" when he deliberately exposed his arm to radium and a burn appeared along with more diffuse symptoms such as fatigue and body aches. The long-term harmful effects of radioactivity were still to be discovered. Indeed, both Marie Curie and her daughter Irene, who later worked with radium, died of leukemia, the cause of their illness being attributed to their lengthy exposure to radium. But if radium could harm, it could also treat. It destroyed not only healthy but diseased tissue, thereby removing tumors. More important than its immediate uses, the discovery of radioactivity—or more precisely, the fact that matter could disintegrate into radiation—led eventually to atomic physics as we know it today.

Reich's first studies were built on a series of discoveries also made in the nineteenth century. During the same years that Röntgen, Becquerel, and the Curies were launching the atomic age, Freud was inaugurating the psychological revolution. There are striking parallels between the two sets of discoveries. Psychoanalysis could look beneath the surface of the mind just as X-rays could penetrate the surface of the body. The energy of libido could be bound in symptoms and character traits analogous to the binding of energy in matter. The release of instinctual energy from its defense mechanisms or armorings could take destructive forms, like radioactive decay from matter. Indeed, for Freud, though not for Reich, it was impossible to conceive of a free flow of energy in civilized man without some anti-instinctual structures (repressions, defense mechanisms). All of Reich's differences with Freud turned on the nature of free-flowing libido, the desirability or undesirability of its blockages, and the proper way to dissolve rigid structures.

Now, in 1950–51, Reich was confronting modern atomic theory. Once again, the issues turned on the relationship between energy and structure, or mass. In the atomic model, mass could be transformed into energy, but the released radiation was destructive to living tissue. Even the electron contained a small amount of mass embodying its charge of negative electricity. Yet orgone energy was life-furthering and mass-free. Whereas in his debates with psychoanalysts Reich was thoroughly conversant with the concepts and clinical data on both sides, he frankly acknowledged his deficiency in physics. In 1945, he wrote: "I have not mastered *mechanistic* physics as well as I might or should."[3] However, his opponents would also have to accept the possibility "that the discovery of cosmic energy may shake the foundations of their special picture of the physical world." Both sides, then, had to risk defeat in an open, honest, paradigmatic debate.

To return to the Oranur experiment: Although the one-milligram units ordered by Reich may seem a small amount, radium emits so powerful a radiation that extreme care must be exercised in its use. Reich kept the radium in a thick shield and his assistants used lead gloves and lead aprons in handling the material.

Before starting the experiment proper, Reich established the "normal radiation" or "background count." According to classical science, normal radiation is present constantly from radioactive materials in rocks and, especially, from cosmic radiation. At Orgonon in December 1950 the background count was approximately 35 counts per minute (CPM), as measured by a Geiger-Müller (GM) counter.[4]

On January 5, 1951, Reich placed one milligram of radium in its lead shielding in a garage outside the laboratory as a control. It was not exposed to any special orgone accumulations. The other, experimental milligram was placed in a small, one-fold orgone charger, which in turn was placed in a twenty-fold accumulator. The radium within the accumulators was then placed in a large room, built of accumulator materials, which served as a "dark room" for the visual observation of orgone energy (hereafter referred to as the OR room). In this way Reich intended to see if the accumulator could neutralize the effects of the treated radium compared to the control.

Five hours after the radium was put in the accumulator, Reich checked the laboratory and found the air charged and oppressive. Objectively, the GM counter "jammed," that is, the impulses were faster than the GM could measure when it was brought near the accumulator in the OR room. That it was not a failure in the battery of the meter which caused the "jamming" became apparent when Reich removed the meter to the fresh air, whereupon it once again gave the normal background count of about 35 CPM.

Reich was not prepared to relinquish the experiment, but he did want to reduce the ominous charge inside the laboratory. The experimental radium, still in its small orgone charger, was removed from the OR room and taken to a shed some 150 feet away from the laboratory. The laboratory was aired with the hope that the high charge would dissipate quickly. But ventilation did not seem to help. Nor was the radium per se causing the heaviness, for one could get very close to the removed radium without feeling any of the ill effects —heaviness in the air, a sense of oppression, headaches, nausea—that one felt in the laboratory.

After ventilating the laboratory, the background count diminished. It is interesting that the GM count was only one index Reich used in determining a new, puzzling, and possibly dangerous development in his experiment. The *quantitative* count was not sufficient to establish the *qualitative* meaning of the phenomenon. Earlier, in 1948, Reich had found that a GM counter allowed to soak for several months in an orgone-charged atmosphere could register very high counts when in or near orgone accumulators with no subjective ill effects.[5] In this instance, however, the background count diminished but the subjective sensations continued, even growing more intense as the days passed. Reich paid close attention to the sensations he and many of his co-workers experienced, such as a salty taste on the tongue; a severe pressure in the depth of the cheekbone; nausea; loss of appetite; sensations of weakness; a ringlike pressure around the forehead; sensitivity in the diaphragmatic segment; pallor; and feelings of cold shivers alternating with hot flashes.

I was assisting Reich in various tasks connected with the Oranur experiment. He was tremendously excited as the Geiger-Müller count increased after the radium was put in the laboratory. I remember his excitement, concern, and curiosity about the subjective reactions. He would ask his assistants repeatedly: "What do you feel now?"

Reich rapidly conceptualized the first surprising results of the Oranur experiment: Contrary to expectations, orgone energy had not counteracted nuclear energy but rather nuclear energy had altered orgone energy. The signs of this transformation were the high background count even after the radium had been removed and the unpleasant subjective sensations. The first day's effects were so great that all but the most necessary work in the building was stopped immediately.

Not long after January 5, Reich gave two names to orgone energy that had been altered by nuclear radiation. One was DOR (Deadly ORgone); the other was simply "Oranur," derived from the experiment itself but now emphasizing the effects of nuclear energy on orgone energy rather than the other way around as expected. Reich would use both terms interchangeably.

Despite the various subjective reactions of his assistants, Reich with his usual daring continued the experiment. For the next six days he placed the experimental radium in the twenty-fold accumulator for an hour each day. On January 12, it remained there for only half an hour. Soon after the radium was deposited, Reich and several persons with him noted that the atmosphere in the laboratory had become clouded. It showed a blue to purplish color through the glass windows. Reich felt sick to his stomach and dizzy. Dr. Tropp had similar reactions.

At this point the experiment was interrupted although, as we shall see, many aspects Reich was to note about the interaction between orgone energy and nuclear energy continue today in the interaction between orgone energy and diverse forms of pollution. The orgone-treated radium was placed a half mile away from the laboratory, buried in the ground of an unused field.

After describing his own and Tropp's intense reactions, Reich's main report touched on a variety of reactions and interpretations of events that occurred in the aftermath of the experiment. Unlike many of his writings, it was completed swiftly, most of it by the end of April 1951, and published that October. The points made below are drawn largely from this report:

Workers who were in contact with Oranur reacted in a highly specific manner, each being attacked at his or her weakest point physically. All had recurrent attacks of their symptoms during the Oranur experiment.

The most dramatic example of the Oranur effect exacerbating a specific, existing symptom involved Eva Reich. She had long suffered from bradycardia, or a slow heartbeat. In February after the experiment she was cleaning out a metal-lined cabinet in the laboratory; she "smelled" something like Oranur and in order to make sure, put her head into the cabinet. Thereupon it "hit her like a wall." She lost her balance and was brought up to the Observatory. Reich saw her and found her pulse rate to be very slow, about 46 per minute. He was also alarmed because her heartbeat continued to weaken and she had difficulty breathing. He gave her some cognac and urged her to keep talking, all the while prodding her to stay in contact with him.[6]

After two hours she began to recover. However, for some months she continued to suffer Oranur effects in milder form.

In May of that year Ilse, who had previously suffered from uterine symptoms, had an operation because tests indicated uterine cancer. Afterward her surgeon informed her that she was indeed fortunate to have had the operation since the pathological process was quite advanced.[7] Connections between this illness and her relationship with Reich will be discussed in the next chapter, but here it is important to stress that she attributed her illness then, as she attributes it now, to Oranur. Her judgment carries all the more weight because of her skepticism vis-à-vis certain aspects of the Oranur experiment.

I myself experienced fatigue, pressure around the eyes, and headaches—symptoms I had also experienced previously under stress. Indeed, that Oranur brought out or exacerbated what was already present meant that there was no specific Oranur illness. As discussed in Chapter 2, my relationship with Reich was worsening at this time and I was inclined to attribute my symptoms to my emotional upset with him rather than to Oranur. In retrospect, I believe both factors were operative.

Some further findings:

Periods of unusual well-being seemed to alternate with periods of Oranur or DOR-sickness.

Persons who had been in the Oranur experiment from the beginning reacted less severely to its effects than visitors to Orgonon.

These two factors led Reich to hypothesize an immunization effect from exposure to Oranur. He thought the original goal of immunization might still be achievable. However, on February 11, thirty experimental mice died suddenly with symptoms of radiation sickness (e.g., disturbances in the blood system). This finding, combined with Eva's severe reaction a few days later, persuaded Reich to give up the idea temporarily of seeing if Oranur had any immunization effect. He was more concerned with stopping the reaction, which he now perceived as dangerous. So he took the following steps:

(1) All accumulators at Orgonon were dismantled. This posed problems since in certain instances of DOR-sickness the accumulator usage had been helpful. But, again, stopping the reaction took priority.

(2) Reich banned any radioactivity whatsoever, however slight, in his environment. Peter Reich has narrated a poignant incident here. By sending in cereal boxtops, Peter had obtained a Lone Ranger glow-in-the-dark ring and was very proud of it. When Reich found out about the ring, he insisted it be removed: "The glow in the dark substance may harm you. It may be very dangerous. Right now we are [conducting] an experiment to help us understand it. I'm sorry. I know you like it as a toy, but we must get rid of it."

Peter's response was: "I tried to look angry at him, but I couldn't even see him because my eyes were so blurry and mad. He didn't even want me to play with it a little bit. All he thought about was his energy."[8]

"All he thought about was his energy"—and now especially its reaction to radioactive substances. Eva, too, was very sensitive to the emanations from radium-dial watches, fluorescent lights, and even TV. It is important to emphasize that for Reich the danger lay not in the radiation effects per se but in their action upon orgone energy.

(3) Other health measures Reich advocated strongly were frequent airing of rooms, the use of fans to keep the air moving, daily baths with prolonged soaking, and intake of fluids. Reich had long emphasized that water absorbed orgone energy, but now he noted that it absorbed DOR at an even faster rate.

What was and remains most impressive is the rapid and profound way Reich conceptualized the many observations he made, starting on January 5. He had begun with the hypothesis that orgone energy would neutralize nuclear energy. Given the high background count and the sensations that persisted after the removal of the radium, he quickly moved to hypothesizing the trigger effect of nuclear energy on atmospheric and organismic orgone energy. As far as the human organism is concerned, he had begun with the conventional idea of specific radiation symptoms, such as nausea, fatigue, and diseases of the blood system, although all of these dysfunctions can be found without over-irradiation as the cause. He had also begun with the idea of a high orgone energy charge serving as resistance to radiation sickness. However, he was surprised by the way people reacted to Oranur through their own specific vulnerabilities. Again, he conceptualized radiation sickness in a new way: not, basically, as due to the effects of nuclear energy, but to the effects of nuclear energy *acting* upon organismic orgone energy. In short, nuclear energy caused both atmospheric and organismic energy "to run amok," with the latter "running amok" specifically in ways it had reacted under stress in the past.

Reich also posited a three-phase reaction of orgone energy to nuclear energy. The first reaction to sudden, unexpected radiation was prostration, shock, helplessness, as it were. The second phase involved orgone energy fighting back, becoming "angry, a killer itself, attempting to kill the irritating nuclear radiation. In this struggle it deteriorates into a killer of the organism which it governs." Then he postulated a third phase in which orgone energy, if available in sufficient fresh supply, overcame nuclear radiation and the triggering of an Oranur chain reaction. Reich based his assumption of OR energy triumphant on his observations of periods of very good health enjoyed by some Oranur workers. It was also based on the fact that some small samples of nuclear radiation which Reich had had for years seemed to be rendered innocuous by prolonged exposure to orgone energy; they had, for example, lost their ionizing capacity to conduct electricity. However, during the Oranur experiment itself, Reich was far more impressed by the reality of the first and second phases than by any real hope for the third.

These positive results paled in comparison to his surprise at finding a deadly quality in orgone energy, hitherto seen as entirely benign. However, Reich recalled other phenomena where healthy organisms turned malignant. For example, in fighting sick T-bacilli, healthy PA bions can themselves be transformed into destructive T-bacilli. Most striking of all for Reich was the fact that a healthy person, when fighting evil, might himself change and develop the same characteristics he was fighting against.

Indeed, as I shall discuss in the next chapter, under the twin pressures of Oranur and the worsening FDA situation, Reich himself became more destructive than ever in his personal relationships. During the Oranur experiment, I had the opportunity to observe how badgering he could be when embarking on new terrain. (In my view, this tendency was heightened by the effect of Oranur upon him.) He wanted everybody to respond strongly to his newest, beloved child—now Oranur. In the face of the avalanche of new observations, Reich was undoubtedly not as secure in his convictions as he appeared. His need for a confirmatory response from others was akin to Oliver Cromwell's plea: "Believe and help me in my unbelief!" After a research advance had been consolidated, he could be more relaxed (within limits!) toward skepticism and criticism.

As always, Reich's natural-scientific work interacted strongly with his social concepts. He began to see the "emotional plague chain reaction" as analogous to Oranur. The emotional plague reaction was comparable to nuclear radiation. It infected others, and the weaker the energy system, the more easily it was paralyzed by the noxious poison. Even healthy persons were often first paralyzed by the shock of their encounter with the plague before they fought back.

Finally, in retrospect one is struck by how prescient Reich was. Today, atomic tests, nuclear wastes, and harmful X-rays can produce public outrage. But such was not the case in 1951. Within weeks of the Oranur experiment, Reich was concerned about the effects of all kinds of toxic influences (chemical offal, electromagnetic pollution) on atmospheric and organismic orgone energy. I recall thinking, back in 1951, that his concern with minute traces of radium on watch dials and TV emissions was excessive, if not insane. Today, the use of radium in watches is rapidly declining,[9] effects of fluorescent lights have been noted,[10] and people are advised not to sit too close to TV sets.[11]

With the surge of ecological interest in the late 1960s and 1970s, we are more aware that there is a limit to the "insults" our planet—this "fragile blue biosphere"—can survive and that we are fast approaching it. Reich had his ecological consciousness raised during the Oranur experiment. He became concerned not only with the dangers of nuclear radiation but also with chemical pollution and the danger from nonnuclear forms of electromagnetic emissions. The latter too, he noted, could in sufficient dosage "irritate" orgone energy in a noxious way. Since the 1960s, the classical theory of radiation sickness has grown more similar to Reich's in its recognition that relatively low levels of nuclear radiation and nonnuclear emissions (e.g., from microwaves) can have harmful cumulative results.[12] However, there remains little awareness of Reich's basic conceptual thrust: that it is not pollution per se—chemical or energetic—that is the main menace, but rather its effect on atmospheric and organismic orgone energy. Classical theory, moreover, focuses entirely on mechanical factors, the amount of radiation one is exposed to in a given period, or the part of the body affected by the radiation, in assessing the risk factor. Characteristically, as we have seen in his work on cancer, Reich focused on both the specific toxic agent and the individual's particular energetic vulnerability. Thus the debate between Reich's Oranur concepts and classical theories of radiation sickness has yet to occur.

By March 1952, Orgonon was evacuated; the high Geiger-Müller counts persisted, as did the subjective malaise. Reich's assistants worked out of their apartments or homes and had only brief meetings at the Observatory with him. Ilse and Peter went to an apartment in Rangeley. Reich moved around a great deal (as we shall see in Chapter 27), occasionally staying at the Observatory but never for very long.

By this time, he was concerned with a new development. He noted a quality of "stillness" and "bleakness" over the landscape.[13] Reich's description of this "bleakness" closely resembles Rachel Carson's in *Silent Spring*, written some ten years after the Oranur experiment.

Reich was especially impressed by what he called "DOR-clouds." These bore a remarkable similarity to what would later be called air pollution or smog. DOR-clouds, black and bleak, could be present even in the midst of sunshine. When they were, the motility of animals was diminished, the atmosphere felt "suffocating," and the sky seemed to lose its sparkle.*

---

*Reich describes the "emotional flavor" (his words) of DOR-clouds in a manner reminiscent of the nineteenth-century art critic John Ruskin. Indeed, the comparison goes further since Ruskin was, to my knowledge, the first writer to comment on the atmospheric effects of intensive coal usage in England in the 1880s. Ruskin noted with horror a new kind of cloud, which he termed the "plague cloud."(!) The "plague cloud" was in sharp contrast to good weather clouds, which were "either white or golden, adding to, not abating, the lustre of the sky." It also contrasted with the clouds of wet weather, which were of two types: "Those of beneficent rain . . . and, those of storm, usually charged highly with electricity. The beneficent rain cloud was indeed often extremely dull and grey for days together, but gracious nevertheless, felt to be doing good, and . . . capable also of the most exquisite colouring. . . . The storm cloud [was] always majestic . . . and felt also to be beneficent in its own way, affecting the mass of the air with vital agitation, and purging it from the impurity of all morbific elements." The plague cloud, on the other hand, was "grey . . . not rain-cloud but a dry, black veil which no ray of sunshine can pierce. . . . That thin, scraggy, filthy, mangy miserable cloud can't turn the sun red, as a good, business-like fog does with a hundred feet or so of itself." Ruskin's description of various kinds of clouds, including pollution clouds, merits attention because, in my view, painters and art critics anticipated many of Reich's descriptions of the atmosphere just as novelists and poets anticipated his psychological findings. John Ruskin, "The Storm Cloud of the Nineteenth Century," *Norton Anthology of English Literature* (New York: W. W. Norton, 1974), 445–454. For interested readers, my quotes give only a suggestion of the wealth of this article, which should be read in its entirety.

In an effort to do something about these debilitating clouds, Reich hit upon the idea of trying to "draw off" energy from the clouds by means of long metal pipes, directed toward the DOR-clouds and connected through cables to a deep well. Here Reich was making use of an observation common to orgone energy and DOR: both were attracted to water. And, indeed, when he aimed the pipes toward the clouds, they began to dissipate and the oppressive atmosphere was alleviated.

Out of this initial work grew what Reich later called "cloud-busting," an operation not limited to DOR-clouds. (The interested reader can turn to the literature for more detail on the subject.) Briefly, Reich became concerned with influencing the dispersal of orgone energy in the atmosphere. By varying his method of drawing, he claimed to be able to influence the atmospheric potential either in the direction of concentration of energy (cloud formation) or in the direction of dispersal of energy (cloud dissipation).

Reich likened the action of the "cloud-buster" (as he came to call his pipes grounded in water) to the lightning rod. For Reich, the lightning rod, too, functioned according to orgone energy principles, since "lightning" is a concentrated atmospheric energy discharge in a very narrow space. The pointed rod, reaching into the atmosphere, attracted the lightning discharge and conducted it through heavy wires into the ground.

Let us jump ahead a little to see why this work may be of real significance. By July 6, 1953, or just over a year after his first experiments with weather modification, Reich felt sufficiently confident to test his work outside the Orgonon area. At the invitation of two Maine blueberry growers who wanted rain to save their crops from persistent drought, Reich conducted an operation with his draw tubes, by now a rather elaborate device mounted on a truck. The results were reported in the Bangor *Daily News* of July 24:

> Dr. Reich and three assistants set up their "rain-making" device off the shore of Grand Lake, near the Bangor hydro-electric dam, at 10:30 on Monday morning 6 July. The device, a set of hollow tubes, suspended over a small cylinder, connected by a cable, conducted a "drawing" operation for about an hour and ten minutes.
>
> The scientist and a small group of spectators then left the lake to await results.
>
> According to a reliable source in Ellsworth the following climactic changes took place in that city on the night of 6 July and the early morning of 7 July: "Rain began to fall shortly after ten o'clock Monday evening, first as a drizzle and then by midnight as a gentle, steady rain. Rain continued throughout the night, and a rainfall of 0.24 inches was recorded in Ellsworth following morning."
>
> A puzzled witness to the "rain-making" process said: "The queerest looking clouds you ever saw began to form soon after they got the thing rolling." And later the same witness said the scientists

were able to change the course of the wind by manipulation of the device.

The growers who contacted Rangeley claimed that they were perfectly satisfied with the results, and one man said if severe drought were to strike again, he would call on the "rain makers" a second time. They paid the agreed-upon fee for the operation.*

Reich conducted other weather modification efforts over a broad area. By 1954 he had several cloud-busters, and at least one functioning in the New York City area. In July of that year there had been a severe drought in the Northeast. Notifying the Weather Bureau of his intentions, Reich began the first of a series of drought-breaking operations. He was successful in New York and also in several other operations.

In assessing Reich's work in this field, there is always the problem of chance. As James McDonald, a professor at the Institute of Atmospheric Physics at the University of Arizona, commented: "The presence of natural variability in atmospheric events, which cannot be controlled or suppressed, may lead to effects twice as great as the one [the researcher] sought to induce experimentally."[14]

However much the need for caution in evaluating Reich's weather work, the initial results still remain impressive. He announced when he would engage in weather modification and I know of no instance where he failed. Weather modification following Reich's principles and techniques has subsequently been carried out by several investigators with positive results.[15] Indeed, one of the first replications of Reich's experimental work under university auspices dealt with cloud-busting. In his master's thesis on cloud-busting for the Department of Geography/Meteorology, University of Kansas, James DeMeo noted that his efforts were successful in decreasing clouds when the cloud-buster was used for that goal, and in enhancing clouds when that was his

---

*The blueberry cloud-busting was Reich's first effort motivated in part by a desire for publicity; it was also the first "contingency fee" he ever received. He thereby gave the appearance of joining an unsavory tradition of nineteenth- and early twentieth-century Americans who promised rain for drought-stricken farmers with a similar "cash on delivery" agreement. None of these rainmaking forays was based on solid concepts or was replicable before cloudseeding with dry ice was introduced in 1946. See Clark C. Spencer, *The Rainmakers: America's "Pluviculture" to World War II* (Lincoln, Nebr.: University of Nebraska Press, 1980).

Other aspects of Reich's work lent themselves to association with scandalous traditions, e.g., his "body therapy" with the sexually arousing massages of some nineteenth-century hypnotists, his accumulator with quack cancer cures. Throughout his scientific career, Reich took great pains to separate not only the content but also the tone of his work from such misalliances; he scrupulously avoided advertising or any other kind of promotional activity. However, by 1953, desperate in the face of growing opposition from the FDA and various professional organizations, he wanted to go straight to the public through dramatic, well-publicized achievements.

intent. He concluded: "While a high degree of statistical significance was not achieved in this preliminary study, the data and phenomena observed do fit comfortably with a positive interpretation of the device's efficacy."[16]

Despite these promising replications, with cloud-busting as with all of Reich's natural-scientific work we lack the broad-based research that could validate or disprove his hypotheses and shed light on the theoretical constructs underlying those hypotheses.

During March 1952, while Reich was concerned with "DOR-clouds," he noticed changes taking place in the rocks at the fireplace of the Observatory. They appeared to be blackening and undergoing a process of progressive crumbling and disintegration. "In many rocks the surfaces have lost their smoothness; the rock surface looks 'spongy' as if the rock has been drilled and innumerable holes of about 1/16th or 1/8th of an inch in diameter and depth had been hewn into the surface."[17]

One particular rock developed small holes with a powder-like substance that could be removed by wiping off the surface with a finger. Observing this rock carefully, Reich saw the steady increase in the number of holes on its surface. He also noted that the white powdery substance became streaked with blackish particles.*

Of this blackening, Reich wrote that he severely doubted himself when he first saw the phenomenon. He went so far as to deny the observation. This was the kind of skepticism Reich could permit himself but not his assistants.[18]

The DOR process and the cloud-busting together led Reich to believe that he had found important leads to the comprehension of desert development and desert fructification. (Four years after the start of Oranur and two and a half years after observing the blackening rocks, Reich would test these hypotheses when he made an expedition to Arizona in the late fall of 1954.)

Almost concurrently with the discovery of orgone energy in 1940, Reich had begun to formulate armor blocks as consisting of immobilized orgone energy. Again around March 1952, he started thinking of the frozen energy in the armor as DOR, which was a new insight stimulated by his observation of atmospheric DOR. When the armor prevented the unimpeded flow of energy, a person's healthy energy was blocked. Orgone energy, trapped within the armor or muscular spasms, became transformed into DOR, quite apart from

---

*"The same kind of phenomena Reich noted in his fireplace was to become of intense concern in the art world a few years later. Although the effects of pollution on stone art works had been noticed from the beginning of the industrial age, this problem did not become a menace until the late 1950s. Then it was noted in Italy, for example, that the fourteenth-century frescos of Giotto were being lost to posterity as the walls on which the murals were painted crumbled away. A specialist on the restoration of American stone buildings declared in 1965 that century-old structures had suffered more decay in the last twenty or so years than in the previous eighty." Howard Lewis, *With Every Breath You Take* (New York: Crown, 1965), 119.

any atmospheric influence. Here again Reich was establishing one of his sweeping connections—an identity between the black DOR-clouds and the "black" DOR in the human organism.[19]

Black was more than a metaphor for Reich, even though the color neatly fitted the metaphysical concept of evil or the Devil. His hypothesis of DOR-clouds and their removal was tested through the use of the cloud-buster. So also was his notion or armor containing DOR. About a year after the development of the cloud-buster, Reich had the idea of using the same principle, indeed the same device but on a smaller scale, in the treatment of human beings. Pipes connected with water were applied to the human body. Once again, it sounds utterly improbable that such a device should have any therapeutic efficacy. However, about fifteen psychiatrists trained in orgonomic therapy have used the device, along with more traditional Reichian methods, in the treatment of patients. There has been only one good controlled study of the DOR-buster, in the treatment of cancer mice; positive results were obtained.[20]

When Reich discovered orgone energy, he made it the basis for a synthesis of creative forces in the organism and the atmosphere. Between 1940 and 1950 he had the opportunity to explore this synthesis in physics, biology, psychiatry, medicine, education, and sociology.

In 1951, he started with a "simple" experiment—to see whether orgone energy could reduce harmful nuclear radiation. In the ensuing process he believed he had discovered a sweeping view of the destructive forces in man and in the environment. In Reich's view, atmospheric and organismic orgone energy had to be irritated or *blocked* before DOR emerged in virulent pathological form. Still, in a "normal" state, DOR was part of life. In a way that Reich was just beginning to conceptualize, DOR was part of the process of death. In Reich's view, the common functioning principle of diverse kinds of death was blocked life energy.

The most practical implications of the whole Oranur experiment, incomplete as it may have been, concern its relevance for understanding and mastering the growing pollution of the environment. Reich only began a few empirical investigations, as with the cloud-buster. It is worth repeating that for Reich what ultimately mattered was not a new abstract synthesis but concepts that generated testable hypotheses. He could not continue his DOR investigations for long because a different "investigation," the FDA's, was yielding its own fruit—a kind Reich would perceive as yet another manifestation of DOR in the form of the emotional plague.

27

Personal Life and Other Developments: 1950–1954

The Oranur years marked a huge upheaval in Reich's personal life. From 1940 to 1950, his existence had been much as he had described Freud's: "He lived a very calm quiet, decent family life."[1] In her biography of Reich, Ilse Ollendorff was reluctant to describe the more intimate aspects of her marriage. The outward impression remained one of a couple united by work rather than intense love. Peter was an important bond between them. However, Reich's main energies were clearly devoted to his work. It is my belief that *some* of his pessimism about adults and his devotion to infants and children, to the unarmored, reflected not only his accurate appraisal of adult humanity but also a dissatisfaction with his own life.

In any case, during the Oranur experiment Reich erupted. In part this eruption was stimulated by Oranur itself. During the spring of 1951, he was unable to stay at the Observatory for any prolonged periods due to the effects of Oranur. He began to move around, sometimes staying at the lower family cabin; however, even there the atmosphere was affected by Oranur. Reich would occasionally take overnight trips to Farmington, Maine, about forty miles from Rangeley, to escape the Orgonon atmosphere. And he took many more drives than he had previously, partly again for relief from the atmosphere, partly to observe the nature and extent of Oranur effects.

Oranur contributed in other ways to the spirit of change and dislocation. As noted in Chapter 26, Reich emphasized that Oranur brought out not only latent physical vulnerabilities in people but also hidden emotional problems.

And what Oranur started, Reich tried to complete. When he felt that people were not straightforward with him or were ambivalent, his response was to be more badgering.

An especially dramatic interaction of this kind occurred with his daughter Eva about a month after her severe Oranur reaction. On March 24 (Reich's fifty-fourth birthday), he gave Eva the present of a fine, expensive microscope. Eva was ambivalent about the gift, saying that she was uncertain where she would be living and that it might be difficult for her to care properly for the instrument. That he gave her this present on *his* birthday may have made her feel, with some resentment, that he wanted her to be exactly like him—to share his devotion to orgonomy and to orgonomic microscopy in particular. Reich became enormously enraged, inferring in her hesitation hostility toward him and his work.[2]

Both Eva's and Reich's behavior may have been amplified by Oranur effects, triggering her old fear of closeness to Reich and his tendency, when disappointed, to outbursts of excessive rage. In any case, Reich told her to leave Orgonon, which she did for about a year, taking a residency in pediatrics in New York City. She also had some therapeutic sessions with Baker.

The Oranur period coincided with a major reorganization of Reich's life, as so often happened after a new scientific development. The discovery of orgone energy in 1940 had launched a period of quiet scientific work, undistracted by the intense emotional involvements with people that had characterized the Oslo stay. But in the process, Reich had made certain renunciations he was no longer prepared to endure. The high-pitched excitement of the Oranur experiment escalated his own emotional needs for a more intense personal life.

Ilse's uterine operation took place in early May 1951. She was away from Orgonon for about six weeks. Reich used her absence from work to insist that she initiate divorce proceedings.[3] He wanted to try to maintain their relationship, but believed it had a better chance of surviving without a marriage license. He had never felt happy with the legalization of their relationship, which had been dictated by outside factors.

Upset by her illness and her conflicts with Reich, Ilse had some therapeutic sessions with Baker, who was becoming the family physician; she also stayed at Baker's home during the convalescent period in May. In early June, she submitted to Reich's plan and went to Arkansas to initiate the proceedings. The divorce became final on September 13, 1951. With Reich's consent, Baker as a witness submitted an affidavit, testifying to Reich's neglect of Ilse, and citing his unwillingness to go out socially to parties or to entertain Ilse's relatives and friends in the Reich home. These complaints are a good example of how Reich found behaviors acceptable to the court as grounds for divorce that did not impugn his character. Indeed, he took pride in his commitment to basic natural-scientific research, which prevented his participation in normal social life.

Ilse, who had submitted to the divorce in the hope of saving the relationship, deeply resented its timing in connection with an operation that had left her feeling vulnerable and depressed. It was one of the major grievances that, along with Reich's insistence on her abortion in the early 1940s and his sexual double standard, she continued to hold against him long after their separation.[4]

In the spring of 1951, Reich began a sexual relationship with Lois Wyvell, then in charge of the business aspects of the Orgone Institute Press. Wyvell had worked for the Press for five years and was one of Reich's most devoted assistants. Thirty-eight and divorced, she had moved to Orgonon in 1950 when the work became concentrated there, even though it presented a lonely life for a single person.

For many years Reich had been a lonely man, but he was especially so after the Oranur experiment. Ilse's emotional inaccessibility was particularly painful to him now. And with Oranur he felt intellectually isolated as well, since Ilse did not bring the same enthusiasm to this phase that she had brought to earlier research. On her part, she felt badgered by his insistence that she respond to this or that phenomenon and withdrew even more, thereby closing the vicious circle. With Lois Wyvell, as with Lia Laszky in the late 1920s and Gerd Bergersen in the late 1930s, Reich found a port in the storm, a haven from the domestic warfare that had become enmeshed with his battles with the world. Moreover, Lois, unlike Gerd, was keenly interested in and supportive of Reich's work, even if she lacked the scientific background to follow it fully. And she could respond to Reich's human predicament.

Reich was drawn to her honesty, her vivacity, and her commitment to orgonomy. Wyvell loved Reich's warmth, excitement, and genius. She learned and grew through him—intellectually, emotionally, sexually. However, according to Wyvell, Reich was not in love with her nor she with him. He would sometimes say, "At this moment I love you," with some emphasis on the first phrase, so there would be no misunderstanding.[5] Wyvell had similar sentiments. Only on rare occasions would she feel Reich's full contact with her, an experience of incredible warmth as she described it. In his words to her: "Usually my mind is partly with my work."

As with everyone else, Reich carried out a kind of informal character analysis with Wyvell. He would tease her about her mystical attitude toward him and orgonomy. At times, he would liken her persistent attitude to a bumblebee buzzing around him. Still, they had a free and comradely exchange of views and feelings.

Upon her return to Orgonon on June 9, Ilse was hurt and angry about Reich's relationship with Lois Wyvell. He justified it on the grounds of various dissatisfactions with Ilse, but he was not prepared to end his relationship with Ilse nor she with him. For some three years they continued a very difficult life together, sometimes far apart, sometimes closer to one another.

Whatever Ilse's unhappiness, Reich's own conflicts about the situation, or the inevitable gossip and local scandal, Reich was determined not to relinquish the relationship with Lois Wyvell for the wrong reasons. Right around the time of this affair, Reich wrote *The Murder of Christ,* which we will later discuss in detail. Here it is pertinent to note the work's emphasis on people's need to foist an ascetic image on their leader and then compel him to live up to that image. According to Reich, the "new leader," the leader who refuses to be mystified, will insist upon his right to lead a healthy sexual life. In 1951, Reich insisted.

But the freedom Reich took for himself was not granted to others. On the contrary, his sexual double standard, his jealous rages became worse than ever after the Oranur experiment, perhaps because it exacerbated his conflicts. A particularly malignant episode was the resurgence of his old suspicions about Ilse and Theo Wolfe having had an affair while Reich was detained at Ellis Island in 1941 (see Chapter 20). Just as Reich's jealousy toward Ilse can be viewed as one symptom of their deteriorating marriage, so his suspicions of Wolfe were rooted in the increasing distance between the two men.

Wolfe's assiduous efforts on behalf of orgonomy during the war years began to decline around 1947. He had become tired of his tedious tasks of translating, editing, and publishing orgonomic literature, tasks he had carried out superbly for seven hard years. Moreover, by that time Reich was writing in English, so the more creative side of Wolfe's function was no longer needed. Reich repeatedly urged him to do some scientific work, for example, to conduct research on cancer. But Wolfe was not willing or able to undertake such a task; besides, his chief interest lay in the therapy of neuroses. Yet Wolfe, who was a shy, distant man, had difficulties tolerating the expansion and excitement connected with orgonomy and with Reich. He made a valiant effort for many years because the emotional and intellectual depth of the work meant so much to him. But it was at considerable cost; for example, Wolfe experienced a psychotic episode during his treatment with Reich in Oslo in the late 1930s.[6]

To all these factors Reich added another hypothesis: Wolfe's orgonomic zeal was being undermined by his wife, Gladys Meyer. Reich's relationship with Meyer and his concern about her influence on Wolfe were of sufficient importance that I must backtrack a few years to give a fuller picture here.

Not long after his relationship with Jo Jenks ended, Theo met Gladys Meyer, on New Year's Eve, 1943. Gladys was thirty-four at the time, Wolfe forty-one. They quickly became involved with each other, but Reich was not interested in meeting her until the relationship was a serious one. He did not want to see Theo's casual women friends.

A few years later Gladys Meyer became a member of the sociology department at Barnard College (where she would remain a beloved teacher until she retired in 1976). A tall, empathic, and immensely thoughtful (in both senses of the word) person, Meyer could also be bitingly critical and had a slight air of *hauteur.* During the summer of 1944, she spent time at Theo's cabin on Mooselookmeguntic Lake; by that point their relationship was serious. Meyer's first sight of Reich was in front of the Rangeley Post Office. Reich was in his car with Ilse and their infant son Peter. Ilse and Reich were quarreling slightly as to whether there was too much sun on the baby. They seemed a very European family to Meyer.

In other ways, too, Reich, as she got to know him, was quite European in Meyer's eyes. At times he reminded her of a "great vigorous Austrian peasant." In his domineering moods, he evoked memories of professors from the Frankfurt school in Germany where she had studied in the early 1930s.

During those summers of the 1940s, Reich and Wolfe consulted with each other often. More occasionally, the Wolfes and the Reichs would visit socially, although no meeting with Reich was "social" in the usual sense. Meyer recalls sitting on the porch with Reich and discussing the youth movement he had known in Germany and Austria. Reich had wondered if there would ever be a similar kind of movement in America. Meyer had not thought there would be, but she was impressed by his searching questions.

In 1945, Meyer went into treatment with Reich, partly at Wolfe's urging since he felt that if she experienced therapy, she would better understand why he was so absorbed in orgonomy. She found therapy "only rewarding." Reich was a disciplined therapist, though at times he could provoke her very directly. In one session she had remembered her childhood distress when a boy threatened to attack her with a knife. Reich took some deer antlers he had in his office and moved toward her, simulating the original incident to elicit her emotions. Meyer jumped off the couch.

The therapy only lasted a few months. As with so many people, Gladys Meyer's time in treatment coincided with her most intense interest in orgonomy. She contributed several excellent book reviews to the *International Journal for Sex-Economy and Orgone-Research*. Whatever her later difficulties with Reich, she never wavered in her conviction that he had been a great innovator in the human disciplines. She took a more neutral position toward his natural-scientific research since she lacked the training and experience to evaluate these investigations.

For his part, Reich valued highly Meyer's use of orgonomic findings in her own work, but was suspicious of her lack of a deeper commitment. An advantage of Meyer's position was that she was more disinterested—in the good sense of the word—than many of his followers. She never gave off the odor of belonging to a "smelly little orthodoxy" (to use George Orwell's phrase) as do so many "Reichians." With her warm, judicious interest in the lives of others, she had a profound influence on hundreds of students, and she introduced some of them to the psychological and sociological aspects of orgonomy.

Her position on the periphery of the orgonomic movements had its disadvantages, too. When Reich entered new domains, she could be more aware of his excesses than his contributions. Critical-minded intellectuals like Gladys Meyer often viewed Reich as an extremely creative but erratic person (child-peasant). With his keen emotional antennae, Reich would pick up the slightest hint of such an attitude and reject it. I recall once going over some documents with Reich when I was in a critical mood toward him. He wrote a note and passed it to me. The note read: "What is disturbing now? *Your* fantasy of managing *me*"—a comment that caught the exact quality of my critical attitude.

But the main issue of controversy between Meyer and Reich concerned Wolfe. Around 1948, Reich began to feel that Meyer was undermining Theo's relationship with Reich and orgonomy. Wolfe had some of the same feeling. Meyer vigorously denied this. Wolfe suggested that she see Reich for further therapy to determine the truth, and Meyer agreed. During a number of sessions Reich and Meyer "waged a battle," in her words. Meyer kept insisting she only wanted Theo to do what he wanted to do. In the end, Reich partly accepted Meyer's explanation, but kept to himself his own interpretation.[7] Thereafter he was much more distant toward her.

Gladys Meyer may well have resented the extent of Theo's involvement with orgonomy, although this feeling never went so far as Reich surmised. When I interviewed her, I said that Wolfe must have given a great deal of money to the Orgone Institute Press. Meyer said bitterly: "He [Reich] took every cent Wolfe had." She then altered this statement to express the same idea but emphasizing that Wolfe wanted to help orgonomy wherever possible. Still the resentment was there, all the more when Wolfe died in 1954, leaving her with no sources of money other than her own income to support their young daughter. Nor was her bitterness mitigated by Reich's total lack of concern for her financial plight. Even after Reich's death he gave her cause for anger, since his will made no provision for the Wolfe family to share in the royalties from Reich's publications. According to Meyer, Reich and Wolfe had had an understanding that should orgonomic literature ever make money, they would share the proceeds.

The seeds of her later resentments may have been sown long before Wolfe's death, in the years when she saw Wolfe so zealously devoting his energy and money to support the development of orgonomy. In many instances, the less involved mate resented the extent of Reich's significance to a more involved partner. As Sigurd Hoel commented: "Reich wanted your whole soul."

For his part, Wolfe's withdrawal from orgonomy continued as his zeal faded. Lois Wyvell took over the business aspects of the Press entirely. During the same year I was responsible for much of the editorial work Wolfe had previously done. So Reich had less interest in him as a colleague and adviser, although on important issues he still sought out Wolfe's counsel.

In the summer of 1949, Wolfe was so depressed about his growing distance from Reich that he rarely left the cabin. Gladys worried, went to see Reich at the Students' Laboratory where he was working. At first, Reich was angry at the unexpected interruption. Gladys said firmly: "I'm sorry, but this is important." So Reich sat down and talked with her. She expressed her concern about Wolfe. In one of his sudden moments of self-criticism, Reich said, "I worked with him too fast in therapy. I needed him as a worker so badly." And he added: "Don't undermine his critical ability. It is his best characteristic."

In these few sentences Reich delivered several messages to Wolfe and to Gladys Meyer: How much Wolfe had meant to him as a colleague and how valuable his criticism was (including, by implication, his criticism of Reich). He took some responsibility for Theo's continuing personal problems. He also let Gladys Meyer know in a gentle way that he still believed she had a capacity to undermine.

Matters worsened when Wolfe, Baker, and Raphael visited Orgonon on February 15, 1951, at the height of Oranur. According to Reich, Wolfe was "out of contact" with the experiment; I do not know exactly what he meant by this description. But, as suggested earlier, one effect of Oranur may have been to exacerbate Reich's jealousy. In any case, by early June, when Ilse was recovering from her operation at the Baker home and Reich had begun his affair with Lois Wyvell, his old suspicions about Ilse and Theo were rekindled. At Reich's instigation, part of Ilse's therapy with Baker dealt with her feelings toward Wolfe.[8] Reich began badgering Wolfe about the matter, and Wolfe took up the issue with Baker.[9] Baker and Wolfe had considerable respect for each other.

Wolfe was understandably incensed that Reich would not accept his word that no affair had taken place. And on June 7, he wrote Reich: "I gathered from your telephone call . . . that you still believe I did not tell the truth in January 1942 or that I am telling the truth now . . . I resent being called a liar . . . and I am not going to be a scapegoat. Last but not least, I hate to see a fine woman driven toward her death because a man will not rid himself of a groundless, foolish idea. . . ."

Reich described Wolfe's letter as "ugly and impertinent." However, the missive, combined with Baker's insistence that no affair had taken place, led Reich to retreat to allegations of Ilse's "fantasies" about Wolfe. (Be this as it may, Baker's defense of Reich's outrageous jealousy on the grounds that Ilse had "fantasies" toward this one or that one[10] would place us but a step from the "thought crimes" of *1984*.)

Wolfe was to celebrate his forty-ninth birthday on September 2, and Gladys planned a party for him. Reich told workers at Orgonon not to attend. (This was the only instance I know of where he issued an edict to his employees not to attend a social function.) I no longer recall his reasons, but I remember —with shame—that I for one did not say I would attend no matter what Reich's feelings. In any case, we were spared a final test because Theo was so depressed by Reich's attitude that Gladys called off the party.[11]

The relationship between the two men must have improved somewhat because Wolfe attended a business meeting at Orgonon in the late fall of 1951. On this occasion, Wolfe and Reich disagreed about a minor issue; to make matters worse, Ilse sided with Theo. The next day Reich called Wolfe in, bringing up the old allegations of an affair. That proved the final straw. Wolfe resigned from the work on the spot, returning to Reich all the papers he still had in his possession.[12]

In April 1952, Wolfe's doctors discovered he had an advanced tuberculosis. He gave up his practice and, without Gladys, went to New Mexico in an effort to recover. Baker arranged for Wolfe's patients to be transferred to other therapists and some of the fees to be sent to Wolfe, who by this point had practically no financial resources.

There is no evidence that Reich moved substantially to help Wolfe at any time after the latter finally left. When Wolfe wrote Reich from New Mexico asking if he, Theo, could be helpful in making atmospheric observations, Reich replied brusquely: Wolfe should do what he wanted to do and not be dependent upon him. A few weeks before Wolfe's death, knowing that his illness was terminal and the end could come at any time, Theo again wrote Reich and this time received a warm reply.

About this time, too, an important relationship between Theo and a woman in New Mexico came to an end. In late July 1954 Wolfe was found dead by his friends, some pills and a half-finished drink near him and a phonograph still playing. One speculation—certainly believed by Reich—was that Wolfe had committed suicide.

Reich had endeavored to keep Wolfe actively engaged in the work; but once he saw that Wolfe was no longer able to be fully involved, he, in effect, cut the strings. How can we understand such ruthless behavior toward a man who had done so much for orgonomy? We recall that Reich had failed to visit his younger brother Robert when the latter was terminally ill with tuberculosis (see Chapter 8). In Theo's as well as in Robert's case, Reich may well have felt guilty toward a person who had done so much to help him. Once again Reich handled guilt as he so often did, by throwing himself into his work and suppressing or repressing personal considerations. He had always been a man in a hurry, and now—hounded, ignored, but knowing that great discoveries still beckoned—he was in a relentless hurry. Furthermore, Reich was now suffering from a heart condition. He had no time for persons who withdrew from orgonomy.

Wolfe had not only withdrawn. He had got caught up in Reich's fantasies about a usurping man (tutor) and an unfaithful woman (mother). In Wolfe's case, Reich's competitiveness with male colleagues is revealed with special vividness. He could relate to men well only when they were clearly subordinate or when they were at a distance (Neill in England and Raknes in Norway). With more independent, nearby men, Reich's fears of being usurped got in the way.

Put differently, the macho side of Reich led to an exaggerated and persistent stress on his preeminence in work and sex. In my view, this problem was connected with his unresolved homoerotic feelings. I do not mean this only in the narrowly sexual sense, but in the larger context of close, tender, at times dependent feelings toward men. Reich's failure to deal with these themes led to their reemergence in distorted and destructive form. For example, jealous, groundless preoccupations often indicate a wish for the apparently feared event. The targets of Reich's jealousy were frequently like Wolfe—handsome, clean-cut, non-Jewish—men different from Reich in ways that he with his acne had always envied. To share a woman with such a man is to be closer to him, in a sense to be more like him.

My interpretation is supported by the moralistic distaste Reich could express about homosexuality. Once in therapy I recall telling him about how an overture from a homosexual made me feel very uncomfortable. Reich replied proudly: "No homosexual has ever approached me. They don't sense it in my structure."

At the time, I thought there was something wrong with me. Today, I am struck not only by how untherapeutic Reich's remark was, blocking as it did my further thoughts and feelings on the subject, but even more by the reflection: Methinks he did protest too much!

Reich's behavior toward Wolfe can be understood, but it certainly cannot be condoned. In a set of photos now displayed at the Orgonon Observatory, there is a picture of Wolfe with a caption supplied by Reich: "Victim of the emotional plague." Reich undoubtedly meant the emotional plague of others, not his own. But Wolfe was also the victim of Reich's emotional plague.

Concomitant with the Oranur experiment, Reich developed an interest in painting during the late spring of 1951. He painted very quickly, ten canvasses in his first two weeks of painting. Like the rest of his work, his artistic themes dealt with life, death, and nature. Ilse Ollendorff has written: "His pictures have a very definite character, use brilliant colors, and I find them very fascinating not as great art but as a characteristic expression of the man Reich. . . . There was much influence of Munch in color and choice of subjects."[13]

In a letter to Neill, Reich half-facetiously related his interest in painting to Oranur: "If art is a disease, Oranur has brought out the artist in me . . . I just enjoy painting tremendously."[14] It is noteworthy that Reich could allow himself so seemingly tangential a pastime as painting under the tremendous stress of Oranur. But his "play" was closely related to the development of his work: Oranur required a careful eye for the details of the natural world, for the "sparkle" or "bleakness" of the atmosphere.

Through his painting, Reich became more acutely aware of a unity between art and science—in general and in himself in particular. The artist in him was evident at the beginning of a research enterprise, when he would permit the aesthetic, qualitative aspects of what he dealt with (a patient, a bion, dots in the sky) to impress him. The scientist was manifest when he went on to conceptualize his observations and find ways to test his hypotheses. As he expressed it around the time he began to paint:

Newton and Goethe are, with their respective world pictures, no longer as much antipodes as they used to be. Their points of view can and will be reconciled. The *scientist* and the *artist* are no longer keepers of two disparate, unmixable worlds, as they still seem to be. Intellect and intuition are no longer irreconcilable opposites in scientific work. As a matter of fact, they have never been so in basic natural-scientific research.[15]

In August 1951, the FDA renewed its investigation. A patient reported that an official had come to his home, taken a picture of the accumulator, and asked various questions about it.[16] Reich reacted sharply. He told accumulator users they were not legally obligated to give the FDA any information. They should refer inspectors directly to his Foundation. (Irritated by its high legal fees, Reich had dropped the legal services of the Hays office in New York.) Reich took the position that since orgone energy was neither a food, a drug, nor a cosmetic, it lay beyond the FDA's jurisdiction. On the other hand, he still offered to cooperate with the FDA if it would proceed seriously, by studying the literature first, then seeking more information directly from the Foundation rather than from patients.

In the battle between Reich and forces inimical to him, the accumulator was his most vulnerable point. He had stated that the accumulator had certain preventive and curative properties, however qualified his assertions. The FDA was mandated to protect the public against false medical claims. The Reich Foundation was renting accumulators to the public. With Reich having largely given up his private practice at the time of his move to Orgonon, the accumulator income became an important source of financial independence.

The FDA flurry in 1951 was soon over, at least in manifestations Reich could discern; however, the agency did confirm that it was continuing the investigation. Reich chose not to regard this information seriously. As in 1948, he preferred to believe that the waning of such activity as visits to patients meant that the investigation itself was finished. This strategy permitted him to turn his attention to other matters and lessened his anxiety. Unfortunately, it also prevented him from formulating a clear line of action in anticipation of a more formidable offensive.

In October 1951, Reich suffered a major heart attack. At one point he experienced tachycardia with a pulse rate of 150–160.[17] Reich himself believed that Oranur had brought out his specific physical vulnerability since he had previously suffered some tachycardia.

He also attributed the attack to his use of an orgone energy funnel over his heart just after he had experienced some mild discomfort. That he used the funnel at all reflects the ambiguity of his thinking. Reich posited that the radium had irritated orgone energy into DOR, a reaction especially strong near orgone accumulators. He still maintained that the accumulator could be helpful, though he did warn people against having any radioactive substances, however minute, near the accumulator. Even at Orgonon he held open the possibility the accumulator might help (although he was not certain of this) in the treatment of illness when Oranur effects were not strong.

Reich was bedridden for four weeks. The heart attack exacerbated his depression and anxiety over the disruption of his work, his upheavals with Ilse, and his general sense of things coming apart. Ilse Ollendorff has described the problems:

> . . . Although it was suggested by those physicians who were at Orgonon at that time that he might be better taken care of in a hospital or that he should at least have an oxygen tent at his disposal or that he should see a heart specialist he absolutely refused, and insisted on curing himself with orgone therapy; but he gave up smoking for good. I took care of him in the beginning, but he became increasingly suspicious of my good will and during the last two weeks of his convalescence had his daughter Eva come back to take care of him.[18]

On November 12, Ilse wrote Dr. Baker:

> He [Reich] is so terrifically sensitive to the least irrationality that it seems almost unavoidable that one of us here gets him upset. If it is not me, it is Tropp, or Mickey [Sharaf], or Grethe or Lois or Tom or Eva, or Peter or the radio, and you cannot keep him completely isolated. . . . He fluctuates very much between wanting to die, not wanting to die and being afraid of dying, and it is impossible to pretend anything to him or to have "bedside manners." I think that he and Dr. Tropp have decided that his sickness could be diagnosed in classical terms as myocarditis which, according to Tropp, has a very hopeful prognosis, if we can just manage to keep him quiet and resting.

Reich's refusal to see a heart specialist reflected his long-held suspicion of classical medicine. But his giving up cigarettes was a big step. He had smoked all his adult life, at least since the Army period. His cigarettes were as dear to him as cigars were to Freud, but clearly his heavy smoking had taken its toll. During the period I knew him, he suffered from a racking cough that at times was like a seizure; one became afraid he would pass out. In the days following his decision to quit, someone asked him if it was hard to stop. He simply replied: "I have considerable self-discipline when I want to exert it."[19]

The growing tension between Reich and Ilse was reflected in his decision to have Eva visit Orgonon and care for him during the last weeks or so of his illness. In the spring of 1951 she returned to Maine along with her lover, William Moise, a painter, teacher, and student of orgonomy. Sometimes living in Rangeley, sometimes in Hancock, Maine (some four hours from Orgonon),

Eva and Bill were both to participate in diverse aspects of Reich's work and remain close to him until the end of his life.

The friction between Reich and Eva continued. Eva had many qualities in common with her father—she was lively, open, domineering, and brilliant, with an intuitive as well as scientific flair for orgonomy. Unlike her father, she could also be scattered, confused, and provocative. She knew exactly how to irritate him, for example, by indulging her penchant for certain mystical notions. As his daughter, she had more leeway from Reich than others, but sometimes he would be mercilessly hard on her. They engaged in frequent battles, triggered at times by his heavy hand. For example, at one point she strongly resented his forbidding her to see her mother. He believed this was a necessary antidote to the years when she had been pressured by her mother's circle not to see Reich. She felt that Reich's step was dictatorial. Later, she very much regretted that she had yielded to his influence, just as she regretted submitting earlier to the influence against him. In one sense, she never entirely lost her feeling of being torn apart by these opposing forces.[20]

By mid-November, Reich was on his feet and back at work. I saw no sign of any reduced work schedule once he recovered. Indeed, his heart attack seemed to add to his urgency about eliminating the Oranur reaction at Orgonon and bringing his affairs in order. He also mentioned at the time that he thought many heart attacks stemmed from heartbreak.

Throughout the winter of 1951–52, the effects of Oranur persisted. The Observatory was only usable for brief periods of time and the Students' Laboratory was closed. I worked in my apartment in Rangeley. By March of 1952, Peter and Ilse had moved to a small apartment in Rangeley. Reich stayed sometimes at the Observatory, sometimes at a motel or with Ilse. For several weeks the three lived together again in Dr. Tropp's home in Rangeley when Tropp and his family left for a vacation.

There was a grimness and restlessness about Reich in those days. I recall his coming into my apartment and being annoyed that the windows weren't open. His comments were often uncommonly curt; he appeared more easily angered than ever.

Yet, however embroiled Reich was with Oranur and its unsettling effects on his existence, his work proceeded. Several major publications were prepared in 1951, the contents of which will be discussed shortly. The *Orgone Energy Bulletin* continued to appear. Although Reich had transferred considerable responsibility for the training of physicians to Baker, he never lost his zealous concern for what was happening to his work, the possible ruination of which by followers as well as enemies was a constant fear. For instance, in 1951 certain examples of "cocktail orgone therapy" occurred, in which some therapists at social gatherings made inappropriate interpretations to strangers about, say, their orgastic potency or their body armor. Reich was furious and said that such behavior betrayed a complete lack of contact with the spirit of orgonomy.

While Reich was plunging forward into new domains through the Oranur experiment, he was also moving backward to survey the body of his work in its entirety. He conceived of publishing a series of volumes to present the essential documentary material on all phases of his life and work. Reich had a deep and abiding fear of distortion of the historical record, a fear that his work and name would somehow be slandered and defamed, not just currently but into posterity. Also, he was increasingly impressed by the unity of his work and he wanted to have its different phases ordered in such a way as to reveal this unity and to reflect the historical perspective. And, as he commented at the time, he did not quite trust himself to make the right interpretations because of his emotional involvement in everything that had occurred. For all these reasons, he wanted to have complete, accurate documents for later historians to study—historians he fervently hoped would be objective in their analysis.

During late 1951 and early 1952, I spent considerable time helping Reich to order his material. He was a very careful archivist and did a great deal of painstaking work in setting up the cataloguing system for his papers. Sometimes when he was carefully pressing out a crumpled newspaper article from the 1930s or pasting up material, he would say with a touch of irony: "When I retire, I can at least get a job at the Library of Congress." Historical work often brought out a mellow, musing side in him. His references to Freud were frequent, especially when he went over the documents from the psychoanalytic years. He was still very pleased by the warmth of some of Freud's letters to him.

Some documents from Reich's Marxist period made him wince, as he reread radical political utterances in his letters and publications with which he now violently disagreed. But he insisted that however much he would love to tear some of them up, all must remain unchanged as part of the historical record. If his emotions grew too strong, he would dictate a note under the heading, "Silent Observer," which recorded his present-day observations about the material.

From the historical material Reich published only one volume, *People in Trouble* (1953). This work, which was mainly written in the 1930s and deals largely with Reich's social concepts, was described in Chapter 11. During 1950 and 1951, I translated the manuscript from the German and Reich added to it in English many of his "Silent Observer" comments. I can thus vouch for the fact that he did not delete a line or change a phrase from the German material, much as he may have liked to downplay his participation in the Communist Party.

Oranur and the revived FDA investigation soon overwhelmed Reich's time and energies, but he did have the chance to put in order most of his archival material. I remember his wanting to get in touch with Harvard University with an eye to their storing his documents. I thought there was little likelihood of Harvard's being interested. Perhaps my judgment was correct at the time. Today, his papers are in the Countway Library of Harvard Medical School.

Although *The Murder of Christ* was not published until 1953, it was written during the summer of 1951 at the height of the Oranur reaction. Reich had long been interested in the Christ story, noting in 1948 when he wrote *Ether, God and Devil:* "It remains to be investigated from where the Christ legend draws its greatness, its emotional force, and its endurance."[21]

Oranur jolted Reich into giving his version of this "legend"—one he had been preparing over the years by reading all the major books on Christ and his times that he could find. *The Murder of Christ* was a long time in gestation, but Reich actually wrote it in a few months. Oranur had impressed him as never before with the power of evil: evil in man and evil in nature. Now he felt a special urgency to tell the quintessential story of human evil and tell it quickly.

The Murder of Christ was not primarily a historical study. In his characteristic way, Reich utilizes the Jesus story—the parables, the gospel narratives, the historical information—to make his own points. At the same time, he writes with the conviction that much of what he describes was actually experienced by the historical Christ, his followers, and his enemies. Reich does not utilize the kind of ironic, distancing device Freud employed when he introduced as a "Just So" story his seriously held hypothesis that a patricide and its sequelae formed the origin of civilization. Reich was writing chiefly in a prophetic vein. Read one way, the combination of historical and prophetic modes of discourse weaken each other: the reader wonders how true the history is and receives no careful answers; he also wonders what the allegorical digressions have to do with the history of Jesus. Read another way, the combination enhances both elements: the Christ story is illuminated by Reich's concepts, while the latter was vivified by their embodiment in the life and death of Jesus. Reich's prose is concordant with his aims. It is forceful, incantatory, alive, and simple. As in *Listen, Little Man!,* he was also at times repetitious, frenzied, and self-pitying. Withal, it stands as a fine example of the best of his late writings, wherein he dropped his academic garb and showed, in Yeats's phrase, "there's more enterprise in walking naked."

Reich took Christ as the supreme example of unarmored life. His is a Christ who loves children, forgives sinners, and has healing powers. Christ can heal because he has a strong energy field capable of exciting the sluggish, "dead" energy systems of the wretched. Most controversially, Reich's Christ is a lover of women, as evinced by their devotion to him and by such remarks as: "Let him who is free of sin cast the first stone." The sex-repressive side of Christianity Reich ascribed to Jesus' rational dislike of pornography and to a rigidification of this notion by Saint Paul. For Reich, Saint Paul, the organizer, was to Christ what Stalin was to Marx—the distorter of the original truth.

Reich dealt with the diverse roles and motivations played by Judas, Pontius Pilate, and the Pharisees in the murder of Christ. But, basically, he indicted armored man. Average men and women flock to Christ in expectation of a miraculous deliverance from their armor. When he cannot rescue them in the way they expect, they turn against him. If they do not lead the crucifixion, they do not stop it—indeed, they support it. In turn, Christ is disappointed in the people, even his closest disciples. Reich quotes Christ citing Isaiah in what amounts to a description of the armor:

> You shall indeed hear but never understand,
> and you shall indeed see but never perceive.
> For this people's heart has grown dull,
> and their ears are heavy of hearing,
> and their eyes have been closed.

For Reich, the murder of Christ goes on continually. Every child is Christ, its spontaneity and genuine curiosity deadened by destructive familial and social practices. Every adult who somehow manages to preserve his or her liveliness and who has also the talent to produce works that challenge man's immobility risks sharing Christ's fate. In Ernest Hemingways's words: "If people bring so much courage to this world the world has to kill them to break them, so of course it kills them. . . . It kills the very good and the very gentle and the very brave impartially. If you are none of these you can be sure it will kill you too but there will be no special hurry."[22]

Thus, Christ is the most vivid example of the murder of the living. Moving freely through history, Reich cites instances everywhere. Giordano Bruno, burned at the stake by the Inquisition, becomes a poignant example. Reich sees himself as another, and reviews the persecution he has suffered from "the people" as well as from various "orthodoxies." At the time of writing *The Murder of Christ,* Reich felt hunted by the Food and Drug Administration, increasingly misunderstood by and isolated from even his closest followers. In my view, he knew somehow that he was facing his own Gethsemane. This awareness saturates the book, giving it a haunting power.

Reich's bold self-references together with discussions of the historical Christ have led to the mistaken conclusion that Reich identified with him in a literal, psychotic fashion. Such a diagnosis does not so much miss the point as collide with it, to use a phrase the critic John Leonard employed in another context. Of course, Reich "identified" with Christ if Christ represented the unimpeded flow of life—precisely the point Reich was trying to make.

Reich's most tragic conclusion is that the killing of Christ and of orgonomy, if not by literal murder then by silence, made sense from the viewpoint of armored man. He cannot live in the way that Christ and orgonomy represent. More, the existence of such a life represents the unbearable provocation of being desirable but unattainable. If armored people try to make contact with the teachings of Christ or orgonomy, there is the danger that they will act out secondary, destructive impulses. Conservatives in whatever guise have a point when they call for "law and order" against the messianic message. As Reich put it:

The human race would meet with the worst, the most devastating disaster if it obtained full knowledge of the life function, of the orgasm function or of the secret of the murder of Christ with one stroke as a whole. There is very good reason and sound rationality in the fact that the human race has refused to acknowledge the depth and the true dynamics of its chronic misery. Such a sudden breaking in of knowledge would incapacitate and destroy everything that still somehow keeps society going.[23]

Reich's grim realism here is akin to that of Dostoevski's Grand Inquisitor in *The Brothers Karamazov*. The Inquisitor tells the reincarnated Christ that he erred in offering man truth and freedom. "By showing him so much respect, Thou didst, as it were, cease to feel for him, for Thou didst ask too much from him. . . . Respecting him less Thou wouldst have asked less of him. That would have been more like love, for his burden would have been lighter. He is weak and vile." In seeking freedom, men are like "little children rioting. . . . Though they are rebels, they are impotent rebels unable to keep up their own rebellion."[24] They will gratefully submit to the authoritarian Church, which understands their need for domination. So the living Christ must die again to protect the people from those aspects of his teachings they cannot live.

Reich mainly differs from the Inquisitor in that he sees man's "vileness" as *mutable*, even if the change requires centuries.

I have one major objection to *The Murder of Christ*. Reich does justice to himself as an example of how life is murdered, but he gives insufficient due to the ways he himself could murder life. In some of his earlier publications, usually written during periods of relative peace and success, he frankly acknowledged his own emotional plague, making it clear that he, too, was a child of this authoritarian civilization, that he could be as destructive as the next person. Now, under attack, he defensively omits such references, though in private conversation he occasionally revealed this aspect of his self-awareness.

My other criticism concerns not the book per se but Reich's failure to apply in his life the very lesson that saturates the book, namely, the deep rationale for the world's avoidance of orgonomy. Right around the time Reich was writing *The Murder of Christ*, he was also very intent on arousing the government's interest in the Oranur experiment. Reich sent copies of his *Oranur Report*, which appeared in October 1951, to many governmental agencies. Naively he interpreted their polite thank-you notes as genuine interest. After his detailed description of the fear of the living, how could he conceivably imagine that government officials would look objectively at Oranur, a comprehension of which was exactly what officials and the average citizen feared with a terror no one described better than Reich? Therein lies the enduring paradox: Reich keeps describing why everyone must fear his work, all the while believing that *some* circle—the Communists in the 1930s or parts of the American government in the 1950s—will appreciate his discoveries.

Reich blamed Christ's followers for seducing him into the ride into Jerusalem on an ass. No one but he himself seduced Reich into seeking Washington's support. Indeed, he hoped, figuratively, to march on Washington with Oranur in his fist, confounding his enemies at last in one dramatic showdown. Reich rationalized the urgency with which he approached the government on the basis of the threat of a nuclear war as well as the possible wide-ranging effects of Oranur itself. However, he was untrue to his basic principle of letting the world come to him. With the exception of his approach to Einstein, Reich had waited patiently during the 1940s. In 1951, time was running out. Driven into a corner by mounting opposition, he wanted to strike back with everything at hand. He deluded himself that one of his assets was possible support in high places if he could just get the "truth" to the right people.

The year 1951 also saw the publication of *Cosmic Superimposition. People in Trouble, The Oranur Report,* and *The Murder of Christ* were all loaded with emotion, and often angry emotion. *Cosmic Superimposition,* on the other hand, was a very quiet book, reflecting a loving attentiveness to natural phenomena. Here Reich was primarily concerned with the complex relationship between energy and mass. Starting with the superimposition of two organisms (or energy systems) in the sexual embrace, he moved to the superimposition of two orgone energy particles in the formation of matter. The work included theoretical formulations on the development of galaxies, hurricanes, and the aurora borealis.

Although the bulk of the book dealt with very technical material, Reich finished with a more accessible chapter on "The Rooting of Reason in Nature." Among other things, he dealt with a problem of long-standing concern: the question of the origin of man's armoring. Reich did not attempt to solve the problem of how the armor developed. Rather, he recast the problem. Earlier, consistent with a Marxist interpretation of human history, he had seen the armoring as secondary to socioeconomic influences, especially the hypothesized shift in early human history from matriarchal to patriarchal forms of social existence. Now he changed the sequence: "The process of armoring, most likely, was there first, and the socio-economic processes which today and throughout written history have *reproduced* armored man, were already the first important results of the biological aberration of man."[25]

Reich went on to speculate that man's reasoning, especially in the form of self-awareness, triggered the development of this armor:

> *In thinking about his own being and functioning, man turned involuntarily against himself;* not in a destructive fashion, but in a manner which may well have been the point of origin of his armoring.

> *... Man somehow became frightened and for the first time in the history of his species began to armor against the inner fright and amazement.* Just as in the well-known fable, the milliped could not move a leg and became paralyzed when he . . . started thinking about *which* leg he put first and *which* second, it is quite possible that the turning of reasoning toward itself induced the first emotional blocking in man. It is impossible to say what perpetuated this blocking of emotions and with it the loss of organismic unity and "paradise."[26]

It is fascinating here to see Reich come close to the Freudian thinking that postulated a "mute hostility" between ego and id. The ego feared being overwhelmed by the id and must needs defend against it in order to carry out the tasks of reasoning and self-awareness. But—and the "but" is important—Reich never saw the split between ego and id as inevitable. The few people who were able to maintain the unity of sensation and reason (for Reich, they were the great artists and scientists) provided examples of a way out of the dilemma: "It would become possible, by the most strenuous effort ever made in the history of man, to adjust the majority to the flow of natural processes. Then if our exposition of the armoring blocking is correct, man could return home to nature; and what appears today as exceptional in a very few could become the rule for all."[27]

Supported by the knowledge of orgone energy, man could use his reason to make better contact with his depths, his deep emotions, his currents of pleasure. The split Reich hypothesized as occurring when man began to be aware of himself could be overcome.

Toward the end of 1951, as Reich was preparing source material for the history of orgonomy, he read a notice that the Freud Archives were gathering all available material pertinent to Freud's life and work. Reich wrote offering his cooperation. In his reply, Kurt Eissler, then secretary of the archives, either suggested or agreed to an interview with Reich at Orgonon about Freud and psychoanalysis.

The interview occurred in two sessions, each lasting several hours, on October 18 and 19, 1952. Everything about it was extraordinary: what Reich said, the context within which it was held (the Oranur emergency), Eissler's responses, and the way it was subsequently published.

For Reich, the interview served several purposes. It was an opportunity to set down for the historical record—for the Freud Archives, for his own archives, and for possible publication—his convictions about Freud's contributions, errors, and personal qualities. More important, it gave him a chance to delineate once more one of his constant preoccupations, the relationship between psychoanalysis and orgonomy. Underlying Reich's preparations for the whole interview was a deep concern that rumors and slander in psychoanalytic circles about his work and person would enter the historical record uncorrected.

In the course of the interview, Reich paid eloquent tribute to what he considered the essential tenets of psychoanalysis: the unconscious, infantile sexuality, resistance, actual neurosis, libido theory. He also discussed at some length the possible personal and social reasons for Freud's rejection of Reich's basic concepts, especially the orgasm theory. He offered a variety of explanations, including the efforts of Federn and Jones to influence Freud against Reich. He also stressed Freud's marital unhappiness as a factor: "There is very little doubt that he was very much dissatisfied genitally. . . . He had to give up his personal pleasures, his personal delights in his middle years."[28]

Reich was, I believe, the first person to focus on the influence of Freud's own marriage on the development of his work. Since the interview, much material has appeared, especially the Freud-Jung correspondence, highlighting Freud's marital unhappiness. In his massive biography, the discreet Ernest Jones barely hints at this.

However, it was not with Freud that Reich was primarily concerned. Rather, it was with the way he, Reich, had developed certain aspects of Freudian thought. Again and again during the interview he explained his own ideas about the nature of streamings, and the way his concepts continued but differed from Freud's, as well as the reception they received from Freud and other analysts. Ranging even more widely, Reich talked about the fate of bio-energy in infants when contact with the mother was disturbed. Eissler patiently waited out his subject's excursions, trying to lead Reich back to Freud. Reich wove in and out of Freud, psychoanalysis during the 1920s, and his own particular themes. Always he emphasized the crucial significance of his *own* work, no matter what the analysts thought of it—this at a time when the psychoanalytic establishment was more powerful than it had ever been or would be in subsequent decades.

Part of Reich was concerned with the analysts' reactions to his work and naively yearned for their goodwill, in spite of all the prevailing evidence. Old feelings of camaraderie still existed, old wounds still hurt him. When Eissler mentioned that he had discussed his interviewing Reich with Heinz Hartmann and Arthur Kronold (a student of Reich's in Vienna), both of whom Reich had known quite well, Reich was clearly disappointed to learn that their interest in the interview was peripheral.[29]

Reich was misled by Eissler's interviewing technique, his "fascinatings," and "go ons." He believed Eissler was far more receptive to his work than in fact was the case. Indeed, Eissler was secretly laughing at Reich a good deal of the time. When I interviewed Eissler about the Freud interview, he assumed I was most interested in what diagnosis of mental illness should be ascribed to Reich. He did not think Reich was schizophrenic, but psychopathic with underlying paranoid trends. He added that his colleagues believed that Eissler himself tended to underestimate pathology.[30]

Eissler had not meant the interview to be published soon since it was intended for the Freud Archives, which were to be sealed for many years. Nor did he want it to be published, fearing embarrassment when some analysts read Reich's astringent comments about them, with Eissler's ambiguous asides of "fascinating." However, in 1967, Mary Higgins published this interview, a transcript of which was in the Reich Archives. In so doing she was following Reich's own wishes, or at least one expression of them, for in 1954 he wrote: "It is of crucial importance . . . that the major, factual parts of the Wilhelm Reich interview on Freud be published now."[31]

Eissler's interview was not in fact Reich's last word about Freud. In 1956, on the anniversary of Freud's one hundredth birthday, Baker requested an article from Reich for his journal, *Orgonomic Medicine*. Reich's response was a paper relating his DOR research to Freud's concept of the death instinct. Although Reich firmly believed that his work on orgone energy was quite distinct from psychoanalysis, and although he had always been and still was in strong opposition to death instinct theory, Reich saw certain connections between Freud's ideas and what he conceptualized as DOR.[32]

I find it extremely moving and poignant that in what would prove to be his last theoretical paper, Reich should make connections between his work and that of Freud. Reich had been deeply hurt by Freud, and the death instinct controversy had led ultimately to Reich's expulsion from the International Psychoanalytic Association. In early 1956, Reich was facing a trial for contempt of an FDA injunction. Psychoanalytic organizations, along with other groups, had encouraged the FDA to get rid of Reich's work. Nonetheless, Reich could see where Freud was right in his thinking about a death instinct, although Reich never agreed with the concept itself.

In his last years, the superficial, irrational Reich was separating himself from more and more people. However, during the same years the deep, rational Reich was making more profound connections with the concepts of others than he ever had in the past. Reich was not only putting his papers in order, he was putting his thoughts in order. The symphonic structure of his work had as its basic themes the liberation of life energy in man and the harnessing of atmospheric orgone energy to help man. Now he was adding more fully than ever the counter-themes, or what he called "the obstacles in the way" to the unfolding of life. While continuing with the Oranur experiment, he was using the fruits of that research as well as other findings to appreciate more fully the partial truths in conservative views he had long opposed: Freud's death instinct theory; Freud's emphasis on the difficulties in integrating self-awareness and self-control with full emotional experiencing of the self; the religious emphasis on the tenacity of man's evil; the political conservative's stress on the dangers of too rapid social change; and the rationality in avoidance of orgonomy.

At the same time, Reich never lost sight of the radical aspects of his own work. He did not mechanically add old insights, but rather reinterpreted them. The new connections found their orderly passages within his scientific music. In the sharpness and originality with which he formulated questions about man's present illness and potential health, in the passion and courage with which he sought answers to these questions, in the combination of his attention to detail and his power of comprehensive generalization, his final work stands unsurpassed. Reich's ultimate legacies to those who followed were the most careful guideposts not only to the potentials but also to the perils of the orgonomic journey. It was an awesome achievement, especially from a man so severely beset from without and from within.

Oranur certainly marked a new beginning, and with it a burst of destructive rage in Reich's personal life. For Reich, new beginnings usually entailed new co-workers and often a new geographical location. Surrounded by disapproving Viennese colleagues in the late 1920s, he moved to Berlin, where he found more receptive associates. His relationship with Elsa Lindenberg speeded the end of his increasingly unhappy marriage to Annie. When the situation became strained in Berlin, Hitler's advent to power in 1933 forced his departure for Scandinavia, where again he could match his developing interests in muscular armor and in the bions with a supportive, if not always fully comprehending, network of colleagues. His work continued to advance in Oslo; when the attacks developed against him and his relationship with Elsa had deteriorated, he could emigrate to the United States to begin a new social and scientific existence. And when life in New York with its responsibilities for therapy and training distracted him from natural-scientific research, he could move to Orgonon, which permitted an almost exclusive devotion to basic investigations.

But when upheavals started at Orgonon, there was nowhere to turn. He often said to me and to others, "You can go back"—meaning we could pursue other ways of life—"I have burned my bridges." There was no going back for him. More, the very few people at Orgonon provided little opportunity for human warmth and companionship when his relationship with Ilse deteriorated so markedly. Where he did reach out, as with Lois Wyvell, the small-town gossip in Rangeley added to his sense of strain and bondage.

During these years his relationship with Ilse continued, though with greater emotional distance between them. In the fall of 1952, Ilse and Peter moved into a small house in Rangeley, while Reich tried to live at Orgonon when the atmosphere permitted him to do so. But a final separation was not easy. The ties between them were strong, they had a child in common to whom Reich was devoted, they had work in common. Again rather typically, Reich made the focal issue Ilse's difficulty in following Oranur developments, especially the cloud-busting operations. As with Annie, he could not simply end a relationship he no longer wanted.

Thus, almost from the start of Oranur in January 1951 through the time when she finally left Orgonon in the summer of 1954, Reich waged his battle with Ilse, interspersed with periods of peace. In her biography, Ms. Ollendorff has rendered well the negative sides of Reich during that period—his jealous rages, his insistence on people following his ideas, his taking it out on those near him when the outside attacks mounted. She has also accurately portrayed the positive aspects of her own behavior at the time: her admirable refusal not to agree about matters she sincerely could not understand, her efforts to work things out, her concern for their son, Peter, and above all her sheer endurance under the most difficult of circumstances.

But what is missing from her account is any really deep appreciation of what Reich was going through, his positive qualities during this period and her negative ones. She argues, for example, that one of the reasons she eventually left Reich was that she could not follow such convictions as that "Red Fascists" were behind this or that attack, or that he had powerful friends in high governmental places. Although retrospectively she acknowledges that he may have been on to something with his cloud-busting work, she attributes any failure on her part to grasp this or other valid aspects of his later work to her limited scientific knowledge or talent. Nowhere does she acknowledge irrational emotional factors within herself that inevitably aroused Reich's wrath.

Given Ilse's blind spots, why, then, did Reich fight so hard and often so unfairly to force her into awareness? Why did he extract written, Stalinist-like confessions of her fear and hatred of him? Why on the day of their final separation in August 1954 did he still accuse her of protecting the now dead Wolfe instead of admitting to an affair? Why at this time did he hit her in front of their ten-year-old son Peter? And why did he strike her on several other occasions, once with such force that he punctured her eardrum?[33]

In his jealous rages, his violence, his bullying, his demand for confessions, Reich was under the spell of, and identified with, his introjected father. Leon had behaved exactly the same way toward Cecilia as Reich was now treating Ilse. The young Willy had been present at some of these scenes between Leon and Cecilia, just as Peter was witness to some of Reich's more outrageous explosions against Ilse. And, given Reich's own guilt over his mother's suicide, one can understand how hard it was for Reich to separate from a woman to whom he had been deeply attached and to whom he owed so much. He had a way of forcing the issues—and making a principle out of the separation in the name of his work—so that the woman ultimately left him. At least in her version of events, Annie decided that she could no longer remain married to Reich. Gerd decided she could not retreat to the Norwegian mountains. Elsa decided she could not go to America. Ilse decided to leave Orgonon. But in another sense, Reich forced each of these separations through his own behavior.

Reich was also behaving as the boy Willy had done, eager to win the mother, feeling betrayed and put down by her when she took the tutor (as earlier she had taken the husband). He would prove that he could win her. In many of Reich's relationships with women there was a tremendous battle quality. He just had to make them see he was on the right track, *had* to win their total admiration. And this urgency grew virulently compulsive when he had taken a new, insecure step in his life's work.

I find it significant that all the women I interviewed or corresponded with who had relationships with Reich attributed their difficulties with him to his problems, social difficulties, or their lack of scientific knowledge and skill. None focused on their emotional problems with him. One can speculate that this denial was also shared by his mother with regard to Leon; all the difficulties were his fault, just as he entirely blamed her until her suicide. In this respect at least, Reich chose women like his mother in an effort to make it come out right this time. It never did.

Thus, Reich remained locked in repetitions of his past, even as he transcended them in his ever grander work. Or transmuted them is perhaps the better term. For the "excess" from his personal problems and compulsions undoubtedly contributed to the passion of his scientific comprehension.

The obverse is also true. By channeling so much irrational rage and groundless suspicion into his personal relations and into some distorted, paranoid explanations of animosity against his work, Reich was free to direct an almost unblemished magnaminity toward his great scientific and human themes. As petty as his grudges against Ilse and Theo, as large was his generosity toward Freud, who in fact had "betrayed" him far more than Ilse or Wolfe ever did.

How much was Reich aware of his past as an irrational influence on his actions and beliefs during his last years? I do not know. Once he said to Lois Wyvell: "I fear your mother in you just as I fear my father in me," but he did not expand on that awareness, nor in his later years did he ever criticize his mother, to my knowledge. During this period the only person who suggested the possible role of his family dynamics was Ola Raknes in a letter to Reich. In reply, Reich quickly and without getting angry dismissed Raknes's tentative and sensitively worded interpretation.

One old friend suggested he needed help. Lia Laszky visited Orgonon in 1953 or 1954. Reading some of his publications in the 1950s, she had become worried about his emotional state. With some psychoanalytic colleagues from New York she went up to Orgonon. Reich would not see them, but he did agree to see Lia, who went up to the Observatory by herself. She said to him: "Willy, in the name of our old friendship and love, get help for yourself!" At first Reich was angry, but then he said: "Whom could I go to?" as if he were just barely considering the idea. Lia replied: "I wouldn't even have mentioned it if I hadn't someone in mind who I think is good." She suggested Harry Guntrip, a teacher of hers and a highly respected therapist.[34]

Nothing came of her suggestion. Reich could not see anyone unless he felt that person knew where he was right as well as wrong. There was no such person, though Reich did yearn for someone to whom he could speak with full candor. He once said: "People can come to me with their problems but I have no one to talk to."

In May 1952, I left Orgonon. My explanation at the time for leaving was that I wanted to continue my academic education, and my lack of scientific training hindered my usefulness now that Oranur was so much at the center of the work. These reasons obtained, but of equal importance was the fact that my own relationship with Reich had deteriorated. I was not so open with him as earlier and his behavior toward fearfulness was not helpful, resulting in the destructive interaction described in Chapter 2.

Reich and I parted amicably. I remember waving good-bye to him from my car as he was working—I undoubtedly thought "fiddling"—with his cloud-buster pipes outside the Students' Laboratory. He gave me a hard look, hurt, angry, yet not unfriendly, as if to say: What about all those fine words and ideals of yours now? Did you really mean them?

It is fashionable to describe Reich as a difficult, even impossible man in his last years. That is Ilse Ollendorff's point in her biography, and in one sense it was true. For part of Reich was a bully and he reacted in the same way as he once described the police: Look them in the eye and they leave you alone; hide and they club you. Once one hid, Reich was merciless—in his accusations, his rages, his demands for various acknowledgments that went far beyond actual deeds.

However, I like to think that if I had dealt with Reich more openly and courageously, with a deeper awareness of what he was about, he would have taken criticism with much better grace. In my experience, no one did what I have in mind. Basically, people either went along or they left.

Helen MacDonald and Lee Wylie had already left Orgonon. Lois Wyvell stayed on another year after me, but her intimate relationship with Reich was increasingly difficult. He was still devoting considerable energy to resolving his relationship with Ilse and had become more despairing about his loneliness. The winter of 1952–53 was particularly painful. The Tropps took a long vacation; Eva spent considerable time in Hancock. Of the original group that had moved to Rangeley with such bright hopes in 1950, only Lois and Ilse remained. Ilse was out of contact with Oranur and Lois was professionally engaged only with matters concerning the Press. On occasion, Reich would say: "I have no one." Lois would reply: "You have Dr. Baker," and Reich would very tentatively say: "Yes." Baker and other physicians gave what support they could, but none of them was actively engaged in scientific work in general or Oranur in particular. At a more personal level, Reich felt really close only to Peter. On some occasions, Reich would cry and indicate his need to be held and comforted. Thus by late winter, the combination of Reich's involvement with Ilse and his general despair corroded whatever satisfaction there had been between Lois and him, and the relationship ended.

During the spring of 1953, Lois Wyvell became involved with another man, a person who spent some time in Rangeley. Reich, jealous, felt that the man was using his connection with Lois to try to obtain work at Orgonon or otherwise involve himself in orgonomy. (Reich frequently felt, sometimes correctly, sometimes incorrectly, that people would use his assistants to inveigle something from him.) However, he also acknowledged his own irrational destructive emotions. With some astonishment about his own jealous feelings, he said: "I, too, am sometimes capable of the murder of Christ."[35]

Since her friend could not find work in Rangeley, Lois decided to move to Farmington, a larger city forty miles away. She planned to continue working for Reich, but Reich decided to terminate her employment. Speechless with disappointment and rage, he experienced the throat block he had described in his very first clinical paper—his disguised autobiography. He wrote a note: "You are fired!" Soon after Lois Wyvell left Rangeley in the beginning of July, Reich's stand toward both her and her friend softened. At a later time the question of her working for him again was considered, but this plan never materialized.

Simeon Tropp had been mainly a consultant and friend to Reich in Rangeley. He was one of the few colleagues with whom Reich would share leisure time—have meals and go to the movies. Reich always appreciated Simeon's warmth, his mischievous humor, and helpfulness. He was also fond of Tropp's wife, Helen, who worked for Reich as a secretary for a period. However, Reich became more and more irritated by Tropp's impulsive thinking and his inability to do consistent work. Moreover, he felt that both Helen and Simeon were adversely affected by Oranur. Helen showed certain precancerous symptoms, symptoms Reich believed Tropp did not take with sufficient seriousness. Simeon himself experienced a recurrence of an old liver ailment. Tired of the stress at Orgonon, the long winters, and the Oranur effects, the Tropps left. They settled on Long Island, New York, in the early fall of 1954.*

In August 1954, Ilse Ollendorff left Orgonon to work at the Hamilton School in Sheffield, Massachusetts. The school was run by two students of Reich, Alexander and Eleanor Hamilton.

By 1954, Tom Ross had moved closer to Reich than ever. For Reich, Tom represented an oasis of simple trust in a desert of loneliness. Reich's deep respect for him, together with his independent status as a workman rather than a disciple, spared him Reich's rages and spared Reich any exalted expectations from Tom.

A new assistant had joined Reich in the spring of 1953. Robert McCullough, a biologist, originally from Utah, had long been interested in Reich's work, especially in its biological and physical aspects. Bob was a very serious, modest person, devoted to science. He had already worked for a year in the biology department of the University of New Hampshire, with periodic visits

---

*Helen Tropp died of cancer in 1959 at the age of forty-two. Simeon maintained his commitment to Reich and orgonomy, practicing as a psychiatric orgone therapist with many devoted patients. He also became interested in macrobiotics and exploring lysergic acid (LSD) treatment, pursuits to which he brought the same scattered intensity he gave to orgonomy. In 1968 he died in his mid-seventies of a heart attack.

to Reich in Orgonon. Then Reich offered him a full-time position at a better salary than the university provided, an offer McCullough happily accepted.[36]

In an article entitled "The Rocky Road to Functionalism," McCullough gave a vivid description of Reich at his best—Reich the careful teacher who was still very much in evidence during the last hectic years.[37] Reich and McCullough's joint research concerned (in addition to cloud-busting) certain chemical developments connected with the blackening rocks and the DOR atmosphere. Reich believed that he had identified a number of new chemical substances in the rocks.

My concern here is less with the findings than with the method used. We can see clearly the continuity in Reich from earlier years. For example, when McCullough began working with him, Reich did not assign him a specific research project. Rather, he gave him a broad mandate to work on any interesting problem within the general field of chemical and biological phenomena associated with the Oranur experiment.

Reich would occasionally make suggestions: "What would happen if you just put some earth on a porous plate, added water, and then observed what occurred in this atmosphere?" This kind of approach, so characteristic of his research method, reminds one of Reich's "brew" of vegetables as an initial playful step on the road to the bions.

At the same time that Reich taught an openness in experimental approaches, he also cautioned strongly against random experimentation, especially actions that did not respect the phenomena. McCullough described well his skepticism about the Oranur effects, which again and again led him to overexpose himself in the laboratory atmosphere in spite of Reich's cautions to the contrary. (By 1953, the Students' Laboratory was in use for research again but only for short periods of time.) These overexposures were followed by distress reactions such as swelling of the cervical glands and severe anxiety. Bob commented about his own behavior perceptively, stating that part of him did not believe orgone energy existed and that he would take all kinds of steps to prove that it did. Such a course was futile since the doubting part of him would not accept any proof; he would have done better to bring out his doubts openly and look at them frankly.

On one occasion, McCullough ashed several decigrams of one of the chemical substances he and Reich were studying, just *"to see what the ash looked like!* Before the furnace had even reached full operating temperature, I was forced to turn it off due to a severe organismic reaction."[38]

Reich went to McCullough's home soon after the ashing, to determine why McCullough had done it. His assistant said he did it just to see what would happen. Reich replied that you don't kill living things that way, and you don't fool around with high temperatures in an Oranur atmosphere.

Whatever Reich's annoyance with McCullough for such impulsive actions, he rarely expressed the kind of anger he could to most of the people around. Ilse or I would perceive Oranur as an enormous jump beyond what we knew and were relatively comfortable with. However, McCullough, whatever his doubts about orgone energy or Oranur (and we all had our doubts), entered the work with some knowledge of Oranur and enthusiasm for it. His attitude was different from the start, and Reich responded accordingly.

McCullough also gave me a picture of Reich's daily interactions during this lonely period. Reich would usually come down to the Students' Lab around 10:00 A.M., for he continued his habit of writing during the first few hours of the day. He would ask McCullough what was new. "I felt badly that only occasionally would be there something up, something new." Reich also wanted word of world news, which McCullough listened to each morning on the radio. Reich was especially concerned about hurricanes, earthquakes, atomic tests, and the like.

Reich used to enjoy a kind of Socratic argument with McCullough, as indeed with others. Reich once asked him if he thought that Red China should be admitted to the United Nations, a hotly debated topic in the 1950s. McCullough said no. Reich, who was adamantly opposed to the admission of Red China, took another tack for the moment: "Well, the government represents 700 million people."

This, then, was one Reich—a kind and helpful teacher, a thoughtful man turning ideas around in his head, a lonely man. The New York physicians had given him a complete set of Beethoven's recordings for his fifty-fifth birthday in 1952, knowing that Reich listened to music a good deal in those years. He continued painting.

The other Reich was also in evidence—quick to reach conclusions on slim evidence, prone to wishful thinking. McCullough saw this side, too. Sometime in 1953 or 1954, McCullough was invited to become a member of the New York Academy of Sciences. McCullough attributed this invitation to a recruitment drive, of no particular significance. Reich, for whom in times of stress little happened by chance either to himself or to those associated with him, thought it might be connected with the Academy's interest in orgonomy.

Reich needed to grab desperately at such straws for he was aware that the FDA investigation, still continuing, posed a dangerous threat to his very existence.

The FDA Injunction and Reich's Responses: 1951-1955

None of Reich's work after the Oranur experiment, nor his personal life, can be understood without considering the impact of the FDA investigation as it reemerged around 1951, culminating in the injunction brought against him in February 1954. In August 1951, Reich had learned that the FDA was visiting accumulator users again. But when nothing further was heard about the FDA for the remainder of the year, he once more hoped that the investigation had ceased.

It had not. On July 29, 1952, three men—one regular FDA inspector, one FDA medical director, and one FDA physicist—came unannounced to the Observatory at Orgonon to "inspect the premises." In order to drive to the Observatory, which was at the top of the hill, one had to take down two chains barring vehicular access. The FDA representatives moved the chains and appeared at the Observatory entrance without any prior notification.

In writing and speaking about this encounter, Reich was to refer to it constantly as a prime example of the contemptuous actions against him. He hated to be interrupted by telephone or unannounced visits; he liked written appointments and screened telephone calls. Those working for him had to make very sure that they were confronted with an emergency before they put through a call to him when he was writing or working in the Observatory.

During the Oranur period and the accelerated FDA pressure, his rage over interruptions and violations of his space and time increased greatly. One reason for this was that often there was no one on the property except him. Nathan C. Hale, a sculptor, writer, and supporter of Reich's, remembers calling once to see if there were any orgone therapists in California. He expected a secretary to answer but got Reich, who proceeded to shout at him in a way that left Hale shaking.[1]

Trespassers on the property were frequent. People would just drive on up to see the "orgies" or whatever. Reich was apoplectic about such curiosity and sometimes innocent persons were caught in his rage. Once, some Rangeley citizens were looking over a property for sale adjacent to Orgonon. In the belief that they were on his property, Reich came running out with gun in hand to chase them away. Reports of such incidents, probably made even more eccentric and dangerous in the retelling, did not help his image in Rangeley.

On the afternoon of July 29, Ilse met the FDA representatives on the first floor of the Observatory, saying that Reich did not see people without an appointment. They persuaded her to let Reich know that two of the men had made a special trip from Washington to see him. Hearing this, Reich changed his mind and came down, probably motivated more by his wrath than any desire to accommodate unwelcome visitors. The FDA men later reported his bellowing: "What right do you people have to come here and ask me whether my secretary has a lover? What do you think we are up here, bums?"[2]

To my knowledge, this was the only time Reich met face to face with an FDA physician and physicist. However, little of substance seems to have been said at this tense meeting. Reich made it a precondition of any interaction that they first read his writings. Finally he told the men to leave.

Reich's point about the accumulator not being a "device" represented a shift in his thinking. A year earlier he had acknowledged the FDA's right, if it acted in good faith, to "investigate all devices at the manufacturing plant" to make sure they were correctly labeled.

A week after the visit of the FDA men, Reich wrote: "I am contemplating to suggest that orgone accumulators be built within the respective states and not be shipped in interstate commerce."[3] Reich's idea not to ship accumulators in interstate commerce would have helped to protect him legally, but it would have meant acknowledging some validity to the FDA's position. He never pursued it.

The recurrence of the FDA investigation, added to Reich's other strains, led him to return slander with slander. When the FDA accused him of fraud, of racketeering, Reich began to call the FDA agents Higs (an acronym for "*H*oodlums *i*n *g*overnment"). He also called them Modjus, a term he had begun using in *The Murder of Christ* to describe especially virulent emotional plague characters.* Even worse, he accused FDA agents of being the conscious or unconscious tools of Red Fascists.

Ironically, Reich made his wild accusations at the very time Senator Joseph McCarthy was riding high on similar accusations. McCarthy and his mentality of course contributed to the atmosphere of fear and suspicion that made the attack on Reich possible in the America of the early 1950s, and McCarthy used the very tactics Reich was analyzing as characteristic of the emotional plague. McCarthy relied on the ordinary citizen's fear of being attacked to ensure that no one would stand up against him in his wild assaults. At no time did Reich support McCarthy; but at times he engaged in McCarthyism.

It is a great tragedy that with all the facts in hand, Reich began to emphasize the least factual part of his entire case, and that he stooped to such name-calling. In Reich's emphasis on the "Red Fascists" as instigators of the campaign against his work, we see once again a desperate effort on his part to make contact with a hostile world. At times he believed that "the enemies of my enemies are my friends." However, at no time did Reich participate in what was quite common in the early 1950s—informing on persons he had known as Communists during the 1920s and 1930s. When an FBI agent visited Orgonon and asked Reich for such names, he refused to give them, although he was quite willing to talk about his own past and present political positions.[4]

No one was able to challenge Reich successfully on the Red Fascist question. Wolfe, who would have been best suited to do so, was no longer close to him. In my view, few of his associates entirely shared his conviction, though a larger number tried to convince themselves that Reich was right. Some, including myself, argued with him about it but with little success. Reich was at his most authoritarian on this particular matter, just as decades earlier he had insisted that a true psychoanalyst had to be in the camp of the political left. In the 1950s, Reich would allude to his earlier political experiences with the Communists, which none of us shared—he knew what they were like firsthand, we didn't. There could be no real discussion in such an atmosphere.

Reich's faith in the American government remained strong despite the FDA action and was reinforced by the election of General Dwight Eisenhower

---

*Reich devised the term by combining the first letters of the name *Mo*cenigo, the man who betrayed Giordano Bruno to the Inquisition, and the first letters of Stalin's original name, *Dju*gashvili. Reich always had a penchant for acronyms, but his coinage of them grew in the last desperate years. In part, their usage reflected his desire to overwhelm his opponents with a verbal barrage and to rally his supporters to blind allegiance. George Orwell has perceptively commented on the use of similar abbreviations in the "Newspeak" of *1984:* "In abbreviating a word one narrowed and subtly altered its meaning, by cutting out most of the associations that would otherwise cling to it. ... *Comintern* is a word that can be uttered almost without taking thought, whereas *Communist International* is a phrase over which one is obliged to linger at least temporarily"—George Orwell, *1984* (New York: Harcourt, Brace, 1949), 310.

as President in November 1952. Like millions of other Americans, Reich found Eisenhower's warm, engaging personality very attractive. But his hope of help from somewhere led him into a highly idealized view of what Eisenhower was like. On the night of Eisenhower's election, Reich taped a conversation he had at Orgonon with Drs. Baker, Raphael, Tropp, and Ilse Ollendorff. He was thrilled by the landslide vote given Eisenhower: "Eisenhower has the simplicity, the closeness and contactfulness of genital characters. I do not know him, really, personally; but that is what I feel about him, also his wife. Now that is a sexual revolution."[5]

Reich began to develop the fantasy that Eisenhower was a secret friend, along with other friends in high places. These allies would help him against the Food and Drug Administration, the pharmaceutical industry, the American Medical Association, the American Psychiatric and Psychoanalytic associations, and his political enemies. However, there is not a scintilla of evidence that his notion of powerful friends had any reality. The delusion that such friends existed would cost him dearly in the years to come.

Reich's assumption of powerful governmental friends led him to believe, sometime around 1953, that U.S. Air Force planes were making occasional flights over Orgonon to see what he was doing and to protect him. Ilse could not understand this at all and it exacerbated the tension between them.

Then, in November 1953, Reich read a book on flying saucers by Donald Keyhoe.[6] He was primed to respond, for he had long believed that life had developed in the universe and was not confined to our planet.[7] Not long after reading the report, Reich did more than take flying saucers as fact. He began to use them, sometimes definitely, sometimes tentatively, as a major cause of the DOR emergency. He became convinced that the UFOs were "space ships" powered by orgone energy. He based this interpretation on certain observations that had been made of flying saucers: the bluish light shimmering through the openings of the machines, their comparatively silent motion, and the unusual maneuvers they were capable of making. And he devised an acronym to refer to the drivers of these machines: CORE (Cosmic Orgone Engineering) men.

In April 1952, the time when the most frequent sightings of flying saucers were made, Reich found a reason for the increase in DOR effects. If the saucers used orgone energy, they would give off waste material or exhaust; such "slag" might be DOR. The DOR could be coming into the earth's atmosphere accidentally or as a deliberate action on the part of the navigators. Alternately, the deliberate path of DOR might have malignant or benign intentions behind it. If malignant, we were at war with invaders participating in the creation of deserts. If benign, the navigators might be giving us a cosmic lesson concerning the "immunization" benefits of DOR sickness.[8]

One should bear in mind the growing belief among serious students of UFOs that some sightings have never been satisfactorily explained and that the government has not been frank about the matter.[9] Still, Reich seriously erred in building so elaborate a superstructure on the basis of such scant evidence, exactly the kind of relationship between theory and fact he normally deplored. In my view, Reich speculated far beyond the verifiable facts for the same reason that he idealized Eisenhower: he was desperately looking for support. CORE men who used orgone-fueled ships could be powerful allies who thought as Reich did. (Indeed, in 1954 Reich changed the name of his periodical, *Orgone Energy Bulletin,* to *CORE,* denoting his cloud-busting concern with cosmic orgone engineering.) However, it might take more time than the crisis with the FDA permitted for friendly space travelers to make contact with him. If, on the other hand, these visitors were deliberately poisoning earth's atmosphere, the world would soon need Reich's concepts and techniques in order to wage effective cosmic war. Reich's imagery concerning the CORE men—their orgonomic creativity and destructiveness—represents a vivid externalization of the high-pitched ferment within himself at this time.

Although Reich held some very irrational ideas during this period, most of the time he was functioning on quite a different level. Writing Neill in 1954, he responded to Neill's query as to whether orgonomy would penetrate socially before mechanistic scientists blew up the world. Reich said he did not know but he did believe that our mechanistic-mystical civilization had already died. He remained outside this world and took pride in his separateness from it.[10]

He repeatedly and rightly criticized Neill for looking to various authorities to "accept" orgonomy. As Reich pointed out, it was an *honor* not to be accepted by a destructive status quo. All the sadder, then, was his own seeking of acceptance from the American government.

One can understand Reich's desperate hope for *some* kind of support when one realizes the ferocity and the range of the attacks against him. Hardly a month went by when there was not some new incident. Thus, in the winter of 1953, Bernard Grad was detained at the Canadian border on his journey from Montreal to visit Orgonon and was interrogated about his association with Reich. In February, several medical orgonomists were asked to appear before professional boards to defend their adherence to orgonomy.[11]

Today, when there is widespread public as well as professional interest in Reich's psychiatric treatment but not the accumulator, many people believe that the attacks in the 1950s completely centered on the "box." This was not the case. Reich's entire later work was under a cloud of obloquy. To give one example: in the spring of 1953, Dr. D. Ewen Cameron, then president of the American Psychiatric Association, told a patient who was considering *psychiatric* orgone therapy that such therapy was "pure fake and that the American Psychiatric Association was going to bring charges of fraud against Dr. Reich."[12]

Reich always wished to be informed about such incidents, much as they hurt and enraged him. Yet the most serious threat to orgonomy came not from visible manifestations, but from actions Reich was unaware of: the accumulator tests the FDA was conducting during 1952 and 1953. Since the FDA had not been able to find any dissatisfied users, medical tests conducted under its auspices were to be crucial for evidence.

The FDA never took its task lightly, even though some of the tests were grossly inadequate. It did not have the resources to run its own tests on the validity of the accumulator. Tests were therefore carried out by a variety of hospitals and clinics, including such prestigious institutions as the Mayo and Lahey clinics. Here we will concentrate on the heart of the FDA's evidence— the biomedical tests. (The FDA's replications of the temperature difference and the electroscopic measure—its physical tests—were described in Chapter 21.)

Reich was quite correct in fearing that he would be at a serious disadvantage in any courtroom procedure where scientists with all the right credentials presented inadequately conducted control studies of his findings. Carried out by reputable people, the FDA's tests were just good enough not to be transparently unscientific, but still palpably inadequate as any genuine assessment. Most of the outside replicators of orgonomy were as convinced of its falsity as the FDA was even before embarking on the testing.

Dr. Frank H. Krusen of the Mayo Clinic wrote on August 24, 1953, to the FDA: "It was very difficult for me to bring myself to take the time to prepare this report because of the fact that this quackery is of such a fantastic nature that it hardly seems worthwhile to refute the ridiculous claims of its proponents."[13] Other investigators also indicated their contempt *prior to* any investigation.

Most of the FDA tests bore out Reich's long-standing criticism of controlled replications of orgonomic findings: they violated essential conditions of the original experiments. For this reason, Reich had urged that he or another medical orgonomist participate in the FDA tests. The FDA never acceded to this condition, insisting on the necessity for entirely independent verification. They too had a point; still, for a completely fair assessment, their researchers would have to follow meticulously all conditions of the original experiments. Not only did they not meet these conditions, they often failed to mention their existence.

One striking way the tests failed is that they generally consisted of having patients sit in the accumulator only a few times. At Johns Hopkins Hospital, for example, a sixty-four-year-old woman with cancer of the large intestine and of the pelvis was treated four times with the accumulator for twenty minutes each on June 9, 10, 11, and 12, 1952. She died on June 12. This was no test at all, since Reich never claimed that accumulator usage for so short a time in such a severe illness would have an effect.* Nor was this an exception. At Johns

---

*It is true, as noted in Chapter 22, that Reich reported one case where a tumor was no longer palpable after eight treatment sessions. However, his cancer cases generally required a much longer course of treatment and even in this instance the schedule was twice as long as most of the Johns Hopkins treatments.

Hopkins the average duration of accumulator treatment for nineteen women with malignant tumors was four or five days, with several being treated for only two or three days.[14]

None of the tests showed a proper regard for Reich's emphasis on the fact that various forms of radiation from X-rays to radium dial watches negatively influenced orgone energy. Such forms of radiation were likely to be abundantly present in the medical settings where the FDA conducted their tests.

Here as elsewhere there was room for discussions between Reich and the experimenters making control studies. But such discussions never took place; and there is no evidence that the medical testers were at all familiar with Reich's writings. They lacked any awareness of the clinical signs one might find from even brief accumulator usage. That the FDA cancer patients died says nothing at all about the validity of Reich's findings. Most of his own patients died.

Even the best FDA tests done for the FDA failed badly on the above criteria. George B. Smith, M.D., of the Holy Ghost Hospital in Boston, Massachusetts, treated quite sick cancer patients with the accumulator blanket. Some cases were treated daily for two months. Smith includes in his report one rather mysterious sentence that the patient was treated from "10 to 30 minutes depending on the patient's tolerance."[15] Why a patient should become "intolerant" of a blanket was never explained. Nor does Smith indicate what symptoms the patient manifested to indicate that his or her degree of tolerance had been passed. Yet it is precisely in such reports that one can find some of the subjective evidence for orgone effects, for example, the patient's reporting sensations of heat, prickling, or itching.

Some positive effects, in terms of Reich's criteria, were noted when illnesses of less severity than cancer were treated. William F. Taylor, M.D., of Maine General Hospital, admitted a patient to the accident ward with burns on her face, ears, nose, neck, dorsum of fingers and hands, and volar surface of the wrists, following a stove explosion. The six-inch funnel from the accumulator was placed about four or five inches from the right side of her neck for twenty minutes. Within five minutes of beginning treatment, the patient said that her neck felt better and that it was less painful than her face and hands. The next day there was no evidence of blistering of the neck, but still some blistering in other burned areas. The neck continued to heal nicely, while the other burned areas had further crusting and blistering.[16]

This case has particular significance because the accumulator treatment of burns and wounds was one of the few instances where Reich maintained that rapid and striking results could be obtained. Not surprisingly, the FDA was in doubt whether this particular physician should be called as an expert witness because portions of his testimony would be favorable to the accumulator.

Two cancer studies using mice were conducted by the Jackson Laboratory in Bar Harbor, Maine. The results showed no significant differences between the control groups and the groups treated with the orgone accumulator in rate of death, final age at death, weight gain, or malignancy of the autopsied tissue.[17]

The medical orgonomist Richard Blasband commented on this particular study:

> This test is so different from Reich's mouse experiments that it cannot be considered a valid test of his claims. The Jackson Laboratory used transplanted tumor cells instead of letting the tumors develop spontaneously. Spontaneous tumors grow more slowly and permit a natural development of defensive reactions. . . .
>
> Of greatest importance is the fact that the treatment rooms at the Jackson Laboratory were located only 100 feet away from two X-ray machines which were used at least several times a week. . . . When the investigator in charge of the experiment was informed of this fact, he admitted not having read any of the literature where the Oranur problem was discussed. He said he wished to remain "completely objective."[18]

The FDA carried out a careful replication of the Reich Blood Test. As we have seen, Reich had found that the rate and form of disintegration of red blood cells into bionous vesicles was one indication of the orgonotic vitality of an organism. The FDA test consisted of examining the rate of disintegration of red blood cells from two groups of subjects, those believed to be healthy (all employees of the Nassau Hospital in Mineola, New York) and those with a known diagnosis of malignance of various organs. There were fifteen subjects in each control group.[19]

The FDA made no statistical analysis of the differences found. The researchers attributed their differences to extraneous factors such as problems in covering the preparation between observations and the inconstancy of red blood cell disintegration from day to day. In his subsequent analysis of FDA data, Richard Blasband in fact found the results an impressive confirmation of Reich's findings: two and a half times as many cancer patients as "normals" showed a 50 percent blood cell disintegration within five minutes.[20]

Whether we are dealing with positive or negative replications, the FDA tests opened the way to all kinds of exchanges of views that might have led to further fruitful experimentation. But they were not conducted with this aim in mind. By and large, the FDA's investigators eagerly set about proving the FDA right and were uninterested in any findings that might shake their preconceived judgment. However, these researchers and investigators, usually ineptly and riddled with bias but on occasion more objectively, were attempting to reach the core of the issue—the efficacy of the accumulator. It is by such tests, properly conducted, that Reich's work stands or falls, and he always said as much. It was never, basically, a question of a medical license, whether he carried a gun, or whether the Red Fascists were after him. At issue essentially was whether the accumulator could help heal burns or wounds, and whether or not sick blood disintegrated faster than healthy blood.

A further irony is that for the wrong reasons and usually in the wrong way the investigators (Reich's enemies) were doing what only a few of his friends did: they were making clinical runs, they were measuring the temperature differences, and the like. Reich wanted people to make the tests, not admire or hate him. He might well, like Montessori, have likened his disciples to dogs who look at their trainer rather than at what he is pointing to. His friends were enchanted with him. His enemies hated him and the very idea of what he was talking about. Hardly anyone looked seriously at his work.

Finally, the FDA came up with some very mixed and suggestive findings. At least some of the FDA tests showed some suggestive positive result—not cure-alls, but indices that perhaps something important was at hand here.

David Blasband, a lawyer sympathetic to orgonomy, assessed the approaching legal confrontation, although he was not aware at the time of the FDA test results:

> If Reich had entered a defense . . . I am convinced that the underlying issue would have been the existence and function of orgone energy. The government would have introduced the results of its tests to show the accumulator has no therapeutic effect on mice. Undoubtedly, classical scientists would also have been called by the government as expert witnesses. Reich could then have introduced his own test results as well as evidence of therapeutic experiences. In view of the conflicting testimony, the trier of facts would have been required to determine if a box-shaped structure built only of simple organic and inorganic materials could do what Reich said it could. . . . I think it most unlikely that a judge or jury would have found for Reich. The concept of orgone energy was too new and too simple.[21]

The blow fell on February 10, 1954, when at the FDA's request the U.S. Attorney for the state of Maine filed a complaint for injunction against Wilhelm Reich, Ilse Ollendorff, and the Wilhelm Reich Foundation. On the same day, the federal Attorney General's Office also announced the complaint action for an injunction against interstate shipment of accumulators. It mentioned extensive investigations that proved the nonexistence of orgone energy, and concluded with the charge that the accumulators were "misbranded under the Food, Drug and Cosmetic Act because of false and misleading claims."

The complaint was a twenty-seven-page document containing information about the accumulator and insinuating that Reich was a profiteer on human misery.[22] Orgone energy was declared nonexistent; the accumulator was declared worthless. All Reich's American publications were regarded as promotional material for the accumulator. This was maintained even for works originally published in German prior to the discovery of orgone energy such as *Character Analysis, The Sexual Revolution,* and *The Mass Psychology of Fascism,* since Reich, either in a foreword or in added material, mentioned orgone energy in the English editions of these works.

The complaint argued that although Reich made a disclaimer of a cure from the use of the accumulator, he published case reports where great benefits were reported. However, in many instances the complaint distorted what Reich or others had written. For example, it quoted one of Reich's case histories which stated that a brain tumor was destroyed "as early as two weeks after the beginning of treatment." It omitted the conclusion to the case given in the same paragraph: "But the detritus from the tumor filled and clogged the lymph glands and the patient died."[23]

The complaint concluded with a "prayer for relief," asking that the defendants and "all persons in active concert or participation with any of them, be perpetually enjoined" from shipping accumulators in interstate commerce.

The FDA was entirely within its mandate in this first plea. It was up to Reich in his defense to demonstrate that the FDA's investigation was biased and its tests unscientific. It rested upon him to bring forth his own positive evidence for the accumulator. However, the plaintiff further "prayed" that the defendants and "all persons in active concert or in participation with any of them, be perpetually enjoined from directly or indirectly doing or causing to be done any act, whether oral, written or otherwise in the manner aforesaid or in any other manner, with respect to any orgone energy accumulator device." In this request the FDA demonstrated that it was out to stop not just the accumulator but orgonomic research. For, as Reich later correctly reasoned, almost anything he wrote or said about orgone energy could be construed as being connected, directly or indirectly, with the accumulator. Here the FDA was directly attacking freedom of speech and freedom of the press.

It should be emphasized that the complaint did not in fact seek the destruction or emendation of any of Reich's publications. This goal was revealed, as we shall see, in the injunction decree itself; it was merely inferred by the second part of the complaint's "prayer."

The complaint was signed by Peter Mills, U.S. Attorney for the state of Maine. Here we discern another of the squalid subplots that flicker through Reich's story. For several years, in the late 1940s and early 1950s, Peter Mills had acted as the lawyer for the Wilhelm Reich Foundation. He had even discussed the FDA investigation with Reich. Conceivably, Reich could have made a considerable legal issue of his former lawyer's becoming his prosecutor. But he never chose to do so.

Reich was stunned to receive the complaint from a federal marshal, William Doherty. For three days he could not act. When he recovered from this state of shock, his first response was to consider complying in the eventuality that the Portland court might enjoin the accumulator alone or all of his activities. Initially, Reich was also favorable to the idea of the New York orgonomists, taking over responsibility for the defense of the accumulator in court. According to Baker, "he felt that his responsibility was that of a scientist, making discoveries but not having to defend them in court. However, if the physicians wished to take any action they could." Baker and other orgonomic physicians based in New York obtained an attorney and prepared to enter the case as "friends of the court." Then, says Baker, Reich changed his mind: "I received another call from Reich stating that he had decided to assume charge of the defense himself, and that the accumulators were, after all, his responsibility. He requested that we drop our action, which we did."[24]

Before the injunction hearing, which was scheduled for March 19, Reich sought legal advice from a Maine lawyer. The lawyer said that if he were to represent Reich in court, he would try to have the complaint reduced so that the injunction applied only to the accumulator and not, as it did by implication, to orgonomic literature as well. Reich made it clear immediately that he had no intention of "bargaining" the accumulator for the literature. To do so would be to acknowledge that the FDA was right, even partially.

Thus very early in the actual legal process we see attitudes highly characteristic of Reich. One reaction was to withdraw from the whole matter. In 1935, when Annie was making it difficult for Reich to see his children, he responded with a similar desire to withdraw. Another tendency was to hit wildly at people closest to him. This, too, he showed after the complaint, especially vis-à-vis Ilse, who was still working with him and trying to maintain their relationship. His resolve not to bargain with the FDA or to try to win on technicalities was also evident early on. This position was to make his relations with lawyers, for whom bargaining and technicalities comprised the name of the game, extremely difficult.

Another decision—and a fateful one—was how precisely to meet the complaint, and, in particular, whether to appear in court to oppose the injunction directly. Initially, Reich was leaning toward a court appearance. Here he would have a chance to show the faults in the logic, the methods, the biases of the FDA. Here was his chance to bring forth his own evidence and the evidence of co-workers who had confirmed his findings. Since both the traditionalists, who labeled his device a "fraud," and the innovators could be blinded by self-interest, where else but in a courtroom could a sound judgment be reached? Who else could decide when the new is the future, when it is truly revolutionary science that overturns old paradigms, and when it is a fraud or a delusion?

These were some of the advantages to Reich's appearing in court. Yet from his viewpoint there was one principal reason for not appearing. It involved granting the right of a judge or jury to decide matters of scientific fact. This prospect made Reich exceedingly uncomfortable. However, he was prepared to consider it quite seriously when another factor arose.

Sometime between February 10 and February 24, a meeting took place attended by, among others, Reich, Baker, Chester Raphael, and Michael Silvert. I must here "declare an interest" and comment that I never liked Silvert's fanatical, humorless temperament; he echoed and amplified Reich's belligerent dogmatism but with few of Reich's redeeming virtues. Still, his role in Reich's last years was an important one and I shall try to describe him objectively. Formerly a staff physician at the Menninger Clinic, Silvert had, according to Greenfield, the reputation there of being a talented if somewhat erratic psychiatrist. In his late thirties he left the clinic to undergo training with Reich, but for six years or until around 1954 Reich kept him out of his inner circle. Reich recognized Silvert's destructive characteristics. For example, Silvert commuted frequently between New York and Rangeley, not only because he was still in treatment with Reich but because he wanted to be as close to Reich as possible. He would carry tales of "bad" doings by other orgonomic workers, deeds often distorted or exaggerated in Silvert's retelling. At the same time, Reich was attracted to Silvert's energy, technical intelligence, and dedication. Unlike most orgonomic physicians, Silvert was as interested in Reich's scientific work as he was in his therapy. Also, unlike most of the physicians, who were family men, Silvert lived alone, devoting most of his spare time to orgonomy, and to helping Reich wherever and whenever the latter would permit him to do so. (In turn, some of Silvert's patients, particularly males, were devoted to him and speak well of him to this day.) Where Reich's medical associates were threatened by the possibility of an injunction, Silvert seemed to court such dangers, almost as a kind of exaggeration of Reich's intransigence.

Lois Wyvell, who knew both men well, believes—and I concur—that Reich was fascinated by the challenge of understanding and treating Silvert's destructiveness precisely at a time when the problem of the emotional plague concerned Reich more than any other. If he could help Silvert, Silvert could be a valuable colleague in fighting the plague—Reich always liked (in his image) to put a reformed fox in charge of the chicken coop. If not, Reich hoped he could channel Silvert's gifts and recklessness toward ends of Reich's choosing. However, as we shall see, Silvert's hostile "orgonomic" fanaticism may well have enhanced Reich's irrationality.

Returning to the February meeting, Reich participated in the discussion of alternative ways of dealing with the complaint, and began to lean toward appearing in court. As Baker was later to write,

> the discussion was going smoothly until Dr. Silvert, who was . . . opposed to Reich's appearance in court, asked defiantly: "And what happens to the truth in all this?" The lawyer replied: "It comes out of the embarrassment each side inflicts on the other." Reich became very angry, stopped the discussion, paced the floor and accused those present of trying to entangle him in court action. His appearance in court was no longer considered.[25]

The operative word in this exchange was "embarrassment." Clearly Reich, a proud man, would not like to have mud thrown in his face. And at a trial there would be plenty of it. "Have you a license to practice medicine?

Yes or no, Doctor." Like Freud before him, Reich liked to give, but he deeply resented being "ordered" or "expected" to give. The fact that after doing all that he had done, giving unstintingly of his gifts to science, he should now be called into court and required to face "the embarrassment each side inflicts on the other" was, in his view, unmitigated indecency.

Infuriated, Reich swung hard to the other side: he would not go to court. He then decided on an unusual course of action, and one that was to prove very costly. Instead of appearing in court, Reich opted for a written document entitled "Response." This Response was sent on February 25, 1954, along with a short cover letter, to Judge John D. Clifford, Jr., of the U.S. District Court for the district of Maine, where the complaint had been issued. Reich also sent the court copies of his publications.

The essential position of the Response was that basic natural-scientific research could not be decided in a courtroom. However, Reich was aware of the complications of this position, for his Response stated: "There are conspirators around whose aim is to destroy human happiness and self-government. Is . . . the right of the conspirator to ravage humanity the same as my right to free, unimpeded inquiry? It obviously is *not the same thing.*"[26]

Reich could not resolve the question: Who decides what is basic natural research and what is destructive? His attempt at a solution was unconvincing. To quote in part from his Response:

> It is not permissible, either morally, legally, or factually to force a natural scientist to expose his scientific results and methods of basic research in court. . . .
>
> To appear in court as a *defendant* in matters of basic natural research would in itself appear, to say the least, extraordinary. It would require disclosure of evidence in support of the position of the discovery of the Life Energy. Such disclosure, however, would involve untold complications and *possibly national disaster.*[27]

Reich's threats about disclosure leading to a "national disaster" were irrelevant and histrionic. He could present a substantial defense against the FDA's complaint on the basis of his findings and witnesses and through cross-examination of the government's experts. Nowhere in his Response did Reich deal with the specific FDA complaint, namely, that he made claims regarding the accumulator that were not true. He simply said that the plaintiff "by his mere Complaint already has shown his ignorance in matters of natural science." Since the FDA was saying the same thing about him, who was to decide?

Somehow Reich believed, or at least he hoped, that the judge would be able to tell from his Response and from his literature that Reich was a bona fide scientist, not a quack. Such an unrealistic hope, and such a misunderstanding of the American legal system reveal Reich at his most childishly naive and self-deluding. Had he sent his Response simply as a matter of record, one could respect his principled position even if one sharply disagreed with it. But the combination in Reich of principle plus hope for the principle being understood was as self-deceiving as it was self-destructive.

A third alternative was for Reich to have appeared in court but limited his defense to the constitutional issues. At least he would have had a far greater standing in court than he gained through the written Response. Reich may have thought that his Response was equivalent to this position. It was not taken that way by the court. The judge did give some deliberation to the Response, but then, according to an FDA memo dated March 9, "it appears that the decision has been reached to characterize this document as a 'crank letter.' It will not be construed as an appearance on the part of any one or all the defendants, since . . . there is a waiver to that effect in the document." The waiver referred to is Reich's statement that "I therefore submit, in the name of truth and justice, that I shall not appear in Court as the defendant. . . ."

Judge Clifford, who later proved to be a kindly man in his dealings with Reich, may well have considered informing Reich that his Response had no legal standing prior to the scheduled hearing on the injunction. However, just as Reich was operating in a very ambiguous situation with regard to his own fate, so the judge must have been at a loss to comprehend Reich's Response. Very likely, the FDA representatives painted a picture of Reich as a dangerous manipulator or fanatic who was defying the court. Obviously, their task would be much easier without opposition in the courtroom.

And so it was. When Reich failed to appear, the FDA had a feast of a victory. The resulting injunction itself went further than the complaint in that it specifically included the literature as well as the accumulator.[28] All accumulators leased to patients were to be recalled and destroyed. The FDA seemed to regard the accumulator as simultaneously worthless (accumulating nothing) and dangerous (to be destroyed). The injunction ordered that all in-stock copies of Reich's soft-cover publications, including the *International Journal for Sex-Economy and Orgone-Research,* the *Orgone Energy Bulletin,* and *The Oranur Experiment* should be destroyed. All of Reich's hard-cover books, many of which included only peripheral references to orgone energy, were ordered withheld from further distribution. They could be sold only if Reich deleted "statements and representations pertaining to the existence of orgone energy . . . and allied material." This of course was impossible. As Reich once asked, how would one define "allied material"? Were references to "libido," "bio-electricity," or "streamings" allied material, since in Reich's system all three terms referred to orgone energy?

It is clear that the destruction and withholding of Reich's publications were actions independent of the accumulator. Even after the accumulators were demolished, some literature still had to be destroyed and the rest censored. The rationale for this legalized destructive rage was that the accumulator, though harmless itself, was dangerous because its advocacy could prevent sick people from obtaining effective help. Similarly, Reich's soft-cover publications were treated entirely as instructions for building worthless accumulators, or as promotional material for a fraud. In order to avoid the accusation of book burning, the FDA was glaringly inconsistent. It ordered, for example, the destruction of journals that did not contain as much information about the accumulator as did *The Cancer Biopathy*, a hard-cover book. The latter could still be distributed if Reich deleted references to orgone energy and allied material, albeit an impossible task.

The injunction decree also went slightly further than even the outrageous second part of the complaint's prayer. I shall italicize the significant addition:

> It is ordered . . .
> That the defendants refrain from, either directly or indirectly, in violation of said Act, disseminating information pertaining to the assembly, construction, or composition of orgone energy accumulator devices *to be employed for therapeutic or prophylactic uses by man or for other animals* [italics mine—M.R.S.].

Protecting other species as well as man from the accumulator, the FDA struck a pioneering blow for animal liberation.

In *The Oranur Experiment* Reich wrote that, using the language of emotions, orgone energy responds to nuclear radiation at first with paralysis and later with fury. When he received the complaint, Reich was paralyzed for three days. When he received the injunction, Reich responded with rage.

The particular path of discharge for Reich's rage was a rain-making operation. This plan seems to have been set in motion only hours after he received the injunction decree.[29] He fired off a telegram to Ivan Tannehill of the U.S. Weather Bureau in Washington, D.C., with a copy to Don Kent, weather reporter for WBZ in Boston, announcing his intention:

> According to the Federal Food and Drug Administration, Orgone Energy does not exist. We are drawing east to west from Hancock, Maine, and Orgonon, Rangeley, Maine, to cause storm to prove that orgone energy does exist. Consequences of this action are all your responsibility and that of Federal Judge Clifford of Portland, Maine. We are flooding the East as you are drying out the Southwest. You do not play with serious natural-scientific research.[30]

Snow in Rangeley and rain along the New England coast came after Reich's weather operations; it had not been predicted. As with all of Reich's weather operations, it could be argued that the rain would have come without his intervention. The forecasts may simply have been wrong, as they so often are. In any case, Reich believed he had caused the precipitation. He sent off another telegram declaring this conviction—with copies to the President, J. Edgar Hoover, and the United and Associated presses in Portland, Maine.

Reich's reactions are quite understandable: he wished to demonstrate his power and the reality of orgone energy in as dramatic a way as he could. What is less comprehensible is how he convinced himself that such efforts would have the slightest impact on the authorities. No one knew better than he their capacity to explain away events of this kind.

After Reich calmed down from his initial reaction, he went through a phase of planning to comply with the injunction. On March 30, Ilse Ollendorff, as clerk of the Foundation and one of the defendants, sent a telegram to Mills, advising him that "the Wilhelm Reich Foundation is far advanced in preparing full compliance with injunction."

For a period after the injunction, the Foundation did not send out further accumulators or literature. However, accumulators previously rented were not recalled. The renters were informed of the decree and the decision to keep or return them was left to them. For the most part, the users decided to keep the accumulators.

Reich could have instituted appeal procedures on limited grounds. There was a clear constitutional issue regarding the literature. But he would have none of this. In his eyes, any such appeal would have meant granting the constitutionality of the ban on the accumulator.

Reich's tight linkage of his literature and the accumulator was understandable but ill-advised. It was understandable because Reich had always stressed the unity of thought and action. If birth control was desirable, for example, a true physician did not limit himself to talking or writing about it; he did what Reich did in the 1920s and 1930s—he distributed devices to those, unmarried or married, fourteen or forty, who sought them, whether such distribution was legal or not. Similarly, one not only wrote about or experimented with orgone energy; one made available a device that accumulated the energy's healing properties to those who wished to use it. Paraphrasing Marx, Reich wanted not only to understand the world but to change it. As he wrote in 1942 in an issue of a journal destroyed by the FDA and today a collector's item:

> ... We cannot find consolation in the expectation that our work will "somehow and some day" find general recognition. Our work is neither of the other world, like that of the church, nor of some distant future, as people would like to see it; no, it has its roots in contemporary life, here, today, and in a practical way. We do not intend to wait until, fifty or a hundred years from now, the existence of the orgone may finally be conceded. It is up to us, and not to any so-called "authority," to see that the existence of the biological energy is recognized.[31]

At the same time, Reich's all-or-nothing approach was misconceived. The device for which he claimed certain curative and preventive properties required a legal defense. He had had his opportunity for a "day in court" and he had not taken it. There was no way for the defendants to reopen the injunction decree banning the accumulator. Nevertheless, freedom of speech and freedom of the press are constitutionally guaranteed save under the most exceptional circumstances, such as disclosure of military secrets. Those aspects of the injunction that called for the destruction or censorship of orgonomic literature were unconstitutional and could have been fought on that ground. But Reich chose not to see it that way.

Reich shifted his stance on one issue. Before that injunction he alone took responsibility for the handling of the case; now he adopted the position that the accumulators were the responsibility of the physicians who prescribed them. This led to a new development.

On May 15, 1954, fifteen orgonomic physicians moved to intervene in the government's case against Reich. They argued that their right to practice medicine as they deemed wise was violated by the injunction since they could not prescribe the accumulator to patients. The government had mailed copies of the injunction to them, thereby binding them to its conditions.

"The Court held that the orgonomists did not have the absolute right to intervene since the injunction was *in personam* against Reich, the foundation, and Isle Ollendorff."[32]

An extraordinary inconsistency had now crept into the government's position—and into that of the court. Presumably, their intent was to protect the public from a "misbranded" article, the accumulator. However, the new ruling made it legal for the orgonomists to use the accumulator so long as they did not act "in concert" with Reich or the Foundation. Clearly, the government was less interested in stopping the accumulator than in stopping Reich personally.

The orgonomists' case was appealed through higher courts, including the U.S. Supreme Court. It lost in every hearing. While the first appeal was being heard, Judge Clifford ruled that the part of the injunction ordering the destruction of publications and accumulators be delayed until "final determination of the . . . appeal . . . or . . . further order from this Court." Reich took heart from this ruling. He notified the court that he intended to resume all activities. As Baker commented: "A lack of protest from the court he interpreted as consent and, with the passage of time, acquired a false sense of security, even believing that the case had been won. When reminded that he was only temporarily protected by the orgonomists' action, he could not believe it."[33]

How did the world in general react? The response was an intellectual disgrace. First, there was very little publicity about the injunction itself—brief newspaper or magazine articles stating that the decree had been passed. There was no outrage about the book-burning or book-banning provisions of the injunction. And from professional organizations came more than neglect; they rendered the FDA effusive thanks. To give but a few examples:

Dr. Daniel Blain, medical director of the American Psychiatric Association, wrote the FDA: "We are delighted to hear of the successful prosecution of your action against the Wilhelm Reich Foundation, and I know that I speak for the profession at large in expressing our deep appreciation of the good work of the Food and Drug Administration."[34]

Dr. Richard L. Frank, secretary of the American Psychoanalytic Association, expressed his appreciation as follows:

> . . . The American Psychoanalytic Association wishes to commend the Food and Drug Administration for their effective action in this situation.
>
> Dr. Reich and his associates are not members of the American Psychoanalytic Association and their theories and activities are completely foreign to all of our theories and practices. . . . Unfortunately, we were never in a position to exercise any control over or to influence his activities in any way.[35]

Mildred Brady, whose article had triggered the FDA investigation in the first place, waited until Reich's trial before she wrote to the FDA: "There is a kind of journalistic excitement in learning that an article you wrote years ago has been instrumental in bearing such fruit."[36]

Some institutions responded to the injuction more in relief than in gladness. Charles L. Dunham of the Atomic Energy Commission wrote in part: "I appreciate very much your making this [news of the injunction decree] available to me, as you know only too well what a thorn in the side he [Reich] has been to many of us."[37]

It is sad and ironic to hear Dunham dismiss Reich as some kind of crank. Reich had diligently sent copies of his publications to the AEC. While he maintained orgone energy did not lie within the jurisdiction of the FDA, if it belonged under the jurisdiction of any agency, it was the AEC. Little did he know that he was simply a "thorn in the side" to them.

Reich should have known. Yet typically he had to go on believing. In order to preserve his own sanity, he had to believe something that appeared insane—he had to hope that somewhere, somehow, somebody was out there who would comprehend the truth.

The reader may ask: What about professional people who were not part of the establishment, and what about the general public? Did they not react strongly to the ordered destruction and censorship of literature, to what amounted to book burning? And if not, why not?

With a few exceptions they did not, for a variety of reasons. There was relatively little publicity about the injunction. Nor did Reich's refusal to appear in court win him sympathizers, as would have been the case had he put up a spirited, well-publicized defense. Moreover, only a few thousand people at most had any idea of the rich scientific, medical, educational, and sociological material contained in the journals and pamphlets the FDA ordered destroyed. The professional world and the public took the FDA's word for it: these contained instructions for the construction and use of, or advertisements for, worthless accumulators. True, many found it inconvenient to have *Character Analysis* temporarily unavailable while, presumably, Reich deleted references to orgone energy. But well before the injunction, psychiatric teachers had strongly advised young psychiatrists not to read the last, added chapters in the third edition of this book—sections which, as in the case of schizophrenia, made many references to orgone energy. The "silent generation" of the fifties followed this advice. There was no widespread dissatisfaction with the medical and psychiatric establishments, no "holistic medicine," no—or little—questioning of received opinion. And with Joseph McCarthy riding high, civil libertarians had more comprehensible problems on their hands than the eccentric Reich and his ludicrous "box."

However, the atmosphere of the 1950s and Reich's quixotic defense are insufficient explanations for the lack of outrage over the burning of his publications. In the subsequent thirty years, long after the departure of McCarthy and of Reich, few expressions of indignation have been heard. Jerome Greenfield's detailed study of the FDA investigation was greeted in 1972 with few reviews and a small sale. In a study sponsored by Ralph Nader in 1970, James S. Turner gave some details on the FDA's "vicious campaign" to discredit Reich and his ideas,[38] but that is the only substantial reference to the injunction and its aftermath beyond the circle of Reichian adherents.

In short, the Reich case has not entered public consciousness as a civil liberties scandal of the first magnitude. Yet there have been few other instances of the American federal government's instigating, ordering, and, as we shall see, executing the conflagration of serious scientific literature. It can be argued that only a scientist can pass judgment on the efficacy of the accumulator. But one does not need to be a scientist to be outraged by the burning of books. Why the strange apathy? I must conclude once again with Reich's explanation: People's fear of spontaneous movement not only prevents the serious study of his new paradigms; it also blocks anger toward those who take steps to destroy the evidence for the concepts.

The Arizona Desert Expedition:
October 1954–April 1955

Reich's successful cloud-busting efforts to modify mild droughts in the Northeast led him to believe he might be able to do something to reverse the more severe drought and desert development in the Southwest. Consequently, during the summer of 1954 he made plans for a trip to explore the Arizona area, including sending McCullough there in advance. As with so many activities during this period, there was a double motivation for Reich's Arizona mission. On the one hand, he was pursuing an investigation stimulated by earlier findings. On the other hand, desperate for a way out of the FDA dilemma, he was prodded by the wish to achieve something dramatic. He became more interested in publicity than he had ever been in the past. If his work could become widely known, the chances for overcoming the injunction would increase.

The planned trip added to Reich's financial burdens. The estimated costs were about $2,000 per month to cover research expenses as well as the living needs of Reich, Eva, William Moise, Robert McCullough, and eleven-year-old Peter, all of whom were making the trip. In addition, there were maintenance costs at Orgonon, where Tom Ross was to remain as caretaker. In the face of a dwindling income from accumulator rentals, Reich organized a financial committee consisting of Elsworth F. Baker, Michael Silvert, and William Steig.

Baker, as we have seen, always played a quiet, supportive role. He was highly trusted by Reich, even with the most confidential private matters concerning Ilse and Eva. In turn, Baker always treated Reich with great respect. He offered independent views, and, unlike Silvert, was very much in favor of fighting the injunction in court. However, he did not flatly disagree with Reich very often as Wolfe, Reich's most outspoken colleague, had done; nor was he prepared to do anything in opposition to Reich. Ilse Ollendorff has argued that the New York physicians, led by Baker, should have intervened, even without Reich's approval, at the time of the initial complaint to represent their interests as members of the Wilhelm Reich Foundation. However, such an action would have left Reich feeling totally betrayed.

Silvert's role at Orgonon increased with the expedition. His talents at this time were much in need. He was prepared to give considerable time to administrative matters and he was ready to visit in Arizona if necessary. His intense interest in the cloud-busting work also drew him closer to Reich.

William Steig had become a key person in raising funds for orgonomy during the post-injunction period and, especially, for the Arizona expedition. He continued his independent artistic career and remained in New York City, but he had grown closer to Reich after the Oranur experiment, in which he took a great interest. He kept reports on DOR effects or rough approximations of what today would be called pollution levels in New York, which he sent regularly to Reich.

I have not yet described Bill Moise. His quiet, steady, warm temperament, combined with his loyalty and diligence, made him a valuable aide-de-camp to Reich. As a painter, he was sensitive to the atmospheric nuances Reich emphasized during this period. Bill tended to absorb equally Reich's sound and bizarre ideas; in his case, this seemed to be due more to naïveté than a desire to curry favor. Bill provided a fine balance to his more volatile wife, and a solid, playful source of support for young Peter, who loved him dearly.

There was some tension between those who worked closely with Reich in Maine, such as Eva and Bill, or who followed him absolutely, such as Silvert and Steig, and the New York physicians, led by Baker, who were often uncomfortable with certain of Reich's positions, especially his dealings with the FDA. However, when Reich issued orders everybody fell into line, with greater or lesser importance. Increasingly, Reich saw himself as a general with lieutenants, sergeants, and privates in his small army. At the very least they were locked in a life-and-death struggle against the emotional plague on earth; possibly they were at war with space men. Like a general, Reich demanded and usually obtained total obedience from those around him.*

A very proud member of this stalwart group was Reich's son, Peter, eleven years old at the time of the injunction. Peter has so well described his relationship with his father in *A Book of Dreams* that to go into it here would only dilute it. Suffice it to say, they were very close. Reich always or almost always seems to have treated Peter with great tenderness. Peter was the only person who could cajole Reich out of his angry moods. Peter has related the story of coming home with his mother after a movie during the post-injunction period. While they were away, the water pipes had burst. Reich was furious, blaming Ilse for the trouble. Peter quickly said: "Let me take a picture of you while you are angry. You look good"—a move that defused Reich's rage.[39]

Reich burdened Peter with his plight just as he shared his joys with his son. Peter has recalled Reich's showing him a 45-automatic kept in the lower cabin and saying that he might have to use it on himself should he be unable to face imprisonment. Reich cried at the time, and Peter was one of the few people who saw Reich cry in those last years. For all his emphasis on Peter's having his own career, freely chosen, his father undoubtedly encouraged Peter's vision of himself as a member of Reich's army, and a future worker in the field. Just as he saw Eva at ten years old as a Communist youth leader, so he saw Peter as a cosmic engineer in apprenticeship. And Peter relished the role. Moreover, Reich, especially in the last years with Ilse and after the separation, tended to treat Peter in a fashion similar to the way the young Willy had been treated by his father after the mother's death—as his best friend and "closest confidant."

On his side, Peter generally relished the closeness with his father. However, he hated the fights between his mother and father. At Christmas 1952 he was so upset by their quarrels that he gave neither of them a present. Decades after these events he felt the emotional burden of his father's plight: he could cry more easily for Reich's loneliness during the early 1950s than he could for his own childhood pain.[40] It is also sad that for all Reich's emphasis on the

---

*The associations of his name—to Kaiser Wilhelm and the German nation itself—were never more embodied in his behavior than during this time. The Yugoslav film director Dusan Makaveyev, who made a film about Reich in 1971, has remarked that for a German-speaking boy to have a name like "Wilhelm Reich" at the turn of the century is comparable to a French child of the same period bearing the name "Napoleon France."

"children of the future," two of his own children, Eva and Peter, were to be troubled into adulthood by their divided loyalties to and their contrary identifications with very disparate parents.

There was one other person who was very important to Reich during the period of the Arizona trip. That was my wife at the time, Grethe Hoff. As mentioned in Chapter 2, Reich and she had started a relationship during the fall of 1954 which left me feeling upset and doubly betrayed. Much of Reich's situation during that period was reflected in his move toward Grethe Hoff. He was a very lonely man. His social circle was restricted to co-workers and students. (The women around him were likely to have been ex-patients or married to associates; although Lois Wyvell had been in neither category, Grethe Hoff was in both.) Characteristically, Reich was prepared to take the consequences of his actions. He was serious in his commitment to Grethe and had no intention of conducting a casual or illicit affair. At a later time, he wanted to marry her.

Still, Reich's step was a reckless and impulsive one. I describe it thus not simply because he disrupted people's lives, including the life of our one-year-old son. Such a disruption would have been justified had Grethe Hoff truly loved him and vice versa. However, as later became clear, Hoff was more in awe of Reich the teacher and former therapist than in love with Reich the man. It takes no great analytic insight to perceive that the thirty-year-old Grethe saw in the fifty-seven-year-old Reich a substitute for her own powerful, magnetic father, to whom she had always remained inordinately attached. Reich knew all this and did not know it. If love is blind, so also was Reich's need. Deprived of any consideration from the larger world in his last years, Reich in turn could often show a ruthless inconsiderateness and sense of entitlement toward his colleagues and students.

There was another curious aspect to Reich's love life at the time. When Hoff was debating whether to join him in the late fall of 1954, Reich mentioned to her that *he* was debating whether to ask Marguerite Baker, Elsworth's wife, to accompany him on the trip to Arizona. Perhaps he expressed this wish in order to make Grethe jealous.* However, he had earlier indicated a romantic interest in Mrs. Baker. (I have no evidence that she reciprocated these feelings, though she held and holds Reich in high esteem as a scientist.) Under stress, his infantile Oedipal wishes were reignited, with the triangle now consisting of the "father" taking the "sons' " wives.

After an intense emotional upheaval lasting several months, Grethe Hoff decided to live with Reich shortly before Christmas 1954. Reich had already left for Tucson on October 18. He drove west with Eva, while Peter went with Bill Moise in one of the cloud-buster trucks.

The preparations for the trip, the trip itself, and events in Arizona were

---

*Baker only learned of Reich's thoughts about Marguerite when, to compound an already entangled situation, Grethe Hoff consulted with Baker in December as to whether she should join Reich.

written up by Reich in 1955 in an unusual document entitled *Contact with Space* (published in 1957). I say "unusual" because the book was submitted as part of Reich's court appeals of his later "Contempt of Injunction" verdict. Only a very limited number of copies of this work were available. The book was also extraordinary because of its content. Written under great pressure and disorganized in structure, it blended wild speculation about space ships and blasts at the FDA as well as other enemies with remarkably sensitive observations and acute conceptualizations of the relationship between orgone energy and DOR.[41]

In his description of the trip west, Reich is at his very best. He carefully noted the environment—weather, landscape, pollution—en route. Reich had learned to bring to the landscape the same observational acuity which he had long brought to the observation of patients. He could let the expression of the landscape *impress* him and then render it in words. As he put it: "A landscape has an expression and an emotional flavor like a human being or an animal. To learn to know this flavor and *to live with it* in good comfort takes time, patience, absence of prejudice and arrogant know-it-allness, or similar attitudes adverse to learning."[42]

Thus he described traveling down through Virginia:

> From the mountain ridge at the "Skyline Drive" we saw for the first time the *"Desert Armor."* . . . On the ridge, vegetation and trees looked sparkling, healthier, greener than down in the valley. . . . Below the ridge, one could see the DOR-*layer* all formed, covering the earth to the distant horizon like a blanket, with a sharply delineated upper edge; beneath it the details of distant views were hidden in an opaque veil, as it were. . . . As the ridge road rose over peaks and dipped down into passes, one could subjectively feel the abrupt descent into the DOR layer: as a sudden pressure in head or chest, a sour taste in the mouth. . . . One could also observe that while the trees sparkled and stood erect above the DOR ceiling, they drooped, were withered, and looked dark below it. . . .[43]

When Reich arrived in Arizona at the end of October, he rented a house in Tucson with a large amount of land, calling this base of operations "little Orgonon." There he continued with the development of cloud-busting, augmenting it with material called "Orur." Orur was a milligram of radium from the original Oranur experiment contained in a lead casing. Its long soaking in an orgone energy atmosphere had given it particular properties that, in Reich's opinion, vastly augmented the efficiency of the cloud-buster.

Even before the Orur arrived, flown behind a specially chartered plane with Silvert coordinating the shipment, Reich had been busy for some weeks with the cloud-buster. He claimed to have increased the natural humidity considerably. But he found it much harder to make rain in Arizona than in

New England. He described himself at one point as being "angry" that he was not more successful. Again, there was the dual urgency—for scientific achievement and for dispelling the injunction some way, somehow.

By January 1955, there was considerable rain in the Southwest, which Reich attributed to his operations. One day the humidity at Tucson Airport rose to 96 percent. Most of the evidence Reich presented for the increase in rainfall is anecdotal. There is no careful evaluation of the amount of precipitation during the period of his efforts compared to the amount of precipitation in previous years.

January 1955 was also the month of a fateful decision taken in the Northeast. Silvert had a large truckload of accumulators and literature shipped from Orgonon to his own address in New York City. From there, he was later to distribute both accumulators and literature. The rationale for Silvert's action was that the previous November Judge Clifford had declared that the injunction pertained only to Reich, Ilse Ollendorff, and the Foundation, not to the orgonomic physicians unless they acted in concert with Reich. Yet these actions made Silvert along with Reich a defendant in the later trial for contempt of the injunction.

Silvert and Reich argued subsequently that Silvert acted on his own and that Reich knew nothing about his decision prior to the shipment of the materials. I find it hard to accept such a version. It seems incredible to me that Reich knew *nothing* about the plan. That would be inconsistent with the Reich I knew, for whom no event connected with orgonomy could be viewed with anything less than close attention. Had Silvert genuinely taken it upon his own to act as he did without prior consultation with Reich, Reich would probably have had nothing to do with him thereafter.

Bill Moise never knew exactly what went on between Reich and Silvert, but his best reconstruction of events was that Silvert did discuss the transfer in advance with Reich. Moise believed Reich took the position that if Silvert carried out his plan, he was acting on his own responsibility.[44] In short, Reich gave a qualified green light. I also would speculate with some confidence that Silvert pushed hard for the particular course of action he followed. Later, Reich was to say privately that Silvert wanted to kill him. But it was unfair of Reich to blame Silvert then and unfair of Reich's followers now to blame Silvert for the disastrous legal course Reich pursued. If Silvert's "hard-line" policy prevailed over more moderate advice, it was ultimately Reich who chose which advice to follow.

Shortly before Silvert's action, an FDA agent, along with a federal marshal, visited "little Orgonon" on December 30, ostensibly to see if Reich was manufacturing accumulators on the property. Reich refused to see the inspector, telling the marshal that he wanted nothing to do with the FDA, though he had nothing against the marshal or the marshal's office. Reich erroneously attributed the FDA's visit to its desire to gather information about the Orur, which had arrived a few weeks earlier.[45]

During this period, Reich was making many assumptions about his work and about people, some of which would prove realistic while others were the irrational products of old psychic conflicts exacerbated by current emotional stress. Unfortunately, Reich never had the opportunity to correct his illusions of the 1950s in the way he had corrected earlier ones when there was more time for peaceful reflection.

At the end of April 1955 Reich left Tucson, arriving back at Orgonon in early May. The expedition suffered one casualty. Robert McCullough had a stroke in Arizona—attributed by both Reich and McCullough himself to his cloud-busting work—so he withdrew and went home to Utah to recover. His relationship with Reich remained amicable.

Not long after Reich's return to Orgonon a new blow struck, one that he had courted. On June 16, Peter Mills, at the request of the FDA, instituted contempt of injunction charges against Reich in the U.S. District Court for the state of Maine. On the same day, Judge Clifford issued an order to the defendants—now Reich, Silvert, and the Foundation—to appear in court on July 26, 1955, to show cause why legal proceedings should not be initiated against them.

Background to the Trial for Contempt of Injunction: 1955–1956

The summer of 1955 at Orgonon was lonely and harassing for Reich. Eva and Bill Moise were living in Hancock, Maine. Peter had returned to Sheffield, Massachusetts, where his mother now lived. The only associate Reich saw regularly was his devoted caretaker, Tom Ross.

Grethe Hoff left Reich late in June. He had been very loving to her, yet there were episodes of unfounded jealous rage. At times he was furious at her for what he alleged to be her contempt toward various aspects of his work. Like Ilse, Grethe could not understand—nor would she parrot—Reich's mistaken ideas, such as that Air Force planes were protecting him. Indeed, she was so upset by his blatantly erroneous notions that she wondered whether he was equally mistaken in his cloud-busting work, or even in those aspects of his work such as orgone energy itself that she had previously thought sound. Once again Reich reacted negatively to all criticism from someone close, and once again that person was not prepared to work arduously at distinguishing between her rational or irrational reactions (or so he concluded). Hoff was also disturbed by his isolated, endangered situation and by the discrepancy in their ages. She wanted a more normal existence, a desire Reich ascribed to her "will to smallness." Finally, she decided to return to Norway that summer.

For some weeks Reich wrote to her imploring her to return. He apologized for his earlier angry outbursts. Still, he believed her main reason for leaving was that she was "running away," not from him but from herself. When she remained firm in her decision to stay in Oslo, his depression did not last long. Soon enough his energies refocused on his work and legal battles.

First, he had to prepare for the July 26 hearing to show cause why legal proceedings against him for contempt of the injunction should not be initiated. During this period his main legal adviser was Charles Haydon, the one lawyer among several Reich consulted who managed to maintain a relation of some solidity and duration with Reich, a very unusual client.

Haydon had first met Reich in the spring of 1954, when he was being considered by the New York physicians to represent them. On this first visit to Orgonon, he made a favorable impression on Reich by noticing a smell. Reich asked him what he smelled. Haydon described an acrid odor. Since Reich believed this was a characteristic smell of Oranur, he was pleased with Haydon's response. As he said, he could tell that Haydon was quite "open and unarmored."[1]

Thereupon began a long and from Haydon's viewpoint very valuable relationship. The two men argued frequently about how the case should be conducted, but Haydon respected the way Reich pursued the argument even if he didn't always agree with it.

One of the points of contention was Reich's basic tenet that the courts lacked jurisdiction over science. Haydon told Reich that he agreed with the position, but legally it did not work that way and Reich could not change it. Also, there was the problem that somebody had to protect the public against real fraud. Reich's position was that while the courts did not have jurisdiction over "legitimate science," they *did* have jurisdiction over "illegitimate science." In an interview with me, Haydon made the point that Reich never really understood the democratic process; he had an elitist notion of how things should be, with "rational" people like himself determining what was legitimate and illegitimate science.

Given Reich's viewpoint that the courts lacked jurisdiction, he would not accept Haydon's proposal to appeal the original injunction since this would be acknowledging the court's authority. Haydon had wanted Reich to appeal on some kind of "special basis," but for Reich that was just a "technicality." Again and again the issue of technicalities came up between Reich and Haydon. Reich kept saying he wasn't going to play the "game of technicalities," while Haydon maintained it was the only game in town.

What did Haydon learn for his own professional life from Reich? One lesson was that, in Reich's words, "people cannot lie"; one way or another, through grimace, body movement, or whatever, the truth emerges. Reich attributed such revelation to "the energy of truth." Apparently, this affected Haydon's life and his practice of law. For example, in cross-examinations, he found that while witnesses were well prepared to defend themselves on central issues, they would reveal the truth, if questioned cleverly, on peripheral matters. Reich appreciated this technique.

Haydon was also impressed by Reich's critique of the criminal justice system. Reich was against labeling people criminals; that was dealing with symptoms rather than causes. He wanted to see boards of social psychiatry established to get to the root causes.

As for his own case, Reich experienced some dissatisfaction with Haydon's view and attempted to engage another lawyer to represent him at the July 26 hearing, with Haydon representing Silvert and the Foundation. Reich was especially interested in obtaining a lawyer more supportive of his basic position in matters of natural science and more prepared to raise the issue of what Reich regarded as the conspiratorial aspects of the FDA. I am not sure who recommended James St. Clair of the law firm of Hale and Dorr, Boston. In any case, St. Clair decided not to take the case. He believed that Reich had had the opportunity to raise the kinds of issues that concerned him but had not taken it.

St. Clair in turn suggested Frederick Fisher of the same law firm. (A year earlier, at the time of the Army-McCarthy Hearings, Fisher had been viciously attacked by Joseph McCarthy for some youthful left-wing activities, a fact that did not disturb Reich for all his Red Fascist emphasis of those days.) Initially, Fisher was as reluctant to take on the case as St. Clair had been. He believed Reich had defied the injunction and was guilty of contempt. However, after a subsequent telephone conversation with Haydon, Fisher, now intrigued, agreed to appear at the hearing.

The hearing was scheduled for the afternoon, in Portland, Maine. During the morning, Reich met for a conference with a small group of associates—Drs. Baker, Raphael, Duvall, Handelman, Sobey, and Anderson; Michael Silvert, James Willie, Eva, William Steig, the lawyers Haydon and Fisher, and me. I was present because in the late spring of 1955 I had begun working for Reich again, now on a part-time basis from Boston. My main task consisted of preparing material for publication and keeping historical records.

Using notes I made at the time, let me summarize some of the points Reich made. He wanted his lawyers to help him get through to the *factual* issues: the fact of the conspiracy behind the injunction, the fact of orgone energy, the fact that the emotional plague enmeshed everyone. He said that as long as they stuck to legal, procedural issues, they would never get through. Furthermore, the emotional plague was infinitely better at this kind of maneuvering.

Reich emphasized several times that the doctors should be aware that they were the *first physicians* of the emotional plague, that this was an awesome responsibility, that the plague was an epidemic and more devastating than any disease in the history of mankind. What they would have to learn was to bring the plague out into the open, to bring character analysis from "the little therapy office" onto the public scene, and to practice "social psychiatry." He was grateful for the rich experiences he had had in fighting the plague, grateful that decades ago he had broken away from a narrow private practice. Now he felt that he was returning actively to the public fight for these issues, as he had done during his sex-economic period.

One physician raised the question: Given the fact that his opponents were in desperate need of social psychiatry, but were "reluctant patients," how did one get through to them? Reich saw it as a question of hitting through their armor, of "drawing out the human being in them." Whether to do this all at once, or slowly, depended on what transpired. It was a question of knowing how to operate, like a skilled surgeon, and for this operation "no knife has been invented yet."

I am impressed still by Reich's lucidity and depth. With the major exception of his continued assertion of a Red Fascist conspiracy, his remarks—and under this kind of pressure—stand the test of time. Unfortunately, there was no way these particular insights could be raised in court or be effective there.

At the hearing, Reich, Silvert, and Moise (representing the Wilhelm Reich Foundation) were the defendants. About twenty of Reich's supporters were present in the courtroom. Joseph Maguire and Peter Mills represented the government. Maguire was a tall, pale, dour man, though not the vicious-looking creature one might have expected from Reich's delineation of the FDA. It was strange to see Mills—short, bland, and smiling—representing the government after his participation as lawyer for the Foundation in many candid discussions with Reich. Judge Clifford was white-haired, gaunt but kindly-looking.

Haydon presented his arguments first. He also opposed, on constitutional grounds, the FDA's right to subpoena Reich's files. Maguire spoke next— simply and fairly factually. He wanted to get rid of the accumulators, as the injunction had decreed. Reich wouldn't let him, Silvert wouldn't let him; they refused entry to FDA agents who had the job of carrying out the injunction. The FDA wanted to eliminate the "worthless" accumulators. (Reich shot a stern look at Maguire in response to the pejorative adjective.)

Reich and Silvert were asked to stand and plead "guilty" or "not guilty." Reich started to say a few words at this point, but was told by Fisher that his statement should be made after the plea. Reich had an aversion to the legalistic form of the plea, as he was to explain later. He finally said "not guilty," as did Silvert. Then Reich asked to say a few words. The judge nodded.

Reich went to the front of the courtroom and, standing, spoke briefly but forcefully. He began by explaining that it was impossible factually to plead either guilty or not guilty. What the injunction demanded was impossible to fulfill. He could not get the accumulators back even if he asked for them. He could not get the literature back—it was in the hands of publishers all over the world. The accumulators, the books, his discoveries were on their way, far into the world, and it was impossible to fulfill an injunction that ordered him to do anything about it.

Reich also explained why he had not appeared in court originally. Among his reasons was that basic science must remain outside the jurisdiction of the courts, and it was for that principle that he was fighting.

At one point Reich turned directly to Maguire and said: "You are not honest!" Maguire had cited one letter from Reich to Baker, a letter published in a limited edition of *Conspiracy*.[2] He asked Maguire why he had not cited other material, such as the Brady article, from the same volume. He also accused him of deliberately and maliciously using as a courtroom exhibit an old, dilapidated accumulator rather than a new one, in order to make Reich look like a fraud.

Reich's voice shook with emotion when he confronted Maguire directly. As his emotions mounted, Fisher anxiously got up in order to warn Reich not to go too far. However, the judge, who was kindly to Reich throughout, gently beckoned him and Reich quickly restrained himself. He told the judge that he had gone too far and would retract what he had said. Reich went on to tell Maguire that he no longer thought he was the main force behind the injunction and that the FDA was behaving better these days, they were no longer badgering patients.

Reich became very strong and vehement again when, directing his words to Maguire, he said that no matter what they did to him—jail, chains, fine— he would never permit Maguire to say anything about orgone energy and the accumulator. Matters of science were not to be decided in court; the court could not say whether the universe was empty or full of orgone energy. When *that* happened, there was no longer any freedom in the United States—this was the way it was behind the Iron Curtain. Reich spoke movingly of Giordano Bruno's fate, Bruno who had been hunted down for seven years by a man named Mocenigo and who finally died at the hands of the Inquisition. Centuries later, a Pope apologized at Bruno's grave. Amid such courageous sentences Reich also spoke nonsense, with references to his support in high government circles.

There was one very human moment when Reich, talking about the Foundation, turned to Peter Mills and said, smiling: "Do you remember when we formed the Foundation together, Mr. Mills?" After Reich's statement, the judge said he would examine the lawyers' briefs.

I rode back to Boston with Fisher, who remarked that he had never seen a day in court like it. Still, his main objective was to find a way to "settle the case." He thought he could get an agreement with the court permitting Reich to do anything except send accumulators into interstate commerce. Reich would never have agreed to such a plan, but Fisher's stand was: "I'm an expert in law and it is on those grounds that Reich must swim or sink." Fisher's insistence on legally sound procedures soon led to his leaving the case.

A further pre-trial hearing took place on November 4, which I also attended. The same people appeared, with two exceptions: neither Haydon nor Fisher was present, though Haydon continued to serve as a consultant. Reich had decided to be his own counsel.

At this hearing, Reich presented a motion to establish a "Board of Social

Pathology" to examine the whole case on an educational and medical level. The chemically-minded, the orgonomically-minded could sit down together peacefully and assess the facts. In a switch of emphasis, Reich said that this proposal assumed the FDA had acted out of ignorance rather than malice.

The judge asked Maguire if he had anything to say. Maguire said he had not been listening. The judge ruled that he lacked the authority to establish such a board.

Reich's next motion concerned various misrepresentations by the FDA. The judge ruled that all such issues belonged in the original hearing when Reich had not appeared; there was no further recourse.

Reich had taken various other rulings with equanimity. However, this new ruling clearly hurt. He asked, almost pleadingly, if there was no opportunity now to go into these issues. There was not, repeated the judge. Reich said he could not appear at the original injunction hearing without "being smothered," that he had to prepare his evidence. Reich kept changing his reasons for his original nonappearance, an indication to me that he was not presenting his essential motives, namely, his pride and his fear of being humiliated.

The judge also ruled favorably on FDA subpoena requests for various Foundation records. When Reich heard this ruling, he said he did not know whether to obey; issues of conscience were involved. The judge firmly asserted that this was a court order. Reich had always acted with the utmost sincerity, so he did not believe Reich would ever consciously disobey an order of the court. Reich replied: "I understand. I know what the word 'obey' means." He went on to say that if he gave any information to the FDA, he could not take responsibility for what might happen. The judge said he understood and the responsibility would be the FDA's and the court's. He seemed quite relieved that Reich would comply with his ruling on the subpoenas.

In spite of the legal defeats, Reich left the courtroom in surprisingly good spirits. He looked forward to more of the issues coming out in the trial for contempt of injunction, a trial scheduled to come before a full jury because Reich was charged with criminal contempt.

During the summer and fall of 1955, consumed as he was by legal matters, Reich also continued his scientific work, devoting considerable time to the DOR-buster. In late August that year he held a seminar on the subject, at which I was present.

Reich's mood was serious, but I recall being impressed by how little the injunction itself was discussed. He was concerned with DOR and its relationship to unimpeded natural orgone energy, and conducted clinical demonstrations that involved a combination of psychiatric techniques with the use of the medical DOR-buster (see Chapter 26). In those days he was especially alert to gray or "dark" coloring in a person's face or body—for him an indication of the accumulation of DOR. "You look black," was one of the descriptions he would apply to people. There were fewer smiles and jokes than there had been at past conferences; the mood was grim at times. Reich had some kind of throat problem, so he wore a scarf at his neck. The scarf, along with his wool shirt and khaki pants, highlighted his resemblance to a guerrilla chief.

It was at this time that I resigned my part-time position with the Foundation. One factor was my disagreement with Reich over his emphasis on the Red Fascist role in obtaining the injunction; there were also the personal reasons discussed earlier.

I was never aware of Reich's loneliness during the summer of 1955, but others saw it. Gladys Meyer met him inadvertently in the main Rangeley shopping area. When she asked him how he was, he answered with uncharacteristic self-pity that he was eating out of cans. (Reich did not like to cook for himself, nor did he particularly enjoy eating out. He felt stared at in Rangeley restaurants.) Meyer offered to bring dinner to Orgonon. Reich accepted. When she arrived with a picnic-style meal, she found him dressed rather formally in a suit and tie, which was not his usual style. By that time the large first-floor room of the Observatory had been redecorated and included fine furniture and rugs. Reich talked of how high government officials might visit him. He played the organ and spoke of rereading *The New Testament* and Rousseau's *Confessions.* For Meyer, the evening had an elegiac, disturbing quality. She was touched by Reich's reaching out for contact but worried by his illusions concerning prominent visitors.

Gladys Meyer saw not only Reich's loneliness but also his rage. On one occasion they again met accidentally in Rangeley and Reich asked her to go for a drive with him. In the course of the conversation, she mentioned a loan Wolfe had made to Reich. After Wolfe's death, Gladys Meyer had told Reich to forget about it, but upon further reflection she now felt that her daughter (ten at the time) might later need the money. Erupting in rage, Reich took Gladys back to her car. Two hours later he went to her cabin and apologized.[3]

Gladys Meyer's request for the return of her husband's loan joined other indications that many of his students were no longer prepared to give him the degree of support they had once extended. The educator Alexander ("Tajar") Hamilton, who for years had studied with Reich and corresponded warmly and admiringly with him, began to rebel in the post-Oranur period. On June 23, with the trial in the offing, Hamilton wrote Reich that he found "everything that has come out of Orgonon since Oranur . . . rationalized defenses against untenable positions."

This kind of indiscriminate criticism was no more helpful than the attitude of other colleagues who always found Reich right no matter what he did. But responses like Hamilton's indicated to Reich that many were abandoning him.

Ilse Ollendorff has written of Reich's mood that summer:

> With the loneliness and frustration . . . his basic optimism must have faltered. Reich must often have sensed that the final outcome might

be rather grim. His health was not good; his heart was bothering him.
. . . He had always been concerned about what would happen to his
remains if he should die, and he now began to prepare in earnest for
a tomb—or mausoleum—at Orgonon. . . . [There was] one spot on
the hill where the observatory was built, where often before he had
said he would like to be buried. He now had Tom Ross, the caretaker,
begin digging out a place for a tomb.[4]

Reich was not totally without consolation during the summer. At the
seminar on the DOR-buster, he met Aurora Karrer, a woman of thirty-one
at the time. As a biologist who was employed by the National Institute of
Health in Washington, Karrer had long been an admirer of Reich's. I met her
only twice briefly and spoke just a few words with her.[5] She was very attractive,
dark-haired, resembling the Tahitian women in Gauguin's paintings, which
Reich greatly admired.

An intense relationship developed. Aurora Karrer seems to have rekindled a depth of romantic feeling Reich had not experienced for many years,
an intensity heightened by his perilous legal predicament. However, there were
difficulties, the precise nature of which I do not know save that they included
Reich's old problem of jealousy. His angry outbursts were frequent and Karrer
would sometimes leave him unpredictably.[6]

In spite of all Reich's legal strains and personal upheavals in the post-
injunction period, his flow of scientific publications did not cease. As mentioned in Chapter 28, Reich in 1955 changed the name of the *Orgone Energy
Bulletin* to *CORE* (standing for cosmic orgone engineering) to reflect his
continuing work. In 1954, he published one large issue devoted to problems of
weather modification and drought, with a report on his experiences up to the
Arizona expedition; in 1955, two more issues of *CORE* appeared. The first
contained a description of his trip to Arizona. It also included a preliminary
paper by Reich on some of his chemical investigations concerning DOR.

The same issue contained a summary by Chester Raphael of a small
seminar on DOR-sickness that Reich had held at Orgonon on August 26 and
27, 1953. Reich made several important distinctions at this conference that
merit a brief description.

He distinguished between Oranur sickness and DOR-sickness. "Oranur
sickness" referred to the organismic response to the experimental use of radium in an atmosphere (Orgonon) highly charged with orgone energy. The
Oranur experiment provided a way of understanding the global "DOR-sickness." The latter stemmed from a variety of irritants or pollution, which
changed orgone energy into a malignant force.

The effect of pollutants on orgone energy, transforming it into DOR, in
turn led to DOR-sickness in man. Reich also stressed that DOR-sickness
brought out latent and specific emotional vulnerabilities within individuals.

In the second issue of *CORE,* published in December 1955, Reich continued his elaboration of themes presented in Raphael's summary. Reich's emphasis here was on the build-up of DOR through the armor. Orgone energy that could not circulate freely within the organism was transformed into DOR, just as atmospheric orgone energy was when irritated by pollutants. During his Arizona trip, Reich was struck by parallels between the physical desert there and the emotional desert in man. The bristles of desert plants, the prickly outer behavior of armored human beings—this is the kind of analogy Reich was drawn to in his last years.

In Arizona, Reich had seen the desert fight hard, so to speak, against his cloud-busting activities. The removal of DOR, the bringing in of fresh orgone energy meant an end of existing secondary desert vegetation. Similarly, the discovery of orgone energy, as well as of the armor, meant eventually an end to the complex, armored, "secondary" forms of living in man. Reich used his understanding of DOR to comprehend in greater depth one of his earliest clinical concerns, latent negative transference and negative therapeutic reaction. His latest formulation posited that armored people dimly knew the "dirty feelings" their armor contained. The negative transference could be viewed as a heightening of awareness in the face of the threatened therapeutic exposure of the dirtiness. Nonetheless, the road to health required a revelation of this "sequestered realm of the self."[7]

Reich's various selves were functioning to the end, and in his best moments, as in this paper, he could stand aside from pettiness and rage; he could, despite gross harassment, clearly strive for that sober pursuit of truth that characterized all phases of his life in spite of recurrent "little man" outbursts. He could put aside extravagant claims in order to present a lucid argument in a tone that was deep and quiet.

Reich may have been quite wrong about the role of DOR in the atmosphere and the organism. However, I must repeat my conviction: his paradigm, with its unification of man and nature and its energetic model of life and death, holds such possibilities that it behooves us to find out how right or wrong it is. To paraphrase Pascal's wager, we lose more by failing to pursue orgonomic hypotheses with all due speed should they eventually prove to be correct than we do by testing them thoroughly only to find they are worthless.

Another issue of *CORE* contained a compilation by Eva Reich of clinical material for a uterine case Reich had followed since 1942. This was the only medical report on accumulator usage published by Reich after the injunction. He gave the FDA nothing, for the article, in defiance of the injunction, showed positive results from the use of the accumulator. After two months of treatment, the patient felt considerably stronger.[8]

Most significant was Reich's recommendation back in 1943 that the patient's uterus be removed. He had recommended this step on the basis of various orgonomic tests. The patient's gynecologist, who used classical criteria of cancer diagnosis, had been against a hysterectomy. In 1947, an emergency operation was performed on the patient, but the uterus could not be extirpated because by then the tissue had become too brittle for suture. The patient died that same year. Reich believed the outcome confirmed his original diagnosis, but one could not say whether the removal of the uterus in 1943 would have prevented death.[9] At the same time, the outcome was far from optimistic. Perhaps she died because the recommended classical technique (surgery) was *not* used on the advice of a classical physician. Thus, Reich hit the FDA twice: the accumulator worked *and* he was not against other treatments for patients, notwithstanding the FDA's repeated assertion that his patients were deprived of legitimate treatment.

During 1955, at Reich's suggestion, Elsworth Baker began to edit and publish the journal entitled *Orgonomic Medicine*. It was devoted to clinical, social, and educational subjects, leaving *CORE* as the publication for natural-scientific research. Two issues of *Orgonomic Medicine* were published in 1955, one in 1956. Determined to keep track of developments in all his work, Reich remained in close contact with Baker about the journal. The FDA must not stop orgonomy.

In November 1955, Reich took up winter residence in Washington, D.C., living at Alban Towers, 3706 Massachusetts Avenue. Probably the most important reason was to be near Aurora Karrer. Other factors were undoubtedly his absorption with legal issues, his desire to be close to the center of American government, and the fearsome isolation of Rangeley winters. Aurora spent considerable time with him. Eva and Bill Moise often came to Washington to be near Reich, while Peter visited during his school vacations. Reich and Ilse had maintained a friendly relationship after their separation and both participated in any decisions concerning Peter's welfare.

To protect his privacy, Reich lived under the assumed name of Walter Roner.[10] (The court, as well as all his associates, knew his whereabouts.) Living in a large city again gave him an anonymity he enjoyed. Unlike Rangeley, he could now go places without being noticed. And even though the forthcoming contempt trial was imminent, he appears to have sought out relaxation more than at any other time in the American period. He sent Peter a copy of the program for a performance at Constitution Hall of the Westminster Choir on February 25, 1956, which he probably attended with Aurora. Pieces by Mozart, Randall Thompson, and Tom Scott were circled with the notation "very good."

Reich loved the city of Washington. Its classical architecture and total design greatly appealed to him. On Peter's vacations they both enjoyed exploring the city and its suburbs. Reich thought he might one day acquire a home in Maryland or Virginia; Peter even has a photograph of one particular house Reich wanted to buy.

Reich lived quite comfortably in the Alban Towers and ate in good restaurants. Indeed, after the injunction, he permitted himself more creature comforts than he had done for decades. He had already refurnished the first floor of the Observatory, and for his trip to Arizona he bought an expensive white Chrysler convertible.

It was characteristic of Reich to expand his scale of living only after he had been accused of swindling by the FDA. It was as though he were saying: For years I sacrificed everything for my work and now you accuse me of running a moneymaking fraud. So I intend to live well. It was as though the sentence confronting him released personal desires he had long restrained. He embarked on relationships with women (Grethe, Aurora) that were not centered upon work and a quiet routine as his marriage to Ilse had been.

There is also evidence that Karrer was less submissive than most of his American associates. In a letter from Washington to Peter, he commented that "people" now treated him more as they used to treat him in the 1920s. I take that reference to mean that people, especially Aurora Karrer, were less afraid of him.

He was concerned about Aurora's well-being, for example, urging Peter to try to be friendly to her. (Not surprisingly, Peter did not especially take to this woman who had usurped his mother's role.) And he did other things that differed from his usual pattern, letting Aurora drive his car while he was in it, for instance. Usually in the past, with his need for control, he had always insisted on driving.

Reich's attentiveness to Karrer should not be taken to mean that he was about to alter any basic tenets in order to please her. At some point in their relationship, Karrer made clear that she wished to be legally married. But after his various experiences, Reich was wary of legal marriage and the claims partners can exert upon one another, although perhaps with jail as a distinct possibility he now desired this step.

However, he held to his principles about the conditions of any marriage. In January 1957 he had his lawyer draw up an agreement between Aurora Karrer and himself, an agreement covering in detail the financial responsibilities of the two partners. It is illuminating to see Reich, given all his legal burdens, carefully working out a marriage contract with Aurora Karrer, more in the fashion of the 1970s than the 1950s. I do not know if this contract was ever signed; but it never became operative as they never legally married.

Whatever peace Reich found for himself in Washington did not last for long. Toward the end of April 1956 he received news of his forthcoming trial, to be held in Portland, Maine.

30

The Trial: 1956

The trial date, originally scheduled for December 1, 1955, was postponed until March 6, 1956. It was changed once more and a definite date set for April 30. Clifford, whose wife was very ill, asked to be excused from serving as judge; he was replaced by Judge George C. Sweeney.[1]

When Reich received notification of the trial, he was upset that the notification was signed by the clerk of the court rather than by the judge himself. Throughout the legal proceedings Reich became very perturbed by such minor points, to the distress of his lawyers. In this instance, Reich wrote to Judge Sweeney on April 24, stating that if he did not receive a properly signed notification for the new trial date, he would assume he did not have to appear in court. Once again Reich took a judge's failure to respond as a sign of agreement and thought he did not have to appear.

He did have to. Reich was arrested in Washington; Silvert, who complied with Reich's interpretation, in New York on May 1. Reich spent the night of May 1 in a Washington jail. On May 2, both were brought in handcuffs to Portland, where they spent another night in jail. Reich had often said that even if "they" put him in "chains," he would not relinquish his position. Now he had brought this to pass but over a quibble. The judge later found Reich and Silvert in contempt for not appearing on time. He fined Reich $500 and Silvert $300.

The trial itself started at ten o'clock on May 3. Reich served as lawyer for Silvert, the Foundation, and himself. He had always wanted to examine his witnesses and cross-examine the government's should a trial occur, so there was little place for Haydon in the courtroom, though the relationship between the two men remained cordial.

446

About forty of Reich's friends (including Aurora Karrer) and followers were present in the courtroom. I attended the first, third, and fourth days. Much of the following description is based on my notes made at the time.

The jury was speedily seated, with only one juror challenged. It looked like a movie jury—extremely typical of the American populace down to one black person. There were several middle-aged women.

Maguire made his opening address to the jury, stating that he was going to prove that Reich and Silvert had committed contempt. Reich, who along with Silvert pleaded "not guilty," began his opening statement, attempting to convey some of the broader issues he wanted to go into, but the judge soon cut him off, telling him to limit himself to the issue of proving he had not committed contempt. The confusion of the whole trial became manifest here since Reich was clearly not out to deny that he had violated aspects of the injunction and that he felt he had to violate them. He was pleading innocent on deeper grounds—that the injunction was unconstitutional and unfairly brought in the first place.

Judge Sweeney was a round-faced man who resembled Winston Churchill. He was pink, debonair, quick-minded, and there was often a slight irony to his remarks. He seemed a less kindly man than Clifford, yet much stronger and more independent. He struck me as very fair. As impatient as he became with Maguire's long-drawn-out proving of the obvious, he was equally impatient when Reich tried to bring in issues Sweeney thought irrelevant, but he softened toward Reich during the course of the trial.

The first witness called by the government was Ilse Ollendorff. She was a fine witness, perhaps the clearest and most secure of any that took the stand during the trial. She tripped up Maguire on several points: at one time when he tried to link all the literature with the accumulator, she made it clear that only a very few pieces, such as the catalogue of types of accumulators and the instruction sheet, went out to those who ordered the accumulator. Perhaps the weakest part of her testimony in terms of logic was her statement that Reich and she had not complied with the injunction in the immediate months after the decree because the FDA had not sent anyone around to supervise its execution; it later became clear that Reich had no intention of cooperating with any FDA agents. Still, Ms. Ollendorff was testifying to events that took place while she was at Orgonon.

In his cross-examination, Maguire constantly tried to create a picture of a "business" activity with a sinister, racketeering connotation. He used such terms as a "drop in New York" and "big boss" (to describe Reich). In his cross-examination of Ilse Ollendorff, Reich set the style for most of his later cross-examinations: he would ask one or two questions for the purpose of eliciting a factual answer. He asked her, for example, what the money from accumulator rentals was used for and she replied, for research, salary of employees, and so on. The question was objected to and the objection sustained, but the jury heard her answer.

The next witness was an accumulator user from New York. He shuffled to the stand looking like the epitome of a deeply sick neurotic. Maguire spent a very long time (clearly irritating the judge) with this witness in order to elicit the simple point that he had continued paying accumulator rentals after the injunction had been issued. In his cross-examination, Reich asked the witness if the accumulator had helped or hindered him. The witness said it had helped. Maguire objected to the question and the judge ordered it and the answer stricken from the record.

Tom Ross then testified that Silvert had taken books and accumulators from Orgonon, evidence the government needed to establish its case that Silvert had acted "in concert" with Reich in violating the injunction. A man who built accumulators at the Rangeley workshop testified that either Silvert or Ross had taken accumulators out of the workshop after the injunction. In his cross-examination, Reich asked the worker how he tested the accumulators he built. The witness mentioned holding his hand close to the walls and was going to continue when the judge, after an objection from Maguire, ruled the question out of order since it bore on the efficacy of the accumulator rather than on the narrow question: contempt or not contempt. After his testimony, the Maine workman made a point of going over to shake hands warmly with Reich.

A federal marshal from Tucson, Arizona, then testified that he had been permitted entrance to Reich's home in Tucson but the accompanying FDA agent had been barred. The marshal also mentioned looking through a telescope at Reich's property—a glimmer of scientific instruments and events constantly flickered through the morass of technical administrative details (payment of checks, delivery of accumulators, etc.).

On Friday, May 4, I was not present. The day was devoted to government witnesses and to proving the obvious and undisputed. May 5 continued with the government's case. Maguire examined William Moise to show that accumulator rentals, gathered by Silvert after the injunction, were sent to help support Reich's research in Arizona. Silvert was also questioned about his taking books and accumulators from Orgonon, renting accumulators in New York, and the like. In his cross-examination, Reich wanted to have the point brought out that Silvert had been declared exempt from the injunction during the intervention case, in other words, when the injunction applied only to Reich, Ollendorff, and the Foundation. Both Moise and Silvert wished to establish that Reich had *not* known about Silvert's removal of books and accumulators from Orgonon, although this was, as we have seen, a somewhat ambiguous point.

Before the noon recess, Reich began calling his witnesses. There was a brief discussion between Reich and the judge as to what defense material Reich could admit. The judge ruled against Reich's arguing the validity of the original injunction or of anything not pertinent to the fact of obedience or disobedience of the injunction. Reich was allowed a wider range in his summation to the jury but nowhere else.

Reich's total time for questioning defense witnesses was not more than an hour and a half. The essential point he wished to establish was that the injunction had been resisted to the utmost, or, more precisely, that FDA agents were barred from Orgonon. McCullough testified to carrying a gun and being under instructions to keep the FDA agents away. The judge interrogated McCullough as to whether he was actually prepared to use the gun. McCullough emphasized its warning function, but did not preclude the possibility that certain circumstances might have compelled its use. Ross testified along similar lines. Under questioning by Reich, he also told of being asked to dig a grave during the summer of 1955 and said that Reich was prepared to die resisting the injunction.

Albert Duvall, M.D., testified that he would not have requested his patients to return their accumulators even if Reich had asked him to do so, and that Reich had an affidavit from him to this effect.

Perhaps the most interesting examinations occurred when Reich called first Maguire and then Mills to the stand. Reich tried to establish the point that Maguire had in fact read the *Conspiracy* volume. Maguire denied that he had. With Mills, Reich had the following exchanges:

REICH: The fact that I want to establish here is only one. You were for three years—for more than three years—a good friend of ours and a counsellor?
MILLS: That's correct. I was professionally, but not intimately.
REICH: There was some private contact?
MILLS: Yes, a cup of coffee.
THE COURT: With cream and sugar in it?
REICH: That's right![2]

And a few minutes later, during the same examination:

REICH: My question is, under the circumstances, what reasons, or what facts induced Mr. Mills after being our counsel for three years, and I regarded him as a good friend, to be our opponent's counsel, and the one to prosecute me and Dr. Silvert as criminals?
THE COURT: That is a fair question if there is anything.
MR. MILLS: The question is, what prompted me?
REICH: What made you change your mind?
MR. MILLS: I have never changed my mind. I am not conscious of changing my mind.
THE COURT: Wait a minute. The original question was, what prompted you to change sides.

MR. MILLS: I never changed sides . . . I never advised you on matters concerning the Pure Food and Drug Administration.[3]

Later that day, Reich produced minutes of a meeting of the Wilhelm Reich Foundation held in 1952 which Mills attended and at which the FDA investigation was discussed. Maguire tried to make the case that once Mills was district attorney and the Reich matter was referred to him by the Department of Justice, he had no choice but to direct the legal action. The judge curtly commented: "We all know he may have assigned it to someone else if he did not care to sit on it."[4]

Undoubtedly, Mills's role could have been exploited by Reich far more than it was, not only in the trial but in subsequent appeals. It was the one action on the government's side that clearly angered Judge Sweeney. But Reich remained adamant: it was a "technicality."

During a recess on May 5, Ilse Ollendorff asked to speak with the judge.[5] She was much incensed that Maguire had denied seeing the *Conspiracy* volume. While she had been waiting in Portland for the trial to begin, Mills and Maguire had asked her if she would initial some Foundation documents in order to speed up proceedings. She agreed, and in the course of carrying out this request, noticed with surprise that Maguire had a copy of the *Conspiracy* volume.

The judge then advised Ms. Ollendorff to tell Reich about the incident with Maguire, and to have Reich examine her again. Reich did so, and Maguire cross-examined her. Once more Maguire tried to make the point that since the material was contained in a looseleaf binder, he might not have seen an identical volume when Reich showed him one. It was a small matter but it conveyed some of Maguire's evasion of a simple point.

Judge Sweeney also asked Ms. Ollendorff whether he should request a psychiatric examination of Reich. This might provide a way out for Reich; undoubtedly, the judge also thought Reich genuinely disturbed. Judge Sweeney went on to say that in the face of the repeated admission of both defendants that they had violated the injunction, there was no other escape than for them to be found guilty. Sweeney added that he was sorry he had come into the picture so late.

Ilse's response to the idea of a psychiatric examination was strong:

I very vigorously advised against a psychiatric examination. First, because it would have infuriated Reich and all his friends to a great extent, and second, because whatever Reich's delusions may have been in regard to the conspiracy or to the secret nature of his work, I felt that he was absolutely rational in the conduct of the trial so far as his basic premises were concerned, namely that scientific research should be free of political interference, that he had a duty to expose the biased and malevolent intentions of the FDA investigation which he felt to be against the public interest.[6]

The final session on Monday, May 7, was brief. Maguire made a short statement to the effect that if he had known what the defense was to be, his presentation might have been much briefer. However, he had not known and he had prepared himself for any eventuality. For the defense, Silvert read an abbreviated (by the judge) version of Reich's "Atoms for Peace versus the Hig [Hoodlums in Government]" address, which had been printed in April 1956.[7] The statement repeated the arguments about the unconstitutionality of the injunction.

Reich himself concluded with a very few words to the jury. Among other things, he pointed out that he had given $350,000 from his earnings as a psychiatrist to orgone energy research, which made ridiculous Maguire's efforts to prove that a $21.50 bill had been paid by accumulator rentals. He told of his difficulties in fighting this case, how one had the feeling that whatever one did was wrong—wherever one turned there was a closed door. He told of his own experimental nature, how he wanted to see the way this case would develop, how he even went to jail briefly to see what jail was like though he could have been released on bail earlier. Jail was barbarous and the people should do something about it. He thought it would be a good idea if every member of a jury, every member of the bar, including Maguire and Mills, spent a little time in jail to see what it was like. He had found out because it was his method to study firsthand what he dealt with. He wished his opponents had also found out what they were dealing with, had read the orgonomic literature and sat in the accumulator.

Maguire gave a short rebuttal, concentrating on material presented in the "Atoms for Peace" address. To Reich's statement that orgonomy was in the realm of basic research and that the Atomic Energy Commission (AEC) had agreed with this statement, Maguire claimed to have a letter from the AEC indicating otherwise. To Reich's charge that the FDA agents were "hoodlums," he countered citing the years of government service of these agents and accused his opponents of being "hoodlums" for keeping the agents away at gun point. However, the most searing, stunning moment of the whole trial—the moment when the fundamental issues were joined, though they were not issues to be settled in any courtroom—came when Maguire scoffingly said: "They talk about pre-atomic, orgone energy! What's that? We've moved way beyond that—we've got atomic energy and now we are getting the H-bomb!"

In his charge to the jury, the judge spoke very briefly. He again confined the issues succinctly to the question of whether or not Reich, the Foundation, and Silvert had committed contempt by violating the injunction. He described it as a "very simple" case; in the sense that he defined it and as the law defined it at this point, it was indeed "very simple." Yet if the entire case were considered in all its ramifications, it was about as complicated as any case could be.

Given the judge's charge, the jury's verdict was predictable. They returned after only ten or fifteen minutes' deliberation with three verdicts of guilty. Reich looked deadly serious as the jury filed in and his seriousness persisted after the foreman announced the jury's decisions. Reich patted Aurora's arm with great tenderness.

I would like to quote here the last paragraphs of my report on the trial:

It was not simple, it was not totally a scientific situation, admixtures of many things were involved. There was something of the atmosphere of Calvary about the whole business and Reich may have been provoked into doing something parallel to what Christ had done when in desperation he asserted: "I can destroy your temple in three days!" and then all his enemies could gloat and say: Did you hear him? Now we have him! He was surely wrong there. And he was wrong on one level, but not on another, the "followers" huddled around then and they huddle now. Can he really destroy the temple? Is there really espionage? Do they want all the top secret information? Will he be able to show them the importance of it all? And the Maguires smirk and win for the moment, the jury goes home and lives as it lived, the Judge feels concerned and worried, but what can you do? And everybody is as they were, or are they? And here is the actual lunchtime conversation I overheard of three Maine lawyers who followed the trial:

"Say, didn't he let the government get away with murder! Why, Charlie, if you or I were in there as his lawyer, the trial would have lasted at least three weeks. He would have lost anyway but it would have been a lot tougher for the government, you bet it would."

"Yeah. Say what is this 'argonne accumulator' [sic] anyway? Does it have something to do with sex?"

"I think so . . . something about free love. It must be helping him. Did you see that lovely girl with him?"

"Yeah . . . Well, what he should have done is fight it in the beginning. He could have called on all these people to say they believed in it and that it helped them. Oh, he could have done a lot. After all, they called the Wright brothers crazy and Ben Franklin." . . .

I hope he doesn't become another martyr for people to enjoy in the mirror. I hope Reich will live out his days. He has done and suffered enough and it is time others took up the brunt of that burden. The work stands, they can burn the books, but the books are out, the accumulators are out in the world, they can't touch them. Reich found the truths he was looking for when he went into this problem —the emotional desert, the connections involving hiding and spying and manipulating and conniving. The problem may be scientifically exhausted just as the problem of human misery is basically exhausted from a scientific viewpoint, though many details remain to be filled in. To get this across in a big way is, one would guess, just as hopeless as was the attempt to get sex-economy across through mass meetings, and when one tries to get it across with a bang, one gets into things unworthy of its essential grandeur.

Schiller wrote: "The strong man is at his most powerful alone." Reich was basically alone during this whole injunction nightmare because he was willing to risk "contempt" of the law not only in the name of scientific freedom (on that level alone he could have gotten more support), but because he wanted to put the emotional plague's "contempt" for life in the prisoner's dock. He tried many ways—and ways not always to his credit—to give that bottomless contempt a communicable form and shape, to make it into a "case."

Now whatever happens he will be basically alone. If he dies, he will die alone. . . . And if he goes on, somehow, somewhere, elaborating the laws of orgone energy and deadly orgone, with that infinite sweetness, depth and harmony, he will again be alone, waiting for structures to grow that are capable of joining him in that soaring but realistic, sweeping but disciplined search. Out of a quite great ignorance I can only say I hope he does the last, rather than dying or pouring out his strength in an attempt to reach a jury or a judge who will not, who cannot perhaps, reach out of themselves.

The judge set sentencing for May 25, 1956. Reich and Silvert were released on bail. Reich left the courtroom in a very active, somber mood. He said that a "legal scandal" had been committed, that this was just the beginning, and that he was glad at least certain issues had been raised in the courtroom.

As he greeted colleagues, students, and followers in the courthouse corridors, he appeared very much the leader still. He said something reassuring to McCullough, who looked very depressed after the verdict. During the trial, Reich had awarded McCullough a $250 "Oranur prize" for the best orgonomic paper of the year by a student ("The Rocky Road to Functionalism"). He was quick to show his opinion of those around him. He criticized one colleague for a recent book review: "You were too nice to the enemy." Another author received warm praise. And the obnoxious, bullying side of his personality was still in evidence. When approached by one follower with a pale gray complexion, Reich commented angrily, "You look DOR-ish," as though the person had committed a crime.

After the verdict, Reich did something unusual for him: he approached persons he thought were friends but whom he didn't know. In one instance, he went up to a follower from New York, shook hands with him, and asked him if he were "one of . . . " and made a circle with his hand, as if there were no quite appropriate word ("group," "circle," both were inadequate and carried connotations Reich detested). The person, rather shy, said "sort of," and Reich answered, "I know . . . sort of . . . kind of . . . " with a mixture of sweetness and irony.

My last image of Reich on the day of the verdict was of him packing his papers into several briefcases, looking determined and much less depressed and helpless than most of his followers.

The day of Reich's sentencing broke fair, cold and dry. The Boston Weather Bureau reported that the night before was the coldest on record for that date. But only the weather was unusual. Few persons noted or even knew that this was the day of sentencing. The newspapers had nothing about it, hardly anyone outside the little circle of followers talked about it.

One entered the Portland courtroom at 10:00 A.M. to see the characters seated in their usual places. Everyone looked almost the same as when the curtain rang down on the trial itself. Only Peter Mills was different, paler, more fatigued. The judge, pink and unsmiling, entered as usual a little later than everyone else. He asked the government for its recommendations. Maguire rose and declared: Three years sentence for each of the two defendants, a fine of $50,000 for the Wilhelm Reich Foundation (equal to the amount of income from the accumulators since the injunction in March 1954), and legal costs.

Before one knew what had happened, the judge in an unusually low voice for him had passed sentence: two years prison for Reich, one year for Silvert, $10,000 fine for the Foundation. Everyone was stunned: such severity had never been foreseen. A few in the audience cried, but most looked impassive with God knows what inward feelings. Reich's expression hardly flickered. Only afterward could one perceive reflected in his face some bottomlessly deep hurt, but this was not revealed through any of the usual emotional signs. There were no tears, no signs of depression, fear, or guilt.

Reich did not say anything then or at any point during the session. Prior to sentencing, he handed Judge Sweeney a statement which the judge read aloud afterward:

> Your Honor:
> We have lost, *technically only,* to an incomprehensible procedure treadmill. I and my fellow workers have, however, won our case in the true, historical sense. We may be physically destroyed tomorrow; we shall live in human memory as long as this planet is afloat in the endless Cosmic Energy Ocean, as the Fathers of the cosmic, technological age.
> Already today every decent soul knows that truth and wells of new knowledge are on my side. I have won the battle against evil.
> One day the motives and legalistic maneuvers of the technical

winners of today, the drug and cosmetic Hig, will emerge from the archives and see the clean light of day.

I certainly prefer to be in the place where I am instead of being in the shoes of the Hig. I may suffer physical disaster, but shame and dishonor are *not on my face*. It is on the face of the XXth Century Judas Iscariot, Peter Mills, who betrayed his former friends and clients when the Oranur experiment struck us in 1952, and when the Red Fascist Hig, under Moskau [sic] order, was out to get our experimental secrets while, at the same time, they spread poison and slander in our peaceful village about us. Judas hurriedly left the apparently sinking ship; in addition he covered up his tracks by accepting the role of prosecutor for the Moskau inspired drug Hig against his former friends and clients.

In a deep sense, too, we are all guilty, bar none. We were and still are on trial, without exception, in one of the most crucial test crises in the history of man.

This important subject has been presented by me in 1953, during the grave planetary DOR emergency, as if in anticipation of the HIG assault. Here, the Murder of Christ 2000 years ago has been taken as an historical example of the method used by the Emotional Plague of Man to kill Life and Truth.

This time, however, Judas has betrayed and the Hig is killing the scientific hope to cope with the planetary disaster that is upon us. I wish to thank you, Judge Sweeney, for the fairness shown us, within the given bounds. May your knowledge help to improve the American judicial system to secure factual truth.[8]

Silvert requested continuance of bail pending appeal. The judge granted this request, with the proviso that Reich and Silvert not resume the activities for which they had been brought to trial.

Then, suddenly, incongruously, it was all over. Out of the blue, as in a dream, someone spoke in French, representing—I believe—some immigrants who had not obeyed the conditions of their stay in the United States. The sudden shift from the most transcendent issues to the most mundane was breathtaking: Reich's case had ended with the same confusion with which it had begun.

Reich talked to a few associates while still in the courtroom. He mentioned getting a lawyer. His voice was soft. Then he and the others left the courtroom.

Someone wanted to speak with him in the hallway and Reich replied sharply: "Yes, but the *truth, please!*" They talked together while the rest of us, about twenty-five people, walked out and stood in front of the building.

Outside, there was a desultory, helpless quality to the conversations, as was often the case when Reich was not present. Willie was clearly dissatisfied with certain aspects of the way the case had been handled. Tropp complimented him on always having spoken his mind to Reich whereas many others —including himself—had not. Eva Reich talked excitedly about giving talks in the community, which would describe her father's work and the factual history of the FDA case without trying to prove anything. Her points were good ones, but it all sounded too easy. William Steig and his wife, Kari Homestead, who was also very devoted to orgonomy, tried to be helpful. Soon most of Reich's followers, feeling helpless and depressed, dispersed.

At two o'clock in the afternoon I was invited to a discussion held in a conference room at the Lafayette Hotel where Reich was staying. Reich, Raphael, Silvert, Steig, Aurora Karrer, Eva and Bill Moise were sitting around a table. Reich began by stressing how the organized Red Fascist plague played upon the fears and conflicts of the average person to achieve its ends. He could not understand why I did not perceive the connection between Red Fascism and the attacks against orgonomy. My position was that the FDA injunction and other assaults had in common the general fear and hatred of orgonomy, but that I could see no clear evidence of any organized conspiracy. This statement elicited expressions of shock and dismay from some of those present, but Reich quickly silenced them: "He may be right."

I cite this exchange because it so vividly illustrates how Reich could allow a note of dissent from someone like me, who was now not working with him, that was not permitted to those closer to him. It is also an example of how Reich could at times put rein to his more aberrant notions. Finally, I mention it because on this occasion I spoke not only frankly but warmly and Reich could often take that kind of disagreement.

Reich was concerned about whether the sentence would mean "the end." He said at one point: "I know what they will do to me in prison," implying that they would make it intolerable for him. The seriousness combined with the sense of humanity, the concern but absence of self-pity with which Reich discussed this possibility were impressive. I never saw him more human than on that day.

Reich asked whether there was anything irrational in his thinking about the case. His thoughts were focused on the Red Fascist conspiracy, on the one hand, and support in high places, on the other. I said that I thought the irrational element was Reich's deep but unrealistic desire to make contact with present-day social organizations. Reich quietly replied that he had always hoped—"I hoped for the psychoanalysts, I hoped for the communists. I hope for you. Have I been a fool?" The question was addressed more to himself than to anyone else.

May 26 was the last time I saw Reich.

The Destruction of Orgone Energy Accumulators and the Burning of Reich's Publications: 1956-1957

Any hopes that Reich would revise his legal strategy after the trial were soon dashed. He continued with the same kind of arguments he had used in the pre-trial hearings and at the trial itself. He did re-engage Charles Haydon as lawyer, although only to prepare a brief for the Foundation. Silvert was to submit his own brief.

The brief that Reich submitted to the U.S. Court of Appeals in October 1956 contained his old assertions about a conscious, organized conspiracy against his work, although on this occasion he granted a larger role to pharmaceutical and other commercial interests than he did to the Red Fascists. For the first time in a legal paper, he introduced the erroneous notion that the U.S. Air Force was fully aware of a motor power in orgone energy.

Even while Reich was making extremely irrational statements, he was also asserting who he was more plainly than ever: *"The injunction did not concern a routine case of fraudulent production to deceive the public.* It was, on the contrary, the most crucial discovery ever made in natural science by an acknowledged, widely-known scientist and physician, arbitrarily misrepresented to the court as a quack and fraudulent crook."[1]

The briefs by Haydon and Silvert essentially followed Reich's position. In addition, Silvert emphasized that he had not acted "in concert with" Reich in shipping accumulators and orgonomic literature, and that the literature did not constitute "promotional" material for the accumulator.

On December 11, 1956, the Court of Appeals issued a four-page decision affirming the view of the District Court. In answer to the argument of FDA fraud, the decision stated that even a fraudulent injunction had to be obeyed until it was legally overturned.

The rejection by the Court of Appeals hurt and angered Reich, but he soon bounced back with renewed hope for a final appeal to the Supreme Court.

The Supreme Court briefs submitted by Reich, Silvert, and Haydon contained expansions on previously presented arguments with one major addition: Reich submitted his volume *Contact with Space*, as an appendix to the briefs. It is rather extraordinary that he should have done so since *Contact with Space* does not deal at all with the specifics of the FDA case. In his last appeal, Reich maintained his course: the FDA became just one theme in his contrapuntal melody of life against death (or pollution, armored human beings, and emotional plague attacks like the injunction).

Even while the appeals were in process, the destruction of accumulators and Reich's literature began. There was little Reich or Silvert could do to prevent this measure since the stay of execution of their sentences depended upon their compliance with the injunction.

On June 5, 1956, two FDA agents accompanied by a federal marshal arrived at Orgonon to supervise the destruction of accumulators. They were met by Reich, Silvert, and two Maine attorneys who were helping Reich to deal with the immediate problem of executing the destruction.

Reich and Silvert informed the agents that most of the accumulators out on rental had been sold to the users. Ten accumulators plus panels in need of repair for about twenty-five more were in Silvert's possession in New York. There were only three accumulators at Orgonon.

A contretemps then ensued as to who would destroy the three accumulators. Reich and Silvert wanted the agents to take the ax themselves. The agents claimed the injunction required the defendants to carry out the destruction. Reich and Silvert yielded on this point. The agents then wanted the accumulators and panels in Silvert's control in New York returned to Rangeley and destroyed. They also asked that the sold accumulators be recalled. One of Reich's lawyers maintained that this did not have to be done since Reich and Silvert had already been penalized by their sentence for these sales.

Jerome Greenfield has described Reich's attitude during this discussion:

> No doubt from Reich's point of view all this discussion must have seemed like a negotiation of surrender terms between two warring countries. Though he made an effort to remain calm and reasonable, occasionally he broke out into bitter accusations, got up, paced about, went out of the room briefly and returned. "Their attitude," the FDA memo of this operation stated, "seemed to be that of mar-

tyrs. The Food and Drug Administration could take and destroy everything they had."[2]

Moise and Tom Ross carried out the actual destruction. At first they tried to burn the accumulators, but this proved impossible. Then, joined by Peter Reich, now twelve, they took axes and began chopping up the accumulators and panels. In his book, Peter has given a harrowing description of Reich's emotions during the destruction and afterward. When the accumulators had been axed, Reich said: "Well, gentlemen, are you satisfied now?" and Peter continues:

> He waited for a moment. It was perfectly quiet except for some crows on the maple next to the barn.
> "Would you like to burn it now?"
> The marshall took his hands out of his pockets.
> "No, Doctor, I think that will be sufficient."
> "Are you sure?" His cheeks were red and his eyes burned.
> "Yes, Doctor, I think that is plenty."
> "We have gasoline! It would make a nice fire, no?"
> "I think we'd better go now, Doctor. We've done what we were supposed to do."
> The three men started to walk around the pile to the black car. Daddy left us and walked up to the first man, looking at him hard all the time.
> "What about books? Not all the books are in New York! There are some here you can burn too! Why not?"
> "No, Doctor, please." The three men tried to walk away from him but they would have walked right into the woods so they kind of walked sideways to their car. One of them took a handkerchief out of his pocket and wiped his forehead. He looked at the sky. The other man licked his lips. The marshall kept trying to look at Daddy but his eyes kept dropping.
> "I have more instruments!" Daddy's voice was sharper and made them wince. "Yes, gentlemen. Instruments. Scientific equipment. Would you like to see that on the pile too? No?"
> The marshall and one of the men walked around the far side of the black car and got in quickly. The other man, the driver, tried to walk around to the door but Daddy was in front of him. He stood in front of Daddy with his head lowered. Daddy just looked at him. After a long time, the driver raised his head and looked at Daddy and then he dropped his head again.
> "Excuse me, Doctor. Please."
> "Yes, I'll excuse you. Of course." He stepped aside and the man twisted past him and got into the car.
> Daddy turned around and looked at him in the window.

The driver leaned out. His face was white.

"Doctor. I . . . I'm sorry."

"Yes. You're sorry. Of course. Aren't we all? Goodbye, gentlemen. Someday you will understand."[3]

The next destruction occurred on June 26. The FDA's records list 251 pieces of literature burned on that day. A memo by an FDA agent states: "We went into the students' laboratory and Reich said, 'There they are, burn them.' " The actual burning was carried out by a workman from the company of S. A. Collins and Sons, the firm that had originally built the accumulators.

The items burned included copies of the *Orgone Energy Bulletin, The Orgone Energy Accumulator,* the *International Journal of Sex-economy and Orgone Research, Emotional Plague versus Orgone Biophysics, Annals of the Orgone Institute, The Oranur Experiment,* and *Ether, God and Devil.*

The FDA agent's report commented: "During the burning, Dr. Reich found himself just about to throw some of the literature on the fire. He stopped short and remarked, 'I promised myself that I would have nothing to do with the burning of this literature.' "[4] Reich told the agent that his books had been burned in Germany but he never expected it to happen again.

On July 9, the first non-Reichian organization attempted to stop the destruction of the literature. The American Civil Liberties Union (ACLU) protested this particular part of the injunction in a letter to the FDA. Later, in December 1956, the ACLU issued a press release criticizing the burning of Reich's books. The release was never published by any major U.S. newspaper. (The same "death by silence" occurred in England, where a letter of protest signed by A. S. Neill, Sir Herbert Read, and others was not published in any newspaper.)

Reich himself stopped further intervention by the ACLU. That organization had approached Reich and Haydon to be of help during the period of the Supreme Court appeal, but Reich told Haydon to have nothing to do with it.[5] He refused help for several reasons. In his mind, the ACLU was connected with suspect leftist causes. Furthermore, Reich was irritated by persons who became upset by the destruction of literature but who accepted the destruction of accumulators. Finally, Reich never fully agreed with—or he had serious reservations about—a basic tenet of the ACLU, free speech for *all* ideas, right or wrong, rational or irrational. As ever, Reich stressed the protection of the rational in human discourse.

About fifty accumulators, those that Silvert had in New York and had shipped to Rangeley, were destroyed by the S. A. Collins and Sons on July 23.

The next destruction of orgonomic materials occurred on August 23 in New York City, when six tons of literature, valued at around $15,000, were burned. The materials included many of Reich's hard-cover books (e.g., *The Sexual Revolution, The Mass Psychology of Fascism*), which the injunction had only ordered withheld until references to orgone energy were "deleted." Now, on the grounds that the books had been "shipped in interstate commerce" when Silvert originally moved them from Rangeley to New York, the FDA also ordered these books consigned to the flames. Greenfield has commented: "In making this decision, apparently at his own discretion, Maguire illegally abrogated to himself the function of interpretation that properly belonged to the court that had issued the injunction."[6]

Silvert and some others actually did the book burning since again the FDA agents were only supposed to supervise the operation. Victor Sobey, a medical orgonomist who participated, described the scene in a letter on September 24, partly as follows: "I arrived at the stockroom at 7:30 A.M. on August 23. . . . All the expenses and labor had to be provided by the [Orgone Institute] Press. A huge truck with three to help was hired. I felt like people who, when they are to be executed, are made to dig their own graves first and are then shot and thrown in. We carried box after box of the literature."[7]

Like Freud, Reich always perceived the depth of the hatred toward his work as a sign that it touched vital nerves. In the summer of 1956 that hatred raged in very visible, concrete acts of destruction.

Reich was in direct regular contact with only a few people after his sentencing on May 26. He kept up his correspondence with Baker, Raknes, Hoppe, and Neill, but his letters were few. His withdrawal from people was increasing.

Tom Ross was with him for only part of the summer; there were no longer funds to pay for a caretaker. In addition, with the general decline of research activity there was less need for his services. Reich had to scrape up money to pay legal costs, although the New York physicians continued to help out. On June 21, Baker made a note: "Reich today called to say he is selling WRF [Wilhelm Reich Foundation] assets to place in a legal fund . . . to pay counsel and fine." Reich sold at least one fine Reichert microscope, as well as other pieces of scientific equipment.

During the summer of 1956, Aurora Karrer was with Reich a good deal of the time. However, there continued to be severe quarrels when she would leave unexpectedly and stay away from him for several days. Reich experienced considerable anguish as a result of these separations.[8]

There were tense moments with others close to him, such as A. S. Neill. During the summer of 1956, Ilse and Peter visited England, where they saw Neill often. At the time, the twelve-year-old Peter was very much under the influence of his father's beliefs in potential danger from Red Fascists and space ships. The boy also shared his father's conviction about the benevolent protection of the U.S. Air Force. Neill and Ilse's brother Robert Ollendorff (a physician deeply interested in orgonomy) were especially concerned when Peter would say on sighting some U.S.A.F. planes above: "They are there to protect me; they are looking after me."[9]

Neill wrote Reich that he found Peter too serious, too far removed from boyish pleasures. At first Reich seemed to have taken this letter in stride, simply counseling Peter later that the two of them were aware of things Neill was not. However, Neill's reaction to Peter—probably combined with other differences of opinion between the two friends—ate into him. That October, Neill was visiting Norway where he saw Grethe Hoff. Reich wired Hoff that Neill was no longer to be trusted.

With his usual integrity Neill wrote Reich on October 1, saying how much it saddened him that Reich no longer found him trustworthy. He went on to add that he was not a disciple or an enemy but one of Reich's few real friends. And he spoke his mind frankly in expressing his concern about Peter.[10]

It was not the end of their friendship. On October 15, Reich replied to Neill's letter: "Can you be patient for a while until I am free to talk to you? Do not worry." It is unfortunate that Reich did not get more letters like the one from Neill; he needed them.

There was only one close colleague, Ola Raknes, who suggested seriously to Reich that his personal conflicts might be affecting his legal position. But Raknes' advice came late, after Baker had telegrammed him the news of Reich's sentence. On May 29, Raknes wrote Reich a letter, parts of which went as follows:

> . . . I have on a couple of points had the feeling that your estimates were not rationally founded. The documents published . . . have not convinced me that there is a "conspiracy" in the literal sense of that word (a "breathing together"). Your enemies and persecutors no doubt have several sources of inspiration in common . . . but I do not think they have concerted their action so as to make it a conspiracy. On the other hand, I have never seen sufficient reason to believe that Eisenhower or other high officials of the U.S. were in agreement or sympathy with you. . . . When I began to ponder on your attitude to the communists, on the one hand, to Eisenhower and the U.S. government, on the other, I imagined to sense some sort of unsolved child-parent conflict behind. I am fully aware that I knew too little about your infancy and childhood to make the "explanation" I hit upon more than a mere conjecture. But I mention it all the same, hoping that if there is any truth in it, it may be of help to you, and if not that it can do you no harm. What I figured was that at some time in your childhood you had felt rejected by your beloved mother (as later you were by the communists) and had then turned for affection to your father, who out of fear for an open conflict with your mother dared not show openly that he was on your side; little by little the strain of such a situation became too much for you and you had to repress it. If and how such a latent conflict has influenced your attitude in later conflictual situations in life, I think you will know better than I if you just try to find out. . . .

On June 22, Reich replied that Raknes was wrong in denying a conspiracy between the pharmaceutical companies in the United States and Red Fascism. Early in January 1957 (when Reich's appeal was before the Supreme Court), Raknes commented that "every honest means is permissible if you can thereby free yourself from the dirty tricks of the FDA." Reich replied on January 14 that he refused to employ "legal tricks."

On January 17, Reich wrote his last letter to Raknes. Its main point concerned a reference in a paper by Raknes to the fact that Reich's father was "Jewish-born."[11] Reich acknowledged this but described at length how his father had moved away from "Jewish chauvinism" and reared his children in a progressive, international way. Reich himself did not follow Jewish customs or beliefs and he did not wish to be categorized as a Jew despite the conventional practice in this matter.

It is interesting that Reich, facing an imminent jail sentence, should have devoted such attention to the question of being "Jewish-born." In part, it belongs to his final effort to clarify the historical record; it is also another manifestation of his angry reaction against being forced into any position not of his own choosing. However, in addition, it seems to reflect some unresolved feelings about being Jewish, particularly when he was under severe attack. Part of Reich never really wanted to be an "outsider," the quintessential Jewish role, as he had been from his medical school days on as an eastern European immigrant in Vienna. He was never more an outsider than during his last years even while he yearned for acceptance by "high government officials." And he never wanted more not to be a "Jew."

In November 1956, Reich left Orgonon, never to see it again. He settled in Alban Towers for another winter. Eva and Bill also lived in Washington for the winter, and Peter visited Reich during the Christmas vacation.

Most of Reich's efforts went into preparing briefs for the Supreme Court after the negative decision of the Court of Appeals on December 11. It was a grim and lonely period. Peter has mentioned the quality of "waiting" that suffused their mood—waiting for some kind of intervention that would dispel the nightmare of Reich's imminent prison sentence.[12] Reich often said that if he went to jail, he would die there. He was preparing his last will during late 1956 and early 1957.

There were moments of relaxation. Peter recalls seeing two western movies with his father in one day. Ilse and Reich continued to talk on the telephone and correspond. Reich wanted Peter to carry on in public school. Ilse agreed in principle but thought that under the circumstances a private Quaker school in Poughkeepsie, New York, would be better. Ilse's wish prevailed.

Reich always liked to celebrate Christmas, but the celebration of 1956 was a sad one. Reich, Aurora Karrer, Bill, Eva, and Peter spent at least part of Christmas Eve in Reich's suite. There is a snapshot of Reich during that evening, dressed in a tuxedo. He has a highball in his hand and a bottle of liquor on the desk in front of him; the desk is covered with books and papers and a tall plant stands in front of it. Reich's look in the photo is indescribable.

There is just a trace of a smile, but it is a very tentative one. His eyes are bright yet questioning and plaintive. Their expression reminds one of the last scene in *City Lights:* Chaplin has helped a blind girl obtain an operation through which she has recovered her sight. Now for the first time she sees her tramp-benefactor. Chaplin watches. What will her reaction be? He hopes for the best, but fears the worst. So it is in this photo of Reich. Yet he would remain his own man to the end.

The sense of abiding by his principles and winding up his affairs in as clean a way as possible was apparent from Reich's dealings with the orgonomic physicians in his last meetings with them. In January 1957, Reich arranged to see about twelve doctors (in some cases singly, in others two at a time) to discuss their future role in orgonomy and any problems.

Morton Herskowitz, who saw Reich with Dr. Charles Oller, told me about his last visit with his teacher.[13] One of the issues Reich emphasized was the length of patient treatment. He asked the two men how many patients they had had in treatment longer than three years. Each gave his answer. Reich then asked them to consider terminating those cases. He implied that to keep patients in treatment more than three years without significant change was a mistake. Herskowitz was amazed that Reich could be concerned about this on the verge of going to jail.

He wanted to know what problems both had. They mentioned one physician who they felt was destructive. Reich said: "Why don't you get rid of him?" According to Herskowitz, this question was consistent with Reich's general attitude toward the doctors; they should make their own decisions and govern themselves.

Baker, who saw Reich alone toward the end of January, put a different construction on Reich's handling of the particular interpersonal problem Herskowitz and Oller had raised. According to Baker, Reich himself told this physician and one other that they did not "belong in orgonomy."[14]

Both Herskowitz and Baker found him quite calm in their last meetings together. Baker felt that for Reich his organizational involvement in orgonomy had come to an end, regardless of whether he went to jail or not. Reich had in mind taking a long vacation, perhaps in the American West, perhaps in Switzerland. He would continue to think and write but he would not lead an organization.

Most of the physicians Reich had trained remained loyal, helping with the heavy financial legal costs even though many of them felt his particular way of fighting the case was doomed to failure. Reich expressed little personal bitterness toward them, but generally he felt that most of them did not really have contact either with his essential orgonomic themes or with him. At bottom, despite all his resilience, he was very tired of people and wanted peace for his own thoughts.

Given the situation, Reich conveyed a sense of "the end" to Baker in their last meeting. With Wolfe gone, Baker was the orgonomic therapist destined to carry on the traditions of Reich's treatment. According to Baker, Reich asked him at that meeting if Baker would assume responsibility "for the future of orgonomy." Baker said he would. Reich asked him whom he would like to help him. Baker proposed one physician. Reich vetoed this choice and instead proposed Albert Duvall and Eva. Baker accepted. That was the last time Baker was to see Reich.

Reich left considerable ambiguity about his official intentions as to which people were to carry on leadership in orgonomy and the extent of their responsibilities. Thus, in his last written will, signed February 10, 1957, Reich designated Eva as the executrix of his archives, a powerful position since the executrix controlled the republication of Reich's books as well as the unpublished papers. In prison, Reich appears to have reconsidered Eva as executrix.[15]

Reich could not entirely envision orgonomy without him; he often said he wanted no successor. This aversion stemmed in part from his fear that anyone with power in orgonomy might build up an organization inconsistent with the truths of orgonomy, as he believed the Church to have done to Christ's principles, the Communist parties to Marx's, and the psychoanalytic organizations to Freud's.

More was involved, for Reich could not let go of the work. Although he often said he would die in jail, he was optimistic for the future, as we shall see. And in the early months of 1957, part of him refused to believe he was going to prison.

That part of Reich was wrong. On February 25, 1957, the Supreme Court decided against reviewing the decision of the lower courts. Reich and Silvert sought for suspension or reduction of their sentences. Judge Sweeney ordered a hearing for March 11, with jail to follow if suspension was rejected.

Even before the Supreme Court decision, Reich seems to have become more desperate than ever to strike back at his opponents, especially Maguire and Mills. Eva, Bill Moise, Silvert, and Reich himself phoned and appeared at FBI offices to convince the agency that espionage was involved in this case and that Maguire and Mills had committed perjury. Reich sought a personal meeting with J. Edgar Hoover. None was forthcoming. The FBI simply informed Mills and Maguire of each move.[16]

On March 10, Reich and his associates took rooms at the Lafayette Hotel in Portland, where the hearing was to be held the next day. William Steig and Moise asked the local police if a cell was available to make a citizen's arrest. They undoubtedly had Mills and Maguire in mind. The officials tried to get Steig and Moise to back off from this plan, which only reinforced the government's conviction that extra security precautions should be taken for the hearing itself. According to Greenfield: "A federal marshall and his three deputies, a deputy and guard from Bangor, Maine, two FBI agents, a number of employees in the Federal Building and men from the Immigration Division were consequently interspersed among the people in the spectator seats. Besides this precaution, Maguire, after the hearing, was escorted by two FBI agents to the Maine Turnpike for his trip back to Washington."[17]

At the hearing, each side was given fifteen minutes to present its argument. The Portland *Evening Express* of March 11 reported Reich's words as follows:

> He pleaded against being imprisoned, saying that if the sentence were carried out, it inevitably would deprive the U.S. and the world at large of his equations on space and negative gravity.
>
> These equations, he said more specifically in his written motion, are carried only in my head, known to no one on this planet. This knowledge will go down with me, maybe for millennia, should mankind survive the present planetary DOR emergency.
>
> It would mean certain death in prison of a scientific pioneer at the hands of psychopathic persons who acted in the service of treason against mankind in a severe planetary emergency.
>
> It would amount to gross neglect of duty of the court with regard to all legal facts on official record in this case.

Reich also asserted that he and Silvert were devoted to the promotion of new knowledge, not a cancer cure. "We are not crooks, not criminals," he concluded, "but courageous people."

Judge Sweeney ordered that Reich and Silvert undergo psychiatric examinations within sixty days, after which the motion for reduction of sentence would be considered.

We know that Judge Sweeney had been considering such a psychiatric examination for Reich during the trial. The psychoanalyst John Murray, an admiring student of Reich's in the 1920s (see Chapter 6), has also told me that Sweeney, who was his neighbor and golfing companion, devoted considerable thought to what he should do about Reich's sentence. The judge liked Reich, but he was deeply committed to the American system of justice, and Reich had flagrantly and knowingly violated the law. Sweeney sought Murray's advice about Reich's mental status. From what Sweeney said, and from seeing some of Reich's recent writings, Murray concluded that Reich was paranoid and an "adamant crusader."[18]

Judge Sweeney later wrote to the U.S. Board of Parole that he had been strongly inclined to suspend or reduce the sentence but the government (Maguire and Mills) convinced him that Reich and Silvert would continue the "orgone business" if not sent to jail.[19] There is one further bit of information bearing on Judge Sweeney's thinking about Reich's future intentions for the accumulator. According to Moise, Reich signed a statement prior to being transferred to a federal prison.[20] The statement was to the effect that orgone accumulators would not be distributed *if* his sentence was suspended or reduced. (Moise's memory is not exact as to what this statement said.)

I have not been able to confirm whether or not Judge Sweeney ever received anything from Reich about accumulators prior to the imprisonment. Indeed, it is impossible to confirm absolutely that there was such a document. We do know that Maguire and Mills kept pushing their view of the future— "they will continue the orgone business"—on Judge Sweeney and that he bowed to it.

After a night in the Portland jail, Reich and Silvert were driven on March 12 to the federal prison in Danbury, Connecticut, by two deputy marshals. Greenfield has commented on the trip to the federal prison: "In the car, Reich and Silvert sat handcuffed in the back, discussing weather conditions and observing the state of vegetation they passed."[21]

32

Prison and Death: 1957

Reich stayed at Danbury Federal Prison for ten days. On March 22, he was moved to the federal penitentiary in Lewisburg, Pennsylvania, while Silvert remained at Danbury.

At Danbury, Reich had had his first psychiatric examination, carried out by Richard C. Hubbard, M.D., a psychiatrist who was a consultant to the prison staff.[1] According to Greenfield, "the examination consisted of an interview lasting about an hour." A young psychiatrist at the time, Hubbard was an admirer of Reich's. It must have been a strange experience for him to "evaluate" so renowned a psychiatric teacher.

They spoke about orgonomy and about the conspiracy against it. At one point in the conversation, Reich heard the sound of an airplane. He rose and went to the window. Then, turning to Hubbard, he "informed him that the plane was flying overhead because of his presence in the prison, as a sign that he was being protected. Hubbard did not know what to make of this. He had had prisoners deliberately say outlandish things to be thought unbalanced so as to invalidate a sentence, but he did not believe Reich would try such a trick." At the same time Hubbard felt that Reich must surely have realized that any psychiatrist, anybody in fact, would interpret what he had just said as a delusion. Hubbard finally concluded that Reich really believed what he had said about the Air Force plane.

Toward the end of Hubbard's interview, Reich asked him what the diagnosis was going to be. Hubbard apologetically explained that, "given Hubbard's background, he could only conclude that there was a definite disturbance." Reich's response was a thoughtful nod, as if in agreement with Hubbard

468

that within traditional realms (psychoanalysis, classical physics), many of his concepts and findings would have to be considered insane. Reich still could not grasp that some of his ideas could not be construed as rational at all.

Hubbard's brief report on Reich went as follows:

Diagnosis:
Paranoia manifested by delusions of grandiosity and persecution and ideas of reference.

The patient feels that he has made outstanding discoveries. Gradually over a period of many years he has explained the failure of his ideas in becoming universally accepted by the elaboration of psychotic thinking. "The Rockerfellows (sic) are against me." (Delusion of grandiosity.) "The airplanes flying over prison are sent by Air Force to encourage me." (Ideas of reference and grandiosity.)

The patient is relatively intact in the greater part of his personality though there is enough frank psychotic thinking to raise the question as to whether the diagnostic label might more appropriately be Schizophrenic Paranoid type. In general his emotional responses and behavior are consistent with his ideas. No hallucinations were elicited.
Discussion:
In my opinion the patient is mentally ill both from a legal and psychiatric viewpoint, hence should not stand convicted of criminal charge.
Treatment:
Observation in a mental hospital.

So at Hubbard's recommendation Reich was moved to the federal penitentiary in Lewisburg, where there were better psychiatric facilities, and where he was examined once more. The Lewisburg Board of Examiners stated:

During the interview, Reich's emotional responses and general demeanor were consistent with his expressed ideation. On occasions he elaborated upon certain theories which are not accepted generally by scientific circles but are adhered to by certain groups which appear to be in the minority. . . .

The following represents the consensus of the Board of Examiners. . . .

1. During the interrogation, Reich gave no concrete evidence of being mentally incompetent. He is capable of adhering to the right and refraining from the wrong.

2. Although he expressed some bizarre ideation, his personality appears to be essentially intact.

3. In our opinion, it is felt that Reich could easily have a frank break with reality, and become psychotic, particularly if the stresses and environmental pressures become overwhelming.[2]

Ilse Ollendorff offered a charitable interpretation of the conclusion made by the Board of Examiners:

> The psychiatrists did not feel that much could be gained by re-opening the entire case for reasons of legal insanity, and second, they felt that a man of Reich's standing should not be made to suffer from the label of legal insanity. I think this latter decision was an honorable one, and I am convinced that Reich himself would have fought very hard against re-opening the case with a plea of legal insanity.[3]

Reich was not alone in opposing the idea of insanity; Maguire and Mills also were against it. On this one point the three stood in total accord. For the prosecution it would have been very embarrassing to find they had convicted a mentally ill person. Indeed, Maguire went to great lengths to prove Reich's behavior sane.

Greenfield believes the Lewisburg Board of Examiners was more concerned with protecting the FDA than it was with protecting Reich's feelings. Greenfield is probably right. If one believed, as the Board of Examiners did, that there was nothing valid in Reich's scientific discoveries—orgone energy and the orgone accumulator—then their diagnosis was easy. Reich had a major psychosis, with delusions such as protective air planes only the peaks on a mountain chain of gross emotional disturbance. It speaks for the depth of the hatred not only of the FDA but of the Board of Examiners that they could come up with any other assessment.

The same vindictive spirit was evident in the Classification Study made of Reich upon his arrival in Lewisburg Prison. The social worker's report stressed that Reich, a "60-year-old divorced white offender, does not embrace any religion nor is he a member of any church." The case worker also emphasized that "family ties are almost nonexistent," a statement that required a peculiar definition of "family ties" since the report also stated that two of the three most important people to Reich were his daughter Eva and his son Peter (the third person being Aurora). The case worker must have based this judgment on Reich's statement that "he does not believe in the marriage laws of the U.S.A. and that they should not apply to him. He should be free to live with whomever he pleases."[4]

The chief probation officer for Maine had conducted an inquiry on Reich prior to his imprisonment. In his report, the officer warned: "It is noted that while operating in other countries the defendant always had contacts which would allow him to move to new territory. It is understood that he has developed contacts in Canada and South America, possibly in anticipation of exhausting all means of carrying on further in this country."[5]

This misreading of Reich's motivations by the probation officer continued the Maguire tradition of viewing Reich as a kind of Mafia chief looking for "new turf."

The probation officer concluded his report:

> He [Reich] is a man of great ego and vanity. He cannot submit to seeing his little kingdom destroyed. The only means he seems to find of perpetuating himself at this point is to present himself to his followers as a martyr to the theory of orgone energy. The defendant has openly defied the court. In the course of this investigation it was learned that there are many accumulators in different places which the defendant has made no attempt to destroy, dismantle, or recall.
>
> There are no attenuating circumstances and the defendant states openly that he will continue to violate the order of the court.[6]

The FDA continued to hound and defame Reich even after he was imprisoned. The warden of the Lewisburg prison, J. C. Taylor, requested a report on Reich from the FDA to assist in determining how Reich should be treated in prison. The FDA report, which would be used when Reich came up for parole, consisted of an eight-page letter written by G. S. Goldhammer, an assistant director.

In an intentional effort to influence the prison officials to take a tough line with Reich, Goldhammer thoroughly distorted the information his own agency, the FDA, had collected in cooperation with the U.S. Department of State about Reich's Norwegian troubles. In 1952, a member of the U.S. Embassy in Oslo had conducted quite careful and objective interviews with Reich's friends and foes in that country.[7] He came to the conclusion that much of Reich's work was held in high professional esteem, although his bion research was generally considered invalid. Yet all the complexity of the embassy officer's report was dropped by Goldhammer.

Reich's day-to-day relations in the prison community were far less tempestuous than any of these reports would indicate. For example, the social worker said Reich was "contemptuous of authority." However, the prison record cited no evidence of his disobeying prison rules or failing to meet any of the requirements of prison life. Nor was there any evidence that he made a habit of asking for "special treatment," as the Classification Study had predicted. All he asked for was Vaseline for his skin condition, which had erupted again, and the opportunity to take baths several times a week during a period when he was bothered by the heavy DOR atmosphere. Both of these requests were granted. The prison personnel seem to have treated Reich quite decently. He was given a work assignment in the prison library, a fitting task.[8]

The one member of the staff Reich talked with at some length was the Protestant chaplain, Frederick Silber, who later became Chief Chaplain for the Federal Bureau of Prisons. In 1972, I interviewed Reverend Silber after he had retired.[9]

Silber saw Reich frequently, as the latter often sought him out. The chaplain's office was on a main pathway and the prisoners would go by it several times a day. The men could drop in freely. Silber did not know much about Reich's concepts and the little he did know, he "didn't buy." However, he enjoyed his talks with him. Reich did not discuss his "sexual theories," and Silber indicated he would not have agreed with them anyway. Nor did Reich talk much about orgone energy. He talked about human nature. Reich occasionally referred to a "conspiracy" against him, but did not belabor this theme. For Silber, it was no different from what many prisoners said about being "railroaded" into jail. Except for the conspiracy theme, Silber found Reich quite rational in their discussions.

Reich was generally quiet and apart from others. "Not many people knew him or what his theories were. He obeyed the rules and went about his business quietly. He got along with the guards." Silber does not remember Reich being openly angry, though at times his withdrawal and preoccupation could be interpreted as reflecting anger.

Emotionally, Silber said, Reich was most preoccupied with Aurora Karrer and visiting and writing privileges, especially as they related to her. Reich and Karrer very much wanted to marry, but this was not possible according to the prison rules of that time.

Silber had not noted any signs of physical deterioration in Reich save for a "shuffling" when he walked down the corridor.

At the end of the interview, I asked Silber if there was any final comment he would like to make. He replied:

"In retrospect what most impresses me was the loneliness of the man. And his dependency on the young lady. He could be vibrant when he talked about her. We didn't appreciate him sufficiently—how much he needed us. Of course, all prisoners needed more of us, there wasn't enough time to go around. But it was harder for Reich than for many others who were used to prison as a way of life." (Reich's co-prisoners had also committed federal crimes, ranging from income tax evasion to kidnapping, but unlike him, many were serving long sentences or were repeat offenders.)

Silber's information bears on two cloudy points. According to Ilse Ollendorff, Reich's letters from prison to Peter "showed a kind of religious fervor—somewhat difficult to understand in the man who for so many decades of his life had fought very articulately any kind of organized religion. He spoke about the need for 'Harbors for Life,' 'Churches for Life,' 'Sanctuaries for Life.' "[10] Reading the same letters, I find no evidence of any major difference in Reich's attitude toward religion in prison than before prison, nor any change in his opposition to "organized religion." Essentially, in his last months Reich repeated what he had been saying for years—that what was called "God" and what he had formulated as "orgone energy" were identical. We should revere "God" or "orgone energy," and allow our lives to be governed by its laws. In the stress and bleakness of prison life, the prison chapel and religious metaphors no doubt had a special appeal for Reich. Silber did not discuss specific theological issues with him. It seems clear that Reich was not planning any conversion to a religious creed.

The second hazy point concerns Reich's writings in prison. Various persons have commented that in prison Reich was working on a book entitled *Creation.* This manuscript was never found after his death. Given Reich's fear that his work might be stolen, one must question how much he would commit to paper, especially mathematical equations. During the prison period, as before, he said that valuable equations were "in his head," to be shared with the world only after the FDA ceased persecuting him.

Silber remembers Reich writing a good deal of the time. He showed the chaplain some pages which Silber believed were more of an "unburdening himself of his thoughts," especially about the legal situation, than a scientific manuscript. At that time, all Reich's letters and any other writings had to go through the educational office.

The Lewisburg prison files yield considerable evidence of Reich's writings. In June 1957, he was preparing an appeal for a presidential pardon; he had engaged a new lawyer, Roy St. Lewis, to help him with his legal efforts. (I believe he had heard about St. Lewis through Eva Reich.) On June 5, he wrote this lawyer stating that he was considering renouncing his U.S. citizenship if "crimes by the FDA were not fully undone."

In August, when the chairman of Silvert's parole board wrote Reich for information about Silvert, Reich replied: "I cannot speak for Dr. Silvert. . . . He has no connection with my basic position in functional logic and basic research. My case should be considered entirely separate from his." The board denied Silvert's application. (Earlier, Dr. Hubbard had declared Silvert legally sane, but under Reich's spell, in a kind of "folie à deux."[11] Hubbard recommended that Silvert should be kept in a different institution.) Silvert was a difficult prisoner, strongly protesting, for example, the lack of conjugal rights at Danbury and Judge Sweeney's reference to the "orgone business." He was not released until December 12, 1957, after having served three quarters of his one-year sentence.[12]

Nothing came of Reich's presidential appeal, so he turned his energies to preparing for the parole hearing. He wrote a document entitled "My Unlawful Imprisonment," which he sent to various prison officials and to the parole board. This document maintained exactly the same principles he had enunciated prior to prison, and is entirely consistent with much that he had been saying throughout his career. However, his dominant tone was that of the intrepid discoverer who will not recant or limit himself to Galileo's whisper: "The earth does move." Thus, his 1957 eccentricities were basically no different from his errors of the late 1920s. To concentrate on his minor errors, to laugh at them or to defend them is entirely to miss the point and to demonstrate again the "little man's" attitude toward greatness Reich so well described.

A few key passages from this prison document show both Reich's continuing grandeur and his pettiness:

1. Cosmic aspect of my discovery.
I have "done wrong" to have disclosed to mankind the cosmic primordial mass-free energy which fills the universe. This energy rules all living processes and the lawful behavior of celestial functions. It determines our emotions, our first sense of orientation, judgment and balance. I have "done wrong" in having discovered and made accessible the basic force in nature which for millennia was called "God" in many tongues. . . .
The scope of the discovery of this primal cosmic energy is of course not my fault. I was imprisoned because my work has given the impression that either I was a dangerous lunatic or a criminal faker to my foes; a genius and a founder of a new hope for this world to my friends. I am neither a lunatic nor a faker. My discovery obeys simple natural laws. It was anticipated by many scientists, philosophers and writers. . . .

These paragraphs show Reich proud but clear. The following quotation reveals the delusional, childish Reich:

My technological achievements in the global atmosphere have already been adapted by special departments of the U.S. Air Force and were developed further. I have heretofore hesitated for reasons of planetary security to call upon these friends in the U.S. Government to clarify for the world and confirm my cosmic energy research. . . . I am certain my implicit trust in "my friends in the U.S. Government" will never be disappointed. Working as I am at the outer frontiers toward space they are doubtless in agreement with me that trust must be maintained among free men or be restored where shaken by the enemies of mankind.

Reich continued to maintain that there was a conspiracy to destroy him and then steal his discoveries for commercial and political interests.

Reich was eligible for parole on November 10, 1957, at which time he would have served a third of his sentence. In answer to questions in his parole application, Reich stated that upon release he intended to spend the summers at Orgonon and winters in Washington. His wife (as he now referred to Aurora Karrer, although they were not legally married) was looking for a home in the Washington area. He would earn money through teaching (at the rate of $200 per two-hour course). In addition, he would receive $3,000 yearly from a fund administered by William Steig for Reich's work on the DOR emergency.[13] (To his final days Reich kept the distinction of charging a high fee for the dissemination of established knowledge and a low salary for himself for new research.)

Reich made his position clear as to whether he would obey or disobey the injunction after his release from prison. This issue was decisive since the FDA's and the probation officer's construction of his position had determined to a significant degree Judge Sweeney's earlier refusal to suspend or reduce Reich's sentence, as we have seen.

Reich now made plain that he would *not*—he twice underlined the word in his application—rebuild the organizations which distributed the accumulators and which he had dissolved. He steadfastly maintained that he, personally, had never distributed accumulators. He made the distinction here between a research activity and a moneymaking fraud with "sex boxes," the latter being the FDA's misrepresentation of what was going on. Since his income would be derived from teaching and research, since he would not rebuild his organization, he had no intention after his release of involving himself with the distribution of accumulators.

Thus, Reich was prepared to obey the injunction's legal sense, that is, to stop the distribution of accumulators. However, as we know, the injunction contained much more: the defendants (Reich, Ollendorff, and the Foundation) were ordered to "refrain from, either directly or indirectly . . . disseminating information pertaining to the assembly, construction, or composition of orgone energy accumulator devices." And in another part of the injunction, Reich was supposed to delete from his publications "statements and representations pertaining to the existence of orgone energy."

Reich made it clear that he would continue to teach and do research and that his subject matter would deal with orgone energy. The reference to DOR research, financed in part by Steig's fund, was evidence of his courageous, unyielding devotion to truth-seeking. He did not say that he would only teach "philosophy" or "character analysis." He did not say he would not mention orgone energy. On the contrary, he continued proudly to assert the scientific and moral rightness of his stance. Reich went on: "I have no attitude of revenge, only pity—the hurt that hurts so very much. The heartbreak caused by raw injustice can never be erased, of course. The assailants have suffered their well-deserved moral defeat. I have won my case."

Implicit in Reich's stance was his inability to stop others from doing what they wished. In Reich's view, orgone energy and the orgone accumulator were nothing to be ashamed of—on the contrary. Yet his parole statement made it clear that he would not act "in concert" with anyone or any organization distributing accumulators. Still, from his pride in his discovery, from his insistence that he would go on thinking and talking about and doing research on orgone energy, one can understand, not condone, what Maguire, Mills, and the probation officer may well have earlier told the judge and now the parole board. My own construction of their thinking goes: "This tricky customer is unrepentant. He says he is going to teach and in the process he'll talk about the worthless orgone energy. Then his doctors, for whom he is the big boss, will go ahead and rent the boxes and then give him the money. He says he can get $100 an hour. Keep him in jail."

From the prison material, the deepest part of Reich emerged in extremely touching letters to his son. On March 24, 1957, shortly after his arrival at Lewisburg, Reich wrote Peter:

> . . . I am in Lewisburg. I am calm, certain in my thoughts, and doing mathematics most of the time. I am kind of "above things," fully aware of what is up. Do not worry too much about me, though anything might happen. I know, Pete, that you are strong and decent. At first I thought you should *not* visit me here. I do not know. With the world in turmoil I now feel that a boy your age should experience what is coming his way—fully digest it without getting a "belly ache," so to speak, nor getting off the right track of truth, fact, honesty, fair play, and being above board—*never a sneak.* . . .

Reich wrote this on his sixtieth birthday. We know how much he liked to note the decades. He had parties—a rare event for him—on the occasion of his fortieth and fiftieth birthdays. He had looked forward to publishing the documentary material on his life and work by his sixtieth birthday. Now he was experiencing that birthday alone in jail.

On several occasions Peter visited Reich in prison. One of Peter's most haunting memories is of Reich waving from the distance as he walked down the prison corridor away from the visitor's room. He also recalls Reich's telling him that when he was Peter's age (thirteen), he had lost his mother; his father was about to die from grief over his mother's death and he himself was about to move into the turmoil of war. Still, he had accomplished much. Even his jail sentence was, in a way, an honor since he was held on the basis of an unconstitutional court order.

He also told Peter that he cried a good deal and he wanted Peter to let himself cry fully, too.

So Reich, who for decades had said that "crying is the great softener," was practicing the same faith to the end. It says a great deal for Reich's integrity that, true to himself, his comments to Peter emphasize crying not in a self-pitying way, but in terms of its deep emotional value. Where Reich found the solitude within prison to cry "with sound," as he used to say in therapy —for sound was important if the sobbing was to be healing—I do not know. Outside prison only a few very trusted people ever saw him cry.

In one of Peter's conversations with his father, he made a positive reference to Joseph McCarthy, linking McCarthy and his father because of their common anti-Communist zeal. Reich replied that Peter should not compare his fate with McCarthy's. McCarthy had no solutions. But Reich had made a discovery with which to fight evil.

Eva visited Reich while he was in prison. There was generally a good relationship between the two, although at one point Reich became quite upset because Eva had reported to Aurora (who lived in Lewisburg during part of Reich's confinement) some local gossip about them as a couple. Aurora in turn was annoyed and Reich angry at Eva for reporting such gossip.[14]

Eva believes that during his prison stay, Reich wanted to name Aurora Karrer as executrix of his estate rather than herself. The reasons for this were never made clear. In any case, no will later than the one Reich had signed on March 8, 1957, before going to jail, was ever found.

On October 22, 1957, in good spirits Reich wrote in his last letter to Peter that the date of his possible release was November 10, with a parole hearing scheduled for a few days before. Reich concluded by requesting his son to find a good hotel in Poughkeepsie to stay in on visits. He asked Peter to find a place without chlorinated water. And he agreed that they had a "date" for a meal at the Howard Johnson's restaurant near Peter's school.

They were never able to keep it. Around October 22, Reich felt ill but he would not reveal it to the prison authorities for fear his sickness might delay the parole.[15] Undoubtedly his distrust of physicians was even higher within prison. He intended to recuperate in a sanatarium after his release.

To the end, Reich was hoping and planning for the future. But that part of him that had believed he would die in prison prevailed. When he failed to appear for the roll call on November 3, the prison staff found him at 7:00 A.M. He had died in his sleep. His shoes were off, but otherwise he was fully clothed and lying on top of the bed.

Upon examination, a physician placed the time of death several hours earlier. His death was attributed to heart complications—"myocardial insufficiency with sudden heart failure associated with generalized arteriosclerosis and sclerosis of the coronary vessels."[16] Sometime during the early morning of November 3, Reich's vital spark, his orgone energy, could no longer bounce back. He had been pushed beyond the limits of his endurance. He died of heartbreak.

Epilogue

When Reich died, the future of his work was in peril. His books were banned, the accumulator outlawed. Most of his students felt disheartened and were leaderless. Few had the training or the motivation to continue his scientific momentum.

This bleak state of affairs was not reflected in Reich's will. Looking into the future, he had envisioned royalties from his books and inventions, royalties sufficient to pay for the expense of maintaining Orgonon. All of Orgonon, but particularly the Observatory, should constitute the Wilhelm Reich Museum, which would preserve for visitors "some of the atmosphere in which the Discovery of Life Energy has taken place over the decades."[1]

Moreover, Reich envisioned that maintaining Orgonon would only require a small part of the royalty income. The bulk, he directed, should go to the Wilhelm Reich Infant Trust Fund, to be established for "the care of infants everywhere" but not specifically for research on infants and children. Reich added that part of the income could also be used for basic orgonomic investigations. It is interesting that Reich gave such priority to the care of infants. Undoubtedly, this decision reflected his love of children. Yet his relegating basic orgonomic research to a secondary place reflects, in my view, his distrust of the capacity of his students to carry on such research and his difficulty envisioning such an enterprise without him.

When Eva Reich assumed the trusteeship in late 1957, there were no royalties for anything. Moreover, she was depressed about her father's death and uncertain about her own legitimacy as executrix. In prison Reich had expressed some distrust of her and seemed inclined to want Aurora Karrer to be the trustee. Although Eva made some efforts to involve Karrer in the trusteeship, the latter proved unable or unwilling to fulfill this function. Eva continued to want someone else to assume the role. In 1959 she heard from Dr. Raphael about a former patient of his, Mary Higgins, who had never met Reich but who was intensely interested in his work and, it turned out, in the trusteeship. After speaking with Higgins, Eva offered her the role. She accepted and since 1959 has fulfilled the responsibilities involved.[2]

A woman of independent means, Higgins was able to devote herself fully to the trusteeship and to make a loan to the trust fund to start bringing Orgonon, which had deteriorated after Reich's death, into better shape. In 1960, she arranged for publication of Reich's books by Farrar, Straus & Giroux, the small but distinguished New York publisher. As of this date (1982) some sixteen works have appeared, covering almost the full scope of his investigations. They enjoy the kind of steady sale Reich always wished for his publications.

The injunction decree against Reich's books applied only to Reich, the Wilhelm Reich Foundation, Ilse Ollendorff, Silvert, and persons "acting in concert" with them. The Foundation was dissolved prior to Reich's death. In May 1958, five months after his release from prison, Silvert committed suicide. He was sick, his license to practice medicine had been revoked, he was working as a bellhop captain.[3] I would speculate that guilt over his role in Reich's last years may have been an additional motive for his action. In any case, by 1959 all the defendants in the FDA case had passed from the scene.

The Higgins trusteeship has not been without dissension. Her most controversial decision concerns the accessibility to scholars of Reich's unpublished papers. Higgins has interpreted Reich's statement in his will that his papers should be "stored" for fifty years after his death (i.e., until 2007) to mean that no one should see them except her. This interpretation has been legally opposed by Eva Reich, but so far the courts have upheld Higgins.

I, too, disagree with Higgins' interpretation and with another manifestation of her possessive tendency toward Reich's work—her reluctance to give permission to authors to quote extensively from Reich's publications. A final disagreement is that I believe Reich's later unavailable articles deserve publishing priority over early analytic papers that have been reissued. Yet on balance I believe that she has done a good job as trustee. Of particular value has been her insistence on publishing Reich's important books, regardless of the question of their salability. Her orderly procedures are also manifest when one visits Orgonon; the setting closely resembles that of Reich's days.

Following Reich's death, Elsworth Baker continued the training of physicians in orgonomic therapy, a role he performed several years prior to Reich's demise. Today there are about twenty psychiatrists working with him. In 1967 the semi-annual *Journal of Orgonomy*, which deals with all aspects of orgonomy, began appearing under Baker's editorship. In 1968 Baker and his associates founded the College of Orgonomy as an umbrella organization for orgonomic research as well as educational activities. In 1981 the college started a fund-raising campaign with a goal of $2 million to finance a building in Princeton, New Jersey, where all the functions of the college can be centralized. As of 1982 the campaign has raised $1 million, a far cry from the financial plight of orgonomy immediately after Reich's death.

Another activity related to the College has been a course on Reich's work given by Paul Mathews and John Bell since 1968 through the Division of Continuing Study at New York University. It is the longest-running course in this particular Division. A different approach to a wider public was started by Lois Wyvell in 1980 when she published the first issue of *Offshoots of Orgonomy*. The articles are written in clear popular language and are addressed to the interested layman. The first three issues have included valuable material on child upbringing and two outstanding studies of the use of orgone energy to stimulate plant growth.[4]

It is true that Baker and his students have tended to devalue much of Reich's earlier sociological work whenever it conflicts or appears to conflict with his later, more conservative emphases. They have also angrily dismissed any contributions from Neo-Reichians and others. However, the cause of orgonomy has been handsomely served by Baker and the college. They have kept Reich's central concepts clearly in focus and have developed many of them. Some orgonomists have done important original research which expands Reich's ideas.

Reich's impact on the professional and intellectual community beyond his close adherents can be clearly seen in a number of fields. The growth of psychoanalytic ego psychology since the 1950s owes much to *Character Analysis*. Reich's advice to proceed always from the most superficial layer of the personality and to penetrate gradually to the unconscious, his urgings not to overlook a latent negative transference that is masked by a superficial positive transference—these and other aspects of his early contributions are an integral part of the present-day theory of analytically oriented treatment.

Reich's later work on the muscular armor has been developed by two Neo-Reichians in particular—Alexander Lowen and John Pierrakos. Both studied with Reich before collaboration, under Lowen's leadership in the late 1950s, in the development of "bio-energetics," or their amplifications of Reichian techniques. Pierrakos later made independent modifications and started his own school of "core-energetics." They have both made many pioneering contributions, for example, Lowen's use of the standing position ("grounding") in therapy, self-help techniques, and Pierrakos' development of a community setting to facilitate the liberation of the "core" self. Unlike the Baker group, however, Lowen and Pierrakos have altered Reich's therapeutic paradigm by de-emphasizing the concept of orgastic potency and omitting the connections between Reich's therapy and his studies of orgone energy.

Other popular, body-oriented approaches such as primal therapy and Gestalt therapy borrow considerably from Reich with little acknowledgment of his contribution. We have, then, the phenomenon of Reich's therapeutic work spreading ever more widely but in highly diluted forms and with its source unacknowledged.

The particular conceptual thrust of Reich's research on infants and children has not entered the social scene. Yet some aspects of his emphases can be found in many medical and educational developments we see today: the Leboyer method of delivery, the growing opposition to circumcision, the stress on mother-infant "bonding," and increased affirmation of childhood and adolescent genitality.

There remains a profound silence about Reich's experimental work, broken every now and then by a call for serious appraisal of scientific orgonomy. Thus, Philip Rieff wrote in 1960: "Competent scientific opinion has yet seriously to confront [Reich's] work. . . . The brilliance of his vision is such that he can no longer be dismissed as a figure of fun. . . . Leaving Freud at the edge of the last desert, littered, as [Reich] saw it, with dying gods and murder machines, Reich stepped across, as few men do, into the very heaven of an idea."[5]

In a review of *The Mass Psychology of Fascism,* the critic Christopher Lehmann-Haupt wrote in *The New York Times* for January 4, 1971: "Perhaps it is time to reconsider all of Wilhelm Reich . . . and to reopen the question of cosmic orgone energy, its effect on cancer, and the other theories Reich died in Lewisburg Penitentiary defending."[6]

In an address given at the Boston Museum of Science in May 1977, William Tiller, chairman of the Department of Material Physics at Stanford University, argued for the existence of an as yet unknown energy, which he asserted "may be the same as, for example, what Reich called orgone."[7]

However, a few swallows do not a summer make. The weight of scientific opinion still considers Reich's experimental work unworthy of serious investigation. The FDA still cites the banning of the accumulator as one of the prize feathers in its enforcement cap. Persons studying or working in academic institutions who do orgonomic research on their own often feel they must use a pseudonym when they publish their findings in the *Journal of Orgonomy;* they fear their interest in Reich will be held against them by their superiors. Needless to say, such an atmosphere has a chilling effect on orgonomic inquiry. It also serves as a self-fulfilling prophecy, for a long-held argument against the validity of orgonomy is that so little research has been conducted since Reich's death twenty-five years ago.

Many of the people who knew Reich well and who have figured prominently in these pages are now dead; for example, Ottilie Reich Heifetz, Annie Reich, Grete Bibring, Lia Laszky, Otto Fenichel, Berta Bornstein, A. S. Neill, Ola Raknes, Theodore Wolfe, and Walter Hoppe. Some, like Arthur Koestler, are still alive but have never, to my knowledge, been closely interviewed about their relationship with and opinion of Reich. Many of these persons are quite aged and an important part of history may slip past us unless their recollections are soon recorded.

Others who were significant moved on to nonorgonomic undertakings.

Ilse Ollendorff taught high-school French and German until her retirement in the late 1970s. Peter Reich works as a public health professional, influenced by but by no means highly committed to his father's investigations. (Of the family members, only Eva Reich actively works in orgonomy, reaching a large number of people through her worldwide lectures and workshops.) Dr. James Willie and Dr. A. Allan Cott (who worked closely with Reich in the late 1940s) have left the field of orgonomy entirely. Dr. Cott is now prominent in nutritional therapy.

This biography began by raising such questions as how Reich became what he was and how much of what he did was true. Although I may not have answered these questions fully, my work will hopefully serve as one of the beginnings. In pursuing Reich and his work, I have tried to keep in mind George Steiner's words quoted in the Introduction: "The inner lives of Shakespeare and Michelangelo are our heritage; we feed our smaller sensibilities on their donations and excess. There can be no other thanks than extreme precision, than the patient, provisional, always inadequate attempt to get each case right, to map its commanding wealth."

Let me conclude by repeating Reich's conviction, and my own, that the main problem in evaluating Reich's work and person lies not with him but with ourselves—above all, in our tendency to "run" from what he studied.

NOTES

It would require a separate volume to give a full history of the various editions of Reich's publications. Suffice it here to say that it is extremely difficult to obtain many of his works with their original content. Reich was himself partly responsible for this deplorable state of affairs. Although he sometimes insisted on English translations of earlier German publications or manuscripts that adhered to the original text, he would on other occasions make changes without clarifying what the alterations were.

Mary Higgins and Chester M. Raphael are serving as editors for what appears to be a standard edition of all of Reich's writings, published through Farrar, Straus & Giroux. In my view, it is fortunate that they did not follow Reich's wish to change the term "dialectical materialism" to "energetic functionalism" when they supervised the preparation of *The Bion Experiments* (1979) from the German monograph *Die Bione* (1938). It is unfortunate that their English edition (1981) of *Die Funktion des Orgasmus* (1927) adheres to Reich's emendations, made in the 1940s, without explaining how the original text was changed. Nor can one obtain the original publications: they are out of print and very few libraries have them. We sorely need an accurate and available record of the *development* of Reich's thought and work.

However, these textual problems are a small matter compared to the fact that many of Reich's late publications went "out of print" when unsold copies were burned by the Food and Drug Administration in the 1950s. The holder of the copyright, Mary Higgins, can now reissue them, but she and the publisher have apparently decided to publish earlier works first. In the interim we are deprived of some of Reich's most important contributions, especially a number of articles on his method of thought ("orgonomic functionalism"), on Oranur and its aftermath, and on infants and children. These and other articles are unavailable save for microfilm copies that were generously donated by Eva Reich to some libraries in this country and abroad.

In citing Reich's publications, I have used the translations by Theodore P. Wolfe, although only one of these is in print. I do so because their literary verve is superior to the translations done for the available Higgins edition. Moreover, Wolfe's work had the benefit of Reich's careful review. In my citations of Wolfe's translations, I have used chapter rather than page references so that the interested reader may more readily find them in the available edition.

Abbreviations

Interviews
AI: Author's Interview
AC: Author's Conversation
Tel. Int.: Telephone Interview

Names
WR: Wilhelm Reich
ER: Eva Reich
IOR: Ilse Ollendorff Reich
EL: Elsa Lindenberg
LL: Lia Laszky
OH: Ottilie Heifetz

Publications
JO: Journal of Orgonomy
JAMA: Journal of the American Medical Association
IZP: Internationale Zeitschrift für Psychoanalyse
ZPS: Zeitschrift für Politische Psychologie und Sexualökonomie
OEB: Orgone Energy Bulletin
IJSO: International Journal of Sex-Economy and Orgone-Research
FO: The Function of the Orgasm
SR: The Sexual Revolution
MPF: The Mass Psychology of Fascism
CB: The Cancer Biopathy
PIT: People in Trouble
RSF: Reich Speaks of Freud
CHAR. ANAL: Character Analysis
IOR, WR:BIO: Ilse Ollendorff Reich, Wilhelm Reich: A Personal Biography

Publishers
OIP: Orgone Institute Press
FSG: Farrar, Straus & Giroux

Chapter 1: Introduction

1. H. M. Matusow, "The Day Reich Died," *The East Village Other,* Feb. 5–15, 1966.

2. "Milestones: Died—Wilhelm Reich," *Time,* Nov. 18, 1957.

3. "Dr. Wilhelm Reich," Nov. 9, 1957.

4. Lawrence Barth, "Reich as a Pioneer," *The Village Voice,* Nov. 20, 1957.

5. Letter from Richard L. Frank, Secretary of the American Psychoanalytic Association, to Irvin Kerlan, Acting Medical Director, FDA, April 19, 1954 (from the FDA file on WR); letter from Daniel Blain, Med. Dir., Amer. Psychoanalytic Assoc., to Irvin Kerlan, April 5, 1954 (FDA file).

6. AI with Charles Haydon, July 6, 1972.

7. Ilse Ollendorff Reich, *Wilhelm Reich: A Personal Biography* (New York: St. Martin's Press, 1969; cited hereafter as IOR, *WR: BIO*), 199.

8. Elsworth F. Baker, "Wilhelm Reich," *JO,* 1, 1967, 23.

9. Baker, Elsworth F., *Man in the Trap* (New York: The Macmillan Company, 1967).

10. WR, *Selected Writings* (New York: FSG, 1960), viii.

11. WR, *People in Trouble* (Rangeley, Me.: OIP, 1953; cited hereafter as PIT), Ch. V. This book is available in another translation through FSG.

12. Charles Rycroft, *Wilhelm Reich* (New York: The Viking Press, 1969), 90.

13. John Mack, *A Prince of Our Disorder* (Boston: Little, Brown, 1966), xix.

14. Eric H. Erikson, *Gandhi's Truth* (New York: W. W. Norton, 1969), 66–67, and *Young Man Luther* (New York: W. W. Norton, 1958).

15. Eric Fromm, *Sigmund Freud's Mission* (New York: Grove Press, 1963).

16. WR, "Über einen Fall von Durchbruch der Inzestschranke in der Pubertät," *Zeitschrift für Sexualwissenschaft,* VII, 1920.

17. WR, *Der Triebhafte Charakter* (Vienna: Internationaler Psychoanalytischer Verlag, 1924).

18. The relationship between self-knowing and self-experiencing is discussed in my doctoral dissertation: Myron R. Sharaf, *An Approach to the Theory and Measurement of Intraception,* Harvard University, 1959.

19. WR, *Ether, God and Devil* (New York: OIP, 1949). This book is available through FSG in another translation.

20. Daniel J. Levinson, The Seasons of a Man's Life (New York: Alfred A. Knopf, 1978), 48.

21. Erikson, *Gandhi's Truth,* 66–67.

22. James Agee, *Let Us Now Praise Famous Men* (Boston: Houghton Mifflin, 1941).

23. I am indebted to Ernest Jones not only for the phrase but also for many suggestive insights on this theme. Cf. his *Sigmund Freud: Four Centenary Addresses* (New York: Basic Books, 1956).

24. WR, *Listen, Little Man!* (New York: OIP, 1948), 14. This work is available in another translation through FSG.

25. George Steiner, *The New Yorker,* Feb. 28, 1977, 99–100.

Chapter 2: My Relationship with Reich

1. Myron R. Sharaf and Daniel J. Levinson, "The Quest for Omnipotence in Professional Training," *Psychiatry,* 27, 1964, 135–149; Myron R. Sharaf, *An Approach to the Theory and Measurement of Intraception* (Doctoral dissertation, Harvard University, 1959).

2. Joel Kotin and Myron Sharaf, "Management Succession and Administrative Style," *Psychiatry,* 30, 1967, 237–248; Milton Greenblatt, Myron R. Sharaf, and Evelyn Stone, *Dynamics of Institutional Change* (Pittsburgh: University of Pittsburgh Press, 1971).

3. Leon Edel, *Literary Biography* (New York: Doubleday, Anchor Books, 1959), 11.

Chapter 3: Reich's Childhood and Youth: 1897–1917

1. AI with ER, Aug. 2, 1972.

2. AI with OH, May 22, 1971.

3. Ibid.

4. WR, "Über einen Fall von Durchbruch der Inzestschranke in der Pubertät," *Zeitschrift fur Sexualwissenschaft,* VII, 1920, 221. (Translation by the author.)

5. IOR, WR: BIO, 24.

6. AI with OH, May 22, 1971.

7. AI with Gladys Myer, July 16, 1971.

8. AI with EL, Aug. 27–28, 1962.

9. AI with Lois Wyvell, Sept. 11, 1981.

10. WR, "Background and Scientific Development of Wilhelm Reich," *Orgone Energy Bulletin (OEB),* V, 1953, p. 6. (For persons interested in looking up these references, it is important to note that all *OEB*s were burned by the FDA, as well as many of WR's other publications. Much of this material has not been republished. However, it is available on microfilm in many libraries in the United States and abroad.)

11. AI with ER, Aug. 2, 1971.

12. WR, "Inzest in der Pubertät," 222–223.

13. AI with OH, Aug. 21, 1971. There are different versions of this event. According to Lois Wyvell (AI on Dec. 6, 1978), WR told her around 1952 that he informed the father about the mother's liaison and, in addition, the father beat a confession from the mother, although according to the mother it was with an earlier tutor. Elsa Lindenberg and Ilse Ollendorff both recount that Reich told the father of the affair, but do not mention the father's "forcing" the truth from anyone.

14. Interview with OH, Aug. 21, 1971. I would stress again that we do not know the time interval between the father's detection of the affair and the mother's suicide. In his "case history," Reich appears to make himself about a year younger than he was when he discovered the liaison, for we now know with some certainty that Reich was thirteen at the time of his mother's suicide. This is the age given by Beverly R. Placzek, the editor of the Reich-Neill correspondence (New York: FSG, 1981). Since Mary Higgins, the executrix of the Reich estate, cooperated with this venture and searched out "relevant material" for the editor, we can assume that Ms. Higgins drew on Reich's personal papers to authenticate his age.

    In describing himself as around eleven and a half or twelve at the time of the affair, Reich may well have been making himself over a year younger than he actually was. He also dates his first sexual intercourse as taking place earlier than it did. However, again I must caution that we do not know the length of the interval between the father's awareness of the affair and the mother's suicide. I have lingered on these details because of the overwhelming significance Reich attaches— as I do—to this childhood tragedy for his later work and development.

15. AI with OH, Aug. 21, 1971.

16. Ibid.

17. AI with EL, Aug. 27–28, 1962.

18. AI with ER, Aug. 22, 1971.

19. Erikson, *Gandhi's Truth*, 128.

20. WR, "Background and Scientific Development of Wilhelm Reich," 7.

21. WR, "Inzest in der Pubertät."

22. IOR, WR: BIO, 26–27.

23. WR, "Background and Scientific Development," 6–7.

24. AI with ER, Aug. 2, 1971.

25. IOR, WR: BIO, 26–27.

26. AI with Sigurd Hoel, Aug. 25, 1957. In the late 1930s Reich told Hoel, then a distinguished Norwegian novelist, of his end-of-the-war feelings. Hoel's relationship with WR will be described later, when it will become apparent why WR confided in him.

Chapter 4: Becoming a Psychoanalyst: 1918–1920

1. AI with OH, Aug. 21, 1971.

2. Tel. Int. with Gisela Stein, Oct. 10, 1971.

3. AI with LL, July 15, 1971.

4. Ernest Jones, *The Life and Work of Sigmund Freud,* Vol. 1 (New York: Basic Books, 1953), 42.

5. *The Function of the Orgasm* (New York: OIP, 1942; cited hereafter as FO), Ch. 1. This book is also available in another translation through FSG.

6. Ibid.

7. AI with Grete Bibring, April 10, 1971.

8. FO, Ch. I.

9. Ibid.

10. Ibid.

11. In *The Seasons of a Man's Life,* Daniel J. Levinson and his associates have best conceptualized the importance of "mentoring" in early adulthood. Cf. 97–101 in particular.

12. FO, Ch. I.

13. Dr. Bibring emphasized that Edward, unlike Willy, was "clean." I took this to be a reference to Reich's skin condition.

14. AI with Grete Bibring, May 30, 1971.

15. AI with LL, July 15, 1971. Laszky was one of the most vivid and forthcoming interviewees. However, some of her ambivalence about Reich and his work was reflected in her desire for me to use her maiden name when referring to her in this book rather than her married name, which she employed professionally as an analyst. Her wish for some anonymity was further revealed when I asked her if I had spelled her maiden name correctly. She said I had it slightly wrong but she preferred it that way.

16. In my July 15 interview with LL, she told me that she and Reich had had an affair during their medical school days and that he had been a clumsy lover. When I wrote a first draft of this chapter, which included the story of their relationship, I sent it to her. On further reflection, she gave me by telephone the revised version of their relationship included here.

17. AI with Grete Bibring, May 30, 1971, and LL, Aug. 2, 1971. Both interviewees were somewhat vague about the relationship between WR and the teacher, but their stories generally coincided.

18. AI with LL, Aug. 2, 1971.

19. AI with LL, May 15, 1971.

20. AI with Grete Bibring, May 30, 1971.

21. Paul Roazen, *Brother Animal* (New York: Alfred A. Knopf, 1969), 64. This book gives an unusually vivid picture of the analytic community ca. 1919.

Chapter 5: Reich's Work on the Impulsive Character: 1922–1924

1. WR, *Der Triebhafte Charakter.* I am using the translation by Barbara Koopman, *The Impulsive Character and Other Writings* (New York: New American Library, 1974), 1–81. A translation is also available through FSG, WR, *Early Writings,* 1975.

2. AI with Ernst Federn, July 11, 1971. Ernst Federn is Paul Federn's son.

3. Koopman, 38.

4. Letter from Freud to Paul Federn. This and other letters from Freud to P. Federn were translated for me by Ernst Federn. I am very grateful to him for his generous assistance.

5. Letter from John Mack to the author, Oct. 14, 1972.

6. Ibid.

Chapter 6: Reich's Early Work on Character Analysis: 1920–1926

1. FO, Ch. II.

2. WR, *Reich Speaks of Freud,* ed. Mary Higgins and Chester M. Raphael (New York: FSG, 1969; cited hereafter as RSF), 40.

3. FO, Ch. II.

4. Ibid., Ch. V.

5. Ibid.

6. Karl Abraham, "A Particular Form of Neurotic Resistance Against the Psychoanalytic Method," *Selected Papers* (London: The Hogarth Press, 1958), 303–311.

7. WR, *Character Analysis* (New York: OIP, 1949; hereafter referred to as CHAR. ANAL), Ch. IV. This edition is an expanded, English development of *Charakter Analyse* (1933).

8. Ibid.

9. Richard Sterba, "Clinical and Therapeutic Aspects of Character Resistance," *Psychoanalytic Quarterly,* 24, 1953, 1–17.

10. CHAR. ANAL., Ch. III.

11. Ibid., Ch. VIII.

12. AI with George Gerö, July 10, 1971.

13. Otto Fenichel, "Concerning the Theory of Psychoanalytic Technique," *Collected Papers*, first series (New York: W. W. Norton, 1953), 339.

14. RSF, 150–151.

15. Ibid., 42.

16. Ibid., 152.

17. These letters from Freud were shown to me and translated for me by Ernst Federn, Paul's son, during an interview on July 11, 1971.

18. Ibid.

19. AI with Ernst Federn, July 11, 1971.

20. Ibid.

21. FO. Ch. II.

Chapter 7: Reich's Work on Orgastic Potency: 1922–1926

1. WR, *Ether, God and Devil*, Ch. I.

2. WR, "Über Spezifität der Onanieformen," *Internationale Zeitschrift für Psychoanalyse* (cited hereafter as IZP), VIII, 1922. The summarizing statement I quoted is taken from FO, Ch. III. The article is available in English in WR: *Early Writings*, Vol. 1 (New York: FSG, 1975).

3. *IZP*, IX, 1923.

4. Sigmund Freud, "Sexuality in the Aetiology of the Neuroses," *Collected Papers*, I (London: The Hogarth Press, 1924), 276.

5. FO, Ch. IV.

6. Rycroft, WR, 25–26.

7. FO, Ch. IV.

8. *IZP*, X, 1924.

9. Sigmund Freud, "Civilized Sexual Morality and Modern Nervousness," *Collected Papers*, II (London: The Hogarth Press, 1924) 76–99.

10. *Zeitschrift für Ärtzliche Psychotherapie*, I, 1925.

11. FO, Ch. IV. The original description, which has some minor differences, appeared in WR, *Die Funktion des Orgasmus* (Vienna: Internationaler Psychoanalytischer Verlag, 1927). An English translation is also contained in WR, *Genitality* (New York: FSG, 1981).

12. Friedrich Nietzsche, *Thoughts out of Season* (New York: The Macmillan Company, 1924), 144.

13. Conrad Aiken, *Collected Poems* (New York: Oxford University Press, 1970).

14. Rycroft, *Wilhelm Reich*, 28.

15. WR, "Die Rolle der Genitälitat in der Neurosentherapie," *Zeitschrift für Ärztliche Psychotherapie,* 1, 1925. English translation: "The Role of Genitality in the Therapy of the Neuroses," *Orgonomic Medicine,* 2, 1956, 20.

16. Tel. Int. with Richard Sterba, Oct. 25, 1971.

17. "The Role of Genitality in the Therapy of the Neuroses," 20–21.

18. FO, Ch. IV.

19. "The Role of Genitality in the Therapy of the Neuroses," 17–18.

20. Helena Deutsch, *Confrontations with Myself* (New York: W. W. Norton, 1973), 157–158.

21. FO, Ch. V.

22. RSF, 15.

23. AI with LL, July 15, 1971.

24. FO, Ch. V.

25. Ibid.

26. Ibid.

27. Ernst Pfeifer, ed., *Sigmund Freud and Lou-Andreas Salomé: Letters* (New York: Helen and Kurt Wolf, 1966), 174.

28. Ibid., 23.

29. Tel. Int. with Richard Sterba, Oct. 25, 1971.

30. Freud, "On the History of the Psychoanalytic Movement," *Collected Papers,* I, 294.

31. Ibid., 295.

32. *Esquire,* July 1961, 114.

33. O. Fenichel, *The Psychoanalytic Theory of the Neuroses* (New York: W. W. Norton, 1945), 87, 572.

34. Erik Erikson, *Childhood and Society* (New York: W. W. Norton, 1950), 230.

35. Seymour Fisher, *The Female Orgasm* (New York: Basic Books, 1973).

36. Norman O. Brown, *Life Against Death* (New York: Columbia University Press, 1959), 140–141.

Chapter 8: Personal Life: 1920–1926

1. AI with ER, Aug. 2, 1971.

2. Tel. Int. with Edith Buxbaum, Feb. 8, 1973.

3. AI with Ernst Federn, July 11, 1971.

4. AI with LL, July 15, 1971.

5. RSF, 103.

6. AI with ER, Aug. 2, 1971.

7. Ibid.

8. Letter to the author from Lore Reich Ruben, Feb. 3, 1973.

9. AI with ER, Aug. 2, 1971.

10. Ibid.

11. Ibid.

12. AI with OH, Aug. 21, 1971.

13. IOR, WR: BIO, 35. It is hard to evaluate the financial aspect of the relationship between WR and his brother. OH seems to have given somewhat different versions of the relationship to IOR and to me.

14. AI with OH, Aug. 21, 1971.

15. Ibid.

16. Ibid.

17. Ibid.

Chapter 9: Reich's Illness and Sanatarium Stay in Davos, Switzerland: Winter 1927

1. AI with ER, Aug. 2, 1971.

2. IOR, WR: BIO, 37.

3. AI with Ola Raknes, July 5, 1972.

4. AC with WR, Summer 1950.

5. AI with EL, Aug. 27, 1962.

6. *The Season's of a Man's Life,* 84ff.

7. WR, *The Sexual Revolution* (New York: OIP, 1945; cited hereafter as SR). This book is available through FSG.

8. AI with ER, Aug. 2, 1971.

9. IOR, WR:BIO, 38, and AI with ER, Aug. 2, 1971.

10. This chapter is available in English in *Genitality.*

11. AI with Ernst Papanek, Aug. 20, 1971.

Chapter 10: July 15, 1927, and Its Aftermath: 1927–1928

1. WR, PIT (Rangeley, Me. : OIP, 1953).

2. Ibid, Ch. I.

3. Charles A. Gulick, *Austria from Hapsburg to Hitler* (Berkeley: University of California Press, 1948), 717ff.

4. PIT, Ch. II.

5. Ibid.

6. Ibid.

7. Ibid.

8. Ibid.

9. Ibid, Ch. IV.

10. Ibid.

Chapter II: The Application of Sex-economic Concepts on the Social Scene—The Sex-pol: 1927–1930

1. PIT, especially Chs. II, IV, VI, and VII, contains the best description of the Sex-pol movement.

2. AI with LL, July 15, 1971. Much of the detail about Reich's community sex-political work is taken from this interview.

3. Tel. Int. with K. R. Eissler, July 1971.

4. Quoted in Ellen Siersted, *Wilhelm Reich og Orgonomi* (Copenhagen: Niels Bluedel, 1972). I am grateful to Ildri Bie Ginn for translating this quotation.

5. AI with LL, July 15, 1971.

6. WR, *The Mass Psychology of Fascism* (New York: OIP, 1946; cited hereafter as MPF). This book is now available through FSG.

7. MPF, Ch. VIII.

8. PIT, Ch. IV.

9. Ibid.

10. Ibid.

11. As late as 1973, Helena Deutsch was still taking this position, criticizing Reich for his "false propaganda of the orgiastic [sic] 'ideology' among adolescents, without any regard for the crucial process of sublimation" —*Confrontations with Myself*, 66.

12. PIT, Ch. IV.

13. AI with Edith Jacobson, Oct. 15, 1971.

14. WR, "Sexualnot und Sexualreform." This talk was published by the World League for Sexual Reform in 1930. It has been translated into English by Anson G. Rabinbach, "The Sexual Misery of the Working Masses and the Difficulties of Sexual Reform," *New German Critique*, Vol. I, No. 1, Winter 1973–1974, 90–110.

15. WR, *Die Sexualität im Kulturkampf* (Copenhagen: Sexpol Verlag, 1936). English translation: *The Sexual Revolution* (New York: OIP, 1945; cited hereafter as SR). This book is now available through FSG.

16. Benjamin Spock, *Baby and Child Care* (2nd rev. ed., New York: Pocket Books, 1957), 369.

17. Ibid, 371.

18. Anna Freud, *The Ego and the Mechanisms of Defense* (New York: International University Press, 1946), 171.

19. Bronislaw Malinowski, *The Sexual Life of Savages* (New York: Harcourt, Brace, 1929).

20. SR, Ch. IV.

21. Ibid.

22. Mary Breasted, *Oh! Sex Education!* (New York: New American Library, 1971).

23. SR, Ch. VII.

24. Ibid.

25. WR, *Der Sexuelle Kampf der Jugend* (Berlin: Sexpol Verlag, 1932). An English translation, *The Sexual Struggle of Youth,* undated and without a translator's name, was published in the 1960s by Socialist Reproduction, London.

26. "Sexual Misery of the Working Masses . . .", 107.

27. Lee Baxandall's collection, *Sex-pol Essays* (New York: Random House, 1966) gives a good representation of Reich's theoretical work during the late 1920s and early 1930s.

Chapter 12: Personal Life and Relations with Colleagues: 1927–1930

1. PIT, Ch. IV.

2. AI with LL, July 15, 1971.

3. Ibid.

4. AI with OH, Aug. 21, 1971.

5. AI with ER, Aug. 2, 1971.

6. Tel. Int. with Richard Sterba, Oct. 25, 1971.

7. AI with OH, Aug. 21, 1971.

8. Ottilie and Reich never saw each other again. When Ottilie came to the United States in 1941, she was married to Alfred Pink, now Reich's former father-in-law since Reich and Annie had divorced in 1934. After her arrival in New York, Reich sent a message to Ottilie that he would like to see her. However, by this time Ottilie had taken Annie's and Alfred's side against him, and she still harbored bitter feelings about the treatment of his grandmother. Thirty years after, she commented ruefully: "I took myself too seriously," wishing, in a way, that she had responded to his friendly overture.

9. Tel. Int. with Edith Buxbaum, Feb. 8, 1973.

10. Freud, " 'Civilized' Sexual Morality and Modern Nervousness," *Collected Papers,* II, 96–97.

11. RSF, 33.

12. Ibid., 34.

13. Freud, *Civilization and Its Discontents* (New York: W. W. Norton, 1961), 23ff.

14. RSF, 56.

15. Tel Int. with Richard Sterba, Oct. 25, 1971.

16. RSF, 51–52.

17. Ibid., 52.

18. Ibid., 66.

19. This and the next letter from Freud were translated by Ernst Federn.

20. RSF, 65–66.

21. Reich's role in the party during this period was unearthed by the historian Anson G. Rabinbach from Viennese newspapers and the archives of the Austrian Social Democratic Party. I am summarizing his account, which appeared as a sidelight in his Ph.D. thesis on "Ernst Fischer and the Left Opposition in Austrian Social Democracy," University of Wisconsin, 1974, 92ff.

22. PIT, 85–86.

Chapter 13: The Sex-political Furor: 1930–1934

1. Karen Horney's esteem for Reich as an analyst is well reflected in a story Fritz Perls has related. After failing to get much help from two analysts, Perls turned to Horney for advice. Her verdict: "The only analyst that I think could get through to you would be Wilhelm Reich." Perls subsequently went into treatment with Reich—Perls, *In and Out of the Garbage Pail* (New York: Bantam Books, 1969), 49.

2. PIT, Ch. VI.

3. AC with WR, Fall 1948.

4. PIT, Ch. VI.

5. A good description of these organizations can be found in Otto Friedrich, *Before the Deluge* (New York: Harper & Row, 1972), 234.

6. These points are taken from David Boadella, *Wilhelm Reich: The Evolution of His Work* (London: Vision, 1973), 83.

7. Berlin: Sexpol Verlag, 1933. (English edition, New York: OIP, 1946.)

8. MPF, Ch. VIII.

9. Erich Fromm, *Escape from Freedom* (New York: Avon, 1971).

10. T. W. Adorno, Else Frankel-Brunswick, Daniel J. Levinson, and R.

Nevitt Sanford, *The Authoritarian Personality* (New York: W. W. Norton, 1969).

11. Konrad Heiden, *Der Führer* (Boston: Houghton Mifflin, 1944), 140.

12. MPF, Ch. IV.

13. MPF, Ch. VIII.

14. FO, Glossary.

15. PIT, Ch. VI.

16. MPF, Ch. VIII.

17. Ibid.

18. Berlin: Sexpol Verlag, 1932.

19. Ibid.

20. Ibid.

21. PIT, Ch. VII.

22. Ibid.

23. Ibid.

24. Ibid.

25. Ibid.

26. Ibid.

27. Ibid.

28. Ibid.

29. Ibid.

30. Ibid.

31. Ibid.

32. MPF, Introduction.

33. PIT, Ch. VII.

Chapter 14: The Psychoanalytic Furor and Reich's Break with the Psychoanalytic Association: 1930–1934

1. AC with WR, Fall 1948.

2. These quotations concerning English's analysis with Reich are taken from an unpublished paper by English, "Some Recollections of a Psychoanalysis with Wilhelm Reich, September, 1929–April, 1932."

3. Leston Havens, "Main Currents of Psychiatric Development," *International Journal of Psychiatry*, V, 1968, 293.

4. WR, CHAR. ANAL., Ch. IX.

5. Ibid.

6. Ibid.

7. Ibid.

8. Ibid., Ch. VIII.

9. FO, Ch. VI.

10. Ibid.

11. Ibid.

12. Ibid.

13. CHAR. ANAL., Ch. XI.

14. Ibid.

15. Ibid.

16. FO, Ch. VII.

17. PIT, Ch. VII.

18. Jones, *Life and Work of Sigmund Freud,* II, 3, 166.

19. PIT, Ch. VII.

20. Ibid.

21. Ibid.

22. Siersted, *Wilhelm Reich og Orgonomi.*

23. PIT, Ch. VII.

24. Ibid.

25. Ibid.

26. PIT, Ch. VIII.

27. Ibid.

28. AI with Grete Bibring, May 30, 1971.

29. Paul Roazen, *Freud and His Followers* (New York: New American Library, 1976), 370.

30. PIT, Ch. VIII.

31. Jones, *Life and Work of Sigmund Freud,* II, 191.

32. Sexpol Verlag, 1935.

33. PIT, Ch. VIII.

34. CHAR. ANAL., Ch. XIV.

35. *ZPS,* I, 1934.

36. CHAR. ANAL., Ch. XIV.

37. Ibid.

38. Ibid.

39. Ibid.

40. Ibid.

Chapter 15: Personal Life: 1930–1934

1. AI with ER, Aug. 2, 1971.

2. Ibid.

3. Ibid.

4. AI with OH, Aug. 21, 1971.

5. Lecture by Michael Stone on Reich, Feb. 27, 1973, Lenox Hill Hospital, New York City.

6. RSF, 112.

7. AI with Edith Jacobson, Oct. 15, 1971.

8. This source wishes to remain anonymous.

9. RSF, 168.

10. AI with EL, Aug. 28, 1977.

11. Arthur Koestler was also a member of this cell. Cf. Koestler, "The Initiates," in Richard Crossman, ed., *The God That Failed* (New York: Bantam Books, 1952).

12. Most of the material in this section pertaining to the Reich-Lindenberg relationship comes from five extended interviews with Lindenberg, starting in 1962 and ending in 1978.

13. AI with OH, Aug. 21, 1971.

14. RSF, 102.

15. AI with ER, Aug. 2, 1971.

16. CHAR. ANAL., Ch. XIV.

17. Berlin: Sexpol Verlag.

18. PIT, Ch. VII.

19. Ibid.

20. Ibid.

21. Most of the information about this visit is taken from my interview with Margaret Fried, July 15, 1971.

22. PIT, Ch. VII.

23. Ibid.

24. Ibid.

25. Ibid.

26. AI with ER, Aug. 2, 1971

27. AI with Fried, July 15, 1971.

28. RSF, 106–107.

29. Tel. Int. with K. R. Eissler, July 1971.

30. AI with Grete Bibring, May 30, 1971.

31. AI with Edith Jacobson, Oct. 15, 1971.

32. PIT, Ch. VIII.

33. Ibid.

34. AI with Rosetta Hurwitz, Oct. 16, 1971.

35. WR, "Work Democracy in Action," *Annals of the Orgone Institute*, I, 1947, 7. (This volume of the *Annals* was destroyed by the FDA.)

36. AI with ER, Aug. 2, 1971.

37. Ibid.

38. AC with WR, Summer 1950.

Chapter 16: The Bio-electrical Experiments: 1934–1935

1. Freud would have taken a dim view of Reich's effort in this direction. A historian of psychoanalysis, Paul Roazen, has stated: "He [Freud] did not have to raise his voice to express displeasure; he almost growled at [Siegfried] Bernfeld's attempt to measure libido quantitatively, and it was known then that Bernfeld must be on his way out with Freud"— *Freud and His Followers*, 502.

2. My summary of Reich's scientific development during this period draws substantially upon David Boadella's fine study of Reich's work, *Wilhelm Reich: The Evolution of His Work*, Ch. 4.

3. L. R. Müller, *Die Lebensnerven* (3rd ed., Berlin: Springer, 1931).

4. Friedrich Kraus, *Allgemeine und Spezielle Pathologie der Person* (Leipzig: Thieme, 1926).

5. WR approached "the function of the orgasm" from diverse viewpoints. For his paper on the subject most relevant to his experimental work of this period, cf. "Der Orgasmus als Elektrophysiologische Entladung," *ZPS*, I, 1934, 29–43. English translation by Barbara Koopman: "The Orgasm as Electrophysiological Discharge," *The Impulsive Character and Other Writings*, 123–138.

6. Koopman, 127.

7. Maxim Gorki, *Reminiscences of Tolstoy, Chekhov and Andreyev* (London: The Hogarth Press, 1934).

8. AC with WR, Summer 1948.

9. I am considerably indebted to Douglas Levinson, psychiatrist and researcher in electrophysiology, for his help with technical aspects of this chapter and its rewriting.

10. Some readers may appreciate a review of the basic concepts in this area. Electric currents consist of electrons flowing along any available con-

ductive path from an area of more negative charge to an area of less negative charge. The "pressure" for electron flow is the amount of the difference in charge between the two areas, measured as *voltage*. For any amount of voltage, the actual current flow in a given time depends on the conducting pathway's *resistance* to current flow (measured in ohms, while current is measured in amperes). If a gradient exists between two areas, one can speak of a *potential* voltage, even if there is no conductive pathway and thus no flow of current.

In electrodermal research, skin resistance can be measured by passing a controlled, imperceptible current through the skin via two electrodes placed a short distance apart. Any change in the current from moment to moment can then be attributed to variation in the skin resistance. Early researchers found that stimuli, particularly frightening or surprising ones, produced discrete, brief (seconds) wavelike reductions in skin resistance, known as the "psychogalvanic response" or "galvanic skin response," or today simply as the "skin resistance response" or its inverse, "skin conductance response."

It was also found that even without externally applied current, the skin would often generate a small current between two electrodes placed on the skin because of unequal charge, i.e., a skin potential. While skin resistance responses are unidirectional, toward lower resistance, skin potential can show either brief (wavelike) or prolonged changes because of the demonstration of spontaneous change in the skin and the two opposite directions of change.

11. For a fuller account of WR's concepts as well as his experimental results, cf. WR, *Experimentelle Ergebnisse über die Elektrische Funktion von Sexualitat und Angst* (Oslo: Sexpol Verlag, 1937). The English translation I have used is by Koopman, "Experimental Investigation of the Electrical Function of Sexuality and Anxiety," *The Impulsive Character and Other Writings,* 139–189. (This monograph is also available through FSG.)

12. Koopman, Ch. 5.

13. Marvin Zuckerman, "Physiological Measures of Sexual Arousal in the Human," *Psychological Bulletin*, Vol. 75, 1971, 297–329.

14. William Hoffmann, "Dr. Reich and His Electrophysiology," *Arbeiderbladet* (Oslo newspaper), June 8, 1938.

15. AC with WR, Summer 1950.

Chapter 17: The Bions: 1936–1939

1. PIT, Appendix.

2. Ibid.

3. WR, *The Bion Experiments* (New York: FSG, 1979), 28. The original German manuscript was published as a monograph, "Die Bione" (Berlin: Sexpol Verlag, 1938).

4. PIT, Appendix.

5. I am here utilizing the framework of analysis provided by Boadella, Ch. 5.

6. Even with regard to structure, R. M. Allen has stated that the observer benefits from magnification up to around 4000x, although the theoretical limit is much lower. Allen adds the proviso that for high magnification, high-quality apochromatic (best color correction) lenses must be used. Reich had such lenses—R. M. Allen, *The Microscope* (Princeton, N.J.: Van Nostrand, 1941).

7. PIT, Appendix.

8. Ibid.

9. John McPhee, *Basin and Range* (New York: FSG, 1981).

10. *The Bion Experiments,* Ch. IV.

11. Reich published these findings some years later in *The Cancer Biopathy* (New York: OIP, 1949; cited hereafter as CB), Ch. II. Copies of this edition, translated by Theodore P. Wolfe, were destroyed by the FDA in 1956; microfilms are available in a number of libraries. A new translation of the work is available through FSG.

12. CB, Ch. IV.

13. Boadella, 136–137.

14. AC with WR, Winter 1949.

15. AI with Ola Raknes, July 5, 1972.

16. AI with Nic Hoel, August 1962.

17. *La Nouvelle République* (Paris), Dec. 27, 1972.

18. Letter from Roger du Tiel to the author, June 26, 1973.

19. CB, Ch. II.

20. Leiv Kreyberg, "Wilhelm Reich's 'Bion' Experiment," *Aftenposten* (Oslo newspaper), April 19, 1938. Nathan Hale, a sculptor and long-time student of orgonomy, gathered together the articles in the Norwegian press on Reich's work. He also had them translated into English. I am grateful to him for making this material accessible to me.

21. Ibid.

22. PIT, Appendix.

23. Ibid.

24. WR, "Proposition of Public Control of Bion Experiments," *Aftenposten,* April 27, 1938.

25. *Aftenposten,* May 31, 1938; *Arbeiderbladet,* June 15, 1938, and June 29, 1938.

26. *Dagbladet* (no exact date available, but most likely between June 15 and June 22, 1938).

27. Ibid.

28. Ibid.

29. Ibid.

30. *Dagbladet* (no exact date available here, but most likely between March and May 1938).

31. Boadella, Appendix III.

32. A. S. Neill, "A Warm Defense of Reich," *Dagbladet,* June 25, 1938.

33. Dean of the Faculty of Medicine, "The Reich Affair," *Dagbladet* (sometime between March and May 1938).

Chapter 18: Psychiatric Developments: 1934–1939

1. AC with Alexander Lowen, Winter 1947.

2. AI with Ola Raknes, July 5, 1972.

3. Sexpol Verlag. Much of this material was included verbatim—but translated into English—in *The Function of the Orgasm,* 1942. I use this translation in my citations.

4. FO, Ch. VIII.

5. Ibid.

6. Ibid.

7. Ibid.

8. Lowen, *Bioenergetics* (Baltimore: Penguin, 1976).

9. WR, *Orgasmusreflex* (Berlin: Sexpol Verlag, 1937), translated by the author.

10. FO, Ch. VIII.

11. Ibid.

12. FO, Ch. V.

13. AC with WR, Summer 1948.

14. FO, Introductory Survey.

Chapter 19: Personal Life and Relations with Colleagues: 1934–1939

1. AI with EL, Aug. 28, 1962.

2. AI with EL, April 1977.

3. IOR, WR:BIO, 59.

4. Fenichel's views about Reich during this time are well conveyed in a series of "Rundbriefe" he wrote to his colleagues during 1935 and 1936. These "circular letters" were designed not for wider distribution but to keep sympathetic colleagues informed. Lore Reich Ruben kindly made available to me the set of letters Fenichel sent to her mother, Annie

Reich. Fenichel's commitment to the psychoanalytic organization is most clearly expressed in his letter of Feb. 12, 1935.

5. Fenichel, "Rundbrief," Feb. 12, 1935.

6. Boadella, Appendix 3.

7. AI with Ola Raknes, July 5, 1972.

8. Tel. Int. with Hanna Fenichel, October 1971.

9. ZPS, III, 1936, 150–156. English translation, *Annals of the Orgone Institute*, I, 1946, 108–114.

10. AI with ER, Aug. 2, 1971.

11. Ibid.

12. Ibid.

13. ER very kindly showed this letter to me and translated it.

14. AI with ER, Aug. 2, 1971.

15. Ibid.

16. Letter translated by ER.

17. AI with IOR, July 1977.

18. AC with WR, Summer 1950.

19. AI with Nic Hoel, Aug. 31, 1957.

20. Ibid.

21. AI with EL, Aug. 28, 1962.

22. Colin Wilson, *The Quest for Wilhelm Reich* (New York: Random House, 1981).

23. Letter from Gerd Bergersen to the author, March 2, 1981.

24. Wilson, 174.

25. Ibid., 177.

26. PIT, Appendix. We have to take with some skepticism Reich's attribution of the initiative for approaching Thjötta. Reich was inclined to blame others when a contact ended badly. I remember around 1950 Reich conceived the idea of donating some of his books to the Rangeley Public Library. He asked me what I thought of the plan. In the face of his enthusiasm I was not inclined to express my doubts about the degree to which the librarian would welcome the gift of *The Function of the Orgasm*. Later, when she returned the books as unacceptable, a very hurt Reich fiercely blamed me for proposing the idea of sending the books.

27. This letter of March 17, 1937, was translated by the author.

28. Charles Péguy, *Basic Verities* (New York: Pantheon, 1943), 53.

29. Gladys Meyer, "America's First Orgonomist," *JO*, 4, 1970, 25.

30. AI with Walter Briehl, March 1972.

31. AI with Gladys Meyer, July 16, 1971.

32. AI with Ola Raknes, July 5, 1972.

33. AI with EL, Aug. 29, 1962.

Chapter 20: Getting Settled in America: 1939–1941

1. AI with Walter Briehl, March 1972.

2. AC with Lillian Bye, December 1954.

3. IOR, WR:BIO, 77.

4. AI with IOR, July 1977.

5. IOR, WR:BIO, 78.

6. WR, "Orgonomic Movement," *OEB*, II, 1950, 148.

7. AC with Gladys Meyer, April 1982.

8. FO.

9. AC with WR, Summer 1948.

10. AC with Christopher Bird, 1973.

11. AC with Sigurd Hoel, August 1956.

12. "Two-year Report of the Orgone Institute Press," *OEB*, IV, 1952, 159.

13. WR, "Orgonomic Movement," *OEB*, II, 1950, 147.

14. Ibid.

15. AC with WR, Summer 1948.

16. AC with Gladys Meyer, July 1971.

17. *JAMA*, Dec. 12, 1942.

18. Abraham Myerson, *American Journal of Psychiatry*, November 1942.

19. Martin Grotjahn, *Psychosomatic Medicine*, 5, 1943.

20. Paul Goodman, "The Political Meaning of Some Recent Revisions of Freud," *Politics*, Vol. 2, 1945.

21. M. L. Berneri, "Sexuality and Freedom," Nov. 5, 1945.

22. AI with Walter Briehl, March 1972.

23. AI with Edith Jacobson, Oct. 15, 1971. I have only her version of her New York encounter with Reich.

24. AI with LL, July 15, 1971.

25. Tel Int. with Gisela Stein, Oct. 10, 1971.

26. This article was prepared in January 1939 by the Sexpol Verlag, but only for select distribution; it was not available for sale.

27. Beverley R. Placzek, ed., *The Record of a Friendship: The Correspondence of Wilhelm Reich and A. S. Neill* (New York: FSG, 1981).

28. IOR, WR:BIO, 88.

29. AI with ER, Aug. 2, 1971.

30. AI with IOR, July 1976.

31. Jerome Greenfield has seen the FBI file on Reich and has ascertained that Reich was in fact detained because of his former "communist" activities. Cf. Greenfield, "Enemy Alien," *JO*, 16, 1982, 91–109.

32. IOR, WR:BIO, 91–92.

33. AI with IOR, July 1977.

34. AI with EL, November 1978.

35. AI with Lillian Bye, December 1954.

36. AI with EL, April 1977.

37. Friedrich Nietzsche, "Schopernhauer as Educator," *Thoughts out of Season* (New York: The Macmillan Company, 1924), 123.

38. AI with EL, November 1978.

Chapter 21: The Discovery of Orgone Energy: 1940

1. WR, CB, Ch. III.

2. Ibid.

3. Ibid.

4. Johann Eckermann, *Conversations with Goethe* (London: Dent, 1930).

5. Boadella, Ch. 6.

6. CB, Ch. IV.

7. Ibid.

8. For this explanation of the electroscope, I have drawn heavily on C. Frederick Rosenblum, "The Electroscope, Part I," *JO*, 3, 1969, 188–197. (Rosenblum is a pseudonym for Courtney Baker, a psychiatrist in training at the time, who feared that publishing an orgonomic article might prejudice his chances for obtaining Board certification in psychiatry.)

9. CB, Ch. IV.

10. Letter from WR to Einstein, Dec. 30, 1940, *The Einstein Affair* (Rangeley, Me.: OIP, 1953). The pages of this slim volume are not numbered.

11. IOR, WR:BIO, 85.

12. Ibid., 85–86.

13. AC with WR, Summer 1948.

14. Ibid.

15. Letter from Einstein to WR, Feb. 7, 1941, *The Einstein Affair*.

16. Letter from WR to Einstein, Feb. 20, 1941, *The Einstein Affair*.

17. Letter from Wolfe to Einstein, Feb. 14, 1944, *The Einstein Affair*.

18. Letter from Einstein to Wolfe, Feb. 15, 1944, *The Einstein Affair.*

19. Letter from WR to Einstein, Feb. 20, 1944, *The Einstein Affair.*

20. Letter from Einstein to WR, Feb. 24, 1944, *The Einstein Affair.*

21. Letter (unsent) from WR to Einstein, March 3, 1944, *The Einstein Affair.* The reasons for Einstein's withdrawal from the "Reich affair" remain unclear. It is entirely possible that Einstein's explanation suffices, i.e., that he did some investigation, received a negative answer, and was not prepared to pursue the matter further, despite Reich's entreaties for a "control of the control." However, from Greenfield's research, cited in Chapter 20, we know that the FBI considered Reich an "enemy alien" right around the time Reich approached Einstein. Einstein was engaged in planning for the development of the atomic bomb. It is quite possible, but by no means verifiable at this time, that the FBI warned Einstein against further contact with Reich. I am indebted to Arthur Efron for making this speculative connection (personal conversation).

22. Ibid.

23. Ronald Clark, *Einstein: Life and Times* (New York: Avon, 1972), 568–569.

24. Courtney Baker, "The Temperature Difference: Experimental Protocol," *JO,* 6, 1972, 61–71. Cf. also Richard Blasband, "Thermal Orgonometry," *JO,* 5, 1971, 175–188; Charles Konia, "Thermical Properties of the ORAC, Part I," *JO,* 8, 1974, 47–64, and "Part II," *JO,* 12, 1978, 244–252; and Gary Mann, "Experiments with the Orgone Accumulator," *International Journal of Life Energy,* 1, 1979, 43–56.

25. Kurt Lion, "Test of the Temperature Difference," FDA file on Reich. (Cf. also Greenfield, 127–129 and 358–362 for a critique of Lion's work taken from an article by Courtney Baker.)

26. Courtney Baker, "The Electroscope III: Atmospheric Pulsation," *JO,* 10, 1976, 57–80.

27. Noel Little, "Test of the Electroscopic Reaction," FDA file; cf. also Greenfield, 128–129.

28. Kurt Lion, "The Electroscopic Reaction," FDA file; cf. also Greenfield, 128–129 and 362–363 for a critique of Lion taken from an article by Courtney Baker.

29. Letter from C. Baker to the author, April 2, 1981. In this letter Baker refers to an article by Reich, "The Swing," which appeared in *Contact with Space* (Rangeley, Me.: Core Pilot Press, 1957), Ch. III. Baker's replication appeared in *JO,* 11, 1977, 176–187.

30. Thomas S. Kuhn, *The Structure of Scientific Revolutions* (2nd enlarged ed. Chicago: University of Chicago Press, 1970).

31. Ibid., 76.

32. Quoted by Kuhn, 151.

33. McPhee, *Basin and Range,* 173.

34. Kuhn, 90.

Chapter 22: The Medical Effects of the Accumulator: 1940–1948

1. CB, Ch. VII.

2. I am following here the analytic framework provided by Boadella, Ch. 8.

3. CB, Ch. VI.

4. W. Edward Mann and Edward Hoffman, *The Man Who Dreamed of Tomorrow* (Los Angeles: Tarcher, 1980).

5. CB, Ch. VI.

6. See Chester M. Raphael and Helen MacDonald, "Orgonomic Diagnosis of Cancer Biopathy," *OEB,* IV, 1952. In the text I imply that this material is "available," but I am using the word only in its loosest meaning. Copies of this *Bulletin* were destroyed by the FDA, like so many other writings by Reich and his associates. This material is only available in the libraries of some major cities; more available similar material can be found in an article on the Reich Blood Tests by Courtney Baker, et al., *JO,* 15, 1981.

7. CB, Ch. VI.

8. Boadella, Ch. 8.

9. Ibid.

10. CB, Ch. X.

11. CB, Ch. V.

12. Ibid.

13. Ibid.

14. Ibid.

15. Ibid.

16. These studies have been summarized by Boadella, Ch. 7, and by Mann and Hoffman, Ch. IV.

17. R. W. Bartrop, *et al.,* "Depressed Lymphocyte Functioning in Bereavement," *Lancet,* I, 1977, 834.

18. Boadella, Ch. 7.

19. CB, Ch. VII.

20. Ibid.

21. Ibid.

22. Ibid.

23. Ibid.

24. Ibid.

25. CB, Ch. X

26. Ibid.

27. Ibid.

28. I heard these remarks at Orgonon, Summer 1950.

29. "Orgone Accumulator," *JAMA,* January 1949.

30. Cf., for example, William A. Anderson, "Orgone Therapy in Rheumatic Fever," *OEB,* II, 1950; Emanuel Levine, "Orgone Therapy in Rheumatic Fever," *OEB,* III, 1951; Walter Hoppe, "Further Experiences with the Orgone Accumulator," *OEB,* II, 1950; A. Allan Cott, "Orgonomic Treatment of Ichthyosis," *OEB,* III, 1951; and N. Wevrick, "Physical Orgone Treatment of Diabetes," *OEB,* III, 1951.

31. Richard A. Blasband, "The Orgone Energy Accumulator in the Treatment of Cancer in Mice," *JO,* 7, 1973, 81–84.

32. Bernard Grad,"Report on the Treatment of Leukemic Mice with the Orgone Acumulator," paper delivered at a conference on Life Energy, York University, Toronto, August 1978.

33. All the information in this paragraph is drawn from Boadella, Ch. VII.

34. On the "Good Morning, America" TV program in Boston, February 4, 1981, an FDA representative displayed the orgone energy funnel and blankets as examples of the quackery the FDA had outlawed.

Chapter 23: Psychiatric, Sociological, and Educational Developments: 1940–1950

1. WR often cited this figure orally, but I have no financial records for this study.

2. *Orgasmusreflex, Muskelhaltung, und Körperausdruck (Orgasm Reflex, Muscular Attitude, and Bodily Expression)* (Oslo: Sexpol Verlag, 1937).

3. CHAR. ANAL., Ch. XV.

4. Ibid.

5. Ibid.

6. AC with WR, 1948.

7. Ibid.

8. CHAR. ANAL., Ch. XVI.

9. Ibid.

10. Ibid.

11. FO, Ch. I.

12. CHAR. ANAL., Ch. XVI.

13. AC with WR, Summer 1948.

14. MPF, Ch. X.

15. MPF, Preface to the 3rd ed.

16. MPF, Ch. X.

17. Taylor Stoehr, ed., *Nature Heals: The Psychological Essays of Paul Goodman* (New York: E. P. Dutton, 1979).

18. MPF, Ch. X.

19. Ibid.

20. Ibid.

21. WR, *Listen, Little Man!* I do not give chapter citations because this slim book is not divided into chapters.

22. AC with WR, Summer 1948.

23. Alfred Kazin, *The Inmost Leaf* (New York: Harcourt, Brace, 1955), 114–115.

24. CHAR. ANAL., Ch. XII.

25. CB, Ch. IX, Section 2.

26. Ibid.

27. Ibid.

28. Ibid.

29. Ibid.

30. Ibid.

31. Ibid.

32. Ibid.

33. *Record of a Friendship,* 268–269.

34. WR, "Children of the Future," *OEB,* II, 1950, 194–206. (Like other papers of Reich in the *OEB,* his articles on children in this journal have been burned by the FDA and are unavailable save on microfilm in some major libraries.)

35. Elsworth F. Baker, "Genital Anxiety in Nursing Mothers," *OEB,* IV, 1952, 19–31, 28. The quote by Reich is taken from the discussion that followed the original presentation of this paper at a conference at Orgonon in August 1951. The paper itself—but not the discussion—was reprinted in Baker, *Man in the Trap,* Ch. 20.

36. Raphael's comments are quoted in *Man in the Trap,* 304–306. Raphael's full report is in "Orgone Treatment During Labor," *OEB,* III, 1951, 90–98.

37. This report on Reich's work with a baby is taken from the author's article, "Remarks of Reich," *JO,* 9, 1975, 105–109.

Chapter 24: Personal Life and Relations with Colleagues: 1941–1950

1. IOR, WR:BIO, 88.

2. Ibid., 90.

3. AI with IOR, July 1976.

4. *Record of a Friendship,* 61.

5. Gunnar Leistikow, "The Fascist Newspaper Campaign in Norway," *IJSO,* I, 1942, 266–273.

6. AI with Alexander Lowen, February 1981.

7. Ilse Ollendorff, "About Self-Regulation in a Healthy Child," *Annals of the Orgone Institute,* I, 1947, 81–90. (This *Annals* was burned by the FDA and is only available on microfilm at some major libraries. A collection of papers on children by Reich and his co-workers is sorely needed.)

8. AI with IOR, July 1976.

9. Ibid.

10. AI with ER, Aug. 2, 1971.

11. AI with Jo Jenks, December 1978.

12. CB, Ch. X.

13. AI with James A. Willie, May 3–4, 1972.

14. AI with Elsworth F. Baker, Aug. 22, 1971.

15. Chester M. Raphael, "The Marlboro Incident," *OEB,* I, 1949, 70–76.

16. Helena Deutsch, "Freud and His Pupils," in Hendrik Ruitenbeck, ed., *Freud As We Knew Him* (Detroit: Wayne State University Press, 1973), 170–179, 175.

17. Elsworth F. Baker, "My Eleven Years with Wilhelm Reich (Part I)," *JO,* 10, 1976, 182–183.

18. AC with WR, Summer 1948.

19. AC with Paul Goodman, Winter 1947.

20. Paul Goodman, *Nature Heals: Psychological Essays,* ed. by Taylor Stoehr (New York: Free Life Edition, 1977).

21. AC with Alfred Kazin, Fall 1958.

22. Cf., especially *Advertisements for Myself* (New York: Berkley, 1976).

23. Isaac Rosenfeld, "From Isaac Rosenfeld's Journal," edited by Mark Shechner, *Partisan Review,* I, 1980, 9–28.

24. AI with James A. Willie, May 3–4, 1972.

25. WR, "Regarding the Founding of *The American Association for Medical Orgonomy,*" *OEB,* I, 1949, 79–116.

26. IOR, WR:BIO, III.

27. See Myron Sharaf, "The First Orgone Conference at Orgonon, August 30 to September 3, 1948," *OEB,* I, 1949, 23–29.

28. AI with Kari Berggrav, July 17, 1971.

29. WR, "Integration of Visible Orgone Energy Functions," *OEB,* III, 1951, 188–200.

30. AC with Grete Hoff, Spring 1955.

31. See Ernest Hartmann, *The Functions of Sleep* (New Haven: Yale University Press, 1973).

32. Donald Hall, *Remembering Poets* (New York: Harper Colophon, 1977), 123.

33. AC with WR, Fall 1949.

Chapter 25: The American Campaign Against Orgonomy—The Beginnings: 1947–1948

1. See Lillian Hellman, *Scoundrel Time* (New York: Bantam Books, 1977).

2. Mildred Edie Brady, "Is the World Sexually Sick?" *Everybody's Digest,* December 1947.

3. Henderson and Shaw, "Greenwich Village," *Collier's,* Dec. 6, 1947.

4. Irwin Ross,"The Strange Case of Wilhelm Reich," *New York Post,* Sept. 5, 1954.

5. Mildred Edie Brady,"The Strange Case of Wilhelm Reich," *Bulletin of the Menninger Clinic,* 12, 1948.

6. FDA file on Reich. How I came upon the FDA file back in the 1960s and prior to the Freedom of Information Act that makes it available to the public says something about the FDA's view of the case. At the time, Nathan C. Hale was planning a study of Reich. He knew the FDA had refused to permit indignant followers of Reich to see the material. Hence he presented himself quite differently, simply asking to see their "six most famous cases" for purposes of an article he was writing, with the correct conviction that they would so define the Reich affair. He was also permitted to Xerox the records on the "six most famous cases," including the material on Reich. When Hale gave up the idea of doing the study, he generously permitted me to use the material.

7. Jerome Greenfield, *Wilhelm Reich Vs. the U.S.A.* (New York: W. W. Norton, 1974), 61–62.

8. Ibid., 62.

9. FDA file.

10. Ibid.

11. Ibid.

12. Ibid.

13. Greenfield, 69.

14. *Conspiracy and Emotional Chain Reaction,* Item 386A. *Conspiracy* was a volume of documents Reich prepared soon after the injunction was issued in 1954. It was quite a thorough record of almost all the attacks against him since his arrival in the United States, with many responses by him and his associates. The various articles, letters, and the like were reproduced by photo offset and then assembled in looseleaf binders; the volume was sold only to associates and students. After the FDA investigation started, Reich was more determined than ever that each attack, slander, or innuendo, written or oral, be carefully recorded in his files, and he drew on this information when he prepared *Conspiracy*.

15. *Conspiracy,* Item 22.

16. Greenfield, 73.

17. Ibid.

18. *Conspiracy.* Item 46.

19. *Conspiracy.* Item 49.

20. Greenfield, 83.

21. Theodore P. Wolfe, *Emotional Plague versus Orgone Biophysics* (New York: OIP, 1948).

22. Nietzsche, "Schopenhauer as Educator," *Thoughts out of Season,* 144.

23. FDA file.

Chapter 26: The Oranur Experiment: 1950–1953

1. WR, "Orgone Biophysics, Mechanistic Science and 'Atomic' Energy," *IJSO,* IV, 1945, 132. (This very valuable article by Reich has never been reissued after the burning of the *Journal* in which it appeared.)

2. WR, "Oranur Project—The Orgonomic Anti-Nuclear Radiation Project (Oranur)" (Rangeley, Me.: OIP, 1950).

3. "Orgone Biophysics," 130.

4. WR, "Orgone Energy (OR) versus Nuclear Energy (NR)—ORANUR (December 1950 – May 1951)," *OEB,* III, 1951, 267–344. Much of the subsequent material is drawn from this report, hereafter referred to as *Oranur.* This report was also destroyed by the FDA but parts of it were reprinted in WR, *Selected Writings.*

5. WR, "The Geiger-Müller Effect of Cosmic Orgone Energy (1947)," *OEB,* III, 1951, 201–266.

6. *Oranur,* 306.

7. AI with IOR, July 1976.

8. Peter Reich, *A Book of Dreams,* 161–162.

9. Martin D. Ecker and Norton J. Bramesco, *All You Need to Know About Radiation* (New York: Vintage, 1981), 59. This text, by a professor of radiology at the Yale School of Medicine and a journalist, is a marvel of concision and readability.

10. James DeMeo, "Effects of Fluorescent Lights and Metal Boxes on Growing Plants," *JO, 9,* 1975, 62–68.

11. Ecker and Bramesco, 62, 161.

12. Ecker and Bramesco, especially Chs. 6 and 7.

13. WR, "DOR Removal and Cloud-Busting," *OEB,* IV, 1952, 171–172.

14. Quoted in Boadella, Ch. 12.

15. Cf., for example, Richard Blasband, "Orgonomic Functionalism: Atmospheric Circulation," *JO,* 4, 1970, 167–182, and his "Core Progress Report, No. 4," *JO,* 8, 1974, 85–89; and Charles Kelley, *A New Method of Weather Control* (Stamford, Conn.: 1961).

16. James DeMeo, "Preliminary Analysis of Changes in Kansas Weather Coincidental to Experimental Operations with a Reich Cloud-Buster," master's thesis, Dept. of Geography/Meteorology, University of Kansas, 1973. This particular quote is taken from the abstract of the thesis.

17. WR, "The Blackening Rocks," *OEB,* V, 1953, 28–59, 41.

18. Ibid., 53.

19. WR, "The Medical DOR-Buster," *CORE,* VII, 1955, 97–113.

20. Richard A. Blasband, "The Medical DOR-Buster in the Treatment of Cancer Mice," *JO,* 8, 1974, 173–180.

Chapter 27: Personal Life and Other Developments: 1950–1954

1. RSF, 20.

2. AI with ER, Oct. 17, 1981.

3. AI with IOR, July 1976.

4. Ibid.

5. AI with Lois Wyvell, December 1978.

6. Most of the information about Wolfe in this chapter is drawn from my interview with Gladys Meyer, July 16, 1971.

7. AI with IOR, July 1976.

8. Ibid.

9. Baker, "My Eleven Years with Wilhelm Reich," *JO,* 12, 1978, 178.

10. Ibid., 179.

11. AI with Gladys Meyer, July 16, 1971.

12. Ibid.

13. IOR, WR:BIO, 140.

14. Ibid.

15. *Oranur,* 328.

16. *Conspiracy.* Item 330.

17. AI with IOR, July 1976.

18. IOR, WR:BIO, 18.

19. AC with WR, Fall 1952.

20. AI with ER, Oct. 17, 1981.

21. WR, *Ether, God and Devil,* Ch. II.

22. Ernest Hemingway, *A Farewell to Arms* (New York: Charles Scribner's Sons, 1924).

23. WR, *The Murder of Christ* (Rangeley, Me.: OIP, 1953), Appendix. This work is also available through FSG.

24. Fyodor Dostoevski, *The Brothers Karamazov* (New York: Random House, 1955).

25. WR, *Cosmic Superimposition* (Rangeley, Me.: OIP, 1953), Ch. VIII. This book is also available through FSG.

26. Ibid.

27. Ibid.

28. RSF, 20.

29. RSF, 118.

30. Tel. Int. with K. R. Eissler, July 1971.

31. RSF, Introductory Note.

32. WR, "Re-emergence of the Death Instinct as 'DOR' Energy," *Orgonomic Medicine,* II, 1956, 2–11.

33. AI with ER, Oct. 17, 1981.

34. AI with LL, July 15, 1971.

35. AI with Lois Wyvell, September 1981.

36. AI with Robert McCullough, July 28, 1972.

37. Robert McCullough, "The Rocky Road to Functionalism," *CORE,* VII, 1955, 144–154.

38. Ibid., 147.

Chapter 28: The FDA Injunction and Reich's Responses: 1951–1955

1. AC with Nathan C. Hale, September 1975.

2. Greenfield, p. 116.

3. *Conspiracy,* Item 364.

4. AI with IOR, July 1976.

5. *Conspiracy,* Item 392B.

6. Donald Keyhoe, *Flying Saucers from Outer Space* (New York: Henry Holt, 1953).

7. WR, "Space Ships, DOR and Drought," *CORE,* VI, 1954, 19.

8. Ibid, 25.

9. Carl Sagan and Thornton Page, eds., *UFOs: A Scientific Debate* (New York: W. W. Norton, 1972).

10. *Record of a Friendship,* 376 (July 17, 1954).

11. *Conspiracy,* Item 412.

12. Greenfield, 98.

13. FDA file.

14. Ibid.

15. Ibid.

16. Ibid.

17. Ibid.

18. Richard A. Blasband, "An Analysis of the U.S. Food and Drug Administration's Scientific Evidence Against Wilhelm Reich, Part One: The Biomedical Evidence," in Greenfield, 349.

19. FDA file.

20. Blasband, op. cit., 35.

21. David Blasband, "United States of America v. Wilhelm Reich (Part II)," *JO,* 2, 1968, 65.

22. *Complaint for Injunction,* Feb. 10, 1954, in Greenfield, 279–299.

23. Greenfield, 132–133.

24. Elsworth F. Baker, "Wilhelm Reich," *JO,* 1, 1967, 48.

25. Ibid.

26. WR, "The Response: OROP DESERT," in Greenfield, 301–303.

27. Ibid., 302.

28. *Decree of Injunction,* Civil Action No. 1056, March 19, 1954, in Greenfield, 304–307.

29. Greenfield, 153–154.

30. WR, *Response to Ignorance* (Rangeley, Me.: OIP, 1955), 20.

31. WR, "Biophysical Functionalism and Mechanistic Natural Science," *IJSO,* I, 1942, 97–107. (The article has been republished in *JO,* 7, 1974, 5–18.)

32. David Blasband, "United States of America v. Wilhelm Reich," *JO,* 1, 1965–69.

33. Baker, "Wilhelm Reich," *JO,* 1, 1967, 49.

34. Letter from Daniel Blain, Med. Dir., Amer. Psychoanalytic Assoc., to Irvin Kerlan, April 5, 1954 (FDA file).

35. Letter from Richard L. Frank, Sec. of the Amer. Psychoanalytic Assoc., to Irvin Kerlan, Act. Med. Dir., FDA, April 19, 1954 (FDA file on WR).

36. FDA file, May 26, 1956.

37. FDA file, April 20, 1954.

38. James S. Turner, *The Chemical Feast* (New York: Grossman, 1970), 30–33.

39. AI with Peter Reich, June 18, 1972.

40. Ibid.

41. WR, *Contact with Space*, Ch. VI. I may note that it was not until some twenty years after its publication that I could bring myself to study *Contact with Space* carefully, so put off was I by its irrational passages. The book highlights the need for great patience on the part of the reader to sort out Reich's wheat from the chaff of his last years.

42. Ibid, Ch. IV.

43. Ibid.

44. Tel. Int. with William Moise, June 12, 1972.

45. *Contact with Space*, Ch. VII.

Chapter 29: Background to the Trial for Contempt of Injunction: 1955–1956

1. AI with Charles Haydon, July 6, 1972.

2. Reich sent a copy of *Conspiracy* to Olveta Culp Hobby, then Secretary of the Department of Health, Education and Welfare, who forwarded it to Maguire.

3. AI with Gladys Meyer, July 16, 1971.

4. IOR, WR:BIO, 164.

5. Aurora Karrer refused to be interviewed by me.

6. AC with Tom Ross, July 1976.

7. WR, "The Medical DOR-Buster," *CORE*, VII, 1955, 112.

8. Eva Reich, ed., "Early Diagnosis of Cancer of the Uterus," *CORE*, VII, 1955, 48–49.

9. Ibid. (WR is being quoted), 50–51.

10. WR also used pseudonyms in the past. In addition to any objective purpose they served, they seem to have met his penchant for the dramatic.

Chapter 30: The Trial: 1956

1. Much of the material in this chapter is taken from notes I kept when attending the trial in 1956. My article from those notes was published in *The Wilhelm Reich Memorial Volume* (Nottingham, England: Ritter Press, 1958). I would like to thank Paul Ritter for giving me permission to publish much of the same material here. An earlier version of this chapter also appeared in Boadella, Appendix 1.

2. IOR, WR:BIO, 178.

3. Greenfield, 217–218.

4. Ibid, 219.

5. IOR, WR:BIO, 179.

6. Ibid, 179–180.

7. WR, "Atoms for Peace versus the Hig: Address to the Jury," *Orgonomic Medicine*, II, 1956, 12–21.

8. Greenfield, 226–227.

Chapter 31: The Destruction of Orgone Energy Accumulators and the Burning of Reich's Publications: 1956–1957

1. Greenfield, 232.

2. Ibid, 244–245.

3. Peter Reich, *A Book of Dreams*, 57–58.

4. FDA file.

5. Greenfield, 250.

6. Ibid, 252.

7. Quoted in *The Jailing of a Great Scientist in the U.S.A.*, 1956, a pamphlet by Raymond R. Rees and Lois Wyvell.

8. AC with Tom Ross, July 1976.

9. IOR, WR:BIO, 185.

10. *Record of a Friendship*, 417–418.

11. A copy of the correspondence between Reich and Raknes was very generously given to me by Ola Raknes.

12. AI with Peter Reich, June 18, 1972.

13. AI with Morton Herskowitz, July 7, 1972.

14. AI with Elsworth F. Baker, Aug. 22, 1971.

15. AI with ER, Aug. 2, 1971.

16. Greenfield, 257.

17. Ibid.

18. AI with John Murray, Nov. 5, 1971. A very likable and humane person, Murray had the highest opinion of Reich as a teacher in the 1920s. Unlike so many analysts, he was not comtemptuous toward the later Reich, even if he judged him "paranoid" on the basis of his conduct of the legal case.

19. Prison file on Reich, Federal Bureau of Prisons, Washington, D.C.

20. AI with William Moise, June 12, 1971.

21. Greenfield, 259.

Chapter 32: Prison and Death: 1957

1. Greenfield, 261–263. All of my information about the encounter between Reich and Hubbard is drawn from Greenfield.

2. Ibid., 263–264.

3. IOR, WR:BIO, 193–194.

4. Prison file on Reich.

5. Ibid.

6. Ibid.

7. FDA file.

8. Prison file.

9. Tel. Int. with the Reverend Frederick Silber, Feb. 25, 1972.

10. IOR, WR:BIO, 196.

11. Greenfield, 263.

12. AC with Greenfield, 273.

13. This information is contained in Reich's parole application in the prison file.

14. AI with ER, Aug. 2, 1971.

15. IOR, WR:BIO, 197.

16. Ibid, 198.

Epilogue

1. WR, *Selected Writings* (New York: FSG, 1960), viii.

2. AI with ER, Aug. 2, 1971.

3. Greenfield, 273.

4. Jutta Espanca, "The Effect of Orgone on Plant Life, Part 1," *Offshoots of Orgonomy*, 3, 1981; "Part 2," *Offshoots*, 4, 1982.

5. Philip Rieff, "Reich's *Selected Writings*," *New York Times*, Sept. 11, 1960.

6. Christopher Lehmann-Haupt, "Back into the Old Orgone Box," *New York Times*, Jan. 4, 1971.

7. Quoted by Arthur Efron in "The Mind-Body Problem in Lawrence, Pepper, and Reich," *Journal of Mind and Behavior*, V, 1980, 249.

BIBLIOGRAPHY

SELECTED AND ANNOTATED LISTING OF REICH'S WRITINGS

In general, the following works of Reich are available. I have listed several, with an asterisk, which are not available: they were burned by the Food and Drug Administration. I briefly describe them here to encourage public pressure for their reissue. Unless otherwise indicated, all the books were edited by Mary Higgins and Chester M. Raphael; they were published by Farrar, Straus, & Giroux of New York City. The first date given refers to the Farrar publication, the second to the earliest publication of the work in whole or in part.

Early Writings, Vol. I, 1975, 1920s. This collection contains two papers of special interest: Reich's monograph on the impulsive character and his disguised autobiographical account, "The Pubertal Breaching of the Incest Taboo," which I have used as a main key to understanding Reich.

Genitality, 1981, 1927. This book is, essentially, a translation of Reich's German study, *Die Funktion des Orgasmus* (not to be confused with the almost totally different later English volume with the same title). It is of great historical importance because it contains Reich's first detailed description of orgastic potency. However, its most important findings are presented more succintly in the later English volume.

The Invasion of Compulsory Morality, 1974, 1932. This represents Reich's attempt to understand the origin of sick attitudes toward sexuality through the use of findings by Malinowski, the Marxist tradition, and his own investigations. It is less clearly written than many of his other books.

The Mass Psychology of Fascism, 1969, 1933. This classic work on the relationship between personality and receptivity to fascism antedates and strikes more deeply than the later, better-known work of Erich Fromm and the authors of *The Authoritarian Personality*.

Character Analysis, 1972, 1933. This book surveys Reich's psychiatric work from the 1920s through the 1940s. Although the first sections are considered classic contributions to psychoanalytic theory and technique, the last parts dealing with the muscular armor and bio-energetic streamings have been shockingly neglected.

The Sexual Revolution, 1974, 1936. This book still represents the most slashing critique of traditional sexuality and the clearest affirmation of the healthy genital impulses of children, adolescents, and adults.

The Biological Foundations of Pleasure and Anxiety, 1982, 1937. This work describes a key transition in Reich's development, his first laboratory studies. It also contains two fine papers that show the theoretical path to these experiments.

The Bion Experiments, 1979, 1938. Although the findings of this book are more concisely summarized in *The Cancer Biopathy*, the first work contains more experimental detail.

The Cancer Biopathy, 1973, 1948. This work is a marvel of concise, clear presentation of Reich's laboratory work from 1938 to the mid-1940s. It shows the path to the discovery of orgone energy and also depicts Reich's many-sided approach to the etiology, treatment, and prevention of cancer.

Ether, God, and Devil and *Cosmic Superimposition*, 1972, 1950 and 1951. The first work in this two-book volume gives the most complete picture available of Reich's functional method of thought. It is as important as it is neglected, even by students of orgonomy. The second work is less accessible to the layman save for the last and important chapter on "the rooting of reason in nature."

Listen, Little Man!, 1975, 1948. This is a forceful, vivid critique of the armor of the average person, written in a way that is accessible to anyone willing to bear the discomfort of its truths, which are often stated belligerently.

People in Trouble, 1976, 1953. This book contains Reich's most personal, vivid account of his participation in the Marxist movement during the late 1920s and early 1930s.

The Murder of Christ, 1979, 1953. In simple, blazing prose, Reich relates the attacks on Christ to those on other pioneers, including himself.

Reich Speaks of Freud, 1967. This is Reich's most vivid statement of the relationship between his work and himself to psychoanalysis and Freud.

Record of a Friendship: The Correspondence between Wilhelm Reich and A. S. Neill, 1982 (Ed. by Beverly R. Placzeck). Neill's light touch and varied interests stand in sharp contrast to Reich's inexorable scientific march. Withal, a fascinating exchange.

Wilhelm Reich, *Sexpol Essays*, 1929–1934 (Ed. by Lee Baxandall, New York: Random House, 1972). This is the only available collection of some of Reich's sex-political papers that were written during his Marxist phase. The book is well translated and a superb contribution.

Reich, "Biophysical Functionalism and Mechanistic Natural Science," *JO*, 8, 1974, 4–18. This is one of Reich's most profound theoretical statements. Reich, "Character and Society," *JO*, 8, 1974, 116–129. This contains one of Reich's finest sociopsychological papers, written with masterful clarity.

*Reich's unavailable articles on his method of thought: Orgonomic Functionalism. *Orgone Energy Bulletin*, II, 1950, 1–16; 49–62; 99–123. *OEB*, IV, 1952, 1–12; 186–196. In these papers Reich presents his work from the viewpoint of his method of thought. These are sharp, profoundly original, and badly needed today.

*Reich's unavailable articles on children: "Children of the Future: I," *OEB*, II, 1950, 194–206. "Armoring in a Newborn Infant," *OEB*, III, 1951, 121–138.

*Reich's unavailable articles on Oranur and its aftermath: "The Oranur Experiment," *OEB,* III, 1951, 267–344; "DOR Removal and Cloud-Busting," *OEB,* IV, 1952, 171–182; "OROP Desert: Space Ships, DOR, and Drought," CORE, VI, 1954, 1–149.

BOOKS ABOUT REICH

Baker, Elsworth F., *Man in the Trap,* New York: Avon Books, 1967. This work is a concise, extremely lucid presentation of Reich's psychiatric concepts and techniques, plus Baker's additions to them.

Bean, Orson, *Me and the Orgone,* New York: St. Martin's Press, 1971. Bean gives a vivid view, written for the layman, of his therapy with Elsworth F. Baker.

Boadella, David, *Wilhelm Reich: The Evolution of His Work,* Chicago: Contemporary Books, Inc., 1973; available in a Dell paperback. This is a fine study of the totality of Reich's work.

Cattier, Michael, *The Life and Work of Wilhelm Reich,* New York: Avon Books, 1971. Cattier deals accurately with Reich's work until about the year 1935, but dismisses it after that.

Greenfield, Jerome, *Wilhelm Reich Vs. the U.S.A.,* New York: W. W. Norton, 1974. This finely researched work studies the investigation of the Food and Drug Administration that ultimately led to the destruction of Reich's accumulators and the burning of his books.

Mann, W. Edward, *Orgone, Reich and Eros,* New York: Simon and Schuster, 1973. This erudite work relates Reich's orgone energy concepts to other energetic theories.

————and Hoffman, Edward, *The Man Who Dreamed of Tomorrow,* Chicago: Tarcher, 1980. As the title indicates, the authors relate Reich's work to current developments in diverse fields.

Meyerowitz, Patricia, *And a Little Child,* New York: rRp Publishers, 1982. This slim poetic book about children contains an absolutely first-rate bibliography of orgonomic literature on infants and children.

Raknes, Ola, *Wilhelm Reich and Orgonomy,* New York: Penguin Books, 1970. Raknes' book is a sensitive, well-informed but somewhat plodding book on Reich's work.

Reich, Ilse Ollendorff, *Wilhelm Reich: A Personal Biography,* New York: St. Martin's Press, 1969. This is a rapid, honest survey of Reich's life and work, written by one who was close but amazingly detached.

Reich, Peter, *A Book of Dreams,* Harper & Row, 1973. This represents an evocative, wrenching account of Reich, as seen by his young son.

Rycroft, Charles, *Wilhelm Reich,* New York: The Viking Press, 1972. What's valuable here is the lucid survey of Reich's therapeutic work *c.* 1930.

Wilson, Colin, *The Quest for Wilhelm Reich,* New York: Doubleday, 1981. This book is a puzzling amalgam of insight and error about Reich's life and work.

PERIODICALS ABOUT ORGONOMY

The Journal of Orgonomy. Editor: Elsworth F. Baker, M.D. Address: Orgonomic Publications, Inc., P. O. Box 565, Ansonia Station, New York, N.Y. 10023. This *Journal* hews closely to and develops orgonomic concepts and findings. It is also often dogmatic in dealing with related therapeutic and social developments.

Energy and Character. Editor: David Boadella. Address: David Boadella, Abbotsbury, Dorset, England. This journal is keenly aware of the broad scientific, social, and therapeutic atmosphere that orgonomy has influenced but it also insufficiently emphasizes the central lines of Reich's thought and work.

Offshoots of Orgonomy. Editor: Lois Wyvell. Address: Offshoots Publications, P. O. Box 1248, Gracie Station, New York, New York 10028. This periodical is frequently marred by dogmatism, but is a brave and often successful attempt to popularize orgonomy without oversimplifying it.

Scienza Orgonomica. Editor: Giuseppe Cammarella, M.D. Pubblicazioni Orgonomische, 215, Via Flaminia, 00196 Roma, Italia. This Italian journal reprints articles from the *Journal of Orgonomy.*

INDEX

Abortion, 4, 60–61, 121, 131, 134, 136,
142, 161, 162, 163, 245, 336, 385
Abraham, Karl, 68, 70, 75, 76, 86–
87, 178, 210
Academie des Sciences, 226, 227
Actual neuroses, 88–90, 96, 97, 100,
108, 120, 143, 152, 207, 401
Adler, Alfred, 85, 229, 240
Adolescent sexuality, 4, 5, 15, 17, 134,
135, 148, 161–2, 169, 306, 321, 482
Adolescents, education of, 168
Adorno, Theodor, 164
The Adventures of Augie March
(Bellow), 347
Aftenposten, 227, 228
Agee, James, 12
Aichorn, August, 113
Aiken, Conrad, 28, 95
Alexander, Franz, 67
American Association for Medical
Orgonomy, 348
The American Civil Liberties
Union, 460
The American Journal of Psychiatry,
268
The American Medical Association
, 362, 413
American press campaign, 360, 366
The American Psychiatric Associa-
tion, 348, 362, 413, 414, 427

The American Psychoanalytic As-
sociation, 427
Amoebae, experiments with, 208,
218, 299, 301
Amoeboid cells in cancer, 297
Anal inhibitions, 182
Anal stage, 68, 86, 88, 181
Anarchism, 319–320, 346
Anderson, Dr., 437
Anderson, Marian, 3
Andreas-Salomé, Lou, 100–101
Anger, 137, 140, 144, 179, 313
Annals of the Orgone Institute, 460
Anorgonia, 328
Anti-semitism, 47, 165
Antithetical relationship, 293, 301
Anxiety, 97, 120, 121, 137, 144, 164,
167, 177, 189, 206–208, 211–212,
234, 241, 299, 303, 304, 306, 316,
318, 326, 331
Arbeiderbladet, 229
Arbeiderblatt, 172
Arizona expedition, 381, 428–429,
431–432, 442–443, 445, 448
Armor, see Character armor; Mus-
cular armor
Armor, segments of body, see Seg-
ments of body armor
Armor blocks, 381
Armor in the genital character, 178

525

Arrest of Silvert, 446
Articles about Reich, USA, 339, 360, 362, 482
Association for Socialist Physicians, Berlin, 160
Astrophysical research, 340
Atmospheric orgone, 280, 285, 288–289, 295, 301, 314, 329, 377–378, 379, 382, 402, 443
Atmospheric pollution, 377–378, 378n., 382, 442–443
Atomic bomb, 280, 322, 370
Atomic Energy Commission, 284, 355, 427, 451
Atomic physics, 371, 372
Atoms for Peace versus the Hig (Reich), 451
Attack of medical orgonomy, 344, 348, 351
Auden, W. H., 273n., 274
Authoritarian societies, 4, 164
Authoritarianism, 9, 138, 164, 285, 398
Autonomic nervous system, 207, 236n.

Baby and Child Care (Spock), 318
Bacterial Institute of Oslo, 228
Baker, Courtney, 288, 289, 290
Baker, Elsworth F., 3, 5, 288, 309, 343–344, 346, 348, 349, 384, 389, 393, 394, 402, 406, 413, 420, 421, 426, 429, 430, 431, 431 n., 437, 439, 444, 461, 462, 464–465, 480, 481
Baker, Marguerite, 431, 431n.
Baldwin, James, 102
Barnard College, 386
The Basic Antithesis of Vegetative Life (Reich), 188
Basic laws of nature, 287
Basic life processes, 243
Beckett, Samuel, 189
Becquerel, Henri, 371

Bell, John, 481
Bellow, Saul, 5, 323, 347
Bergersen, Gerd, 255, 273n., 385, 404
Berggrav, Kari, 351, 352
Bergman, Ingmar, 189
Bergson, Henri, 54
Berle, Adolph, 258
Berlin, 123, 150, 152, 154–155, 157, 160–161, 163, 167, 186, 192–193, 195, 199–200, 202, 245, 262, 403
Berlin, Isaiah, 247
Berneri, Marie-Louise, 268
Bernfeld, Siegfried, 82, 121, 155
Bibring, Edward, 55–56, 59
Bibring, Grete, 55–56, 59, 108, 119, 143, 147–148, 152, 201–202, 482
Binding of anxiety, 208
Bio-electrical experiments, 209–218, 234, 252, 267, 280
Bio-electrical model, 209–210, 212, 214, 239, 295, 310
Bio-energetics, 4, 244, 481
Bio-feedback techniques, 208
Biogenesis, 5, 217, 218, 222–223, 226
Biological Aspects of Character Formation (Reich), 265
Biological core, 4, 299–300, 326, 328
Biological energy, *see* Orgone energy
Bion experiments, 219–222, 408
Bion research, 215, 217, 220–227, 243, 252, 257, 293–294, 301, 471
Die Bione (Reich), 226, 266
Bions, 5, 217–223, 228, 254, 269–270, 276, 280, 285, 295, 302, 326, 340–341, 351, 403, 408
Biopathic contractions, 316
Biopathic shrinking process, 299–301
Biopathy, 298, 305, 306
Birth control, 131, 165, 425
Bizzi, Bruno, 308

Blackening of rocks, *see* DOR, disintegration of rocks
Blain, Daniel, 427
Blasband, David, 418
Blasband, Richard, 308, 417
Blocking of sensations, 25, 120, 237
The Blue Angel (von Sternberg), 131
Blum, Josef, 36, 44, 150
Boadella, David, 224, 279–280, 300–301
Body armor, *see* Muscular armor
Body expression, 234, 236*n.*, 237, 238, 239, 298, 329
Body sensations, 315, 316
Bohr, Niels, 53
Book burning, *see* Destruction of orgonomic publications
A Book of Dreams (Reich), 403
Bornstein, Berta, 248–252, 271, 273, 322, 482
Boston, Mass., 23, 27, 31, 364, 439
Boston State Hospital, 31
Botanical Institute, Oslo, 218
Bowdoin College, 289
Brackett, Mr., 364
Brady, Mildred Edie, 360–364, 366–367, 369, 427, 439
Brandt, Willi, 264, 264*n.*
Braque, Georges, 53
The Breakthrough of the Incest Taboo in Puberty (Reich), 41–46, 63–64, 96, 107, 139, 407
Breuer, Josef, 78, 101, 117
Briehl, Marie, 268
Briehl, Walter, 81, 258, 262, 268–269
Brill, A. A., 18, 187
Brown, Norman O., 103
Brownian movement, 222, 227, 257
Bruno, Giordano, 397, 412*n.*, 439
Brupbacher, Fritz, 142, 198
Bulletin of the Menninger Clinic, 362
Burning eyes expression, 17, 161
Burroughs, William, 5

Buxbaum, Edith, 106, 107, 109, 151–152
Bye, Lillian, 262, 263, 273

Calderone, Mary, 140
Cameron, D. Ewen, 414
Cancer, 227, 294, 296–298, 300, 304, 307, 319, 340, 344, 378, 407*n.*, 482
Cancer, diagnosis, 297, 407, 443
Cancer, etiology of, 294, 299–301, 306, 309
Cancer, prevention of, 306, 307
Cancer, treatment of, 294, 296, 301–305, 382, 415–416, 443–444
Cancer biopathy, 298–299, 306, 378
The Cancer Biopathy (Reich), 299, 301, 424
Cancer cell formation, 294, 295
Cancer cells, live, 228, 295, 297, 301, 322
Cancer patients, 294–296, 298–300, 303–304, 322, 328
Cancer tumor, 296, 298, 299, 300, 301, 302, 304, 305
Cardiovascular biopathies, 299
Carson, Rachel, 378
Carstens, Erik, 185
Castration threats, 68
Catharsis, 97
Catholic Church, 133, 161
Central Committee for Youth, 169
Central nervous system, 207
Centre Universitaire Méditerranée, Nice, 225
Cervical segment, 312, 325
The Chalk Triangle (Reich et al), 168–169
Character analysis, 8, 58, 75–76, 80–81, 85–86, 88, 99, 116, 118, 126, 133, 143, 160, 175, 176, 178–179, 182, 210, 218, 236*n.*, 241, 266, 269, 312, 343, 385, 481

Character Analysis (Reich) 1933, 75 n., 78, 80, 95, 126, 168, 171–172, 183, 226, 266

Character Analysis (Reich) 1945, 188, 268, 313, 322, 419, 428, 481

Character-analytic vegetotherapy, 208, 218, 236, 236n., 237, 241–242, 244, 252, 267

Character armor, 75–77, 79–81, 95, 126, 143, 164, 165, 176, 182, 189, 208, 218, 279, 322, 327, 353, 397

Character neuroses, 68, 75, 102–103, 176, 323

Character structure, 9, 79, 86, 127, 164, 176–178, 237, 244, 299

Character traits, diagnostic, 68, 177, 221, 298, 314

Character types, 177–178

Charcot, Jean Martin, 101

Charge, 210, 211, 213

Charlottenburg, 163

Childhood and Society (Erikson), 102

Childhood sexuality, 136–139, 143, 148, 150, 208, 306, 482

Children, education of, 168, 325

Chiurco, Prof., 308

Christian Socialist Party of Austria, 54, 123, 125, 127, 131, 156, 184

Christianity, 13, 321, 465

Chronic anxiety, 207–208

Chronic muscular spasm, *see* Muscular armor

Circumcision, 330, 332, 482

City Lights (Chaplin), 464

City Opera, Berlin, 194

Civilization and Its Discontents (Freud), 153

Clark, Ronald W., 288

Classification Study of Reich, 470–471

Clifford, Judge John D., 422–424, 426, 433–434, 438–440, 446–447

Cloud-buster, 379–382, 406, 431

Cloud-busting, 379–381, 403–404, 408, 414, 424–425, 428–429, 432, 434–435, 443

Coleridge on Iago, 324

College of Orgonomy, 480, 481

Collier's, 362

Columbia Medical School, 257

Committee of Revolutionary Social Democrats, 156

Common functioning principle, 382

Communism in Russia, 165, 173, 318

Communist movement, 6, 172–173, 192, 240, 395, 412, 430, 456, 462, 465

Communist Party of
America, 361, 366, 367n.
Austria, 125–128, 134, 145–146, 148, 156, 199
Denmark, 172, 184, 196
Germany, 157, 160–163, 165–169, 171, 173, 183, 185, 194, 197, 322, 395

Complaint for Injunction, 418–419

Compulsive character, 80, 177

Compulsive morality, 166, 167

Conference at Orgonon, 30, 349–353

Consequences of Orgone in Vacuum (Reich), 352

Conservatism, 397–398, 402, 481

Conspiracy (Reich et al), 439, 449, 450

Contact, body, 326, 328

Contact, energetic, 328, 332

Contact with the core, 9, 10, 12, 132, 258, 400

Contact with Space (Reich), 432, 458

Contactlessness, 189–191

Contempt of Injunction, 432, 433
preliminary hearings, 438–439
proceedings, 434, 436–439

Contraception, 4, 5, 88, 121, 130, 132, 134–136, 142, 161, 162, 168

Contraction, chronic, *see* Muscular armor

Contraction, sudden, 326, 328, 332
Control over irrationality, 321
Copenhagen, 172, 184–186, 196–197, 200, 245
Copernicus, 291
CORE, 414, 442–444
CORE men, 413–414
Core-energetics, 481
Cosmic orgone energy, 352–353, 482
Cosmic orgone engineering, 413–414, 430
Cosmic rays, 372
Cosmic Superimposition (Reich), 399
Cott, A. Allan, 343, 347, 348, 483
Cotten, Henry, 344
Council on Pharmacy and Chemistry, 308
Course on Reich's work, 481
Co-workers response to FDA attack, 367–368
Creation, function of, 382
Creativity, lack of, 345
Criticism of cancer treatments, 305–306, 308
Criticism of experiments, 215–216, 218, 221–222, 227, 243, 256, 281–282, 286–287, 380n. 415
Crying, 235–236, 238, 244, 311–313, 325, 476
Culver, Julian, 365–366, 368
Curie, Marie and Pierre, 371
Custom-built measuring equipment, 211–212
Czernowitz, Bukovina, 47

Daily News, Bangor, Me., 379–380
Dangers of therapy, 239–240
Danish campaign, 185
Danish government, 184, 196–197
Davos, Switzerland, 116–117, 119–120, 145, 188, 263, 272
Death, process of, 382

Death instinct theory, 120, 180, 182, 183, 187, 188, 247, 402
Decay of stone masonry, 381, 381n.
Defensive character traits, 75, 181, 239
DeMeo, James, 380–381
Demonstration of orgonomic phenomena, 351
Denison, Lucille, 329
Depression, biological, 303–304
Depression, economic, 148, 150, 156
Desert development, 381, 413, 428
Destruction of orgone accumulators, 458–460
Destruction of orgonomic publications, 423–424, 426–428, 458, 460–461
Deutsch, Felix, 153
Deutsch, Helena, 98, 117, 152, 153, 345
Diagnosis in therapy, 88, 313
Dialectical materialism, 252
Diaries of Reich, 6–7, 120
Dickinson, Emily, 357n.
Dietrich, Marlene, 131
Dinesen, Isak, 120
Discharge, 102, 209, 210, 213, 239, 306
Distorted criticism of Reich, 183, 200–201, 216, 227–230, 305–306, 317, 360–362, 366, 419, 471, 475
Distortions of Reich's views, 139, 360–363, 366
Dodge Pond, Maine, 340, 350
Doherty, William, 419
Dollfuss, Engelbert, 171, 184, 199
Donne, John, 182
DOR, 373, 376–377, 379, 381–382, 392, 402, 408, 413, 429, 432, 440, 442–443, 453, 455, 471, 474
DOR, disintegration of rocks, 381, 408

DOR-buster, *see* Cloud-buster; Medical DOR-buster
DOR-clouds, 378, 378*n.*, 379, 381–382
DOR-sickness, 375, 408, 413, 442
Dostoevski, Feodor, 8, 48, 398
Dresden, 163, 169
Dunbar, H. Flanders, 257
Dunham, Charles L., 427
Durrett, J. J., 362–363
Düsseldorf, 162
Duvall, Albert, 437

Edel, Leon, 32–33
Education of children, 138–139, 142–143, 321, 329, 337
Education of Reich's children, 192–193
Ego development, 69–70, 103
Einstein, Albert, 8, 53, 280, 283–288, 288*n.*, 293, 322, 337, 342, 399
Eisenhower, Dwight D., 320, 412–413, 414, 425, 462
Eissler, Kurt, 73, 131, 161, 167, 193, 200–201, 400–402
Eitingon, Max, 183
Electromagnetic pollution, 377
Electroscopic discharge rate, 283–284, 289–290
Electroscopic effects of orgone, 282–284, 288–290, 301
Ellis, Havelock, 53, 142
Ellis Island, 271, 339, 350, 386
Emerson, Ralph Waldo, 98
Emotional behavior, 180–181
Emotional expression of the body, 197, 207, 234, 239, 278, 311, 313, 325, 329
Emotional first aid, 332, 333
Emotional plague, 9, 323–324, 344, 357, 377, 382, 391, 412, 421, 430, 437–438, 453, 455, 458
  analogy with oranur, 377
  organized, 366, 430, 437, 456

Emotional plague character, 323, 324, 411–412, 421
Emotional Plague versus Orgone Biophysics (Wolfe), 367, 460
Emotions, blocked, 77–78, 89, 111, 239, 301, 400
Emotions and Bodily Changes (Dunbar), 257
End phase of therapy, 238–239
Energy, release of, 244, 328, 372
Energy blocks, 314, 317, 319, 325, 372, 381
Energy field, 296, 396
Energy flow, biological, 208–209, 218, 235–236, 236*n.*, 239, 243–244, 296, 326, 328, 329, 343, 372, 381, 382
Engels, Friedrich, 143
English, O. Spurgeon, 81, 175–176
Enterline and Coman, 297, 301
Erikson, Erik, 7, 11, 21, 45, 58, 102
Erogenous zones, 211–215
Escape from Freedom (Fromm), 164
Ether, God and Devil (Reich), 352, 396, 460
Evaluation of Reich's experiments, 214–215
Evasion of truth, 105
Evening Express, Portland, 466
Everybody's Digest, 362
Excreta of cancer patients, 296, 297, 300
Experiments, results of, 212–214, 301–304, 373
Experiments with mice, 293–295, 301–302
Expression of anger in therapy, 76–77
Eye block, 315
Eye contact, 311, 315–316, 327, 332
Eyes, expression of the, 237–239, 311

Facial expression, 237–239, 241
Faith healing, 208

Falling anxiety, 325–329
Family cabin at Orgonon, 340
Farmington, Me., 383
Fascism, 148, 337
The Fascist Newspaper Campaign in Norway (Leistikow), 337
Fascist regime, Italy, 123
FDA, *see* Food and Drug Administration
FDA files, 366, 367*n.*, 458, 460
FDA injunction, 308–309, 368, 402, 418–419, 423, 428–429, 456
FDA test of the accumulator, 414–418
FDA vs. Reich, 3, 402, 423–424, 456, 457–458, 480
Fear of falling, 197, 304, 326
Fear of freedom and responsibility, 319–320, 361, 398, 402
Fear of Reich's work, 195, 248, 353, 362, 365, 368–369, 398, 402, 456, 461, 470, 483
Fear of spontaneous movement, 291–292, 352, 398, 428
Federal Bureau of Investigation, 271, 350, 412, 465
Federal penitentiary, Lewisburg Pa., 2, 468–471, 476, 482
Federal prison, Danbury Ct., 467–468, 473
Federal Trade Commission, 362
Federn, Ernst, 84, 107
Federn, Paul, 64, 68–69, 71, 81–85, 99, 107, 151, 153–155, 183–184, 187, 194, 203, 322, 401
Feeling of tension, 182
Fellini, Frederico, 189
Fenichel, Otto, 5, 56, 61, 77, 80–81, 102, 106, 109, 121, 160–161, 186–187, 194, 196, 200, 202, 224, 241, 246–249, 256, 273, 322, 482
Ferenczi, Sandor, 8, 76–77, 81, 187, 210
Field excitation, orgone, 302, 352

Fisher, Frederick, 437–439
Fisher, Seymour, 102–103
Flaubert, Gustav, 322–323
Food, study of, 221
Food and Drug Administration, 3, 9, 31, 171, 289, 292, 305, 308–309, 348, 357, 361–363, 366–367, 369, 397, 402, 413, 424, 427–428, 430, 432, 434, 437–438, 440, 443–445, 447, 450–451, 460–461, 463, 470–471, 473, 482
Forest Hills, 16, 27, 263–264, 276, 278, 335–336, 339, 349
Forty Years a Heretic (Brupbacher), 198
Frank, Richard L., 427
Freedom, 2
Freedom of Information Act, 367
Freedom-peddlers, 19
Freud, Anna, 107, 137–138, 146, 184, 187, 202, 248
Freud, Sigmund, 2, 5, 7, 9–10, 18–19, 27, 46, 53, 56–58, 60–61, 63–64, 66, 68–69, 71, 73–74, 78, 81–88, 91–92, 97–104, 107–108, 110, 116–118, 120, 122, 130, 143, 152–155, 171, 173, 178–180, 182–185, 187–188, 193, 197, 203, 207, 210, 217, 235, 240, 247–248, 266, 268, 272–273, 284, 287, 323, 343, 345, 364, 371–372, 383, 393, 395–396, 400–402, 405, 422, 465, 482
Freud Archives, 73, 400–401
Fried, Margaret, 198–199
Frigidity, 87
Fromm, Erich, 5, 7, 160, 164, 268
Function of the orgasm, 86, 90–94, 100–103, 113, 116, 130, 146–147, 197, 209, 213, 243, 247, 272, 287, 300, 306, 328–329, 398, 401
The Function of the Orgasm (Reich) 1927, 92, 100, 120–121, 147, 266

The Function of the Orgasm (Reich)
1942, 15, 19, 92, 266–268, 311, 342
Functional identity, 295, 301
Functional principles, 305
Funeral of Reich, 3
Fusion, energetic, 326, 328

Gaasland, Gertrud, 258, 263–264, 270–271, 276
Gag reflex, 312
Gandhi, Mahatma, 7, 11
Geiger-Müller counter, 372–373
General and Special Pathology of the Person (Kraus), 209
Genital anxiety, 149, 306
Genital character, 9, 70, 86, 95, 176, 178–179, 195, 396, 413
Genital disturbances, 88–91, 208
Genital excitation, 97, 208–209, 237–239, 333
  blocking of, 239
Genital gratification, 90–94, 97, 102–104, 133, 143, 178
Genital sensations, 315
Genital stage, 86, 88, 149, 178, 328, 333
Genitality, 25, 66, 84–92, 96–97, 99–100, 102–103, 118–121, 126, 148–150, 178, 183, 237, 247, 252, 325, 331, 482
German Association for Proletarian Sex-Politics, 162–163, 170
German Communist Party, *see* Communist Party of Germany
German resistance movement, 246, 269
Germicidal action of bions, 276
Gerö, George, 80, 186, 187
Gestalt therapy, 4, 204, 481
Gindler, Elsa, 275*n*.
Goal of therapy, 218, 238–239, 244, 311–312
Goethe, J. W. von, 55, 104, 152, 279–280
Gold, Philip, 345

Goldhammer, G. S., 471
Goodman, Paul, 5, 268, 319, 346–347
Gordon, J. B., 344
Gordon, Sam and Jane, 21, 26, 28
Gorki, Maxim, 210
Grad, Bernard, 308, 345, 414
Grass infusions, study of, 219–220
Greenblatt, Milton, 30–31
Greenfield, Jerome, 363, 363*n.*, 367
  n., 421, 428, 458–459, 460, 465, 467–468, 470
Grotjahn, Martin, 15, 268
Grundlsee, 154, 250
Guntrip, Harry, 405
Gymnasium, Czernowitz, 40, 46–47

Hale, Nathan C., 411
Hall, Donald, 356
Hamilton, Alexander, 23, 407, 441
Hamilton, Eleanor, 23, 407
Hamilton School, 23, 26, 407, 435
Hancock, Me., 393, 406, 424, 435
Handelman, Sidney, 343, 437
Hansen, Klaus, 227
Hardoy, Ferrari, 350
Hartmann, Ernest, 356
Hartmann, Heinz, 117, 153, 187, 401
Hartmann, Max, 207–208, 219
Hate, 178–179
Havens, Leston, 176
Havrevold, Odd, 225, 228, 256–257, 259, 352
Haydon, Charles, 3, 436–438, 446, 457–458, 460
Hays, Arthur G., 338, 350, 365, 392
Health, emotional, 17, 87–88, 90–95, 102–103, 138, 179, 244, 324, 330, 333, 386, 396
Heiden, Konrad, 165
Heifetz, Ottilie Reich, 37–38, 40, 47, 49–52, 111–113, 147–151, 269, 275, 482
Heimwehr, 123–124, 127, 156
Helmholtz, Hermann, 55
Hemingway, Ernest, 289*n.*, 397

Henderson the Rain King (Bellow), 347

Herskowitz, Morton, 345, 464

Heterosexual play in childhood, 137–138

Heterosexuality, 87, 102

Hig, 411, 451, 455

Higgins, Mary, 6, 402, 480

Hiroshima, 370

Hirschfeld, Magnus, 162

History of orgonomy, 395, 400

Hitler, Adolph, 9, 150, 163, 165–167, 170–172, 186, 196, 198, 246, 251, 253, 269, 272, 274, 280, 403

Hitler Youth movement, 161, 169

Hitschmann, Eduard, 67, 73, 82, 99

Hodann, Max, 142

Hoel, Nic, 186, 202, 225, 230, 246–248, 348

Hoel, Sigurd, 186, 225, 230–231, 246, 253–254, 259, 267, 388

Hoff, Grethe, 23, 25, 27–31, 330, 333, 393, 431, 431*n.*, 435, 445, 462

Hoffmann, Wilhelm, 215–216, 230, 233

Hofstadter, Richard, 164

Holy Ghost Hospital, Boston, 416

Homestead, Kari, 456

Homosexuality, 84, 87

Hoover, J. Edgar, 271, 324, 425, 465

Hoppe, Walter, 308, 348, 350, 351, 353, 461, 482

Horney, Karen, 103, 160, 186

Hostility toward therapist, 344

How I Lost Eva (Reich), 251

Hubbard, Richard C., 468–469, 473

Hurwitz, Rosetta, 268

Hypnosis, 235

Hysterical character, 177

Ibsen's Peer Gynt (Reich), 58, 62

Idealization, 8–9, 12

Identification, 69

Identity of sensation and potential, 213

Imitation, technique of, 181

Immunity, processes of, 294–295, 297, 300, 306

Impotence, 87, 102, 178, 299

Impulsive character, 9, 67–68, 70, 146, 315

The Impulsive Character (Reich), 67–68, 70–71, 75, 83, 118, 139

Indifference, 10–11, 353

Infant-mother relationship, 325–328, 332, 401, 482

Infant Research Center, 190, 329, 330, 333, 344, 356

Infantile sexuality, 56, 88, 103, 138, 235, 321, 401

Infants, research on, 274, 325–326, 328–330, 333–334, 338, 349, 481–482

Infants and children, therapy for, 326–327, 329, 332, 334

Inhibition of respiration, 213, 236

Injunction decree, 423–424, 426, 429–430, 433, 438, 460, 480

Integration of Freud and Marx, 143–144, 160

International Journal of Psychoanalysis, 169, 183

International Journal of Sex-Economy and Orgone-Research, 20, 267, 283, 337, 356, 387, 423, 460

International Orgonomic Conference, 349–353

International Psychoanalytic Association, 175, 184, 187, 191, 196, 198, 246–247, 257, 269, 364, 402

International Psychoanalytic Congress, Lucerne, 1934, 186–188, 191, 200–201, 234, 246

International Psychoanalytic Publishers, 171, 183

International Research Center on Precancer Conditions, 308

The Invasion of Compulsory Sex-Morality (Reich), 197–198

Investigation by FDA, 361, 363–369, 377, 382, 392, 395, 409–412, 414–419, 427–428, 433, 450
Investigation by medical authorities, 347, 414
Investigation by state police, 357
Involuntary body movements during therapy, 180–181, 238, 243
Involuntary convulsions during intercourse, *see* Orgasm reflex
Involuntary surrender during the orgasm, 91–92, 94–95, 103

Jack, 22–23, 26
Jackson Laboratory, 416–417
Jacobson, Edith, 5, 136, 160–161, 186, 193, 202, 245, 251, 269
Janov, Arthur, 4
von Jauregg, Wagner, 66–67
Jekels, Ludwig, 153
Jenks, Jo, 339–340, 386
Jesus Christ, 396–399, 465
Johns Hopkins Hospital, 415, 415*n.*, 416
Johnson, Alvin, 269
Jokl, Robert, 82–84
Jones, Ernest, 68, 183, 187–188, 198, 288, 401
Journal for Political Psychology and Sex-economy, 186, 206, 225, 227, 230, 240, 252–253, 267
Journal for Psychoanalytic Pedagogy, 172
Journal of the American Medical Association, 268, 308
Journal of Orgonomy, 71, 309, 334, 480, 482
Joyce, James, 53
Jujinetz, Bukovina, 36, 47, 50
Jung, Carl, 85, 240, 401

Kaiser Wilhelm Institute, 215
Karrer, Aurora, 442, 444–445, 447, 456, 461, 463, 470, 472, 474, 477, 479

Kaufman, M. Ralph, 81
Kazin, Alfred, 323, 347
Kerensky, Alexander, 202
Key, Ellen, 142
Keyhoe, Donald, 413
King, Martin Luther, 324
Kinsey, Alfred, 18, 102
Koestler, Arthur, 482
Kokoschka, Oskar, 53
Korean War, 370
Kraepelin, Emil, 176
Kramer, Sol, 345
Kraus, Friedrich, 189 *n.*, 207, 209–210
Kraus, Karl, 53
Kreyberg, Leiv, 227–230, 232–233, 248, 256, 322
Kronold, Arthur, 401
Kropotkin, Peter, 346
Krusen, Frank H., 415
Kuhn, Thomas, 290–292, 314

Laboratory space, 263, 336, 340, 408
Laing, R. D., 8, 315
Lange, August, 246
Lapicque, Louis, 226–227
Laszky, Lia, 59–63, 96, 99, 107–108, 130–132, 146–147, 149, 151, 173, 195–197, 256, 270, 275, 385, 405, 482
Latency period, childhood, 68, 70
Lavater, Johann Kasper, 355
Lawrence, D. H., 53, 95, 135
Lawrence, T. E., 7
Leahy Clinic, Boston, 305
Lehmann-Haupt, Christopher, 482
Leipzig, 163
Leistikow, Gunnar, 337
Leunbach, R. L., 185
Levine, Emanuel, 345
Levinson, Daniel J., 9–10, 30, 119, 125, 273 *n.*
Lewin, Kurt, 354
Lewisburg Board of Examiners, 469–470

Libidinal excitation of the masses, 165–166
Libido, 57, 96–97, 99, 102, 178–179, 206–207, 210, 217, 280, 310, 372, 401
Libido stasis, 179, 372
Life energy, *see* Orgone energy
Life formula, *see* Orgasm formula
Lifton, Robert, 118
Light effects, impressions of, 280
Lightning discharges, 379
Lindenberg, Elsa, 39, 194–197, 199–202, 217, 233–234, 245, 248, 253–256, 258–259, 263–265, 272–275, 273*n.*, 336, 403–404
Lion, Kurt, 289–290
Listen, Little Man! (Reich), 13, 321–322, 341, 346, 396
Little, Noel C., 289–290
London, 185, 197, 339
Los Alamos project, 280
Love, 94, 102, 141, 197, 274–275, 312, 332
Lowen, Alexander, 4–5, 235, 239, 242*n.*, 244, 265–266, 266*n.*, 337, 346, 481
Lucerne Congress, *see* International Psychoanalytic Congress
Lumination of orgone, 302, 326, 352

MacDonald, Dwight, 268, 366
MacDonald, Helen, 345, 406
Mack, John, 7
Maguire, Joseph, 438–440, 447–452, 454, 461, 465–467, 470–475
Mailer, Norman, 5, 347
Maine, 357, 363, 379, 393
Maine General Hospital, 416
Makaveyev, Dusan, 430*n.*
Malinowski, Bronislaw, 138, 179, 185, 197–198, 207, 231, 249
Malmö, 185, 199–200
Man in the trap, concept, 4
Mann, Thomas, 53
Marcuse, Herbert, 103

Marienbad, 250
Marlboro State Hospital, 343–344
Marriage, 136, 139–142, 153
Marx, Karl, 10, 27, 134, 143, 190–191, 207, 210, 273, 396, 399, 425, 465
Marxism, 8–9, 13, 124, 130, 133, 147, 163, 166, 169–170, 173, 240, 252, 270, 310, 318–319, 321, 337, 395
Masochism, 176, 179–183, 188, 316–317
Mass psychology concept, 8, 126–128, 152, 161, 163, 166, 168, 218, 269
The Mass Psychology of Fascism (Reich) 1933, 132, 151, 163–164, 168, 172, 232, 266
The Mass Psychology of Fascism (Reich) 1946, 319, 361, 419, 460, 482
Mass therapy, 167–168
Massachusetts Institute of Technology, 289
Massachusetts Mental Health Center, 30
Masters and Johnson, 215, 243
Masturbation, 87–88, 135–138, 144, 180, 214, 216, 344
Mathews, Paul, 481
McCarthy, Joseph, 362, 412, 428, 437, 476
McCullough, Robert, 407–409, 428–429, 434, 449, 453
McDonald, James, 380
McGill University, 308, 345
McPhee, John, 291
Mechanistic concepts, 55, 57, 352
Medical DOR-buster, 382, 440–441
Medical license, 268–269, 347
Medical orgonomy, 344, 440
Medical practice of therapy, 239, 240
Meeting on the FDA injunction, 420–421

Mein Kampf (Hitler), 272
Memorial to Reich, 3, 442
Menninger Clinic, 362, 421
Mesmer, Franz, 235
Meyer, Gladys, 258, 386–390, 441
Mills, Peter, 419, 425, 434, 438–439, 449–451, 454–455, 465–467, 470, 475
Misch, Käthe, 161
Mitosis, 209, 218, 243
Mocenigo, 412n., 439
Modjus, 411–412, 412n.
Moise, William, 393–394, 429–431, 433, 435, 438, 444, 448, 456, 459, 463, 465–466
Monogamy, compulsive, 119–120, 140–141, 144, 153, 338
Montessori nursery school, 146
Mooselookmeguntic Lake, Me., 278, 280, 340–341, 386
Moralistic defenses, 132, 153, 167, 306
Moreno, Jacob, 8
Mother-infant interaction, 181, 338
Movement of protozoa, 220
Müller, L. R., 207
Müller-Braunschweig, Carl, 186
The Murder of Christ (Reich), 386, 396–398, 411
Murder of Christ concept, 3, 397–398, 407, 455
Murray, John, 81, 466
Muscular armor, 4, 25, 27, 132, 177, 182, 197, 207–208, 217–218, 229, 235, 238, 241–243, 265, 315, 317, 326–328, 332, 343, 394, 403, 443, 481
Muscular spasm, 182, 221, 235, 300, 381
My Life (Trotsky), 272
My Unlawful Imprisonment (Reich), 473–474
Mycoplasmas, 297
Myerson, Abraham, 268

Mystical attitude, 165, 167, 352, 361, 385
Mystical teachings, 133

Nader, Ralph, 428
Nassau Hospital, Mineola, 417
National Institute of Health, 442
National Science Foundation, 26
National Socialism, 166
Natural laws of life, 306
The Natural Organization of Work Democracy (Reich), 270
Naturphilosophie, 55
Nazi conquests, 251, 255, 259, 274
Nazi propaganda, 163, 165–167, 169
Nazi-Soviet pact, 318
Nazism, 62, 132, 163, 165–166, 168, 170, 173, 288
Negative transference, 28, 188, 443
    latent, 74–75, 77–79, 85, 143, 176, 443, 481
Neill, A. S., 19, 23, 231–232, 258, 265, 270, 273, 284, 329–330, 336–338, 349–350, 353, 390–391, 414, 460–462, 482
Neo-Reichians, 481
The Nervous System (Müller), 207
Neuroses, etiology of, 101, 188
Neuroses, social origin, 188
Neuroses, symptom, *see* Character neuroses
Neurotic character, 178–179
Neurotic equilibrium, 77
New Jersey, 262
New Jersey Medical Society, 343, 346
The New Republic, 339, 360–361, 366–367
The New School for Social Research, 258, 262, 265, 269
New York, 27, 258, 262–263, 269, 271, 329–330, 339, 342, 344, 349, 350, 356, 380, 384, 403, 405,

New York *cont.*
407, 421, 429, 433, 446, 453, 458, 460–461
New York Academy of Sciences, 409
New York orgonomists, 419–420, 429, 430, 436, 461
New York *Post*, 362
The New Yorker, 346
News reports of Reich, 185, 215–216, 227, 229, 230, 233, 249, 379–380, 426, 466
Nice, 225
Nietzsche, Friedrich, 10, 20, 62, 77, 95, 100, 178, 182, 274, 368
Night sky observations, 278–279
Nissen, Ingjald, 229
Nobel Prize, 66
Nonverbal behavior of patients, 77, 79–80, 143, 175–177
Norwegian press campaign, 228–233, 253–256, 322, 337, 360, 362
Nuclear energy and orgone, *see* Orgone and nuclear energy
Nuclear radiation, 370, 372, 375–377, 416, 424
Nuclear war, threat of, 399
Nunberg, Hermann, 73, 82, 99, 107, 153

Objective validity, 9
Observatory building, Orgonon, 340–341, 378, 381, 383, 391, 394, 405, 410–411, 441–442, 445, 479
Ocular segment, 311, 315, 326
Oedipal conflict, 10, 56, 87, 98, 121, 136, 138, 142, 154, 178, 181, 193, 198, 431
Offshoots of Orgonomy, 329 *n.*, 481
Oklahoma, 342
Ollendorff, Ilse, 29, 37, 50–51, 69, 109, 111, 116, 246, 256, 263–265, 271–273, 275, 278, 284–285, 335–336, 338–339, 343, 347,

Ollendorff, Ilse *cont.*
349, 351, 356, 367, 374–375, 378, 383–387, 389, 391, 393–394, 403–409, 411, 413, 418, 420, 425–426, 429–430, 433, 435, 441, 444, 447, 450–451, 461, 463, 470, 472, 475, 480, 482
Ollendorff, Robert, 461
Oller, Charles, 345, 464
On Genitality (Reich), 88–90
On the Most Prevalent Form of Degradation in Erotic Life (Freud), 118
O'Neill, Eugene, 48
Oppenheimer, Robert J., 342
Oral orgasm, 325–326, 328–329, 329 *n.*, 333–334
Oral segment, 312, 325, 328
Oral stage, 86, 88, 149
Oranur, 374–378, 384, 392–396, 398–399, 403, 407–409, 411, 416–417, 436
The Oranur Experiment (Reich), 423, 424, 460
Oranur experiment, 29, 370–373, 377, 382–384, 386, 389, 391, 398, 400, 402, 406, 408, 410, 429, 441, 455
    initial intentions, 370–371, 382
    preliminary experiment, 371–373
    results, 373–377
    second stage, 374
    stopping the reaction, 375–376, 394
Oranur prize, 453
Oranur Report (Reich), 398
Oranur sickness, 442
Organismic DOR, 299, 408, 442–443
Organismic orgone energy, 317, 376, 378, 382, 443
Organizational activities, 336, 464
Organized emotional plague, *see* Emotional plague, organized

Orgasm, function of the, *see* Function of the orgasm

Orgasm anxiety, 197, 239, 326

Orgasm formula, 209–210, 213–214, 328

Orgasm in childhood, 333

Orgasm reflex, 218, 238–240, 243–244, 311–312, 328, 333

Orgasm Reflex, Muscular Attitude, and Bodily Expression (Reich), 236

Orgastic convulsions, 243–244

Orgastic impotence, 94, 102, 104, 218, 322

Orgastic potency, 4–5, 9, 17, 24, 39, 52, 66, 84–86, 91–94, 96, 98–99, 101–104, 118, 143, 152, 178–179, 218, 236, 238–239, 243–244, 266, 280, 306, 312, 317–318, 328, 353, 361, 394, 481

Orgone, *see* Orgone energy; Cosmic orgone energy

Orgone, manifestations of, *see* Electroscopic effects of orgone; Field excitation; Lumination of orgone; Thermal effects of orgone; Visible effects of orgone

Orgone accumulator, *see* Orgone energy accumulator

Orgone biophysics, 343

Orgone blanket, 303*n.*, 416

Orgone energy, 4, 17, 25, 30–31, 166, 210, 223, 244, 265–267, 269–270, 276, 278, 280–281, 288, 301–302, 307, 310, 315, 329, 330, 336, 340, 349–350, 352, 367–368, 370, 376, 379, 381–382, 392, 402, 308–409, 413–414, 416, 418–419, 423–425, 428, 432–435, 437–440, 442–443, 451, 453, 460, 470–472, 474–476, 479, 481

    social application, 369

Orgone energy *cont.*

    spontaneous motion of, 244, 280 *n.*, 291

The Orgone Energy Accumulator (Reich), 460

Orgone energy accumulator, 2, 277, 279, 281–284, 289, 301–303, 341, 342, 346, 348, 350, 352, 357, 360–361, 363, 365, 368, 370, 372, 392–393, 414, 418–420, 423–426, 433, 439, 447–449, 451, 458–459, 466–467, 470, 482

Orgone energy accumulator

    action of, 303, 305–306

    construction of, 303

    medical use of, 284, 293–294, 296, 301–302, 304–309, 344, 350–351, 364, 366–367, 392, 416, 426, 443

    production of, 363

Orgone Energy Bulletin, 29, 347, 356, 394, 414, 423, 442, 460

Orgone energy motor, 354, 354*n.*, 355, 357

Orgone energy research, 265, 269, 274, 276–278, 283–284, 289, 291–292, 306–307, 317, 319, 352, 384, 419, 451

Orgone Institute Press, 267, 356, 385, 388, 406, 461

Orgone Institute Research Laboratories, 307, 357, 366

Orgone physics, 343, 352

Orgone shooter, 303*n.*

Orgone therapy, 304–305, 312–316, 329, 343, 348, 350, 386, 414

Orgonometry, 329, 466, 473, 476

Orgonomic functionalism, 351, 473

Orgonomic Functionalism (Reich), 23

Orgonomic Infant Research Center, *see* Infant Research Center

Orgonomic Medicine, 402, 444

Orgonomic research, 479, 481–482

Orgonomists, medical, 342–345, 365, 406, 409, 426, 433, 464
Orgonomy, 15, 30, 280*n.*, 321, 323, 340, 342–343, 345–347, 349, 353, 361, 384–388, 390, 394, 397–398, 406, 414, 418, 421, 429, 433, 444, 456, 465, 468, 481–483
Orgonon, 3, 13, 24, 28–30, 39, 278, 340–342, 345, 349, 354, 355–357, 363–364, 372, 375, 378, 383–385, 389, 393, 400, 405–408, 411, 412–413, 429, 433–436, 441–442, 447–449, 458, 463, 474, 479–480
  evacuation of, 378
Orgonotic charge, 295, 306
Orgonotic pulsation, 329*n.*
Orgonotic streamings, *see* Streamings
Origin of armoring, 399–400
Orur, 432–433
Orwell, George, 387, 412*n.*
Oslo, 5–6, 185–186, 194, 200, 202, 211, 225–226, 229, 232–233, 245–246, 248–249, 255–256, 258, 273, 275–276, 293, 384, 386, 403, 436, 471
Our Congratulations to Freud on His Birthday (Reich), 248
Overland, Arnulf, 246

PA-bions, 223, 293–294, 297, 376–377
PAP cervical smear test, 297
Papanek, Ernst, 121
Parasympathetic responses, 207, 208, 236*n.*, 303
Paris, 198, 264
The Partisan Review, 347
Passive-feminine character, 80
Pasteur, Louis, 220
Paul, Saint, 396
Pearl Harbor, attack on, 271, 272
Péguy, Charles, 257

Pendulum experiment, 290
Penis anaesthesia, 190, 234, 243
People in Trouble (Reich), 123–126, 156, 171, 173, 217, 395, 399
Perception, distortion of, 315, 317
Perls, Fritz, 4, 5
Permissiveness, 165
Perversion, sexual, 87
Phallic-narcissistic character, 177
Pharmaceutical industry, 362, 413, 457, 463
Philipson, Tage, 184, 185
Physical orgone therapy, 313
Physiology, 206–207
Picasso, Pablo, 53
Pierrakos, John, 481
Pink, Alfred, 106, 108–109, 145–146, 195, 248–249
Pink, Annie, *see* Reich, Annie
Pink, Malva, 106, 108–109, 195, 248
Pinter, Harold, 189
Placebo effect, 208
Plan, 172
Planck, Max, 53, 291
Plasmatic movements, 208, 218, 301
Pleasure, 206–209, 211–213, 215, 234, 238, 328, 400
Pleasure anxiety, 208, 238
Polarities, biological, 208–209
Political behavior, 164
Politics, 268
Pollution of atmospheric orgone, *see* Atmospheric pollution
Pornography, 162, 172, 235, 364–365, 368, 396
Portland Me., 419, 424, 437, 445–446, 450, 454, 465, 467
Post-sentencing statement, 454–455
Pound, Ezra, 356
Prague, 195, 199, 202, 248, 251, 256, 269
Pregenital expression, 102
Pregenital fixations, 99, 110
Pregenital impulses, 178

Pregenital stages, 103, *see* Oral stage, Anal stage
Pregnancy, 330–331, 333
Prevention of
armoring, 330, 343
cancer, *see* Cancer, prevention of
neuroses, 135, 142, 154, 183, 306, 325
sexual repression, 105, 136
Primal scene, 68, 139
Primal therapy, 4, 244, 481
Princeton, 283, 285
Prison sentence, 454, 466
Prison writings, 473
Probation report, 470–471
Program for GAPSP (Reich), 162
Projections of perception, 315, 317
Protection of
children & adolescents, 163
the newborn, 321
Protozoa, study of, 217–221, 295, 297, 299, 340, 351
Proust, Marcel, 53
Psychiatric establishment, 2–3, 7–8, 15, 427
Psychiatric orgone therapy, *see* Orgone therapy
Psychiatry, traditional, 240
Psychic Contact and Vegetative Current (Reich), 188, 191, 234
Psychoanalysis, 2–5, 13, 32, 53–58, 67, 72–73, 87–89, 102, 207, 210, 229, 232, 234–235, 236n., 241, 246–247, 268, 310, 314, 372, 400–402
Psychoanalysts, 240, 372, 456
Psychoanalytic Association of Vienna, 183
Psychoanalytic Institute of New York, 262
Psychoanalytic Institute of Norway, 247

Psychoanalytic movement, 5, 8, 58, 66, 71, 81–84, 86, 102, 117–119, 148, 157, 171, 173, 185–188, 246–248, 257, 361, 401–402, 427, 465
Psychoanalytic Society of Berlin, 157, 161, 183, 186–187
Psychoanalytic Society of Norway, 186–188, 191
Psychoanalytic Society of Vienna, 58, 71, 73, 81–83, 90, 122, 155
The Psychoanalytic Theory of the Neuroses (Fenichel), 102
Psychobiography, 11–12
Psychodrama, 8
Psychological Research Institute, Oslo, 211, 225, 254
Psychoneuroses, 88–89, 97, 207
Psychoses, 68, 103, 315
Psychosomatic Medicine, 268

Qualitative observations, 373–375
The Quest for Wilhelm Reich (Wilson), 255

Rabinbach, Anson, 156
Racialism, 165
Radiation effects of SAPA bions, 223–224
Radiation sickness, 371, 375–378, 383
Radium, 371, 416, 432, 442
Radium in oranur experiment, 371–374, 392
Rado, Sandor, 155, 193–194
Rage, 235, 237, 244, 312
The Rainmakers: America's "Pluviculture" to World War II (Spencer), 380n.
Raising Two Children (Vahkup), 329n.
Raknes, Ola, 117, 225, 230, 235, 239, 246–248, 258–259, 285, 348–

Raknes, Ola *cont.*
350, 352–353, 390, 405, 461–463, 482
Rangeley Me., 29–30, 123, 147, 278, 307, 329, 335–336, 340, 342, 345, 347, 351, 356, 364, 378, 393–394, 406–407, 411, 421, 424, 441, 444, 458, 460
Rangeley School System, 356–357, 357*n.*
Rank, Otto, 83, 85
Raphael, Chester M., 331–332, 343–344, 389, 413, 420, 437, 442–443, 456, 480
Read, Sir Herbert, 460
Record of a Friendship (ed. Placzek), 357*n.*
Red blood cells, disintegration of, 295–296, 300–301
Red fascism, 404, 412, 437–438, 441, 455–457, 461–463
Red thread, 266
Reich, Annie, 106–108, 116, 119–120, 122, 124, 142, 145–147, 149–151, 161, 170, 184, 192–194, 196–203, 248–252, 255–256, 264–265, 269, 271, 273, 404, 420, 482
Reich, Cecilia, 36–38, 44, 57, 63, 79, 96, 107, 150, 241, 404–405
Reich, Eva, 6, 47, 50, 108–111, 120, 146, 149–150, 192–193, 195, 198–200, 202–203, 248–252, 271, 338–339, 356, 374–375, 384, 393–394, 406, 429–431, 435, 437, 443–444, 456, 463, 465, 470, 473, 477, 479–480, 483
Reich, Leon, 10, 36–39, 44, 47–48, 57–58, 63, 69, 79, 241, 404–405
Reich, Lore, III, 122, 149, 193, 195, 198, 200, 202–203, 248–249, 271, 338–339
Reich, Ottilie, *see* Heifetz, Ottilie Reich

Reich, Peter, 150, 252, 325–329, 330, 337–338, 357, 375, 378, 383, 387, 393–394, 403–404, 406, 429, 430–431, 435, 444–445, 459, 461–463, 470, 472, 476–477, 483
Reich, Robert, 36–38, 40, 44, 47–50, 54–55, III–II3, 149, 390
Reich, Sigrid, III
Reich, Tony, 149–150
Reich, Wilhelm
acceptance of orgonomy, 345–346, 353, 425
adolescent love life, 43, 47, 49
ailments, 47–48, 50, 96, 116, 390, 392, 441–442
American government, 398–399, 412, 414, 444, 462, 474
in analysis, 64, 82, 193
appearance, 16, 110, 116, 119, 148–149, 188, 352, 361, 363, 441, 454, 463–464
as an archivist, 395, 400, 437
arrest by FBI, 271
arrest for Contempt, 446
assessing the FDA's investigation, 366–369
association with Communism, 125, 127, 182–183
association with psychoanalysis, 55–58, 66–67, 81–83, 119, 127, 130, 146, 152, 154–155, 160, 169, 182–184, 186–187, 342
attracts talented followers, 184–186, 217, 342–346, 353
authoritarianism, 346, 351, 354, 389, 412
behavior, 26–29, 31, 46–47, 49–50, 69, 79, 107, III–II3, 145, 147, 149–151, 195, 241, 243, 250, 252–256, 273*n.*, 349, 352, 368, 384, 389–391, 404–406, 430*n.*, 444, 458–460

Reich, Wilhelm *cont.*
benchmark experiences, 44, 57–
58, 125–126, 174
birth of, 36
birth process, 331–334, 482
capacity to cross boundaries, 8,
190–191, 294, 297, 304, 314, 381–
382
character, 10, 20, 26–27, 29, 40–
41, 44–46, 51, 69, 78–79, 90, 149–
150, 390–391
childhood, 20, 37–40, 51
child rearing, 141–143, 168, 306,
325, 330, 338
clinical research, 87–88, 91, 92–94,
97–98, 122–123, 126, 146, 171,
180, 182, 189, 209, 218, 234
competitiveness, 59, 62, 110, 390
contactfulness, 196, 387–388, 432,
476
contribution to Psychoanalysis.
4–5, 58, 81, 86, 88, 91–92, 146
contribution to radical politics,
128
core contact, 9–10
in court, 438–440, 446–452
creativity, 62–63, 70, 91, 120, 152,
210, 256, 274, 314, 356, 391–392,
402–403, 443
criticism of Marxist practices,
163–164
criticism of Psychoanalytic practices, 81–83, 108, 130, 148, 163–
164, 182, 195
criticized by Communists, 169–
170, 172–173
criticized by Nazis, 170
criticized by psychoanalysts, 81,
86, 95, 98–102, 108, 119, 139, 144,
147, 154–155, 167, 171, 182–184,
187–188, 194, 200–201, 224
cultural activities, early, 62–63
death of, 2–3, 31, 477

Reich, Wilhelm *cont.*
death of brother, 112, 113, 116, 118,
390
death of father, 48
divergence from Freudian theory,
118, 180, 182, 184, 186–187, 201,
247, 288, 401
divorce, 245, 338–339, 384–385
early education, 40, 44–47
education, university & after, 53–
54, 66–67, 82, 99, 117
emotional plague expression, 398,
458
everyday expressions, 209
expulsion from Communist
Party, 6, 169–173, 188, 203, 318
expulsion from Psychoanalytic
movement, 5, 84, 186–188, 201,
203, 207, 364, 402
expulsion from Social Democratic Party, 5–6, 156, 171
family crisis, 40–46, 96, 109, 118,
241, 267
as a father, 249–252, 337–339,
394, 430
feeling of being different, 66–67,
118, 120, 414
feelings for Freud, 57–58, 83, 99–
101, 116, 154–155, 188, 203, 248,
285, 287
finances, 132, 156, 161, 211, 224,
284, 310–311, 345, 364, 367, 380
n., 388, 429, 451, 464, 474–475,
479, 480–481
first published paper, *see The
Breakthrough of the Incest
Taboo in Puberty* (Reich)
Freud, character of, 117
friendship versus work, 151, 201–
202, 224–225, 230–231, 243,
273, 349, 387–388
functional health, 27, 49, 63, 79,
95, 97, 138, 140, 171, 179, 244, 310

Reich, Wilhelm *cont.*
functional observations, 78–80, 88–89, 190, 295, 298, 301, 432
functional thinking, 25, 33, 55, 79, 87–89, 97–98, 139, 212, 252, 296, 353
fury, 250, 256, 274, 323, 350, 353, 384, 394, 411, 422, 424, 430, 435
grandmother Roniger, *see* Roniger, Josephine
heart attack, 392–394, 477
heroic actions, 134
his own accomplishments, 395
his own work, 66–67, 330, 395, 457, 474
income, 54–55, 60, 64, 145–146, 192, 392
independence, early, 49, 55
individual therapy, 318, 464
jealousy, 60, 63, 109, 254–255, 272–275, 339, 386, 389, 391, 403, 406–407, 435, 442
Jewish origin, 463
journey through Europe, 198–199
laboratory work, 8, 27–28, 215, 227, 409
later aversion to politics, 167
law and its application, 236–437
leader, natural, 31, 48, 73–74, 82, 132, 161, 152, 346, 453, 464
loneliness, 284–285, 405–406, 430–431, 441, 472
love relationships, 30, 52, 59–61, 63, 84, 95–96, 140–142, 144, 146–147, 194–197, 200–201, 210, 217, 234, 245, 253–254, 263, 273, 275, 338–339, 385–386, 431, 435, 442, 445, 461
marriage, 119–120, 140–141, 245, 338, 384, 445, 470
marriage to Annie, 108–109, 113, 116, 119, 122, 142, 144–146, 149,

Reich, Wilhelm *cont.*
157, 170, 173, 184, 192, 194–196, 245, 403
marriage to Ilse, 338–339, 384–386, 445
meetings with Freud, 57–58, 153–156
method of research, 91, 98, 126, 144, 150, 179, 213–214, 221, 279, 281, 330–331, 373, 408, 415
method of writing, 123, 126, 214, 250–251, 266–267, 324–325, 286, 296, 409
money, feelings about, 60, 69, 109–110, 132, 145–146, 150, 195, 224–225, 269, 339, 441
naiveté, 124, 128, 167, 278, 398–399, 422–423
naturalization as U.S. citizen, 338–339
neuroses, 9, 253–254, 297–298, 315, 322, 328
nudity, 138–139, 234–235, 239–240
optimism, 171, 240, 305, 369, 398, 400, 441, 465
organizations, 174, 186, 354, 460, 465
organize a subject clearly, 131
organizer of work, 28–29, 39, 48, 73–74, 329–330, 333, 402, 410
originality, 208, 215, 247, 402–403
paintings, 391–392, 409
paranoia, 355–366
parents, *see* Reich, Cecilia; Reich, Leon
pedagogics, 70, 325
at play, 196–198, 200, 245–246, 336, 444
political activities, early, 54, 59, 61, 173
political education lectures, 130–131, 160, 183

Reich, Wilhelm *cont.*
political involvement, 123, 125–
127, 129, 132, 156, 160, 173, 183
politics, 167, 270, 318–320
preferences, early, 54–57
premarital sexuality, 121, 142
presentation of papers, 58, 87–88,
91–92, 118, 153–154, 156, 188, 252,
352–352
primacy of work, 203, 224–225,
245, 252, 259, 273, 336, 340,
346, 383
priority of discoveries, 240–241,
351–352
private practice of psychoanalysis, 72–73, 76, 106–107, 122,
127, 184
professional education, 67, 332
protection of work method, 380*n.*,
395
psychiatric examination of, 466,
468–470
as a psychoanalyst, 46, 58, 64, 66,
72, 82, 110, 180–181
psychoanalytic education lectures, 129
as a publisher, 169, 171–172, 186,
206, 226, 252–253, 267, 395,
423, 437, 442
recorded statements, 17, 21–22
relation to associates, 246, 252,
256–257, 259, 273, 336, 342–
343, 345–346, 349, 350–351, 354,
367, 386, 388–389, 390, 407, 421,
431, 445
relation to co-workers, 27, 38, 60,
111–112, 151, 170, 225, 233, 253,
265, 267, 340, 353, 356, 403,
408–409
relation to Federn, 82–85, 154–
155
relation to Freud, 82, 85, 99–102,
116–119, 122, 152–154, 171, 173,
182–183, 185, 193, 202

Reich, Wilhelm *cont.*
relation to political ideology, 4,
125, 173–174, 270, 318–319
relation to workmen, 341–342,
403, 448
research questions, basic, 207,
209, 211, 218–219, 221, 276, 294,
330
response to criticism, 102–104,
139, 152, 182–183, 232–233, 243,
256, 337
response to criticism of research,
98–99, 215, 222–223, 228–229,
286–287
response to FDA investigations,
364–369, 411, 419–423, 429
response to Injunction decree,
424–426
responses, 27, 31, 48–49, 116–117,
145, 149–150, 160, 169, 207, 210,
243, 248, 253–254, 344, 347,
354, 395, 407, 421–422, 456,
459–460, 462
responsiveness, 17, 20, 26, 28–29,
69, 99, 101, 149, 195–196, 249–
252, 453–454
sanity, 5–10, 84, 119–120, 147, 193–
194, 201–202, 217, 248, 271, 286,
294, 344, 348, 350, 355, 360,
450, 468–470
self-analysis, 69, 179
self-awareness, 69–70, 83, 96, 98–
99, 171, 196, 225, 274, 354, 372,
398, 405, 407
self-criticism, 389, 398, 407
seminars, 247, 249, 263, 265, 440–
442
sense of mission, 51, 58, 110, 120,
146, 148, 151, 196, 225, 240, 259,
336, 346
sex education lectures, 121, 130
sexual experiences, early, 30, 52,
62
sexual impulses of adolescents, 121

Reich, Wilhelm *cont.*
  sexual impulses of children, 120–
    121, 138
  skin condition, 47–48, 50, 63, 272,
    391, 471
  social analysis, 164, 191, 337
  social attitudes, 120, 126, 153, 183,
    201
  social involvement, 110, 121, 337
  social observations, 96, 126, 143,
    190, 199, 318–320, 333
  social revolution, 126–127, 129–
    130, 143, 173, 318–319, 337
  socializing, 89, 110, 119–120, 148,
    444
  speaking style, 131, 353
  student life, 59, 61–62, 146, 463
  study of adolescents, 135–136, 138
  study of child development, 136–
    139, 150
  study of Marx & Engels, 124
  suicide of mother, 44, 96, 118
  support of patients, 243, 265
  as a teacher, 73–74, 78–79, 81–82,
    143, 152, 175–176, 202*n.*, 310,
    312, 346, 408–409, 440
  technical seminar, leader of, *see*
    Technical seminar in psychoa-
    nalysis, Berlin; Vienna
  tendencies, 49, 56, 59–60, 63, 128,
    147, 240, 253–254, 305, 337,
    355–356, 377, 384
  therapeutic techniques, 207, 217,
    229, 234–244, 307, 311, 316, 326–
    327, 329, 332
  as a therapist, 22, 24–26, 80, 152,
    175–177, 181–182, 189, 242–243,
    253, 310–311, 314, 317, 336, 343,
    356, 387
  transitions of understanding, 182,
    210, 316, 376–377, 382
  trial for Contempt of Injunction,
    402, 440, 444–452
  tuberculosis attack, 116, 121

Reich, Wilhelm *cont.*
  unpublished papers, 480
  vitality, 179
  vulnerability, 49, 59, 116–118, 173,
    196, 233, 253–256, 272, 355–
    356, 384, 430, 476
  warmth, 352, 385
  work, approach to, 12, 24, 26, 28–
    29, 91, 118–119, 265, 267, 278,
    336, 408, 474–475
  work capacity, 48, 63, 66, 143,
    274, 384
  World War I, 20, 22, 37, 46, 48,
    50, 52–53, 124, 146, 173
Reich archives, 6, 29, 351, 402, 465
Reich blood tests, 295–296, 298, 301,
    340, 417
Reich's impact outside orgonomy,
    481
Reichstag fire, 170
Reik, Theodore, 81, 99
Relation of energy to structure, 372
Relation of psychoanalysis & or-
    gonomy, 400
Relaxation, 210, 213
Release of emotion, 235, 239, 244
Release of energy, *see* Energy, re-
    lease of,
Religion and masochism, 182
Research volunteers, assessing, 330
Resignation, 299–300
Resistance to change in science,
    290–291
Resistances, analysis of, 73–81, 85,
    89, 97, 99, 107, 176, 181, 189, 301,
    401
Respiration, 236–239, 298, 300, 311,
    313
Response (Reich), 422
Response to attacks on orgonomy,
    348
Reviews of Reich's publications, 15,
    169, 268, 361, 482
Rhumbler, Ludwig, 208, 219

Riefenstahl, Leni, 166
Rieff, Philip, 482
Rights of adolescents, 134–135, 143
Rilke, Rainer Maria, 21, 100
Rockefeller Foundation, 225
The Rocky Road to Functionalism (McCullough), 408, 453
The Role of Genitatlity in the Therapy of the Neuroses (Reich), 92
Roner, Walter, alias Wilhelm Reich
Roniger, Josephine, 37–38, 44, 50–51, 150–151
Röntgen, Wilhelm, 371
Roosevelt, Franklin D., 270–271, 280, 320
Rosenfeld, Isaac, 347
Ross, Irwin, 362
Ross, Tom, 341, 364–365, 393, 407, 429, 435, 442, 448–449, 459, 461
Roter Sport, 170
Rubinstein, Annie, 271, 272, *see* Reich, Annie
Rubinstein, Thomas, 202, 250, 271
Rumormongering attacks, 357, 360
Ruskin John, 378*n*.
Russell, Bertrand, 53, 142
Russian invasion of Bukovina, 50
Rycroft, Charles, 7, 90, 95

Sachter, Dr., 40
Sadger, Isidor, 64, 69, 107–108
Sadism, 180, 183
St. Lewis, Roy, 473
Sanatarium at Davos, 116, 119
SAPA-bions, 223–224, 276–277, 280–281, 285, 301–302
Sartre, Jean Paul, 104
Scandinavian Psychoanalytic Institute, 246
Scharffenberg, Johann, 229–230, 231–233, 248, 256, 322
Schattendorf, 124
Schiller, J. von, 210–211, 453

Schizophrenia, 66, 215, 327, 428
study of, 314–319
Schjelderup, Harold, 186, 211, 225, 230, 246, 248, 254, 257, 259
Schmidt, Vera, 143
Schönberg, Arnold, 53, 62
Schutzbund, 123, 125, 156
Science and Sanity (Korzybski), 17
Scientific observer, 9, 373
Secondary layer drives, 397
Segments of body armor, 182, 235, 238, 244, 300, 311–314, 318
Self-experiencing, 9, 402
Self-regulation, 110, 149, 231, 338
Sensations as a tool, 280, 373, 416
Sensations due to accumulated orgone, 281, 283, 301, 416
Settlement House, 337
Sex-counseling clinics, 161
Sex-economy, 166–167, 171, 173, 248, 306, 319, 321, 337, 352, 453
Sex hygiene clinics, 133–136, 145, 151, 156
Sex Information and Educational Council of the United States, 140
Sex-political propaganda, 132, 165–166
Sex-politics, 146–148, 151–152, 160–163, 166–168, 170–171, 174, 182–183, 197, 206–207, 240, 266, 305, 318
Sex-pol movement, 129, 131–134, 136, 139, 143, 146, 163, 167, 171, 174, 211, 240
Sex reform movement, 161, 163, 167
Sexual abstinence, 299
Sexual behavior, 180
Sexual disturbances as epidemic, 136, 306
Sexual energy, 88–89, 92, 96–97, *see* Orgone energy
Sexual excitation, 120, 190, 240, 299, 306

Sexual intercourse, study of, 213–214, 216
The Sexual Life of Savages (Malinowski), 249
Sexual needs, 133
Sexual pleasure, 209
The Sexual Revolution (Reich) 1936, 20, 266, 419
The Sexual Revolution (Reich) 1945, 268, 460
The Sexual Struggle of Youth (Reich), 168–169, 183, 199
Sexual suppression, 103, 132, 139, 153–154, 162, 164, 179, 306
Sexuality, 56, 66, 86–88, 103, 217, 231, 235, 244, 298
Sharaf, Myron, 356–357, 366, 373, 375, 388, 393–395, 401, 405–406, 408–409, 437, 439, 440–441, 447, 452–453, 456
  adolescence, 19–20
  association with W. Washington, 354–355
  character structure, 24–25, 31–32
  childhood, 20
  competence for assessing Reich's work, 206, 305
  emotional health, 104
  father, 18–19
  first marriage, 23, 25, 28–31, 431
  first meeting with Reich, 16–17
  mother, 18–19, 22–23, 26
  notes on Reich, 22, 27–29
  at Orgonon, 24
  practice of therapy, 22, 32
  in psychoanalysis, 31
  relation to Reich, 24–32, 388, 406, 431, 441
  summary of Reich's findings, 104, 305
  therapy with Reich, 24–28, 311, 314
  translator of Reich's writings, 23–24, 295

Sharaf, Myron *cont.*
  university studies, 20–23, 25, 27, 30
  working for Reich, 29, 31, 356, 373, 375, 388, 394–395, 437
  writing this book, 32–33, 401
Sharaf, Peter, 30
Shaw, G. B., 53
Siersted, Ellen, 186
Silber, Frederick, 471–473
Silent Observer, 395
Silent Spring (Carson), 378
Silvert, Michael, 345, 420–421, 429–430, 432–434, 437–438, 446–448, 451, 453–458, 460–461, 465–468, 473, 480
Skin, potentials at the, 211–215
Skin excitation, 181
Sletten, 200
Smith, George B., 416
Smythe, Austin, 308
Sobey, Victor, 345, 437, 461
Social criticism, 132, 140, 143, 153
Social Democratic Party of Austria, 5–6, 53–54, 61–62, 121, 123–128, 130–131, 134, 145, 152, 156, 171, 185, 199
Social structure, 9, 143
Socialist Association for Sex Hygiene and Sexological Research, 133
Socialist Workers Party of Germany, 264
Society, sexual repression by, 103
Solar plexus, 213, 236
Sorrow, 237
Soviet Union, 142, 249, 259, 318, 320
Soviet Union and sexual issues, 142–143, 153, 163, 183, 318
Spartacus uprising, Berlin, 194
The Specificity of Forms of Masturbation (Reich), 87
Spock, Benjamin, 137, 318

Spontaneous feelings, 126, 221
Spontaneous movement, *see* Orgone energy, spontaneous motion of; Orgastic convulsions; Plasmatic movements; Bions; Atmospheric orgone; Fear of spontaneous movement
Sputum of cancer patients, 296–297, 300
Stalin, Joseph, 198, 322, 396, 412*n.*
Stalinist sympathies, 361–362, 366, 367*n.*
Stalinists in the U.S.A., 362
Stasis neurosis, *see* Actual neurosis
State Department of the U.S.A., 258, 471
Statement Regarding Competence in Matters of Orgone Energy (Reich), 365–366
Static electricity, 281, 283
Steig, William, 322, 346–347, 429–430, 437, 456, 465, 474
Stein, Gisela, 62, 69, 99, 270
Stein, Paul, 62, 99, 270
Stein, Peter, 200
Steiner, George, 14, 483
Sterba, Richard, 78–79, 81, 96, 110, 147, 152, 154
Stettin, 163
Stocker, Helena, 142
The Storm Cloud of the Nineteenth Century (Ruskin), 378*n.*
The Strange Case of Wilhelm Reich (Brady), 360–362, 439
Streamings, 30, 189, 206, 218, 235–236, 239, 310, 314–317, 400–401 perception of, 5, 23–24, 31–32, 189, 213, 315
Student laboratory at Orgonon, 340, 388, 394, 406, 408–409, 460
Sublimation, concept of, 96, 121, 135, 153–154, 180
Substitute contact, 190–191
Suckling, function of, 325–326, 328

Suicide, 344, 390
Summerhill school, 231
Summer school, 1935, 246
Superimposition, 399
Survivor guilt, 118
Swarowski, Hans, 60
Swedish government, 185,
Sweeney, Judge George C., 446–451, 454–455, 465–467, 473, 475
Sympathetic responses, 207–208, 236*n.*

Taylor, J. C., 471
Taylor, William, 416
T-bacilli, 223, 293–297, 301, 324, 376–377
Technical Seminar in Psychoanalysis, Berlin, 160, 183
Technical Seminar in Psychoanalysis, Vienna, 73–74, 77–78, 82, 84, 89, 98, 122, 132, 143, 146, 152, 154–155
du Teil, Roger, 222, 225–226, 256
Templeton, Cista, 363–364
Templeton, Herman, 307, 341, 363
Tension, 209, 213
Thälmann, Ernst, 166
Therapeutic concepts, 311, 315–316, 325
The Therapeutic Significance of Genital Libido (Reich), 91
Thermal effects of orgone, 282–285, 288–301
Thinking, productive, 95
Thjötta, Prof., 228–229, 232, 256
Thoracic segment, 312
Thorburn, William, 342–343
Thoreau, Henry, 218, 321, 324–325
Throat, block, 313, 316–317, 407
Tiller, William, 482
Time-lapse photomicrographs, 219–220
Time, 2, 309

Tivoli Gardens, Copenhagen, 197
Tolstoy, Leo, 210
Tomb at Orgonon, 442
Touching the patient, 234–236, 240, 244
Training of physicians, 310, 318, 394, 480
Training of teachers, 329
Transference, 12, 75, 97, 107, 180, 224, 234–235
Transitional states, 220–223, 239
Trobriand Islanders, 138, 179, 197
Tropp, Helen, 356–357, 406–407, 407n.
Tropp, Jimmy, 356, 406
Tropp, Oscar, 345
Tropp, Simeon J., 344–345, 350, 356, 364, 367, 374, 393–394, 406–407, 407n., 413, 456
Trotsky, Leon, 198, 232
Trotsky's Fourth International, 174, 198
Truman, Harry S., 322, 361
Trustee of Wilhelm Reich's estate, 479–480
Tucson, Ariz., 431–434, 448
Tufts Medical School, 31
Turner, James S., 428
Tyrol, Austrian Alps, 198

UFOs, 413, 461
Un-American activities, 262
Unconscious memories, 241–242
Union Theological Seminary, 337
United States of America, 251, 257–259, 262, 269, 318, 320, 403
  Air Force, 413, 435, 457, 461, 468, 474
  Attorney for the state of Maine, 418–419, 434
  Board of Parole, 466, 473, 475
  Court of Appeals, 457–458
  Department of State, 258, 471

United States cont.
  District Court for the state of Maine, 422, 434, 458
  Supreme Court, 426, 458, 460, 463, 465
  Weather Bureau, 380, 424
Unity of sensation and reason, 400
University of
  Arizona, 380
  California, 345
  Chicago, 15–17, 20, 354
  Harvard, 21–23, 25, 27, 30, 395–396
  Kansas, 380
  New Hampshire, 407–408
  New York, 481
  Oslo, 186, 211
  Stanford, 482
  Vienna, 54, 106
  Wisconsin, 345
University of Vienna Clinic, 66–67
Vaginal orgasm, 103
Vaginal secretions of cancer patients, 296
Vahkup, Mary, 329n.
Vegetative energy, 188–189
Vegetative nervous system, see Autonomic nervous system
Vegetotherapy, see Character-analytic vegetotherapy
Verlag fur Sexualpolitik, 169, 172
Vesicles in food brews, 221
Vesicles in grass infusions, 219–221
Vienna, 5, 47–48, 50–51, 53–54, 62, 81, 108, 111, 113, 117, 119, 122–125, 128, 130–131, 133, 148, 150, 152, 155–156, 160, 170, 172, 183, 192, 195–196, 199–200, 202, 248–250, 262, 270, 403, 463
Vienna Psychoanalytic Polyclinic, 67, 91, 110, 117, 122
Vienna uprising, July 15, 1927, 124–126, 145

Village Voice, 2
Visible effects of orgone, 276–279, 281–282, 286, 301
Vitalist view of life, 54, 57
Voice, expression of the, 312
Volkischer Beobachter, 170
Volvo Company, Sweden, 320
Voyeurism, 87

Waal, Nic, 348, 352, *see* Hoel, Nic
Wallace, Henry A., 361, 366
Warburg, Otto, 300
Washington, D.C., 272, 444–446, 463, 474
Washington, William, 354–355
Weather modification, 379–380, 380 *n.,* 432–434, 442
Wegener, Alfred, 291
Weimar Republic, 161–162
Wells, H. G., 284
Wertham, Frederic, 361–362
Wharton, W. R. M., 363–365, 368–369
What Is Class Consciousness (Reich), 174, 198
When Your Child Asks You (Annie Reich), 168–169
Where Does Nudist Education Lead To? (Reich), 172
White House, Washington, 284
Wiener-Neustadt, 127–128
Wilhelm Reich Foundation, 2, 308, 392, 418–419, 425–427, 429,433–434, 437–439, 441, 446, 450–451, 454, 457, 461, 475, 480
Wilhelm Reich Infant Trust Fund, 479
Wilhelm Reich Museum, 479
Wilhelm Reich Vs the U.S.A. (Greenfield), 363*n.*

Will of Wilhelm Reich, 388, 463, 465, 479–480
Willie, James A., 342–343, 347–349, 352, 367, 437, 455–456, 483
Wilson, Colin, 255
With Every Breath You Take (Lewis), 381 *n.*
Wittgenstein, Ludwig, 95
Wolfe, Theodore P, 5, 257–258, 262–263, 265–267, 272, 283–284, 287, 336–340, 342–344, 348, 350–353, 356, 367, 386–390, 404–405, 412, 429, 441, 464, 482
Women's rights, 4, 141, 254
Wood, Charles A., 363–365
Work democracy, 4, 217, 270–271, 319–320, 342, 346, 354
Work product, involvement with, 320
Working class, 124, 127–128, 148, 163–164, 319
Work interwoven with character, 7–9, 12, 80–81, 96, 118–119, 149, 150, 363
World League for Sexual Reform, 136, 154, 162, 185
World War II, 259, 274–275, 284, 320, 342, 349
Wylie, H. Lee, 356, 406
Wyvell, Lois, 356, 385–386, 388–389, 393, 403, 405–407, 421, 431, 481

X-rays, 371–372, 375–376, 416–417

Yeats, William Butler, 396

Zadniker, Mr., 130
Zuckerman, Marvin, 214–215
Zurich, 198